Methods for Achieving Your Purpose in Writing

The Bedford Reader centers on common ways of thinking and writing about all kinds of subjects, from everyday experiences to complex scientific theories. Whatever your purpose in writing, one or more of these ways of thinking—or methods of development—can help you discover and shape your ideas in individual paragraphs or entire papers.

The following list connects various purposes you may have for writing and the methods for achieving those purposes. The blue boxes along the right edge of the page correspond to tabs on later pages where each method is explained.

PURPOSE	METHOD
To tell a story about your subject, possibly to enlighten readers or to explain something to them	Narration
To help readers understand your subject through the evidence of their senses—sight, hearing, touch, smell, taste	Description
To explain your subject with instances that show readers its nature or character	Example
To explain or evaluate your subject by helping readers see the similarities and differences between it and another subject	Comparison and Contrast
To inform readers how to do something or how something works—how a sequence of actions leads to a particular result	Process Analysis
To explain a conclusion about your subject by showing readers the subject's parts or elements	Division or Analysis
To help readers see order in your subject by understanding the kinds or groups it can be sorted into	Classification
To tell readers the reasons for or consequences of your subject, explaining why or what if	Cause and Effect
To show readers the meaning of your subject—its boundaries and its distinctions from other subjects	Definition
To have readers consider your opinion about your subject or your proposal for it	Argument and Persuasion

THE BEDFORD READER

Ninth Edition

THE BEDFORD READER

Ninth Edition

X. J. Kennedy

Dorothy M. Kennedy

Jane E. Aaron

BEDFORD/ST. MARTIN'S   BOSTON ◆ NEW YORK

FOR BEDFORD/ST. MARTIN'S

Developmental Editor: Karin Halbert
Production Editor: Arthur Johnson
Production Supervisor: Jennifer Wetzel
Senior Marketing Manager: Rachel Falk
Editorial Assistants: Stefanie Wortman, Christina Gerogiannis, and Anne Noyes
Production Assistants: Kristen Merrill and Amy Derjue
Copyeditor: Mary Lou Wilshaw-Watts
Text Design: Anna Palchik and Dorothy Bungert/EriBen Graphics
Cover Design: Donna Lee Dennison
Cover Art: Dmitri Cavander, *View Towards Great Spruce Head*, oil on canvas, 40 × 54 inches, 2002, http://www.dcavander.com.
Composition: Stratford Publishing Services, Inc.
Printing and Binding: Haddon Craftsmen, Inc., an R. R. Donnelley & Sons Company

President: Joan E. Feinberg
Editorial Director: Denise B. Wydra
Editor in Chief: Karen S. Henry
Director of Marketing: Karen Melton Soeltz
Director of Editing, Design, and Production: Marcia Cohen
Managing Editor: Elizabeth M. Schaaf

Library of Congress Control Number: 2004118171

Manufactured in the United States of America.

0   9   8   7   6   5
f   e   d   c   b   a

For information, write: Bedford/St. Martin's, 75 Arlington Street, Boston, MA 02116 (617-399-4000)

ISBN: 0-312-43317-4
EAN: 978-0-312-43317-8

PREFACE FOR INSTRUCTORS

"A writer," says Saul Bellow, "is a reader moved to emulate." In a nutshell, the aim of *The Bedford Reader* is to move students to be writers, through reading and emulating the good writing of others.

Like its predecessor, this ninth edition of *The Bedford Reader* works toward its aim both rhetorically and thematically. We present the rhetorical methods realistically, as we ourselves use them — as natural forms that assist invention and fruition and as flexible forms that mix easily for any purpose a writer may have. Further, we forge scores of thematic connections among selections, both in paired essays in each rhetorical chapter and in writing topics after all the selections.

Filling in this outline is a wealth of features, new and old.

NEW FEATURES

ENGAGING NEW READINGS BY REMARKABLE WRITERS. As always, we have been engrossed in freshening the book's selections. Exceptional rhetorical models that also compel students' interest, the twenty-six new selections are by contemporary writers such as Ethan Canin, Bill Bryson, Scott Russell Sanders, Joan Didion, Naomi Klein, Edward Said, Katha Pollitt, and Dagoberto Gilb. Added stories by Shirley Jackson and Daniel Orozco raise the number of literary works to six. And four new student essays increase the student contributions to eighteen.

MORE MODELS OF ACADEMIC WRITING. At the request of instructors who use the book, *The Bedford Reader* now includes more of the kinds of reading and writing that students will do throughout their academic careers. We also offer more opportunities to practice academic writing.

- **More source-based essays.** Throughout the reader, eight documented essays — seven of them new — show both student and professional writers drawing on and acknowledging sources. In Chapter 3 a new annotated student paper illustrates research writing and MLA style in detail.
- **Expanded chapter on argument.** Chapter 13 now offers ten essays to stimulate lively student discussion and writing. Two new pairings and a new four-essay casebook provide multiple viewpoints on current topics: vegetarianism, same-sex marriage, and national security versus civil liberty in the post–9/11 United States.
- **More research-based writing assignments.** To help students practice their research skills, almost every selection now includes a writing suggestion calling for library or Internet research.

MORE HELP WITH WRITING.   The focus on academic writing continues in *The Bedford Reader*'s writing instruction:

- **New focus on sentences and paragraphs.** In the introduction to each rhetorical method, a new "Focus" box highlights an element of writing that is especially relevant to that method — for example, verbs in narration, concrete words in description, sentence variety in example, and tone in argument and persuasion. To show the elements in context, most selections include a question about them.
- **More emphasis on key concepts.** In Chapters 1 and 2 on reading and writing and in the introduction to every rhetorical chapter, we have emphasized and expanded the discussions of audience, purpose, and thesis.
- **New student essay-in-progress.** In Chapter 2 on writing, a new student essay-in-progress now includes peer review. The essay responds to Nancy Mairs's "Disability" by looking at the TV portrayals of persons with disabilities.

NEW TWO-COLOR DESIGN.   As you thumb through *The Bedford Reader*, you'll notice an added blue color that makes the book easier to navigate and highlights key information such as documentation models, revision checklists, and "Focus" boxes. New marginal page tabs in the rhetorical introductions make those sections easier to find.

AN EXPANDED COMPANION WEB SITE.   New Web boxes in the text link to *The Bedford Reader*'s Web site (*bedfordstmartins.com/thebedfordreader*), which has a much broader range of resources. For each selection, the site provides an interactive reading quiz and links to further information on the author and the author's topics. For the new "Focus" boxes, the site offers Exercise Central, a collection of grammar and usage exercises. For research writing, the site links directly to *The Bedford Research Room* and *Diana Hacker's Research and Documentation Online*. And for instructors, the site provides sample syllabi, the complete text of the instructor's manual, a reporting feature for monitoring students' progress on the reading quizzes and Exercise Central, and links to *The Bedford Bibliography for Teachers of Writing* and *The St. Martin's Tutorial on Avoiding Plagiarism*.

TRADEMARK FEATURES

VARIED SELECTIONS BY WELL-KNOWN AUTHORS.   The selections in *The Bedford Reader* vary in authorship, topics, even length. We offer clear models of the methods of development by noted writers such as Annie Dillard, Judith Ortiz Cofer, E. B. White, and Brent Staples. Half the selections are by women, and a quarter touch on cultural diversity. They range in subject from family to science, from language to disability.

EXCITING VISUAL DIMENSION.   *The Bedford Reader* emphasizes the visual as well as the verbal. Chapter 1 on reading provides a short course in thinking critically about images, with an advertisement serving as a case study. Each rhetorical chapter then opens with a striking image — an ad, a cartoon, a photograph, or a painting. With accompanying text and questions, these openers invite students' own critical reading and show how the rhetorical methods work visually. Finally, several of the book's selections take images as their starting points, modeling the close reading asked of students, and another selection highlights key points visually.

REALISTIC TREATMENT OF THE RHETORICAL METHODS.   *The Bedford Reader* treats the methods of development not as boxes to be stuffed full of verbiage but as tools for inventing, for shaping, and, ultimately, for accomplishing a purpose. Clear, practical chapter introductions link the methods to the range of purposes they can serve and give step-by-step guidance for writing and revising in the method. (For quick reference, the purpose–method links also appear inside the front cover, where they are keyed to the marginal page tabs in each chapter introduction.) In addition, a selection in every rhetorical chapter illustrates the method in practice: A student arrives at the method to achieve a particular writing goal, such as reporting an accident, crafting a résumé, or advertising an apartment for sublet.

Taking this realistic approach to the methods even further, we show how writers freely combine the methods to achieve their purposes: Each rhetorical introduction discusses how that method might work with others, and at least one "Other Methods" question after every selection helps students analyze how methods work together. Most significantly, Part Three provides an anthology of works by well-known writers that specifically illustrate mixed methods. The headnotes for these selections point to where each method comes into play.

THOROUGH COVERAGE OF READING, WRITING, AND RESEARCH.   Part One of *The Bedford Reader* offers detailed advice on the kinds of reading and research writing that students are expected to do in college and beyond. Chapter 1 covers critical reading, including a sample of a student's annotations on a text and practical guidelines for summarizing, analyzing, and interpreting texts and visual images. Chapter 2 covers writing, from ideas through editing, illustrated with a new student work-in-progress.

Chapter 3, "Using and Documenting Sources," helps students evaluate print and online sources, integrate sources, summarize and paraphrase, avoid plagiarism, and document sources using the latest MLA guidelines. A new student research paper, with marginal annotations, provides a model.

EXTENSIVE THEMATIC CONNECTIONS.   *The Bedford Reader* provides substantial topics for class discussion and writing. A pair of essays in each rhetorical chapter addresses the same subject, from the ordinary (housekeeping) to the controversial (globalization), and, as mentioned earlier, the chapter on argument now includes two essay pairs and a four-essay casebook. At least one "Connections" writing topic after every selection suggests links to other selections. And an alternate thematic table of contents arranges the book's selections under more than two dozen topics.

UNIQUE COMMENTS BY WRITERS ON WRITING.   After their essays, poems, or stories, fifty-five of the book's writers offer comments on everything from grammar to revision to how they developed the reprinted piece. Besides providing rock-solid advice, these comments also prove that for the pros, too, writing is usually a challenge. Writers on Writing new to this edition include those by Ethan Canin, Scott Russell Sanders, Naomi Klein, and Dagoberto Gilb.

For easy access, the Writers on Writing are listed in the book's index under the topics they address. Look up *Revision*, for instance, and find that Russell Baker, Gore Vidal, and Maxine Hong Kingston, among others, have something to say about this crucial stage of the writing process.

ABUNDANT EDITORIAL APPARATUS.   As always, we've surrounded the selections with a wealth of material designed to get students reading, thinking,
and writing. To help structure students' critical approach to the selections,
each one comes with two headnotes (on the author and the selection itself),
three sets of questions (on meaning, writing strategy, and language), and at
least five writing topics. One writing topic encourages students to explore
their responses in their journals, another suggests how to develop the journal
writing into an essay, and others emphasize critical writing, research, and connections among selections.

Besides the aids with every selection, the book also includes additional
writing topics for every rhetorical chapter, a glossary ("Useful Terms") that
defines all terms used in the book (including all those printed in SMALL CAPI-
TAL LETTERS), and an index that alphabetizes authors and titles and important
topics (including, as noted earlier, those covered in the Writers on Writing).

EXTENSIVE INSTRUCTOR'S MANUAL.   Available as a separate manual, bound
into the instructor's edition, or through the companion Web site, *Notes and
Resources for Teaching The Bedford Reader* suggests ways to integrate journal
writing and collaboration into writing classes and ways to use the book's
Chapters 1 and 2 on reading and writing. In addition, *Notes and Resources* discusses every method, every selection (with possible answers to all questions),
and every Writer on Writing.

TWO VERSIONS.   *The Bedford Reader* has a sibling. A shorter edition, *The
Brief Bedford Reader*, features fifty selections instead of seventy-two, including
five essays—rather than twelve—in Part Three.

ACKNOWLEDGMENTS

Hundreds of the teachers and students using *The Bedford Reader* over the
years have helped us shape the book. For this edition, the following teachers
offered insights from their experiences that encouraged worthy changes:
Sharon Anthony, Montgomery College, Germantown; Miriam Applebaum,
Baruch College, City University of New York; Mary Baumhover, Western
New Mexico University; Amy Beaudry, Fisher College; Lynette Beers, Saddle-
back College; Robin Bahr Casey, St. Peter-Marian Junior/Senior High School;
Wendi Chen, Minneapolis Community and Technical College; Jodi Cook,
Western Illinois University; Sandra Cooper, Central Florida Community
College; James Cotter, Mount St. Mary College; Janet Eber, County College
of Morris; Roger Ekins, Butte College; Cassandra Falke, Lamar State College,
Port Arthur; Richard Follett, Los Angeles Pierce College; Joanna Fulbright,

Ozarka Technical College; Judith Gardner, University of Texas at San Antonio; Daniel Glynn, Highland Community College; Barbara Goldthwait, Santa Monica College; Kay Grosso, Glendale Community College; Susan Jordan, Fisher College; Eunha Jung, Olympic College; Rita Kranidis, Montgomery College, Takoma Park; Tamara Kuzmenkov, Tacoma Community College; Jane LaRoque, Middlesex Community College; Patricia Leverentz, Pima Community College; Kimmarie Lewis, Lord Fairfax Community College; Joe Lostracco, Austin Community College, Rio Grande Campus; Kimberly Manning, Chaffey College; Manuel Martinez, Santa Fe Community College; Beth Maxfield, Blinn College; Todd McCann, Bay College, Escanaba; Gene McCarthy, Middlesex Community College; Charles McGranaghan, Western Nevada Community College; Richard Miller, Suffolk University; Lee Ann Montagne, Santa Fe Community College; David Moriarty, Middlesex Community College; Bernard Morris, Modesto Junior College; Rhonda Morris, Santa Fe Community College; Patricia Morrow, Middlesex Community College; Stephanie Pesce, Middlesex Community College; Paul Reid, Chippewa Valley Technical College; James Sodon, St. Louis Community College, Florissant Valley; Arlo Stoltenberg, North Iowa Area Community College; Olga Valbuena, Wake Forest University; John Wallman, University High School; Brian Ward, Valdosta State University; Jason Webb, Columbine High School; Jennifer Webb, Lakewood Senior High School; and Dianne Wilcox, Georgia Military College, Robins Air Force Base.

More than ever before, it seems, we owe a huge debt to the creative people at and around Bedford/St. Martin's. Charles Christensen, Joan Feinberg, Denise Wydra, Karen Henry, and Steve Scipione contributed insight and support. Karin Halbert, developing the book, was an imaginative problem solver, a comforting hand holder, a gentle prod, and an all-around angel. Her assistants—Stefanie Wortman, Christina Gerogiannis, and Anne Noyes—provided first-rate research and responded nimbly to any request. Mark Gallaher and Janice Weber helped to shape the book's apparatus and instructor's manual. Anna Palchik and Dorothy Bungert created the beautiful, very functional new design. Donna Dennison created the striking cover. Elizabeth Schaaf planned and oversaw the production of the book. And Arthur Johnson, working on a difficult schedule and yet with uncommon thoroughness and grace, transformed the raw manuscript into the book you hold.

CONTENTS

A writer with multiple sclerosis thinks she knows why the media carry so few images of disabled people like herself: Viewers might conclude, correctly, that "there is something ordinary about disability itself."

Responding to Nancy Mairs's "Disability," a student cites three current television programs to show positive changes in how the media portray people with disabilities.

MARIE JAVDANI   Plata o Plomo: *Silver or Lead*   68

Integrating information from varied sources, a student takes a global view of the US war on drugs.

PART TWO
THE METHODS   73

4   NARRATION: Telling a Story   75

Visual Image: *How Joe's Body Brought Him Fame Instead of Shame,* advertisement for Charles Atlas

DIFFERENCE

MAYA ANGELOU   *Champion of the World*   88

She didn't dare ring up a sale while the epic battle was on. A noted African American writer remembers from her early childhood the night when a people's fate hung on a pair of boxing gloves.

Maya Angelou on Writing   92

PAIRED
SELECTIONS

AMY TAN   *Fish Cheeks*   94

The writer remembers her teenaged angst when the minister and his cute blond son attended her family's Christmas Eve dinner, an elaborate Chinese feast.

Amy Tan on Writing   97

PAIRED
SELECTIONS

PAIRED
SELECTIONS

PERSONALITIES

"Neat people are lazier and meaner than sloppy people," asserts the writer. As she compares and contrasts, she takes up a cudgel and chooses sides.

**PAIRED
SELECTIONS**

An expert at comedic observation takes a humorous swing at the difference between the sexes. It hinges on the importance each sex gives to dirt and baseball.

A popular essayist complains about his "unspeakably dull" childhood, when he might have grown up like his partner, Hugh, amid monkeys and machete-wielding guards.

Face to face at Appomattox, Ulysses S. Grant and Robert E. Lee clearly personified their opposing traditions. But what the two Civil War generals had in common was more vital by far.

Trying to buy a skirt in a US department store leads the author to compare the relative disadvantages of women in Western and Muslim countries. Who's worse off?

In this short story, a mother weighs the interests of her two daughters, one who left home and one who didn't.

9   DIVISION OR ANALYSIS: Slicing into Parts   **335**

Visual Image: *Deconstructing Lunch,* cartoon by Roz Chast

WOMEN AND MEN

In this feminist view of marriage, the work of a wife is divided into its roles and functions. What a wonderful boon a wife is! Shouldn't every woman have one of her own?

**PAIRED
SELECTIONS**

Reading bedtime stories to his daughter, a writer discovers that fictional fathers remain stuck in the old negative molds: sloppy, unnurturing, neglectful.

A missile designer helped create the hard, highly molded Barbie doll. What are the implications for the millions of girls who grow up with this sexy toy?

The ambiguities of a World War II photograph prompt this student to explore a byway of the German Nazis' efforts at racial purification.

Visual Image: *Mounted Nazi Troops on the Lookout for Likely Polish Children,* photograph

In this fictional exchange, a daughter can barely insert two sentences into her mother's litany of instructions on how to become a lady, not a slut.

11　CAUSE AND EFFECT: Asking Why　**429**

Visual Image: *Garbage In...*, cartoon by Mike Thompson

GLOBALIZATION

Visiting an Indonesian sweatshop, this journalist discovers connections between herself and the young women working there—connections bearing the brand names London Fog, Esprit, and, of course, McDonald's.

PAIRED SELECTIONS

Forcing developing countries to put an end to child labor might not be the cure-all it seems. The children themselves, asserts this fiction writer and activist, could suffer much worse fates than working.

A critic and novelist presents an always radical idea for dealing with drug abuse: Legalize drugs. The effects will be less addiction and less crime.

According to a twenty-something writer, those who grew up in the age of AIDS have learned some unintended lessons, among them "chronic dishonesty and fear."

The narrator of this short story wonders: What compels him to watch a videotape of a murder over and over and over again?

With a sharp eye and ear, a native Californian observes how she and others respond to a series of earthquakes. Could this be "the Big One"?

Making war puts human beings in a class with ants and chimpanzees among the earth's species. Abolishing war, argues this critic, requires thinking differently about it.

Mickey Mouse changed over the decades, becoming softer and younger looking. A scientist with a flair for explanation proposes why and finds surprising parallels in human evolution.

Visual Images: *Mickey's Evolution During Fifty Years,* drawing; *The "Evolution" of Mickey Mouse,* chart; *Humans feel affection for animals with juvenile features,* drawing

With force and eloquence, an inspired leader champions the rights of African Americans and equality for all.

An adulterous woman is driven to suicide by her unforgiving family and village in China. A generation later, her American-born niece seeks to understand the story of someone whose name she has never dared to ask.

As a young British police officer, this famous writer faced a killer elephant and the expectations of a gleeful Burmese crowd. He could not take pride in his response.

Recalling both the pleasures and the pains of his boyhood, a Mexican American writer reflects on his two languages, Spanish and English, and his two cultures. His argument against bilingual education may provoke debate.

THEMATIC
CONTENTS

CHILDHOOD AND FAMILY

CLASS

COMMUNICATION

COMMUNITY

CULTURAL DIVERSITY

DEATH

ENVIRONMENT

ETHICS

GLOBALIZATION

HEALTH AND DISABILITY

HISTORY

HOMELESSNESS

HUMOR AND SATIRE

LAW

MANNERS AND MORALS

MARRIAGE

MEDIA

MEMORY

MINORITY EXPERIENCE

THE NATURAL WORLD

PSYCHOLOGY AND BEHAVIOR

READING, WRITING, AND LANGUAGE

SCIENCE AND TECHNOLOGY

SELF-DISCOVERY

SEXUALITY

SOCIAL CUSTOMS

SPORTS AND LEISURE

VIOLENCE

WAR AND NATIONAL SECURITY

WOMEN AND MEN

WORK

INTRODUCTION

WHY READ? WHY WRITE? WHY NOT PHONE?

Many prophets have predicted the doom of the word on paper, and they may yet be proved correct. We may soon be reading books and magazines mainly on pocket computers and communicating exclusively by e-mail. But even if we do discard paper and pens, the basic aims and methods of writing will not fundamentally change. Whether on paper or on screen, we will need to explain our thoughts to others plainly and forcefully.

In almost any career or profession you may enter, you will be expected to read continually and also to write. This book assumes that reading and writing are a unity. Deepen your mastery of one, and you deepen your mastery of the other. The experience of carefully reading an excellent writer, noticing not only what the writer has to say but also the quality of its saying, rubs off (if you are patient and perceptive) on your own writing. "We go to college," said the poet Robert Frost, "to be given one more chance to learn to read in case we haven't learned in high school. Once we have learned to read, the rest can be trusted to add itself *unto us*."

For any writer, reading is indispensable. It turns up fresh ideas; it stocks the mind with information, understanding, examples, and illustrations; it instills critical awareness of one's surroundings. When you have a well-stocked and girded mental storehouse, you tell truths, even small and ordinary truths. Instead of building shimmering spires of words in an attempt to make a reader think, "Wow, what a grade A writer," you write what most readers will find worth reading. Thornton Wilder, playwright and novelist, put this advice memorably: "If you write to *impress* it will always be bad, but if you write to *express* it will be good."

USING *THE BEDFORD READER*

The Selections

In this book, we trust, you'll find at least a few selections you will enjoy and care to remember. *The Bedford Reader* features work by many of the finest nonfiction writers and even a few sterling fiction writers and poets.

The selections deal with more than just writing and literature and such usual concerns of English courses; they cut broadly across a college curriculum. You'll find writings on science, history, business, popular culture, sociology, education, communication, the environment, technology, sports, politics, the media, and minority experience. Some writers recall their childhoods, their families, their problems and challenges. Some explore matters likely to spark controversy: drug use, funerals, sex roles, race relations, civil liberties in an age of terrorism. Some writers are intently serious; others, funny. In all, these seventy-two selections — including five stories and a poem — reveal kinds of reading you will meet in other college courses. Such reading is the usual diet of well-informed people with lively minds — who, to be sure, aren't found only on campuses.

The selections have been chosen with one main purpose in mind: to show you how good writers write. Don't feel glum if at first you find an immense gap in quality between E. B. White's writing and yours. Of course there's a gap: White is an immortal with a unique style that he perfected over half a century. You don't have to judge your efforts by comparison. The idea is to gain whatever writing techniques you can. If you're going to learn from other writers, why not go to the best of them? Do you want to know how to define an idea so that the definition is vivid and clear? Read Dagoberto Gilb's "Pride." Do you want to know how to tell a story about your childhood and make it stick in someone's memory? Read Maya Angelou. Incidentally, not all the selections in this book are the work of professional writers: Students, too, write essays worth studying, as proved by Doug Roberts, Marie Javdani, Jessica Cohen, Brad Manning, Linnea Saukko, Laila Ayad, Christine Leong, and Colleen Wenke.

Not all the selections in this book are solely verbal, either, for much of what we "read" in the world is visual information, such as in photographs and paintings, or visual-with-verbal information, such as in advertisements, films, and Web sites. In all, we include seventeen visual works. Some of them are subjects of writing, as when a poet comments on a painting or a writer analyzes a photograph. Other visual works stand free, offering themselves to be understood, interpreted, and perhaps enjoyed, just as prose and poetry do.

We combine visual material with written texts to further a key aim of *The Bedford Reader*: to encourage you to think critically about what you see, hear, and read, that is, to think with an open, questioning mind. Like everyone else, you face a daily barrage of words and pictures—from the media, from your courses, from relatives and friends. Mulling over the views of the writers, artists, and others represented in this book—figuring out their motives and strategies, agreeing or disagreeing with their ideas—will help you learn to manage, digest, and use, in your own writing, what you read and hear.

The Organization

As a glance over the table of contents will show, the selections in *The Bedford Reader* fall into two parts. In Part Two each of the ten chapters explains a familiar method of developing ideas, such as DESCRIPTION or CLASSIFICATION or DEFINITION, and the selections illustrate the method. Then Part Three offers an anthology of selections by well-known writers that illustrate how, most often, the methods work together.

These methods of development aren't empty jugs to pour full of any old, dull words. Neither are they straitjackets woven by fiendish English teachers to pin your writing arm to your side and keep you from expressing yourself naturally. The methods are tools for achieving your PURPOSE in writing, whatever that purpose may be. They can help you discover what you know, what you need to know, how to think critically about your subject, and how to shape your writing.

Suppose, for example, that you set out to explain what makes a certain popular singer unique. You want to discuss her voice, her music, her lyrics, her style. While putting your ideas down on paper, it strikes you that you can best illustrate the singer's distinctions by showing the differences between her and another popular singer, one she is often compared with. To achieve your purpose, then, you draw on the method of COMPARISON AND CONTRAST, and as you proceed the method prompts you to notice differences between the two singers that you hadn't dreamed of noticing. Using the methods, such little miracles of focusing and creating take place with heartening regularity. Give the methods a try. See how they help you reach your writing goals by giving you more to say, more that you think is worth saying.

Examining *The Bedford Reader*'s selections, you'll discover two important facts about the methods of development. First, they are flexible: Two people can use the same method for quite different ends, and just about any method can point a way into just about any subject in any medium. This flexibility is apparent in every method chapter:

- A photograph, advertisement, cartoon, or other image shows how the method can contribute to visual representation of an idea.
- Two sample paragraphs—one about television, one from a college text-book—illustrate the method's useful range.
- A short example shows the method in practice, as a student solves an actual writing problem such as crafting a résumé or advertising an apartment sublet.
- A pair of essays shows authors using the same method to focus on the same general subject but with different purposes and results.

In addition, half a dozen works of literature show how the methods can guide authors' explorations of subjects as diverse as the feelings depicted in a painting, the experiences of a young girl, or the compulsion to watch real-life crime.

The second point about the methods of development is this: A writer never sticks to just one method all the way through a piece of writing. Even when one method predominates, as in all the essays in Part Two, you'll see the writer pick up another method, let it shape a paragraph or more, and then move on to yet another method—all to achieve some overriding aim. In "Cookies or Heroin?" Marie Winn mainly defines the term *TV addiction*, but she also compares the addiction with drug and alcohol addiction, gives EXAMPLES of the addiction that include description, and examines the CAUSES AND EFFECTS of the addiction. The point is that Winn employs whatever methods suit her dual purpose of explaining what TV addiction is and con-vincing readers that it is, in fact, an addiction.

So the methods are like oxygen, iron, and other elements that make up substances in nature: all around us, indispensable to us, but seldom found alone and isolated, in laboratory-pure states. When you read an essay in a chapter called "Description" or "Classification," don't expect it to describe or classify in every line, but do notice how the method is central to the writer's purpose. Then, when you read the selections in Part Three, notice how the "elements" of description, example, comparison, definition, and so on rise to prominence and recede as the writer's need dictates.

The Journal Prompts, Questions, Writing Topics, and Glossary

After every selection you'll find a suggestion for responding in your journal to what you've just read. (See p. 35 for more on journal writing.) Then you'll find questions on meaning, writing strategy, and language that can help you analyze the selection and learn from it. (You can see a sample of how these questions work when we analyze Nancy Mairs's "Disability," starting on p. 20.) These questions are followed by at least four suggestions for writing, including one that proposes turning your journal entry into an essay, one that links the selection with one or two others in the book, and one that asks you to read the selection and write about it with your critical faculties alert (more on this in Chap. 1). More writing topics conclude each chapter.

In this introduction and throughout the following chapters, certain terms appear in CAPITAL LETTERS. These are words helpful in discussing both the selections in this book and the reading and writing you do. If you'd like to see such a term defined and illustrated, you can find it in the glossary, Useful Terms, at the back of this book. This section offers more than just brief definitions. It is there to provide you with further information and support.

Writers on Writing

We have tried to give this book another dimension. We want to show that the writers represented here do not produce their readable and informative text on the first try, as if by magic, leaving the rest of us to cope with writer's block, awkward sentences, and all the other difficulties of writing. Take comfort and cheer: These writers, too, struggled to make themselves interesting and clear. In proof, we visit their workshops littered with crumpled paper and forgotten coffee cups. In Chapter 2, when we discuss the writing process briefly and include an essay by a student, Doug Roberts, we also include his drafts and his thoughts about them. Then following most of the other selections are statements by the writers, revealing how they write (or wrote), offering their tricks, setting forth things they admire about good writing.

No doubt you'll soon notice some contradictions in these statements: The writers disagree about when and how to think about their readers, about whether outlines have any value, about whether style follows subject or vice versa. The reason for the difference of opinion is, simply, that no two writers follow the same path to finished work. Even the same writer may take the left instead of the customary right fork if the writing situation demands a change.

A key aim of providing Roberts's drafts and the other writers' statements on writing, then, is to suggest the sheer variety of routes open to you, the many approaches to writing and strategies for succeeding at it. At the very end of the book, an index points you toward the writers' comments on such practical matters as drafting, finding your point, and revising sentences.

PART ONE

READING, WRITING, AND RESEARCH

1

READING
CRITICALLY

Whatever career you enter, much of the reading you will do—for business, not for pleasure—will probably be hasty. You'll skim: glance at words here and there, find essential facts, catch the drift of an argument. To cross oceans of print, you won't have time to paddle: You'll need to hop a jet. By skimming, you'll be able to tear through screens full of electronic mail or quickly locate the useful parts of a long report.

But other reading that you do for work, most that you do in college, and all that you do in this book call for closer attention. You may be trying to understand a new company policy, seeking the truth in a campaign ad, researching a complicated historical treaty, or (in using this book) looking for pointers to sharpen your reading and writing skills. To learn from the selections here how to write better yourself, expect to spend an hour or two in the company of each one. Does the essay assigned for today remain unread, and does class start in five minutes? "I'll just breeze through this little item," you might tell yourself. But no, give up. You're a goner.

Good writing, as every writer knows, demands toil, and so does CRITICAL READING—reading that looks beneath the surface of a work, whether written or visual, seeking to understand the creator's intentions, the strategies for achieving them, and their worthiness. Never try to gulp down a rich and potent work without chewing; all it will give you is indigestion. When you're going to read an essay or study a visual image in depth, seek out some quiet place—a library, a study cubicle, your room (provided it doesn't also hold a cranky baby or two roommates playing poker). Flick off the radio, stereo, or television. The fewer the distractions, the easier your task will be and the more you'll enjoy it.

How do you read critically? Exactly how, that is, do you see beneath the surface of a work, master its complexities, gauge its intentions and techniques, judge its value? To find out, we'll model critical-thinking processes that you can apply to the selections in this book, taking a close look at an essay, Nancy Mairs's "Disability" (p. 13), and at an insurance advertisement that mingles the visual and the verbal (p. 28).

READING AN ESSAY

The Preliminaries

Critical reading starts before you read the first word of a piece of writing. Like a pilot circling an airfield, you take stock of what's before you, locating clues to the work's content and the writer's biases.

The Title

Often the title will tell you the writer's subject, as in Suzanne Britt's "Neat People vs. Sloppy People" or Stephanie Ericsson's "The Ways We Lie." Sometimes the title immediately states the THESIS, the main point the writer will make: "I Want a Wife." The title may set forth the subject as a question: "Why Don't We Complain?" Some titles spell out the method a writer proposes to follow: "Grant and Lee: A Study in Contrasts." The TONE of the title may also reveal the writer's attitude toward the material, as "The Plot Against People" or "Live Free and Starve" does.

Some titles reveal more than others. From Nancy Mairs's title, "Disability," we can infer that the author's subject is physical or mental impairment (although the inference could be wrong). Beyond that, we can't say where Mairs might take the subject. That is for us to find out as we read.

Whatever it does, a title sits atop its essay like a neon sign. It tells you what's inside or makes you want to venture in. To pick an alluring title for an essay of your own is a skill worth cultivating.

The Author

Whatever you know about a writer—background, special training, previous works, outlook, or ideology—often will help you guess something about the essay before you read a word of it. Is the writer on new taxes a political conservative? Expect an argument against added "revenue enhancement." Is the writer a liberal? Expect an argument that new social programs are worth the price. Is the writer a feminist? an athlete? an internationally renowned philosopher? a popular television comedian? By knowing something about a writer's background or beliefs, you may know beforehand a little of what he or she will say.

To help provide such knowledge, this book supplies biographical notes. The one on Nancy Mairs, included before "Disability" (p. 13), tells us that Mairs is a poet and nonfiction writer who has multiple sclerosis, a debilitating disease, and who strives to "speak the 'unspeakable'" about sensitive subjects. We can expect that in "Disability" Mairs writes frankly and thought provokingly from her experience as a person with disabilities.

Where the Work Was Published

Clearly, it matters to a writer's credibility whether an article called "Living Mermaids: An Amazing Discovery" appears in *Scientific American*, a magazine for scientists and interested nonscientists, or in a popular tabloid weekly, sold at supermarket checkout counters, that is full of eye-popping sensations. But no less important, examining where a work appears can tell you for whom the writer was writing.

In this book we'll strongly urge you as a writer to think of your AUDIENCE, your readers, and to try looking at what you write as if through their eyes. To help you develop this ability, we tell you something about the sources and thus the original readers of each essay you study, in a note just before the essay. (Such a note precedes "Disability" on p. 13.) After you have read the sample essay, we'll further consider how having a sense of your readers helps you write.

When the Work Was Published

Knowing in what year a work appeared may give you another key to understanding it. A 1988 essay on mermaids will contain statements of fact more recent and more reliable than an essay printed in 1700—although the older essay might contain valuable information, too, and perhaps some delectable language, folklore, and poetry. In *The Bedford Reader* the introductory note on every essay tells you not only where but also when the essay was originally printed. If you're reading an essay elsewhere — say, in one of the writer's books — you can usually find this information on the copyright page.

The First Reading

On first reading an essay, you don't want to bog down over every troublesome particular. Mairs's "Disability" is written for an educated audience, and that means the author may use a few large words when they seem necessary. If you meet any words that look intimidating, take them in your stride. When, in reading a rich essay, you run into an unfamiliar word or name, see if you can figure it out from its surroundings. If a word stops you cold and you feel lost, circle it in pencil; you can always look it up later. (In a little while we'll come back to the helpful habit of reading with a pencil. Indeed, some readers feel more confident with pencil in hand from the start.)

The first time you read an essay, size up the forest; later, you can squint at the acorns all you like. Glimpse the essay in its entirety. When you start to read "Disability," don't even think about dissecting it. Just see what Mairs has to say.

NANCY MAIRS

A self-described "radical feminist, pacifist, and cripple," NANCY MAIRS aims to "speak the 'unspeakable.'" Her poetry, memoirs, and essays deal with many sensitive subjects, including her struggles with the debilitating disease of multiple sclerosis. Born in Long Beach, California, in 1943, Mairs grew up in New Hampshire and Massachusetts. She received a BA from Wheaton College in Massachusetts (1964) and an MFA in creative writing (1975) and a PhD in English literature (1984) from the University of Arizona. While working on her advanced degrees, Mairs taught high school and college writing courses and served as project director at the Southwest Institute for Research on Women, where she is now a research associate. Her second book of poetry, *In All the Rooms of the Yellow House* (1984), received a Western States Arts Foundation book award. Her essays are published in *Plaintext* (1986), *Remembering the Bone-House* (1988), *Carnal Acts* (1990), *Ordinary Time* (1993), *Waist High in the World: A Life Among the Nondisabled* (1996), and *A Troubled Guest* (2001). Mairs reads two of her essays on the CD *Essays Out Loud* (2004).

Disability

As a writer afflicted with multiple sclerosis, Nancy Mairs is in a unique position to examine how the culture responds to people with disabilities. In this essay from *Carnal Acts*, she examines the media's depiction of disability and argues with her usual unsentimental candor that the media must treat disability as normal. The essay was first published in 1987 in the *New York Times*.

For months now I've been consciously searching for representation of myself in the media, especially television. I know I'd recognize this self because of certain distinctive, though not unique, features: I am a forty-three-year-old woman crippled with multiple sclerosis; although I can still totter short distances with the aid of a brace and a cane, more and more of the time I ride in a wheelchair. Because of these appliances and my peculiar gait, I'm easy to spot even in a crowd. So when I tell you I haven't noticed any women like me on television, you can believe me.

Actually, last summer I did see a woman with multiple sclerosis portrayed on one of those medical dramas that offer an illness-of-the-week like the daily special at your local diner. In fact, that was the whole point of the show: that this poor young woman had MS. She was terribly upset (understandably, I assure you) by the diagnosis, and her response was to plan a trip to Kenya while she was still physically capable of making it, against the advice of the young, fit, handsome doctor who had fallen in love with her. And she almost did it.

13

At least, she got as far as a taxi to the airport, hotly pursued by the doctor. But at the last she succumbed to his blandishments and fled the taxi into his manly protective embrace. No escape to Kenya for this cripple.

Capitulation into the arms of a man who uses his medical powers to strip one of even the urge toward independence is hardly the sort of representation I had in mind. But even if the situation had been sensitively handled, according to the woman her right to her own adventures, it wouldn't have been what I'm looking for. Such a television show, as well as films like *Duet for One* and *Children of a Lesser God*, in taking disability as its major premise, excludes the complexities that round out a character and make her whole. It's not about a woman who happens to be physically disabled; it's about physical disability and the determining factor of a woman's existence.

Take it from me, physical disability looms pretty large in one's life. But it doesn't devour one wholly. I'm not, for instance, Ms. MS, a walking, talking embodiment of a chronic incurable degenerative disease. In most ways I'm just like every other woman of my age, nationality, and socioeconomic background. I menstruate, so I have to buy tampons. I worry about smoker's breath, so I buy mouthwash. I smear my wrinkling skin with lotions. I put bleach in the washer so my family's undies won't be dingy. I drive a car, talk on the telephone, get runs in my pantyhose, eat pizza. In most ways, that is, I'm the advertisers' dream: Ms. Great American Consumer. And yet the advertisers, who determine nowadays who will get represented publicly and who will not, deny the existence of me and my kind absolutely.

I once asked a local advertiser why he didn't include disabled people in his spots. His response seemed direct enough: "We don't want to give people the idea that our product is just for the handicapped." But tell me truly now: If you saw me pouring out puppy biscuits, would you think these kibbles were only for the puppies of the cripples? If you saw my blind niece ordering a Coke, would you switch to Pepsi lest you be struck sightless? No, I think the advertiser's excuse masked a deeper and more anxious rationale: To depict disabled people in the ordinary activities of daily life is to admit that there is something ordinary about disability itself, that it may enter anybody's life. If it is effaced completely, or at least isolated as a separate "problem," so that it remains at a safe distance from other human issues, then the viewer won't feel threatened by her or his own physical vulnerability.

This kind of effacement or isolation has painful, even dangerous consequences, however. For the disabled person, these include self-degradation and a subtle kind of self-alienation not unlike that experienced by other minorities. Socialized human beings love to conform, to study others and then mold themselves to the contours of those whose images, for good reasons or bad, they come to love. Imagine a life in which feasible others—others you can hope to be like—don't exist. At the least you might conclude that there is something queer about you, something ugly or foolish or shameful. In the extreme, you might feel as though you don't exist, in any meaningful social sense, at all. Everyone else is "there," sucking breath mints and splashing cologne and swigging wine coolers. You're "not there." And if not there, nowhere.

But this denial of disability imperils even you who are able-bodied, and not just by shrinking your insight into the physically and emotionally complex world you live in. Some disabled people call you TAPs, or Temporarily Abled Persons. The fact is that ours is the only minority you can join involuntarily, without warning, at any time. And if you live long enough, as you're increasingly likely to do, you may well join it. The transition will probably be difficult from a physical point of view no matter what. But it will be a good bit easier psychologically if you are accustomed to seeing disability as a normal characteristic, one that complicates but does not ruin human existence. Achieving this integration, for disabled and able-bodied people alike, requires that we insert disability daily into our field of vision: quietly, naturally, in the small and common scenes of our ordinary lives.

———————————

Writing While Reading

In giving an essay a going-over, many readers find a pencil in hand as good as a currycomb for a horse's mane. The pencil (or pen or computer keyboard) concentrates the attention wonderfully, and, as often happens with writing, it can lead you to unexpected questions and connections. (Some readers favor markers that roll pink or yellow ink over a word or line, making the eye jump to that spot, but you can't use a highlighter to note *why* a word or an idea is important.) You can annotate your own books, underlining essential ideas, scoring key passages with vertical lines, writing questions in the margins about difficult words or concepts, venting feelings ("Bull!" "Yes!" "Says who?"). Here, as an example, are the jottings of one student, Doug Roberts, on a paragraph of Mairs's essay:

> I once asked a local advertiser why he didn't include disabled people in his spots. His response seemed direct enough: "We don't want to give people the idea that our product is just for the handicapped." But tell me truly now: If you saw me pouring out puppy biscuits, would you think these kibbles were only for the puppies of the cripples? If you saw my blind niece ordering a Coke, would you switch to Pepsi lest you be struck sightless? No, I think the advertiser's excuse masked a deeper and more anxious rationale: To depict disabled people in the ordinary activities of daily life is to admit that there is something ordinary about disability itself, that it may enter anybody's life. If it is effaced completely, or at least isolated as a separate "problem," so that it remains at a safe distance from other human issues, then the viewer won't feel threatened by her or his own physical vulnerability.

Marginal notes: Also would distract from purely commercial message — Offensive word — why? — ☆ Important — key to essay — ?

If a book is borrowed, you can accomplish the same thing by making notes on a separate sheet of paper or on your computer.

Whether you own the book or not, you'll need separate notes for responses that are lengthier and more substantial than the margins can contain, such as the informal responses, summaries, detailed analyses, and evaluations discussed below. For such notes, you may find a JOURNAL handy. It can be a repository of your ideas, a comfortable place to record meandering or direct thoughts about what you read. You may be surprised to find that the more you write in an unstructured way, the more you'll have to say when it's time to write a structured essay. (For more on journals, see p. 35.)

Writing and reading help you behold the very spine of an essay, as if in an X-ray view, so that you, as much as any expert, can judge its curves and connections. You'll develop an opinion about what you read, and you'll want to express it. While reading this way, you're being a writer. Your pencil tracks or keystrokes will jog your memory, too, when you review for a test, when you take part in class discussion, or when you want to write about what you've read.

Summarizing

It's usually good practice, especially with more difficult essays, to SUMMA-RIZE the content in writing to be sure you understand it or, as often happens, to come to understand it. We use summary all the time to fill friends in on the gist of a story—shrinking a two-hour movie to a single sentence, "This woman is recruited to be a spy, and she stops a ring of double agents." In summarizing a work of writing, you digest, *in your own words*, what the author says: You take the essence of the author's meaning, without the supporting evidence and other details that make that gist convincing or interesting. When you are practicing reading and the work is short (the case with the reading you do in this book), you may want to make this a two-step procedure: First write a summary sentence for every paragraph or related group of paragraphs; then summarize those sentences in two or three others that capture the heart of the author's meaning.

Here is a two-step summary of "Disability." (The numbers in parentheses refer to paragraph numbers in the essay.) First, the longer version:

(1) Mairs searches the media in vain for depictions of women like herself with disabilities. (2) One TV movie showed a woman recently diagnosed with multiple sclerosis, but she chose dependence over independence. (3) Such shows oversimplify people with disabilities by making disability central to their lives. (4) People with disabilities live lives and consume goods like everyone else, but the media ignore them. (5) Showing disability as ordinary would remind nondisabled viewers that they are vulnerable. (6) The media's exclusion of others like themselves deprives people with disabilities of role models and makes them feel undesirable or invisible. (7) Nondisabled viewers lose an understanding that could enrich them and would help them adjust to disability of their own.

Now the short summary:

Mairs believes that the media, by failing to depict disability as ordinary, both marginalize viewers with disabilities and impair the outlook and coping skills of the "temporarily abled."

(We're suggesting that you write summaries for yourself, but the technique is also useful when you discuss other people's works in your writing. Then you must use your own words or use quotation marks for the author's words, and either way you must acknowledge the source in a citation. See pp. 53 and 55–56.)

Thinking Critically

Summarizing will start you toward understanding the author's meaning, but it won't take you as far as you're capable of going, or as far as you'll need to go in school or work or just to live well in our demanding Information Age. Passive, rote learning (such as memorizing the times tables in arithmetic) won't do. You require techniques for comprehending what you encounter. But more: You need tools for discovering the meaning and intentions of an essay or case study or business letter or political message. You need ways to discriminate between the trustworthy and the not so and to apply what's valid in your own work and life.

We're talking here about critical thinking—not "negative," the common conception of *critical*, but "thorough, thoughtful, question asking, judgment forming." When you approach something critically, you harness your faculties, your fund of knowledge, and your experiences to understand, appreciate, and evaluate the object. Using this book—guided by questions on meaning, writing strategy, and language—you'll read an essay and ask what the author's purpose and main idea are, how clear they are, and how well supported. You'll isolate which writing techniques the author has used to special advantage, what hits you as particularly fresh, clever, or wise—and what *doesn't* work, too. You'll discover exactly what the writer is saying, how he or she says it, and whether, in the end, it was worth saying. In class discussions and in writing, you'll tell others what you think and why.

Critical thinking is a process involving several overlapping operations: analysis, inference, synthesis, and evaluation.

Analysis

Say you're listening to a new album by a band called the Alley Cats. Without thinking much about it, you isolate melodies, song lyrics, and instrumentals—in other words, you ANALYZE the album by separating it into its parts. Analysis is a way of thinking so basic to us that it has its own chapter (9) in this book. For reading in this book, you'll consciously analyze essays by looking at the author's main idea, support for the idea, special writing strategies, and other elements.

Analysis underlies many of the other methods of development discussed in this book, so that while you are analyzing a subject you might also (even unconsciously) begin classifying it, or comparing it with something else, or fig-uring out what caused it. For instance, you might compare the Alley Cats' new instrumentals with those on their earlier albums, or you might notice that the lyrics seem to be influenced by another band's. Similarly, in analyzing a poem you might compare several images of water, or in analyzing a journal article in psychology you might consider how the author's theories affect her interpre-tations of behavior.

Inference

Say that after listening to the Alley Cats' new album, you conclude that it reveals a preoccupation with traditional blues music and themes. Now you are using INFERENCE, drawing conclusions about a work based on your store of information and experience, your knowledge of the creator's background and biases, and your analysis. When you infer, you add to the work, making explicit what was only implicit.

In critical thinking, inference is especially important in discovering a writer's ASSUMPTIONS: opinions or beliefs, often unstated, that direct the writ-er's choices of ideas, support, writing strategies, and language. A writer who favors gun control may assume without saying so that some individual rights (such as the right to bear arms) may be infringed for the good of the commu-nity. A writer who opposes gun control may assume the opposite—that in this case the individual's right is superior to the community's.

Synthesis

What are the Alley Cats trying to accomplish with their new album? Is it different from their previous album in its understanding of the blues? Answer-ing such questions leads you into SYNTHESIS, linking elements into a whole, or linking two or more wholes. During synthesis, you use your special aptitudes, interests, and training to reconstitute the work so that it now contains not just the original elements but also your sense of their underpinnings and relation-ships. About an essay you might ask why the author elicits contradictory feel-ings from readers, or what this essay has to do with that other essay, or what this essay has to do with your life.

Analysis, inference, and synthesis overlap—so much so that it's often impossible to distinguish one from the other during critical thinking. To stave off confusion, in this book we use the word *analysis* to cover all of these oper-ations: identifying elements, drawing conclusions about them, *and* reconsti-tuting them.

Evaluation

Not all critical thinking involves EVALUATION, or judging the quality of the work. You'll probably form a judgment of the Alley Cats' new album (Is the band getting better or just standing still?), but often you (and your teachers) will be satisfied with a nonjudgmental reading of a work. ("Nonjudgmental" does not mean "uncritical": You will still be expected to analyze, infer, and synthesize.) When you *do* evaluate, you determine adequacy, significance, value. You answer a question such as whether an essay moves you as it was intended to, or whether the author has proved a case, or whether the argument is even worthwhile.

Analyzing "Disability"

The following comments on Nancy Mairs's "Disability" show how a critical reading can work. The headings "Meaning," "Writing Strategy" (p. 22), and "Language" (p. 24) correspond to those organizing the questions at the end of each essay.

Meaning

Purpose   "No man but a blockhead," declared Samuel Johnson, "ever wrote except for money." Perhaps the eighteenth-century critic, journalist, and dictionary maker was remembering his own days as a literary drudge in London's Grub Street; but surely most people who write often do so for other reasons.

When you read an essay, you'll find it rewarding to ask, "What is this writer's PURPOSE?" By purpose, we mean the writer's apparent reason for writing: what he or she was trying to achieve with readers. A purpose is as essential to a good, pointed essay as a destination is to a trip. It affects every choice or decision the writer makes. (On vacation, of course, carefree people sometimes climb into a car without a thought and go happily rambling around. A writer may ramble like that in an early draft, with good results. But in a final draft such wandering will leave the reader pleading, "Let me out!")

In making a simple statement of a writer's purpose, we might say that the writer writes *to entertain* readers, or *to explain* something to them, or *to persuade* them. To state a purpose more fully, we might say that a writer writes not just to persuade but "to tell readers a story to illustrate the point that when you are being cheated it's a good idea to complain," or not just to entertain but "to tell a horror story to make chills shoot down readers' spines." If the essay is an argument meant to convince, a fuller statement of its writer's purpose might be "to win readers over to the writer's opinion that San Antonio is the most livable city in the United States," or "to persuade readers to take action by writing their representatives and urging more federal spending for the rehabilitation of criminals."

"But," the skeptic might object, "how can I know a writer's purpose? I'm no mind reader, and even if I were, how could I tell what E. B. White was trying to do? He's dead and buried." And yet writers living and dead have revealed their purposes in their writing, just as visibly as a hiker leaves footprints.

What is Nancy Mairs's purpose in writing? If you want to be more exact, you can speak of her *main purpose* or *central purpose*, for "Disability" fulfills more than one. Mairs clearly wants to explain her view of the media as a person with disabilities, and she is not averse to entertaining with amusing details and wry language. But Mairs's larger purpose seems to be persuading "you who are able-bodied" that by omitting or marginalizing people with disabilities the media hurt the nondisabled as much as they do the disabled. She wants change.

How can you tell a writer's purpose? This is where analysis, inference, and synthesis come in. Mairs gives a glimpse of her purpose in her opening line: "For months now I've been consciously searching for representation of myself in the media, especially television." For several paragraphs she contrasts herself and what she *does* see in the media, but then she closes on her main point, her THESIS, through which she makes her purpose very clear.

Thesis   Every essay has—or should have—a point, a main idea the writer wants to communicate for a purpose. Some writers come right out and sum up this idea in a sentence or two, a THESIS STATEMENT. Mairs, for instance, builds her thesis over the course of the essay and then states it in paragraph 7:

> Achieving this integration [of seeing disability as normal], for disabled and able-bodied people alike, requires that we insert disability daily into our field of vision: quietly, naturally, in the small and common scenes of our ordinary lives.

Mairs holds a statement of her thesis for the end of her essay, but other authors state the thesis outright in the first or second paragraph, or they provide it in the middle, or they release it part by part, paragraph by paragraph. And some writers don't state a thesis at all, although it remains in the background controlling the essay and can be inferred by a critical reader.

Questioning the work   It's part of your job as an active reader to answer questions like these: What is the writer's purpose? How does it govern the writer's choices? Is it actually achieved? Does the thesis come through? How is it supported? Is the support adequate to convince you of the author's sincerity and truthfulness? (Such conviction is a basic transaction between writer and reader, even when the writer isn't seeking the reader's outright agreement or action.) Sometimes you'll be confused by a writer's point—"What *is* this about?"—and sometimes your confusion won't yield to repeated careful readings. That's when you'll want to toss the book or magazine aside in exasperation, but you won't always have the choice: A school or work assignment or just an urge to understand the writer's problem may keep you at it. Then it'll be up to you to figure out why the writer fails—in essence, to clarify what's unclear—by, say, digging for buried assumptions that you may not agree with or by spotting where facts and examples fall short.

We think Nancy Mairs supports her thesis well. At least as we see it, she achieves her apparent purpose of persuading us who are not disabled that the media should normalize disability for our own sakes. We appreciate the twist Mairs gives to the usual call for more representation of minorities in the media: Sure it will help the group depicted, she says, but no more than it helps the majority. If we are put off by the reminder that we may someday become disabled ourselves, that seems intentional on Mairs's part: Disability makes us uncomfortable because we are unfamiliar with it, and we shouldn't be.

Analyzing writers' purposes and their successes and failures makes you an alert and critical reader. Applied to your own writing, this analysis also gives you a decided advantage, for when you write with a clear-cut purpose in mind, aware of your assumptions, you head toward a goal. Of course, sometimes you just can't know what you are going to say until you say it, to echo the English novelist E. M. Forster. In such a situation, your purpose emerges as you write. But the earlier and more exactly you define your purpose, the easier you'll find it to fulfill.

Writing Strategy

To the extent that Nancy Mairs holds our interest and makes us think, it pays to ask, "How does she succeed?" (When a writer bores or angers us, we ask why he or she fails.) Conscious writers make choices intended to get their audience on their side so that they can achieve their purpose. These choices are what we mean by STRATEGY in writing.

Audience   Almost all writing is a *transaction* between a writer and an audience, maybe one reader, maybe millions. The success or failure of writing depends on the extent to which the writer achieves his or her purpose with the intended audience.

Mairs's original audience was the readers of the *New York Times*. She could assume educated readers with diverse interests. She could assume readers who, like the general population, are not themselves disabled or even familiar with disability, so she fills them in: "Take it from me, physical disability looms pretty large in one's life" (par. 4); "Imagine a life in which feasible others—others you can hope to be like—don't exist" (6). She could also assume readers who do not know her situation, so she takes pains to describe her disability (1) and her life (4).

For this thoughtful but somewhat blinkered audience, Mairs mixes a range of attitudes: plain talk ("I am a forty-three-year-old woman crippled with multiple sclerosis," par. 1), humor ("I put bleach in the washer so my family's undies won't be dingy," 4), and insistence ("...the advertisers, who determine nowadays who will get represented publicly and who will not, deny the existence of me and my kind absolutely," 4). The blend gives readers the facts they need, wins them over with common humanity and lightness, and conveys the gravity of the problem.

Methods of development   Part of a writer's strategy—Mairs's, too—is the methods used to discover and arrange ideas and information. Mairs notably uses several methods:

- With COMPARISON AND CONTRAST Mairs shows the similarities and differences between herself and a woman in a TV drama (pars. 2–4), between herself and nondisabled people (1, 4, 5), and between the effects on the disabled and on the nondisabled of not showing disability as ordinary (6–7).
- With EXAMPLES Mairs illustrates dramas she dislikes (2–3), the products she buys (4), and the ads in which people with disabilities might appear (5).
- With DESCRIPTION Mairs shows the helplessness of the woman in the TV drama (2), the flavor of her own daily life (4), and the bad feelings experienced by people with disabilities (6).
- With CAUSE AND EFFECT Mairs explains why disability is "effaced" (or rubbed out) from the media (5), how that affects people with disabilities (6), and how treating disability as ordinary could help the nondisabled (7).
- With ARGUMENT AND PERSUASION overall, Mairs presents and supports an opinion she hopes her readers will accept and perhaps even act on.

In drawing on a range of methods, Mairs is typical of nonfiction and even fiction writers. As we noted earlier, one method or another may predominate in a piece of writing (as argument does in Mairs's essay or NARRATION usually does in fiction), but other methods will help the writer explore the subject in paragraphs or shorter passages.

Structure   Aside from considering an audience's needs and attitudes and choosing the methods for developing ideas, probably no writing strategy is as crucial to success as finding an appropriate structure. Writing that we find interesting and clear and convincing almost always has UNITY (everything relates to the main idea) and COHERENCE (the relations between parts are clear). When we find an essay wanting, it may be because the writer got lost in digressions or couldn't make the parts fit together.

Sometimes structure almost takes care of itself. In NARRATION, for instance, events usually follow a chronological sequence, as they occurred in time. But when subject or method don't dictate a structure, then the writer must mold and arrange ideas to pique, hold, and direct our interest.

Nancy Mairs's structure is complex for a short essay: She introduces herself and her complaint that the media do not show people with disabilities (par. 1); dismisses a TV movie and other films centering on disability that don't satisfy her (2, 3); establishes her credentials as a consumer, someone advertisers *should* be appealing to (4); takes issue with an advertiser's view and suggests her own (5); describes the negative effects of "effacement" on people with disabilities (6); and describes the positive effects that normalizing disability would have on presently nondisabled people (7).

As often occurs in arguments, Mairs's organization builds to her main idea, her thesis, which readers might find difficult to accept at the outset. For much of the essay, Mairs prepares us to accept her opinion by establishing her credentials as a disabled woman, a TV and film viewer, a normal consumer, and a humorous (not bitter), sensitive, thoughtful person.

Whether gradually unfolding the main idea or hitting us with it right away, and however the support is arranged, the decisions come out of the writer's purpose: What is the aim? What do I want readers to think or feel? What's the best way to achieve that? As you'll see in this book, there are as many options as there are writers.

Language

To examine the element of language is often to go even more deeply into an essay and how it was made. Mairs, you'll notice, is a writer whose language is rich and varied. It isn't bookish. Many expressions from common speech lend her prose vigor and naturalness: "I can still totter" (par. 1), "the daily special at your local diner" (2), "Take it from me" (4), "sucking breath mints and

splashing cologne and swigging wine coolers" (6). These and other expressions lighten the essay. At the same time, Mairs is serious about her argument,
and she puts it in serious, firm words: "deny the existence of me and my kind
absolutely" (4), "This kind of effacement or isolation has painful, even dangerous consequences" (6), "this denial of disability imperils even you who are
able-bodied" (7).

Mairs's language not only animates and weights her meaning but also conveys her attitudes and elicits them from readers. It creates a TONE, the equivalent of tone of voice in speaking. Whether it's angry, sarcastic, or sad, joking
or serious, tone carries almost as much information about a writer's purpose as
the words themselves do. Mairs's tone, like her words, mixes lightness with
gravity, humor with intensity. Sometimes she uses IRONY, saying one thing but
meaning another, as in "If you saw my blind niece ordering a Coke, would you
switch to Pepsi lest you be struck sightless?" (par. 5). She's blunt, too, revealing intimate details about her personal hygiene and her feelings. Honest and
wry, she invites us to see the media's exclusion as ridiculous and then leads us
to her discomforting conclusion.

With everything you read, as with "Disability," it's instructive to study the
writer's tone so that you are aware of whether and how it affects you. Pay particular attention to the CONNOTATIONS of words—their implied meanings,
their associations. When one writer calls the homeless "society's downtrod-
den" and another calls them "human refuse," we know something of their attitudes and can use that knowledge to analyze and evaluate what they say about
homelessness. In Mairs's essay, the word with the strongest connotations may
be "cripple" (pars. 2, 5) because it calls up old, insensitive attitudes toward
people with disabilities. Mairs's use of the word reinforces her bluntness and
her frankness about her own condition. But perhaps she's also suggesting that
the old attitudes are still alive, still determining what we see in the media and
what we ask to see.

One other use of language is worth noting in Mairs's essay and in many
others in this book: FIGURES OF SPEECH, bits of colorful language not meant to
be taken literally. In one instance, Mairs says that people "study others and
then mold themselves to the contours of those whose images . . . they come to
love" (par. 6). That image of molding to contours is a *metaphor*, stating that
one thing (behavioral change) is another (physical change). Elsewhere Mairs
uses *understatement* ("Take it from me, physical disability looms pretty large in
one's life," 4) and *simile*, or stating that one thing is *like* another ("medical dramas that offer an illness-of-the-week like the daily special at your local diner,"
2). All the figures give Mairs's essay flavor and force. (More examples of figures
of speech can be found in Useful Terms, p. 701.)

Many questions in this book point to figures of speech, to oddities of tone, or to troublesome or unfamiliar words. We don't wish to swamp you in details or make you a slave to your dictionary; we only want to get you thinking about how meaning and effect begin at the most basic level, with the word. As a writer, you can have no traits more valuable to you than a fondness and respect for words and a yen to experiment with them.

THINKING CRITICALLY ABOUT VISUAL IMAGES

Does a particular billboard always catch your eye when you drive by it? Does a certain television commercial irritate you or make you smile? Do you look at the pictures in a magazine before you read the articles? If so, you're like everyone else in that you are subject to the visual representations coming at you continually, unbidden, from all around.

Much of the flood of visual information just washes over us, like noise to the eyes. Sometimes we do focus on an image or a whole sequence that interests us — maybe it tweaks our emotions or tells us something we want to know. But even then we aren't always thinking that an image, just as much as a sentence of words, was created by somebody for a reason. No matter what it is — Web advertisement, TV commercial, painting, music video, photograph, cartoon — a visual image originated with a creator or creators who had a purpose, an intention for how the image should look and how we, the viewers, should respond to it.

In their purposefulness, then, visual images are not much different from written texts, and they are no less open to critical thinking that will uncover their meanings and effects. To a great extent, the method for critically "reading" visuals parallels the one for essays outlined on pages 10–20. In short:

- *Get the big picture:* As when scoping out a written work, survey the image or sequence for a view of the whole and clues about its origins and purposes.
- *Analyze:* Discern the elements of the image or sequence.
- *Infer:* Interpret the underlying meanings of the elements and the ASSUMPTIONS and intentions of the work's creators.
- *Synthesize:* Understand how the elements function together to produce a whole and to deliver a message.
- Often, *evaluate:* Judge the quality, significance, or value of the work.

One other important parallel with critical reading of written works: Always write while examining a visual image or images. Jotting down responses, questions, and other notes will not only help you remember what you were thinking but also jog further thoughts into being.

To show the critical method in action, we'll look closely at the advertisement on page 28, which appeared in the magazine *US News & World Report*. Further examples of analyzing visual works appear elsewhere in *The Bedford Reader* as well. See pages 178 (a painting), 359 (a photograph), and 615 (drawings). In addition, Chapters 4–13 each open with a visual image that gives you a chance to try out the method yourself.

The Big Picture

To examine any visual representation, it helps first to get an overview, a sense of the whole. Try making some inquiries of the work:

- What is the source of the work? Who created it—for instance, a painter, a teacher, an advertiser—and when?
- What does the work show overall? What appears to be happening?
- At a glance, why was the work created—for instance, to educate, to sell, to shock, to entertain?

The example on the next page is obviously an advertisement, which we can assume was created by an advertising agency to suit the client, the St. Paul Companies (now called St. Paul Travelers). Like most advertisements, this one has a clear purpose: to encourage readers of *US News & World Report* to consider St. Paul for insurance. (Grasping the purpose of visual images is not always this easy. Sometimes you'll have to proceed through layers of thinking to grasp it.) The main selling tools in the ad, each occupying about half the page, are a photograph and a block of text. The photograph shows a young girl petting a huge rhinoceros. The text emphasizes the word *Trust*.

Analysis

After you've gained an overview of the visual work, begin focusing on the elements that contribute to the whole—not just the people, animals, or objects depicted but the background and what might be called the artistic elements of lighting, color, shape, and balance.

- Which elements of the image stand out? What is distinctive about each one?
- What does the composition of the image emphasize?
- If spoken or written words accompany the work, what do they say? How are they sized and placed in relation to the visual elements?

In the insurance advertisement, three elements are especially prominent: the improbable image of a little girl and a rhinoceros and the words *Trust* and

Trust is not being afraid even if you're vulnerable.

Is there someone who understands how frightening a situation can be? Someone who

believes fear can be dismantled when we are armed with confidence? Is there an insurance

company that is consistently rated superior by independent rating services – a company

with a 148 year history of providing strength in the face of uncertainty? Without Question.

Without Question. **The St Paul**
Property and Liability Insurance

St. Paul. In this context, we notice details as well: the girl wearing what seems to be a homespun dress, her head bent affectionately, her smooth hand against the rhinoceros's rough face; the relatively huge size of the rhinoceros, the dangerous upward thrust of its horn, the bright look of its eye; the waving grass at the figures' feet, receding to the stormy-looking horizon; the direct connection between the image and the word *Trust*; the small and sedate italic type for the rest of the written copy, which requires the viewer to concentrate on reading in order to get more information.

Inference

Identifying the elements of the visual representation leads you to consider what they mean and how the image's creator has selected and arranged them so that viewers will respond in certain ways. As when reading a written text critically, you make explicit what may only be implicit in the work.

- What do the elements of the work say about the creator's intentions and assumptions? In particular, what does the creator seem to assume about viewers' backgrounds, needs, interests, and values?
- If the work includes written or spoken words, how do they interact with the visual components?

We can guess at the intentions of the St. Paul ad's creators: Use an arresting image to grab the attention of *US News* readers, link image to copy so they'll read the copy, encourage them to look into buying St. Paul insurance so that ultimately they'll invest in it. We can infer the basic meaning of the ad without difficulty: Trust = St. Paul; St. Paul = Trust. But the message is also more complicated than that. In the photograph, the girl's homespun dress, the grassy savannah-like setting, the beastly rhino, and the very idea of a rhino responding tamely to a girl all suggest a primitive feeling or experience. The small-type copy elaborates on the message Trust = St. Paul by introducing another primitive feeling, fear. Trust = fearlessness despite vulnerability and uncertainty = confidence = St. Paul. The ad's creators seem to assume that viewers are well heeled (they read *US News*; they have assets to insure) and that they're anxious and cautious about their assets (they understand fear; they want insurance; they need to trust).

Synthesis

Linking the elements and your inferences about them, you'll move into a new conception of the visual representation, a sense of its overall intentions and effect.

- What general appeal does the work make to viewers? For instance, does it emphasize logical argument, emotion, or the creator's or subject's worthiness?
- What feelings, memories, moods, or ideas does the work seem intended to summon from viewers' own store of experiences? Why, given the purpose of the work, would its creator try to establish these associations?

The St. Paul ad appeals mainly to viewers' emotions—most obviously, their need for trust, less obviously (but more interestingly) their fear. Look again at the rhino's great size and its prominent and scary horn: The animal represents a clear threat to physical security and by extension to financial security. The girl—representing St. Paul—disarms the fearsome beast. The small-type copy asks its readers to act in part from logic (the company has a superior rating and performance history), but it and the photograph work hardest to stir up fear so that the audience will take refuge in St. Paul insurance. Backed up, no doubt, by plenty of market research, the ad's creators see strong anxiety among the prosperous readers of US News.

When using synthesis, you may often go outside the work itself to explore its cultural context. For instance, the St. Paul ad might be compared with other ads that use images of tamed nature or that play to fear.

Evaluation

Often in criticizing visual works, you'll take one step beyond synthesis to evaluate success or significance or value.

- Does the work seem to fulfill its creator's intentions? Does it do what the creator wanted?
- Apart from the creator's intentions, how does the work affect you? Does it move you? amuse you? bore you? offend you?
- Was the work worth creating?

The St. Paul ad seems to fulfill at least one of its creators' intentions: The image of the girl and the rhino is arresting. To us, the message of fear is culturally interesting—a typical insurance sales pitch, here worked especially hard. Whether it's successful, though, only the company can say. It doesn't sell us, but then we're not in the market for insurance.

2

WRITING
EFFECTIVELY

The CRITICAL THINKING discussed in the previous chapter will serve you in just about every role you'll play in life—consumer, voter, friend, parent. As a student and a worker, though, you'll find critical thinking especially important as the foundation for writing. Whether to demonstrate your competence or to contribute to discussions and projects, writing will be the main way you communicate with teachers, supervisors, and peers.

Like critical thinking, writing is no snap: As this book's Writers on Writing attest, even professionals do not produce thoughtful, detailed, attention-getting prose in a single draft. Writing well demands, and rewards, a willingness to work recursively—to begin tentatively, perhaps, and then to double back, to welcome change and endure frustration, to recognize and exploit progress. The path can be rocky and confusing, but you'll find it was worth following when your readers respond just as you hoped they would.

THE WRITING SITUATION

Any writing you do will occur in a specific situation: What are you writing about? Whom are you writing to? Why are you writing about this subject to these people? Subject, audience, and purpose are the main components in the writing situation, although others may figure as well, such as length or deadline.

Subject

Your subject may be specified or at least suggested in the writing assignment you receive. "Discuss one of the works we've read this semester in its historical and social context," reads a literature assignment; "Can you draw me up a proposal for holiday staffing?" asks your boss. If you're left to your own devices and nothing occurs to you, try the discovery techniques explained on pages 34–37 to find a subject that interests you.

In *The Bedford Reader* we've provided ideas for writing about the selections that will also give you practice in working with writing assignments. Immediately after each selection, a "Journal Writing" prompt encourages you to respond to the selection just for yourself. (See p. 35 for a discussion of journal writing.) Then, in "Suggestions for Writing," one assignment proposes turning that journal writing into an essay for others to read. Of the three or four other suggestions, one labeled "Critical Writing" asks you to take a deliberate, critical look at the selection, and another labeled "Connections" helps you relate the selection to one or two others in the book. You may not wish to take any of our suggestions as worded; they may merely urge your own thoughts toward what you want to say.

To give you an idea of the writing suggestions we provide, here are possibilities for Nancy Mairs's "Disability," the essay reprinted in the preceding chapter (p. 13):

Journal Writing

Do you agree that many people respond with discomfort to those who are disabled? What do you feel when you see a stranger using a wheelchair: pity? sympathy? curiosity? uncertainty? admiration? fear? something else? In your journal, set down your answers to these questions as honestly as you can. What do you think causes these feelings? Consider how they are colored by your experiences with disability— whether you are disabled yourself, know someone who is disabled, or have no first-hand experience with disability.

Suggestions for Writing

1. **FROM JOURNAL TO ESSAY.** Based on your journal reflections, write an essay that explains how your own responses to people with disabilities lead you to accept or dispute Mairs's call for depicting "disabled people in the ordinary activities of daily life."

2. Have media depictions of people with disabilities changed since Mairs wrote her essay in 1987? If so, how? If not, why? Write an essay in which you ANALYZE current media representations of disability, using specific examples to support your ideas.

3. Choose another group you think has been "effaced" in television advertising and programming—a racial, ethnic, or religious group, for instance. Write an essay detailing how and why that group is overlooked. How could representations of the group be incorporated into the media? What effects might such representation have?

4. **CRITICAL WRITING.** Reread this essay carefully. Mairs tells us about herself through details and through tone (for example, through IRONY, intensity, and humor). Write an essay on how Mairs's self-revelations do or do not help further her THESIS.

5. **CONNECTIONS.** In "On Compassion" (p. 195), Barbara Lazear Ascher writes about the way people who are comfortable tend to respond to homeless people on the street, and she suggests that compassion must be "learned by having adversity at our window." Does what Ascher asks in relation to homeless people resemble what Mairs asks in relation to disabled people? In an essay, discuss the similarities and differences between these two writers' views of how people's attitudes could or should change.

Audience and Purpose

We looked at AUDIENCE and PURPOSE in the previous chapter, as concerns of writers that can help us readers analyze their works. When you are *doing* the writing, considering audience and purpose moves from informative to necessary: Knowing whom you're addressing and why tells you what approach to take, what EVIDENCE to gather, how to arrange ideas, even what words to use.

You can conceive of your audience generally (your classmates? the readers of a newspaper?), but usually you'll want to think about the characteristics of readers that will affect how they respond to you:

- What do readers expect from writing like yours? A particular format or organization? Certain kinds of information? A customary level of formality?

- What do readers need to know if they are to understand you or agree with you? How much background should you provide? How thoroughly should you support your ideas? What kinds of evidence will be most effective?

- What in readers' own makeup will influence their responses? How old are they? Are they educated? Do they share your values? Are they likely to have some misconceptions about your subject?

While you are considering readers' backgrounds and inclinations, you'll also be refining your purpose. You may know early on whether you want to explain something about your subject or argue something about it—a general purpose. To be most helpful, though, your idea of purpose should include what you want readers to think or do as a result of reading your writing. For instance:

> To explain two treatments for autism in young children so that readers clearly understand the similarities and differences
>
> To defend term limits for state legislators so that readers who are now undecided on the issue will support limits
>
> To analyze Shakespeare's *Macbeth* so that readers see the strengths as well as the flaws of the title character
>
> To propose an online system for scheduling work shifts so that company managers decide to explore the options

We have more to say about audience and purpose in the introduction to each rhetorical method (Chaps. 4–13).

THE WRITING PROCESS

"The writing process" is not really a single process at all, not even for an individual writer. Some people work out meticulous plans before beginning to compose sentences; others find plans stifling and prefer to just start writing; still others will work one way for one project and a different way for another. Generally, though, writers do move through three rough stages between assignment or initial idea and finished work: discovery, drafting, and revision.

In examining these stages, we'll have the help of a student, Doug Roberts. Roberts wrote an essay for *The Bedford Reader* responding to Nancy Mairs's essay "Disability." Along with the final draft of his essay (pp. 46–47), Roberts also provided his notes and earlier drafts and his comments on his progress at each stage.

Discovery

During the first phase of the writing process, DISCOVERY, you'll feel your way into an assignment. This is the time when you critically examine any text or image that is part of the assignment and begin to generate ideas for writing. When writing about selections in this book, you'll be reading and rereading and writing, coming to understand the work, figuring out what you think of it, figuring out what you have to *say* about it. From notes during reading to jotted phrases, lists, or half-finished paragraphs after reading, this stage should always be a writing stage. You may even produce a rough draft. The important thing is to let yourself go: Do not, above all, concern yourself with making beautiful sentences or correcting errors. Such self-consciousness at this stage will only jam the flow of thoughts. If your idea of "audience" is "teacher with sharp pencil" (not, by the way, a fair picture), then temporarily blank out your audience, too.

Several techniques can help you let go and open up during the discovery stage, among them writing in a journal, freewriting, and using the methods of development.

Journal Writing

A JOURNAL is a notebook or tablet or computer file where you record your thoughts *for yourself.* (Teachers sometimes assign journals and periodically collect them to see how students are doing, but even in these situations the journal is for yourself.) In keeping a journal, you don't have to worry about being understood by a reader or making mistakes: You are free to write however you want to get your thoughts down.

Kept faithfully — say, for ten or fifteen minutes a day — a journal can limber up your writing muscles, giving you more confidence and flexibility as a writer. It can also provide a place to work out personal difficulties, explore half-formed ideas, make connections between courses, or respond to reading. Here, for instance, is Doug Roberts's initial journal entry on Nancy Mairs's "Disability":

> *Mairs is so right — I never thought of it that way, that seeing more people with disabilities and seeing disabilities as ordinary could really help people without disabilities. But aren't things a little better on TV now? What about the character in JAG, the one who lost his leg? His disability isn't "ordinary" exactly, but his character isn't all about his disability either. Need to think of more examples.*

Freewriting

Another technique for limbering up, but more in response to specific writing assignments than as a regular habit, is *freewriting.* When freewriting, you write without stopping for ten or fifteen minutes, not halting to reread, criticize, edit, or admire. You can use partial sentences, abbreviations, question marks for uncertain words. If you can't think of anything to write about, jot "can't think" over and over until new words come (they will).

You can use this technique to find a subject for writing or to explore ideas on a subject you already have. Of course, when you've finished, you'll need to separate the promising passages from the dead ends, using those promising bits as the starting place for more freewriting or perhaps a freely written first draft.

The Methods of Development

Since each method of development provides a different perspective on your subject, you can use the methods singly or together to discover possible ideas or directions. Say you already have a sense of your purpose for writing: Then you can search the methods for one or more that will help you achieve that purpose by revealing and focusing your ideas. Or say you're still in the dark about your purpose: Then you can apply each method of development systematically to throw light on your subject, as a headlight illuminates a midnight road, so that you see its possible angles.

The introductions to Chapters 4–13 suggest the purposes each method is suited for and some specific ways the method can open up your subject. For now, we've given some examples of how the methods can reveal responses, either direct or indirect, to Mairs's "Disability."

- *Narration:* Tell a story about the subject, possibly to enlighten or entertain readers or to explain something to them. Answer the journalist's questions: who, what, when, where, why, how? For instance, relate a day in the life of a person with a disability.
- *Description:* To explain or evoke the subject, focus on its look, sound, feel, smell, taste—the evidence of the senses. For instance, describe Mairs's feelings about her subject as revealed in her use of language.
- *Example:* Point to instances, or illustrations, of the subject that clarify and support your idea about it. For instance, give examples that illustrate the media's current representation of people with disabilities.
- *Comparison and contrast:* Set the subject beside something else, noting similarities or differences or both, for the purpose of either explaining or evaluating. For instance, compare and contrast characters with disabilities in two movies or TV shows.
- *Process analysis:* Explain step by step how to do something or how something works—in other words, how a sequence of actions leads to a particular result. For instance, explain a process for convincing advertisers to use people with disabilities in TV commercials.
- *Division or analysis:* Slice the subject into its parts or elements in order to show how they relate and to explain your conclusions about the subject. For instance, analyze Mairs's tone and its relation to her purpose.
- *Classification:* To show resemblances and differences among many related subjects, or the many forms of a subject, sort them into kinds or groups. For example, classify attitudes toward people with disabilities, physical and mental.

- *Cause and effect:* Explain why or what if, showing reasons for or consequences of the subject. For instance, explain how someone's life changed, and didn't change, as a result of disability.
- *Definition:* Trace a boundary around the subject to pin down its meaning. For instance, define *disability*.
- *Argument and persuasion:* Formulate an opinion or make a proposal about the subject. For instance, argue for a change in grocery or department stores to accommodate people who use wheelchairs.

Drafting

Sooner or later, the discovery stage yields to DRAFTING: writing out sentences and paragraphs, linking ideas, focusing them. For most writers, drafting is the occasion for exploring the relations among ideas, filling in the details to support them, beginning to work out the shape and aim of the whole. During drafting, you may clarify your purpose, try out different arrangements of material, or experiment with tone. Sometimes, though, you may find that just spelling out thoughts into complete sentences is challenge enough for a first draft, and you'll leave issues of purpose, structure, and tone for another round.

A few suggestions for drafting:

- Give yourself time, at least a couple of hours.
- Work in a place where you won't be disturbed.
- Stay loose so that you can wander down intriguing avenues or consider changing direction altogether.
- Don't feel compelled to follow a straight path from beginning to end. If the introduction is giving you fits, skip it until later.
- Keep your eyes on what's ahead, not on the pebbles underfoot—the possible mistakes, "wrong" words, and bumpy sentences that you can attend to later. This is an important message that many inexperienced writers miss: It's okay to make mistakes. You can fix them later.

The Thesis and the Thesis Statement

One important element that should receive some attention during drafting, or shortly after, is the THESIS, often stated in a THESIS STATEMENT of one or two sentences. The thesis, to recap page 21, is the main idea of a piece of writing, its focus. Without a focus, either expressed or implied, an essay wanders and irritates and falls flat. With a focus, an essay is much more likely to click.

On page 21 we gave one example of a thesis statement, from Nancy Mairs's "Disability." Here are some other examples from the essays in this book:

> These were two strong men, these oddly different generals [Ulysses S. Grant and Robert E. Lee], and they represented the strengths of two conflicting currents that, through them, had come into final collision.
> —Bruce Catton, "Grant and Lee: A Study in Contrasts"

> Inanimate objects are classified into three major categories—those that don't work, those that break down and those that get lost.
> —Russell Baker, "The Plot Against People"

> It is possible to stop most drug addiction in the United States within a very short time. Simply make all drugs available and sell them at cost.
> —Gore Vidal, "Drugs"

These diverse examples share a few important qualities:

- The authors assert opinions, taking positions on their subjects. They do not merely state facts, as in "Grant and Lee both signed the document ending the Civil War" or "Grant and Lee were different men."
- Each thesis statement projects a single idea. The thesis may have parts (such as Baker's three categories of objects), but the parts fit under a single umbrella idea.
- As you will see when you read the essays themselves, each thesis statement accurately forecasts the scope of its essay, neither taking on too much nor leaving out essential parts.
- Each thesis statement hints about the writer's purpose—we can tell that Catton and Baker want to explain, whereas Vidal wants mainly to persuade. (Explaining and persuading overlap a great deal; we're talking here about the writer's *primary* purpose.)

Every single essay in this book has a *thesis* because a central, controlling idea is a requirement of good writing. But we can give no rock-hard rules about the *thesis statement*—how long it must be or where it must appear in an essay or even whether it must appear. Indeed, the essays in this book demonstrate that writers have great flexibility in these areas, even within a given method. For your own writing, we advise stating your thesis explicitly and putting it near the beginning of your essay—at least until you've gained experience as a writer. The stated thesis will help you check that you have that necessary focus, and the early placement will tell your readers what to expect from your writing.

Revision

If it helps you produce writing, you may want to view your draft as a kind of dialog with readers, fulfilling their expectations, answering the questions you imagine they would ask. But some writers save this kind of thinking for the next stage, REVISION. Literally "re-seeing," revision is the price you pay for the freedom to experiment and explore. Initially the work centers on you and your material, but gradually it shifts into that transaction we spoke of earlier between you and your reader. And that means stepping outside the intense circle of you-and-the-material to see the work as a reader will, with whatever qualities you imagine that reader to have. Questions after most essays in this book ask you to analyze how the writers' ideas of their readers have influenced their writing strategies, and how you as a reader react to the writers' choices. These analyses will teach you much about responding to your own readers.

Like many writers, you will be able to concentrate better if you approach revision as at least a two-step process. First you question fundamental matters, using a checklist like this one:

QUESTIONS FOR REVISION

Will my purpose be clear to readers? Have I achieved it?
What is my thesis? Have I proved it?
Is the essay unified (all parts relate to the thesis)?
Is the essay coherent (the parts relate clearly)?
Will readers be able to follow the organization?
Have I given enough details, examples, and other specifics for readers to
     understand me and stay with me?
Is the tone appropriate for my purpose?
Have I used the methods of development to full advantage?

When these deeper issues are resolved, you then look at the surface of the writing in the step called *editing*:

QUESTIONS FOR EDITING

Do PARAGRAPH breaks help readers grasp related information?
Do TRANSITIONS tell readers where I am making connections, additions,
     and other changes?
Are sentences smooth and concise? Do they use PARALLELISM, EMPHASIS,
     and other techniques to clarify meaning?
Do words say what I mean, and are they as vivid as I can make them?
Are my grammar and punctuation correct?
Are any words misspelled?

Two-step revision is like inspecting a ship before it sails. First check under the water for holes to make sure the boat will stay afloat. Then look above the water at what will move the boat and please the passengers: intact sails, sparkling hardware, gleaming decks.

Collaboration

Your writing teacher may ask you to spend some time talking with your classmates, as a whole class or in small groups or pairs. You may analyze the essays in this book (perhaps answering the end-of-essay questions), read each other's journals or drafts, or plot revision strategies. Such conversation and collaboration—voicing, listening to, and arguing about ideas—can help you develop more confidence in your writing and give you a clearer sense of audience. One classmate may show you that your introduction, which you thought was lame, really worked to get her involved in your essay. Another classmate may question you in a way that helps you see how the introduction sets up expectations in the reader, expectations you're obliged to fulfill. Doug Roberts received classmates' comments on the first draft of his paper about Nancy Mairs's "Disability" (see p. 43).

You may at first be anxious about collaboration: How can I judge others' writing? How can I stand others' criticism of my own writing? These are natural worries, and your teacher will try to help you with both of them—for instance, by providing a checklist to guide your critique of your classmates' writing. (The first checklist on the previous page works for reading others' drafts as well as your own.) With practice and plentiful feedback, you'll soon appreciate how much you're learning about writing and what a good effect that knowledge has on your work. You're writing for an audience, after all, and you can't beat the immediate feedback of a live one.

AN ESSAY-IN-PROGRESS

In the following pages, you have a chance to watch Doug Roberts as he develops an essay through journal notes and several drafts. His topic is the second of the writing suggestions given on pages 32–33—about current media representations of people with disabilities—which he had already started exploring in his journal (p. 35). Roberts's journal notes during each stage enlighten us about his thinking as he proceeds through the writing process.

Reading and Drafting

Journal Notes on Reading

Essay first published in 1987. What would Mairs think of today's portrayals of disability?

"For months now I've been consciously searching for representation of myself in the media" (¶ 1)
     —"representation of myself" = multidimensional character, not flat, dependent character with MS from "illness-of-the-week" medical drama (¶ 2).
     —Criticizes characters with disability as "determining factor" (¶ 3). Instead wants characters who just happen to have a disability.

Ads are afraid to show people with disabilities as normal bec. a threat to viewers — would make them "admit that there is something ordinary about disability itself, that it may enter anybody's life" (¶ 5).

Negative effects of media's treatment of disability:
     —for disabled people: "self-degradation and a subtle kind of self-alienation" (¶ 6)
     —for "Temporarily Abled Persons": "imperils" them — they won't be accustomed to seeing disability as a "normal characteristic" (¶ 7)

I agree we should "insert disability daily into our field of vision: quietly, naturally, in the small and common scenes of our ordinary lives" (¶ 7). Has it happened in today's media?
     —Lt. Roberts, guy who lost his leg on JAG: not quite what Mairs wants, because his struggle with his new disability was a major issue. But he's rounded out with other important plot lines.
     —Joey, deaf character on West Wing: Mairs would like that her deafness isn't the focus. We do see her interpreter, though.
     —Also the character in a wheelchair on Malcolm in the Middle? Christopher Reeve and Michael J. Fox?

I think I have some evidence here to answer question 2, about current media depictions of disability. The characters of Joey and Roberts are an improvement over the character Mairs criticizes in ¶ 2. Their disabilities aren't the "determining factor" in their lives. But does Mairs think disability should always be treated as background? Wouldn't that be unrealistic? I want to look at how a character's struggle with disability can sometimes make for a positive image.

First Draft

Nancy Mairs trashes movies, television shows, and commercials for rarely featuring characters who just happen to be disabled. Advertisements ignore disability altogether, and when movies and television feature characters with disabilities, they focus on the disability. The examples Mairs gives do seem to support her argument--especially the show she calls "one of those medical dramas that offer an illness-of-the-week like the daily special at your local diner"--but this is from 1987.

Since then, the media has begun treating disability more sensitively. Take for example Stevie Kenarban (Malcolm in the Middle), Lieutenant Bud Roberts (JAG), and Joey Lucas (The West Wing). Stevie uses a wheelchair, wheezes, labors to speak, and struggles to live a "normal" teenage life. Bud, who lost the lower half of his leg during the series, is preoccupied with adjusting to his new disability, and frustrated by how it affects his job. Joey, a deaf polling expert, has a sign language interpreter who "translates" her signs and the other characters' speech. But while disability is always present for these characters, it is not the only thing that is important in their lives. Stevie's life is in many ways like every teenager's. Bud eventually regains his professional status and does well at his job. Joey is indispensable to the White House.

Maybe Mairs would appreciate Joey, whose disability is never much of a focus, but she would probably take issue with Stevie and Bud, for the reason that their disabilities aren't background. But is it very realistic for her to expect the programs to ignore the very real difficulties these characters face? Even Joey needs to accommodate constantly with the use of a sign language interpreter. And Bud and Stevie naturally have more problems, showing them represents a positive image of disability as surmountable like divorce, addiction, financial peril, etc.

The media gives the same message through its depiction of former actor Michael J. Fox as a man who deals with his disability (Parkinson's Disease) in an uplifting manner. When former Superman Christopher Reeve was still alive, his ability to cope with his paralysis from a riding accident was treated with similar respect. These portraits may leave plenty of blind spots, but the media's focus on their struggles shows us that disability isn't necessarily devastating.

The media still has far to go, but in the two decades since Mairs wrote, progress has been made.

Revising

Peer Responses to First Draft

Is the first sentence of para. 2 your thesis? It's pretty vague--"things have changed a bit." Maybe you could spell this out. What things? Changed how?

—Michael Spellmyer

I like the examples you've thought of from today's media, but can you add more details about Stevie, Bud, and Joey? I haven't seen West Wing or Malcolm in the Middle, so I don't know anything about the characters on those shows.

—Jessie Wang

You do a good job showing how the media's portrayal of disability has changed since Mairs wrote her essay, but do you really need to include Fox and Reeve? They don't seem to fit--they're not fictional characters. Also, your conclusion seems abrupt.

—Julia Gomez

Journal Notes on First Draft

This is a good start, but it has some big holes. As Michael pointed out, my thesis isn't very clear, and then I jump right into discussing today's TV shows. The idea is there—that the media have made progress—but I need to state this more clearly in ¶ 1. Also, the word "trashes" isn't right—too slangy and strong.

The next paragraph covers too much ground and not very well—need more detail for readers like Jessie who don't know the shows. Do 2 paragraphs—one to introduce each character, and the next to discuss how the shows handle disability.

I'm glad Julia said to omit Michael J. Fox and Christopher Reeve. They don't really relate. The lame conclusion needs a rewrite, too—it's tacked on and incomplete (mention Joey—just the type of character Mairs calls for).

Revised Draft

Disability in the Media

In her essay "Disability,"   *points out that*
∧ Nancy Mairs ~~trashes~~ movies, television shows, and commercials ~~for~~ rarely
      e
featur~~ing~~ characters who just happen to be disabled. Advertisements ignore disability altogether, and when movies and television feature characters with
                                                                                        flat
disabilities, they focus on the disability. The examples Mairs gives do seem ~~to~~
                                character in the
~~support her argument~~--especially the ∧ show she calls "one of those medical

dramas that offer an illness-of-the-week like the daily special at your local
diner"~~—but this is from 1987.~~ *(p. no.).*

But Mairs wrote her essay in 1987. Since then the media has begun treating disability more sensitively. We have a long way to go until we see "something ordinary about disability itself" (p. no.), but some recent shows have presented characters for whom disability "complicates but does not ruin human existence" (p. no.).

Three recent TV series—JAG, Malcolm in the Middle, and The West Wing— feature complex characters with disabilities. JAG's Lieutenant Bud Roberts is a loyal and diligent attorney who lost his leg during the series. Malcolm's Stevie Kenarban is a sensitive, brilliant teenager who has asthma and uses a wheelchair. And West Wing's Joey Lucas is an insightful polling expert who is deaf and uses sign language to communicate with the White House staff.

~~Since then, the media has begun treating disability more sensitively.~~

~~Take for example Stevie Kenarban (Malcolm in the Middle), Lieutenant Bud~~
For Stevie, Bud, and Joey, disability is always present.
~~Roberts (JAG), and Joey Lucas (The West Wing).~~ Stevie ~~uses a wheelchair,~~

wheezes, labors to speak, and struggles to live a "normal" teenage life.

Bud~~, who lost the lower half of his leg during the series,~~ is preoccupied with
the lightweight cases assigned to him while he rehabilitates.
adjusting to his new disability, and frustrated by ~~how it affects his job.~~

Joey~~, a deaf polling expert,~~ has a sign language interpreter who "translates"

her signs and the other characters' speech. But while disability is always

present for these characters, it is not the only thing that is important in
: like his friend
their lives. Stevie's life is in many ways like every teenager's~~. Bud eventually~~
Malcolm, he obsesses over girls, rebels against his parents, and gets into trouble
~~regains his professional status and does well at his job. Joey is indispensable~~
over pranks. Bud eventually returns fully to his job, skillfully handles difficult cases,
~~to the White House.~~
and receives a promotion. Joey is indispensable to the White House, brought in to
help analyze and diffuse crises in the presidency.

essentially background, never discussed by her or
Maybe Mairs would appreciate Joey, whose disability is~~never much of a~~
other characters. But Mairs   find   still unsatisfactory
~~focus, but she~~ would probably ~~take issue with~~ Stevie and Bud, for the reason

that their disabilities aren't background. But is it very realistic for her to
caused by   disabilities
expect the programs to ignore the very real difficulties these characters face?

Even Joey needs to accommodate constantly with the use of a sign language

interpreter. And Bud and Stevie naturally have more problems, showing them

represents a positive image of disability as surmountable like divorce, addic-
and other problems that you often see treated in movie and TV
tion, financial peril, ~~etc.~~
dramas. Disability doesn't necessarily have to be devastating.

~~The media gives the same message through its depiction of former actor Michael J. Fox as a man who deals with his disability (Parkinson's Disease) in an uplifting manner. When former Superman Christopher Reeve was still alive, his ability to cope with his paralysis from a riding accident was treated with similar respect. These portraits may leave plenty of blind spots, but the media's focus on their struggles shows us that disability isn't necessarily devastating.~~

This is precisely the message that both disabled and "temporarily abled" people need to see.

                                                              B
The media still has far to go, but in the two decades since Mairs wrote, *the media has at least made progress.* ~~progress has been made.~~ *in showing characters with disabilities and especially characters like Joey, for whom disability is ordinary.*

Editing

Journal Notes on Revised Draft

This hangs together much better now; more coherent. The thesis is clearer. Every paragraph builds on the last, and each one analyzes how disability is treated in the media, addressing Mairs's concerns.

Clean up errors ("media" is plural), and also clear up some things: In ¶ 1, the "illness-of-the-week" blurs the focus of the intro. In ¶ 4, say why Bud and Stevie "naturally" have more problems than Joey. Also ¶ 4 is awkward—fix sentences.

Add page numbers for Mairs quotations and Works Cited!

Edited Paragraph

                       might
~~Maybe~~ Mairs ~~would~~ appreciate Joey, whose disability is essentially background, never discussed by her or other characters. But Mairs would probably
                                                because
find Stevie and Bud still unsatisfactory, ~~for the reason that~~ their disabilities
                              , though,
aren't background. ~~But~~ is it very realistic ~~for her to expect the programs~~ to ignore the very real difficulties caused by these characters' disabilities? Even Joey needs to accommodate constantly with ~~the use of~~ a sign language inter-
        The other two characters   *: Bud's disability is very*
preter. ~~And Bud and Stevie~~ naturally have more problems, ~~showing them~~
recent, and Stevie is very young. Showing their struggles and successes
represents a positive image of disability as surmountable, like divorce, addic-
              the   sorts of personal
tion, financial peril, and other problems ~~that you often see~~ treated in movie
                    need not
and TV dramas. Disability ~~doesn't necessarily have to~~ be devastating.

Final Draft

We have annotated Roberts's final draft to show something of how it works. Roberts's purpose is to analyze how much progress, if any, the media have made in representing people with disabilities in the way Nancy Mairs calls for. For this purpose, he draws heavily on DIVISION or ANALYSIS, examining the characters in current TV shows. He uses COMPARISON AND CONTRAST to develop his analysis. Detailed EXAMPLES provide his main support.

Disability in the Media

In her essay "Disability," Nancy Mairs points out that television programs, movies, and commercials rarely feature characters who just happen to be disabled. Advertisements ignore the physically challenged altogether, and when movies and television feature characters with disabilities, they focus on the disability. The examples Mairs gives do seem flat, with characters who are defined by their disabilities. But Mairs wrote her essay in 1987, and since then the media have begun treating disability more sensitively. We're a long way from seeing "something ordinary about disability itself" (14), but some recent shows have presented characters for whom disability "complicates but does not ruin human existence" (15).

> *Introduction explains Mairs's viewpoint and sets up Roberts's analysis.*

> *Thesis statement establishes Roberts's main idea.*
>
> *Page numbers in parentheses refer to "Work Cited" at end of paper. (See also p. 57.)*

Three recent TV series--JAG, Malcolm in the Middle, and The West Wing--feature complex characters with disabilities. JAG's Lieutenant Bud Roberts is a loyal and diligent attorney who loses the lower half of a leg during the series. Malcolm's Stevie Kenarban is a sensitive, brilliant teenager who has asthma and uses a wheelchair. And West Wing's Joey Lucas is an insightful polling expert who is deaf and uses sign language to communicate with White House staff.

> *Examples provide support for the thesis.*

For Stevie, Bud, and Joey, disability is always present. Stevie wheezes, labors to speak, and struggles to live a "normal" teenage life. Bud is preoccupied with physical and psychological adjustments to his new disability, and he is frustrated by the lightweight cases assigned to him while he rehabilitates. Joey travels everywhere with a sign-language interpreter who "translates" her signs and the other characters' speech. But present as it is for these characters, disability is not everything. Stevie's life is in many ways every

> *Analysis of examples shows how they support the thesis.*

teenager's: like his friend Malcolm, he obsesses over girls, rebels against his parents, and gets into trouble over pranks. Bud eventually returns fully to his job, skillfully handles difficult cases, and receives a promotion. Joey is indispensable to the White House, brought in to help analyze and diffuse crises in the presidency.

Mairs might appreciate Joey, whose disability is essentially background, never discussed by her or other characters. Mairs might find Bud and Stevie still unsatisfactory because their disabilities aren't background. Is it realistic, though, to ignore the very real difficulties caused by these characters' disabilities? Even Joey needs to accommodate constantly with a sign-language interpreter. The other two characters naturally have more problems: Bud's disability is very recent, and Stevie is very young. Showing their struggles and their successes actually represents a positive image of disability as surmountable, like divorce, addiction, financial peril, and the other sorts of personal problems treated in movie and TV dramas. Disability need not be devastating.

Comparison and contrast highlight similarities and differences in the ways disability is portrayed.

Examples lead to a question about Mairs's viewpoint.

This is precisely the message that both disabled and "temporarily abled" people alike need to see. The media still have far to go in showing characters with disabilities and especially characters like Joey, for whom disability is ordinary. But in the two decades since Mairs wrote, the media have at least made progress.

Conclusion reasserts thesis and summarizes.

Work Cited

Mairs, Nancy. "Disability." The Bedford Reader. Ed. X. J. Kennedy, Dorothy M. Kennedy, and Jane E. Aaron. 9th ed. Boston: Bedford, 2006. 13-15.

"Work Cited" gives complete publication information for Mairs's essay. (See also p. 59.)

3

USING AND DOCUMENTING SOURCES

When you write about them, the selections in this book serve as your sources: Either you ANALYZE them or you use them to support your own ideas. Writing with sources will occupy you for much of your academic career, as you rely on books, periodical articles, interviews, Web sites, electronic databases, and other materials to establish and extend your own ideas.

This chapter introduces the essentials of using sources: evaluating them (below), integrating source material into your own text (p. 52), avoiding plagiarism (p. 55), and documenting sources using the style of the Modern Language Association, or MLA (p. 56).

CRITICAL THINKING ABOUT SOURCES

Working with sources, you have an opportunity and an obligation to think critically—to analyze, infer, synthesize, and evaluate as described on pages 18–20 and 26–30. Of course, you want every potential source to be relevant to your subject and your approach. But you also want it to be reliable— that is, based on good evidence, carefully reasoned. If a source's evidence is shaky or its opinions are strongly biased, you may still be able to use the source, but you'll want to balance it with others that are more reliable.

The following guidelines apply to both print and online sources. Special guidelines for online sources begin on the facing page.

Relevance and Reliability

To determine a source's relevance and reliability, ask yourself a series of questions:

- What is the PURPOSE of the source, and who is the source's intended AUDIENCE?
- Is the material a primary or a secondary source?
- Is the author an expert? What are his or her credentials?
- Does the author's bias affect the reliability of his or her argument?
- Does the author support his or her argument with EVIDENCE that is complete and up to date?

Purpose and Audience

The potential sources you find may have been written for a variety of reasons — for instance, to inform the public, to publish new research, to promote a product or service, to influence readers' opinions about a particular issue. While the first two of these purposes might lead to a balanced approach to the subject, the second two should raise yellow caution flags: Watch for bias that undermines the source's reliability.

A source's intended audience can suggest relevance. Was the work written for general readers? Then it may provide a helpful overview but not much detail. Was the work written for specialists? Then it will probably cover the topic in depth, but it may be difficult to understand.

Primary Versus Secondary Sources

Primary sources are works by people who conducted or saw events first-hand. They include research reports, eyewitness accounts, diaries, and personal essays as well as novels, poems, and other works of literature. Secondary sources, in contrast, present and analyze the information in primary sources and include histories, reviews, and surveys of a field. Both types of source can be useful in research writing. For example, if you were writing about the debate over John F. Kennedy's assassination, you might seek an overview in books that discuss the evidence and propose theories about what happened — secondary sources. But you would be remiss not to read eyewitness accounts and law-enforcement documents — the primary sources.

Author's Credentials and Bias

Before you use a source to support your ideas, investigate the author's background to be sure that he or she is trustworthy. Look for biographical information in the introduction or preface of a book or in a note at the beginning or end of an article. Is the author an expert on the topic? Do other writers cite the author of your source in their work?

Investigating the author's background and credentials will probably uncover any bias as well—that is, the author's preference for a particular view of an issue. Actually, bias itself is not a problem: Everyone has a unique outlook created by experience, training, and even research techniques. What does matter is whether the author deals frankly with his or her bias and argues reasonably despite it. (See Chap. 13 for a discussion of reasoning.)

Evidence

Look for strong and convincing evidence to support the ideas in a source: facts, examples, reported experience, expert opinions. A source that doesn't muster convincing evidence, or much evidence at all, is not a reliable source. For very current topics, such as in medicine or technology, the source's ideas and evidence should be as up to date as possible.

Online Sources

You have two paths to online sources: the Web site of your school's library and your own Web browser. Always start with the library path: It leads to scholarly journals, reputable newspapers, and other sources that you trust because they have passed through filters of verification, editing, and library review. The same is not necessarily true of online sources you reach directly. Anyone can put anything on the Internet, so you're as likely to find the rantings of an extremist or an advertisement posing as science as you are to find reasonable opinions and scholarly research.

Use the criteria discussed above—gauging purpose, audience, bias, and other factors—for all online sources, including those found through the library. But broaden your evaluation when considering sources you reach directly.

Authorship or Sponsorship

Often, you won't be able to tell easily, or at all, who put a potential source on the Internet and thus whether that author or sponsor is credible and reliable. Sometimes an abbreviation in an electronic address contains a clue to the origin of a source: *edu* for educational institution, *gov* for government body, *org* for nonprofit organization, *com* for commercial organization. More specific background on the author or sponsor may require digging. On Web sites look for pages that have information about the author or sponsor or links to such information on other sites. In discussion groups ask anonymous authors for information about themselves. If you can't identify an author or a sponsor at all, you probably should not use the source.

Links or References to Sources

Most reliable sources will acknowledge borrowed evidence and ideas and tell you where you can find them. Some but not all online sources will do the same: A Web site, for instance, may provide links to its sources. Check out source citations that you find to be sure they represent a range of views. Be suspicious of any online work that doesn't acknowledge sources at all.

Currency

Online sources tend to be more current than print sources, which can actually be a disadvantage: The most current information may not have been tested by others and so may not be reliable. Always seek to verify recent information in other online sources or in print sources.

If they aren't tended regularly by their authors or sponsors, online sources can also be deceptive — that is, they may seem current but actually be out of date. Look for a date of copyright, publication, or last revision to gauge currency. If you don't find a date (and often you won't), compare the source with others you know to be recent before using its information.

INTEGRATING SOURCE MATERIAL

Use the ideas and information in sources to support your own ideas, not to direct or overwhelm them. Depending on the importance and complexity of source material, you may summarize it, paraphrase it, or quote it directly. Then you want to work it into your own text smoothly and informatively.

Summary, Paraphrase, and Quotation

When you summarize or paraphrase a source, you express its ideas in your own words. When you quote, you use the source's exact words, in quotation marks. *All summaries, paraphrases, and quotations must be acknowledged in source citations.*

Summary

With SUMMARY you use your own words to condense a paragraph, an entire article, or even a book into a few lines that convey the source's essential meaning. We discuss summary as a reading technique on pages 17–18, and the advice and examples there apply here as well. For another example, here is a summary of Barbara Lazear Ascher's "On Compassion," which appears on pages 195–97.

> SUMMARY   Ascher shows how contact with the homeless can be unsettling and depressing. Yet she also suggests that these encounters are useful because they can teach others to be more compassionate (195–97).

Notice how the summary identifies the source author and page numbers and uses words that are *not* the author's. (Any of Ascher's distinctive phrasing would have to be placed in quotation marks.)

Paraphrase

A PARAPHRASE usually restates a specific passage, again in words different from those of the original author. Use paraphrase when a source's idea or data but not its exact words will strengthen your own idea. Here is a quotation from Ascher's essay and a paraphrase of it:

> ORIGINAL QUOTATION   "Could it be that the homeless, like [Greek dramatists], are reminding us of our common humanity? Of course, there is a difference. This play doesn't end—and the players can't go home."

> PARAPHRASE   Ascher points out an important distinction between the New York City homeless and the characters in Greek tragedies: The homeless are living real lives, not performing on a stage (197).

As with a summary, note that a paraphrase cites the original author and page number. Here is another example of paraphrase, this from an essay about immigration by David Cole.

> ORIGINAL QUOTATION   "If we are collectively judged by how we treat immigrants—those who appear to be 'other' but will in a generation be 'us'—we are not in very good shape."

> PARAPHRASE   Cole argues that the way native-born Americans deal with immigrants reflects badly on the native-born citizens themselves. He also points out that today's immigrants will be part of tomorrow's mainstream society (110).

Quotation

Quotations from sources can both support and enliven your own ideas—
if you choose them well. When analyzing a primary source, such as a work of
literature or a historical document, you may need to quote many passages in
order to give the flavor of the author's words and evidence for your analysis.
With secondary sources, however, too many quotations will clutter an essay
and detract from your own voice. Select quotations that are relevant to the
point you are making, that are concise and pithy, and that use lively, bold, or
original language. Sentences that lack distinction—for example, a statement
providing statistics on economic growth between 1999 and 2004—should
almost always be paraphrased.

Always enclose quotations in quotation marks and cite the source author
and page number.

Introduction of Source Material

When you summarize, paraphrase, or quote a source, you want to introduce the borrowed material so that it fits into your sentences and readers
know what to make of it. In the passage below, the writer drops a quotation
awkwardly into her sentence and doesn't clarify how the quotation relates to
her idea.

> NOT INTRODUCED   The problem of homelessness is not decreasing, and "It is
> impossible to insulate ourselves against what is at our very doorstep" (Ascher
> 197).

In the following revision, however, the writer indicates with "As Ascher says"
that she is using the quotation to reinforce her point. These words also link
the quotation to the writer's sentence.

> INTRODUCED   The problem of homelessness is not decreasing, nor is our
> awareness of it, however much we wish otherwise. As Ascher says, "It is
> impossible to insulate ourselves against what is at our very doorstep" (197).

You can introduce source material into your sentence by interpreting it
and by mentioning the author in your text—both techniques illustrated in
the previous example. The introductory phrase "As Ascher says" has a number of variations:

> According to one authority . . .
>
> John Eng maintains that . . .
>
> The author of an important study, Hilda Brown, observes that . . .
>
> Ascher, the author of "On Compassion," has a different view, claiming . . .

For variety, such a phrase can also fall elsewhere in the quotation.

> "It is impossible," Ascher says, "to insulate ourselves against what is at our very doorstep" (197).

When you omit something from a quotation, signal the omission with the three spaced periods of an ellipsis mark as shown:

> "It is impossible to insulate ourselves . . . ," says Ascher (197).
> In Ascher's view, "Compassion . . . must be learned . . ." (197).

PLAGIARISM

Take a look at this attempt to paraphrase the quotation we saw earlier by David Cole.

> ORIGINAL QUOTATION   "If we are collectively judged by how we treat immigrants—those who appear to be 'other' but will in a generation be 'us'—we are not in very good shape."
>
> ATTEMPTED PARAPHRASE   Cole argues that if we are judged as a group by how we treat immigrants—those who seem to be different but eventually will be the same—we are in bad shape (110).

This is PLAGIARISM—the theft of someone's ideas or written work. Even though the writer identifies Cole as the source of the information, the language essentially remains the same. It is not enough to change a few words—"collectively" to "as a group," "in a generation" to "eventually," "not in very good shape" to "in bad shape." A paraphrase or summary must express the original idea in an entirely new way, both in word choice and in sentence structure. Even more blatant plagiarism, of course, would have repeated Cole's statement exactly as he wrote it, without quotation marks *or* a source citation. Plagiarism also occurs when a writer neglects to cite a source at all—if, for example, a writer paraphrased Ascher's comparison of the homeless with actors in a Greek drama, as on page 53, but did not mention Ascher's name.

Plagiarism and the Internet

The Internet has made plagiarism both easier and riskier. Whether accidentally or deliberately, you can download source material directly into your own document with a few clicks of a mouse. And you can buy complete papers from term-paper sites. *Using downloaded material without credit, even accidentally, or turning in someone else's work as your own, even if you paid for it, is plagiarism.*

The chances of being caught plagiarizing from the Internet have also increased. Teachers can use search engines and plagiarism-detection programs to match phrases in students' papers with the same words anywhere on the Internet.

Common Knowledge

Not all information from sources must be cited. Some falls under the category of common knowledge—facts so widely known or agreed upon that they are not attributable to a specific source. The statement "World War II ended after the United States dropped atomic bombs on Hiroshima and Nagasaki, Japan" is an obvious example: Most people recognize this statement as true. But some lesser-known information is also common knowledge. You may not know that President Dwight Eisenhower coined the term *military-industrial complex* during his 1961 farewell address; still, you could easily discover the information in encyclopedias, in books and articles about Eisenhower, and in contemporary newspaper accounts. The prevalence of the information and the fact that it is used elsewhere without source citation tell you that it's common knowledge.

In contrast, a scholar's argument that Eisenhower waited too long to criticize the defense industry, or the president's own comments on the subject in his diary, or an opinion from a Defense Department report in 1959—any of these needs to be credited. Unlike common knowledge, each of them remains the property of its author.

SOURCE CITATION USING MLA STYLE

On the following pages we explain the documentation style of the Modern Language Association, as described in the *MLA Handbook for Writers of Research Papers*, 6th edition (2003). This style—used in English, foreign languages, and some other humanities—involves a brief parenthetical citation in the text that refers to an entry in a list of works cited at the end of the text:

PARENTHETICAL TEXT CITATION
The homeless may be to us what tragic heroes were to the ancient Greeks (Ascher 197).

ENTRY IN LIST OF WORKS CITED
Ascher, Barbara Lazear. "On Compassion." The Bedford Reader. Ed. X. J. Kennedy, Dorothy M. Kennedy, and Jane E. Aaron. 9th ed. Boston: Bedford, 2006. 195-97.

By providing the author's name and page number in your text citation, you give the reader just enough information to find the source in the list of works cited and then find the place in the source where the borrowed material appears.

MLA Parenthetical Citations

When citing sources in your text, you have two options:

- You can identify both the author and the page number within parentheses, as in the Ascher example on the preceding page.
- You can introduce the author's name into your own sentence and use the parentheses only for the page number, as here:

Wilson points out that sharks, which have existed for 350 million years, are now more diverse than ever (301).

A work with two or three authors

More than 90 percent of the hazardous waste produced in the United States comes from seven major industries, all energy-intensive (Romm and Curtis 70).

A work with more than three authors

With more than three authors, name all the authors, or name only the first author followed by "et al." ("and others"). Use the same form in your list of works cited.

Gilman herself created the misconception that doctors tried to ban her story "The Yellow Wallpaper" when it appeared in 1892 (Dock, Allen, Palais, and Tracy 61).

Gilman herself created the misconception that doctors tried to ban her story "The Yellow Wallpaper" when it appeared in 1892 (Dock et al. 61).

An entire work

Reference to an entire work does not require a page number.

Postman argues that television is destructive because of the nature of the medium itself.

An electronic source

Most electronic sources can be cited like print sources, by author's name or, if there is no author, by title. If a source numbers screens or paragraphs instead of pages, give the reference number as in the following model, after "par." (one paragraph), "pars." (more than one paragraph), "screen," or "screens." For a source with no reference numbers at all, use the preceding model for an entire work.

> One nurse questions whether doctors are adequately trained in tending patients' feelings (Van Eijk, pars. 6-7).

A work in more than one volume

If you cite two or more volumes of the same work, identify the volume number before the page number. Separate volume number and page number with a colon.

> According to Gibbon, during the reign of Gallienus "every province of the Roman world was afflicted by barbarous invaders and military tyrants" (1: 133).

Two or more works by the same author(s)

If you cite more than one work by the same author or authors, include the work's title. If the title is long, shorten it to the first one or two main words. (The full title for the first citation below is Death at an Early Age.)

> In the 1960s Kozol was reprimanded by his principal for teaching the poetry of Langston Hughes (Death 83).

> Kozol believes that most people do not understand the effect that tax and revenue policies have on the quality of urban public schools (Savage Inequalities 207).

An unsigned work

Cite an unsigned work by using a full or shortened version of the title.

> In 1995 concern about Taiwan's relationship with China caused investors to transfer capital to the United States ("How the Missiles Help" 45).

An indirect source

Use "qtd. in" ("quoted in") to indicate that you found the source you quote within another source.

> Despite his tendency to view human existence as an unfulfilling struggle, Schopenhauer disparaged suicide as "a vain and foolish act" (qtd. in Durant 248).

A literary work

Because novels, poems, and plays may be published in various editions, the page number may not be enough to lead readers to the quoted line or passage. For a novel, specify the chapter number after the page number and a semicolon.

> Among South Pacific islanders, the hero of Conrad's Lord Jim found "a totally new set of conditions for his imaginative faculty to work upon" (160; ch. 21).

For a verse play or a poem, omit the page number in favor of line numbers.

> In "Dulce Et Decorum Est," Wilfred Owen undercuts the heroic image of warfare by comparing suffering soldiers to "beggars" and "hags" (lines 1-2) and describing a man dying in a poison-gas attack as "guttering, choking, drowning" (17).

If the work has parts, acts, or scenes, cite those as well (below: act 1, scene 5, lines 16–17).

> Lady Macbeth worries about her husband's ambition: "Yet I do fear thy nature; / It is too full o' the milk of human kindness" (1.5.16-17).

More than one work

> In the post-Watergate era, journalists have often employed aggressive reporting techniques not for the good of the public but simply to advance their careers (Gopnik 92; Fallows 64).

MLA List of Works Cited

Your list of works cited is a complete record of your sources. Follow these guidelines for the list:

- Title the list "Works Cited." Do not enclose the title in quotation marks.
- Double-space the entire list.
- Arrange the sources alphabetically by the last name of the first author.
- Begin the first line of each entry at the left margin. Indent the subsequent lines of the entry one-half inch or five spaces.

Following are the essentials of a works-cited entry:

- Reverse the names of the author, last name first, with a comma between. If there is more than one author, give the others' names in normal order.

- Give the full title of the work, capitalizing all important words. Underline the titles of books and periodicals; use quotation marks for the titles of parts of books and articles in periodicals.
- Give publication information. For books, this information includes city of publication, publisher, date of publication. For periodicals, this information includes volume number, date of publication, and page numbers for the article you cite. For online sources such as Web sites, this information includes the date you consulted the source and the URL, or electronic address. (See pp. 63–66 for more on electronic sources.)
- Use periods between parts of each entry.

You may need to combine the models below for a given source—for instance, combine "A book with two or three authors" and "A book with an editor" for a book with two or three editors.

Books

A book with one author

Tuchman, Barbara W. <u>The March of Folly: From Troy to Vietnam</u>. New York: Knopf, 1984.

A book with two or three authors

Silverstein, Olga, and Beth Rashbaum. <u>The Courage to Raise Good Men</u>. New York: Viking, 1994.

Trevor, Sylvia, Joan Hapgood, and William Leumi. <u>Women Writers of the 1920s</u>. New York: Columbia UP, 1998.

A book with more than three authors

You may list all authors or only the first author followed by "et al." ("and others"). Use the same form in your parenthetical text citation.

Kippax, Susan, R. W. Connel, G. W. Dowsett, and June Crawford. <u>Gay Communities Respond to Change</u>. London: Falmer, 2004.

Kippax, Susan, et al. <u>Gay Communities Respond to Change</u>. London: Falmer, 2004.

More than one work by the same author(s)

Kozol, Jonathan. <u>Death at an Early Age: The Destruction of the Hearts and Minds of Negro Children in the Boston Public Schools</u>. Boston: Houghton, 1967.

---. <u>Savage Inequalities: Children in America's Schools</u>. New York: Crown, 1991.

A book with an editor

Gwaltney, John Langston, ed. <u>Drylongso: A Self-Portrait of Black America</u>. New York: Random, 1980.

A book with an author and an editor

Orwell, George. <u>The Collected Essays, Journalism and Letters of George Orwell</u>. Ed. Sonia Orwell and Ian Angus. New York: Harcourt, 1968.

A later edition

Mumford, Lewis. <u>Herman Melville: A Study of His Life and Vision</u>. 2nd ed. New York: Harcourt, 1956.

A work in a series

Hall, Donald. <u>Poetry and Ambition</u>. Poets on Poetry. Ann Arbor: U of Michigan P, 1988.

An anthology

Glantz, Michael H., ed. <u>Societal Responses to Regional Climatic Change</u>. London: Westview, 2004.

Cite an entire anthology only when you are citing the work of the editor or you are cross-referencing it, as in the Ascher and Quindlen models below and on the next page.

A selection from an anthology

The numbers at the end of the following entry are the page numbers on which the entire cited selection appears.

Kellog, William D. "Human Impact on Climate: The Evolution of an Aware-ness." <u>Societal Responses to Regional Climatic Change</u>. Ed. Michael H. Glantz. London: Westview, 2004. 283-96.

If you cite more than one selection from the same anthology, you may give the anthology as a separate entry and cross-reference it by the editor's or editors' last names in the selection entries.

Ascher, Barbara Lazear. "On Compassion." Kennedy, Kennedy, and Aaron 195-97.

Kennedy, X. J., Dorothy M. Kennedy, and Jane E. Aaron, eds. <u>The</u>
<u>Bedford Reader</u>. 9th ed. Boston: Bedford, 2006.

Quindlen, Anna. "Homeless." Kennedy, Kennedy, and Aaron 200-02.

A reference work

Cheney, Ralph Holt. "Coffee." <u>Collier's Encyclopedia</u>. 2004 ed.

"Versailles, Treaty of." <u>The New Encyclopaedia Britannica: Macropaedia</u>.
15th ed. 1990.

Periodicals: Journals, Magazines, and Newspapers

An article in a journal with continuous pagination throughout the annual volume

In many journals the pages are numbered consecutively for an entire
annual volume of issues, so that the year's fourth issue might run from pages
240 to 320. For this type of journal, give the volume number after the journal
title, followed by the year of publication in parentheses, a colon, and the page
numbers of the article.

Clayton, Richard R., and Carl G. Leukefeld. "The Prevention of Drug
Use Among Youth: Implications of Legalization." <u>Journal of Primary</u>
<u>Prevention</u> 12 (2004): 289-301.

An article in a journal that pages issues separately

Some journals begin page numbering at 1 for each issue. For this kind of
journal, give the issue number after the volume number and a period.

Vitz, Paul C. "Back to Human Dignity: From Modern to Postmodern Psychology." <u>Intercollegiate Review</u> 31.2 (2002): 15-23.

An article in a monthly or bimonthly magazine

Fallows, James. "Why Americans Hate the Media." <u>Atlantic Monthly</u> Feb.
2001: 45-64.

An article in a weekly magazine

Gopnik, Adam. "Read All About It." <u>New Yorker</u> 12 Dec. 2002: 84-102.

An article in a newspaper

Gorman, Peter. "It's Time to Legalize." <u>Boston Sunday Globe</u> 28 Aug.
2004, late ed.: 69+.

The page number "69+" means that the article begins on page 69 and continues on a later page. If the newspaper is divided into lettered sections, give both section letter and page number, as in "A7."

An unsigned article

"How the Missiles Help California." Time 1 Apr. 2001: 45.

A review

Bergham, V. R. "The Road to Extermination." Rev. of Hitler's Willing
    Executioners, by Daniel Jonah Goldhagen. New York Times Book
    Review 14 Apr. 1996: 6.

CD-ROMs and Other Portable Media

For portable databases (CD-ROMs as well as diskettes and magnetic tapes), the content of the citation depends on whether the database is a periodical.

For a periodical, follow the models given earlier to provide full publication information. Add the title of the electronic source, the medium (for instance, "CD-ROM"), the name of the vendor or distributor, and the date of electronic publication:

Rausch, Janet. "So Late in the Day." Daily Sun 10 Dec. 2003, late ed.: C1.
    Daily Disk. CD-ROM. Cybernews. Jan. 2004.

Treat a portable database that is not a periodical as if it were a book, but provide the medium and any edition or version after the title.

"China." Concise Columbia Encyclopedia. CD-ROM. 2004-05 ed. Redmond:
    Microsoft, 2004.

Online Sources

Online sources vary greatly, and they may be and often are updated. Your aim in citing such a source should be to tell what version you used and how readers can find it for themselves. The following example includes (1) author's name, (2) the title of the work used, (3) information for the print version of the source, (4) the title of the online site, (5) the date of electronic publication, (6) the date the source was consulted, and (7) the source's complete URL (electronic address) in angle brackets (<>).

Loewenstein, Andrea Freud. "My Learning Disability: A (Digressive) Essay."
College English 66 (2004): 585-602. National Council of Teachers
of English. July 2004. 3 Aug. 2004 <http://www.ncte.org/portal/
30_view.asp?id+=117302>.

The following models show various kinds of additional information to be inserted between these basic elements. If some information is unavailable, list what you can find.

A work from a library subscription service

Library subscription services are usually available over your library's Web site and include EBSCOhost, LexisNexis, ProQuest, and InfoTrac. Provide basic information for sources you obtain from these services, as in the preceding example. In addition, provide (1) the name of the database, (2) the name of the subscription service, (3) the name of the subscribing institution (most likely your school), and (4) the name of the library. If the subscription service provides source URLs that are temporary or are unique to the subscribing library, give the URL of the service's home page (as in the example) or end with the date of your access.

Conway, Daniel W. "Reading Henry James as a Critic of Modern Moral
Life." Inquiry 45 (2002): 319-30. Academic Search Elite. EBSCOhost.
Santa Clara U, Orradre Lib. 20 Apr. 2004 <http://www.epnet.com>.

An online scholarly project or professional site

Include the names, if any, of the editor and of the institution or organization that sponsors the project or site.

Shanks, Thomas, "The Case of the Cyber City Network." Markkula Network
for Applied Ethics. Ed. Kirk Hanson. 14 Aug. 2004. Santa Clara U.
12 Dec. 2004 <http://www.scu.edu/ethics/cybercity.html>.

If you are acknowledging the entire project or site rather than a short work within it, begin the entry with the project or site title.

An online personal site

Provide the date of electronic publication if it differs from the date of your access.

McClure, Mark. "Speakers." <u>Online Calendar of Shakespeare Conferences</u>.
     18 Apr. 2004. 23 May 2004 <http://www.mwc.edu/~mcclure/
     sa_spkrs.html>.

An online book

For a book published independently, after the title add any editor's or
translator's name, either the publication information for a print version (as in
the following model) or the date of electronic publication, and any sponsor-
ing institution or organization.

Murphy, Bridget. <u>Fictions of the Irish Emigration</u>. Cambridge: Harvard UP,
     1998. 5 Apr. 2003 <http://www.historicalfictions.unv.edu/
     irel_murph.html>.

For a book published as part of a scholarly project, give any information about print publication and then follow the model on the previous page
for a scholarly project.

An article in an online journal

Base an entry for an online journal article on one of the models on
page 62 for a print journal article.

Sjostrand, Odile. "Law Philosophy in <u>Mansfield Park</u>." <u>Jane Austen Quar-</u>
     <u>terly</u> 33.1 (1999). 12 Oct. 2004 <http://facstaff.uww.edu/JAusten/
     home.html>.

Omit page numbers (as in the example) if the journal does not provide them.
If instead it provides another indication of length (sections, screens, paragraphs), give the total for the article (for instance, "15 pars.").

An article in an online newspaper

Base an entry for an online newspaper article on the model on page 62 for
a print newspaper article.

Smith, Craig S. "A French Employee's Work Celebrates the Sloth Ethic."
     <u>New York Times on the Web</u> 3 June 2004. 26 Nov. 2004 <http://
     www.nytimes.com/2004/06/03/france.html?8hpib>.

An article in an online magazine

Base an entry for an online magazine article on one of the models on
pages 62–63 for a print magazine article.

Brus, Michael. "Proxy War." <u>Slate</u> 9 July 2004. 12 July 2004 <http://
    www.slate.com/Features/profile/profile.html>.

Electronic mail

Give as the title the text of the e-mail's subject line, in quotation marks.
"To the author" in the example means to you, the author of the paper.

Dove, Chris. "Re: Bishop's Poems." E-mail to the author. 7 May 2004.

A posting to an online discussion group

For a posting to a discussion group, give the posting's subject line as the
title, and follow the title with "Online posting," the date of the posting, and
the title of the group (without underlining or quotation marks).

Forrester, Jane. "Embracing Mathematics." Online posting. 21 Sept. 2004.
    Math Teaching Discussion List. 22 Sept. 2004 <http://www.acc.edu/
    gargantuan/smart/mathteach.html>.

An online painting, sculpture, or photograph

Matisse, Henri. <u>La Musique</u>. 1939. Albright-Knox Gallery, Buffalo. <u>Web
    Museum</u>. 3 Mar. 2003 <http://www.ibiblio.org/wm/paint/matisse/
    matisse.musique.jpg>.

An online television or radio program

Niebur, Gustav. "John Paul's Activist Legacy." <u>All Things Considered</u>.
    National Public Radio. 1 Oct. 2003. 5 Oct. 2003 <http://
    www.npr.org/programs/commentaries/2003/oct>.

An online sound recording or clip

Roosevelt, Eleanor. Address to the United Nations. 9 Dec. 1955. <u>Vincent
    Voice Library</u>. Digital and Multimedia Center, U of Michigan. 16 Nov.
    2004 <http://www.lib.msu.edu/vincent/RooseveltE.xml>.

An online film or film clip

<u>San Francisco Earthquake and Fire</u>. 4 Apr. 1906. <u>American Memory</u>. Library
    of Congress. 22 Sept. 2004 <http://memory.loc.gov/cgi-bin/
    D?papr:17/ammem_gBGh>.

Other Sources

A musical composition or work of art

Dvořák, Antonín. String Quartet in E-flat, op. 97.

Hockney, David. Nichols Canyon. 1980. Private collection. David Hockney:
    A Retrospective. By Maurice Tuchman and Stephanie Barron. Los
    Angeles: Los Angeles County Museum of Art, 1988. 205.

A television or radio program

Irving, John, guest. "Movies into Books." Talk of the Nation. PBS. KQED,
    San Francisco. 20 Nov. 2004.

A sound recording

Mendelssohn, Felix. A Midsummer Night's Dream. Cond. Erich Leinsdorf.
    Boston Symphony Orch. RCA, 1982.

A film, video, or DVD

Achbar, Mark, and Peter Wintonick, dirs. Manufacturing Consent: Noam
    Chomsky and the Media. Zeitgeist, 1992.

A letter

List a published letter under the author's name, and provide full publication information.

Hemingway, Ernest. Letter to Grace Hemingway. 15 Jan. 1920. In
    Ernest Hemingway: Selected Letters. Ed. Carlos Baker. New York:
    Scribner's, 1981. 44.

For a letter that you receive, list the source under the writer's name, add "to
the author," and provide the date of the correspondence.

Dove, Chris. Letter to the author. 7 May 2004.

An interview

Kesey, Ken. Interview. "The Art of Fiction." Paris Review 130 (1994):
    59-94.

Macedo, Donaldo. Personal interview. 13 May 2004.

SAMPLE RESEARCH PAPER

Marie Javdani wrote the following paper for her freshman writing course and revised and updated it for *The Bedford Reader*. We reprint the paper for two reasons: It illustrates many techniques of using and documenting sources, which are highlighted in marginal comments; and it shows a writer working with a topic that interests her in a way that arouses the reader's interest as well.

<u>Plata o Plomo:</u>

Silver or Lead

At 8:00 on a Friday night, Eric walks down the street in his American hometown whistling. Tonight, for the first time in almost a week, Eric does not have to do homework or chores. Tonight Eric is a free spirit. Best of all, tonight Eric has scored some drugs. He and his friends will trade their bland, controlled existence for some action and a little bit of fun.

Profiles invented by Javdani pique readers' interest and establish contrasting experiences of the drug trade. No source citation needed for Javdani's own material.

At 8:00 on a Friday night, Miguel creeps down the road in his Colombian village praying. Tonight, for the last time in his life, Miguel will have to watch where he is going and listen anxiously for distant gunshots. Tonight Miguel will die. The guerillas who have been threatening him and his father will end his life for some coca and a lot of money.

Eric and Miguel represent opposite poles in what the United States government refers to as the "war on drugs." Miguel's home is where it starts. In his little village, drug production is the only possible way of life. Eric's home is where it ends. In his suburban paradise, the stress of home-work and ex-girlfriends requires weekend breaks for drugs. All but ignoring both youths, congresspeople, governors, and presidents talk about how their actions will combat the flow of drugs into our homeland. In an attempt to find the quick-est route around a complicated problem, the United States sends billions in aid dollars every year to the governments of Latin American "drug-source" countries such as Colombia, Ecuador, Bolivia, and Peru (Carpenter 205). But the solution isn't working: Political turmoil and violence continue to plague

Transition connects opening profiles to larger concern of paper.

Parenthetical citation includes author's name and page number.

the countries to which we are sending aid, and illegal drug use in the United States remains fairly constant (Vásquez 571-75). To begin to solve the problem, we need to understand what's happening in drug-source countries, how the United States can and can't help there, and what, instead, can be done at home.

Thesis statement.

Miguel's country, Colombia, is one of the top recipients of US money and military weaponry and equipment. According to the US Department of State, Colombia produces nearly 80 percent of the world's cocaine as well as a significant amount of the US heroin supply. Drug production has become a way of life for Colombians. Some call it the plata o plomo mentality. As Gonzalo Sanchez explains it, plata o plomo is literally translated as "silver or lead" and means that one can either take the money--drug money, bribe money, and so on-- or take a bullet (7). Since 1964, the country has been essentially run by drug lords and leftist extremists, mainly the FARC (the military wing of the Colombian Communist Party), whose guerilla presence is much stronger and more threatening than that of the actual government. In response, extreme right-wing paramilitary forces act in an equally deadly manner. Both of these groups raid villages continually, looking to root out "traitors" and executing whomever they please (Sanchez 12-15).

Background on Colombian drug trade.

No parenthetical citation because author (US Department of State) is named in the text and online source has no page numbers.

Citation of a paraphrase. Citation includes only page number because author is named in the text.

Citation of Sanchez in middle and at end of paragraph clarifies boundaries of information drawn from Sanchez.

According to the humanitarian organization Human Rights Watch, US aid money has helped fund, supply, and train Colombian military units that maintain close alliances with paramilitary groups. Although Colombia has recently taken a tougher stance toward the paramilitaries and peace negotiations are in progress, the US State Department, major human rights organizations, and the United Nations claim that the Colombian government is still linked to illicit paramilitary activities. For example, government forces have often invaded, emptied, and then left a guerilla-held area, clearing the way for paramilitary fighters to take control (Carpenter 162). Human rights groups also criticize what Adam Isacson calls a "forgive and forget" government policy toward paramilitary leaders accused of crimes, including

US involvement in Colombia.

No parenthetical citation because author (Human Rights Watch) is named in the text and online source has no page numbers.

promises of amnesty in return for gradual demobilization
(251-52). Although the US has threatened to suspend aid if
Colombia does not break such ties with paramilitary groups,
the full amount of promised aid continues to be granted
(Human Rights Watch).

For the past forty years, the people of Colombia have
found themselves between a rock and a hard place over the
production of coca, the plant used for making cocaine and
heroin. Under threats from the rebel drug lords, who now
control many areas, civilians must either allow their land to
be cultivated for the growth of coca or put themselves and
their families at deadly risk. At the same time, however, the
consequence of "cooperation" with the rebels is execution by
paramilitary groups or even by the Colombian government.
Some coca farmers, fearful of the government, willingly form
alliances with rebels who offer to protect their farms for a
fee (Vásquez 572).

Entire villages get caught in the crossfire between paramilitaries and rebels. In the past ten years, over 35,000 civilians have lost their lives in the conflict and hundreds of
thousands have been forced from their homes (Carpenter 215).
A terrible incident in the town of Bellavista was reported in
the New York Times in 2002 (Forero, "Colombian War"). Paramilitary forces took over the town in an attempt to gain control of jungle smuggling routes. When leftist rebels arrived
ready to fight a battle, the paramilitaries fled, leaving the
civilians trapped and defenseless. Most of the villagers huddled
together in their church, and 117 were killed when a stray
rocket destroyed the church.

What is to be done to prevent such atrocities? The
United States rushes aid to Colombia, hoping to stop the violence and the drugs. Unfortunately, the solutions attempted
so far have had their own bad results. For instance, eradicat-
ing coca fields has alienated peasants, who then turn to the
rebels for support, and it has also escalated violence over
the reduced coca supply (Vásquez 575). Money intended
to help peasants establish alternative crops has ended up
buying weapons for branches of the military that support

paramilitary operations (Human Rights Watch). Not long ago
$2 million intended for the Colombian police just disappeared
(Forero, "Two Million").

Obviously, the United States needs to monitor how its
dollars are used in Colombia. It can continue to discourage
the Colombian government from supporting the paramilitaries
and encourage it to seek peace among the warring factions.
But ultimately the United States is limited in what it can do
by international law and by the tolerance of the US people
for foreign intervention.

Instead, the United States should be looking to its
homefront and should focus on cutting the demand for drugs.
Any economist will affirm that where there is demand, there
will be supply. A report by the United Nations Office on Drugs
and Crime connects this basic economic principle to illegal
drugs:

> Production of illicit drugs is market driven. In the
> United States alone, illicit drugs are an $80 billion
> market. More than $70 billion of that amount goes
> to traffickers, those who bring the drugs to market.
> Stopping the demand would stop their business. (26)

The United States should reduce demand by dramatically
increasing both treatment and education. The first will help
people stop using drugs. The second will make users aware of
the consequences of their choices.

The war on drugs is not fought just in the jungles of
some distant country. It takes place daily at our schools, in
our homes, and on our streets. People my age who justify
their use of illegal drugs by saying "It's my life, and I can do
with it what I please" should be made aware that they are
funding drug lords and contributing to the suffering of
people across the globe, including in Colombia. Eric's "little
bit of fun" is costing Miguel his life.

Writer's own conclusions: continued US role in Colombia.

Writer's own conclusions: reduced demand in the US.

Quotation of more than 4 typed lines is set off and indented 5 spaces or 1 inch.

Parenthetical citation for set-off quotation falls outside final period.

Conclusion returns to opening profiles of Eric and Miguel.

Works Cited

Carpenter, Ted Galen. <u>Peace and Freedom: Foreign Policy for a Constitutional Republic</u>. Washington: Cato, 2002.

Forero, Juan. "Colombian War Brings Carnage to Village Altar." <u>New York Times</u> 9 May 2002. <u>LexisNexis Academic</u>. LexisNexis. U Oregon, Knight Lib. 18 Mar. 2004 <http://www.lexisnexis.com>.

---. "Two Million in US Aid to Colombia Missing from Colombian Police Fund." <u>New York Times</u> 11 May 2002. <u>LexisNexis Academic</u>. LexisNexis. U Oregon, Knight Lib. 18 Mar. 2004 <http://www.lexisnexis.com>.

Human Rights Watch. <u>World Report 2003</u>. 2004. <u>Human Rights Watch</u>. 9 Mar. 2004 <http://www.hrw.org/wr2k3.html>.

Isacson, Adam. "Optimism, Pessimism, and Terrorism: The United States and Colombia in 2003." <u>Brown Journal of World Affairs</u> 10.2 (2004): 245-55.

Sanchez, Gonzalo. <u>Violence in Colombia</u>. Wilmington: Scholarly Resources, 1992.

United Nations. Office on Drugs and Crime. <u>Drug Consumption Stimulates Cultivation and Trade</u>. 3 Dec. 2003. 18 Mar. 2004 <http://www.unodc.org/unodc/report2003-12-3.html>.

United States. Dept. of State. <u>International Narcotics Control Strategy Report, 2003</u>. Jan. 2004. 12 Mar. 2004 <http://www.state.gov/g/inl/rls/nrcrpt/2003/>.

Vásquez, Ian. "The International War on Drugs." <u>Cato Handbook for Congress: Policy Recommendations for the 108th Congress</u>. Ed. Edward H. Crane and David Boaz. Washington: Cato, 2003. 567-76. <u>Cato Institute</u>. 2003. 18 Mar. 2004 <http://www.cato.org/pubs/handbook/hb108/hb108-56.pdf>.

"Works Cited" begins on a new page.
A book.

A newspaper article from a library subscription service.

The second of two works by the same author.

A report from a Web site.

An article from a print journal that pages issues separately.

A government report from a Web site.

An essay in an online book that is also available in print.

PART TWO

THE METHODS

4

NARRATION

Telling a Story

THE METHOD

"What happened?" you ask a friend who sports a luminous black eye. Unless he merely grunts "A golf ball," he may answer you with a narrative—a story, true or fictional.

"Okay," he sighs, "you know The Tenth Round? That nightclub down by the docks that smells of formaldehyde? Last night I heard they were giving away $500 to anybody who could stand up for three minutes against this karate expert, the Masked Samurai. And so . . . ."

You lean forward. At least, you lean forward *if* you love a story. Most of us do, particularly if the story tells us of people in action or in conflict, and if it is told briskly, vividly, and with insight into the human heart. NARRATION, or storytelling, is therefore a powerful method by which to engage and hold the attention of listeners—readers as well. A little of its tremendous power flows to the public speaker who starts off with a joke, even a stale joke ("A funny thing happened to me on my way over here . . ."), and to the preacher who at the beginning of a sermon tells of some funny or touching incident. In its opening paragraph, an article in a popular magazine ("Vampires Live Today!") will give us a brief, arresting narrative: perhaps the case history of a car dealer who noticed, one moonlit night, his incisors strangely lengthening.

The term *narrative* takes in abundant territory. A narrative may be short or long, factual or imagined, as artless as a tale told in a locker room or as artful as a novel by Henry James. A narrative may instruct and inform, or simply divert and regale. It may set forth some point or message, or it may be no more significant than a horror tale that aims to curdle your blood.

At least a hundred times a year, you probably resort to narration, not always for the purpose of telling an entertaining story, but often to explain, to illustrate a point, to report information, to argue, or to persuade. That is, although a narrative can run from the beginning of an essay to the end, more often in your writing (as in your speaking) a narrative is only a part of what you have to say. It is there because it serves a larger purpose. In truth, because narration is such an effective way to put across your ideas, the ability to tell a compelling story—on paper, as well as in conversation—may be one of the most useful skills you can acquire.

A novel is a narrative, but a narrative doesn't have to be long. Sometimes an essay will include several brief stories. See, for instance, "Why Don't We Complain?" by William F. Buckley, Jr. (p. 538). A type of story often used to illustrate a point is the ANECDOTE, a short, entertaining account of a single incident. Anecdotes add color and specifics to history and to every issue of *People* magazine, and they often help support an ARGUMENT by giving it the flesh and blood of real life. Besides being vivid, an anecdote can be deeply revealing. In a biography of Samuel Johnson, the great eighteenth-century critic and scholar, W. Jackson Bate uses an anecdote to show that his subject was human and lovable. As Bate tells us, Dr. Johnson, a portly and imposing gentleman of fifty-five, had walked with some friends to the crest of a hill, where the great man,

> delighted by its steepness, said he wanted to "take a roll down." They tried to stop him. But he said he "had not had a roll for a long time," and taking out of his pockets his keys, a pencil, a purse, and other objects, lay down parallel at the edge of the hill, and rolled down its full length, "turning himself over and over till he came to the bottom."

However small the event it relates, this anecdote is memorable — partly because of its attention to detail, such as the exact list of the contents of Johnson's pockets. In such a brief story, a superhuman figure comes down to human size. In one stroke, Bate reveals an essential part of Johnson: his boisterous, hearty, and boyish sense of fun.

An anecdote may be used to explain a point. Asked why he had appointed to a cabinet post Josephus Daniels, the harshest critic of his policies, President Woodrow Wilson replied with an anecdote of a woman he knew. On spying a strange man urinating through her picket fence into her flower garden, she invited the offender into her yard because, as she explained to him, "I'd a whole lot rather have you inside pissing out than have you outside pissing in." By telling this story, Wilson made clear his situation in regard to his political enemy more succinctly and pointedly than if he had given a more abstract explanation.

THE PROCESS

Purpose and Shape

Every good story has a purpose, and we've suggested several in the preceding section. A narrative without a purpose is bound to irritate readers, as a young child's rambling can vex an unsympathetic adult.

Whatever the reason for its telling, an effective story holds the attention of readers or listeners; and to do so, the storyteller shapes that story to appeal to its audience. If, for instance, you plan to tell a few friends of an embarrassing moment you had on your way to campus — you tripped and spilled a load of books into the arms of a passing dean — you know how to proceed. Simply to provide a laugh is your purpose, and your listeners, who need no introduction to you or the dean, need to be told only the bare events of the story. Perhaps you'll use some vivid words to convey the surprise on the dean's face when sixty pounds of literary lumber hit her. Perhaps you'll throw in a little surprise of your own. At first, you didn't take in the identity of this passerby on whom you'd dumped a load of literary lumber. Then you realized: It was the dean!

The Thesis

In writing a news story, a reporter often begins with the conclusion, placing the main event in the opening paragraph (called the *lead*) so that readers get the essentials up front. Similarly, in using an anecdote to explain something or to argue a point, you'll want to tell readers directly what you think the story demonstrates. But in most other kinds of narration, whether fiction or nonfiction, whether to entertain or to make an idea clear, the storyteller refrains from revealing the gist of the story, its point, right at the beginning. In fact, many narratives do not contain a THESIS STATEMENT, an assertion of the idea behind the story, because such a statement can rob the reader of the very pleasure of narration, the excitement of seeing a story build. That doesn't mean the story lacks a thesis, however—far from it. The writer has every obligation to construct the narrative as if a thesis statement showed the way at the start, even when it didn't.

By the end of the story, that thesis should become obvious, as the writer builds toward a memorable CONCLUSION. In a story Mark Twain liked to tell aloud, a woman's ghost returns to claim her artificial arm made of gold, which she wore in life and which her greedy husband had unscrewed from her corpse. Carefully, Twain would build up suspense as the ghost pursued the husband upstairs to his bedroom, stood by his bed, breathed her cold breath on him, and intoned, *"Who's got my golden arm?"* Twain used to end his story by suddenly yelling at a member of the audience, *"You've got it!"*—and enjoying the victim's shriek of surprise. That final punctuating shriek may be a technique that will work only in oral storytelling; yet, like Twain, most storytellers like to end with a bang if they can. For another example, take specific notice in this chapter of Shirley Jackson's ending for "The Lottery" (*after* you've read the whole story, that is). The final impact need not be as dramatic as Twain's and Jackson's, either. As Maya Angelou demonstrates in her narrative in this chapter, you can achieve a lot just by leading to your point, stating your thesis at the very end. You can sometimes make your point just by saving the best incident—the most dramatic or the funniest—for last.

The Narrator in the Story

Narratives often report personal experience, whether in reality or in fiction. The NARRATOR (or teller) of such a personal experience is the speaker, the one who was there. (Five of the selections in this chapter tell of such experiences. All use the first-PERSON *I*.) The telling is usually SUBJECTIVE, with details and language chosen to express the writer's feelings. Of course, a personal experience told in the first person can use some artful telling and some structuring. (In the course of this discussion, we'll offer advice on telling stories of different kinds.)

When a story isn't your own experience but a recital of someone else's, or of events that are public knowledge, then you proceed differently as narrator. Without expressing opinions, you step back and report, content to stay invisible. Instead of saying, "I did this; I did that," you use the third person, *he, she, it,* or *they*: "The runner did this; he did that." You may have been on the scene; if so, you will probably write as a spectator, from your own POINT OF VIEW (or angle of seeing). If you put together what happened from the testimony of others, you tell the story from the point of view of a nonparticipant (a witness who didn't take part). Generally, a nonparticipant is OBJECTIVE in setting forth events: unbiased, as accurate and dispassionate as possible.

When you narrate a story in the third person, you aren't a character central in the eyes of your audience. Unlike the first-person writer of a personal experience, you aren't the main actor; you are the camera operator, whose job is to focus on what transpires. Most history books and news stories are third-person narratives, and so is much fiction. (In this chapter, the story by Shirley Jackson illustrates third-person narration.) In telling of actual events, writers stick to the facts and do not invent the thoughts of participants (historical novels, though, do mingle fact and fancy in this way). And even writers of fiction and anecdote imagine the thoughts of their characters only if they want to explore psychology. Look back at the anecdote by Woodrow Wilson on page 77, and notice how much would be lost if Wilson had gone into the thoughts of his characters: "The woman was angry and embarrassed at seeing the stranger. . . ."

A final element of the narrator's place in the story is verb tense, whether present (*I stare, he stares*) or past (*I stared, he stared*). The present tense is often tempting because it gives events a sense of immediacy. Told as though everything were happening right now, Wilson's story might have begun, "Peering out her window, a woman spies a strange man. . . ." But the present tense can seem artificial because we're used to reading stories in the past tense, and it can be difficult to sustain throughout an entire narrative. (See p. 83 on consistency in tenses.) The past tense may be more removed, but it is still powerful: Just look at Maya Angelou's gripping "Champion of the World," beginning on page 88.

What to Emphasize

Discovery and Choice of Details

Whether you tell of your own experience or of someone else's, even if it is brief, you need a whole story to tell. If the story is complex, do some searching and discovering in writing. One trusty method to test your memory (or to make sure you have all the necessary elements of a story) is that of a news reporter. Ask yourself:

1. *What* happened?
2. *Who* took part?
3. *When?*
4. *Where?*
5. *Why* did this event (or these events) take place?
6. *How* did it (or they) happen?

That last *how* isn't merely another way of asking what happened. It means: In exactly what way or under what circumstances? If the event was a murder, how was it done—with an ax or with a bulldozer? Journalists call this handy list of questions "the five *W*'s and the *H*."

Well-prepared storytellers, those who first search their memories (or do some research and legwork), have far more information on hand than they can use. The writing of a good story calls for careful choice. In choosing, remember your purpose and your audience. If you're writing that story of the dean and the books to give pleasure to readers who are your friends, delighted to hear about the discomfort of a pompous administrator, you will probably dwell lovingly on each detail of her consternation. You would tell the story differently if your audience were strangers who didn't know the dean from Eve. They would need more information on her background, reputation for stiffness, and appearance. If, suspected of having deliberately contrived the dean's humiliation, you were writing a report of the incident for the campus police, you'd want to give the plainest possible account of the story—without drama, without adornment, without background, and certainly without any humor whatsoever.

Scene Versus Summary

Your purpose and your audience, then, clearly determine which of the two main strategies of narration you're going to choose: to tell a story by SCENE or to tell it by SUMMARY. When you tell a story in a scene, or in scenes, you visualize each event as vividly and precisely as if you were there—as though it were a scene in a film, and your reader sat before the screen. This is the strategy of most fine novels and short stories—and of much excellent nonfiction as well. Instead of just mentioning people, you portray them. You recall dialog as best you can, or you invent some that could have been spoken. You include DESCRIPTION (a mode of writing to be dealt with fully in our next chapter).

For a lively example of a well-drawn scene, see Maya Angelou's account of a tense crowd's behavior as, jammed into a small-town store, they listen to a fight broadcast (in "Champion of the World"). Angelou prolongs one scene for almost her entire essay. Sometimes, though, a writer will draw a scene in only two or three sentences. This is the brevity we find in W. Jackson Bate's glimpse of the hill-rolling Johnson (p. 77). Unlike Angelou, Bate evidently seeks not to weave a tapestry of detail but to show, in telling of one brief event, a trait of his hero's character.

When, in contrast, you tell a story by the method of summary, you relate events concisely. Instead of depicting people and their surroundings in great detail, you set down just the essentials of what happened. Most of us employ this method in most stories we tell, for it takes less time and fewer words. A summary is to a scene, then, as a simple stick figure is to a portrait in oils. This is not to dismiss simple stick figures as inferior. The economy of a story told in summary may be as effective as the lavish detail of a story told in scenes.

Again, your choice of a method depends on your answer to the questions you ask yourself: What is my purpose? Who is my audience? How fully to flesh out a scene, how much detail to include—these choices depend on what you seek to do and on how much your audience needs to know to follow you. Read the life of some famous person in an encyclopedia, and you will find the article telling its story in summary form. Its writer's purpose, evidently, is to recount the main events of a whole life in a short space. But glance through a book-length biography of the same celebrity, and you will probably find scenes in it. A biographer writes with a different purpose: to present a detailed portrait roundly and thoroughly, bringing the subject vividly to life.

To be sure, you can use both methods in telling a single story. Often, summary will serve a writer who passes briskly from one scene to the next or hurries over events of lesser importance. Were you to write, let's say, the story of a man's fiendish passion for horse racing, you might decide to give short shrift to most other facts of his life. To emphasize what you consider essential, you might begin a scene with a terse summary: "Seven years went by, and after three marriages and two divorces, Lars found himself again back at Hialeah." (A detailed scene might follow.)

Good storytellers know what to emphasize. They do not fall into a boring drone: "And then I went down to the club and I had a few beers and I noticed this sign, Go 3 Minutes with the Masked Samurai and Win $500, so I went and got knocked out and then I had pizza and went home." In this lazily strung-out summary, the narrator reduces all events to equal unimportance. A more adept storyteller might leave out the pizza and dwell in detail on the big fight.

In *The Bedford Reader* we are concerned with the kind of writing you do every day in college: nonfiction writing in which you generally explain ideas, organize information you have learned, analyze other people's ideas, or argue a case. In fiction, though, we find an enormously popular and appealing use of narration and certain devices of storytelling from which all storytellers can learn. For these reasons, this chapter includes one celebrated short story by a master storyteller, Shirley Jackson. But fiction and fact barely separate Jackson's story and the equally compelling true memoirs in this chapter. All of the authors strive to make people and events come alive for us. All of them also use a tool that academic writers generally do not: dialog. Reported speech, in quotation marks, is invaluable for revealing characters' feelings.

Organization

In any kind of narration, the simplest approach is to set down events in CHRONOLOGICAL ORDER, the way they happened. To do so is to have your story already organized for you. A chronological order is therefore an excellent sequence to follow unless you can see some special advantage in violating it. Ask: What am I trying to do? If you are trying to capture your readers' attention right away, you might begin *in medias res* (Latin, "in the middle of things") and open with a colorful, dramatic event, even though it took place late in the chronology. If trying for dramatic effect, you might save the most exciting or impressive event for last, even though it actually happened early. By this means, you can keep your readers in suspense for as long as possible. (You can return to earlier events by a FLASHBACK, an earlier scene recalled.) Let your purpose be your guide.

The writer Calvin Trillin has recalled why, in a narrative titled "The Tunica Treasure," he deliberately chose not to follow a chronology:

> I wrote a story on the discovery of the Tunica treasure which I couldn't begin by saying, "Here is a man who works as a prison guard in Angola State Prison, and on his weekends he sometimes looks for buried treasure that is rumored to be around the Indian village." Because the real point of the story centered around the problems caused when an amateur wanders onto professional territory, I thought it would be much better to open with how momentous the discovery was, that it was the most important archeological discovery about Indian contact with the European settlers to date, and *then* to say that it was discovered by a prison guard. So I made a conscious choice *not* to start with Leonard Charrier working as a prison guard, not to go back

to his boyhood in Bunkie, Louisiana, not to talk about how he'd always been interested in treasure hunting—hoping that the reader would assume I was about to say that the treasure was found by an archeologist from the Peabody Museum at Harvard.

Trillin, by saving the fact that a prison guard made the earthshaking discovery, effectively took his reader by surprise.

No matter what order you choose, either following chronology or departing from it, make sure your audience can follow it. The sequence of events has to be clear. This calls for TRANSITIONS of time, whether they are brief phrases that point out exactly when each event happened ("Seven years later," "A moment earlier"), or whole sentences that announce an event and clearly locate it in time ("If you had known Leonard Charrier ten years earlier, you would have found him voraciously poring over every archeology text he could lay his hands on in the public library"). See *Transitions* in Useful Terms for a list of possibilities.

FOCUS ON VERBS

Narration depends heavily on verbs to clarify and enliven events. Strong verbs sharpen meaning and encourage you to add other informative details:

WEAK   The wind <u>made</u> an awful noise.

STRONG   The wind <u>roared</u> around the house and <u>rattled</u> the trees.

Forms of *make* (as in the example above) and forms of *be* (as in the next example) can sap the life from narration:

WEAK   The noises <u>were</u> alarming to us.

STRONG   The noises <u>alarmed</u> us.

Verbs in the ACTIVE VOICE (the subject does the action) usually pack more power into fewer words than verbs in the PASSIVE VOICE (the subject is acted upon):

WEAK PASSIVE   We <u>were besieged</u> in the basement by the wind, as the water at our feet <u>was swelled</u> by the rain.

STRONG PASSIVE   The wind <u>besieged</u> us in the basement, as the rain <u>swelled</u> the water at our feet.

While strengthening verbs, also ensure that they're consistent in tense. The tense you choose for relating events, present or past, should not shift unnecessarily.

INCONSISTENT TENSES   We <u>held</u> a frantic conference to consider our options. It <u>takes</u> only a minute to decide to stay put.

CONSISTENT TENSE   We <u>held</u> a frantic conference to consider our options. It <u>took</u> only a minute to decide to stay put.

For exercises on verbs, visit Exercise Central at *bedfordstmartins.com/ thebedfordreader.*

CHECKLIST FOR REVISING A NARRATIVE

✔ **THESIS.** What is the point of your narrative? Will it be clear to readers by the end? Even if you don't provide a thesis statement, your story should focus on a central idea. If you can't risk readers' misunderstanding—if, for instance, you're using narration to support an argument or explain a concept—then have you stated your thesis outright?

✔ **POINT OF VIEW.** Is your narrator's position in the story appropriate for your purpose and consistent throughout the story? Check for awkward or confusing shifts in point of view (participant or nonparticipant; first, second, or third person) and in the tenses of verbs (present to past or vice versa).

✔ **SELECTION OF EVENTS.** Have you selected and emphasized events to suit your audience and fulfill your purpose? Tell the important parts of the story in the greatest detail. Summarize the less important, connective events.

✔ **ORGANIZATION.** If your organization is not strictly chronological (first event to last), do you have a compelling reason for altering it? If you start somewhere other than the beginning of the story or use flashbacks at any point, will your readers benefit from your creativity?

✔ **TRANSITIONS.** Have you used transitions to help clarify the order of events and their duration?

✔ **DIALOG.** If you have used dialog, quoting participants in the story, is it appropriate for your purpose? Is it concise, telling only the important, revealing lines? Does the language sound like spoken English?

✔ **VERBS.** Do strong, active verbs move your narrative from event to event? Are verb tenses consistent?

NARRATION IN PARAGRAPHS

Writing About Television

The following paragraph was written for *The Bedford Reader* as a kind of mini-essay. But it is easy to see how it might have worked in the context of a full essay about, say, the emotional effects of television on children. Recounting events vividly, moment by moment, the writer gives evidence for a rather dramatic effect on one little girl.

Oozing menace from beyond the stars or from the deeps, televised horror powerfully stimulates a child's already frisky imagination. As parents know, a "Creature Double Feature" has an impact that lasts long after the click of the *off* button. Recently a neighbor reported the strange case of her eight-year-old. Discovered late at night in the game room watching *The Exorcist*, the girl was

— Claim to be supported by narrative

Transitions (underlined) clarify sequence and pace of events

promptly sent to bed. <u>An hour later</u>, her parents could hear her
chanting something in the darkness of her bedroom. On tiptoe,
they stole to her door to listen. The creak of springs told them that
their daughter was swaying rhythmically to and fro, and the smell of
acrid smoke warned them that something was burning. <u>At once</u>,
they shoved open the door to find the room flickering with shadows
cast by a lighted candle. Their daughter was sitting in bed, rocking
back and forth as she intoned over and over, "Fiend in human
form . . . Fiend in human form . . ." This case may be unique; still, it
seems likely that similar events take place each night all over the
screen-watching world.

Anecdote builds suspense:

Mystery

Warnings

Crisis

Conclusion broadens claim

Writing in an Academic Discipline

In this paragraph from a geology textbook, the authors use narration to
illustrate a powerful geological occurrence. Following another paragraph that
explains landslides more generally, the narrative places the reader at an actual
event.

The news media periodically relate the terrifying and often grim
details of landslides. On <u>May 31, 1970</u>, one such event occurred
when a gigantic rock avalanche buried more than 20,000 people in
Yungay and Ranrahirca, Peru. There was little warning of the
impending disaster; it began and ended in just <u>a matter of a few
minutes</u>. The avalanche started 14 kilometers from Yungay, near
the summit of 6,700-meter-high Nevados Huascaran, the loftiest
peak in the Peruvian Andes. Triggered by the ground motion from
a strong offshore earthquake, a huge mass of rock and ice broke free
from the precipitous north face of the mountain. <u>After plunging
nearly one kilometer</u>, the material pulverized on impact and immediately began rushing down the mountainside, made fluid by trapped
air and melted ice. The initial mass ripped loose additional millions
of tons of debris <u>as it roared downhill</u>. The shock waves produced
by the event created thunderlike noise and stripped nearby hillsides
of vegetation. Although the material followed a previously eroded
gorge, a portion of the debris jumped a 200–300-meter-high bed-
rock ridge that had protected Yungay from past rock avalanches and
buried the entire city. <u>After inundating another town in its path</u>,
Ranrahirca, the mass of debris <u>finally</u> reached the bottom of the valley where its momentum carried it across the Rio Santa and tens of
meters up the opposite bank.

—Edward J. Tarbuck and Frederick K. Lutgens,
The Earth: An Introduction to Physical Geology

Generalization illustrated by narrative

Anecdote helps explain landslides:

Sudden beginning

Fast movement

Irresistible force

Transitions (underlined) clarify sequence and pace of events

NARRATION IN PRACTICE

Robert Guzman was on his way to class at Cañada College when his car was hit at an intersection. He reported the accident to his insurance company, and the claims adjuster asked him to supplement the standard police report with a letter explaining what happened.

"What happened?" prompted Guzman to write the following narrative. Since the accident was uncomplicated, he had little difficulty getting the events down in chronological order. In editing, though, he did add some clarifying TRANSITIONS, such as "After the light turned green" and "When I was midway through the intersection."

> Robert Guzman
> 415 Washington St., Apt. 5
> San Carlos, CA 94070
> June 7, 2004

David McClure
MDN Insurance
2716 El Camino Real
San Carlos, CA 94072

Dear Mr. McClure:

Thanks for your call about my claim. Here is the report you requested about the accident I was involved in.

At about 7:30 on the morning of June 4, I was driving south on Laurel Street in San Carlos. The traffic light at the corner of Laurel and San Carlos Avenue was red and I stopped at it, the first car in the stop line.

After the light turned green, I looked to my left and right. Although I saw a car approaching from the right on San Carlos, it seemed to be slowing for the light. Since my light was green, I proceeded through the intersection.

The car, which I later found out was driven by Mr. Henry, did not stop for its red light. When I was midway through the intersection, I heard the other car's tires squeal and felt an impact. Mr. Henry's car hit the rear fender and bumper on my passenger side. My car spun clockwise and came to a stop facing north, in the northbound lane of Laurel.

Mr. Henry parked in a lot across the street, and I pulled in after him. I called the police on my cell phone, and we waited for the police to arrive. No one was injured, but my passenger-side rear fender is severely dented and my bumper is twisted like a pretzel.

As you can see, I was not at fault in this accident. I believe Mr. Henry will confirm as much. Please let me know if you have any questions or if I can help my claim in any other way.

Sincerely,

Robert Guzman

Robert Guzman

MAYA ANGELOU

MAYA ANGELOU was born Marguerite Johnson in Saint Louis in 1928. After an unpleasantly eventful youth by her account ("from a broken family, raped at eight, unwed mother at sixteen"), she went on to join a dance company, star in an off-Broadway play (*The Blacks*), write six books of poetry, produce a TV series on Africa, act in the television series *Roots*, serve as a coordinator for the Southern Christian Leadership Conference, direct a feature film, win the Presidential Medal of Freedom, and secure lifetime membership in the National Women's Hall of Fame. Angelou may be best known, however, for the six books of her searching, frank, and joyful autobiography—beginning with *I Know Why the Caged Bird Sings* (1970), which she adapted for television, through *A Song Flung Up to Heaven* (2002). Her most recent book is *Hallelujah! The Welcome Table: A Lifetime of Memories with Recipes* (2004). She is Reynolds Professor of American Studies at Wake Forest University.

Champion of the World

"Champion of the World" is the nineteenth chapter in *I Know Why the Caged Bird Sings*; the title is a phrase taken from the chapter. Remembering her childhood, the writer tells how she and her older brother, Bailey, grew up in a town in Arkansas. The center of their lives was Grandmother and Uncle Willie's store, a gathering place for the black community. On the night when this story takes place, Joe Louis, the "Brown Bomber" and the hero of his people, defends his heavyweight boxing title against a white contender. Angelou's telling of the event both entertains us and explains what it was like to be African American in a certain time and place.

Amy Tan's "Fish Cheeks," following Angelou's essay, also explores the experience of growing up an outsider in mainly white America.

The last inch of space was filled, yet people continued to wedge themselves along the walls of the Store. Uncle Willie had turned the radio up to its last notch so that youngsters on the porch wouldn't miss a word. Women sat on kitchen chairs, dining-room chairs, stools, and upturned wooden boxes. Small children and babies perched on every lap available and men leaned on the shelves or on each other.

The apprehensive mood was shot through with shafts of gaiety, as a black sky is streaked with lightning.

"I ain't worried 'bout this fight. Joe's gonna whip that cracker like it's open season."

"He gone whip him till that white boy call him Momma."   4

At last the talking finished and the string-along songs about razor blades   5
were over and the fight began.

"A quick jab to the head." In the Store the crowd grunted. "A left to the   6
head and a right and another left." One of the listeners cackled like a hen and
was quieted.

"They're in a clinch, Louis is trying to fight his way out."   7

Some bitter comedian on the porch said, "That white man don't mind   8
hugging that niggah now, I betcha."

"The referee is moving in to break them up, but Louis finally pushed the   9
contender away and it's an uppercut to the chin. The contender is hanging on,
now he's backing away. Louis catches him with a short left to the jaw."

A tide of murmuring assent poured out the door and into the yard.   10

"Another left and another left. Louis is saving that mighty right . . ."   11
The mutter in the Store had grown into a baby roar and it was pierced by the
clang of a bell and the announcer's "That's,the bell for round three, ladies and
gentlemen."

As I pushed my way into the Store I wondered if the announcer gave any   12
thought to the fact that he was addressing as "ladies and gentlemen" all the
Negroes around the world who sat sweating and praying, glued to their "Master's voice."[1]

There were only a few calls for RC Colas, Dr Peppers, and Hires root beer. 13
The real festivities would begin after the fight. Then even the old Christian
ladies who taught their children and tried themselves to practice turning the
other cheek would buy soft drinks, and if the Brown Bomber's victory was a
particularly bloody one they would order peanut patties and Baby Ruths also.

Bailey and I laid the coins on top of the cash register. Uncle Willie didn't 14
allow us to ring up sales during a fight. It was too noisy and might shake up the
atmosphere. When the gong rang for the next round we pushed through the
near-sacred quiet to the herd of children outside.

"He's got Louis against the ropes and now it's a left to the body and a right 15
to the ribs. Another right to the body, it looks like it was low . . . Yes, ladies
and gentlemen, the referee is signaling but the contender keeps raining the
blows on Louis. It's another to the body, and it looks like Louis is going down."

My race groaned. It was our people falling. It was another lynching, yet   16
another Black man hanging on a tree. One more woman ambushed and raped.
A Black boy whipped and maimed. It was hounds on the trail of a man running
through slimy swamps. It was a white woman slapping her maid for being for-
getful.

[1]"His master's voice," accompanied by a picture of a little dog listening to a phonograph,
was a familiar advertising slogan. (The picture still appears on some RCA recordings.) — EDS.

The men in the Store stood away from the walls and at attention. Women 17 greedily clutched the babes on their laps while on the porch the shufflings and smiles, flirtings and pinching of a few minutes before were gone. This might be the end of the world. If Joe lost we were back in slavery and beyond help. It would all be true, the accusations that we were lower types of human beings. Only a little higher than apes. True that we were stupid and ugly and lazy and dirty and, unlucky and worst of all, that God Himself hated us and ordained us to be hewers of wood and drawers of water, forever and ever, world without end.

We didn't breathe. We didn't hope. We waited. 18

"He's off the ropes, ladies and gentlemen. He's moving towards the center 19 of the ring." There was no time to be relieved. The worst might still happen.

"And now it looks like Joe is mad. He's caught Carnera with a left hook to 20 the head and a right to the head. It's a left jab to the body and another left to the head. There's a left cross and a right to the head. The contender's right eye is bleeding and he can't seem to keep his block up. Louis is penetrating every block. The referee is moving in, but Louis sends a left to the body and it's an uppercut to the chin and the contender is dropping. He's on the canvas, ladies and gentlemen."

Babies slid to the floor as women stood up and men leaned toward the radio. 21

"Here's the referee. He's counting. One, two, three, four, five, six, 22 seven . . . Is the contender trying to get up again?"

All the men in the store shouted, "NO." 23

"—eight, nine, ten." There were a few sounds from the audience, but they 24 seemed to be holding themselves in against tremendous pressure.

"The fight is all over, ladies and gentlemen. Let's get the microphone over 25 to the referee . . . Here he is. He's got the Brown Bomber's hand, he's holding it up . . . Here he is . . ."

Then the voice, husky and familiar, came to wash over us—"The win- 26 nah, and still heavyweight champeen of the world . . . Joe Louis."

Champion of the world. A Black boy. Some Black mother's son. He was 27 the strongest man in the world. People drank Coca-Colas like ambrosia and ate candy bars like Christmas. Some of the men went behind the Store and poured white lightning in their soft-drink bottles, and a few of the bigger boys followed them. Those who were not chased away came back blowing their breath in front of themselves like proud smokers.

It would take an hour or more before the people would leave the Store 28 and head for home. Those who lived too far had made arrangements to stay in town. It wouldn't do for a Black man and his family to be caught on a lonely country road on a night when Joe Louis had proved that we were the strongest people in the world.

*For a reading quiz, sources on Maya Angelou, and annotated links to further readings on Joe Louis and on the history of segregation in the South, visit **bedfordstmartins** .com/thebedfordreader.*

Journal Writing

How do you respond to the group identification and solidarity that Angelou writes about in this essay? What groups do you belong to, and how do you know you're a member? Consider groups based on race, ethnic background, religion, sports, hobbies, politics, friendship, kinship, or any other ties. (To take your journal writing further, see "From Journal to Essay" on the next page.)

Questions on Meaning

1. What do you take to be the author's PURPOSE in telling this story?
2. What connection does Angelou make between the outcome of the fight and the pride of African Americans? To what degree do you think the author's view is shared by the others in the store listening to the broadcast?
3. To what extent are the statements in paragraphs 16 and 17 to be taken literally? What function do they serve in Angelou's narrative?
4. Primo Carnera was probably *not* the Brown Bomber's opponent on the night Maya Angelou recalls. Louis fought Carnera only once, on June 25, 1935, and it was not a title match; Angelou would have been no more than seven years old at the time. Does the author's apparent error detract from her story?

Questions on Writing Strategy

1. What details in the opening paragraphs indicate that an event of crucial importance is about to take place?
2. How does Angelou build up SUSPENSE in her account of the fight? At what point were you able to predict the winner?
3. Comment on the IRONY in Angelou's final paragraph.
4. What EFFECT does the author's use of direct quotation have on her narrative?
5. **OTHER METHODS.** Besides narration, Angelou also relies heavily on the method of DESCRIPTION. Analyze how narration depends on description in paragraph 27 alone.

Questions on Language

1. Explain what the author means by "string-along songs about razor blades" (par. 5).
2. Point to some examples in the essay of Angelou's use of strong verbs.

3. How does Angelou's use of NONSTANDARD ENGLISH contribute to her narrative?
4. Be sure you know the meanings of these words: apprehensive (par. 2); assent (10); ambushed, maimed (16); ordained (17); ambrosia, white lightning (27).

Suggestions for Writing

1. **FROM JOURNAL TO ESSAY.** From your journal entry, choose one of the groups you belong to and explore your sense of membership through a narrative that tells of an incident that occurred when that sense was strong. Try to make the incident come alive for your readers with vivid details, dialogue, and tight sequencing of events.
2. Write an essay based on some childhood experience of your own, still vivid in your memory.
3. Do some research about the boxing career of Joe Louis. Then write an essay in which you discuss popular attitudes toward the Brown Bomber in his day.
4. **CRITICAL WRITING.** Angelou does not directly describe relations between African Americans and whites, yet her essay implies quite a lot. Write a brief essay about what you can INFER from the exaggeration of paragraphs 16–17 and the obliqueness of paragraph 28. Focus on Angelou's details and the language she uses to present them.
5. **CONNECTIONS.** Angelou's "Champion of the World" and the next essay, Amy Tan's "Fish Cheeks," both tell stories of children who felt like outsiders in predominantly white America. COMPARE AND CONTRAST the two writers' perceptions of what sets them apart from the dominant culture. How does the event each reports affect that sense of difference? Use specific examples from both essays as your EVIDENCE.

Maya Angelou on Writing

Maya Angelou's writings have shown great variety: She has done notable work as an autobiographer, poet, short-story writer, screenwriter, journalist, and song lyricist. Asked by interviewer Sheila Weller, "Do you start each project with a specific idea?" Angelou replied:

It starts with a definite subject, but it might end with something entirely different. When I start a project, the first thing I do is write down, in longhand, everything I know about the subject, every thought I've ever had on it. This may be twelve or fourteen pages. Then I read it back through, for quite a few days, and find—given that subject—what its rhythm is. 'Cause everything in the universe has a rhythm. So if it's free form, it still has a rhythm. And once I hear the rhythm of the piece, then I try to find out what are the salient points that I must make. And then it begins to take shape.

I try to set myself up in each chapter by saying: "This is what I want to go from — from B to, say, G-sharp. Or from D to L." And then I find the hook. It's like the knitting, where, after you knit a certain amount, there's one thread that begins to pull. You know, you can see it right along the cloth. Well, in writing, I think: "Now where is that one hook, that one little thread?" It may be a sentence. If I can catch that, then I'm home free. It's the one that tells me where I'm going. It may not even turn out to be in the final chapter. I may throw it out later or change it. But if I follow it through, it leads me right out.

For Discussion

1. How would you define the word *rhythm* as Maya Angelou uses it?
2. What response would you give a student who said, "Doesn't Angelou's approach to writing waste more time and thought than it's worth?"

AMY TAN

AMY TAN is a gifted storyteller whose first novel, *The Joy Luck Club* (1989), met with critical acclaim and huge success. The relationships it details between immigrant Chinese mothers and their Chinese American daughters came from Tan's firsthand experience. She was born in 1952 in Oakland, California, the daughter of immigrants who had fled China's civil war in the late 1940s. She majored in English and linguistics at San Jose State University, where she received a BA in 1973 and an MA in 1974. After two more years of graduate work, Tan became a consultant in language development for disabled children and then started her own company writing reports and speeches for business corporations. Tan began writing fiction to explore her ethnic ambivalence and to find a voice for herself. Since *The Joy Luck Club*, she has published three more novels — *The Kitchen God's Wife* (1991), *The Hundred Secret Senses* (1995), and *The Bonesetter's Daughter* (2001) — as well as children's books and *The Opposite of Fate* (2003), a collection of autobiographical essays. She also sings in the Rock Bottom Remainders, a rock band of writers.

Fish Cheeks

"Fish Cheeks" is a very brief narrative, almost an anecdote, but still it deftly portrays the contradictory feelings and the advantages of a girl with feet in different cultures. The essay first appeared in *Seventeen*, a magazine for teenage girls and young women, in 1987.

For a complementary view of growing up "different," read the preceding essay, Maya Angelou's "Champion of the World."

I fell in love with the minister's son the winter I turned fourteen. He was 1 not Chinese, but as white as Mary in the manger. For Christmas I prayed for this blond-haired boy, Robert, and a slim new American nose.

When I found out that my parents had invited the minister's family over 2 for Christmas Eve dinner, I cried. What would Robert think of our shabby Chinese Christmas? What would he think of our noisy Chinese relatives who lacked proper American manners? What terrible disappointment would he feel upon seeing not a roasted turkey and sweet potatoes but Chinese food?

On Christmas Eve I saw that my mother had outdone herself in creating 3 a strange menu. She was pulling black veins out of the backs of fleshy prawns.

The kitchen was littered with appalling mounds of raw food: A slimy rock cod with bulging eyes that pleaded not to be thrown into a pan of hot oil. Tofu, which looked like stacked wedges of rubbery white sponges. A bowl soaking dried fungus back to life. A plate of squid, their backs crisscrossed with knife markings so they resembled bicycle tires.

And then they arrived — the minister's family and all my relatives in a clamor of doorbells and rumpled Christmas packages. Robert grunted hello, and I pretended he was not worthy of existence.   4

Dinner threw me deeper into despair. My relatives licked the ends of their chopsticks and reached across the table, dipping them into the dozen or so plates of food. Robert and his family waited patiently for platters to be passed to them. My relatives murmured with pleasure when my mother brought out the whole steamed fish. Robert grimaced. Then my father poked his chopsticks just below the fish eye and plucked out the soft meat. "Amy, your favorite," he said, offering me the tender fish cheek. I wanted to disappear.   5

At the end of the meal my father leaned back and belched loudly, thanking my mother for her fine cooking. "It's a polite Chinese custom to show you are satisfied," explained my father to our astonished guests. Robert was looking down at his plate with a reddened face. The minister managed to muster up a quiet burp. I was stunned into silence for the rest of the night.   6

After everyone had gone, my mother said to me, "You want to be the same as American girls on the outside." She handed me an early gift. It was a miniskirt in beige tweed. "But inside you must always be Chinese. You must be proud you are different. Your only shame is to have shame."   7

And even though I didn't agree with her then, I knew that she understood how much I had suffered during the evening's dinner. It wasn't until many years later — long after I had gotten over my crush on Robert — that I was able to fully appreciate her lesson and the true purpose behind our particular menu. For Christmas Eve that year, she had chosen all my favorite foods.   8

*For a reading quiz, sources on Amy Tan, and annotated links to further readings on Chinese Americans, visit **bedfordstmartins.com/thebedfordreader**.*

Journal Writing

Do you sympathize with the shame Tan feels because of her family's differences from their non-Chinese guests? Or do you think she should have been more proud to share her family's customs? Think of an occasion when, for whatever reason, you were acutely aware of being different. How did you react? Did you try to hide your difference in order to fit in, or did you reveal or celebrate your uniqueness? (To take your journal writing further, see "From Journal to Essay" below.)

Questions on Meaning

1. Why does Tan cry when she finds out that the boy she is in love with is coming to dinner?
2. Why does Tan's mother go out of her way to prepare a disturbingly traditional Chinese dinner for her daughter and guests? What one sentence best sums up the lesson Tan was not able to understand until years later?
3. How does the fourteen-year-old Tan feel about her Chinese background? about her mother?
4. What is Tan's PURPOSE in writing this essay? Does she just want to entertain readers, or might she have a weightier goal?

Questions on Writing Strategy

1. How does Tan draw the reader into her story right from the beginning?
2. How does Tan use TRANSITIONS both to drive and to clarify her narrative?
3. What is the IRONY of the last sentence of the essay?
4. **OTHER METHODS.** Paragraph 3 is a passage of pure DESCRIPTION. Why does Tan linger over the food? What is the EFFECT of this paragraph?

Questions on Language

1. The simile about Mary in the second sentence of the essay is surprising. Why? Why is it amusing? (See *Figures of speech* in Useful Terms for a definition of *simile*.)
2. How does the narrator's age affect the TONE of this essay? Give EXAMPLES of language particularly appropriate to a fourteen-year-old.
3. In which paragraph does Tan use strong verbs most effectively?
4. Make sure you know the meanings of the following words: prawns, tofu (par. 3); clamor (4); grimaced (5); muster (6).

Suggestions for Writing

1. **FROM JOURNAL TO ESSAY.** Using Tan's essay as a model, write a brief narrative based on your journal sketch about a time when you felt different from others. Try to imitate the way Tan integrates the external events of the dinner with her own

feelings about what is going on. Your story may be humorous, like Tan's, or more serious.

2. Take a perspective like that of the minister's son, Robert: Write a narrative essay about a time when you had to adjust to participating in a culture different from your own. It could be a meal, a wedding or other rite of passage, a religious cere- mony, a trip to another country. What did you learn from your experience, about yourself and others?

3. **CRITICAL WRITING.** From this essay one can INFER two very different sets of ASSUMPTIONS about the extent to which immigrants should seek to integrate themselves into the culture of their adopted country. Take either of these posi- tions, in favor of or against assimilation (cultural integration), and make an ARGUMENT for your case.

4. **CONNECTIONS.** Both Tan and Maya Angelou, in "Champion of the World" (p. 88), write about difference from white Americans, but their POINTS OF VIEW are not the same: Tan's is a teenager's lament about not fitting in; Angelou's is an oppressed child's excitement about proving the injustice of oppression. In an essay, ANALYZE the two authors' uses of narration to convey their perspectives. What details do they focus on? What internal thoughts do they report? Is one essay more effective than the other? Why, or why not?

Amy Tan on Writing

In 1989 Amy Tan delivered a lecture titled "Mother Tongue" at the State of the Language Symposium in San Francisco. The lecture, later published in *The Threepenny Review* in 1990, addresses Tan's own experience as a bilingual child speaking both Chinese and English. "I do think that the language spoken in the family, especially in immigrant families, which are more insular, plays a large role in shaping the language of the child. And I believe that it affected my results on achievement tests, IQ tests, and the SAT. While my English skills were never judged as poor, compared to math English could not be con- sidered my strong suit. . . . This was understandable. Math is precise; there is only one correct answer. Whereas, for me at least, the answers on English tests were always a judgment call, a matter of opinion and personal experience."

Tan goes on to say that the necessity of adapting to different styles of expression may affect other children from bilingual households. "I've been asked, as a writer, why there are not more Asian-Americans represented in American literature. Why are there few Asian-Americans enrolled in creative- writing programs? Why do so many Chinese students go into engineering? Well, these are broad sociological questions I can't begin to answer. But I have noticed in surveys . . . that Asian students, as a whole, always do significantly better on math achievement tests than in English. And this makes me think that there are other Asian-American students whose English spoken in the home might also be described as 'broken' or 'limited.' And perhaps they also have teachers who are steering them away from writing and into math and science, which is what happened to me."

Tan admits that when she first began writing fiction, she wrote "what I thought to be wittily crafted sentences, sentences that would finally prove I had mastery over the English language." But they were awkward and self-conscious, so she changed her tactic. "I later decided I should envision a reader for the stories I would write. And the reader I decided upon was my mother, because these were stories about mothers. So with this reader in mind—and in fact, she did read my early drafts—I began to write stories using all the Englishes I grew up with: the English I spoke to my mother, . . . the English she used with me, . . . my translation of her Chinese, . . . and what I imagined to be her translation of her Chinese if she could speak in perfect English, her internal language, and for that I sought to preserve the essence, but not either an English or a Chinese structure. I wanted to capture what language ability tests can never reveal: her intent, her passion, her imagery, the rhythms of her speech and the nature of her thoughts.

"Apart from what any critic had to say about my writing, I knew I had succeeded where it counted when my mother finished reading my book and gave me her verdict: 'So easy to read.'"

For Discussion

1. How could growing up in a household of "broken" English be a handicap for a student taking an achievement test?
2. What does the author suggest is the reason why more Asian Americans major in engineering than major in writing?
3. Why did Amy Tan's mother make a good reader?

ANNIE DILLARD

ANNIE DILLARD is accomplished as a prose writer, poet, and literary critic. Born in 1945, she earned a BA (1967) and an MA (1968) from Hollins College in Virginia. Dillard's first published prose, *Pilgrim at Tinker Creek* (1974), is a work alive with close, intense, and poetic descriptions of the natural world. It won her a Pulitzer Prize and comparison with Thoreau. Since then, Dillard's entranced and entrancing writing has appeared regularly in *Harper's, American Scholar, The Atlantic Monthly,* and other magazines and in her books: *Tickets for a Prayer Wheel* (1975), poems; *Holy the Firm* (1978), a prose poem; *Living by Fiction* (1982), literary criticism; *Teaching a Stone to Talk* (1982), nonfiction; *Encounters with Chinese Writers* (1984), an account of a trip to China; *An American Childhood* (1987), an autobiography; *The Writing Life* (1989), anecdotes and metaphors about writing; *The Living* (1992), a historical novel set in the Pacific Northwest; *Mornings Like This: Found Poems* (1995); and *For the Time Being* (1999), an exploration of how God and evil can coexist. In 1999 Dillard was inducted into the American Academy of Arts and Letters.

The Chase

In this chapter from her autobiography, *An American Childhood*, Dillard leads us running desperately through snow-filled backyards. Like all of Dillard's writing, this romp shows an unparalleled enthusiasm for life and skill at expressing it.

Some boys taught me to play football. This was fine sport. You thought up 1
a new strategy for every play and whispered it to the others. You went out for a pass, fooling everyone. Best, you got to throw yourself mightily at someone's running legs. Either you brought him down or you hit the ground flat on your chin, with your arms empty before you. It was all or nothing. If you hesitated in fear, you would miss and get hurt: you would take a hard fall while the kid got away, or you would get kicked in the face while the kid got away. But if you flung yourself wholeheartedly at the back of his knees — if you gathered and joined body and soul and pointed them diving fearlessly — then you likely wouldn't get hurt, and you'd stop the ball. Your fate, and your team's score, depended on your concentration and courage. Nothing girls did could compare with it.

Boys welcomed me at baseball, too, for I had, through enthusiastic prac- 2
tice, what was weirdly known as a boy's arm. In winter, in the snow, there was neither baseball nor football, so the boys and I threw snowballs at passing cars. I got in trouble throwing snowballs, and have seldom been happier since.

On one weekday morning after Christmas, six inches of new snow had
just fallen. We were standing up to our boot tops in snow on a front yard on
trafficked Reynolds Street, waiting for cars. The cars traveled Reynolds Street
slowly and evenly; they were targets all but wrapped in red ribbons, cream
puffs. We couldn't miss.

I was seven; the boys were eight, nine, and ten. The oldest two Fahey boys
were there—Mikey and Peter—polite blond boys who lived near me on
Lloyd Street, and who already had four brothers and sisters. My parents
approved Mikey and Peter Fahey. Chickie McBride was there, a tough kid,
and Billy Paul and Mackie Kean too, from across Reynolds, where the boys
grew up dark and furious, grew up skinny, knowing, and skilled. We had all
drifted from our houses that morning looking for action, and had found it here
on Reynolds Street.

It was cloudy but cold. The cars' tires laid behind them on the snowy
street a complex trail of beige chunks like crenellated castle walls. I had
stepped on some earlier; they squeaked. We could have wished for more traffic. When a car came, we all popped it one. In the intervals between cars we
reverted to the natural solitude of children.

I started making an iceball—a perfect iceball, from perfectly white snow,
perfectly spherical, and squeezed perfectly translucent so no snow remained
all the way through. (The Fahey boys and I considered it unfair actually to
throw an iceball at somebody, but it had been known to happen.)

I had just embarked on the iceball project when we heard tire chains
come clanking from afar. A black Buick was moving toward us down the
street. We all spread out, banged together some regular snowballs, took aim,
and, when the Buick drew nigh, fired.

A soft snowball hit the driver's windshield right before the driver's face. It
made a smashed star with a hump in the middle.

Often, of course, we hit our target, but this time, the only time in all of
life, the car pulled over and stopped. Its wide black door opened; a man got
out of it, running. He didn't even close the car door.

He ran after us, and we ran away from him, up the snowy Reynolds sidewalk. At the corner, I looked back; incredibly, he was still after us. He was
in city clothes: a suit and tie, street shoes. Any normal adult would have
quit, having sprung us into flight and made his point. This man was gaining
on us. He was a thin man, all action. All of a sudden, we were running for our
lives.

Wordless, we split up. We were on our turf; we could lose ourselves in the
neighborhood backyards, everyone for himself. I paused and considered.
Everyone had vanished except Mikey Fahey, who was just rounding the cor-

ner of a yellow brick house. Poor Mikey, I trailed him. The driver of the Buick sensibly picked the two of us to follow. The man apparently had all day.

He chased Mikey and me around the yellow house and up a backyard path 12
we knew by heart: under a low tree, up a bank, through a hedge, down some snowy steps, and across the grocery store's delivery driveway. We smashed through a gap in another hedge, entered a scruffy backyard and ran around its back porch and tight between houses to Edgerton Avenue; we ran across Edgerton to an alley and up our own sliding woodpile to the Halls' front yard; he kept coming. We ran up Lloyd Street and wound through mazy backyards toward the steep hilltop at Willard and Lang.

He chased us silently, block after block. He chased us silently over picket 13
fences, through thorny hedges, between houses, around garbage cans, and across streets. Every time I glanced back, choking for breath, I expected he would have quit. He must have been as breathless as we were. His jacket strained over his body. It was an immense discovery, pounding into my hot head with every sliding, joyous step, that this ordinary adult evidently knew what I thought only children who trained at football knew: that you have to fling yourself at what you're doing, you have to point yourself, forget yourself, aim, dive.

Mikey and I had nowhere to go, in our own neighborhood or out of it, but 14
away from this man who was chasing us. He impelled us forward; we compelled him to follow our route. The air was cold; every breath tore my throat. We kept running, block after block; we kept improvising, backyard after backyard, running a frantic course and choosing it simultaneously, failing always to find small places or hard places to slow him down, and discovering always, exhilarated, dismayed, that only bare speed could save us—for he would never give up, this man—and we were losing speed.

He chased us through the backyard labyrinths of ten blocks before he 15
caught us by our jackets. He caught us and we all stopped.

We three stood staggering, half blinded, coughing, in an obscure hilltop 16
backyard: a man in his twenties, a boy, a girl. He had released our jackets, our pursuer, our captor, our hero: He knew we weren't going anywhere. We all played by the rules. Mikey and I unzipped our jackets. I pulled off my sopping mittens. Our tracks multiplied in the backyard's new snow. We had been breaking new snow all morning. We didn't look at each other. I was cherishing my excitement. The man's lower pants legs were wet; his cuffs were full of snow, and there was a prow of snow beneath them on his shoes and socks. Some trees bordered the little flat backyard, some messy winter trees. There was no one around: a clearing in a grove, and we the only players.

It was a long time before he could speak. I had some difficulty at first 17
recalling why we were there. My lips felt swollen; I couldn't see out of the sides of my eyes; I kept coughing.

"You stupid kids," he began perfunctorily.   18

We listened perfunctorily indeed, if we listened at all, for the chewing out   19
was redundant, a mere formality, and beside the point. The point was that he
had chased us passionately without giving up, and so he had caught us. Now
he came down to earth. I wanted the glory to last forever.

But how could the glory have lasted forever? We could have run through   20
every backyard in North America until we got to Panama. But when he
trapped us at the lip of the Panama Canal, what precisely could he have done
to prolong the drama of the chase and cap its glory? I brooded about this for
the next few years. He could only have fried Mikey Fahey and me in boiling
oil, say, or dismembered us piecemeal, or staked us to anthills. None of which
I really wanted, and none of which any adult was likely to do, even in the
spirit of fun. He could only chew us out there in the Panamanian jungle, after
months or years of exalting pursuit. He could only begin, "You stupid kids,"
and continue in his ordinary Pittsburgh accent with his normal righteous
anger and the usual common sense.

If in that snowy backyard the driver of the black Buick had cut off our   21
heads, Mikey's and mine, I would have died happy, for nothing has required
so much of me since as being chased all over Pittsburgh in the middle of
winter—running terrified, exhausted—by this sainted, skinny, furious redheaded man who wished to have a word with us. I don't know how he found
his way back to his car.

---

*For a reading quiz, sources on Annie Dillard, and annotated links to further read-
ings on play for children and adults, visit **bedfordstmartins.com/thebedfordreader**.*

Journal Writing

Why do you suppose Dillard remembers in such vivid detail the rather insignificant
event she describes? What incidents from your childhood seem momentous even
now? List these incidents, along with some notes about their importance. (To take
your journal writing further, see "From Journal to Essay" on the facing page.)

Questions on Meaning

1. What is Dillard's PURPOSE in this essay? Obviously, she wants to entertain readers,
   but does she have another purpose as well?

2. Does the persistence of the pursuer seem reasonable to you, given the children's prank?
3. What does the pursuer represent for the narrator? How do her feelings about him change after the chase is over, and why?
4. Why does Dillard describe the "chewing out," seemingly the object of the chase, as "redundant, a mere formality, and beside the point" (par. 19)?

Questions on Writing Strategy

1. Why does Dillard open her story with a discussion of football? In what way does the game of football serve as a metaphor in the story? (Hint: Look at par. 13, as well as the sentence "It was all or nothing" in par. 1.) (See *Figures of speech* in Useful Terms for a definition of *metaphor*.)
2. Identify the two rapid TRANSITIONS in paragraph 2. Do they contribute to or detract from the COHERENCE of the essay?
3. Why does Dillard interrupt the story of the chase with an "immense discovery" (par. 13)? Does this interruption weaken the narrative?
4. Discuss Dillard's POINT OF VIEW. Is her perspective that of a seven-year-old girl, or that of an adult writer reflecting on her childhood experience?
5. **OTHER METHODS.** Dillard's story implicitly COMPARES AND CONTRASTS a child's and an adult's way of looking at life. What are some of the differences that Dillard implies?

Questions on Language

1. Look up the meaning of any of the following words you don't already know: crenellated (par. 5); translucent (6); nigh (7); impelled, compelled (14); prow (16); perfunctorily (18); redundant (19); piecemeal, exalting, righteous (20).
2. Explain the contradiction in this statement: "I got in trouble throwing snowballs, and have seldom been happier since" (par. 2). Can you find other examples of paradox in what the narrator says? How is this paradox related to the narrator's apparent view of children? (See *Figures of speech* in Useful Terms for a definition of *paradox*.)
3. Why are the strong verbs Dillard uses in paragraph 20 especially appropriate?
4. What is the EFFECT of the last sentence of the essay?

Suggestions for Writing

1. **FROM JOURNAL TO ESSAY.** Choose one significant incident from the list of childhood experiences you wrote in your journal, and narrate the incident as vividly as you can. Include the details: Where did the event take place? What did people say? How were they dressed? What was the weather like? Follow Dillard's model in putting CONCRETE IMAGES to work for an idea, in this case an idea about the significance of the incident to you then and now.
2. From what you have seen of children and adults, do you agree with Dillard's characterization of the two groups (see "Writing Strategy" question 5)? Write an essay comparing and contrasting children's and adults' attitudes toward play. (You will

have to GENERALIZE, of course, but try to keep your broad statements grounded in a reality your readers will share.)

3. **CRITICAL WRITING.** Dillard's narration of the chase is only six paragraphs long (pars. 10–15), but it seems longer, as if almost in real time. What techniques does Dillard use in these paragraphs to hold our attention and re-create the breathlessness of the chase? Look at concrete details, repetition, PARALLELISM, and the near absence of time-marking transitions. In ANALYZING Dillard's techniques, use plenty of quotations from the essay.

4. **CONNECTIONS.** Dillard's essay and Brad Manning's "Arm Wrestling with My Father" (p. 144) both deal with childhood values and how they are transformed as one grows older. In an essay, compare and contrast the two writers' treatment of this subject. How does the TONE of each essay contribute to its effect?

Annie Dillard on Writing

Writing for *The Bedford Reader,* Dillard has testified to her work habits. Rarely satisfied with an essay until it has gone through many drafts, she sometimes goes on correcting and improving it even after it has been published. "I always have to condense or toss openings," she affirms; "I suspect most writers do. When you begin something, you're so grateful to have begun you'll write down anything, just to prolong the sensation. Later, when you've learned what the writing is really about, you go back and throw away the beginning and start over."

Often she replaces a phrase or sentence with a shorter one. In one essay, to tell how a drop of pond water began to evaporate on a microscope slide, she first wrote, "Its contours pulled together." But that sentence seemed to suffer from "tortured abstraction." She made the sentence read instead, "Its edges shrank." Dillard observes, "I like short sentences. They're forceful, and they can get you out of big trouble."

For Discussion

1. Why, according to Dillard, is it usually necessary for writers to revise the opening paragraphs of what they write?
2. Dillard says that short sentences "can get you out of big trouble." What kinds of "big trouble" do you suppose she means?

SHERMAN ALEXIE

SHERMAN ALEXIE is a poet, fiction writer, and filmmaker known for witty and frank explorations of the lives of contemporary Native Americans. A Spokane/Coeur d'Alene Indian, Alexie was born in 1966 and grew up on the Spokane Indian Reservation in Wellpinit, Washington. He spent two years at Gonzaga University before transferring to Washington State University in Pullman. The same year he graduated, 1991, Alexie published *The Business of Fancydancing*, a book of poetry that led the *New York Times Book Review* to call him "one of the major lyric voices of our time." Since then Alexie has published many more books of poetry, including *I Would Steal Horses* (1993) and *One Stick Song* (2000); the novels *Reservation Blues* (1995) and *Indian Killer* (1996); and the story collections *The Lone Ranger and Tonto Fistfight in Heaven* (1993), *The Toughest Indian in the World* (2000), and *Ten Little Indians* (2003). Alexie also wrote and produced *Smoke Signals*, a film that won awards at the 1998 Sundance Film Festival, and he wrote and directed *The Business of Fancydancing* (2002), a film about the paths of two young men from the Spokane reservation. Living in Seattle with his wife and children, Alexie occasionally performs as a stand-up comic and holds the record for the most consecutive years as World Heavyweight Poetry Bout Champion.

Indian Education

Alexie attended the tribal school on the Spokane reservation through the seventh grade, when he decided to seek a better education at an off-reservation all-white high school. As this year-by-year account of his schooling makes clear, he was not firmly at home in either setting. The essay first appeared in Alexie's *The Lone Ranger and Tonto Fistfight in Heaven*.

First Grade

My hair was too short and my US Government glasses were horn-rimmed, ugly, and all that first winter in school, the other Indian boys chased me from one corner of the playground to the other. They pushed me down, buried me in the snow until I couldn't breathe, thought I'd never breathe again.

They stole my glasses and threw them over my head, around my outstretched hands, just beyond my reach, until someone tripped me and sent me falling again, facedown in the snow.

I was always falling down; my Indian name was Junior Falls Down. Sometimes it was Bloody Nose or Steal-His-Lunch. Once, it was Cries-Like-a-White-Boy, even though none of us had seen a white boy cry.

Then it was a Friday morning recess and Frenchy SiJohn threw snowballs at me while the rest of the Indian boys tortured some other *top-yogh-yaught* kid, another weakling. But Frenchy was confident enough to torment me all by himself, and most days I would have let him.

But the little warrior in me roared to life that day and knocked Frenchy to the ground, held his head against the snow, and punched him so hard that my knuckles and the snow made symmetrical bruises on his face. He almost looked like he was wearing war paint.   5

But he wasn't the warrior. I was. And I chanted *It's a good day to die, it's a good day to die*, all the way down to the principal's office.   6

Second Grade

Betty Towle, missionary teacher, redheaded and so ugly that no one ever had a puppy crush on her, made me stay in for recess fourteen days straight.   7

"Tell me you're sorry," she said.   8

"Sorry for what?" I asked.   9

"Everything," she said and made me stand straight for fifteen minutes, eagle-armed with books in each hand. One was a math book; the other was English. But all I learned was that gravity can be painful.   10

For Halloween I drew a picture of her riding a broom with a scrawny cat on the back. She said that her God would never forgive me for that.   11

Once, she gave the class a spelling test but set me aside and gave me a test designed for junior high students. When I spelled all the words right, she crumpled up the paper and made me eat it.   12

"You'll learn respect," she said.   13

She sent a letter home with me that told my parents to either cut my braids or keep me home from class. My parents came in the next day and dragged their braids across Betty Towle's desk.   14

"Indians, indians, indians." She said it without capitalization. She called me "indian, indian, indian."   15

And I said, *Yes, I am. I am Indian. Indian, I am.*   16

Third Grade

My traditional Native American art career began and ended with my very first portrait: *Stick Indian Taking a Piss in My Backyard*.   17

As I circulated the original print around the classroom, Mrs. Schluter intercepted and confiscated my art.   18

Censorship, I might cry now. *Freedom of expression*, I would write in editorials to the tribal newspaper.   19

In third grade, though, I stood alone in the corner, faced the wall, and waited for the punishment to end.   20

I'm still waiting.   21

Fourth Grade

"You should be a doctor when you grow up," Mr. Schluter told me, even   22
though his wife, the third grade teacher, thought I was crazy beyond my years.
My eyes always looked like I had just hit-and-run someone.

"Guilty," she said. "You always look guilty."   23

"Why should I be a doctor?" I asked Mr. Schluter.   24

"So you can come back and help the tribe. So you can heal people."   25

That was the year my father drank a gallon of vodka a day and the same   26
year that my mother started two hundred different quilts but never finished
any. They sat in separate, dark places in our HUD[1] house and wept savagely.

I ran home after school, heard their Indian tears, and looked in the mir-   27
ror. *Doctor Victor,* I called myself, invented an education, talked to my reflection. *Doctor Victor to the emergency room.*

Fifth Grade

I picked up a basketball for the first time and made my first shot. No. I   28
missed my first shot, missed the basket completely, and the ball landed in the
dirt and sawdust, sat there just like I had sat there only minutes before.

But it felt good, that ball in my hands, all those possibilities and angles. It   29
was mathematics, geometry. It was beautiful.

At that same moment, my cousin Steven Ford sniffed rubber cement from   30
a paper bag and leaned back on the merry-go-round. His ears rang, his mouth
was dry, and everyone seemed so far away.

But it felt good, that buzz in his head, all those colors and noises. It was   31
chemistry, biology. It was beautiful.

Oh, do you remember those sweet, almost innocent choices that the   32
Indian boys were forced to make?

Sixth Grade

Randy, the new Indian kid from the white town of Springdale, got into a   33
fight an hour after he first walked into the reservation school.

Stevie Flett called him out, called him a squawman, called him a pussy,   34
and called him a punk.

Randy and Stevie, and the rest of the Indian boys, walked out into the   35
playground.

[1] Housing and Urban Development, a US government department. —EDS.

"Throw the first punch," Stevie said as they squared off. 36

"No," Randy said. 37

"Throw the first punch," Stevie said again. 38

"No," Randy said again. 39

"Throw the first punch!" Stevie said for the third time, and Randy reared 40
back and pitched a knuckle fastball that broke Stevie's nose.

We all stood there in silence, in awe. 41

That was Randy, my soon-to-be first and best friend, who taught me the 42
most valuable lesson about living in the white world: *Always throw the first punch*.

Seventh Grade

I leaned through the basement window of the HUD house and kissed the 43
white girl who would later be raped by her foster-parent father, who was also
white. They both lived on the reservation, though, and when the headlines
and stories filled the papers later, not one word was made of their color.

Just Indians being Indians, someone must have said somewhere and they 44
were wrong.

But on the day I leaned through the basement window of the HUD 45
house and kissed the white girl, I felt the good-byes I was saying to my entire
tribe. I held my lips tight against her lips, a dry, clumsy, and ultimately stupid kiss.

But I was saying good-bye to my tribe, to all the Indian girls and women I 46
might have loved, to all the Indian men who might have called me cousin,
even brother.

I kissed that white girl and when I opened my eyes, she was gone from the 47
reservation, and when I opened my eyes, I was gone from the reservation, living in a farm town where a beautiful white girl asked my name.

"Junior Polatkin," I said, and she laughed. 48

After that, no one spoke to me for another five hundred years. 49

Eighth Grade

At the farm town junior high, in the boys' bathroom, I could hear voices 50
from the girls' bathroom, nervous whispers of anorexia and bulimia. I could
hear the white girls' forced vomiting, a sound so familiar and natural to me
after years of listening to my father's hangovers.

"Give me your lunch if you're just going to throw it up," I said to one of 51
those girls once.

I sat back and watched them grow skinny from self-pity. 52

Back on the reservation, my mother stood in line to get us commodities. 53
We carried them home, happy to have food, and opened the canned beef that
even the dogs wouldn't eat.

But we ate it day after day and grew skinny from self-pity. 54

There is more than one way to starve. 55

Ninth Grade

At the farm town high school dance, after a basketball game in an over- 56
heated gym where I had scored twenty-seven points and pulled down thirteen
rebounds, I passed out during a slow song.

As my white friends revived me and prepared to take me to the emergency 57
room where doctors would later diagnose my diabetes, the Chicano teacher
ran up to us.

"Hey," he said. "What's that boy been drinking? I know all about these 58
Indian kids. They start drinking real young."

Sharing dark skin doesn't necessarily make two men brothers. 59

Tenth Grade

I passed the written test easily and nearly flunked the driving, but still 60
received my Washington State driver's license on the same day that Wally Jim
killed himself by driving his car into a pine tree.

No traces of alcohol in his blood, good job, wife and two kids. 61

"Why'd he do it?" asked a white Washington State trooper. 62

All the Indians shrugged their shoulders, looked down at the ground. 63

"Don't know," we all said, but when we look in the mirror, see the history 64
of our tribe in our eyes, taste failure in the tap water, and shake with old tears,
we understand completely.

Believe me, everything looks like a noose if you stare at it long enough. 65

Eleventh Grade

Last night I missed two free throws which would have won the game 66
against the best team in the state. The farm town high school I play for is
nicknamed the "Indians," and I'm probably the only actual Indian ever to play
for a team with such a mascot.

This morning I pick up the sports page and read the headline: INDIANS   67
LOSE AGAIN.

Go ahead and tell me none of this is supposed to hurt me very much.   68

Twelfth Grade

I walk down the aisle, valedictorian of this farm town high school, and my   69
cap doesn't fit because I've grown my hair longer than it's ever been. Later, I
stand as the school-board chairman recites my awards, accomplishments, and
scholarships.

I try to remain stoic for the photographers as I look toward the future.   70

Back home on the reservation, my former classmates graduate: a few can't   71
read, one or two are just given attendance diplomas, most look forward to the
parties. The bright students are shaken, frightened, because they don't know
what comes next.

They smile for the photographer as they look back toward tradition.   72

The tribal newspaper runs my photograph and the photograph of my for-   73
mer classmates side by side.

Postscript: Class Reunion

Victor said, "Why should we organize a reservation high school reunion?   74
My graduating class has a reunion every weekend at the Powwow Tavern."

For a reading quiz, sources on Sherman Alexie, and annotated links to further
readings on Native American education and reservation life, visit **bedfordstmartins
.com/thebedfordreader**.

Journal Writing

Alexie mingles positive and negative school experiences, each seeming almost to
grow out of the other. Write down some of your own memorable school experiences,
positive or negative. Which kind of memories seem to dominate? Are the experiences connected? (To take your journal writing further, see "From Journal to Essay" on
p. 112.)

Questions on Meaning

1. What overall impression does Alexie create of life on the reservation? Point to specific EXAMPLES in the text that contribute to this impression.
2. Notice those places in the essay where Alexie describes how Native Americans face prejudice and negative stereotyping. What does this focus suggest about his PURPOSE?
3. The title "Indian Education" refers here to more than just formal schooling. What are some other implications of the title?
4. Alexie refers to his hair in the opening sentence of the essay and in the sections on second grade and twelfth grade. How, and of what, is his hair a SYMBOL?

Questions on Writing Strategy

1. In this essay Alexie offers thirteen scenes: one for each school grade and a post-script reunion. Why do you think he set these scenes up in separate sections and labeled them with headings, instead of, say, running the sections together and introducing each with a phrase like "During first grade" or "When I was in second grade"? What is the EFFECT of Alexie's narrative technique?
2. Each section of the essay ends with a brief paragraph, usually a single sentence. What common function do all of these conclusions perform? How do their functions vary, and why?
3. How does the section on the seventh grade, almost exactly in the middle of the essay, serve as a thematic TRANSITION?
4. Why do you think Alexie ends with the section "Postscript: Class Reunion"? What is the effect of this final image?
5. **OTHER METHODS.** At several points in the essay, Alexie uses COMPARISON AND CONTRAST. Locate at least two examples, and explain what each contributes to the essay.

Questions on Language

1. In paragraph 15 Alexie writes that his teacher said of him and his parents " 'Indians, indians, indians' . . . without capitalization." What is his point?
2. At the end of the seventh grade section (par. 49), Alexie writes that "no one spoke to me for another five hundred years." What does he mean? What is the effect of this hyperbole? (See *Figures of speech* in Useful Terms if you need a definition of *hyperbole*.)
3. Describe the IRONY in paragraphs 67 and 68.
4. Notice the similarities between the pairs of sentences composing paragraphs 29 and 31 and paragraphs 70 and 72. What point does Alexie make with the similarities?
5. If any of the following words are unfamiliar, be sure to look them up in a dictionary: horn-rimmed (par. 1); symmetrical (5); scrawny (11); circulated, intercepted, confiscated (18); ultimately (45); anorexia, bulimia (50); commodities (53); diabetes (57); valedictorian (69).

Suggestions for Writing

1. **FROM JOURNAL TO ESSAY.** Write an essay about a particularly memorable aspect of your life as a student, whether positive, negative, or a mix of both. You might focus on a single event, a series of events over years, or perhaps an entire school year. As you relate your story, try to give your personal experience meaning for your readers.

2. Using Alexie's essay as a model, write an essay about significant moments that occurred in your life and that had in common a challenge or a struggle or an achievement that is or was important to you. You need not organize according to school years, nor need the events be school related. Do make sure that the common theme in the events and the significance of each event is clear to readers.

3. One of Alexie's underlying themes in this essay is the difficulties Native Americans often face on reservations. Do some research about the conditions of reservation life. Then write an essay in which you report your findings.

4. **CRITICAL WRITING.** Alexie is well known for injecting humor, sometimes very dark humor, into tales that might otherwise be unrelievedly bleak. Where do you see humor in "Indian Education"? Who or what, if anything, does Alexie poke fun at? How effective is the humor? Write an essay analyzing Alexie's use of humor, focusing your analysis on a single central idea of your own and supporting it with plenty of examples from Alexie's essay.

5. **CONNECTIONS.** Like Alexie's "Indian Education," Maya Angelou's "Champion of the World" (p. 88) and Amy Tan's "Fish Cheeks" (p. 94) also report experiences of being culturally and racially different from mainstream white America. Earlier "Connections" writing topics ask you to compare and contrast Angelou's and Tan's perceptions of what sets them apart from the dominant culture (p. 92) or their uses of narration to convey their differing POINTS OF VIEW (p. 97). Now bring Alexie into one of these comparisons with Angelou or Tan or both. Be sure to use examples from the essays to support your main idea.

Sherman Alexie on Writing

The humor woven into his work sometimes surprises first-time readers of Sherman Alexie. "One of the biggest misconceptions about Indians is that we're stoic," Alexie told Pam Lambert of *People Weekly*. "But humor is an essential part of our culture." The humor in Alexie's writing reflects its role in the lives of contemporary Native Americans, for whom, Alexie told Doug Marx of *Publishers Weekly*, "laughter is a ceremony. It's the way people cope."

Alexie does not avoid depicting the poverty, alcoholism, and despair faced by many Indians. Sometimes criticized by other Indians for portraying reservation life as hopeless, Alexie responded to Doug Marx: "I write what I know and I don't try to mythologize myself, which is what some seem to want, and which some Indian women and men writers are doing, this Earth Mother and Shaman Man thing, trying to create these 'authentic, traditional' Indians. We don't live our lives that way."

Alexie believes that as an American Indian writer he has a special responsibility "to tell the truth," as he put it to E. K. Caldwell in another interview. But, he continued, "Part of the danger in being an artist of whatever color is that you fall in love with your wrinkles. The danger is that if you fall in love with your wrinkles then you don't want to get rid of them. You start to glorify them and perpetuate them. If you write about pain, you can end up searching for more pain to write about, that kind of thing, that self-destructive route. We need to get away from that. We can write about pain and anger without having it consume us."

Alexie doesn't mind being typecast as a Native American writer. Speaking to Joel McNally of *The Writer* magazine, Alexie said, "If you object to being defined by your race and culture, you are saying there is something wrong with writing about your race and your culture. I'm not going to let others define me. . . . If I write it, it's an Indian novel. If I wrote about Martians, it would be an Indian novel. If I wrote about the Amish, it would be an Indian novel. That's who I am."

For Discussion

1. What do you think Alexie means by the "Earth Mother and Shaman Man thing" that he disparages in the work of some Indian writers? Why does he disapprove of it?
2. Judging from his essay "Indian Education," how would you say Alexie follows his own advice to "write about the pain and anger without having it consume us"?

JESSICA COHEN

JESSICA COHEN was born in 1981 in Brussels, Belgium. The child of a journalist, she traveled extensively while growing up but now calls St. Paul, Minnesota, her hometown. Cohen graduated from Yale University in 2003 with a degree in history. She currently works in publishing, reads "voraciously," and plays competitive ultimate Frisbee.

Grade A:
The Market for a Yale Woman's Eggs

When she was a junior in college, Cohen answered an intriguing advertisement in the school newspaper. In this essay she both narrates her unsettling experience and reports the information she unearthed to help interpret her experience. The essay appeared first in 2001 in *The New Journal*, a Yale undergraduate magazine, and then in 2002 in *The Atlantic Monthly*, after Cohen won the magazine's competition for student essayists.

Early in the spring of last year a classified ad ran for two weeks in the *Yale Daily News*: "EGG DONOR NEEDED." The couple that placed the ad was picky, and for that reason was offering $25,000 for an egg from the right donor.

As a child I had a book called *Where Did I Come From?* It offered a full biological explanation, in cartoons, to answer those awkward questions that curious tots ask. But the book is now out of date. Replacing it is, for example, *Mommy, Did I Grow in Your Tummy?: Where Some Babies Come From*, which explains the myriad ways that children of the twenty-first century may have entered their families, including egg donation, surrogacy, in vitro fertilization,[1] and adoption. When conception doesn't occur in the natural way, it becomes very complicated. Once all possible parties have been accounted for—egg donor, sperm donor, surrogate mother, paying couple—as many as five people can be involved in conceiving and carrying a child. No wonder a new book is necessary.

The would-be parents' decision to advertise in the *News*—and to offer a five-figure compensation—immediately suggested that they were in the market for an egg of a certain rarefied type. Beyond their desire for an Ivy League donor, they wanted a young woman over five feet five, of Jewish heritage, athletic, with a minimum combined SAT score of 1500, and attractive. I was curious—and I fit all the criteria except the SAT score. So I e-mailed Michelle and David (not their real names) and asked for more information

---

[1] Fertilization of an egg outside the body. In Latin, *in vitro* means "in glass." —EDS.

114

about the process and how much the SAT minimum really meant to them. Then I waited for a reply.

Donating an egg is neither simple nor painless. Following an intensive 4 screening and selection process the donor endures a few weeks of invasive medical procedures. First the donor and the woman who will carry the child must coordinate their menstrual cycles. Typically the donor and the recipient take birth-control pills, followed by shots of a synthetic hormone such as Lupron; the combination suppresses ovulation and puts their cycles in sync. After altering her cycle the donor must enhance her egg supply with fertility drugs in the same way an infertile woman does when trying to conceive. Shots of a fertility hormone are administered for seven to eleven days, to stimulate the production of an abnormally large number of egg-containing follicles. During this time the donor must have her blood tested every other day so that doctors can monitor her hormone levels, and she must come in for periodic ultrasounds. Thirty-six hours before retrieval day a shot of hCG, human chorionic gonadotropin, is administered to prepare the eggs for release, so that they will be ready for harvest.

The actual retrieval is done while the donor is under anesthesia. The tool 5 is a needle, and the product, on average, is ten to twenty eggs. Doctors take that many because "not all eggs will be good," according to *Surrogate Mothers Online*, an informational Web site designed and maintained by experienced egg donors and surrogate mothers. "Some will be immature and some over-ripe."

Lisa, one of the hosts on *Surrogate Mothers Online* and an experienced egg 6 donor, described the process as a "rewarding" experience. When she explained that once in a while something can go wrong, I braced myself for the fine print. On very rare occasions, she wrote, hyperstimulation of the ovaries can occur, and the donor must be hospitalized until the ovaries return to normal. In even rarer cases the ovaries rupture, resulting in permanent infertility or possibly even death. "I must stress that this is very rare," Lisa assured prospective donors. "I had two very wonderful experiences. . . . The second [time] I stayed awake to help the doctor count how many eggs he retrieved."

David responded to my e-mail a few hours after I'd sent it. He told me 7 nothing about himself, and only briefly alluded to the many questions I had asked about the egg-donation process. He spent the bulk of the e-mail describing a cartoon, and then requested photos of me. The cartoon was a scene with a "couple that is just getting married, he a nerd and she a beauty," he wrote. "They are kvelling about how wonderful their offspring will be with his brains and her looks." He went on to describe the punch line: The next panel showed a nerdy-looking baby thinking empty thoughts. The following paragraph was more direct. David let me know that he and his wife were flexible on most criteria but that Michelle was "a real Nazi" about "donor looks and donor health history."

This seemed to be a commentary of some sort on the couple's situation   8
and how plans might go awry, but the message was impossible to pin down. I thanked him for the e-mail, asked where to send my pictures, and repeated my original questions about egg donation and their criteria.

In a subsequent e-mail David promised to return my photos, so I sent him   9
dorm-room pictures, the kind that every college student has lying around. Now they assumed a new level of importance. I would soon learn what this anonymous couple, somewhere in the United States, thought about my genetic material as displayed in these photographs.

Infertility is not a modern problem, but it has created a modern industry.   10
Ten percent of American couples are infertile, and many seek treatment from the $2-billion-a-year infertility industry. The approximately 370 fertility clinics across the United States help prospective parents to sift through their options. I sympathize with women who cannot use their own eggs to have children. The discovery must be a sober awakening for those who have always dreamed of raising a family. When would-be parents face this problem, however, their options depend greatly on their income. All over the world most women who can't have children must simply accept the fact and adopt, or find other roles in society. But especially here in the United States wealth can enable such couples to have a child of their own and to determine how closely that child will resemble the one they might have had—or the one they dream of having.

The Web site of Egg Donation, Inc., a program based in California, con-   11
tains a database listing approximately 300 potential donors. In order to access the list interested parties must call the company and request the user ID and the password for the month. Once I'd given the receptionist my name and address, she told me the password: *colorful*. I hung up and entered the database. Potential parents can search for a variety of features, narrowing the pool as much as they like according to ethnic origin, religion of birth, state of residence, hair color, eye color, height, and weight. I typed in the physical and religious characteristics that Michelle and David were looking for and found four potential donors. None of them had a college degree.

The standard compensation for donating an egg to Egg Donation is $3,500   12
to $5,000, and additional funds are offered to donors who have advanced degrees or are of Asian, African-American, or Jewish descent. Couples searching for an egg at Egg Donation can be picky, but not as picky as couples advertising in the *Yale Daily News*. Should couples be able to pay a premium on

an open market for their idea of the perfect egg? Maybe a modern-day Social Darwinist would say yes.[2] Modern success is measured largely in financial terms, so why shouldn't the most successful couples, eager to pay more, have access to the most expensive eggs? Of course, as David illustrated in his first e-mail, input does not always translate perfectly into output — the donor's desirable characteristics may never actually be manifested in the child.

If couples choose not to find their eggs through an agency, they must do so   13 independently. An Internet search turned up a few sites like *Surrogate Mothers Online*, where would-be donors and parents can post classified ads. More than 500 classifieds were posted on the site: a whole marketplace, an eBay for genetic material.

"Hi! My name is Kimberly," one of the ads read. "I am 24 years old, 5'11"   14 with blonde hair and green eyes. I previously donated eggs and the couple was blessed with BIG twin boys! The doctor told me I have perky ovaries! . . . The doctor told me I had the most perfect eggs he had ever seen." The Web site provided links to photographs of Kimberly and an e-mail address. Would-be parents on the site offered "competitive" rates, generally from $5,000 to $10,000 for donors who fit their specifications.

About a week after I sent my pictures to David and Michelle, I received a   15 third e-mail: "Got the pictures. You look perfect. I can't say this with any authority. That is my wife's department." I thought back to the first e-mail, where he'd written, "She's been known to disregard a young woman based on cheekbones, hair, nose, you name it." He then shifted the focus. "My department is the SAT scores. Can you tell me more about your academic performance? What are you taking at Yale? What high school did you attend?"

The whole thing seemed like a joke. I dutifully answered his questions,   16 explaining that I was from a no-name high school in the Midwest, I couldn't do math or science, and my academic performance was, well, average; I couldn't help feeling a bit disconcerted by his particular interest in my SAT score.

Michelle and David now had my educational data as well as my photos.   17 They were examining my credentials and trying to imagine their child. If I was accepted, a harvest of my eggs would be fertilized by the semen of the author of the disturbing e-mails I had received. A few embryos would be implanted; the remaining, if there were any, would be frozen; and then I would be out of the picture forever.

The modern embryo has been frozen, stolen, aborted, researched, and   18 delivered weeks early, along with five or six instant siblings. The summer of

---

[2] In the late nineteenth century, social Darwinism misapplied Charles Darwin's evolutionary theory of the survival of the fittest to human relations, maintaining that the wealthy are naturally more fit than the poor for economic and social life. — EDS.

2001 was full of embryo news, and the first big story was President Bush's deliberation on stem-cell research. The embryos available for genetic research include those frozen by fertility clinics for later use by couples attempting in vitro fertilization.

Embryos took the spotlight again when Helen Beasley, a surrogate mother   19
from Shrewsbury, England, decided to sue a San Francisco couple for parental rights to the twin fetuses she was carrying. The couple and Beasley had agreed that they would pay her $20,000 to carry one child created from a donated egg and the father's sperm. The agreement also called for selective reduction — the abortion of any additional embryos. Beasley claimed that there had been a verbal agreement that such reduction would occur by the twelfth week. The problem arose when Beasley, who had discovered she was carrying twins, was told to abort one, but the arrangements for the reduction weren't made until the thirteenth week. Fearing for her own health and objecting to the abortion of such a highly developed fetus, she refused. At that time she was suing for the right to put the babies up for adoption. She was also seeking the remainder of the financial compensation specified in the contract. The couple did not want the children, and yet had the rights to the genetic material; Beasley was simply a vessel. The case is only one of a multitude invited by modern fertility processes. On August 15, 2001, the *New York Times* reported that the New Jersey Supreme Court had upheld a woman's rights to the embryos that she and her ex-husband had created and frozen six years before. A strange case for child-custody lawyers.

Nearly ten years ago, at the University of California at Irvine's Center for   20
Reproductive Health, doctors took the leftover frozen embryos from previous clients and gave them without consent to other couples and to research centers. Discovery of the scam resulted in more than thirty prosecutions: A group of children had biological parents who hadn't consented to their existence and active parents who had been given stolen goods. Who can say whether throwing the embryos away would have been any better?

Even if Michelle and David liked my data, I knew I'd have a long way to   21
go before becoming an actual donor. The application on Egg Donation's Web site is twelve pages long — longer than Yale's entrance application. The first two pages cover the basics: appearance, name, address, age, and other mundane details. After that I was asked if I'd ever filed for bankruptcy or ever had counseling, if I drank, what my goals in life were, what two of my favorite books were, what my paternal grandfather's height and weight were, what hobbies I had, what kind of relationship I would want to have with the parents and child, and so forth. A few fill-in-the-blanks were thrown in at the end: "I feel strongly about _____. I am sorry I did not _____. In ten years I

want to be _____." Not even my closest friends knew all these things about me. If Egg Donation, offering about a fifth what Michelle and David were offering, wanted all this information, what might Michelle and David want?

Michelle and David were certainly trying hard. On one classified-ad site   22
I came across a request that was strangely familiar: "Loving family seeks exceptional egg donor with 1500 SAT, great looks, good family health history, Jewish heritage and athletic. Height 5'4"–5'9", Age 18–29. We will pay EXTREMELY well and will take care of all expenses. Hope to hear from you." The e-mail address was David and Michelle's familiar AOL account. Theirs was the most demanding classified on the site, but also the only one that offered to pay "EXTREMELY well."

I kept dreaming about all the things I could do with $25,000. I had gone   23
into the correspondence on a whim. But soon, despite David's casual tone and the optimistic attitude of all the classifieds and information I read, I realized that this process was something I didn't want to be a part of. I understand the desire for a child who will resemble and fit in with the family. But once a couple starts choosing a few characteristics, shooting for perfection is too easy—especially if they can afford it. The money might have changed my life for a while, but it would have led to the creation of a child encumbered with too many expectations.

After I'd brooded about these matters, I received the shortest e-mail of the   24
correspondence. The verdict on my pictures was in: "I showed the pictures to [my wife] this AM. Personally, I think you look great. She said ho-hum."

David said he might reconsider, and that he was going to keep one of my   25
pictures. That was it. No good-bye, no thanks for my willingness to be, in effect, the biological mother of their child. I guess I didn't fit their design; my genes weren't the right material for their *chef d'oeuvre*.[3] So I was rejected as a donor. I keep imagining the day when David and Michelle's child asks where he or she came from. David will describe how hard they both worked on the whole thing, how many pictures they looked at, and how much money they spent. The child will turn to them and say, "Ho-hum."

For a reading quiz and annotated links to further readings on egg and sperm donation, visit **bedfordstmartins.com/thebedfordreader**.

---

[3] French, "masterpiece."—EDS.

Journal Writing

Would you consider offering your eggs or your sperm to a person or a couple who could not have a biological child? Would money be important to you? Would you be more willing to donate to an individual or to a couple? to acquaintances or relatives or to strangers? Would you be willing to be screened and selected on the basis of your appearance, intelligence, and personality? If a child resulted, would you want to be involved or not in his or her life? In your journal, answer these questions or any others that occur to you about egg or sperm donation. (To take your journal writing further, see "From Journal to Essay" on the facing page.)

Questions on Meaning

1. Why did Cohen respond to the ad for an egg donor? Do you think she seriously considered donating her eggs to the couple who placed the ad?
2. According to Cohen, conception via a donor can result in a variety of complications and difficulties. What are some of these?
3. What seems to be Cohen's primary PURPOSE in this essay?
4. Cohen states her THESIS near the end of her essay. What is this thesis?

Questions on Writing Strategy

1. Cohen intersperses narration of her own experiences with information gleaned from research into egg donation. Which paragraphs focus on narration? How would the essay have been different if Cohen had first presented the narrative and then the research, or vice versa? Why do you think she mixes the two?
2. Cohen specifically lays the groundwork for her thesis at two points earlier in the essay. Where are these two points?
3. What is the EFFECT of Cohen's final paragraph?
4. **OTHER METHODS.** Where in the essay does Cohen rely on PROCESS ANALYSIS? Why is process analysis appropriate at this point?

Questions on Language

1. Why do you think Cohen quotes the word *rewarding* in paragraph 6?
2. What is the IRONY in the husband's referring to his wife as "'a real Nazi' about 'donor looks and donor health history'" (par. 7)?
3. Why do you think Cohen quotes so extensively from Kimberly's advertisement as an egg donor (par. 14)?
4. The term *egg donation* is not really accurate because most "donors" are in fact paid for their services. Why do you think this is the common term rather than, say, *egg marketing*?
5. Consult a dictionary if you need help defining the following: myriad, surrogacy (par. 2); rarefied (3); synthetic, ovulation, follicles (4); rupture, infertility (6); kvelling (7); embryos (17); deliberation (18); vessel (19); brooded (24).

Suggestions for Writing

1. **FROM JOURNAL TO ESSAY.** Based on your earlier journal writing, draft an essay in which you explain your attitudes toward egg or sperm donation. You might expand your thinking to include advice you would give to a friend or relative who was considering trying to conceive a child using donated sperm or eggs.
2. Have you ever initiated a course of action but then, as events unfolded, developed second thoughts? What changed your mind? Write a narrative essay in which you relate that experience.
3. Conceiving a child by purchasing eggs or sperm raises a number of moral questions. For instance: Are there moral limits on our use of biotechnology to achieve our wishes? Is it ethical to transfer genetic material between strangers? Is it ethical to buy or sell genetic material? Should buyers be able to select "donors" for their appearance and intelligence? Research one of these questions or any other that interests you, and write an essay in which you report the various positions on the issue and defend your view.
4. **CRITICAL WRITING.** Write an essay in which you ANALYZE Cohen's TONE in this essay. You might consider how Cohen manages to suggest, without explicitly arguing, that she disapproves of egg donation as it is currently practiced.
5. **CONNECTIONS.** In "A Measure of Restraint" (p. 212), Chet Raymo writes about "breakthrough[s] in science that harbored potential for danger as well as good" (par. 10). How do you think Cohen might respond to Raymo's concerns? How do you respond? In an essay, consider egg donation and egg selection in light of their "potential for danger as well as good." Research can extend and test your thinking.

Jessica Cohen on Writing

Jessica Cohen wrote "Grade A" because she couldn't get her experience out of her head. Putting her thoughts on paper helped confirm her decision not to pursue egg donation. "When you figure something out for yourself," Cohen says, "there is a high likelihood that someone else might like to read about it."

Cohen believes that writing "is about sitting down and doing it." "Grade A" came fairly easily to her once she put pencil to paper, probably because she cared about her topic: "It was exciting to do research on a topic I was invested in." Such topics are everywhere, Cohen points out: "Strange things happen to us all the time. We notice interesting and quirky things and wonder why they exist or how they came to exist. The kind of nonfiction writing that I like best comes from these questions."

For Discussion

1. What are some examples of the questions Cohen refers to at the end of the second paragraph? What questions have prompted your own writing?
2. Discuss a time when writing helped you figure out something about yourself.

SHIRLEY JACKSON

SHIRLEY JACKSON was a fiction writer best known for horror stories that probe the dark side of human nature and social behavior. But she also wrote humorously about domestic life, a subject she knew well as a wife and the mother of four children. Born in 1919 in California, Jackson moved as a teenager to Syracuse, New York, and graduated from Syracuse University in 1940. She started writing as a young girl and was highly disciplined and productive all her life. She began publishing stories in 1941, and eventually her fiction appeared in *The New Yorker, Harper's, Good Housekeeping,* and many other magazines. Her tales of family life appeared in two books, *Life among the Savages* (1953) and *Raising Demons* (1957). Her more popular (and to her more significant) suspense novels included *The Haunting of Hill House* (1959) and *We Have Always Lived in the Castle* (1962). After Jackson's death in 1965, her husband, the literary critic Stanley Edgar Hyman, published two volumes of her stories, novels, and lectures, *The Magic of Shirley Jackson* (1966) and *Come Along with Me* (1968).

The Lottery

By far Jackson's best-known work and indeed one of the best-known short stories ever, "The Lottery" first appeared in *The New Yorker* in 1948 to loud applause and louder cries of outrage. Jackson's husband, denying that her work purveyed "neurotic fantasies," argued instead that it was fitting "for our distressing world of concentration camps and The Bombs." Is it still relevant today?

1   The morning of June 27th was clear and sunny, with the fresh warmth of a full-summer day; the flowers were blossoming profusely and the grass was richly green. The people of the village began to gather in the square, between the post office and the bank, around ten o'clock; in some towns there were so many people that the lottery took two days and had to be started on June 26th, but in this village, where there were only about three hundred people, the whole lottery took less than two hours, so it could begin at ten o'clock in the morning and still be through in time to allow the villagers to get home for noon dinner.

2   The children assembled first, of course. School was recently over for the summer, and the feeling of liberty sat uneasily on most of them; they tended to gather together quietly for a while before they broke into boisterous play, and their talk was still of the classroom and the teacher, of books and reprimands. Bobby Martin had already stuffed his pockets full of stones, and the other boys soon followed his example, selecting the smoothest and roundest stones; Bobby and Harry Jones and Dickie Delacroix—the villagers pro-

nounced this name "Dellacroy"—eventually made a great pile of stones in one corner of the square and guarded it against the raids of the other boys. The girls stood aside, talking among themselves, looking over their shoulders at the boys, and the very small children rolled in the dust or clung to the hands of their older brothers or sisters.

Soon the men began to gather, surveying their own children, speaking of planting and rain, tractors and taxes. They stood together, away from the pile of stones in the corner, and their jokes were quiet and they smiled rather than laughed. The women, wearing faded house dresses and sweaters, came shortly after their menfolk. They greeted one another and exchanged bits of gossip as they went to join their husbands. Soon the women, standing by their husbands, began to call to their children, and the children came reluctantly, having to be called four or five times. Bobby Martin ducked under his mother's grasping hand and ran, laughing, back to the pile of stones. His father spoke up sharply, and Bobby came quickly and took his place between his father and his oldest brother.

The lottery was conducted—as were the square dances, the teenage club, the Halloween program—by Mr. Summers, who had time and energy to devote to civic activities. He was a round-faced, jovial man and he ran the coal business, and people were sorry for him, because he had no children and his wife was a scold. When he arrived in the square, carrying the black wooden box, there was a murmur of conversation among the villagers, and he waved and called, "Little late today, folks." The postmaster, Mr. Graves, followed him, carrying a three-legged stool, and the stool was put in the center of the square and Mr. Summers set the black box down on it. The villagers kept their distance, leaving a space between themselves and the stool, and when Mr. Summers said, "Some of you fellows want to give me a hand?" there was a hesitation before two men, Mr. Martin and his oldest son, Baxter, came forward to hold the box steady on the stool while Mr. Summers stirred up the papers inside it.

The original paraphernalia for the lottery had been lost long ago, and the black box now resting on the stool had been put into use even before Old Man Warner, the oldest man in town, was born. Mr. Summers spoke frequently to the villagers about making a new box, but no one liked to upset even as much tradition as was represented by the black box. There was a story that the present box had been made with some pieces of the box that had preceded it, the one that had been constructed when the first people settled down to make a village here. Every year, after the lottery, Mr. Summers began talking again about a new box, but every year the subject was allowed to fade off without anything's being done. The black box grew shabbier each year; by now it was no longer completely black but splintered badly along one side to show the original wood color, and in some places faded or stained.

Mr. Martin and his oldest son, Baxter, held the black box securely on the   6
stool until Mr. Summers had stirred the papers thoroughly with his hand.
Because so much of the ritual had been forgotten or discarded, Mr. Summers
had been successful in having slips of paper substituted for the chips of wood
that had been used for generations. Chips of wood, Mr. Summer had argued,
had been all very well when the village was tiny, but now that the population
was more than three hundred and likely to keep on growing, it was necessary
to use something that would fit more easily into the black box. The night
before the lottery, Mr. Summers and Mr. Graves made up the slips of paper and
put them in the box, and it was then taken to the safe of Mr. Summers' coal
company and locked up until Mr. Summers was ready to take it to the square
next morning. The rest of the year, the box was put away, sometimes one
place, sometimes another; it had spent one year in Mr. Graves's barn and
another year underfoot in the post office, and sometimes it was set on a shelf
in the Martin grocery and left there.

There was a great deal of fussing to be done before Mr. Summers declared   7
the lottery open. There were the lists to make up — of heads of families, heads
of households in each family, members of each household in each family.
There was the proper swearing-in of Mr. Summers by the postmaster, as the
official of the lottery; at one time, some people remembered, there had been a
recital of some sort, performed by the official of the lottery, a perfunctory,
tuneless chant that had been rattled off duly each year; some people believed
that the official of the lottery used to stand just so when he said or sang it, others believed that he was supposed to walk among the people, but years and
years ago this part of the ritual had been allowed to lapse. There had been,
also, a ritual salute, which the official of the lottery had had to use in addressing each person who came up to draw from the box, but this also had changed
with time, until now it was felt necessary only for the official to speak to each
person approaching. Mr. Summers was very good at all this; in his clean white
shirt and blue jeans, with one hand resting carelessly on the black box, he
seemed very proper and important as he talked interminably to Mr. Graves
and the Martins.

Just as Mr. Summers finally left off talking and turned to the assembled   8
villagers, Mrs. Hutchinson came hurriedly along the path to the square, her
sweater thrown over her shoulders, and slid into place in the back of the
crowd. "Clean forgot what day it was," she said to Mrs. Delacroix, who stood
next to her, and they both laughed softly. "Thought my old man was out back
stacking wood," Mrs. Hutchinson went on, "and then I looked out the window and the kids was gone, and then I remembered it was the twenty-seventh
and came a-running." She dried her hands on her apron, and Mrs. Delacroix
said, "You're in time, though. They're still talking away up there."

Mrs. Hutchinson craned her neck to see through the crowd and found her   9
husband and children standing near the front. She tapped Mrs. Delacroix
on the arm as a farewell and began to make her way through the crowd. The
people separated good-humoredly to let her through; two or three people said,
in voices just loud enough to be heard across the crowd, "Here comes your
Missus, Hutchinson," and "Bill, she made it after all." Mrs. Hutchinson
reached her husband, and Mr. Summers, who had been waiting, said cheerfully, "Thought we were going to have to get on without you, Tessie." Mrs.
Hutchinson said, grinning, "Wouldn't have me leave m'dishes in the sink,
now, would you, Joe?" and soft laughter ran through the crowd as the people
stirred back into position after Mrs. Hutchinson's arrival.

"Well now," Mr. Summers said soberly, "guess we better get started, get   10
this over with, so's we can go back to work. Anybody ain't here?"

"Dunbar," several people said. "Dunbar, Dunbar."   11

Mr. Summers consulted his list. "Clyde Dunbar," he said. "That's right.   12
He's broke his leg, hasn't he? Who's drawing for him?"

"Me, I guess," a woman said, and Mr. Summers turned to look at her.   13
"Wife draws for her husband," Mr. Summers said. "Don't you have a grown
boy to do it for you, Janey?" Although Mr. Summers and everyone else in the
village knew the answer perfectly well, it was the business of the official of the
lottery to ask such questions formally. Mr. Summers waited with an expression
of polite interest while Mrs. Dunbar answered.

"Horace's not but sixteen yet," Mrs. Dunbar said regretfully. "Guess I gotta   14
fill in for the old man this year."

"Right," Mr. Summers said. He made a note on the list he was holding.   15
Then he asked, "Watson boy drawing this year?"

A tall boy in the crowd raised his hand. "Here," he said. "I'm drawing for   16
m'mother and me." He blinked his eyes nervously and ducked his head as several voices in the crowd said things like "Good fellow, Jack," and "Glad to see
your mother's got a man to do it."

"Well," Mr. Summers said, "guess that's everyone. Old Man Warner make it?"   17

"Here," a voice said, and Mr. Summers nodded.   18

A sudden hush fell on the crowd as Mr. Summers cleared his throat and   19
looked at the list. "All ready?" he called. "Now, I'll read the names — heads of
families first — and the men come up and take a paper out of the box. Keep
the paper folded in your hand without looking at it until everyone has had a
turn. Everything clear?"

The people had done it so many times that they only half listened to   20
the directions, most of them were quiet, wetting their lips, not looking
around. Then Mr. Summers raised one hand high and said, "Adams." A man

disengaged himself from the crowd and came forward. "Hi, Steve," Mr. Summers said, and Mr. Adams said, "Hi, Joe." They grinned at one another humorlessly and nervously. Then Mr. Adams reached into the black box and took out a folded paper. He held it firmly by one corner as he turned and went hastily back to his place in the crowd, where he stood a little apart from his family, not looking down at his hand.

"Allen," Mr. Summers said, "Anderson. . . . Bentham."   21

"Seems like there's no time at all between lotteries anymore," Mrs. Delacroix said to Mrs. Graves in the back row. "Seems like we got through with the last one only last week."   22

"Time sure goes fast," Mrs. Graves said.   23

"Clark. . . . Delacroix."   24

"There goes my old man," Mrs. Delacroix said. She held her breath while her husband went forward.   25

"Dunbar," Mr. Summers said, and Mrs. Dunbar went steadily to the box while one of the women said, "Go on Janey," and another said, "There she goes."   26

"We're next," Mrs. Graves said. She watched while Mr. Graves came around from the side of the box, greeted Mr. Summers gravely, and selected a slip of paper from the box. By now, all through the crowd there were men holding the small folded papers in their large hands, turning them over and over nervously. Mrs. Dunbar and her two sons stood together, Mrs. Dunbar holding the slip of paper.   27

"Harburt . . . Hutchinson."   28

"Get up there, Bill," Mrs. Hutchinson said, and the people near her laughed.   29

"Jones."   30

"They do say," Mr. Adams said to Old Man Warner, who stood next to him, "that over in the north village they're talking of giving up the lottery."   31

Old Man Warner snorted. "Pack of crazy fools," he said. "Listening to the young folks, nothing's good enough for *them*. Next thing you know, they'll be wanting to go back to living in caves, nobody work anymore, live *that* way for a while. Used to be a saying about 'Lottery in June, corn be heavy soon.' First thing you know, we'd all be eating stewed chickweed and acorns. There's *always* been a lottery," he added petulantly. "Bad enough to see young Joe Summers up there joking with everybody."   32

"Some places have already quit lotteries," Mrs. Adams said.   33

"Nothing but trouble in *that*," Old Man Warner said stoutly. "Pack of young fools."   34

"Martin." And Bobby Martin watched his father go forward. "Overdyke. . . . Percy."   35

"I wish they'd hurry," Mrs. Dunbar said to her older son. "I wish they'd   36
hurry."

"They're almost through," her son said.   37

"You get ready to run tell Dad," Mrs. Dunbar said.   38

Mr. Summers called his own name and then stepped forward precisely and   39
selected a slip from the box. Then he called, "Warner."

"Seventy-seventh year I been in the lottery," Old Man Warner said as he   40
went through the crowd. "Seventy-seventh time."

"Watson." The tall boy came awkwardly through the crowd. Someone   41
said, "Don't be nervous, Jack," and Mr. Summers said, "Take your time, son."

"Zanini."   42

After that, there was a long pause, a breathless pause, until Mr. Summers   43
holding his slip of paper in the air, said, "All right, fellows." For a minute, no
one moved, and then all the slips of paper were opened. Suddenly, all the
women began to speak at once, saying, "Who is it?" "Who's got it?" "Is it the
Dunbars?" "Is it the Watsons?" Then the voices began to say, "It's Hutchinson.
It's Bill," "Bill Hutchinson's got it."

"Go tell your father," Mrs. Dunbar said to her older son.   44

People began to look around to see the Hutchinsons. Bill Hutchinson was   45
standing quiet, staring down at the paper in his hand. Suddenly, Tessie
Hutchinson shouted to Mr. Summers, "You didn't give him time enough to
take any paper he wanted. I saw you. It wasn't fair!"

"Be a good sport, Tessie," Mrs. Delacroix called, and Mrs. Graves said,   46
"All of us took the same chance."

"Shut up, Tessie," Bill Hutchinson said.   47

"Well, everyone," Mr. Summers said, "that was done pretty fast, and now   48
we've got to be hurrying a little more to get done in time." He consulted his
next list. "Bill," he said, "you draw for the Hutchinson family. You got any
other households in the Hutchinsons?"

"There's Don and Eva," Mrs. Hutchinson yelled. "Make *them* take their   49
chance!"

"Daughters drew with their husband's families, Tessie," Mr. Summers said   50
gently. "You know that as well as anyone else."

"It wasn't *fair*," Tessie said.   51

"I guess not, Joe," Bill Hutchinson said regretfully. "My daughter draws   52
with her husband's family, that's only fair. And I've got no other family except
the kids."

"Then, as far as drawing for families is concerned, it's you," Mr. Summers   53
said in explanation, "and as far as drawing for households is concerned, that's
you, too. Right?"

"Right," Bill Hutchinson said.   54

"How many kids, Bill?" Mr. Summers asked formally.   55

"Three," Bill Hutchinson said. "There's Bill, Jr., and Nancy, and little   56
Dave. And Tessie and me."

"All right, then," Mr. Summer said. "Harry, you got their tickets back?"   57

Mr. Graves nodded and held up the slips of paper. "Put them in the box,   58
then," Mr. Summers directed. "Take Bill's and put it in."

"I think we ought to start over," Mrs. Hutchinson said, as quietly as she   59
could. "I tell you it wasn't *fair*. You didn't give him time enough to choose.
Everybody saw that."

Mr. Graves had selected the five slips and put them in the box, and he   60
dropped all the papers but those onto the ground, where the breeze caught
them and lifted them off.

"Listen, everybody," Mrs. Hutchinson was saying to the people around her.   61

"Ready, Bill?" Mr. Summers asked, and Bill Hutchinson, with one quick   62
glance around at his wife and children, nodded.

"Remember," Mr. Summers said, "take the slips and keep them folded   63
until each person has taken one. Harry, you help little Dave." Mr. Graves took
the hand of the little boy, who came willingly with him up to the box. "Take
a paper out of the box, Davy," Mr. Summers said. Davy put his hand into the
box and laughed. "Take just *one* paper," Mr. Summers said. "Harry, you hold it
for him." Mr. Graves took the child's hand and removed the folded paper from
the tight fist and held it while little Dave stood next to him and looked up at
him wonderingly.

"Nancy next," Mr. Summers said. Nancy was twelve, and her school   64
friends breathed heavily as she went forward, switching her skirt, and took a
slip daintily from the box. "Bill, Jr.," Mr. Summers said, and Billy, his face red
and his feet overlarge, nearly knocked the box over as he got a paper out.
"Tessie," Mr. Summers said. She hesitated for a minute, looking around defi-
antly, and then set her lips and went up to the box. She snatched a paper out
and held it behind her.

"Bill," Mr. Summers said, and Bill Hutchinson reached into the box and   65
felt around, bringing his hand out at last with the slip of paper in it.

The crowd was quiet. A girl whispered, "I hope it's not Nancy," and the   66
sound of the whisper reached the edges of the crowd.

"It's not the way it used to be," Old Man Warner said clearly. "People ain't   67
the way they used to be."

"All right," Mr. Summers said. "Open the papers. Harry, you open little   68
Dave's."

Mr. Graves opened the slip of paper and there was a general sigh through   69
the crowd as he held it up and everyone could see that it was blank. Nancy

and Bill, Jr., opened theirs at the same time, and both beamed and laughed, turning around to the crowd and holding their slips of paper above their heads.

"Tessie," Mr. Summers said. There was a pause, and then Mr. Summers looked at Bill Hutchinson, and Bill unfolded his paper and showed it. It was blank.   70

"It's Tessie," Mr. Summers said, and his voice was hushed. "Show us her paper, Bill."   71

Bill Hutchinson went over to his wife and forced the slip of paper out of her hand. It had a black spot on it, the black spot Mr. Summers had made the night before with the heavy pencil in the coal-company office. Bill Hutchinson held it up and there was a stir in the crowd.   72

"All right, folks," Mr. Summers said. "Let's finish quickly."   73

Although the villagers had forgotten the ritual and lost the original black box, they still remembered to use stones. The pile of stones the boys had made earlier was ready; there were stones on the ground with the blowing scraps of paper that had come out of the box. Mrs. Delacroix selected a stone so large she had to pick it up with both hands and turned to Mrs. Dunbar. "Come on," she said. "Hurry up."   74

Mrs. Dunbar had small stones in both hands, and she said, gasping for breath, "I can't run at all. You'll have to go ahead and I'll catch up with you."   75

The children had stones already, and someone gave little Davy Hutchinson a few pebbles.   76

Tessie Hutchinson was in the center of a cleared space by now, and she held her hands out desperately as the villagers moved in on her. "It isn't fair," she said. A stone hit her on the side of the head.   77

Old Man Warner was saying, "Come on, come on, everyone." Steve Adams was in front of the crowd of villagers, with Mrs. Graves beside him.   78

"It isn't fair, it isn't right," Mrs. Hutchinson screamed and then they were upon her.   79

---

*For a reading quiz, sources on Shirley Jackson, and annotated links to further readings on the psychology of conformity, visit **bedfordstmartins.com/thebedfordreader**.*

Journal Writing

Think about rituals in which you participate, such as those involving holidays, meals, religious observances, family vacations, sporting events—anything that is repeated and traditional. List some of these in your journal and write about their significance to you. (To take your writing further, see "From Journal to Essay" on the facing page.)

Questions on Meaning

1. The PURPOSE of all fiction might be taken as entertainment or self-expression. Does Jackson have any other purpose in "The Lottery"?
2. When does the reader know what is actually going to occur?
3. Describe this story's community on the basis of what Jackson says of it.
4. What do the villagers' attitudes toward the black box indicate about their feelings toward the lottery?

Questions on Writing Strategy

1. Jackson uses the third PERSON (*he, she, it, they*) to narrate the story, and she does not enter the minds of her characters. Why do you think she keeps this distant POINT OF VIEW?
2. On your first reading of the story, what did you make of the references to rocks in paragraphs 2–3? Do you think they effectively forecast the ending?
3. Jackson has a character introduce a controversial notion in paragraph 31. Why does she do this?
4. **OTHER METHODS.** Jackson is exploring—or inviting us to explore—CAUSES AND EFFECTS. Why do the villagers participate in the lottery every year? What does paragraph 32 hint might have been the original reason for it?

Questions on Language

1. Dialog provides much information not stated elsewhere in the story. Give three examples of such information about the community and its interactions.
2. Check a dictionary for definitions of the following words: profusely (par. 1); boisterous, reprimand (2); jovial, scold, paraphernalia (4); perfunctory, duly, interminably (7); petulantly (32).
3. In paragraph 64 we read that Mrs. Hutchinson "snatched" the paper out of the box. What does this verb suggest about her attitude?
4. Jackson admits to setting the story in her Vermont village in the present time (that is, 1948). Judging from the names of the villagers, where did these people's ancestors originally come from? What do you make of the names Delacroix and Zanini? What is their significance?
5. Unlike much fiction, "The Lottery" contains few FIGURES OF SPEECH. Why do you think this is?

Suggestions for Writing

1. **FROM JOURNAL TO ESSAY.** Choose one of the rituals you wrote about in your journal, and compose a narrative about the last time you participated in this ritual. Use DESCRIPTION and dialog to convey the significance of the ritual and your own and other participants' attitudes toward it.

2. Write an imaginary narrative, perhaps set in the future, of a ritual that demonstrates something about the people who participate in it. The ritual can be but need not be as sinister as Jackson's lottery; yours could concern bathing, eating, dating, going to school, driving, growing older.

3. In his 1974 book *Obedience to Authority*, the psychologist Stanley Milgram reported and analyzed the results of a study he had conducted that caused a furor among psychologists and the general public. Under orders from white-coated "experimenters," many subjects administered what they believed to be life-threatening electric shocks to other people whom they could hear but not see. In fact, the "victims" were actors and received no shocks, but the subjects thought otherwise and many continued to administer stronger and stronger "shocks" when ordered to do so. Find *Obedience to Authority* in the library and compare and contrast the circumstances of Milgram's experiment with those of Jackson's lottery. For instance, who or what is the order-giving authority in the lottery? What is the significance of seeing or not seeing one's victim?

4. **CRITICAL WRITING.** In a 1960 lecture (which we quote more from in "Shirley Jackson on Writing"), Jackson said that a common response she received to "The Lottery" was "What does this story mean?" (She never answered the question.) In an essay, interpret the meaning of the story as *you* understand it. (What does it say, for instance, about social customs, conformity, guilt, obliviousness, or good and evil?) You will have to INFER meaning from such features as Jackson's own TONE as narrator, the tone of the villagers' dialog, and, of course, the events of the story. Your essay should be supported with specific EVIDENCE from the story.

5. **CONNECTIONS.** As its title might suggest, "Why Don't We Complain?" by William F. Buckley, Jr. (p. 538) touches on some of the same issues as "The Lottery." Write an essay applying Buckley's explanations for why we don't complain to the situation in Jackson's story — or arguing that they don't apply.

Shirley Jackson on Writing

Come Along with Me, a posthumous collection of her work, contains a lecture by Shirley Jackson titled "Biography of a Story" — specifically, a biography of "The Lottery." Far from being born in cruelty or cynicism, the story had quite benign origins. Jackson wrote the story, she recalled, "on a bright June morning when summer seemed to have come at last, with blue skies and warm sun and no heavenly signs to warn me that my morning's work was anything but just another story. The idea had come to me while I was pushing my daughter up the hill in her stroller—it was, as I say, a warm morning, and the hill was steep, and beside my daughter the stroller held the day's groceries— and perhaps the effort of that last fifty yards up the hill put an edge on the story; at any rate, I had the idea fairly clearly in my mind when I put my daughter in her playpen and the frozen vegetables in the refrigerator, and, writing the story, I found that it went quickly and easily, moving from begin- ning to end without pause. As a matter of fact, when I read it over later I decided that except for one or two minor corrections, it needed no changes, and the story I finally typed up and sent off to my agent the next day was almost word for word the original draft. This, as any writer of stories can tell you, is not a usual thing. All I know is that when I came to read the story over I felt strongly that I didn't want to fuss with it. I didn't think it was perfect, but I didn't want to fuss with it. It was, I thought, a serious, straightforward story, and I was pleased and a little surprised at the ease with which it had been writ- ten; I was reasonably proud of it, and hoped that my agent would sell it to some magazine and I would have the gratification of seeing it in print."

After the story was published, however, Jackson was surprised to find both it and herself the subject of "bewilderment, speculation, and plain old-fashioned abuse." She wrote that "one of the most terrifying aspects of publishing stories and books is the realization that they are going to be read, and read by strangers. I had never fully realized this before, although I had of course in my imagination dwelt lovingly upon the thought of the millions and millions of people who were going to be uplifted and enriched and delighted by the sto- ries I wrote. It had simply never occurred to me that these millions and mil- lions of people might be so far from being uplifted that they would sit down and write me letters I was downright scared to open; of the three-hundred-odd letters that I received that summer I can count only thirteen that spoke kindly to me, and they were mostly from friends."

Jackson's favorite letter was one concluding, "Our brothers feel that Miss Jackson is a true prophet and disciple of the true gospel of the redeeming light. When will the next revelation be published?" Jackson's answer: "Never. I am out of the lottery business for good."

For Discussion

1. What lesson can we draw about creative inspiration from Jackson's anecdote about the origins of "The Lottery"?
2. What seems to have alarmed Jackson about readers' reactions to her story? Do you think she was naive in expecting otherwise?

ADDITIONAL WRITING TOPICS

Narration

1. Write a narrative with one of the following as your subject. It may be (as your instructor may advise) either a first-PERSON memoir or a story written in the third person, observing the experience of someone else. Decide before you begin what your PURPOSE is and whether you are writing (1) an anecdote; (2) an essay consisting mainly of a single narrative; or (3) an essay that includes more than one story.

   A memorable experience from your early life
   A lesson you learned the hard way
   A trip into unfamiliar territory
   An embarrassing moment that taught you something
   A monumental misunderstanding
   An accident
   An unexpected encounter
   A story about a famous person or someone close to you
   A conflict or contest
   A destructive storm
   An assassination attempt
   A historical event of significance

2. Tell a true story of your early or recent school days, either humorous or serious, relating a struggle you experienced (or still experience) in school.

Note: Writing topics combining narration and description appear on page 185.

5

DESCRIPTION

Writing with Your Senses

◄ **Description in a photograph**

Margaret Morton photographs homeless communities in New York City. This photograph, titled Doug and Mizan's House, East River, 1993, *depicts a makeshift dwelling on a Manhattan riverbank. Consider Morton's photograph as a work of description— revealing a thing through the perceptions of the senses. What do you see through her eyes? What is the house made of? What do the overhanging structure on the upper left and the bridge behind the house add to the impression of the house? If you were standing in the picture, in front of the house, what might you hear or smell? If you touched the house, what textures might you feel? What main idea do you think Morton wants this photograph to convey?*

THE METHOD

Like narration, DESCRIPTION is a familiar method of expression, already a working part of you. In any talk-fest with friends, you probably do your share of describing. You depict in words someone you've met by describing her clothes, the look on her face, the way she walks. You describe somewhere you've been, something you admire, something you just can't abide. In a diary or in e-mail to a friend, you describe your college (cast concrete buildings, crowded walks, pigeons rattling their wings); or perhaps you describe your brand-new secondhand car, from the snakelike glitter of its hubcaps to the odd antiques in its trunk, bequeathed by its previous owner. You hardly can live a day without describing (or hearing described) some person, place, or thing. Small wonder that, in written discourse, description is almost as indispensable as paper.

Description reports the testimony of your senses. It invites your readers to imagine that they, too, not only see but perhaps also hear, taste, smell, and touch the subject you describe. Usually, you write a description for either of two PURPOSES: (1) to convey information without bias or emotion; or (2) to convey it with feeling.

In writing with the first purpose in mind, you write an OBJECTIVE (or *impartial, public,* or *functional*) description. You describe your subject so clearly and exactly that your reader will understand it or recognize it, and you leave your emotions out. Technical or scientific descriptive writing is usually objective: a manual detailing the parts of an internal combustion engine, a biology report on a species of frog. You write this kind of description in sending a friend directions for finding your house: "Look for the green shutters on the windows and a new garbage can at the front door." Although in a personal letter describing your house you might very well become emotionally involved with it (and call it, perhaps, a "fleabag"), in writing an objective description your purpose is not to convey your feelings. You are trying to make the house easily recognized.

The other type of descriptive writing is SUBJECTIVE (or *emotional, personal,* or *impressionistic*). This is the kind included in a magazine advertisement for a new car. It's what you write in your e-mail to a friend setting forth what your college is like—whether you are pleased or displeased with it. In this kind of description, you may use biases and personal feelings—in fact, they are essential. Let us consider a splendid example: a subjective description of a storm at sea. Charles Dickens, in his memoir *American Notes,* conveys his passenger's-eye view of an Atlantic steamship on a morning when the ocean is wild:

> Imagine the ship herself, with every pulse and artery of her huge body swollen and bursting . . . sworn to go on or die. Imagine the wind howling, the sea roaring, the rain beating; all in furious array against her. Picture the

sky both dark and wild, and the clouds in fearful sympathy with the waves, making another ocean in the air. Add to all this the clattering on deck and down below; the tread of hurried feet; the loud hoarse shouts of seamen; the gurgling in and out of water through the scuppers; with every now and then the striking of a heavy sea upon the planks above, with the deep, dead, heavy sound of thunder heard within a vault; and there is the head wind of that January morning.

　　I say nothing of what may be called the domestic noises of the ship; such as the breaking of glass and crockery, the tumbling down of stewards, the gambols, overhead, of loose casks and truant dozens of bottled porter, and the very remarkable and far from exhilarating sounds raised in their various staterooms by the seventy passengers who were too ill to get up to breakfast.

Notice how many *sounds* are included in this primarily ear-minded description. We can infer how Dickens feels about the storm. It is a terrifying event that reduces the interior of the vessel to chaos; and yet the writer (in hearing the loose barrels and beer bottles merrily gambol, in finding humor in the seasick passengers' plight) apparently delights in it. Writing subjectively, he intrudes his feelings. Think of what a starkly different description of the very same storm the captain might set down—objectively—in the ship's log: "At 0600 hours, watch reported a wind from due north of 70 knots. White-caps were noticed, in height two ells above the bow. Below deck, much gear was reported adrift, and ten casks of ale were broken and their staves strewn about. Mr. Liam Jones, chief steward, suffered a compound fracture of the left leg. . . ." But Dickens, not content simply to record information, strives to ensure that the mind's eye is dazzled and the mind's ear regaled.

　　Description is usually found in the company of other methods of writing. Often, for instance, it will enliven NARRATION and make the people in the story and the setting unmistakably clear. Writing an ARGUMENT in his essay "Why Don't We Complain?" (p. 538), William F. Buckley, Jr., begins with a description of eighty suffering commuters perspiring in an overheated train; the description makes the argument more powerful. Description will help a writer in examining the EFFECTS of a flood, or in COMPARING AND CONTRAST-ING two towns. Keep the method of description in mind when you come to try expository and argumentative writing.

THE PROCESS

Purpose and Audience

　　Understand, first of all, why you are writing about your subject and thus what kind of description is called for. Is it appropriate to perceive and report without emotion or bias—and thus write an objective description? Or is it appropriate to express your personal feelings as well as your perceptions — and thus write a subjective description?

Give a little thought to your AUDIENCE. What do your readers need to be told, if they are to share the perceptions you would have them share, if they are clearly to behold what you want them to? If, let's say, you are describing a downtown street on a Saturday night for an audience of fellow students who live in the same city and know it well, then you need not dwell on the street's familiar geography. What must you tell? Only those details that make the place different on a Saturday night. But if you are remembering your home city, and writing for readers who don't know it, you'll need to establish a few central landmarks to sketch (in their minds) an unfamiliar street on a Saturday night.

Before you begin to write a description, go look at your subject. If that is not possible, your next best course is to spend a few minutes imagining the subject until, in your mind's eye, you can see every flyspeck on it. Then, having fixed your subject in mind, ask yourself which of its features you'll need to report to your particular audience, for your particular purpose. Ask, "What am I out to accomplish?"

Dominant Impression and Thesis

When you consider your aim in describing, you'll begin to see what impression you intend your subject to make on readers. Let your description, as a whole, convey this one DOMINANT IMPRESSION. If you plan to write a subjective description of an old house, laying weight on its spooky atmosphere for readers you wish to make shiver, then you might mention its squeaking bats and its shadowy halls, leaving out any reference to its busy swimming pool and the stomping dance music that billows from its interior. If, however, you are describing the house in a classified ad, for an audience of possible buyers, you might focus instead on its eat-in kitchen, working fireplace, and proximity to public transportation. Details have to be carefully selected. Feel no grim duty to include every perceptible detail. To do so would only invite chaos — or perhaps, for the reader, mere tedium. Pick out the features that matter most.

Your dominant impression is like the THESIS of your description — the main idea about your subject that you want readers to take away with them. When you use description to explain or to argue, it's usually a good strategy to state that dominant impression outright, tying it to your essay's thesis or a part of it. In a biology report on a species of frog, for instance, you might preface your description with a statement like this one:

A number of unique features distinguish this frog from others in the order Anura.

Or in an argument in favor of cleaning a local toxic-waste site, you might begin with a description of the site and then state your point about it:

> This landscape is as poisonous as it looks, for underneath its barren crust are enough toxic chemicals to sicken a small village.

When you use subjective description more for its own sake—to show the reader a place or a person, to evoke feelings—you needn't always state your dominant impression as a THESIS STATEMENT, as long as the impression is there dictating the details.

Organization

You can organize a description in several ways. In depicting the storm at sea—a subjective description—Charles Dickens sorts out the pandemonium for us. He groups the various sounds into two classes: those of sea and sailors, and the "domestic noises" of the ship's passengers—their smashing dishes, their rolling bottles, the crashing of stewards who wait on them.

Other writers of description rely on their POINT OF VIEW to help them arrange details—the physical angle from which they're perceiving and describing. In the previous chapter, on narration, we spoke of point of view: how essential it is for a story to have a narrator—one who, from a certain position, reports what takes place. A description, too, needs a consistent point of view: that of an observer who stays put and observes steadily. From this point of view, you can make a carefully planned inspection tour of your subject, moving spatially (from left to right, from near to far, from top to bottom, from center to periphery), or perhaps moving from prominent objects to tiny ones, from dull to bright, from commonplace to extraordinary—or vice versa.

The plan for you is the one that best fulfills your purpose, arranging details so that the reader firmly receives the impression you mean to convey. If you were to describe, for instance, a chapel in the middle of a desert, you might begin with the details of the lonely terrain. Then, as if approaching the chapel with the aid of a zoom lens, you might detail its exterior and then go on inside. That might be a workable method to write a description *if* you wanted to create the dominant impression of the chapel as an island of beauty and feeling in the midst of desolation. Say, however, that you had a different impression in mind: to emphasize the spirituality of the chapel's interior. You might then begin your description inside the structure, perhaps with its most prominent feature, the stained glass windows. You might mention the surrounding desert later in your description, but only incidentally.

Whatever method you follow in arranging details, stick with it all the way through. Don't start out describing a group of cats by going from old cats to kittens, then switch in the middle of your description and line up the cats according to color. If your arrangement would cause any difficulty for the reader, you need to rearrange your details. If a writer, in describing a pet shop, should skip about wildly from clerks to cats to customers to cat food to customers to cat food to clerks, the reader may quickly be lost. Instead, the writer might group clerks together with customers, and cats together with cat food (or in some other clear order). But suppose (the writer might protest) it's a wildly confused pet shop I'm trying to describe? No matter—the writer nevertheless has to write in an orderly manner, if the reader is to understand. Dickens describes a scene of shipboard chaos, yet his prose is orderly.

Details

Luckily, to write a memorable description, you don't need a storm at sea or any other awe-inspiring subject. As Sarah Vowell demonstrates in "Shooting Dad" later in this chapter, you can write about your family as effectively as you write about a tornado. The secret is in the vividness, the evocativeness of the details. Like most good describers, Vowell uses many IMAGES (language calling up concrete sensory experiences), including FIGURES OF SPEECH (expressions that do not mean literally what they say, often describing one thing in terms of another). For instance, using *metaphor* Vowell writes that "the respective work spaces governed by my father and me were jealously guarded totalitarian states in which each of us declared ourselves dictator." Using *similes*, Vowell describes shooting a pistol as a six-year-old: "The sound it made was as big as God. It kicked little me back to the ground like a bully, like a foe."

FOCUS ON SPECIFIC AND CONCRETE LANGUAGE

When you write effective description, you'll convey your experience as exactly as possible. You may use figures of speech, as discussed above, and you'll definitely rely on language that is specific (tied to actual things) and concrete (tied to the senses of sight, hearing, touch, smell, and taste). Specific and concrete language enables readers to behold with the mind's eye—and to feel with the mind's fingertips.

The first sentence below shows a writer's first-draft attempt to describe something she saw. After editing, the second sentence is much more vivid.

VAGUE   Beautiful, scented wildflowers were in the field.

CONCRETE AND SPECIFIC   Backlighted by the sun and smelling faintly sweet, an acre of tiny lavender flowers spread away from me.

When editing your description, keep a sharp eye out for vague words such as *delicious, handsome, loud,* and *short* that force readers to create their own impressions or, worse, leave them with no impression at all. Using details that call on readers' sensory experiences, say why delicious or why handsome, how loud or how short. When stuck for a word, conjure up your subject and see it, hear it, touch it, smell it, taste it.

Note that *concrete* and *specific* do not mean "fancy": Good description does not demand five-dollar words when nickel equivalents are just as informative. The writer who uses *rubiginous* instead of *rusty red* actually says less because fewer readers will understand the less common word and all readers will sense a writer showing off.

For exercises on language, visit Exercise Central at *bedfordstmartins.com/ thebedfordreader.*

CHECKLIST FOR REVISING A DESCRIPTION

✔ **SUBJECTIVE OR OBJECTIVE.** Given your purpose and audience, is your description appropriately subjective (emphasizing feelings) or objective (unemotional)?

✔ **DOMINANT IMPRESSION.** What is the dominant impression of your subject? If you haven't stated it, will your readers be able to express it accurately to themselves?

✔ **POINT OF VIEW AND ORGANIZATION.** Do your point of view and organization work together to make your subject clear in readers' minds? Are they consistent?

✔ **DETAILS.** Have you provided all the details—and just those—needed to convey your dominant impression? What needs expanding? What needs condensing or cutting?

✔ **SPECIFIC AND CONCRETE LANGUAGE.** Have you used words that pin down your meaning exactly and appeal to the senses of sight, hearing, touch, taste, and smell?

DESCRIPTION IN PARAGRAPHS

Writing About Television

In the following paragraph written especially for *The Bedford Reader*, description works with narration to create suspense. Without even knowing the cause of the suspense, we gather tension from the details. Such a paragraph might pull us into an essay on the subject that is finally revealed only in the last sentence.

At 7:59 this Thursday night, a thick hush settles like cigarette smoke inside the sweat-scented TV room of Harris Hall. First to arrive, freshman Lee Ann squashes down into the catbird seat in front of the screen. Soon she is flanked by roommates Lisa and Kate, silent, their mouths straight lines, their upturned faces lit by the nervous flicker of a car ad. To the left and right of the couch, Pete and Anse crouch on the floor, leaning forward like runners awaiting a starting gun. Behind them, stiff standees line up at attention. Farther back still, English majors and jocks compete for an unobstructed view. Fresh from class, shirttail flapping, arm crooking a bundle of books, Dave barges into the room demanding, "Has it started? Has it started yet?" He is shushed. Somebody shushes a popped-open can of Dr Pepper whose fizz is distractingly loud. What do these students so intently look forward to? At last it starts— TV's hottest reality show.

Dominant impression (not stated): tense expectation of something vital

Details (underlined) contribute to dominant impression

Organization proceeds from front of room (at TV) to back

Writing in an Academic Discipline

Description interprets a familiar painting in the following paragraph from a text on art history. The details "translate" the painting, creating a bridge between the reader and the text's reproduction of the great work.

While working on *The Battle of Anghiari*, Leonardo painted his most famous portrait, the *Mona Lisa*. The delicate *sfumato* already noted in the *Madonna of the Rocks* is here so perfected that it seemed miraculous to the artist's contemporaries. The forms are built from layers of glazes so gossamer-thin that the entire panel seems to glow with a gentle light from within. But the fame of the *Mona Lisa* comes not from this pictorial subtlety alone; even more intriguing is the psychological fascination of the sitter's personality. Why, among all the smiling faces ever painted, has this particular one been singled out as "mysterious"? Perhaps the reason is that, as a portrait, the picture does not fit our expectations. The features are too individual for Leonardo to have simply depicted an ideal type, yet the element of idealization is so strong that it blurs the sitter's character. Once again the artist has brought two opposites into harmonious balance. The smile, too, may be read in two ways: as the echo of a momentary mood, and as a timeless, symbolic expression (somewhat like the "Archaic smile" of the Greeks . . .). Clearly, the *Mona Lisa* embodies a quality of maternal tenderness which was to Leonardo the essence of womanhood. Even the landscape in the background, composed mainly of rocks and water, suggests elemental generative forces.

(Sfumato: soft gradations of light and dark)

Main idea (topic sentence) of the paragraph, supported by description of "pictorial subtlety" (above) and "psychological fascination" (below)

Details (underlined) contribute to dominant impression

—H. W. Janson, *History of Art*

DESCRIPTION IN PRACTICE

Edward Johnson was leaving campus for the summer and wanted to sublet his apartment. Scouting around, he discovered that the best place to advertise his apartment was with his college's online "Housing Connection," which served as a network for students, staff, and faculty seeking short- or long-term rentals.

Johnson looked through many of the ads at "The Housing Connection," especially in his category of one-bedrooms, to see how he could make his place seem irresistible compared with the others listed. He noticed that other ads tended to be bare-bones, just the basics on rooms and rent, so he decided to use the twelve lines allotted to him to portray the special qualities of his apartment. In just a couple of drafts, he summoned the descriptive details that would attract a tenant. Here is the actual online posting:

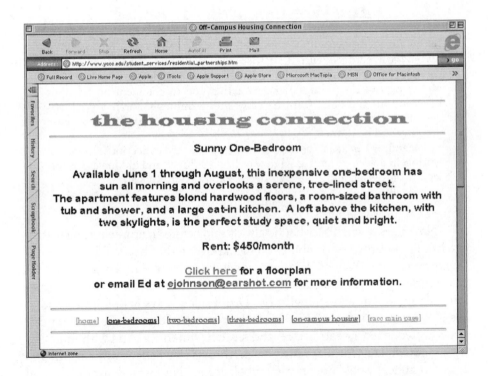

BRAD MANNING

BRAD MANNING was born in Little Rock, Arkansas, in 1967 and grew up near Charlottesville, Virginia. He attended Harvard University, graduating in 1990 with a BA in history and religion. At Harvard he played intramural sports and wrote articles and reviews for the *Harvard Independent*. After graduation Manning wrote features and news stories for the *Charlotte Observer* and then attended law school at the University of Virginia, graduating in 1995. Now living in Charlottesville with his wife and three children, Manning is a resident in the University of Virginia's department of psychiatric medicine.

Arm Wrestling with My Father

In this essay written for his freshman composition course, Manning explores his physical contact with his father over the years, perceiving gradual changes that are, he realizes, inevitable. For Manning, description provides a way to express his feelings about his father and to comment on relations between sons and fathers. In the essay after Manning's, Sarah Vowell uses description for similar ends, but her subject is the relationship between a daughter and her father.

Manning's essay has been published in a Harvard collection of students' writing; in *Student Writers at Work: The Bedford Prizes*; and in *Montage*, a collection of Russian and American stories published in Russian.

"Now you say when" is what he always said before an arm-wrestling match.   1
He liked to put the responsibility on me, knowing that he would always control the outcome. "When!" I'd shout, and it would start. And I would tense up, concentrating and straining and trying to push his wrist down to the carpet with all my weight and strength. But Dad would always win; I always had to lose. "Want to try it again?" he would ask, grinning. He would see my downcast eyes, my reddened, sweating face, and sense my intensity. And with squinting eyes he would laugh at me, a high laugh, through his perfect white teeth. Too bitter to smile, I would not answer or look at him, but I would just roll over on my back and frown at the ceiling. I never thought it was funny at all.

That was the way I felt for a number of years during my teens, after I had   2
lost my enjoyment of arm wrestling and before I had given up that same intense desire to beat my father. Ours had always been a physical relationship,

I suppose, one determined by athleticism and strength. We never communicated as well in speech or in writing as in a strong hug, battling to make the other gasp for breath. I could never find him at one of my orchestra concerts. But at my lacrosse games, he would be there in the stands, with an angry look, ready to coach me after the game on how I could do better. He never helped me write a paper or a poem. Instead, he would take me outside and show me a new move for my game, in the hope that I would score a couple of goals and gain confidence in my ability. Dad knew almost nothing about lacrosse and his movements were all wrong and sad to watch. But at those times I could just feel how hard he was trying to communicate, to help me, to show the love he had for me, the love I could only assume was there.

His words were physical. The truth is, I have never read a card or a letter   3
written in his hand because he never wrote to me. Never. Mom wrote me all the cards and letters when I was away from home. The closest my father ever came, that I recall, was in a newspaper clipping Mom had sent with a letter. He had gone through and underlined all the important words about the dangers of not wearing a bicycle helmet. Our communication was physical, and that is why we did things like arm wrestle. To get down on the floor and grapple, arm against arm, was like having a conversation.

This ritual of father-son competition in fact had started early in my life,   4
back when Dad started the matches with his arm almost horizontal, his wrist an inch from defeat, and still won. I remember in those battles how my tiny shoulders would press over our locked hands, my whole upper body pushing down in hope of winning that single inch from his calm, unmoving forearm. "Say when," he'd repeat, killing my concentration and causing me to squeal, "I did, I did!" And so he'd grin with his eyes fixed on me, not seeming to notice his own arm, which would begin to rise slowly from its starting position. My greatest efforts could not slow it down. As soon as my hopes had disappeared I'd start to cheat and use both hands. But the arm would continue to move steadily along its arc toward the carpet. My brother, if he was watching, would sometimes join in against the arm. He once even wrapped his little legs around our embattled wrists and pulled back with everything he had. But he did not have much and, regardless of the opposition, the man would win. My arm would lie at rest, pressed into the carpet beneath a solid, immovable arm. In that pinned position, I could only giggle, happy to have such a strong father.

My feelings have changed, though. I don't giggle anymore, at least not   5
around my father. And I don't feel pressured to compete with him the way I thought necessary for years. Now my father is not really so strong as he used to be and I am getting stronger. This change in strength comes at a time when I am growing faster mentally than at any time before. I am becoming less my father and more myself. And as a result, there is less of a need to be set apart

from him and his command. I am no longer a rebel in the household, wanting to stand up against the master with clenched fists and tensing jaws, trying to impress him with my education or my views on religion. I am no longer a challenger, quick to correct his verbal mistakes, determined to beat him whenever possible in physical competition.

I am not sure when it was that I began to feel less competitive with my 6 father, but it all became clearer to me one day this past January. I was home in Virginia for a week between exams, and Dad had stayed home from work because the house was snowed in deep. It was then that I learned something I never could have guessed.

I don't recall who suggested arm wrestling that day. We hadn't done it for 7 a long time, for months. But there we were, lying flat on the carpet, face to face, extending our right arms. Our arms were different. His still resembled a fat tree branch, one which had leveled my wrist to the ground countless times before. It was hairy and white with some pink moles scattered about. It looked strong, to be sure, though not so strong as it had in past years. I expect that back in his youth it had looked even stronger. In high school he had played halfback and had been voted "best-built body" of the senior class. Between college semesters he had worked on road crews and on Louisiana dredges. I admired him for that. I had begun to row crew in college and that accounted for some small buildup along the muscle lines, but it did not seem to be enough. The arm I extended was lanky and featureless. Even so, he insisted that he would lose the match, that he was certain I'd win. I had to ignore this, however, because it was something he always said, whether or not he believed it himself.

Our warm palms came together, much the same way we had shaken hands 8 the day before at the airport. Fingers twisted and wrapped about once again, testing for a better grip. Elbows slid up and back making their little indentations on the itchy carpet. My eyes pinched closed in concentration as I tried to center as much of my thought as possible on the match. Arm wrestling, I knew, was a competition that depended less on talent and experience than on one's mental control and confidence. I looked up into his eyes and was ready. He looked back, smiled at me, and said softly (did he sound nervous?), "You say when."

It was not a long match. I had expected him to be stronger, faster. I was 9 conditioned to lose and would have accepted defeat easily. However, after some struggle, his arm yielded to my efforts and began to move unsteadily toward the carpet. I worked against his arm with all the strength I could find. He was working hard as well, straining, breathing heavily. It seemed that this time was different, that I was going to win. Then something occurred to me, something unexpected. I discovered that I was feeling sorry for my father. I wanted to win but I did not want to see him lose.

It was like the thrill I had once experienced as a young boy at my grand-   10
father's lake house in Louisiana when I hooked my first big fish. There was
that sudden tug that made me leap. The red bobber was sucked down beneath
the surface and I pulled back against it, reeling it in excitedly. But when my
cousin caught sight of the fish and shouted out, "It's a keeper," I realized that
I would be happier for the fish if it were let go rather than grilled for dinner.
Arm wrestling my father was now like this, like hooking "Big Joe," the old fish
that Lake Quachita holds but you can never catch, and when you finally think
you've got him, you want to let him go, cut the line, keep the legend alive.

Perhaps at that point I could have given up, letting my father win. But it   11
was so fast and absorbing. How could I have learned so quickly how it would
feel to have overpowered the arm that had protected and provided for me all
of my life? His arms have always protected me and the family. Whenever I am
near him I am unafraid, knowing his arms are ready to catch me and keep me
safe, the way they caught my mother one time when she fainted halfway
across the room, the way he carried me, full grown, up and down the stairs
when I had mononucleosis, the way he once held my feet as I stood on his
shoulders to put up a new basketball net. My mother may have had the words
or the touch that sustained our family, but his were the arms that protected us.
And his were the arms now that I had pushed to the carpet, first the right arm,
then the left.

I might have preferred him to be always the stronger, the one who carries   12
me. But this wish is impossible now; our roles have begun to switch. I do not
know if I will ever physically carry my father as he has carried me, though I
fear that someday I may have that responsibility. More than once this year I
have hesitated before answering the phone late at night, fearing my mother's
voice calling me back to help carry his wood coffin. When I am home with
him and he mentions a sharp pain in his chest, I imagine him collapsing onto
the floor. And in that second vision I see me rushing to him, lifting him onto
my shoulders, and running.

A week after our match, we parted at the airport. The arm-wrestling   13
match was by that time mostly forgotten. My thoughts were on school. I had
been awake most of the night studying for my last exam, and by that morning
I was already back into my college-student manner of reserve and detachment. To say goodbye, I kissed and hugged my mother and I prepared to shake
my father's hand. A handshake had always seemed easier to handle than a
hug. His hugs had always been powerful ones, intended I suppose to give me
strength. They made me suck in my breath and struggle for control, and the
way he would pound his hand on my back made rumbles in my ears. So I
offered a handshake; but he offered a hug. I accepted it, bracing myself for the
impact. Once our arms were wrapped around each other, however, I sensed a

different message. His embrace was softer, longer than before. I remember how it surprised me and how I gave an embarrassed laugh as if to apologize to any-one watching.

I got on the airplane and my father and mother were gone. But as the   14
plane lifted my throat was hurting with sadness. I realized then that Dad must have learned something as well, and what he had said to me in that last hug was that he loved me. Love was a rare expression between us, so I had denied it at first. As the plane turned north, I had a sudden wish to go back to Dad and embrace his arms with all the love I felt for him. I wanted to hold him for a long time and to speak with him silently, telling him how happy I was, telling him all my feelings, in that language we shared.

In his hug, Dad had tried to tell me something he himself had discovered.   15
I hope he tries again. Maybe this spring, when he sees his first crew match, he'll advise me on how to improve my stroke. Maybe he has started doing pushups to rebuild his strength and challenge me to another match — if this were true, I know I would feel less challenged than loved. Or maybe, rather than any of this, he'll just send me a card.

For a reading quiz and annotated links to further readings on fathers and sons, visit **bedfordstmartins.com/thebedfordreader.**

Journal Writing

Manning expresses conflicting feelings about his father. How do you respond to his conflict? When have you felt strongly conflicting emotions about a person or an event, such as a relative, friend, breakup, ceremony, move? Write a paragraph or two exploring your feelings. (To take your journal writing further, see "From Journal to Essay" on the facing page.)

Questions on Meaning

1. In paragraph 3 Manning says that his father's "words were physical." What does this mean?
2. After his most recent trip home, Manning says, "I realized then that Dad must have learned something as well" (par. 14). What is it that father and son have each learned?

3. Manning says in the last paragraph that he "would feel less challenged than loved" if his father challenged him to a rematch. Does this statement suggest that he did not feel loved earlier? Why, or why not?
4. What do you think is Manning's PURPOSE in this essay? Does he want to express love for his father, or is there something more as well?

Questions on Writing Strategy

1. Why does Manning start his essay with a match that leaves him "too bitter to smile" and then move backward to earlier bouts of arm wrestling?
2. In the last paragraph Manning suggests that his father might work harder at competing with him and pushing him to be competitive, or he might just send his son a card. Why does Manning present both of these options? Are we supposed to know which will happen?
3. Explain the fishing ANALOGY Manning uses in paragraph 10.
4. **OTHER METHODS.** Manning's essay is as much a NARRATIVE as a description: The author gives brief stories, like video clips, to show the dynamic of his relationship with his father. Look at the story in paragraph 4. How does Manning mix elements of both methods to convey his powerlessness?

Questions on Language

1. Manning uses the word *competition* throughout this essay. Why is this a more accurate word than *conflict* to describe Manning's relationship with his father?
2. What is the EFFECT of "the arm" in this line from paragraph 4: "But the arm would continue to move steadily along its arc toward the carpet"?
3. In paragraph 9 Manning writes, "I wanted to win but I did not want to see him lose." What does this apparent contradiction mean?
4. If any of these words is unfamiliar, look it up in a dictionary: embattled (par. 4); dredges, crew (7); conditioned (9); mononucleosis (11).

Suggestions for Writing

1. **FROM JOURNAL TO ESSAY.** Expand your journal entry into a descriptive essay that brings to life your mixed feelings about a person or an event. Focus less on the circumstances and events than on emotions, both positive and negative.
2. Write an essay that describes your relationship with a parent or another close adult. You may want to focus on just one aspect of your relationship, or one especially vivid moment, in order to give yourself the space and time to build many sensory details into your description.
3. Arm wrestling is a highly competitive sport with a long history. Research the sport in the library or on the Internet. Then write a brief essay that traces its history and explains its current standing.
4. **CRITICAL WRITING.** In paragraph 12 Manning writes, "our roles have begun to switch." Does this seem like an inevitable switch, or one that this father and son have been working to achieve? Use EVIDENCE from Manning's essay to support

your answer. Also consider whether Manning and his father would respond the same way to this question.

5. **CONNECTIONS.** Like "Arm Wrestling with My Father," the next essay, Sarah Vowell's "Shooting Dad," depicts a struggle for communication between child and parent. In an essay, COMPARE AND CONTRAST the two essays on this point. What impedes positive communication between the two authors and their fathers? In what circumstances are they able to communicate?

Brad Manning on Writing

For *The Bedford Reader*, Brad Manning offered some valuable concrete advice on writing as a student.

You hear this a lot, but writing takes a long time. For me, this is especially true. The only difference between the "Arm Wrestling" essay and all the other essays I wrote in college (and the only reason it's in this book and not thrown away) is that I rewrote it six or seven times over a period of weeks.

If I have something to write, I need to start early. In college, I had a bad habit of putting off papers until 10 PM the night before they were due and spending a desperate night typing whatever ideas the coffee inspired. But putting off papers didn't just lower my writing quality; it robbed me of a good time.

I like starting early because I can jot down notes over a stretch of days; then I type them up fast, ignoring typos; I print the notes with narrow margins, cut them up, and divide them into piles that seem to fit together; then it helps to get away for a day and come back all fresh so I can throw away the corny ideas. Finally, I sit on the floor and make an outline with all the cutouts of paper, trying at the same time to work out some clear purpose for the essay.

When the writing starts, I often get hung up most on trying to "sound" like a good writer. If you're like me and came to college from a shy family that never discussed much over dinner, you might think your best shot is to sound like a famous writer like T. S. Eliot and you might try to sneak in words that aren't really your own like *ephemeral* or *the lilacs smelled like springtime*. But the last thing you really want a reader thinking is how good or bad a writer you are.

Also, in the essay on arm wrestling, I got hung up thinking I had to make my conflict with my father somehow "universal." So in an early draft I wrote in a classical allusion — Aeneas lifting his old father up onto his shoulders and carrying him out of the burning city of Troy.[1] I'd read that story in high school

---

[1] In the *Aeneid*, by the Roman poet Vergil (70–19 BC), the mythic hero Aeneas escaped from the city of Troy when it was sacked by the Greeks and went on to found Rome. — EDS.

and guessed one classical allusion might make the reader think I knew a lot more. But Aeneas didn't help the essay much, and I'm glad my teacher warned me off trying to universalize. He told me to write just what was true for me.

But that was hard, too, and still is—especially in the first draft. I don't know anyone who enjoys the first draft. If you do, I envy you. But in my early drafts, I always get this sensation like I have to impress somebody and I end up overanalyzing the effects of every word I am about to write. This self-consciousness may be unavoidable (I get self-conscious calling L. L. Bean to order a shirt), but, in this respect, writing is great for shy people because you can edit all you want, all day long, until it finally sounds right. I never feel that I am being myself until the third or fourth draft, and it's only then that it gets personal and starts to be fun.

When I said that putting off papers robbed me of a good time, I really meant it. Writing the essay about my father turned out to be a high point in my life. And on top of having a good time with it, I now have a record of what happened. And my ten-month-old son, when he grows up, can read things about his grandfather and father that he'd probably not have learned any other way.

For Discussion

1. What did Manning miss by writing his college papers at the last minute?
2. Why does Manning say that "writing is great for shy people"? Have you ever felt that you could express yourself in writing better than in speech?

SARAH VOWELL

SARAH VOWELL is best known for the smart, witty spoken essays she delivers on public radio. Born in Muskogee, Oklahoma, in 1969, Vowell grew up in Oklahoma and Montana. After graduating from Montana State University, she earned an MA in art history and criticism from the School of the Art Institute of Chicago. Radio has played a large part in Vowell's life: She worked as a DJ for her college station in Montana; she published a day-by-day diary of one year spent listening to the radio, *Radio On: A Listener's Diary* (1996); and in 1996 she became a contributing editor for *This American Life* on Public Radio International. She is a frequent guest on television talk shows as well, including David Letterman's and Jon Stewart's. Many of her essays from *This American Life* appear in her book *Take the Cannoli: Stories from the New World* (2000). Her most recent books are *Partly Cloudy Patriot* (2002) and *Assassination Vacation* (2005). Vowell is also a regular columnist for the online magazine *Salon*, and her writing has appeared in numerous print periodicals, including *Time, Esquire, GQ*, and *Spin*. She lives in New York City.

Shooting Dad

Like the previous essay, Brad Manning's "Arm Wrestling with My Father," Vowell's "Shooting Dad" explores the relationship between child and father. Engaged in a lifelong opposition to her father's politics, interests, and even his work, Vowell discovers with a jolt how much she has in common with him. Vowell read this essay, in slightly different form, on *This American Life* and then included it in *Take the Cannoli*.

If you were passing by the house where I grew up during my teenage years   1
and it happened to be before Election Day, you wouldn't have needed to come inside to see that it was a house divided. You could have looked at the Democratic campaign poster in the upstairs window and the Republican one in the downstairs window and seen our home for the Civil War battleground it was. I'm not saying who was the Democrat or who was the Republican—my father or I—but I will tell you that I have never subscribed to *Guns & Ammo*, that I did not plaster the family vehicle with National Rifle Association stickers, and that hunter's orange was never my color.

About the only thing my father and I agree on is the Constitution, though   2
I'm partial to the First Amendment, while he's always favored the Second.

I am a gunsmith's daughter. I like to call my parents' house, located on a   3
quiet residential street in Bozeman, Montana, the United States of Firearms.
Guns were everywhere: the so-called pretty ones like the circa 1850 walnut
muzzleloader hanging on the wall, Dad's clients' fixer-uppers leaning into corners, an entire rack right next to the TV. I had to move revolvers out of my
way to make room for a bowl of Rice Krispies on the kitchen table.

I was eleven when we moved into that Bozeman house. We had never   4
lived in town before, and this was a college town at that. We came from Oklahoma—a dusty little Muskogee County nowhere called Braggs. My parents'
property there included an orchard, a horse pasture, and a couple of acres of
woods. I knew our lives had changed one morning not long after we moved to
Montana when, during breakfast, my father heard a noise and jumped out of
his chair. Grabbing a BB gun, he rushed out the front door. Standing in the
yard, he started shooting at crows. My mother sprinted after him screaming,
"Pat, you might ought to check, but I don't think they do that up here!" From
the look on his face, she might as well have told him that his American citizenship had been revoked. He shook his head, mumbling, "Why, shooting
crows is a national pastime, like baseball and apple pie." Personally, I preferred
baseball and apple pie. I looked up at those crows flying away and thought, I'm
going to like it here.

Dad and I started bickering in earnest when I was fourteen, after the 1984   5
Democratic National Convention. I was so excited when Walter Mondale
chose Geraldine Ferraro as his running mate that I taped the front page of the
newspaper with her picture on it to the refrigerator door. But there was some
sort of mysterious gravity surge in the kitchen. Somehow, that picture ended
up in the trash all the way across the room.

Nowadays, I giggle when Dad calls me on Election Day to cheerfully   6
inform me that he has once again canceled out my vote, but I was not always
so mature. There were times when I found the fact that he was a gunsmith
horrifying. And just *weird*. All he ever cared about were guns. All I ever cared
about was art. There were years and years when he hid out by himself in the
garage making rifle barrels and I holed up in my room reading Allen Ginsberg
poems, and we were incapable of having a conversation that didn't end in an
argument.

Our house was partitioned off into territories. While the kitchen and the   7
living room were well within the DMZ,[1] the respective work spaces governed
by my father and me were jealously guarded totalitarian states in which each
of us declared ourselves dictator. Dad's shop was a messy disaster area, a
labyrinth of lathes. Its walls were hung with the mounted antlers of deer he'd

[1] Abbreviation for *demilitarized zone*, an area off-limits to war making. —EDS.

bagged, forming a makeshift museum of death. The available flat surfaces were buried under a million scraps of paper on which he sketched his mechanical inventions in blue ballpoint pen. And the floor, carpeted with spiky metal shavings, was a tetanus shot waiting to happen. My domain was the cramped, cold space known as the music room. It was also a messy disaster area, an obstacle course of musical instruments—piano, trumpet, baritone horn, valve trombone, various percussion doodads (bells!), and recorders. A framed portrait of the French composer Claude Debussy was nailed to the wall. The available flat surfaces were buried under piles of staff paper, on which I penciled in the pompous orchestra music given titles like "Prelude to the Green Door" (named after an O. Henry short story by the way, not the watershed porn flick *Behind the Green Door*) I started writing in junior high.

It has been my experience that in order to impress potential suitors, skip   8
the teen Debussy anecdotes and stick with the always attention-getting line "My dad makes guns." Though it won't cause the guy to like me any better, it will make him handle the inevitable breakup with diplomacy—just in case I happen to have any loaded family heirlooms lying around the house.

But the fact is, I have only shot a gun once and once was plenty. My twin   9
sister, Amy, and I were six years old—six—when Dad decided that it was high time we learned how to shoot. Amy remembers the day he handed us the gun for the first time differently. She liked it.

Amy shared our father's enthusiasm for firearms and the quick-draw   10
cowboy mythology surrounding them. I tended to daydream through Dad's activities—the car trip to Dodge City's Boot Hill, his beloved John Wayne Westerns on TV. My sister, on the other hand, turned into Rooster Cogburn Jr., devouring Duke movies with Dad. In fact, she named her teddy bear Duke, hung a colossal John Wayne portrait next to her bed, and took to wearing one of those John Wayne shirts that button on the side. So when Dad led us out to the backyard when we were six and, to Amy's delight, put the gun in her hand, she says she felt it meant that Daddy trusted us and that he thought of us as "big girls."

But I remember holding the pistol only made me feel small. It was so   11
heavy in my hand. I stretched out my arm and pointed it away and winced. It was a very long time before I had the nerve to pull the trigger and I was so scared I had to close my eyes. It felt like it just went off by itself, as if I had no say in the matter, as if the gun just had this *need*. The sound it made was as big as God. It kicked little me back to the ground like a bully, like a foe. It hurt. I don't know if I dropped it or just handed it back over to my dad, but I do know that I never wanted to touch another one again. And, because I believed in the devil, I did what my mother told me to do every time I felt an evil presence. I looked at the smoke and whispered under my breath, "Satan, I rebuke thee."

It's not like I'm saying I was traumatized. It's more like I was decided. Guns: 12
Not For Me. Luckily, both my parents grew up in exasperating households
where children were considered puppets and/or slaves. My mom and dad were
hell-bent on letting my sister and me make our own choices. So if I decided
that I didn't want my father's little death sticks to kick me to the ground
again, that was fine with him. He would go hunting with my sister, who
started calling herself "the loneliest twin in history" because of my reluctance
to engage in family activities.

Of course, the fact that I was allowed to voice my opinions did not mean 13
that my father would silence his own. Some things were said during the Reagan administration that cannot be taken back. Let's just say that I blamed Dad
for nuclear proliferation and Contra aid. He believed that if I had my way, all
the guns would be confiscated and it would take the commies about fifteen
minutes to parachute in and assume control.

We're older now, my dad and I. The older I get, the more I'm interested 14
in becoming a better daughter. First on my list: Figure out the whole gun
thing.

Not long ago, my dad finished his most elaborate tool of death yet. A can- 15
non. He built a nineteenth-century cannon. From scratch. It took two years.

My father's cannon is a smaller replica of a cannon called the Big Horn 16
Gun in front of Bozeman's Pioneer Museum. The barrel of the original has
been filled with concrete ever since some high school kids in the '50s pointed
it at the school across the street and shot out its windows one night as a prank.
According to Dad's historical source, a man known to scholars as A Guy at the
Museum, the cannon was brought to Bozeman around 1870, and was used by
local white merchants to fire at the Sioux and Cheyenne Indians who blocked
their trade access to the East in 1874.

"Bozeman was founded on greed," Dad says. The courthouse cannon, 17
he continues, "definitely killed Indians. The merchants filled it full of nuts,
bolts, and chopped-up horseshoes. Sitting Bull could have been part of these
engagements. They definitely ticked off the Indians, because a couple of years
later, Custer wanders into them at Little Bighorn. The Bozeman merchants
were out to cause trouble. They left fresh baked bread with cyanide in it on
the trail to poison a few Indians."

Because my father's sarcastic American history yarns rarely go on for 18
long before he trots out some nefarious ancestor of ours—I come from a long
line of moonshiners, Confederate soldiers, murderers, even Democrats—he
cracks that the merchants hired some "community-minded Southern soldiers
from North Texas." These soldiers had, like my great-great-grandfather John
Vowell, fought under pro-slavery guerrilla William C. Quantrill. Quantrill is
most famous for riding into Lawrence, Kansas, in 1863 flying a black flag and

commanding his men pharaohlike to "kill every male and burn down every house."

"John Vowell," Dad says, "had a little rep for killing people." And since he abandoned my great-grandfather Charles, whose mother died giving birth to him in 1870, and wasn't seen again until 1912, Dad doesn't rule out the possibility that John Vowell could have been one of the hired guns on the Bozeman Trail. So the cannon isn't just another gun to my dad. It's a map of all his obsessions—firearms, certainly, but also American history and family history, subjects he's never bothered separating from each other.   19

After tooling a million guns, after inventing and building a rifle barrel boring machine, after setting up that complicated shop filled with lathes and blueing tanks and outmoded blacksmithing tools, the cannon is his most ambitious project ever. I thought that if I was ever going to understand the ballistic bee in his bonnet, this was my chance. It was the biggest gun he ever made and I could experience it and spend time with it with the added bonus of not having to actually pull a trigger myself.   20

I called Dad and said that I wanted to come to Montana and watch him shoot off the cannon. He was immediately suspicious. But I had never taken much interest in his work before and he would take what he could get. He loaded the cannon into the back of his truck and we drove up into the Bridger Mountains. I was a little worried that the National Forest Service would object to us lobbing fiery balls of metal onto its property. Dad laughed, assuring me that "you cannot shoot fireworks, but this is considered a firearm."   21

It is a small cannon, about as long as a baseball bat and as wide as a coffee can. But it's heavy—110 pounds. We park near the side of the hill. Dad takes his gunpowder and other tools out of this adorable wooden box on which he has stenciled "PAT G. VOWELL CANNONWORKS." Cannonworks: So that's what NRA members call a metal-strewn garage.   22

Dad plunges his homemade bullets into the barrel, points it at an embankment just to be safe, and lights the fuse. When the fuse is lit, it resembles a cartoon. So does the sound, which warrants Ben Day dot[2] words along the lines of *ker-pow!* There's so much Fourth of July smoke everywhere I feel compelled to sing the national anthem.   23

I've given this a lot of thought—how to convey the giddiness I felt when the cannon shot off. But there isn't a sophisticated way to say this. It's just really, really cool. My dad thought so, too.   24

Sometimes, I put together stories about the more eccentric corners of the American experience for public radio. So I happen to have my tape recorder   25

---

[2] Ben Day dots are colored dots in various sizes, used in comics to intensify words for actions and loud sounds. —EDS.

with me, and I've never seen levels like these. Every time the cannon goes off, the delicate needles which keep track of the sound quality lurch into the bad, red zone so fast and so hard I'm surprised they don't break.

The cannon was so loud and so painful, I had to touch my head to make   26
sure my skull hadn't cracked open. One thing that my dad and I share is that we're both a little hard of hearing—me from Aerosmith, him from gun-smith.

He lights the fuse again. The bullet knocks over the log he was aiming at.   27
I instantly utter a sentence I never in my entire life thought I would say. I tell him, "Good shot, Dad."

Just as I'm wondering what's coming over me, two hikers walk by. Appar-   28
ently, they have never seen a man set off a homemade cannon in the middle of the wilderness while his daughter holds a foot-long microphone up into the air recording its terrorist boom. One hiker gives me a puzzled look and asks, "So you work for the radio and that's your dad?"

Dad shoots the cannon again so that they can see how it works. The other   29
hiker says, "That's quite the machine you got there." But he isn't talking about the cannon. He's talking about my tape recorder and my microphone—which is called a *shotgun* mike. I stare back at him, then I look over at my father's can-non, then down at my microphone, and I think, Oh. My. God. My dad and I are the same person. We're both smart-alecky loners with goofy projects and weird equipment. And since this whole target practice outing was my idea, I was no longer his adversary. I was his accomplice. What's worse, I was liking it.

I haven't changed my mind about guns. I can get behind the cannon   30
because it is a completely ceremonial object. It's unwieldy and impractical, just like everything else I care about. Try to rob a convenience store with this 110-pound Saturday night special, you'd still be dragging it in the door Sun-day afternoon.

I love noise. As a music fan, I'm always waiting for that moment in a song   31
when something just flies out of it and explodes in the air. My dad is a one-man garage band, the kind of rock 'n' roller who slaves away at his art for no reason other than to make his own sound. My dad is an artist—a pretty driven, idiosyncratic one, too. He's got his last *Gesamtkunstwerk*[3] all planned out. It's a performance piece. We're all in it—my mom, the loneliest twin in history, and me.

When my father dies, take a wild guess what he wants done with his ashes.   32
Here's a hint: It requires a cannon.

"You guys are going to love this," he smirks, eyeballing the cannon. "You   33
get to drag this thing up on top of the Gravellies on opening day of hunting

---

[3] German, "total work of art," specifically a work that seeks to unify all the arts.—EDS.

season. And looking off at Sphinx Mountain, you get to put me in little paper bags. I can take my last hunting trip on opening morning."

I'll do it, too. I will have my father's body burned into ashes. I will pack   34 these ashes into paper bags. I will go to the mountains with my mother, my sis-ter, and the cannon. I will plunge his remains into the barrel and point it into a hill so that he doesn't take anyone with him. I will light the fuse. But I will not cover my ears. Because when I blow what used to be my dad into the earth, I want it to hurt.

*For a reading quiz, sources on Sarah Vowell, and annotated links to further readings on fathers and daughters, visit **bedfordstmartins.com/thebedfordreader**.*

Journal Writing

How do you respond to Vowell's eccentric, even obsessive, father? Do you basically come to sympathize with him or not? Who in your life has quirky behavior that you find charming or annoying or a little of both? Write a paragraph or two about this per-son, focusing on his or her particular habits or obsessions. (To take your journal writ-ing further, see "From Journal to Essay" on the facing page.)

Questions on Meaning

1. In her opening sentence, Vowell describes growing up in "a house divided." What does she mean? Where in the essay does she make the divisions in her household explicit?
2. Why, given Vowell's father's love of guns, was it "fine" with him that his daugh-ter decided as a young child that she wanted nothing to do with guns (par. 12)? What does this attitude suggest about his character?
3. What motivated Vowell to come home to watch her father shoot off his homemade cannon? Why, given her aversion to guns, does she regard this cannon positively?
4. What do paragraphs 18–19, about her father's family history, contribute to Vowell's portrait of him?
5. What seems to be Vowell's PURPOSE in writing here? What DOMINANT IMPRESSION of her father does she create?

Questions on Writing Strategy

1. Why is the anecdote Vowell relates in paragraph 4 an effective introduction both to her father and to their relationship?

2. Paragraph 8 is sort of an aside in this essay—not entirely on the main topic. What purpose does it serve?
3. What does Vowell's final sentence mean? Do you find it a satisfying conclusion to her essay? Why, or why not?
4. **OTHER METHODS.** Throughout her essay, Vowell relies on COMPARISON AND CONTRAST to express her relationship with her father (and with her twin sister in pars. 9–12). Find examples of comparison and contrast. Why is the method important to the essay? How does the method help reinforce Vowell's main point about her relationship with her father?

Questions on Language

1. In paragraph 4 Vowell shows her father "mumbling" that "shooting crows is a national pastime, like baseball and apple pie," while she notes that she herself "preferred baseball and apple pie." How does the language here illustrate IRONY?
2. Pick out five or six concrete and specific words in paragraph 7. What do they accomplish?
3. In paragraph 9 Vowell writes, "My twin sister, Amy, and I were six years old—six—when Dad decided that it was high time we learned how to shoot. Amy remembers the day he handed us the gun for the first time differently. She liked it." What are the EFFECTS of the repetition of the word *six* in the first sentence and of the three-word final sentence?
4. Study the FIGURES OF SPEECH Vowell uses in paragraph 11 to describe the gun she shot. What is their effect?
5. Consult a dictionary if you need help in defining the following: muzzleloader (par. 3); revoked (4); bickering (5); partitioned, respective, totalitarian, labyrinth, lathes, pompous (7); colossal (10); traumatized (12); proliferation, confiscated (13); cyanide (17); nefarious, moonshiners, guerrilla, pharaohlike (18); ballistic (20); giddiness (24); adversary, accomplice (29); unwieldy (30); idiosyncratic (31).

Suggestions for Writing

1. **FROM JOURNAL TO ESSAY.** Based on your journal writing, compose an essay that uses description to portray your subject and his or her personal quirks. Be sure to include specific incidents you've witnessed and specific details to create a vivid dominant impression of the person. You may, like Vowell, focus on the evolution of your relationship with this person—whether mainly positive or mainly negative.
2. Conflict between generations is common in many families—whether over music, clothing, hair styles, friends, or larger issues of politics, values, and religion. Write an essay about generational conflicts you have experienced in your family or that you have witnessed in other families. Are such conflicts inevitable? How can they be resolved?
3. Gun ownership is a divisive issue in the United States. Research and explain the main arguments for and against gun control. Whatever your own position, strive for an objective presentation, neither pro nor con.

4. **CRITICAL WRITING.** Vowell's essay divides into several fairly distinct sections: paragraphs 1–4, 5–7, 8, 9–12, 13, 14–31 (which includes an aside in pars. 17–19), and 32–34. In an essay, analyze what happens in each of these sections. How do they fit together to help develop Vowell's dominant impression? How does the relative length of each section contribute to your understanding of her evolving relationship with her father?

5. **CONNECTIONS.** Both Vowell and Brad Manning, in "Arm Wrestling with My Father" (p. 144), describe their fathers. In an essay, examine words Manning and Vowell use to convey their feelings of distance from their fathers and also their feelings of closeness. Use quotations from both essays to support your analysis.

Sarah Vowell on Writing

Writing for both radio and print, Sarah Vowell has discovered differences in listening and reading audiences. On *Transom.org*'s Internet discussion board, she explained how she writes differently for the two media.

[S]ometimes I feel like I'm so much more manipulative on the radio. I know how to use my voice to make you feel a certain way. And that's not writing—that's acting. I get tired of acting sometimes. Which is why it's nice to be able to go back to the cold old page. Also, real time is an unforgiving medium. I still maintain a little academic streak, and any time I read something on the air or out loud, I have to cut back on the abstract, thinky bits. I have to read a story out loud in front of an audience this week and I had to lop it off by half, to prune it of its dull information and, sometimes, its very point. Those things for you the listener, are bonuses—the listener doesn't get as much filler, the listener gets to feel more. Readers are more patient. . . .

The only real drawback I think from moving between verbal and print media is punctuation. I'm working on another book right now, and there are so many things I want to say that I have to normalize on the page because I do not think in complete, fluid sentences. I seem to think in stopgaps and asides. Which the listener doesn't notice. But the reader, I think, becomes antsy when there are too many dashes and parentheses. So that is a constant battle—(dash!) trying to retain my casual, late twentieth-century (it's where I'm from), American-girl cadences, but without driving the reader crazy with a bunch of marks all over the place. Also, I love the word *and*. And I start too many sentences with *and*. Again, no one notices out loud because that's normative speech. But do that too much on the page and it's distracting and stupid.

For Discussion

1. What does Vowell mean by having to "normalize [her thoughts] on the page"?
2. What difficulties or rewards have you encountered trying to put ideas into written words for others to read?
3. In your experience as a speaker and a writer, what are the advantages of each form of communication? What are the disadvantages of each?

JUDITH ORTIZ COFER

A native of Puerto Rico who has lived most of her life in the United States, JUDITH ORTIZ COFER writes poetry, fiction, and essays about her heritage and the balancing of two cultures. Born in Hormigueros, Puerto Rico, in 1952, she earned a BA from Augusta College in 1974 and an MA from Florida Atlantic University in 1977. Cofer started out as a bilingual teacher in the schools of Palm Beach County, Florida, and she is now a professor of English and creative writing at the University of Georgia. Her publications include collections of poetry, among them *Peregrina* (1986) and *Terms of Survival* (1987); three novels, *The Line of the Sun* (1989), *The Meaning of Consuelo* (2003), and, for young adults, *Call Me Maria* (2004); two books of essays, *Silent Dancing* (1990) and *Woman in Front of the Sun* (2000); a book of stories for young people, *An Island Like You: Stories of the Barrio* (1995); and two collections of nonfiction, fiction, and poetry, *The Latin Deli* (1993) and *The Year of Our Revolution* (1998). As a native Spanish speaker who challenged herself to learn English, she is always experimenting, she says, with "the 'infinite variety' and power of language."

Silent Dancing

Cofer immigrated to New Jersey from Puerto Rico when she was three years old. In this much-reprinted essay, she links views of old home movies and bits of dreams with her adult recollections to describe her family's and her own immigrant experience. The essay first appeared in *The Georgia Review* and then as the title essay in Cofer's collection *Silent Dancing.*

We have a home movie of this party. Several times my mother and I have watched 1
it together, and I have asked questions about the silent revelers coming in and out of focus. It is grainy and of short duration, but it's a great visual aid to my memory of life at that time. And it is in color — the only complete scene in color I can recall from those years.

We lived in Puerto Rico until my brother was born in 1954. Soon after, 2 because of economic pressures on our growing family, my father joined the United States Navy. He was assigned to duty on a ship in Brooklyn Yard — a place of cement and steel that was to be his home base in the States until his retirement more than twenty years later. He left the Island first, alone, going to New York City and tracking down his uncle who lived with his family across the Hudson River in Paterson, New Jersey. There my father found a tiny apartment in a huge tenement that had once housed Jewish families but was just being taken over and transformed by Puerto Ricans, overflowing from New York City. In 1955 he sent for us. My mother was only twenty years old,

I was not quite three, and my brother was a toddler when we arrived at El Building, as the place had been christened by its newest residents.

My memories of life in Paterson during those first few years are all in shades of gray. Maybe I was too young to absorb vivid colors and details, or to discriminate between the slate blue of the winter sky and the darker hues of the snow-bearing clouds, but that single color washes over the whole period. The building we lived in was gray, as were the streets, filled with slush the first few months of my life there. The coat my father had bought for me was similar in color and too big; it sat heavily on my thin frame.

I do remember the way the heater pipes banged and rattled, startling all of us out of sleep until we got so used to the sound that we automatically shut it out or raised our voices above the racket. The hiss from the valve punctuated my sleep (which has always been fitful) like a nonhuman presence in the room—a dragon sleeping at the entrance of my childhood. But the pipes were also a connection to all the other lives being lived around us. Having come from a house designed for a single family back in Puerto Rico—my mother's extended-family home—it was curious to know that strangers lived under our floor and above our heads, and that the heater pipe went through everyone's apartment. (My first spanking in Paterson came as a result of playing tunes on the pipes in my room to see if there would be an answer.) My mother was as new to this concept of beehive life as I was, but she had been given strict orders by my father to keep the doors locked, the noise down, ourselves to ourselves.

It seems that Father had learned some painful lessons about prejudice while searching for an apartment in Paterson. Not until years later did I hear how much resistance he had encountered with landlords who were panicking at the influx of Latinos into a neighborhood that had been Jewish for a couple of generations. It made no difference that it was the American phenomenon of ethnic turnover which was changing the urban core of Paterson, and that the human flood could not be held back with an accusing finger.

"You Cuban?" one man had asked my father, pointing at his name tag on the navy uniform—even though my father had the fair skin and light brown hair of his northern Spanish background, and the name Ortiz is as common in Puerto Rico as Johnson is in the United States.

"No," my father had answered, looking past the finger into his adversary's angry eyes. "I'm Puerto Rican."

"Same shit." And the door closed.

My father could have passed as European, but we couldn't. My brother and I both have our mother's black hair and olive skin, and so we lived in El Building and visited our great-uncle and his fair children on the next block. It was their private joke that they were the German branch of the family. Not many years later that area too would be mainly Puerto Rican. It was as if the heart of the city map were being gradually colored brown—*café con leche*[1] brown. Our color.

The movie opens with a sweep of the living room. It is "typical" immigrant 10
Puerto Rican decor for the time: The sofa and chairs are square and hard-looking,
upholstered in bright colors (blue and yellow in this instance) and covered with the
transparent plastic that furniture salesmen then were so adept at convincing women
to buy. The linoleum on the floor is light blue; where it had been subjected to spike
heels, as it was in most places, there were dime-size indentations all over it that can-
not be seen in this movie. The room is full of people dressed up: dark suits for the
men, red dresses for the women. When I have asked my mother why most of the
women are in red that night, she has shrugged and said, "I don't remember. Just a
coincidence." She doesn't have my obsession for assigning symbolism to everything.
The three women in red sitting on the couch are my mother, my eighteen-year- 11
old cousin, and her brother's girlfriend. The novia[2] is just up from the Island, which
is apparent in her body language. She sits up formally, her dress pulled over her
knees. She is a pretty girl, but her posture makes her look insecure, lost in her full-
skirted dress, which she has carefully tucked around her to make room for my gor-
geous cousin, her future sister-in-law. My cousin has grown up in Paterson and is in
her last year of high school. She doesn't have a trace of what Puerto Ricans call la
mancha *(literally, the stain: the mark of the new immigrant—something about the*
posture, the voice, or the humble demeanor that makes it obvious to everyone the
person has just arrived on the mainland). My cousin is wearing a tight, sequined,
cocktail dress. Her brown hair has been lightened with peroxide around the bangs,
and she is holding a cigarette expertly between her fingers, bringing it up to her mouth
in a sensuous arc of her arm as she talks animatedly. My mother, who has come up
to sit between the two women, both only a few years younger than herself, is some-
where between the poles they represent in our culture.

It became my father's obsession to get out of the barrio, and thus we were 12
never permitted to form bonds with the place or with the people who lived there. Yet El Building was a comfort to my mother, who never got over yearn-ing for *la isla*.[3] She felt surrounded by her language: The walls were thin, and voices speaking and arguing in Spanish could be heard all day. *Salsas* blasted out of radios, turned on early in the morning and left on for company. Women seemed to cook rice and beans perpetually—the strong aroma of boiling red kidney beans permeated the hallways.

---

[1] Spanish for "coffee with milk."—EDS.
[2] Fiancée, or a girl just arrived from Puerto Rico.—EDS.
[3] The island.—EDS.

Though Father preferred that we do our grocery shopping at the super-   13
market when he came home on weekend leaves, my mother insisted that she
could cook only with products whose labels she could read. Consequently,
during the week I accompanied her and my little brother to La Bodega—a
hole-in-the-wall grocery store across the street from El Building. There we
squeezed down three narrow aisles jammed with various products. Goya and
Libby's—those were the trademarks that were trusted by her *mamá*, so my
mother bought many cans of Goya beans, soups, and condiments, as well as
little cans of Libby's fruit juices for us. And she also bought Colgate toothpaste
and Palmolive soap. (The final *e* is pronounced in both these products in
Spanish, so for many years I believed that they were manufactured on the
Island. I remember my surprise at first hearing a commercial on television in
which "Colgate" rhymed with "ate.") We always lingered at La Bodega, for it
was there that Mother breathed best, taking in the familiar aromas of the
foods she knew from Mamá's kitchen. It was also there that she got to speak to
the other women of El Building without violating outright Father's dictates
against fraternizing with our neighbors.

Yet Father did his best to make our "assimilation" painless. I can still see   14
him carrying a real Christmas tree up several flights of stairs to our apartment,
leaving a trail of aromatic pine. He carried it formally, as if it were a flag in a
parade. We were the only ones in El Building that I knew of who got presents
on both Christmas and *día de Reyes*, the day when the Three Kings brought
gifts to Christ and to Hispanic children.

Our supreme luxury in El Building was having our own television set. It   15
must have been a result of Father's guilt feelings over the isolation he had
imposed on us, but we were among the first in the barrio to have one. My
brother quickly became an avid watcher of Captain Kangaroo and Jungle Jim,
while I loved all the series showing families. By the time I started first grade, I
could have drawn a map of Middle America as exemplified by the lives of
characters in *Father Knows Best, The Donna Reed Show, Leave It to Beaver, My
Three Sons*, and (my favorite) *Bachelor Father*, where John Forsythe treated his
adopted teenage daughter like a princess because he was rich and had a Chinese houseboy to do everything for him. In truth, compared to our neighbors
in El Building, *we* were rich. My father's navy check provided us with financial security and a standard of living that the factory workers envied. The only
thing his money could not buy us was a place to live away from the barrio—
his greatest wish, Mother's greatest fear.

In the home movie the men are shown next, sitting around a card table set up in   16
one corner of the living room, playing dominoes. The clack of the ivory pieces was a
familiar sound. I heard it in many houses on the Island and in many apartments in

Paterson. In Leave It to Beaver, the Cleavers played bridge in every other episode; in my childhood, the men started every social occasion with a hotly debated round of dominoes. The women would sit around and watch, but they never participated in the games.

Here and there you can see a small child. Children were always brought to par- 17 *ties and, whenever they got sleepy, were put to bed in the host's bedroom. Babysitting was a concept unrecognized by the Puerto Rican women I knew: A responsible mother did not leave her children with any stranger. And in a culture where children are not considered intrusive, there was no need to leave the children at home. We went where our mother went.*

Of my preschool years I have only impressions: the sharp bite of the wind 18 in December as we walked with our parents toward the brightly lit stores downtown; how I felt like a stuffed doll in my heavy coat, boots, and mittens; how good it was to walk into the five-and-dime and sit at the counter drinking hot chocolate. On Saturdays our whole family would walk downtown to shop at the big department stores on Broadway. Mother bought all our clothes at Penney's and Sears, and she liked to buy her dresses at the women's specialty shops like Lerner's and Diana's. At some point we'd go into Woolworth's and sit at the soda fountain to eat.

We never ran into other Latinos at these stores or when eating out, and it 19 became clear to me only years later that the women from El Building shopped mainly in other places—stores owned by other Puerto Ricans or by Jewish merchants who had philosophically accepted our presence in the city and decided to make us their good customers, if not real neighbors and friends. These establishments were located not downtown but in the blocks around our street, and they were referred to generically as La Tienda, El Bazar, La Bodega, La Botánica. Everyone knew what was meant. These were the stores where your face did not turn a clerk to stone, where your money was as green as anyone else's.

One New Year's Eve we were dressed up like child models in the Sears cat- 20 alogue: my brother in a miniature man's suit and bow tie, and I in black patent-leather shoes and a frilly dress with several layers of crinoline underneath. My mother wore a bright red dress that night, I remember, and spike heels; her long black hair hung to her waist. Father, who usually wore his navy uniform during his short visits home, had put on a dark civilian suit for the occasion: We had been invited to his uncle's house for a big celebration. Everyone was excited because my mother's brother—Hernan—a bachelor who could indulge himself with luxuries—had bought a home movie camera, which he would be trying out that night.

Even the home movie cannot fill in the sensory details such a gathering   21
left imprinted in a child's brain. The thick sweetness of women's perfumes
mixing with the ever-present smells of food cooking in the kitchen: meat and
plantain *pasteles,* as well as the ubiquitous rice dish made special with pigeon
peas—*gandules*—and seasoned with precious *sofrito* sent up from the Island
by somebody's mother or smuggled in by a recent traveler. *Sofrito* was one of
the items that women hoarded, since it was hardly ever in stock at La Bodega.
It was the flavor of Puerto Rico.

The men drank Palo Viejo rum, and some of the younger ones got weepy.   22
The first time I saw a grown man cry was at a New Year's Eve party: He had
been reminded of his mother by the smells in the kitchen. But what I remember most were the boiled *pasteles,* plantain or yucca rectangles stuffed with
corned beef or other meats, olives, and many other savory ingredients, all
wrapped in banana leaves. Everybody had to fish one out with a fork. There
was always a "trick" *pastel*—one without stuffing—and whoever got that one
was the "New Year's Fool."

There was also the music. Long-playing albums were treated like precious   23
china in these homes. Mexican recordings were popular, but the songs that
brought tears to my mother's eyes were sung by the melancholy Daniel Santos,
whose life as a drug addict was the stuff of legend. Felipe Rodríguez was a particular favorite of couples, since he sang about faithless women and broken-
hearted men. There is a snatch of one lyric that has stuck in my mind like a
needle on a worn groove: *De piedra ha de ser mi cama, de piedra la cabezera . . .*
la mujer que a mi me quiera . . . ha de quererme de veras. Ay, Ay, Ay, corazón,
porque no amas . . . I must have heard it a thousand times since the idea of a
bed made of stone, and its connection to love, first troubled me with its disturbing images.

The five-minute home movie ends with people dancing in a circle—the   24
creative filmmaker must have set it up, so that all of them could file past him.
It is both comical and sad to watch silent dancing. Since there is no justification for the absurd movements that music provides for some of us, people
appear frantic, their faces embarrassingly intense. It's as if you were watching
sex. Yet for years, I've had dreams in the form of this home movie. In a recurring scene, familiar faces push themselves forward into my mind's eye, plaster-
ing their features into distorted close-ups. And I'm asking them: "Who is *she?*
Who is the old woman I don't recognize? Is she an aunt? Somebody's wife? Tell
me who she is."

"See the beauty mark on her cheek as big as a hill on the lunar landscape   25
of her face—well, that runs in the family. The women on your father's side
of the family wrinkle early; it's the price they pay for that fair skin. The young

girl with the green stain on her wedding dress is *la novia*—just up from the Island. See, she lowers her eyes when she approaches the camera, as she's supposed to. Decent girls never look at you directly in the face. *Humilde,* humble, a girl should express humility in all her actions. She will make a good wife for your cousin. He should consider himself lucky to have met her only weeks after she arrived here. If he marries her quickly, she will make him a good Puerto Rican–style wife; but if he waits too long, she will be corrupted by the city, just like your cousin there."

"She means me. I do what I want. This is not some primitive island I live   26
on. Do they expect me to wear a black mantilla on my head and go to mass every day? Not me. I'm an American woman, and I will do as I please. I can type faster than anyone in my senior class at Central High, and I'm going to be a secretary to a lawyer when I graduate. I can pass for an American girl anywhere—I've tried it. At least for Italian, anyway—I never speak Span-ish in public. I hate these parties, but I wanted the dress. I look better than any of these *humildes* here. My life is going to be different. I have an Ameri-can boyfriend. He is older and has a car. My parents don't know it, but I sneak out of the house late at night sometimes to be with him. If I marry him, even my name will be American. I hate rice and beans—that's what makes these women fat."

"Your *prima*[4] is pregnant by that man she's been sneaking around with.   27
Would I lie to you? I'm your *tía política,*[5] your great-uncle's common-law wife—the one he abandoned on the Island to go marry your cousin's mother. *I* was not invited to this party, of course, but I came anyway. I came to tell you that story about your cousin that you've always wanted to hear. Do you remember the comment your mother made to a neighbor that has always haunted you? The only thing you heard was your cousin's name, and then you saw your mother pick up your doll from the couch and say: 'It was as big as this doll when they flushed it down the toilet.' This image has bothered you for years, hasn't it? You had nightmares about babies being flushed down the toilet, and you wondered why anyone would do such a horrible thing. You didn't dare ask your mother about it. She would only tell you that you had not heard her right, and yell at you for listening to adult conversations. But later, when you were old enough to know about abortions, you suspected.

"I am here to tell you that you were right. Your cousin was growing an   28
americanito in her belly when this movie was made. Soon after, she put some-thing long and pointy into her pretty self, thinking maybe she could get rid of the problem before breakfast and still make it to her first class at the high school. Well, *niña,*[6] her screams could be heard downtown. Your aunt, her *mamá,* who had been a midwife on the Island, managed to pull the little

[4] Cousin.—EDS.
[5] Aunt-in-law.—EDS.
[6] Child.—EDS.

thing out. Yes, they probably flushed it down the toilet. What else could they do with it—give it a Christian burial in a little white casket with blue bows and ribbons? Nobody wanted that baby—least of all the father, a teacher at her school with a house in West Paterson that he was filling with real children, and a wife who was a natural blonde.

"Girl, the scandal sent your uncle back to the bottle. And guess where   29
your cousin ended up? Irony of ironies. She was sent to a village in Puerto Rico to live with a relative on her mother's side: a place so far away from civilization that you have to ride a mule to reach it. A real change in scenery. She found a man there—women like that cannot live without male company—but believe me, the men in Puerto Rico know how to put a saddle on a woman like her. *La gringa*,[7] they call her. Ha, ha, ha. *La gringa* is what she always wanted to be . . ."

The old woman's mouth becomes a cavernous black hole I fall into. And   30
as I fall, I can feel the reverberations of her laughter. I hear the echoes of her last mocking words: *la gringa, la gringa!* And the conga line keeps moving silently past me. There is no music in my dream for the dancers.

When Odysseus visits Hades to see the spirit of his mother,[8] he makes an   31
offering of sacrificial blood, but since all the souls crave an audience with the living, he has to listen to many of them before he can ask questions. I, too, have to hear the dead and the forgotten speak in my dream. Those who are still part of my life remain silent, going around and around in their dance. The others keep pressing their faces forward to say things about the past.

My father's uncle is last in line. He is dying of alcoholism, shrunken and   32
shriveled like a monkey, his face a mass of wrinkles and broken arteries. As he comes closer I realize that in his features I can see my whole family. If you were to stretch that rubbery flesh, you could find my father's face, and deep within *that* face—my own. I don't want to look into those eyes ringed in purple. In a few years he will retreat into silence, and take a long, long time to die. *Move back, Tío, I tell him. I don't want to hear what you have to say. Give the dancers room to move. Soon it will be midnight. Who is the New Year's Fool this time?*

For a reading quiz, sources on Judith Ortiz Cofer, and annotated links to further readings on Puerto Ricans' experience in the United States, visit **bedfordstmartins .com/thebedfordreader.**

---

[7] Foreigner or outsider, especially a North American or Briton.—EDS.
[8] An episode in the *Odyssey*, usually attributed to Homer, who flourished in the ninth or eighth century BC. In Greek mythology, Hades rules the underworld.—EDS.

Journal Writing

In paragraphs 24–33 Cofer describes a recurring dream she has had for years. Think of a dream you've had that stays with you for some reason. Write down as many details of the dream as you can. (To take your journal writing further, see "From Journal to Essay" on the facing page.)

Questions on Meaning

1. What do you think is Cofer's PURPOSE in this essay? Does she have something specific she wants the reader to understand?
2. Of her father, Cofer writes, "The only thing his money could not buy us was a place to live away from the barrio—his greatest wish, Mother's greatest fear" (par. 15). Why was moving her father's greatest wish? Why did her mother fear it? What passages from the essay support your answer?
3. Are the quoted speeches in paragraphs 25–29 real or imagined? Use EVIDENCE from the essay to support your answer.

Questions on Writing Strategy

1. What are the contents of the passages in italics (pars. 1, 10–11, 16–17) and the ones in smaller type (25–29)? How do these passages work with those in regular type? What is their EFFECT?
2. How well does the observation in paragraph 24, "It is both comical and sad to watch silent dancing," convey the dominant impression of Cofer's essay? What, if anything, would you add to "comical and sad"?
3. What does the dialog contribute to Cofer's TONE?
4. What does Cofer's description of Paterson and her childhood apartment (pars. 3–4) tell us about Cofer herself as a child?
5. **OTHER METHODS.** Paragraph 11 offers three EXAMPLES of Puerto Rican women: Cofer's mother, her assimilated cousin, and the cousin's brother's girlfriend. How do these three examples illustrate a cultural shift Puerto Rican immigrants were experiencing at the time the home movie was made?

Questions on Language

1. Cofer uses concrete language to appeal to all five of the senses: sight, sound, taste, smell, touch. Find examples of each appeal.
2. How might "silent dancing" serve as a metaphor for memory? (See *Figures of speech* in Useful Terms for a definition of *metaphor*.)
3. What larger meaning can we INFER from this sentence in paragraph 23: "Long-playing albums were treated like precious china in these homes"?
4. Consult a dictionary if you need help in defining the following words: influx (par. 5); adept (10); animatedly (11); barrio (12); assimilation (14); avid (15); plantain (22); mantilla (26).

Suggestions for Writing

1. **FROM JOURNAL TO ESSAY.** In an essay, describe the dream you wrote about in your journal (previous page), but also do more: Try to interpret the dream in the context of your life when you had it. What do you think it meant? Why did you have it when you did? What did it tell you?

2. Have you had the experience of being isolated from your surroundings, whether because of language or culture or because of some other barrier—being new in town, feeling friendless, or even just having to study when everyone else was having fun? Describe the experience in an essay, using plenty of details to help your readers understand your feelings.

3. Research the influx of Puerto Rican families to New York City and its surroundings during the 1950s. What prompted this migration? What quality of life did the newcomers face on arrival? What tensions did their arrival create? In an essay, consider these questions and others your research may lead you to. You may prefer to focus on a different migration—such as those during the nineteenth and twentieth centuries of Irish to the eastern United States, Chinese to the western United States, or African Americans from the southern to the northern United States.

4. **CRITICAL WRITING.** ANALYZE the different tones of Cofer herself, her cousin (par. 26), and her *tía política* (25, 27–29). How do their tones convey the different experiences and expectations of these three women?

5. **CONNECTIONS.** Several other writers in this book focus on the struggle to assimilate into mainstream American culture while maintaining one's ethnic ties: for example, Amy Tan in "Fish Cheeks" (p. 94), Sherman Alexie in "Indian Education" (p. 105), Dagoberto Gilb in "Pride" (p. 503), and Richard Rodriguez in "Aria: A Memoir of a Bilingual Childhood" (p. 655). Based on "Silent Dancing" and one or more of these other essays, consider this aspect of the immigrant experience in the United States—the challenges of assimilation, the effects of prejudice, and the role of family ties and cultural loyalty.

Judith Ortiz Cofer on Writing

In the 1980s Cofer told *Contemporary Authors* why she so often chooses her family as her writing subject. She was speaking of her poetry, but the same could be said of her stories and essays as well. "My family is one of the main topics of my poetry," Cofer explained, "the ones left behind on the island of Puerto Rico, and the ones who came to the United States. In tracing their lives, I discover more about mine. The place of birth itself becomes a metaphor for the things we all must leave behind; the assimilation of a new culture is the coming into maturity by accepting the terms necessary for survival. My poetry is the study of this process of change, assimilation, and transformation."

For Discussion

1. What does Cofer mean when she says that "the assimilation of a new culture is the coming into maturity by accepting the terms necessary for survival"? Does this statement apply only to immigrants or to nonimmigrants as well? Why?

2. If you have ever written about your family or a relative, what did the experience tell you about your kin? What did it tell you about yourself?

ETHAN CANIN

ETHAN CANIN was born in Ann Arbor, Michigan, in 1960 and grew up in San Francisco. Beginning Stanford University as an engineering major, he graduated with a BA in English. He went on to receive an MFA from the Iowa Writers' Workshop in 1984, but after producing only two short stories in two years he thought himself a failure as a writer and entered Harvard Medical School. There he managed to keep writing, publishing his first story collection, *Emperor of the Air* (1988), as a fourth-year medical student. His first novel, *Blue River* (1991), appeared the year he earned his MD. Making his living as a doctor, Canin wrote on the side until the publication of *The Palace Thief: Stories* (1994), when he decided to concentrate exclusively on writing. His other books include the novels *For Kings and Planets* (1998) and *Carry Me Across the Water* (2001). His short fiction has appeared in *The Atlantic Monthly*, *Esquire*, *Ploughshares*, *The New Yorker*, and a number of anthologies. Canin returned to the Iowa Writers' Workshop as a faculty member in 1988. He and his wife and daughters divide their time between Iowa and California.

Fly-Fishing for Doctors

Published in *The New Yorker* in 1998, this essay is a rare work of nonfiction by Canin. Recalling a summer during medical school, Canin describes a tiny moment of natural chaos in an otherwise orderly, antiseptic operating room.

This was the summer of 1986, a hot one in Boston, but I never knew that it was summer, exactly, because in the mornings I left before dawn. The walk to my car along the sleeping street was my only time out in the world—a few moments in the dark, when the warm sidewalks were still giving off the evidence of yesterday's heat and walking on them was like passing by the oven in a kitchen. I drove to work along the river, where, by daylight, I knew lovers would come to spread out blankets along the shore, to pilot the little rented sailboats that tacked back and forth beneath the shining bridges, to lie arm in arm under the spreading oaks as lovers do in summertime. My own girlfriend had recently moved into my small apartment, but she was still just two unpacked suitcases and a lump on the other side of the bed. By the time I made it home, every second night, I was too exhausted to talk.

I was a third-year medical student, and in the hospital we were cutting people open. This was my rotation in surgery, the first real rotation I had done, and I was terrified and enthralled. I remember leaning in close while the vilest thing I had ever seen—the cracking of a man's chest—was performed by two surgeons, on either side of the table. The sternum was first split with an electric saw; then a steel spreader was inserted and its gears cranked apart until the ribs opened like a bear trap and revealed the shining organs inside, pulsing to a steady beat. That beat was where we were going.

At the time, I thought I wanted to become a surgeon. I was drawn to oper- 3 ating the way I was drawn to the Boston-style boxing matches that occurred nearly every weekend in my neighborhood — big, tight-shirted brawls outside the pubs in Kenmore Square. Surgery seemed, in a way, like a sport: a simple physical pastime that shot me full of adrenaline. And, though it horrified me, I loved it.

But I was also beginning to suspect — correctly, it turned out — that I 4 would not spend my life in a hospital. Every second morning as I drove by the river, I felt the exquisite urge to keep on going, along Route 2 and straight out of Boston, past the suburbs and onward to the sweet country ponds where I had recently been teaching myself to fly-fish. Even then I must have known that this longing would turn out to be stronger than my ambition. The hospi- tal was death. Summer was life.

I was still learning what is called aseptic technique — the ritual cleanli- 5 ness that surrounds the operating room. This involved washing one's hands and arms with scrub brushes, donning mask and gown and gloves without touching them anywhere on the outside, and then, while assisting in surgeries that could take half a day, never allowing one's hands to move below the waist or above the shoulders. This last part was the most difficult, for the untrained hand reaches every few moments to the face — to brush back hair, to cough — and against these transgressions the scrub nurse stood careful watch, like a guard at a prison. Whenever my hand strayed — as every beginner's did — she instantly raised her finger and barked, in a satisfied voice, "Contamination!" Embarrassed, I would retreat to the scrub room, to rewash, reglove, and regown.

It was hot in the hospital, but the operating rooms were cool, and the 6 coolest of all were the ones where heart surgery took place. These patients had to be kept chilled. Their open chests were packed with ice, and their blood, which was pumped through a bypass machine, was refrigerated before being returned to the arteries. My job was to hold the suction wand that pulled the blood out of the operating field. I was standing there one day, dreaming of water, of standing waist-deep in a sun-drenched pond in the woods, of arcing a frog-green popper across the cloudless New England sky, when I looked up and saw an ant crawl out of the surgeon's mask.

Nature! Summer! I was the only one who had noticed it, because I was the 7 only one whose gaze was not fixed on the open heart in front of us. But then, seconds later, the ant turned around and disappeared. I wasn't quite sure that it hadn't been a hallucination. I kept my eyes on the surgeon's face, but noth- ing reappeared. Why did I want it to? What instinct for disorder was this?

Oh, how I longed then to be outside — to be at Baddacook Pond while the   8
grasshoppers and dragonflies and honeybees made their crazy thrumming on the
shore. It was blasphemous, I thought, to spend an entire summer inside. By
evening, all the world would be pouring out onto the banks of the river — the
lightning bugs would be blinking, the girls would be walking bare-armed in their
summer dresses — and I would be in an operating room, scrubbed and masked.

A moment later, from beneath the surgeon's mask, a set of black feelers   9
appeared again; then, after a pause, the ant itself emerged, not an illusion after
all. It stood perched on the narrow brim of the mask, like a goat on a cliff. It
paused there, tested the descent with its forelegs, then changed its mind and
headed north, out onto the bridge of the surgeon's nose. I watched his head
jerk back; I saw his eyes dart away from the beating heart and then cross as
they squinted downward. The scrub nurse snatched her hand to her mouth in
surprise. (Contamination! Contamination!) In a flash, she reached up and
squashed the thing. Seconds later, she had replaced the surgeon's mask, then
her own gown and gloves, then his entire gown. A moment after that we were
back at work again. Oh, ant! Oh, summer!

*For a reading quiz, sources on Ethan Canin, and annotated links to further readings
on medical training and on fly-fishing, visit* **bedfordstmartins.com/thebedfordreader.**

Journal Writing

What memories does summer conjure up for you? Is summer the prominent season of
your childhood memories? Was a particular summer special in some way — whether
positively or negatively? In your journal, write about your summer memories, focusing
on recalling striking details. (To take your journal writing further, see "From Journal
to Essay" on the next page.)

Questions on Meaning

1. What does Canin say was his attraction to surgery? Why, while pursuing his surgical rotation in medical school, did he begin to doubt that he was destined for
   life as a surgeon?
2. Why does Canin give so much attention to "aseptic technique" in paragraph 5?
3. Why is Canin the first person in the operating room to notice the ant? What
   point is he making about himself?

4. In what way does the ant serve as a SYMBOL for Canin? How does this symbol contribute to his main point?

Questions on Writing Strategy

1. Why do you think Canin begins this essay by describing his predawn commute to the hospital and imagining what daylight will bring?
2. What DOMINANT IMPRESSIONS does Canin create of summer outside the operating room and of the operating room itself? How do these two contrast?
3. Canin uses exclamation points in paragraphs 5, 7, and 9. What EFFECT do these have?
4. **OTHER METHODS.** Where does the NARRATION that ends the essay actually begin? How does Canin signal to readers that he is beginning a specific ANECDOTE?

Questions on Language

1. Much of Canin's description relies on visual IMAGES, but he does appeal to other senses as well. Point to language that evokes bodily sensation and sound.
2. Point out some similes in the essay. What metaphors does Canin offer in paragraph 4? (See *Figures of speech* in Useful Terms for definitions of *simile* and *metaphor*.)
3. Why do you suppose Canin chooses to use the adjective *blasphemous* in paragraph 8?
4. Consult a dictionary if you are unsure about the meanings of any of the following: enthralled, vilest, sternum (par. 2); brawls (3); exquisite, fly-fish (4); donning, transgression, contamination (5); hallucination (7).

Suggestions for Writing

1. **FROM JOURNAL TO ESSAY.** Based on your journal writing, compose an essay in which you share with readers your memories of summers in general or of a specific summer. Your essay may include narration, but be sure to ground it in descriptive details that contribute to a dominant impression.
2. The long hospital hours required of medical students and residents have sparked significant controversy in recent years. Research why long hours are traditional in medical training and why some doctors and patient advocates believe the hours should be shortened. Then write an essay in which you summarize your findings. If your research—or your experience as a medical worker or patient—leads you to form an opinion for or against change, present and support that as well.
3. **CRITICAL WRITING.** Write a brief essay that ANALYZES Canin's mingling of description and narration. You could focus just on paragraphs 6–9, on how Canin moves back and forth from operating room to pond while building the story about the ant.
4. **CONNECTIONS.** In his essay "Once More to the Lake" (p. 686), E. B. White also describes the joys of summer. In fact, Canin's "Nature! Summer!" and "Oh, summer!" echo White's "Summertime, oh, summertime" (par. 8). In an essay, COMPARE AND CONTRAST White's description of summer with Canin's. What similar pleasures do they find? What distinguishes each author's experience?

Ethan Canin on Writing

Ethan Canin thought he could never make it as a writer. As he explains in an interview for the Commonwealth Club of California, self-doubt, "an ever present and looming ghost," drove him to quit writing for a time and go to medical school. What saved him was a single book by the fiction writer John Cheever. "Suddenly this world opened up to me and all I wanted to do was write. It's as though you hear someone sing and you want to sing, like a mockingbird.

"You have to learn a lot of things to be a writer," Canin says. "First is the prose style; second is how to get up after you've been knocked down; third is how to keep inventing things. Maybe the fourth is how to deal with envy. That's true for any profession. The only way I've learned to do it—and it's enormously freeing—is to really be devoted to writing. It sounds a little too good to be true, but it works: to be moved by something that's well done."

For Discussion

1. Canin calls his self-doubt as a writer an "ever present and looming ghost." Do you have similar doubts about your own writing? If so, what are they? What other kinds of "ghosts" might bother a writer? How might these ghosts be banished?
2. What is the difference between envy and the kind of admiration that Canin says motivates him as a writer? Why would a writer need to "deal with envy"?

JOYCE CAROL OATES

One of America's most respected and prolific contemporary authors, JOYCE CAROL OATES was born in 1938 in Lockport, New York. After graduating from Syracuse University in 1960, she earned a master's degree from the University of Wisconsin. In 1963 she published her first book, a collection of short stories, and she has published an average of two books a year since then. (To the charge that she publishes too much, Oates replies that her critics may be "secretly afraid that someone will accuse them of having done too little with their lives.") With the novel *them* (1969), Oates became one of the youngest writers to receive the National Book Award for fiction. Other notable novels include *Wonderland* (1971), *Because It Is Bitter, and Because It Is My Heart* (1990), and, most recently, *Rape: A Love Story* (2003). Oates has also written more than a dozen volumes of poetry, a score of plays, and many works of nonfiction, including literary criticism and a study of boxing. In almost every novel, short story, poem, play, literary analysis, or essay, Oates remains, she says, "concerned with only one thing: the moral and social conditions of my generation." Since 1978 Oates has taught writing and literature at Princeton University.

Edward Hopper's Nighthawks, *1942*

First published in Oates's poetry collection *The Time Traveler* (1989), this poem responds to a well-known painting by the American Edward Hopper (1882–1967). The painting, *Nighthawks*, is reproduced on the facing page, both in full view and in detail.

> The three men are fully clothed, long sleeves,
> even hats, though it's indoors, and brightly lit,
> and there's a woman. The woman is wearing
> a short-sleeved red dress cut to expose her arms,
> a curve of her creamy chest; she's contemplating   5
> a cigarette in her right hand, thinking that
> her companion has finally left his wife but
> can she trust him? Her heavy-lidded eyes,
> pouty lipsticked mouth, she has the redhead's
> true pallor like skim milk, damned good-looking   10
> and she guesses she knows it but what exactly
> has it gotten her so far, and where?—he'll start
> to feel guilty in a few days, she knows
> the signs, an actual smell, sweaty, rancid, like
> dirty socks; he'll slip away to make telephone calls   15

Edward Hopper, American, 1882–1967, *Nighthawks* (full painting and detail), 1942, oil on canvas, 84.1 × 152.4 cm, Friends of American Art Collection, 1942.51. © 2002 The Art Institute of Chicago. All rights reserved.

and she swears she isn't going to go through that
again, isn't going to break down crying or begging
nor is she going to scream at him, she's finished
with all that. And he's silent beside her,
not the kind to talk much but he's thinking   20
thank God he made the right move at last,
he's a little dazed like a man in a dream—
is this a dream?—so much that's wide, still,
mute, horizontal, and the counterman in white,
stooped as he is and unmoving, and the man   25
on the other stool unmoving except to sip
his coffee; but he's feeling pretty good,
it's primarily relief, this time he's sure
as hell going to make it work, he owes it to her
and to himself, Christ's sake. And she's thinking   30
the light in this place is too bright, probably
not very flattering, she hates it when her lipstick
wears off and her makeup gets caked, she'd like
to use a ladies' room but there isn't one here
and Jesus how long before a gas station opens?—   35
it's the middle of the night and she has a feeling
time is never going to budge. This time
though she isn't going to demean herself—
he starts in about his wife, his kids, how
he let them down, they trusted him and he let   40
them down, she'll slam out of the goddamned room
and if he calls her *Sugar* or *Baby* in that voice,
running his hands over her like he has the right,
she'll slap his face hard, *You know I hate that: Stop!*
And he'll stop. He'd better. The angrier   45
she gets the stiller she is, hasn't said a word
for the past ten minutes, not a strand
of her hair stirs, and it smells a little like ashes
or like the henna she uses to brighten it, but
the smell is faint or anyway, crazy for her   50
like he is, he doesn't notice, or mind—
burying his hot face in her neck, between her cool
breasts, or her legs—wherever she'll have him,
and whenever. She's still contemplating
the cigarette burning in her hand,   55
the counterman is still stooped gaping

at her, and he doesn't mind that, why not,
as long as she doesn't look back, in fact
he's thinking he's the luckiest man in the world
so why isn't he happier?   60

For a reading quiz, sources on Joyce Carol Oates, and annotated links to further read-
*ings on Edward Hopper and reproductions of his paintings, visit **bedfordstmartins***
.com/thebedfordreader.

Journal Writing

In this poem Oates describes what she sees in Hopper's painting and also what she
imagines, particularly about the woman. Most of us have unobtrusively observed
strangers in a public place and imagined what they were thinking or what was going
on between them. Write a paragraph or two on why such observation can be interesting or what it can (or can't) reveal. (To take your journal writing further, see "From
Journal to Essay" on the next page.)

Questions on Meaning

1. What story does Oates imagine about the couple in *Nighthawks?* How are the
   man's and the woman's thoughts different?
2. Line 23 of the poem asks, "*is this a dream?*" Who is posing this question? What
   about the painting is dreamlike?
3. Throughout the poem, Oates emphasizes the silence and stillness of the scene in
   the coffee shop—for instance, "The angrier / she gets the stiller she is, hasn't said
   a word / for the past ten minutes" (lines 45–47). What meanings about the painting and the people in it might Oates be emphasizing?

Questions on Writing Strategy

1. Where in the poem does Oates use concrete language to describe what can actually be seen in the painting, as opposed to what she imagines? How does she use
   the former to support the latter? What does the mixture suggest about Oates's
   PURPOSE?
2. The thoughts of the woman include some vivid sensory images. What are some
   examples? How do these thoughts contrast with the man's?
3. What techniques of sentence structure does Oates use in lines 12–19 and 30–45
   to suggest the woman's rising anger?

4. **OTHER METHODS.** Where does Oates use NARRATION in the poem? Where does she imply a narrative? Why is narration important to her analysis of Hopper's painting?

Questions on Language

1. Oates uses just a few words that might be unfamiliar. Make sure you know the meanings of contemplating (line 5); rancid (14); budge (37); demean (38); henna (49).
2. The man's and woman's thoughts are peppered with strong language that some might find offensive. What does this suggest about how Oates sees the characters?
3. In lines 27–28 Oates writes that the man is "feeling pretty good, / primarily relief." How does the word "relief" undercut the notion of "feeling pretty good"?

Suggestions for Writing

1. **FROM JOURNAL TO ESSAY.** Find a public place where you can observe strangers unobtrusively from a distance—a park, for example, or a plaza, campus quad, dining hall, restaurant, bus, train. Take notes about what you observe—what your subject or subjects look like, how they behave, how they interact with each other. Then write an essay based on your notes that incorporates both actual description of your subjects and what the details lead you to imagine the subjects are thinking to themselves and saying to each other. Make sure the link between actual and imaginary is clear to your readers.
2. In a local gallery or museum, in a library art book, or on a Web site such as *WebMuseum* (*ibiblio.org/wm/paint*), find a painting that seems to you particularly intriguing or appealing. Then write a prose essay or a poem that expresses the painting's appeal to you. You may but need not imitate Oates by focusing on the thoughts of any figures in the painting. Describe the details of the painting and how they work together to create meaning for you. If you write a poem, don't worry about the technical aspects of poetry (meter, rhyme, and the rest). Think instead about your choice of words and IMAGES, building the poem through description.
3. **CRITICAL WRITING.** Throughout her poem, Oates interweaves description of the painting and its figures with what she imagines the figures are thinking. Mark each kind of material in the poem, and then analyze the shifts from one to the other. How does Oates make readers aware that she is moving from one to the other? Are the shifts always clear? If not, are the blurrings deliberate or a mistake? What do you think of this technique overall?
4. **CONNECTIONS.** In "But What Do You Mean?" (p. 390), Deborah Tannen outlines differences in the ways women and men communicate. Read that essay, and ANALYZE which of the differences seem to apply to Hopper's woman and man, either as Oates imagines them or as you see them. In an essay, explain how Tannen might view each as typifying his or her gender.

Joyce Carol Oates on Writing

For a 1997 book titled *Introspections: American Poets on One of Their Own Poems,* Joyce Carol Oates did us the valuable service of writing an essay about her poem "Edward Hopper's *Nighthawks,* 1942." She tells us why and how the painting sparked her own work of imagination.

The attempt to give concrete expression to a very amorphous impression is the insurmountable difficulty in painting.

These words of Edward Hopper's apply to all forms of art, of course. Certainly to poetry. How to evoke, in mere words, the powerful, inchoate flood of emotions that constitute "real life"? How to take the reader into the poet's innermost self, where the poet's language becomes the reader's, if only for a quicksilver moment? This is the great challenge of art, which even to fail in requires faith.

Insomniac nights began for me when I was a young teenager. Those long, lonely stretches of time when no one else in the house was awake (so far as I knew); the romance of solitude and self-sufficiency in which time seems not to pass or passes so slowly it will never bring dawn.

Always there was an air of mystery in the insomniac night. What profound thoughts and visions came to me! How strangely detached from the day-self I became! Dawn brought the familiar world, and the familiar self; a "self" that was obliged to accommodate others' expectations, and was, indeed, defined by others, predominantly adults. *Yes but you don't know me,* I would think by day, in adolescent secrecy and defiance. *You don't really know me!*

Many of Edward Hopper's paintings evoke the insomniac's uncanny vision, none more forcefully than *Nighthawks,* which both portrays insomniacs and evokes their solitude in the viewer. In this famous painting, "reality" has undergone some sort of subtle yet drastic alteration. The immense field of detail that would strike the eye has been reduced to smooth, streamlined surfaces; people and objects are enhanced, as on a lighted stage; not life but a nostalgia for life, a memory of life, is the true subject. Men and women in Hopper's paintings are somnambulists, if not mannequins, stiffly posed, with faces of the kind that populate our dreams, at which we dare not look too closely for fear of seeing the faces dissolve.

Here is, not the world, but a memory of it. For all dreams are memory: cobbled-together sights, sounds, impressions, snatches of previous experience. The dream-vision is the perpetual present, yet its contents relate only to the past.

There is little of Eros in Hopper's puritanical vision, *Nighthawks* being the rare exception. The poem enters the painting as a way of animating what cannot be animated; a way of delving into the painting's mystery. *Who are these people, what has brought them together, are they in fact together?* At the time of writing the poem I hadn't read Gail Levin's definitive biography of Hopper, and did not know how Hopper had made himself into the most methodical and premeditated of artists, continuously seeking, with his wife Jo (who would have posed for the redheaded nighthawk), scenes and tableaux to paint. Many of Hopper's canvases are elaborately posed, and their suggestion of movie stills is not accidental. This is a visual art purposefully evoking narrative, or at least the opening strategies of narrative, in which a scene is "set," "characters" are presented, often in ambiguous relationships.

Nighthawks is a work of silence. Here is an Eros of stasis, and of melancholy. It is an uncommonly beautiful painting of stark, separate, sculpted forms, in heightened juxtapositions, brightly lit and yet infinitely mysterious. The poem slips into it with no transition, as we "wake" in a dream, yearning to make the frozen narrative come alive; but finally thwarted by the painting's measured void of a world, in which silence outweighs the human voice, and the barriers between human beings are impenetrable. So the poem ends as it begins, circling upon its lovers' obsessions, achieving no crisis, no confrontation, no epiphany, no release, time forever frozen in the insomniac night.

For Discussion

1. For Oates, as well as for Hopper, what is the "great challenge of art"?
2. Why, according to Oates, did she write a poem about Hopper's painting?
3. Why is the poem circular, ending where it began?

ADDITIONAL WRITING TOPICS

Description

1. This is an in-class writing experiment. Describe another person in the room so clearly and unmistakably that when you read your description aloud, your subject will be recognized. (Be OBJECTIVE. No insulting descriptions, please!)
2. Write a paragraph describing one subject from *each* of the following categories. It will be up to you to make the general subject refer to a particular person, place, or thing. Write at least one paragraph as an objective description and at least one as a SUBJECTIVE description.

PERSON

A friend or roommate
A typical hip-hop, jazz, or
   country musician
One of your parents
An elderly person you know
A prominent politician
A historical figure

THING

A car
A dentist's drill
A painting or photograph
A foggy day
A season of the year
A musical instrument

PLACE

An office
A classroom
A college campus
A vacation spot
A hospital emergency room
A forest

3. In a brief essay, describe your ideal place—perhaps an apartment, a dorm room, a vacation spot, a restaurant, a gym, a store, a garden, a golf course. With concrete details, try to make the ideal seem actual.

Narration and Description

4. Use a combination of NARRATION and description to develop any one of the following topics:

Your first day on the job
Your first day at college
Returning to an old neighborhood
Getting lost
A brush with a celebrity
Delivering bad (or good) news

6

EXAMPLE

Pointing to Instances

◄ **Examples in a cartoon**

This cartoon by Barry Blitt, from Mother Jones *magazine, uses
the method of example in a complex way. Most simply, the
drawings-with-text propose instances or illustrations of the general category stated in the title—not every conceivable future
cell phone but a few possibilities. At the same time, the humor
of the examples reveals other, sharper observations by the
artist—ideas about current and future uses of cell phones,
our expectations for technology, and the results of technology
whether we expect them or not. What are some of these general ideas? How, for instance, would you state the artist's opinion of the usefulness or necessity of innovations in telephone
technology?*

THE METHOD

"There have been many women runners of distinction," a writer begins, and quickly goes on, "among them Joan Benoit, Grete Waitz, Florence Griffith Joyner, and Marion Jones."

You have just seen examples at work. An EXAMPLE (from the Latin *exemplum*: "one thing selected from among many") is an instance that reveals a whole type. By selecting an example, a writer shows the nature or character of the group from which it is taken. In a written essay, examples will often serve to illustrate a general statement, or GENERALIZATION. Here, for instance, the writer Linda Wolfe makes a point about the food fetishes of Roman emperors (Domitian and Claudius ruled in the first century AD).

> The emperors used their gastronomical concerns to indicate their contempt of the country and the whole task of governing it. Domitian humiliated his cabinet by forcing them to attend him at his villa to help solve a serious problem. When they arrived he kept them waiting for hours. The problem, it finally appeared, was that the emperor had just purchased a giant fish, too large for any dish he owned, and he needed the learned brains of his ministers to decide whether the fish should be minced or whether a larger pot should be sought. The emperor Claudius one day rode hurriedly to the Senate and demanded they deliberate the importance of a life without pork. Another time he sat in his tribunal ostensibly administering justice but actually allowing the litigants to argue and orate while he grew dreamy, interrupting the discussions only to announce, "Meat pies are wonderful. We shall have them for dinner."

Wolfe might have allowed the opening sentence of her paragraph — the TOPIC SENTENCE — to remain a vague generalization. Instead, she supports it with three examples, each a brief story of an emperor's contemptuous behavior. With these examples, Wolfe not only explains and supports her generalization but also animates it.

The method of giving examples — of illustrating what you're saying with a "for instance" — is not merely helpful to practically all kinds of writing, it is indispensable. Bad writers — those who bore us, or lose us completely — often have an ample supply of ideas; their trouble is that they never pull their ideas down out of the clouds. A dull writer, for instance, might declare, "The emperors used food to humiliate their governments," and then, instead of giving examples, go on, "They also manipulated their families," or something — adding still another large, unillustrated idea. Specific examples are *needed* elements in effective prose. Not only do they make ideas understandable, but they also keep readers awake. (The previous paragraphs have tried — by giving examples from Linda Wolfe and from "a dull writer" — to illustrate this point.)

Example   **189**

THE PROCESS

The Generalization and the Thesis

Examples illustrate a generalization, such as Linda Wolfe's opening state-ment about the Roman emperors. Any example essay is bound to have such a generalization as its THESIS, expressed in a THESIS STATEMENT. Here are a few examples from the essays in this chapter:

> Sometimes I think we would be better off [in dealing with social problems] if we forgot about the broad strokes and concentrated on the details.
> —Anna Quindlen, "Homeless"

> That first encounter, and those that followed, signified that a vast, unnerving gulf lay between nighttime pedestrians—particularly women—and me.
> —Brent Staples, "Black Men and Public Space"

The thesis statement establishes the backbone, the central idea, of an essay de-veloped by example. Then the specifics bring the idea down to earth for readers.

The Examples

An essay developed by example will often start with an example or two. That is, you'll see something—a man pilfering a quarter for bus fare from a child's Kool-Aid stand, a friend dating another friend's fiancé (or fiancée)— and your observation will suggest a generalization (perhaps a statement about how people mishandle ethical dilemmas). But a mere example or two proba-bly won't demonstrate your generalization for readers and thus won't achieve your PURPOSE. For that you'll need a range of instances.

Where do you find more? In anything you know—or care to learn. Start close to home. Seek examples in your own immediate knowledge and experi-ence. Explore your conversations with others, your studies, and the storehouse of information you have gathered from books, newspapers, radio, TV, and the Internet as well as from popular hearsay: proverbs and sayings, popular songs, bits of wisdom you've heard voiced in your family.

Now and again, you may feel an irresistible temptation to make up an example out of thin air. This procedure is risky, but with imagination can work wonderfully. When Henry David Thoreau, in *Walden*, attacks Americans' smug pride in the achievements of nineteenth-century science and industry, he wants to illustrate that kind of invention or discovery "which distracts our attention from serious things." And so he makes up the examples— far-fetched at the time, but pointed—of a transatlantic speaking tube and what it might convey: "We are eager to tunnel under the Atlantic and bring the Old World some weeks nearer to the New; but perchance the first news that will leak through into the broad, flapping American ear will be that the Princess Adelaide has the whooping cough." (Thoreau would be appalled at what we know of the British Royal Family via just the sort of communication he imagined.)

Thoreau's examples (and the sarcastic phrase about the American ear) bespeak genius; but, of course, not every writer can be a Thoreau—or needs to be. A hypothetical example may well be better than no example at all; yet, as a rule, an example from fact or experience is likely to carry more weight. Suppose you have to write about the benefits—any benefits—that recent science has conferred upon the nation. You might imagine one such benefit: the prospect of one day being able to vacation in outer space and drift about in free-fall like a soap bubble. That imagined benefit would be all right, but it is obviously a conjecture that you dreamed up without going to the library. Do a little digging on the Internet or in recent books and magazines. Your reader will feel better informed to be told that science—specifically, the NASA space program—has produced useful inventions. You add:

> Among these are the smoke detector, originally developed as Skylab equipment; the inflatable air bag to protect drivers and pilots, designed to cushion astronauts in splashdowns; a walking chair that enables paraplegics to mount stairs and travel over uneven ground, derived from the moonwalkers' surface buggy; the technique of cryosurgery, the removal of cancerous tissue by fast freezing.

By using specific examples like these, you render the idea of "benefits to society" more concrete and more definite. Such examples are not prettifications of your essay; they are necessary if you are to hold your readers' attention and convince them that you are worth listening to.

When giving examples, you'll find other methods useful. Sometimes, as in the paragraph by Linda Wolfe, an example takes the form of a NARRATIVE (Chap. 4): a brief story, an ANECDOTE, or a case history. Sometimes an example embodies a vivid DESCRIPTION of a person, place, or thing (Chap. 5).

Lazy writers think, "Oh well, I can't come up with any example here—I'll just leave it to the reader to find one." The flaw in this ASSUMPTION is that the reader may be as lazy as the writer. As a result, a perfectly good idea may be left suspended in the stratosphere. The linguist and writer S. I. Hayakawa tells the story of a professor who, in teaching a philosophy course, spent a whole semester on the theory of beauty. When students asked him for a few examples of beautiful paintings, symphonies, or works of nature, he refused, saying, "We are interested in principles, not in particulars." The professor himself may well have been interested in principles, but it is a safe bet that his classroom resounded with snores. In written EXPOSITION, it is undoubtedly the particu-

Example   **191**

lars—the pertinent examples—that keep a reader awake and having a good time, and taking in the principles besides.

FOCUS ON SENTENCE VARIETY

While accumulating and detailing examples during drafting, you may find yourself writing strings of similar sentences:

UNVARIED   One example of a movie about a disease is *In the Forest.* Another example is *The Beating Heart.* Another is *Tree of Life.* These three movies treat misunderstood or little-known diseases in a way that increases the viewer's sympathy and understanding. *In the Forest* deals with a little boy who suffers from cystic fibrosis. *The Beating Heart* deals with a middle-aged woman who is weakening from multiple sclerosis. *Tree of Life* deals with a father of four who is dying from AIDS. All three movies show complex, struggling human beings caught blamelessly in desperate circumstances.

The writer of this paragraph was clearly pushing to add examples and to expand them—both essential tasks—but the resulting passage needs editing so that the writer's labor isn't so obvious. In the more readable and interesting revision, the sentences vary in structure, group similar details, and distinguish the specifics from the generalizations:

VARIED   Three movies dealing with disease are *In the Forest, The Beating Heart,* and *Tree of Life.* In these movies people with little-known or misunderstood diseases become subjects for the viewer's sympathy and understanding. A little boy suffering from cystic fibrosis, a middle-aged woman weakening from multiple sclerosis, a father of four dying from AIDS—these complex, struggling human beings are caught blamelessly in desperate circumstances.

For exercises on sentence variety, visit Exercise Central at *bedfordstmartins.com/thebedfordreader.*

CHECKLIST FOR REVISING AN EXAMPLE ESSAY

✔ **GENERALIZATION.** What general statement do your examples illustrate? Will it be clear to readers what ties the examples together?

✔ **SUPPORT.** Do you have enough examples to establish your generalization, or will readers be left needing more?

✔ **SPECIFICS.** Are your examples detailed? Does each capture some aspects of the generalization?

✔ **RELEVANCE.** Do all your examples relate to your generalization? Should any be cut because they go off track?

✔ **SENTENCE VARIETY.** Have you varied sentence structures for clarity and interest?

EXAMPLES IN PARAGRAPHS

Writing About Television

This paragraph appears in an essay maintaining that television merely simulates, or imitates, real problems, events, activities, and institutions. The essay offers many examples of programming that only seem to represent what's real, such as morning news shows, small-claims courts, and wrestling. (Although the essay predates the recent explosion of "reality" TV, from *Survivor* to *Wife Swap*, it would apply to those shows as well.) Here the author uses specific examples of TV wrestling to show how it simulates televised football, basketball, and other sports.

To sustain the simulation, wrestling must construct and main- ⎤ *Generalization to be*
tain a little universe of the simulated. To do this, its discourse refers ⎟ *illustrated*
in its every enunciation to the apparatus used to broadcast conven- ⎦
tional sport. Wrestling features the same style of ringside commen- ⎤
tary, the same interpolation of interviews, the same mystification of ⎟
sporting expertise, the same freeze-frame and instant replay formats, ⎬ *Six examples*
the same faintly prurient interest in the wrestlers' private lives (not ⎟
to mention parts), the same cults of personality, and so on. This sys- ⎦
tem of understanding, however, is marshaled in the service of an
event which is a parody of its originating source: "real" sport.
                              —Michael Sorkin, "Faking It,"
                      in *Watching Television*, ed. Todd Gitlin

Writing in an Academic Discipline

The following paragraph from an economics textbook appears amid the author's explanation of how markets work. To dispel what might seem clouds of theory, the author here brings an abstract principle down to earth with a concrete and detailed example.

The primary function of the market is to bring together suppli- ⎤
ers and demanders so that they can trade with one another. Buyers ⎟ *Generalization to be*
and sellers do not necessarily have to be in face-to-face contact; ⎬ *illustrated*
they can signal their desires and intentions through various inter- ⎦
mediaries. For example, the demand for green beans in California is ⎤
not expressed directly by the green bean consumers to the green ⎟
bean growers. People who want green beans buy them at a grocery ⎟
store; the store orders them from a vegetable wholesaler; the whole- ⎟
saler buys them from a bean cooperative, whose manager tells local ⎬ *Single extended example*
farmers of the size of the current demand for green beans. The de- ⎟
manders of green beans are able to signal their demand schedule to ⎟
the original suppliers, the farmers who raise the beans, without any ⎟
personal communication between the two parties. ⎦
                              —Lewis C. Solmon, *Microeconomics*

Example   **193**

Example

EXAMPLES IN PRACTICE

As a college sophomore, Kharron Reid was applying for a summer internship implementing computer networks for businesses. He put together a résumé structured to present his previous work experience and his education for this kind of job. (See the résumé on p. 383.)

In drafting a cover letter for the résumé, Reid at first found himself repeating all his background in a very long letter. On the advice of his school's placement office, he rewrote the letter to emphasize just what the prospective employer would most need to know: the work, courses, and computer skills that qualified him for the opening it had. The rewritten letter, below, focuses on examples from the résumé to support the statement (in the second-to-last paragraph) that "my education and my hands-on experience with networking prepare me for the opening you have."

Kharron Reid
137 Chester St., Apt. E
Allston, MA 02134
February 23, 2004

Ms. Dolores Jackson
Human Resources Director
E-line Systems
75 Arondale Avenue
Boston, MA 02114

Dear Ms. Jackson:

I am applying for the networking internship in your information technology department, advertised in the career services office of Boston University.

I have considerable experience in networking from summer internships at NBS Systems and at Pioneer Networking. At NBS I planned and laid the physical platforms and configured the software for seven WANs on a Windows NT server. At Pioneer, I laid the physical platforms and configured the software to connect eight workstations into a LAN. Both internships gave me experience in every stage of networking.

In the fall I will be entering my third year in Boston University's School of Management, majoring in business administration and information systems. I have completed courses in computers (including programming), information systems, and business. In addition to my experience and coursework, I am proficient in Unix, Windows NT/2000/2003, and Linux.

As the enclosed résumé indicates, my education and my hands-on experience with networking prepare me for the opening you have.

I am available for an interview at your convenience. Please call me at (617) 555-4009 or e-mail me at kreid@bu.edu.

Sincerely,

Kharron Reid

Kharron Reid

BARBARA LAZEAR ASCHER

BARBARA LAZEAR ASCHER was born in 1946 and educated at Bennington College and Cardozo School of Law. She practiced law for two years in a private firm, where she found herself part of a power structure in which those on top resembled "the two-year-old with the biggest plastic pail and shovel on the beach. It's a life of nervous guardianship." Ascher quit the law to devote herself to writing, to explore, as she says, "what really matters." Her essays have appeared in the *New York Times*, the *Yale Review*, *Vogue*, and other periodicals and have been collected in *Playing After Dark* (1986) and *The Habit of Loving* (1989). She has also published *Landscape Without Gravity: A Memoir of Grief* (1993), about her brother's death from AIDS; and *Dancing in the Dark: Romance, Yearning, and the Search for the Sublime* (1999), about our quest for romance. Ascher is a contributing editor of *Self* magazine, a reviewer for the *Washington Post Book World*, and an essayist on National Public Radio.

On Compassion

Ascher often writes about life in New York City, where human problems sometimes seem larger and more stubborn than in other places. In this essay Ascher uses examples from the city to address a universal need: compassion for those who require help. First published in *Elle* magazine in 1988, the essay was later reprinted in *The Habit of Loving*. The essay following this one, Anna Quindlen's "Homeless," addresses the same issue.

The man's grin is less the result of circumstance than dreams or madness.   1
His buttonless shirt, with one sleeve missing, hangs outside the waist of his baggy trousers. Carefully plaited dreadlocks bespeak a better time, long ago. As he crosses Manhattan's Seventy-ninth Street, his gait is the shuffle of the forgotten ones held in place by gravity rather than plans. On the corner of Madison Avenue, he stops before a blond baby in an Aprica stroller. The baby's mother waits for the light to change and her hands close tighter on the stroller's handle as she sees the man approach.

The others on the corner, five men and women waiting for the crosstown   2
bus, look away. They daydream a bit and gaze into the weak rays of November light. A man with a briefcase lifts and lowers the shiny toe of his right shoe, watching the light reflect, trying to catch and balance it, as if he could hold

and make it his, to ease the heavy gray of coming January, February, and March. The winter months that will send snow around the feet, calves, and knees of the grinning man as he heads for the shelter of Grand Central or Pennsylvania Station.

But for now, in this last gasp of autumn warmth, he is still. His eyes fix on the baby. The mother removes her purse from her shoulder and rummages through its contents: lipstick, a lace handkerchief, an address book. She finds what she's looking for and passes a folded dollar over her child's head to the man who stands and stares even though the light has changed and traffic navigates about his hips.   3

His hands continue to dangle at his sides. He does not know his part. He does not know that acceptance of the gift and gratitude are what make this transaction complete. The baby, weary of the unwavering stare, pulls its blanket over its head. The man does not look away. Like a bridegroom waiting at the altar, his eyes pierce the white veil.   4

The mother grows impatient and pushes the stroller before her, bearing the dollar like a cross. Finally, a black hand rises and closes around green.   5

Was it fear or compassion that motivated the gift?   6

Up the avenue, at Ninety-first Street, there is a small French bread shop where you can sit and eat a buttery, overpriced croissant and wash it down with rich cappuccino. Twice when I have stopped here to stave hunger or stay the cold, twice as I have sat and read and felt the warm rush of hot coffee and milk, an old man has wandered in and stood inside the entrance. He wears a stained blanket pulled up to his chin, and a woolen hood pulled down to his gray, bushy eyebrows. As he stands, the scent of stale cigarettes and urine fills the small, overheated room.   7

The owner of the shop, a moody French woman, emerges from the kitchen with steaming coffee in a Styrofoam cup, and a small paper bag of . . . of what? Yesterday's bread? Today's croissant? He accepts the offering as silently as he came, and is gone.   8

Twice I have witnessed this, and twice I have wondered, what compels this woman to feed this man? Pity? Care? Compassion? Or does she simply want to rid her shop of his troublesome presence? If expulsion were her motivation she would not reward his arrival with gifts of food. Most proprietors do not. They chase the homeless from their midst with expletives and threats.   9

As winter approaches, the mayor of New York City is moving the homeless off the streets and into Bellevue Hospital. The New York Civil Liberties Union is watchful. They question whether the rights of these people who live in our parks and doorways are being violated by involuntary hospitalization.   10

I think the mayor's notion is humane, but I fear it is something else as well. Raw humanity offends our sensibilities. We want to protect ourselves   11 from an awareness of rags with voices that make no sense and scream forth in inarticulate rage. We do not wish to be reminded of the tentative state of our own well-being and sanity. And so, the troublesome presence is removed from the awareness of the electorate.

Like other cities, there is much about Manhattan now that resembles   12
Dickensian London. Ladies in high-heeled shoes pick their way through poverty and madness. You hear more cocktail party complaints than usual, "I just can't take New York anymore." Our citizens dream of the open spaces of Wyoming, the manicured exclusivity of Hobe Sound.

And yet, it may be that these are the conditions that finally give birth to   13
empathy, the mother of compassion. We cannot deny the existence of the helpless as their presence grows. It is impossible to insulate ourselves against what is at our very doorstep. I don't believe that one is born compassionate. Compassion is not a character trait like a sunny disposition. It must be learned, and it is learned by having adversity at our windows, coming through the gates of our yards, the walls of our towns, adversity that becomes so familiar that we begin to identify and empathize with it.

For the ancient Greeks, drama taught and reinforced compassion within   14
a society. The object of Greek tragedy was to inspire empathy in the audience so that the common response to the hero's fall was: "There, but for the grace of God, go I." Could it be that this was the response of the mother who offered the dollar, the French woman who gave the food? Could it be that the homeless, like those ancients, are reminding us of our common humanity? Of course, there is a difference. This play doesn't end—and the players can't go home.

*For a reading quiz, sources on Barbara Lazear Ascher, and annotated links to further readings on homelessness, visit **bedfordstmartins.com/thebedfordreader**.*

Journal Writing

Using Ascher's essay as a springboard, consider a personal experience that involved misfortune. Have you ever needed to beg on the street, been evicted from an apartment, or had to scrounge for food? Have you ever been asked for money by beggars, worked in a soup kitchen, or volunteered at a shelter or public hospital? Write about such an experience in your journal. (To take your journal writing further, see "From Journal to Essay" on the next page.)

Questions on Meaning

1. What do the two men in Ascher's essay exemplify?
2. What is Ascher's THESIS? What is her PURPOSE?
3. What solution to homelessness is introduced in paragraph 10? What does Ascher think of this possibility?
4. How do you interpret Ascher's last sentence? Is she optimistic or pessimistic about whether people will learn compassion?

Questions on Writing Strategy

1. Which comes first, the GENERALIZATIONS or the supporting examples? Why has Ascher chosen this order?
2. What assumptions does the author make about her AUDIENCE?
3. Why do the other people at the bus stop look away (par. 2)? What does Ascher's DESCRIPTION of their activities say about them?
4. Look at the sentences in paragraph 13. How does the variety in their structures reinforce Ascher's meaning?
5. **OTHER METHODS.** Ascher explores CAUSES AND EFFECTS. Do you agree with her that exposure to others' helplessness increases our compassion? Why, or why not?

Questions on Language

1. What is the difference between empathy and compassion? Why does Ascher say that "empathy [is] the mother of compassion" (par. 13)?
2. Find definitions for the following words: plaited, dreadlocks, bespeak (par. 1); stave, stay (7); expletives (9); inarticulate, electorate (11).
3. What are the implications of Ascher's ALLUSION to "Dickensian London" (par. 12)?
4. Examine the language Ascher uses to describe the two homeless men. Is it OBJECTIVE? sympathetic? negative?

Suggestions for Writing

1. **FROM JOURNAL TO ESSAY.** Write an essay on the experience you explored in your journal, using examples to convey the effect the experience had on you.
2. Write an essay on the problem of homelessness in your town or city. Use examples to support your view of the problem and a possible solution.
3. In paragraph 10 Ascher refers to the involuntary hospitalization of homeless people and the concerns such government action raises among supporters of individual rights, such as the American Civil Liberties Union. What is your opinion of the rights of homeless people to live on the streets? How do you distinguish among the individual's rights, the community's responsibilities to the individual, and the community's rights? (For instance, what if a homeless person seems sick? What if he or she seems unstable, if not violent?) You may work solo on this assignment—stating your ideas and supporting them with EVIDENCE from your own observations and experience—or you may conduct research to discover legal and other arguments and data to support your ideas.

4. **CRITICAL WRITING.** In her last paragraph, Ascher mentions but does not address another key difference between the characters in Greek tragedy and the homeless on today's streets: The former were "heroes"—gods and goddesses, kings and queens—whereas the latter are placeless, poor, anonymous, even reviled. Does this difference negate Ascher's comparison between Greek theatergoers and ourselves or her larger point about how compassion is learned? Answer in a brief essay, saying why or why not.

5. **CONNECTIONS.** The next essay, Anna Quindlen's "Homeless," also uses examples to make a point about homelessness. What are some of the differences in the examples each writer uses? In a brief essay, explore whether and how these differences create different TONES in the two works.

Barbara Lazear Ascher on Writing

A lawyer before she was a full-time writer, Barbara Lazear Ascher thinks that her legal training helped her become a stronger writer.

"I believe there is a kind of legal thinking that becomes part of your own thinking," she told Jean W. Ross of *Contemporary Authors*. "What it did for me was help me to become quite a tight writer. My pieces are very short, and I think a lot of that has to do with the training in law, which is to tell the facts and the theories, and then put it all together and close it up. I might have been a more excessive writer if I hadn't had the legal training."

For Ascher, the essay is the ideal form of expression. "I'm quite impatient, so it's very satisfying to have a small space in which to tell what it was you wanted to tell. You get to the point right away instead of having to drag it out and slowly reveal it."

For Discussion

1. How did her legal training help Ascher when she became a writer? How does a "tight writer" help readers as well?
2. How might an "excessive writer" have trouble with the essay form? What, in your view, is "excessive" writing?

ANNA QUINDLEN

ANNA QUINDLEN was born in 1952 and graduated from Barnard College in 1974. She worked as a reporter for the *New York Post* and the *New York Times* before taking over the *Times*'s "About New York" column, serving as the paper's deputy metropolitan editor, and in 1986 creating her own weekly column, "Life in the Thirties." Between 1989 and 1994 Quindlen wrote a twice-weekly op-ed column for the *Times* on social and political issues, earning a Pulitzer Prize in 1992. In 1999 she began writing a biweekly "My Turn" column for *Newsweek* magazine. Her essays and columns are collected in *Living Out Loud* (1988), *Thinking Out Loud* (1993), and *Loud and Clear* (2004). Quindlen has also published two books about children, two for children, and four successful novels: *Object Lessons* (1991), *One True Thing* (1994), *Black and Blue: A Novel* (1998), and *Blessings* (2002).

Homeless

In this essay from *Living Out Loud,* Quindlen uses examples to explore the same topic as Barbara Lazear Ascher (p. 195), but with a different slant. Typically for Quindlen, she mingles a reporter's respect for details with a passionate regard for life.

Her name was Ann, and we met in the Port Authority Bus Terminal several Januarys ago. I was doing a story on homeless people. She said I was wasting my time talking to her; she was just passing through, although she'd been passing through for more than two weeks. To prove to me that this was true, she rummaged through a tote bag and a manila envelope and finally unfolded a sheet of typing paper and brought out her photographs.

They were not pictures of family, or friends, or even a dog or cat, its eyes brown-red in the flashbulb's light. They were pictures of a house. It was like a thousand houses in a hundred towns, not suburb, not city, but somewhere in between, with aluminum siding and a chain-link fence, a narrow driveway running up to a one-car garage and a patch of backyard. The house was yellow. I looked on the back for a date or a name, but neither was there. There was no need for discussion. I knew what she was trying to tell me, for it was something I had often felt. She was not adrift, alone, anonymous, although her bags and her raincoat with the grime shadowing its creases had made me believe she was. She had a house, or at least once upon a time had had one. Inside

200

were curtains, a couch, a stove, potholders. You are where you live. She was somebody.

I've never been very good at looking at the big picture, taking the global 3 view, and I've always been a person with an overactive sense of place, the legacy of an Irish grandfather. So it is natural that the thing that seems most wrong with the world to me right now is that there are so many people with no homes. I'm not simply talking about shelter from the elements, or three square meals a day or a mailing address to which the welfare people can send the check—although I know that all these are important for survival. I'm talking about a home, about precisely those kinds of feelings that have wound up in cross-stitch and French knots on samplers over the years.

Home is where the heart is. There's no place like it. I love my home with 4 a ferocity totally out of proportion to its appearance or location. I love dumb things about it: the hot-water heater, the plastic rack you drain dishes in, the roof over my head, which occasionally leaks. And yet it is precisely those dumb things that make it what it is—a place of certainty, stability, predictability, privacy, for me and for my family. It is where I live. What more can you say about a place than that? That is everything.

Yet it is something that we have been edging away from gradually during 5 my lifetime and the lifetimes of my parents and grandparents. There was a time when where you lived often was where you worked and where you grew the food you ate and even where you were buried. When that era passed, where you lived at least was where your parents had lived and where you would live with your children when you became enfeebled. Then, suddenly where you lived was where you lived for three years, until you could move on to something else and something else again.

And so we have come to something else again, to children who do not 6 understand what it means to go to their rooms because they have never had a room, to men and women whose fantasy is a wall they can paint a color of their own choosing, to old people reduced to sitting on molded plastic chairs, their skin blue-white in the lights of a bus station, who pull pictures of houses out of their bags. Homes have stopped being homes. Now they are real estate.

People find it curious that those without homes would rather sleep sitting 7 up on benches or huddled in doorways than go to shelters. Certainly some prefer to do so because they are emotionally ill, because they have been locked in before and they are damned if they will be locked in again. Others are afraid of the violence and trouble they may find there. But some seem to want something that is not available in shelters, and they will not compromise, not for a cot, or oatmeal, or a shower with special soap that kills the bugs. "One room," a woman with a baby who was sleeping on her sister's floor, once told me, "painted blue." That was the crux of it; not size or location, but pride of ownership. Painted blue.

This is a difficult problem, and some wise and compassionate people are   8
working hard at it. But in the main I think we work around it, just as we walk
around it when it is lying on the sidewalk or sitting in the bus terminal — the
problem, that is. It has been customary to take people's pain and lessen our
own participation in it by turning it into an issue, not a collection of human
beings. We turn an adjective into a noun: the poor, not poor people; the
homeless, not Ann or the man who lives in the box or the woman who sleeps
on the subway grate.

Sometimes I think we would be better off if we forgot about the broad   9
strokes and concentrated on the details. Here is a woman without a bureau.
There is a man with no mirror, no wall to hang it on. They are not the homeless. They are people who have no homes. No drawer that holds the spoons.
No window to look out upon the world. My God. That is everything.

*For a reading quiz, sources on Anna Quindlen, and annotated links to further read-
ings on homelessness, visit **bedfordstmartins.com/thebedfordreader**.*

Journal Writing

What does the word *home* mean to you? Does it involve material things, privacy, family, a sense of permanence? In your journal, explore your ideas about this word. (To
take your journal writing further, see "From Journal to Essay" on the facing page.)

Questions on Meaning

1. What is Quindlen's THESIS?
2. What distinction is Quindlen making in her CONCLUSION with the sentences
   "They are not the homeless. They are people who have no homes"?
3. Why does Quindlen believe that having a home is important?

Questions on Writing Strategy

1. Why do you think Quindlen begins with the story of Ann? How else might
   Quindlen have begun her essay?
2. What is the EFFECT of Quindlen's examples of her own home?

3. What key ASSUMPTIONS does the author make about her AUDIENCE? Are the assumptions reasonable? Where does she specifically address an assumption that might undermine her view?
4. How does Quindlen vary the sentences in paragraph 7 that give examples of why homeless people avoid shelters?
5. **OTHER METHODS.** Quindlen uses examples to support an ARGUMENT. What position does she want readers to recognize and accept?

Questions on Language

1. What is the effect of "My God" in the last paragraph?
2. How might Quindlen be said to give new meaning to the old CLICHÉ "Home is where the heart is" (par. 4)?
3. What is meant by "crux" (par. 7)? Where does the word come from?

Suggestions for Writing

1. **FROM JOURNAL TO ESSAY.** Write an essay that gives a detailed DEFINITION of *home* by using your own home(s), hometown(s), or experiences with home(s) as supporting examples. (See Chap. 12 if you need help with definition.)
2. Have you ever moved from one place to another? What sort of experience was it? Write an essay about leaving an old home and moving to a new one. Was there an activity or a piece of furniture that helped ease the transition?
3. Estimates of the number of homeless people in the United States vary widely. Research the numbers, and then write an essay in which you present your findings and propose reasons for the variations.
4. **CRITICAL WRITING.** Write a brief essay in which you agree or disagree with Quindlen's assertion that a home is "everything." Can one, for instance, be a fulfilled person without a home? In your answer, take account of the values that might underlie an attachment to home; Quindlen mentions "certainty, stability, predictability, privacy" (par. 4), but there are others, including some (such as fear) that are less positive.
5. **CONNECTIONS.** COMPARE AND CONTRAST the views of homelessness and its solution in Quindlen's "Homeless" and Barbara Lazear Ascher's "On Compassion" (p. 195). Use specific passages from each essay to support your comparison.

Anna Quindlen on Writing

Anna Quindlen started her writing career as a newspaper reporter. "I had wanted to be a writer for most of my life," she recalls in the introduction to her book *Living Out Loud*, "and in the service of the writing I became a reporter. For many years I was able to observe, even to feel, life vividly, but at secondhand. I was able to stand over the chalk outline of a body on a sidewalk dappled with black blood; to stand behind the glass and look down into an operating theater where one man was placing a heart in the yawning chest of another; to sit in the park on the first day of summer and find myself professionally obligated to record all the glories of it. Every day I found answers: who, what, when, where, and why."

Quindlen was a good reporter, but the business of finding answers did not satisfy her personally. "In my own life," she continues, "I had only questions." Then she switched from reporter to columnist at the *New York Times*. It was "exhilarating," she says, that "my work became a reflection of my life. After years of being a professional observer of other people's lives, I was given the opportunity to be a professional observer of my own. I was permitted—and permitted myself—to write a column, not about my answers, but about my questions. Never did I make so much sense of my life as I did then, for it was inevitable that as a writer I would find out most clearly what I thought, and what I only thought I thought, when I saw it written down. . . . After years of feeling secondhand, of feeling the pain of the widow, the joy of the winner, I was able to allow myself to feel those emotions for myself."

For Discussion

1. What were the advantages and disadvantages of news reporting, according to Quindlen?
2. What did Quindlen feel she could accomplish in a column that she could not accomplish in a news report? What evidence of this difference do you see in her essay "Homeless"?

BRENT STAPLES

BRENT STAPLES is a member of the editorial board of the *New York Times*. Born in 1951 in Chester, Pennsylvania, Staples has a BA in behavioral science from Widener University in Chester and a PhD in psychology from the University of Chicago. Before joining the *New York Times* in 1985, he worked for the *Chicago Sun-Times*, the *Chicago Reader*, *Chicago* magazine, and *Down Beat* magazine. At the *Times*, Staples writes on culture, politics, reading, and special education, championing the cause of children with learning disabilities. He has also contributed to the *New York Times Magazine*, *New York Woman*, *Ms.*, *Harper's*, and other magazines. His memoir, *Parallel Time: Growing Up in Black and White*, appeared in 1994.

Black Men and Public Space

"Black Men and Public Space" appeared in the December 1986 issue of *Harper's* magazine and was then published, in a slightly different version, in Staples's memoir, *Parallel Time*. To explain a recurring experience of African American men, Staples relates incidents when he has been "a night walker in the urban landscape."

My first victim was a woman—white, well dressed, probably in her late twenties. I came upon her late one evening on a deserted street in Hyde Park, a relatively affluent neighborhood in an otherwise mean, impoverished section of Chicago. As I swung onto the avenue behind her, there seemed to be a discreet, uninflammatory distance between us. Not so. She cast back a worried glance. To her, the youngish black man—a broad six feet two inches with a beard and billowing hair, both hands shoved into the pockets of a bulky military jacket—seemed menacingly close. After a few more quick glimpses, she picked up her pace and was soon running in earnest. Within seconds she disappeared into a cross street.

That was more than a decade ago. I was twenty-two years old, a graduate student newly arrived at the University of Chicago. It was in the echo of that terrified woman's footfalls that I first began to know the unwieldy inheritance I'd come into—the ability to alter public space in ugly ways. It was clear that she thought herself the quarry of a mugger, a rapist, or worse. Suffering a bout of insomnia, however, I was stalking sleep, not defenseless wayfarers. As a softy who is scarcely able to take a knife to a raw chicken—let alone hold one to a person's throat—I was surprised, embarrassed, and dismayed all at once. Her flight made me feel like an accomplice in tyranny. It also made it clear that I was indistinguishable from the muggers who occasionally seeped into the area from the surrounding ghetto. That first encounter, and those that followed, signified that a vast, unnerving gulf lay between nighttime pedestrians — particularly women — and me. And I soon gathered that being perceived as dangerous is a hazard in itself. I only needed to turn a corner into a dicey situation, or crowd some frightened, armed person in a foyer somewhere, or make an errant move after being pulled over by a policeman. Where fear and weapons meet — and they often do in urban America — there is always the possibility of death.

In that first year, my first away from my hometown, I was to become thoroughly familiar with the language of fear. At dark, shadowy intersections, I could cross in front of a car stopped at a traffic light and elicit the *thunk, thunk, thunk, thunk* of the driver — black, white, male, or female — hammering down the door locks. On less traveled streets after dark, I grew accustomed to but never comfortable with people crossing to the other side of the street rather than pass me. Then there were the standard unpleasantries with policemen, doormen, bouncers, cabdrivers, and others whose business it is to screen out troublesome individuals *before* there is any nastiness. 3

I moved to New York nearly two years ago and I have remained an avid night walker. In central Manhattan, the near-constant crowd cover minimizes tense one-on-one street encounters. Elsewhere — in SoHo, for example, where sidewalks are narrow and tightly spaced buildings shut out the sky — things can get very taut indeed. 4

After dark, on the warrenlike streets of Brooklyn where I live, I often see women who fear the worst from me. They seem to have set their faces on neutral, and with their purse straps strung across their chests bandolier-style, they forge ahead as though bracing themselves against being tackled. I understand, of course, that the danger they perceive is not a hallucination. Women are particularly vulnerable to street violence, and young black males are drastically overrepresented among the perpetrators of that violence. Yet these truths are no solace against the kind of alienation that comes of being ever the suspect, a fearsome entity with whom pedestrians avoid making eye contact. 5

It is not altogether clear to me how I reached the ripe old age of twenty-two without being conscious of the lethality nighttime pedestrians attributed to me. Perhaps it was because in Chester, Pennsylvania, the small, angry industrial town where I came of age in the 1960s, I was scarcely noticeable against a backdrop of gang warfare, street knifings, and murders. I grew up one of the good boys, had perhaps a half-dozen fistfights. In retrospect, my shyness of combat has clear sources. 6

As a boy, I saw countless tough guys locked away; I have since buried several, too. They were babies, really — a teenage cousin, a brother of twenty- 7 two, a childhood friend in his mid-twenties—all gone down in episodes of bravado played out in the streets. I came to doubt the virtues of intimidation early on. I chose, perhaps unconsciously, to remain a shadow—timid, but a survivor.

The fearsomeness mistakenly attributed to me in public places often has a   8
perilous flavor. The most frightening of these confusions occurred in the late 1970s and early 1980s, when I worked as a journalist in Chicago. One day, rushing into the office of a magazine I was writing for with a deadline story in hand, I was mistaken for a burglar. The office manager called security and, with an ad hoc posse, pursued me through the labyrinthine halls, nearly to my editor's door. I had no way of proving who I was. I could only move briskly toward the company of someone who knew me.

Another time I was on assignment for a local paper and killing time before   9
an interview. I entered a jewelry store on the city's affluent Near North Side. The proprietor excused herself and returned with an enormous red Doberman pinscher straining at the end of a leash. She stood, the dog extended toward me, silent to my questions, her eyes bulging nearly out of her head. I took a cursory look around, nodded, and bade her good night.

Relatively speaking, however, I never fared as badly as another black male   10
journalist. He went to nearby Waukegan, Illinois, a couple of summers ago to work on a story about a murderer who was born there. Mistaking the reporter for the killer, police officers hauled him from his car at gunpoint and but for his press credentials would probably have tried to book him. Such episodes are not uncommon. Black men trade tales like this all the time.

Over the years, I learned to smother the rage I felt at so often being taken   11
for a criminal. Not to do so would surely have led to madness. I now take pre-cautions to make myself less threatening. I move about with care, particularly late in the evening. I give a wide berth to nervous people on subway platforms during the wee hours, particularly when I have exchanged business clothes for jeans. If I happen to be entering a building behind some people who appear skittish, I may walk by, letting them clear the lobby before I return, so as not to seem to be following them. I have been calm and extremely congenial on those rare occasions when I've been pulled over by the police.

And on late-evening constitutionals I employ what has proved to be an   12
excellent tension-reducing measure: I whistle melodies from Beethoven and Vivaldi and the more popular classical composers. Even steely New Yorkers hunching toward nighttime destinations seem to relax, and occasionally they even join in the tune. Virtually everybody seems to sense that a mugger wouldn't be warbling bright, sunny selections from Vivaldi's *Four Seasons*. It is my equivalent of the cowbell that hikers wear when they know they are in bear country.

*For a reading quiz, sources on Brent Staples, and annotated links to further readings on racial stereotyping, visit **bedfordstmartins.com/thebedfordreader**.*

Journal Writing

Staples explains how he perceives himself altering public space. Write in your journal about a time when you felt as if *you* altered public space—in other words, you changed people's attitudes or behavior just by being in a place or entering a situation. If you haven't had this experience, write about a time when you saw someone else alter public space in this way. (To take your journal writing further, see "From Journal to Essay" on the facing page.)

Questions on Meaning

1. What is the PURPOSE of this essay? Do you think Staples believes that he (or other African American men) will cease "to alter public space in ugly ways" in the near future? Does he suggest any long-term solution for "the kind of alienation that comes of being ever the suspect" (par. 5)?
2. In paragraph 5 Staples says he understands that the danger women fear when they see him "is not a hallucination." Do you take this to mean that Staples perceives himself to be dangerous? Explain.
3. Staples says, "I chose, perhaps unconsciously, to remain a shadow—timid, but a survivor" (par. 7). What are the usual CONNOTATIONS of the word *survivor*? Is "timid" one of them? How can you explain this apparent discrepancy?

Questions on Writing Strategy

1. The concept of altering public space is relatively abstract. How does Staples convince you that this phenomenon really takes place?
2. Staples employs a large number of examples in a fairly small space. How does he avoid having the piece sound like a list? How does he establish COHERENCE among all these examples? (Look, for example, at details and TRANSITIONS.)
3. **OTHER METHODS.** Many of Staples's examples are actually ANECDOTES—brief NARRATIVES. The opening paragraph is especially notable. Why is it so effective?

Questions on Language

1. What does the author accomplish by using the word *victim* in the essay's first paragraph? Is the word used literally? What TONE does it set for the essay?

2. Be sure you know how to define the following words, as used in this essay: afflu-ent, uninflammatory (par. 1); unwieldy, tyranny, pedestrians (2); intimidation (7); congenial (11); constitutionals (12).
3. The word *dicey* (par. 2) comes from British slang. Without looking it up in your dictionary, can you figure out its meaning from the context in which it appears?

Suggestions for Writing

1. **FROM JOURNAL TO ESSAY.** Write an essay narrating your experience of either alter-ing public space yourself or being a witness when someone else altered public space. What changes did you observe in people's behavior? Was your behavior similarly affected? In retrospect, do you think your reactions were justified?
2. Write an essay using examples to show how a trait of your own or of someone you know well always seems to affect people, whether positively or negatively.
3. The ironic term *DWB* (driving while black) expresses the common perception that African American drivers are more likely than white drivers to be pulled over by authorities for minor infractions—or no infraction at all. Research and write an essay about the accuracy of this perception in one state or municipality: Is there truth to it? If African Americans have been discriminated against, what if anything have the appropriate governments done to address the problem?
4. **CRITICAL WRITING.** Consider, more broadly than Staples does, what it means to alter public space. Staples would rather not have the power to do so, but it *is* a power, and it could perhaps be positive in some circumstances (wielded by a street performer, for instance, or the architect of a beautiful new building on cam-pus). Write an essay expanding on Staples's essay in which you examine the pros and cons of altering public space. Use specific examples as your EVIDENCE.
5. **CONNECTIONS.** Like Staples, Barbara Lazear Ascher, in "On Compassion" (p. 195), considers how people regard and respond to "the Other," the one who is viewed as different. In an essay, COMPARE AND CONTRAST the POINTS OF VIEW of these two authors. How does point of view affect each author's selection of details and tone?

Brent Staples on Writing

In comments written especially for *The Bedford Reader,* Brent Staples talks about the writing of "Black Men and Public Space." "I was only partly aware of how I felt when I began this essay. I knew only that I had this collection of experiences (facts) and that I felt uneasy with them. I sketched out the expe-riences one by one and strung them together. The bridge to the essay—what I wanted to say, but did not know when I started—sprang into life quite unexpectedly as I sat looking over these experiences. The crucial sentence comes right after the opening anecdote, in which my first 'victim' runs away from me: 'It was in the echo of that terrified woman's footfalls that I first began to know the unwieldy inheritance I'd come into—the ability to alter public space in ugly ways.' 'Aha!' I said. 'This is why I feel bothered and hurt and frustrated when this happens. I don't want people to think I'm stalking them. I want some fresh air. I want to stretch my legs. I want to be as anonymous as any other person out for a walk in the night.'"

A news reporter and editor by training and trade, Staples sees much similarity between the writing of a personal essay like "Black Men and Public Space" and the writing of, say, a murder story for a daily newspaper. "The newspaper murder," he says, "begins with standard newspaper information: the fact that the man was found dead in an alley in such-and-such a section of the city; his name, occupation, and where he lived; that he died of gunshot wounds to such-and-such a part of his body; that arrests were or were not made; that such-and-such a weapon was found at the scene; that the police have established no motive; etc.

"Personal essays take a different tack, but they, too, begin as assemblies of facts. In 'Black Men and Public Space,' I start out with an anecdote that crystallizes the issue I want to discuss—what it is like to be viewed as a criminal all the time. I devise a sentence that serves this purpose and also catches the reader's attention: 'My first victim was a woman—white, well dressed, probably in her late twenties.' The piece gives examples that are meant to illustrate the same point and discusses what those examples mean.

"The newspaper story stacks its details in a specified way, with each piece taking a prescribed place in a prescribed order. The personal essay begins often with a flourish, an anecdote, or the recounting of a crucial experience, then goes off to consider related experiences and their meanings. But both pieces rely on reporting. Both are built of facts. Reporting is the act of finding and analyzing facts.

"A fact can be a state of the world—a date, the color of someone's eyes, the arc of a body that flies through the air after having been struck by a car. A fact can also be a feeling—sorrow, grief, confusion, the sense of being pleased, offended, or frustrated. 'Black Men and Public Space' explores the relationship between two sets of facts: (1) the way people cast worried glances at me and sometimes run away from me on the streets after dark, and (2) the frustration and anger I feel at being made an object of fear as I try to go about my business in the city."

Personal essays and news stories share one other quality as well, Staples thinks: They affect the writer even when the writing is finished. "The discoveries I made in 'Black Men and Public Space' continued long after the essay was published. Writing about the experiences gave me access to a whole range of internal concerns and ideas, much the way a well-reported news story opens the door onto a given neighborhood, situation, or set of issues."

For Discussion

1. In recounting how his essay developed, what does Staples reveal about his writing process?
2. How, according to Staples, are essay writing and news writing similar? How are they different?
3. What does Staples mean when he says that "writing about the experiences gave me access to a whole range of internal concerns and ideas"?

CHET RAYMO

Almost every day for forty years, CHET RAYMO walked the same one-mile path from his home in North Easton, Massachusetts, to Stonehill College, where he taught physics and astronomy until his retirement in 2001. In *The Path: A One-Mile Walk Through the Universe* (2003), Raymo observes the ecology of his short commute. Until recently Raymo also wrote a weekly science column for the *Boston Globe*. "That's fifty essays a year for seventeen years," he told an interviewer in 2000, "and I never once ran out of ideas." Raymo continues to write essays on his Web site, *ScienceMusing.com*. His ten other nonfiction books include *365 Starry Nights: An Introduction to Astronomy for Every Night of the Year* (1982), *Biography of a Planet* (1984), and *Climbing Brandon: Science and Faith on Ireland's Holy Mountain* (2004). Raymo has also written three novels, including *The Dork of Cork* (1993), which was adapted as the movie *Frankie Starlight* (1995). Widely anthologized, Raymo's essays earned him the 1998 Lannan Literary Award for nonfiction.

A Measure of Restraint

In this excerpt from his book *The Virgin and the Mousetrap* (1991), Raymo uses three extended examples, both historical and current, to warn of the dangers lurking in the human quest for scientific discovery.

On September 13, 1987, two unemployed young men in search of a fast   1 buck entered a partly demolished radiation clinic in Goiânia, Brazil. They removed a derelict cancer therapy machine containing a stainless steel cylinder, about the size of a gallon paint can, which they sold to a junk dealer for twenty-five dollars. Inside the cylinder was a cake of crumbly powder that emitted a mysterious blue light. The dealer took the seemingly magical material home and distributed it to his family and friends. His six-year-old niece rubbed the glowing dust on her body. One might imagine that she danced, eerily glowing in the sultry darkness of the tropic night like an enchanted elfin sprite. The dust was cesium-137, a highly radioactive substance. The lovely light was the result of the decay of the cesium atoms. Another product of the decay was a flux of invisible particles with the power to damage living cells. The girl is dead. Others died or became grievously sick. More than two hundred people were contaminated.

A beautiful, refulgent dust, stolen from an instrument of healing, had be-   2 come the instrument of death. The junk dealer's niece was not the only child who rubbed the cesium on her body like carnival glitter, and the image of those luminous children will not go away. Their story is a moral fable for our times — a haunting story, touched with dreamlike beauty and ending in death. It evokes another story that took place almost a century ago, another story that illustrates the risks that are sometimes imposed by knowledge. It is a story of Marie and Pierre Curie, the discoverers of radium, as told by their daughter Eve.

The story begins at nine o'clock in the evening at the Curies' house in Paris. Marie is sitting at the bedside of her four-year-old daughter, Irene. It is a nightly ritual; the child is uncomfortable without her mother's presence. Marie sits quietly near the girl until the restless young voice gives way to sleep. Then she goes downstairs to her husband Pierre. Husband and wife have just completed an arduous four-year effort to isolate from tons of raw ore the tiny amount of the new element that will win them fame. The work is still on their minds: the laboratory, the workbenches, the flasks and vials. "Suppose we go down there for a moment," suggests Marie. They walk through the night to the laboratory and let themselves in. "Don't light the lamps," says Marie, in darkness. Before their recent success in isolating a significant amount of the new element, Pierre had expressed the wish that radium would have "a beautiful color." Now it is clear that the reality is better than the wish. Unlike any other element, radium is spontaneously luminous! On the shelves in the dark laboratory precious particles of radium in their tiny glass receivers glow with an eerie blue light. "Look! Look!" says Marie. She sits down in darkness, her face turned toward the glowing vials. *Radium. Their radium!* Pierre stands at her side. Her body leans forward, her eyes attentive; she adopts the posture that had been hers an hour earlier at the bedside of her child. Eve Curie called it "the evening of the glowworms."

Marie and Pierre Curie and their new element became famous. By the middle of the first decade of this century had begun what can only be called a radium craze. A thousand and one uses were proposed for the material with the mysterious emanations. The curative powers of a radium solution—called "liquid sunshine"—were widely touted. It was soon discovered that radium killed bacteria, and suggested uses included mouthwashes and toothpastes. Health spas with traces of radium in the water became popular. Entertainers created "radium dances," in which props and costumes coated with fluorescent salts of radium glowed in the dark. It is said that in New York people played "radium roulette," with a glowing wheel and ball, and refreshed themselves with luminescent cocktails of radium-spiked liquid. The most important commercial application of radium was in the manufacture of self-luminous paint, widely used for the numerals of watches and clocks that could be read in the dark. Hundreds of women were employed applying the luminous compound to the dials. It was a common practice for them to sharpen the tips of their brushes with their lips. Many of these women were later affected by anemia and lesions of the jawbone and mouth; a number of them died.

By 1930 the physiological hazards of radioactivity were recognized by the medical profession and the reckless misuse of radium had mostly ceased. But the mysterious emanations—which properly used are an effective treatment for cancer—had taken their toll. Marie Curie discovered the secret of the stars; her tiny glass vials contained the distilled essence of the force that makes the universe glow with light. She died of radiation-induced leukemia, with cataracts on her eyes and her fingertips marked by sores that would not heal. Like many of the gifts of knowledge, radium had proved a mixed blessing. The poet Adrienne Rich[1] has described Marie Curie's death this way:

> She died   a famous woman   denying
> her wounds
> denying
> her wounds   came   from the same source as her power

The evening of the glowworms! Eve Curie's evocative phrase might also be   6
used to describe the dance of the Brazilian children, their bodies luminous with cesium-137. In these two stories we are drawn at last and emphatically into the circle of the Janus-faced[2] god. Death and beauty, wounds and power: the piercing horns of the dilemma of science, demanding from the seeker of truth a measure of restraint.

As I write these lines, I recall glowworm evenings I experienced as a child   7
in Tennessee, running barefoot with my young companions through the lush green grass of the long sloping lawn, catching up fireflies in our hands. Stars in the silky night glimmered in concert with insect scintillations—tiny flashes of cold brilliance reflected in a canopy of overarching pines, as in dark water. The insect lights seemed a miracle, a conjuration of elfin magic; a dozen fireflies in a bottle made a fairy light. Now, forty-five years later, I have before me as I write the image of another firefly light: a photograph of a tobacco plant made to glow with the phantasmic radiance of the firefly's luciferous gene. I have clipped the photograph from the pages of the journal *Science* and tacked it up on the wall above my desk. It expresses what is best and worst in our quest for knowledge.

To make the autoluminescent tobacco plant, genetic engineers first   8
located the firefly gene—the DNA segment that gives rise to the enzyme that catalyzes the firefly's light-producing chemistry. The purloined gene was then introduced into the cells of tobacco plants, and the plants watered with a solution of the chemicals necessary for the luminescent reaction. The plants then emitted a faint but detectable light. The photograph was made by placing a genetically altered plant in contact with photographic film for twenty-four hours. The result is a scientific artifact that qualifies as a work of art.

---

[1] American poet, born 1929.—EDS.
[2] The ancient Roman god Janus was imagined to have two faces looking in opposite directions.—EDS.

One hardly knows how to react to experiments such as this. One admires   9
the knowledge and skill that enabled the genetic researchers to achieve so
remarkable a transmutation of living matter—a plant made luminous with an
animal's gene. Certainly, one is moved to a deeper respect for the chemical
machinery of life. Still, I turn to the photograph of the genetically altered
plant with a sense of foreboding. The tobacco plant seems to rise out of the
paper like a will-o'-the-wisp or friar's lantern, those flickering phosphorescent
lights that are sometimes seen over marshes and swamps at night, that in folk
legend beckon unwary followers into the mire.

The transgenic researchers do not consider their experiments frivolous or   10
dangerous. They are confident that the firefly's etheric gene can be spliced
with other genes as a valuable marker in genetic experiments. Researchers
need to know quickly if and where transplanted genes have been activated.
The firefly's light, issuing from the cells of another organism—human cancer-
fighting cells, for example—can be an ideal signal. There is no doubt that the
tobacco-cum-firefly experiments, and others like them, will lead to discoveries of potential benefit to society: Grains that are resistant to disease, fruit
trees that defy frost, bacteria that eat oil spills, vaccines for the cure of animal
and human diseases—all these things and more are promised by genetic engineers. Then what is the source of my uneasiness? Certainly, genetic engineering is not the first breakthrough in science that harbored potential for danger
as well as good: The discovery of radium comes too quickly to mind. Radium
beckoned us forward with the promise of cures for disease and inexhaustible
energy resources. Then Janus turned to reveal his other face—terrible weapons of destruction, a plague of nuclear waste, cancers caused, not cured. In
many ways, the fruitful promise of genetic engineering is greater than that of
radioactivity, but so is the potential danger. A gene reproduces. A gene copies
itself into the fabric of life. Nuclear waste remains radioactive for thousands
of years; a gene is potentially immortal. The soft phosphorescent light of the
genetically altered tobacco plant beckons us toward a future bright with health
and plenty, but it also has a spooky Frankensteinian[3] quality that warns us to
proceed with caution. "For Beauty's nothing but the beginning of Terror,"
wrote the poet Rilke,[4] and all too often his words might describe the enterprise of science.

On those sultry nights in Tennessee we caught glowworms in our hands.   11
Sometimes we pinched their tiny bodies to set their gene-activated fires alight.
But we squeezed gently, and then released the insects to take their place again
among the live constellations of the summer night. We recognized, if only in

[3] Uncontrollable, like the monster created by the title character in Mary Wollstonecraft
Shelley's *Frankenstein* (1818).—EDS.
[4] Rainer Maria Rilke (1875–1926), a German poet born in Austria.—EDS.

a childlike way, an integrity and balance within nature that demands of earth's dominant species a judicious self-restraint. The unexamined quest for knowledge is hemmed with peril.

Journal Writing

Think of an exploration, discovery, or invention that some people view positively but that you view differently because of its risks, unintended effects, or wastefulness. Cloning? Stem-cell research? Nuclear power? Space travel? An everyday convenience such as e-mail or cell phones? In your journal, explore your thoughts about this exploration, discovery, or invention. (To take your journal writing further, see "From Journal to Essay" on the facing page.)

Questions on Meaning

1. What is Raymo's THESIS? Where does he state it most directly?
2. What three examples does Raymo give to illustrate his thesis? How is the third example different from the first two? What does this difference suggest about his PURPOSE?
3. The discovery of radium promised "cures for disease and inexhaustible energy resources" (par. 10). What were some of the unforeseen negative consequences of this discovery?
4. Why does Raymo believe that the risks of genetic engineering outweigh those of radium?

Questions on Writing Strategy

1. How does Raymo use the IMAGE of glowworms to unify his essay? How does this image, along with the related image of the glowing will-o'-the-wisp (par. 9), relate to his three examples and to his larger point?
2. In paragraph 4 Raymo offers a number of examples of radium's uses in the early part of the twentieth century. How does he use sentence variety to make this passage interesting to read?
3. Raymo doesn't state his thesis directly until his conclusion, but where earlier does he allude to this thesis as a way to prepare readers for it?
4. How does the excerpt from the poem in paragraph 5 reinforce Raymo's main point?

5. **OTHER METHODS.** Where does Raymo use NARRATION in the essay? What is the EFFECT of these narrative passages?

Questions on Language

1. Raymo uses specialized vocabulary and uncommon words throughout this essay. Consult a dictionary to define the following words: cesium (par. 1); refulgent (2); anemia, lesions (4); scintillations, phantasmic, luciferous (7); autoluminescent, enzyme, catalyzes, luminescent (8); transmutation; phosphorescent (9); trans-genic, etheric (10). Must you know the precise meanings of these words to understand the essay? Do they undermine Raymo's attempt to explain a specialized subject to a general audience?
2. Why does Raymo call the story of the Brazilians contaminated by cesium-137 "a moral fable for our times" (par. 2)? What is a "moral fable"?
3. In paragraph 11 Raymo writes that he and his childhood companions "recognized, if only in a childlike way, an integrity and balance within nature that demands of earth's dominant species a judicious self-restraint." This is certainly not a childlike statement. Why do you think he chose to express his childhood understanding in sophisticated language?
4. Consult a dictionary if you are unsure of the meaning of any of the following: derelict, radioactive, flux, contaminated (par. 1); luminous (2); arduous, flasks, vials (3); craze, emanations, fluorescent (4); leukemia, cataracts (5); dilemma (6); conjuration (7); beckon, unwary (9); frivolous (10); judicious, quest, hemmed (11).

Suggestions for Writing

1. **FROM JOURNAL TO ESSAY.** Compose an essay in which you explain why you believe that the exploration, discovery, or invention you wrote about in your journal has or may have negative consequences ignored by others. Be sure to acknowledge what others see as the benefits. Also keep in mind that some readers may not immediately agree with you, so you will need to defend your views carefully and fully.
2. In books or periodicals intended for general audiences, such as the weekly science section of the *New York Times*, research the current state of genetic engineering. What have genetic engineers already accomplished? What are they working on? What are some predictions for future breakthroughs in the field? Report your findings in an essay. Your report may be neutral, simply explaining what you have learned, or you could take a stand on the value or danger of genetic engineering.
3. **CRITICAL WRITING.** ANALYZE the organization of "A Measure of Restraint." What sections does the essay fall into? How does Raymo make the transition from each section to the next? Do you think this organization helps Raymo make his point clearly and effectively? Why, or why not?
4. **CONNECTIONS.** In "How to Poison the Earth" (p. 294), Linnea Saukko also writes about technological developments that have led to negative consequences. Write an essay in which you discuss how Raymo might respond to Saukko and how Saukko might respond to Raymo.

Chet Raymo on Writing

At an event sponsored by the Lannan Foundation in 2000, Chet Raymo talked with author Scott Russell Sanders, who is also a recipient of the Lannan Literary Award (see p. 219). In the following excerpts from that conversation, Raymo explains why he writes and where his ideas come from.

SANDERS   How far back does the desire to write go?

RAYMO   I didn't really start writing—consciously, deliberately trying to put words on paper—until I was in my thirties. I was trained as a physicist, and somehow I thought I wanted to be a physicist. But, as I got deeper into it, I realized I wasn't really cut out to be a physicist. I found what was increasingly preoccupying me was the business of making connections. Which is, of course, what writers do. Susan Sontag said that the great thing about being a writer is that nothing is irrelevant. If you are interested in making connections in the world, you almost inevitably gravitate toward language and toward writing, and that's what happened to me in my midthirties.

The column [in the *Boston Globe*] has been a wonderful learning experience. Every column begins with something seen or heard or read—a wooly bear caterpillar on the pavement. To turn it into an essay, as you well know, a whole learning process is involved. What is this animal? What has it become? How does it become that?

SANDERS   In writing so many essays, do you have to scour the landscape for ideas, or does the world come to you?

RAYMO   The world constantly comes to you. I've never once in almost fifteen years had to sit around saying, "Now what am I going to write about?" I walk through nature every day, read science journals every week, and there's no end to possible things to write about. I occasionally teach a nonfiction writing class. I tell my students that they can write about anything. The challenge is to find the angle and to discover what connections you want to make.

For Discussion

1. What does Raymo mean by the "business of making connections"? Connections between what and for what purpose?
2. Why does Raymo quote Susan Sontag's line that nothing is irrelevant to a writer? Do you agree or disagree?

SCOTT RUSSELL SANDERS

SCOTT RUSSELL SANDERS writes stories, novels, and essays about plain people who, in his words, "are neither literary nor intellectual." He was born in 1945 in Memphis, Tennessee, and reports a somewhat nomadic childhood. He attended Brown University (BA, 1967) and Cambridge University (PhD, 1971) and for more than three decades has taught English at Indiana University in Bloomington. His books include stories for children, such as *Meeting Trees* (1996) and *Crawdad Creek* (1999); novels for adults, such as *Terrarium* (1985) and *The Invisible Company* (1989); collections of short stories, such as *Fetching the Dead* (1984) and *Hear the Wind Blow* (1985); and collections of essays, such as *Secrets of the Universe* (1991), *Writing from the Center* (1995), and *The Country of Language* (1999). His essays have appeared four times in the annual *Best American Essays*. Sanders's latest book is *The Force of Spirit* (2000), an exploration of nature, family, and everyday life.

Signs

In this essay from *Secrets of the Universe*, Sanders journeys through Bloomington, Indiana, his hometown, exploring the billboards, store signs, graffiti, and other postings that inform, nag, assault, and amuse the passerby. Layering example on example, detail on detail, Sanders reads the signs to reveal a human truth.

We seem compelled to scrawl our words on the mute, impervious world. We label the trees in parks, the caged animals in zoos. We encumber the horizon with billboards. We paste wisdom and wisecracks on the bumpers of cars, wear messages on our T-shirts, leave notes on refrigerators. In hospitals we hang names on the cribs of newborns, and in cemeteries we carve names above the dead. Watch any bare wall or lamppost, and before long it will blossom with signs, posters, the initials of lovers. Look at any map, and see how names crowd the blank spaces.

If you get out the road atlas and flip to the map of Indiana, say, and if you let your finger spiral toward my burg of Bloomington in the southern part of the state, you will trace over Gnaw Bone, Possum Trot, Buddha, Tulip, Handy, Pinhook, Peerless, Hope and New Hope, Beanblossom, Piano, Mount Healthy, Story, and Surprise. Wide places in the road, mostly, but they all carry labels, as do the creeks, the bridges, the government forests, the roads themselves.

Say you fly to Indianapolis, rent a car, drive south on Route 37, a four-lane that bears the name of a dead highway commissioner. After an hour of housing tracts and soybean fields and rumpled woodlands, you approach

Bloomington through the gauntlet of hectoring signs that ring most American cities, billboards urging you to smoke this brand of cigarette, drink that whiskey, sleep in this motel, drive that car, buy and buy, eat, eat, eat. You have been called into the world to devour it, the billboards cry. None of this is local speech. These garish ads for national brands are like distant voices hurled at us through loudspeakers; they are slabs of network culture heaved up on stilts and frozen against the sky. But if you leave the highway and enter the city, you pass through layer after layer of signs, each one more local and quirky than the one before, until, on reaching the downtown alleys, you find painted on brick walls the slogans and hieroglyphs of this particular place.

Turn off the highway, then. Take the College Avenue exit. Cruise past the   4
billboards for lawyers, realtors, restaurants, banks. Check out the titles of this week's teenybopper movies playing at the Y & W drive-in. Slow down. Notice in yards the hand-lettered rectangles of plywood and cardboard and tin, signs offering to pull stumps, read palms, figure taxes, clean septic tanks, upholster chairs, weave rugs, sell porch swings and quilts. You can almost hear the seethe of enterprise. On more official signs, twenty flavors of churches invite you to worship. Service clubs—Moose, Lions, Elk, the whole menagerie— invite you to lunch. Funeral homes invite you to think ahead. Tune us in, beg the radio stations. Read us, beg the newspapers. Remember us, beg the charities. The air is filled with seductive babble.

Where woods give way to the spreading hem of houses, the city greets you   5
with a sign for the Cascades Softball Complex (which sounds engagingly Freudian), and then, because every crossroads aspires to be the center of *something,* Bloomington introduces itself as the Home of the Children's Organ Transplant Association. All over town you will see COTA fund-raising banners, from which bald infants in need of livers or kidneys gaze at you hopefully.

You reach the outermost traffic light. On your right is the first of three   6
Big Red Liquor stores you will pass within two minutes. Go straight on College Avenue, which runs along one flank of the courthouse square. A mile from the square, the round sign of the Big Wheel Restaurant flashes in sequence its neon spokes, creating the illusion of a spinning wheel. The electronic marquee of a savings & loan spells out the time, temperature, interest rates, and news about the Girl Scout cookie sale. A mural on the second Big Red Liquor shows the Hoosier hills in autumn, scarlet maple and golden poplar. Drink, drink, and be mellow. On slotted plastic signs that shoulder for space along the avenue, a car dealer pleads "Come on Rain," Fantasy Lingerie offers "Adult Models," a pizza palace boasts "No Fooling, We're Number One," a burger joint confesses "We've Never Sold Millions of Anything," and a gas station promises, with spelling that gives one pause, "Mechantic on Duty."

Four blocks from the courthouse, a cartoon sign above Custom Grooming   7
shows a cheerful woman with curly blond hair and ruby lips, the fingers of one
uplifted hand signaling V-for-Victory, the other hand grasping the leash of a
beige poodle. You cannot tell without going inside that the grooming is for
dogs, not women. Pleazure Hours Adult Bookstore beckons from the right,
across the street from Big Red Liquor number three. Even on so brief an
acquaintance with our city, you realize that no one possessed of cash need go
hungry or lonely or dry.

Pull into one of the angled spaces beside the courthouse and park. Get out   8
and stretch. You might puzzle at seeing a copper fish atop the courthouse
dome. Everybody does, but no one can say for sure why an aquatic weather-
vane presides over this town so far from the sea. On the courthouse lawn, next
to the Women's Christian Temperance Union fountain ("Drink and Be
Grateful"), a plywood sheet braced with two-by-fours marks the "Future Site
of Vietnam Veterans Memorial." It has been a future site for so long, the dona-
tions accumulating so sluggishly, that the wood has begun to warp, the paint
to peel. Awaiting their memorial, the veterans do not let the war end, for their
sign shows a map of Vietnam still sharply divided between north and south,
the north stained a demonic red and the south a tranquil green.

Milder struggles are played out in the downtown's welter of signs and   9
countersigns. Take an hour, walk the streets and alleys within two or three
blocks of the courthouse, and you will see other traces of embattled visions.
To begin with, head west from the square along Sixth, past the Ben Franklin
five-and-dime. Halfway down the block you come to the dingy office of Yellow Cab, on whose roof there is a billboard-size imitation of Leonardo's *Last
Supper,* done in splotches of bright primary colors like a gigantic paint-by-
numbers project. On a traffic signal box out front of Yellow Cab, someone has
written "Trust Jesus," and above this injunction another hand has written
"Don't."

A mural of the holy supper comes as no surprise here, for Bloomington is   10
a notch in the Bible belt, the seat of a county whose barns and silos are apt to
proclaim "Get Right with God!" or "Jesus Is Lord!" But the contrary impulse,
the mocking voice that adds "Don't" before "Trust Jesus," is also native to the
place. On bridges and underpasses and in the shadows of alleys, where the
devout have scrawled "He Is Risen" or "He Is Coming," ribald skeptics draw
erupting phalluses. "Jesus Saves" is amended with the words, "in His Piggy
Bank." Wags repeatedly steal the "S" from the SHELL signs. Adherents of a
more furtive faith chalk up notices that "Good Witchcraft Is Alive." Walk
another half block past the paint-by-numbers Leonardo and, within sight of
two churches, you will discover on the back of a grocery store the warning,
"Don't Love Gods!"

In your stroll around the square, time and again you will see this pattern, 11
an official vision fronting the street and a rebel vision flickering in the alley.
Behind the fattest of our several fat banks, critics have spray-painted "Lance
That Boil" and "Pride Kills." On the front of the Knights of Columbus building, this month's antiabortion broadside proclaims "Always Choose Life,"
while on the rear someone has written in small, fierce letters, "Choose
Choice!" A downtown cinema known for running the more witless breed of
movies has been inscribed with "Post No Dreams" and "100% Unconscious by
the Year 2000." A record store has inspired the milder and wittier protest, "I'm
Not Your Groovy Thing!" When a grassy vacant lot—favorite hangout for
skateboarders and singers and Frisbee flingers—vanished recently under a
new gimcrack store, the fresh paint on the alley was soon emblazoned with
"Town for Sale!"

Stick to the alleys and you begin to see clashes, not only between official 12
and rebel visions, but among the dissidents themselves. "Kill Art!" appears
behind Pygmalion's Art Supplies, but so does the rival claim that "Artists
Control the Means of Expression!" A pastel mural of frolicking citizens has
been smirched with paintings of houseflies the size and color of crows. Behind Bloomingfood's vegetarian co-op, a carnivore has painted "Raw Meat!"
in bloody tones, but a gentler spirit has replied with "Love All Beings, Only
Life Is Holy." Elsewhere, the call to "Stop CIA Terrorism" is answered by
"Off the Gooks," and the rare, nostalgic peace symbol is answered by a
swastika.

Despite the efforts at cheer, the dominant tone in the alleys is grim, 13
reflecting the histrionic postures but also the confusion and despair of the
young people who paint most of the graffiti. The skull and crossbones is a
common motif, often accompanied by "Shatter Yourself" or "Life Sucks."
Keep walking, and you read: "Give me drugs!" "Born to lose!" "It just doesn't
matter!" "Can't wait to be extinct!" The stenciled silhouettes of women,
headless and ghostly white, cling to the brick walls like the shadows of pedestrians cast by the nuclear flash onto the walls of Hiroshima. The blunt four-
letter word for lovemaking appears frequently, but more as curse than
exhortation. "Sex = Death" appears on the back of Nick's English Hut, written by a metaphysician who was perhaps frightened by AIDS, perhaps moved
by intimations of the link between loving the flesh and leaving it. The voices
are local, but they speak of universal things.

In the alleys, on the cindery edges of parking lots, in the gloomy back pas- 14
sageways, tokens of hope never go unchallenged. On a mailbox near the
Lutheran Church a moving hand has written "Just Believe," but another has
countered with "Big Daddy in the Sky's a Bum!" Rosy letters cry "Love Now!"
from the delivery door of a boutique, and black ones answer:

> It's not allowed to be unkind,
> But still hate lives in my mind.

That is bleak enough, and yet, in such strangled poetry, in puns and rhymes, in outbursts of wackiness and whimsy, the alleys offer an antidote to their own bitter messages. Here and there on the gray cement a mushroom cloud has been redrawn into the humped shell of a snail, above the caption, "Slugs are friends." The score of a composition for brass quintet marches across the wall of a music store in notes a yard high. Sidewalks and dumpsters are embellished with a simple visual pun:

> MOM
> WOW

A rental house is labeled "Roach Motel." The windows of apartments over shops bear the warnings "Guard Snake on Duty" or "Beware of Canary." Next to dreary mottoes of ennui, you find the fluttering peacock-bright posters for dances, concerts, revivals, lessons in meditation, motorcycles for sale, kittens for free. Amid the gloomy pronouncements about sex, you read the perennial news that "Fred loves Nancy," Jack loves Jill.

The alleys become our caves. We paint on their walls the symbols of what   15 we love and hate, what we fear and worship, what we hunt and what we feel ourselves hunted by. With pictures, poems, and slogans, we gesture at mysteries. Like the cave artists who traced the outlines of their hands on the ceiling of Lascaux,[1] we leave marks that say of us: Here I am, the one who sees, the one who shapes. The power of naming our grief gives us leverage over despair, the power of voicing our confusion gives us a grip on chaos. Another couplet sums up the equivocal mood of the alleys:

> I opened my mouth to vomit,
> But all I got were words.

At least it is an individual mouth, not the great maw of a corporation or an advertising firm. And at least, against the silence, words do come. Words, the outbreathings of mind, the shadows cast by inwardness: They cover the walls of my city, and no doubt of yours, they blot out chunks of sky, they make the unspoken world speakable.

When your eyes grow weary of symbols or your feet of pavement, look for   16 the copper fish gliding atop the courthouse dome, and make your way back to the car. To leave Bloomington, hang two lefts around the square, then take Walnut north to 37, from which you can easily retrace your path to the airport. Signs will shout and whisper at you all the way.

---

[1] The cave paintings in Lascaux, France, are about 15,000 years old. — EDS.

*For a reading quiz, sources on Scott Russell Sanders, and annotated links to further readings on the history and means of written expression, visit **bedfordstmartins .com/thebedfordreader**.*

Journal Writing

"The power of naming our grief gives us leverage over despair," Sanders writes in paragraph 15, "the power of voicing our confusion gives us a grip on chaos." In your journal, reflect on these lines. Have you ever found that expressing yourself in speech or writing has helped you understand yourself more clearly? (To take your journal writing further, see "From Journal to Essay" on the facing page.)

Questions on Meaning

1. In what two sentences of the essay does Sanders state his main GENERALIZATION, his THESIS, most explicitly?
2. What point is Sanders making in paragraph 2? How does this point relate to his thesis?
3. What is the difference between the signs Sanders details in paragraph 3 and those he details in paragraphs 4–7?
4. What point unifies Sanders's presentation of signs in paragraphs 9–12? in paragraphs 13–14?
5. What does Sanders mean by "The alleys become our caves" (par. 15)?

Questions on Writing Strategy

1. In paragraphs 1 and 15, Sanders uses the first-person plural *we*. Everywhere else he uses the second person, either explicitly (*you*) or implicitly (with verbs of command, as in "Turn off the highway"). What is the EFFECT of the first person in paragraphs 1 and 15? of the second person in paragraphs 3–14 and 16?
2. Almost any paragraph in Sanders's essay demonstrates effective sentence variety, but look just at paragraph 1. How does sentence structure here add interest to the paragraph?
3. What is your response to Sanders's concluding paragraph?
4. **OTHER METHODS.** Sanders uses DESCRIPTION throughout the essay. Why is this method appropriate for his subject?

Questions on Language

1. How would you describe Sanders's TONE? Does it vary at all?

2. The second sentence in paragraph 15 offers three oppositions. What is the effect of these oppositions?
3. Consult a dictionary if you are unsure of the meanings of any of the following: impervious, encumber (par. 1); gauntlet, hectoring, garish, quirky, hieroglyphs (3); seethe, enterprise (4); demonic, tranquil (8); embattled (9); ribald, phalluses, adherents (10); gimcrack, emblazoned (11); dissidents, frolicking, carnivore, nostalgic, swastika (12); histrionic, metaphysician, intimations (13); antidote, ennui, perennial (14); leverage, equivocal (15).

Suggestions for Writing

1. **FROM JOURNAL TO ESSAY.** Based on your journal writing, write an essay in which you explore your beliefs about the power of words to help us understand ourselves and control our circumstances. If you like, you can relate a situation when speaking or writing helped you, or failed to help you.
2. Take Sanders's advice, and explore the signs in your own neighborhood—around your campus, for example, or along nearby streets if you live in a place where signs appear. Take notes about what you find. Then write an essay in which, like Sanders, you reflect on the significance of the various signs you encounter.
3. Scrawling on walls—writing graffiti—has a long history. Research the behavior to discover who has practiced it, why, and how it has changed over the centuries. Report your findings in an essay.
4. **CRITICAL WRITING.** Sanders offers a great number of examples in "Signs." In an essay, ANALYZE how he presents these many examples. Do you think he succeeds in both differentiating them and unifying them? Why, or why not?
5. **CONNECTIONS.** While Sanders writes about verbal expression, Laila Ayad, in "The Capricious Camera" (p. 359), writes about the ability of both visual and verbal expression to communicate. Based on your reading of both essays and on your own experience, write an essay that examines the similarities and differences between words and pictures as effective means of communication. Use specific examples to support your ideas.

Scott Russell Sanders on Writing

In exchanges with *Contemporary Authors* over the years, Scott Russell Sanders has explained his impulse to write.

I do not much value experimentation in form and style, if it is not engendered by new insights into human experience. I do value clarity of language and vision. . . . I believe that a writer should be a servant of language, community, and nature. Language is the creation and sustenance of community; and any community, if it is to be healthy and durable, must be respectful of the natural order which makes life possible. Because there is no true human existence apart from family and community, I feel a deep commitment to my region, to the land, to the people and all other living things with which I share this place. My writing is driven by a deep regard for particular places and voices, persons and tools, plants and animals, for human skills and stories, for the small change of daily life—a regard compounded of grief and curiosity and love. If my writing does not help my neighbors to live more alertly, pleasurably, or wisely, then it is worth little.

For Discussion

1. What does Sanders mean by "Language is the creation and sustenance of community"? What does language do for a community? Could a community exist without some form of language?
2. Do you think "Signs" achieves the goal Sanders states in his last sentence: Will he help *you* "live more alertly, pleasurably, or wisely"? Why, or why not?

ADDITIONAL WRITING TOPICS

Example

1. Select one of the following general statements, or set forth a general statement of your own that one of these inspires. Making it your central idea (or THESIS), support it in an essay full of examples. Draw your examples from your reading, your studies, your conversation, or your own experience.

   Voice mail is a great convenience (or a great inconvenience) for the caller.
   Electronic mail provides a form of communication that letters and the telephone don't.
   People one comes to admire don't always at first seem likable.
   Fashions this year are loonier than ever before.
   Good (or bad) habits are necessary to the nation's economy.
   Each family has its distinctive lifestyle.
   Certain song lyrics, closely inspected, promote violence.
   Comic books are going to the dogs.
   At some point in life, most people triumph over crushing difficulties.
   Churchgoers aren't perfect.
   TV commercials suggest that buying the advertised product will improve your love life like crazy.
   Home cooking can't win over fast food.
   Ordinary lives sometimes give rise to legends.
   Some people I know are born winners (or losers).
   Books can change our lives.
   Certain machines *do* have personalities.
   Some road signs lead drivers astray.

2. In a brief essay, make a GENERALIZATION about the fears, joys, or contradictions that members of minority groups seem to share. To illustrate your generalization, draw examples from personal experience, from outside reading, or from two or three of the essays in this book by the following authors: Nancy Mairs (p. 13), Maya Angelou (p. 88), Amy Tan (p. 94), Sherman Alexie (p. 105), Judith Ortiz Cofer (p. 162), Brent Staples (p. 205), Gloria Naylor (p. 486), Christine Leong (p. 492), Dagoberto Gilb (p. 503), Sandra Cisneros (p. 596), Martin Luther King, Jr. (p. 625), and Richard Rodriguez (p. 655).

7

COMPARISON AND CONTRAST

Setting Things Side by Side

◀ **Comparison and contrast in a painting and a photograph**

*Created just five years apart, these works relate in time as well
as subject. On the top, the painting* American Gothic, *by the
Iowan Grant Wood (1892–1942), depicts farmers in 1930, before the Great Depression was fully under way. On the bottom,
the photograph* Rural Rehabilitation Client, *by the Lithuanian-
born New Jerseyan Ben Shahn (1899–1969), depicts recipients
of a federal aid program in Arkansas in 1935, at the Depression's low point. Closely examine the people in each image
(clothes, postures, expressions) and their settings. What striking
and not-so-striking similarities do you notice? What is the most
obvious difference? What are some more subtle differences?
What does the medium of each work (painting versus photography) contribute to the differences? How would you summarize
the visions of rural folk conveyed by Wood and Shahn?*

THE METHOD

Should we pass laws to regulate pornography or just let pornography run wild? Which team do you place your money on, the Cowboys or the Forty-Niners? To go to school full-time or part-time: What are the rewards and drawbacks of each way of life? How do the Republican and the Democratic platforms stack up against each other? How is the work of Picasso like or unlike that of Matisse? These are questions that may be addressed by the dual method of COMPARISON AND CONTRAST. In comparing, you point to similar features of the subjects; in contrasting, to different features. (The features themselves you identify by the method of DIVISION or ANALYSIS; see Chap. 9.)

With the aid of comparison and contrast, you can show why you prefer one thing to another, one course of action to another, one idea to another. In an argument in which you support one of two possible choices, a careful and detailed comparison and contrast of the choices may be extremely convincing. In an expository essay, it can demonstrate that you understand your subjects thoroughly. That is why, on exams that call for essay answers, often you will be asked to compare and contrast. Sometimes the examiner will come right out and say, "Compare and contrast nineteenth-century methods of treating drug addiction with those of the present day." Sometimes, however, comparison and contrast won't even be mentioned by name; instead, the examiner will ask, "What resemblances and differences do you find between John Updike's short story 'A & P' and the Grimm fairy tale 'Godfather Death'?" Or, "Explain the relative desirability of holding a franchise as against going into business as an independent proprietor." But those—as you realize when you begin to plan your reply—are just other ways of asking you to compare and contrast.

In practice, the two methods are usually inseparable. A little reflection will show you why you need both. Say you intend to write a portrait-in-words of two people. No two people are in every respect exactly the same or entirely dissimilar. Simply to compare them or to contrast them would not be true to life. To set them side by side and portray them accurately, you must consider both similarities and differences.

A good essay in comparing and contrasting serves a PURPOSE. Most of the time, the writer of such an essay has one of two purposes in mind:

1. *The purpose of showing each of two subjects distinctly by considering both, side by side.* Writing with such a purpose, the writer doesn't necessarily find one of the subjects better than the other. In "Grant and Lee" in this chapter, Bruce Catton examines the characters of two Civil War generals. His

conclusion is not that either was a better man but that each reflected strong currents of American society.

2. *The purpose of choosing between two things*. In daily life, we often EVALUATE two possibilities to choose between them: which college course to elect, which movie to see, which luncheon special to take—chipped beef over green noodles or fried smelt on a bun? Our thinking on a matter such as the last is quick and informal: "Hmmmm, the smelt *looks* better. Red beef, green noodles—ugh, what a sight! Smelt has bones, but the beef is rubbery. Still, I don't like the smell of that smelt. I'll go for the beef (or maybe just grab a hamburger after class)." In essays, too, a writer, by comparing and evaluating points, decides which of two things is more admirable: "Organic Gardening, Yes; Gardening with Chemical Fertilizers, No!"— or "Skydiving Versus the Safe, Sane Life." In writing, as in thinking, you need to consider the main features of both subjects, the positive features and the negative, and to choose the subject whose positive features more clearly predominate.

THE PROCESS

Subjects for Comparison

When you find yourself considering two subjects side by side or preferring one subject over another, you have already embarked on comparison and contrast. Just be sure that your two subjects display a clear basis for comparison. In other words, they should have something significant in common. Comparison usually works best with two of a kind: two means of reading for the visually impaired, two ways of gardening, two California wines, two mystery writers, two schools of political thought.

It can sometimes be effective to find similarities between evidently unlike subjects—a city and a country town, say—and a special form of comparison, ANALOGY, always equates two very unlike things, explaining one in terms of the other. (In an analogy you might explain how the human eye works by comparing it to a simple camera, or you might explain the forces in a thunderstorm by comparing them to armies in battle.) In any comparison of unlike things, you must have a valid reason for bringing the two together. In "Grant and Lee," Bruce Catton compares two Civil War generals. But in an essay called "General Grant and Mick Jagger" you would be hard-pressed to find any real basis for comparison. Although you might wax ingenious and claim, "Like Grant, Jagger posed a definite threat to Nashville," the ingenuity would wear thin and soon the yoking together of general and rock star would fall apart.

Basis for Comparison and Thesis

Beginning to identify the shared and dissimilar features of your subjects will get you started, but the comparison won't be manageable for you or interesting to your readers unless you also limit it. You would be overly ambitious to try to compare and contrast the Russian way of life with the American way of life in five hundred words; you couldn't include all the important similarities and differences. In a brief paper, you would be wise to select a single basis for comparison: to show, for instance, how day-care centers in Russia and the United States are both like and unlike each other.

This basis for comparison will eventually underpin the THESIS of your essay—the claim you have to make about the similarities and dissimilarities of two things or about one thing's superiority over another. Here, from essays in this chapter, are THESIS STATEMENTS that clearly lay out what's being compared and why:

> Neat people are lazier and meaner than sloppy people.
> —Suzanne Britt, "Neat People vs. Sloppy People"

> These were two strong men, these oddly different generals, and they represented the strengths of two conflicting currents that, through them, had come into collision.
> —Bruce Catton, "Grant and Lee: A Study in Contrasts"

Notice that each author not only identifies his or her subjects (neat and sloppy people, two generals) but also previews the purpose of the comparison, whether to evaluate (Britt) or to explain (Catton).

Organization

Even with a limited basis for comparison, the method of comparison and contrast can be tricky without some planning. We suggest that you make an outline (preferably in writing), using one of two organizations described below. Say you're writing an essay on two banjo-pickers, Jed and Jake. Your purpose is to explain the distinctive identities of the two players, and your thesis statement might be the following:

> Jed and Jake are both excellent banjo-pickers whose differences reflect their training.

Here are the two ways you might arrange your comparison:

1. *Subject by subject.* Set forth all your facts about Jed, then do the same for Jake. Next, sum up their similarities and differences. In your conclusion, state what you think you have shown.

1. *Jed*
   Training
   Choice of material
   Technical dexterity
   Playing style
2. *Jake*
   Training
   Choice of material
   Technical dexterity
   Playing style

   SUMMARY
   CONCLUSION

This procedure works for a paper of a few paragraphs, but for a longer one, it has a built-in disadvantage: Readers need to remember all the facts about subject 1 while they read about subject 2. If the essay is long and lists many facts, this procedure may be burdensome.

2. *Point by point.* Usually more workable in writing a long paper than the first method, the second scheme is to compare and contrast as you go. You consider one point at a time, taking up your two subjects alternately. In this way, you continually bring the subjects together, perhaps in every paragraph. Notice the differences in the outline:

1. *Training*
   Jed: studied under Earl Scruggs
   Jake: studied under Bela Fleck

2. *Choice of material*
   Jed: bluegrass
   Jake: jazz-oriented

3. *Technical dexterity*
   Jed: highly skilled
   Jake: highly skilled

4. *Playing style*
   Jed: rapid-fire
   Jake: impressionistic

For either the subject-by-subject or the point-by-point scheme, your conclusion might be: Although similar in skill, the two differ greatly in aims and in personalities. Jed is better suited to the Grand Ol' Opry and Jake to a concert hall.

No matter how you group your points, they have to balance; you can't discuss Jed's on-stage manner without discussing Jake's too. If you have nothing to say about Jake's on-stage manner, then you might as well omit the point. A surefire loser is the paper that proposes to compare and contrast two subjects but then proceeds to discuss quite different elements in each: Jed's playing style and Jake's choice of material, Jed's fondness for smelt on a bun and Jake's hobby of antique-car collecting. The writer of such a paper doesn't compare and contrast the two musicians at all, but provides two quite separate discussions.

By the way, a subject-by-subject organization works most efficiently for a *pair* of subjects. If you want to write about *three* banjo-pickers, you might first consider Jed and Jake, then Jake and Josh, then Josh and Jed—but it would probably be easiest to compare and contrast all three point by point.

Flexibility

As you write, an outline will help you see the shape of your paper and keep your procedure in mind. But don't be the simple tool of your outline. Few essays are more boring to read than the long comparison and contrast written mechanically. The reader comes to feel like a weary tennis spectator whose head has to swivel from side to side: now Jed, now Jake; now Jed again, now back to Jake. You need to mention the same features of both subjects, it is true, but no law decrees *how* you must mention them. You need not follow your outline in lockstep order, or cover similarities and differences at precisely the same length, or spend a hundred words on Jed's banjo-picking skill just because you spend a hundred words on Jake's. Your essay, remember, doesn't need to be as symmetrical as a pair of salt and pepper shakers. What is your outline but a simple means to organize your account of a complicated reality? As you write, keep casting your thoughts upon a living, particular world—not twisting and squeezing that world into a rigid scheme, but moving through it with open senses, being patient and faithful and exact in your telling of it.

FOCUS ON PARAGRAPH COHERENCE

With several points of comparison and alternating subjects, a comparison will be easy for your readers to follow only if you frequently clarify what subject and what point you are discussing. Two techniques, especially, can help you guide readers through your comparison: transitions and repetition or restatement.

- Use TRANSITIONS as signposts to tell readers where you, and they, are headed. Some transitions indicate that you are shifting between subjects, either finding resemblances between them (*also, like, likewise, similarly*) or finding differences (*but, however, in contrast, instead, unlike, whereas, yet*). Other transitions indicate that you are moving on to a new point (*in addition, also, furthermore, moreover*).

Traditional public schools depend for financing, of course, on tax receipts and on other public money like bonds, and as a result they generally open enrollment to all students without regard to background, skills, or special needs. Magnet schools are similarly funded by public money. But they often require prospective students to pass a test or other hurdle for admission. In addition, whereas traditional public schools usually offer a general curriculum, magnet schools often focus on a specialized program emphasizing an area of knowledge or competence, such as science and technology or performing arts.

- Use repetition or restatement of subjects and points of comparison to clarify and link sentences. Here is the same passage on schools with its repetitions and restatements underlined:

Traditional public schools depend for financing, of course, on tax receipts and on other public money like bonds, and as a result they generally open enrollment to all students without regard to background, skills, or special needs. Magnet schools are similarly funded by public money. But they often require prospective students to pass a test or other hurdle for admission. In addition, whereas traditional public schools usually offer a general curriculum, magnet schools often focus on a specialized program emphasizing an area of knowledge or competence, such as science and technology or performing arts.

For exercises on transitions, visit Exercise Central at *bedfordstmartins.com/ thebedfordreader.*

CHECKLIST FOR REVISING A COMPARISON AND CONTRAST

✔ **PURPOSE.** What is the aim of your comparison: to explain two subjects or to evaluate them? Will the purpose be clear to readers from the start?

✔ **SUBJECTS.** Are the subjects enough alike, sharing enough features, to make comparison worthwhile?

✔ **THESIS.** Does your thesis establish a limited basis for comparison so that you have room and time to cover all the relevant similarities and differences?

✔ **ORGANIZATION.** Does your arrangement of material, whether subject by subject or point by point, do justice to your subjects and help readers follow the comparison?

✔ **BALANCE AND FLEXIBILITY.** Have you covered the same features of both subjects? At the same time, have you avoided a rigid back-and-forth movement that could bore or exhaust a reader?

✔ **COHERENCE.** Have you used transitions and repetition or restatement to clarify which subjects and which points you are discussing?

COMPARISON AND CONTRAST IN PARAGRAPHS

Writing About Television

The following example, written especially for *The Bedford Reader*, uses point-by-point comparison for a clear purpose: to evaluate television drama, then and now, and to express a preference for one over the other. Notice that the writer is fair—acknowledging (toward the end) that today's dramas also have fine actors and have none of the primitiveness of yesterday's dramas.

Though written to be freestanding, this paragraph on drama might do good work in a full essay about, say, the chief differences between TV programming in the medium's early days and programming now.

Seen on aged 16-millimeter film, the original production of Paddy Chayevsky's *Marty* makes clear the differences between television drama of 1953 and that of today. Today there's no weekly Goodyear Playhouse to showcase original one-hour plays by important authors; most scriptwriters collaborate, all but anonymously, on serials about familiar characters. *Marty* features no bodice ripping, no drug busts, no deadly illness, no laugh track. Instead, it simply shows the awakening of love between a heavyset butcher and a mousy high-school teacher: both single, lonely, and shy, never twice dating the same person. Unlike the writer of today, Chayevsky couldn't set scenes outdoors or on location. In one small studio, in slow lingering takes (some five minutes long—not eight to twelve seconds, as we now expect), the camera probes the faces of two seated characters as Marty and his pal Angie plan Saturday night ("What do you want to do?"—"I dunno. What do *you* want to do?"). Oddly, the effect is spellbinding. To bring such scenes to life, the actors must project with vigor; and like the finer actors of today, Rod Steiger as Marty exploits each moment. In 1953, plays were telecast live. Today, well-edited videotape may eliminate blown lines, but a chill slickness prevails. Technically, *Marty* is primitive, yet it probes souls. Most televised drama today displays a physically larger world—only to nail a box around it.

Point-by-point comparison supporting this topic sentence

1. *Original plays vs. serials*

2. *Simple love story vs. violence and sex*

3. *Studio sets with long takes vs. locations with short takes*

4. *Good acting vs. good acting*

5. *Live vs. videotaped*

6. *Primitive and probing vs. big and limited*

Transitions (underlined) clarify the comparison

Writing in an Academic Discipline

Taken from a textbook on architectural history, the following subject-by-subject comparison explains the differences between two competing theories of architecture in Russia in the 1920s and 1930s. The paragraph is one of several in which the author demonstrates how modernist architects divided into those concerned mainly with form and those concerned mainly with social progress.

In Russia, too, modernists fell into two camps. They squared off against each other in public debate and in Vkhutemas, a school of architecture organized in 1920 along lines parallel to the Bauhaus. "The measure of architecture is architecture," went the motto of one camp. They believed in an unfettered experimentalism of form. The rival camp had a problem-solving orientation. The architect's main mission, in their view, was to share in the common task of achieving the transformation of society promised by the October Revolution [of 1917]. They were keen on standardization, user interviews, and ideological prompting. They worked on new building programs that would consolidate the social order of communism. These they referred to as "social condensers."

                    —Spiro Kostof, *A History of Architecture*

Subject-by-subject comparison supporting this topic sentence

1. First camp: experimental

2. Second camp: problem solving (receives more attention because it eventually prevailed)

COMPARISON AND CONTRAST IN PRACTICE

In her sophomore year in college, Susan Wheeler was running for president of her dormitory. She prepared a campaign statement for the student newspaper's coverage of the election, and she also created the flier on the next page for posting throughout the dorm.

Wheeler believed that her campaign platform was much stronger than her opponent's, and she decided to highlight the differences by showing her ideas alongside her opponent's (in a point-by-point arrangement). But her draft needed work to make the points more concise and to give them PARALLEL wording that would clarify and stress the contrasts. Originally, the first three points read as follows:

Susan Wheeler
- A supporter of all extracurricular activities
- Actively participates in student government association
- The food plans should be more flexible for all students

Matt Parker
- Supports mainly sports and cheerleading
- He is not in the student government association
- Does not mention the food plans

In Wheeler's final draft (next page), the parallel wording (each point beginning with a verb) is both easier to read and more emphatic.

Susan Wheeler

for

Dorm President

Here are the reasons why:

Susan Wheeler

- Supports all extracurricular activities
- Participates actively in student government association
- Wants to make food plans more flexible for all students
- Wants to extend bookstore hours
- Wants to increase quantity and accessibility of copiers
- Wants a 24-hour computer lab in the dorm
- Has made Dean's List every semester

Matt Parker

- Supports mainly sports and cheerleading
- Does not participate in student government association
- Does not mention the food plans
- Does not mention extending bookstore hours
- Does not mention copier problems
- Does not mention a computer lab
- Has not made Dean's List

Vote May 2

SUSAN WHEELER FOR PRESIDENT . . . WE'LL DO IT TOGETHER!

SUZANNE BRITT

SUZANNE BRITT was born in Winston-Salem, North Carolina, and studied at Salem College and Washington University, where she earned an MA in English. Britt has written for *Sky Magazine*, the *New York Times*, *Newsweek*, the *Boston Globe*, and many other publications. She teaches English at Meredith College in North Carolina and has published a history of the college and two English textbooks. Her other books are collections of her essays: *Skinny People Are Dull and Crunchy like Carrots* (1982) and *Show and Tell* (1983).

Neat People
vs.
Sloppy People

"Neat People vs. Sloppy People" appears in Britt's collection *Show and Tell*. Mingling humor with seriousness (as she often does), Britt has called the book a report on her journey into "the awful cave of self: You shout your name and voices come back in exultant response, telling you their names." In this essay, Britt uses comparison mainly to entertain by showing us aspects of our own selves, awful or not. For another approach to a similar subject, see the next essay, by Dave Barry.

I've finally figured out the difference between neat people and sloppy people. The distinction is, as always, moral. Neat people are lazier and meaner than sloppy people.

Sloppy people, you see, are not really sloppy. Their sloppiness is merely the unfortunate consequence of their extreme moral rectitude. Sloppy people carry in their mind's eye a heavenly vision, a precise plan, that is so stupendous, so perfect, it can't be achieved in this world or the next.

Sloppy people live in Never-Never Land. Someday is their métier. Someday they are planning to alphabetize all their books and set up home catalogs. Someday they will go through their wardrobes and mark certain items for tentative mending and certain items for passing on to relatives of similar shape and size. Someday sloppy people will make family scrapbooks into which they will put newspaper clippings, postcards, locks of hair, and the dried corsage from their senior prom. Someday they will file everything on the surface of their desks, including the cash receipts from coffee purchases at the snack shop. Someday they will sit down and read all the back issues of *The New Yorker*.

For all these noble reasons and more, sloppy people never get neat. They 4 aim too high and wide. They save everything, planning someday to file, order, and straighten out the world. But while these ambitious plans take clearer and clearer shape in their heads, the books spill from the shelves onto the floor, the clothes pile up in the hamper and closet, the family mementos accumulate in every drawer, the surface of the desk is buried under mounds of paper, and the unread magazines threaten to reach the ceiling.

Sloppy people can't bear to part with anything. They give loving atten- 5 tion to every detail. When sloppy people say they're going to tackle the surface of a desk, they really mean it. Not a paper will go unturned; not a rubber band will go unboxed. Four hours or two weeks into the excavation, the desk looks exactly the same, primarily because the sloppy person is meticulously creating new piles of papers with new headings and scrupulously stopping to read all the old book catalogs before he throws them away. A neat person would just bulldoze the desk.

Neat people are bums and clods at heart. They have cavalier attitudes 6 toward possessions, including family heirlooms. Everything is just another dust-catcher to them. If anything collects dust, it's got to go and that's that. Neat people will toy with the idea of throwing the children out of the house just to cut down on the clutter.

Neat people don't care about process. They like results. What they want 7 to do is get the whole thing over with so they can sit down and watch the rasslin' on TV. Neat people operate on two unvarying principles: Never handle any item twice, and throw everything away.

The only thing messy in a neat person's house is the trash can. The 8 minute something comes to a neat person's hand, he will look at it, try to decide if it has immediate use and, finding none, throw it in the trash.

Neat people are especially vicious with mail. They never go through their 9 mail unless they are standing directly over a trash can. If the trash can is beside the mailbox, even better. All ads, catalogs, pleas for charitable contributions, church bulletins, and money-saving coupons go straight into the trash can without being opened. All letters from home, postcards from Europe, bills, and paychecks are opened, immediately responded to, then dropped in the trash can. Neat people keep their receipts only for tax purposes. That's it. No sentimental salvaging of birthday cards or the last letter a dying relative ever wrote. Into the trash it goes.

Neat people place neatness above everything, even economics. They are 10 incredibly wasteful. Neat people throw away several toys every time they walk through the den. I knew a neat person once who threw away a perfectly good dish drainer because it had mold on it. The drainer was too much trouble to wash. And neat people sell their furniture when they move. They will sell a La-Z-Boy recliner while you are reclining in it.

Neat people are no good to borrow from. Neat people buy everything in   11
expensive little single portions. They get their flour and sugar in two-pound bags. They wouldn't consider clipping a coupon, saving a leftover, reusing plastic nondairy whipped cream containers, or rinsing off tin foil and draping it over the unmoldy dish drainer. You can never borrow a neat person's newspaper to see what's playing at the movies. Neat people have the paper all wadded up and in the trash by 7:05 AM.

Neat people cut a clean swath through the organic as well as the inorganic   12
world. People, animals, and things are all one to them. They are so insensitive. After they've finished with the pantry, the medicine cabinet, and the attic, they will throw out the red geranium (too many leaves), sell the dog (too many fleas), and send the children off to boarding school (too many scuff-marks on the hardwood floors).

*For a reading quiz, sources on Suzanne Britt, and annotated links to further readings on personality traits, visit **bedfordstmartins.com/thebedfordreader**.*

Journal Writing

Britt suggests that grouping people according to oppositions, such as neat versus sloppy, reveals other things about them. Write about the oppositions you use to evaluate people. Smart versus dumb? Fit versus out of shape? Hip versus clueless? Rich versus poor? Outgoing versus shy? Open-minded versus narrow-minded? (To take your journal writing further, see "From Journal to Essay" on the next page.)

Questions on Meaning

1. "Suzanne Britt believes that neat people are lazy, mean, petty, callous, wasteful, and insensitive." How would you respond to this statement?
2. Is the author's main PURPOSE to make fun of neat people, to assess the habits of neat and sloppy people, to help neat and sloppy people get along better, to defend sloppy people, to amuse and entertain, or to prove that neat people are morally inferior to sloppy people? Discuss.

3. What is meant by "as always" in the sentence "The distinction is, as always, moral" (par. 1)? Does the author seem to be suggesting that any and all distinctions between people are moral?

Questions on Writing Strategy

1. What is the general TONE of this essay? What words and phrases help you determine that tone?
2. Britt mentions no similarities between neat and sloppy people. Does that mean this is not a good comparison and contrast essay? Why might a writer deliberately focus on differences and give very little or no time to similarities?
3. Consider the following GENERALIZATIONS: "For all these noble reasons and more, sloppy people never get neat" (par. 4) and "The only thing messy in a neat person's house is the trash can" (8). How can you tell that these statements are generalizations? Look for other generalizations in the essay. What is the EFFECT of using so many?
4. How does Britt use repetition to clarify her comparison?
5. **OTHER METHODS.** Although filled with generalizations, Britt's essay does not lack for EXAMPLES. Study the examples in paragraph 11, and explain how they do and don't work the way examples should: to bring the generalizations about people down to earth.

Questions on Language

1. Consult your dictionary for definitions of these words: rectitude (par. 2); métier, tentative (3); accumulate (4); excavation, meticulously, scrupulously (5); salvaging (9).
2. How do you understand the use of the word *noble* in the first sentence of paragraph 4? Is it meant literally? Are there other words in the essay that appear to be written in a similar tone?

Suggestions for Writing

1. **FROM JOURNAL TO ESSAY.** From your journal entry, choose your favorite opposition for evaluating people, and write an essay in which you compare and contrast those who pass your "test" with those who fail it. You may choose to write your essay tongue-in-cheek, as Britt does, or seriously.
2. Write an essay in which you compare and contrast two apparently dissimilar groups of people: for example, blue-collar workers and white-collar workers, people who write a lot of e-mail and people who don't bother with it, runners and football players, readers and TV watchers, or any other variation you choose. Your approach may be either lighthearted or serious, but make sure you come to some conclusion about your subjects. Which group do you favor? Why?
3. ANALYZE the similarities and differences between two characters in your favorite novel, story, film, or television show. Which aspects of their personalities make them work well together, within the context in which they appear? Which char-

acteristics work against each other, and therefore provide the necessary conflict to hold the reader's or viewer's attention?

4. **CRITICAL WRITING.** Britt's essay is remarkable for its exaggeration of the two types. Write a brief essay analyzing and contrasting the ways Britt characterizes sloppy people and neat people. Be sure to consider the CONNOTATIONS of the words, such as "moral rectitude" for sloppy people (par. 2) and "cavalier" for neat people (6).

5. **CONNECTIONS.** Neither Suzanne Britt nor the author of the next essay, Dave Barry, seems to have much sympathy for neat people. Write a brief essay in which you explain why neatness matters. Or if you haven't a clue why, then write a brief essay in which you explain the benefits of dirt and disorder.

Suzanne Britt on Writing

Asked to tell how she writes, Suzanne Britt contributed the following comment to *The Bedford Reader*.

The question "How do you write?" gets a snappy, snappish response from me. The first commandment is "Live!" And the second is like unto it: "Pay attention!" I don't mean that you have to live high or fast or deep or wise or broad. And I certainly don't mean you have to live true and upright. I just mean that you have to suck out all the marrow of whatever you do, whether it's picking the lint off the navy-blue suit you'll be wearing to Cousin Ione's funeral or popping an Aunt Jemimah frozen waffle into the toaster oven or lying between sand dunes, watching the way the sea oats slice the azure sky. The ominous question put to me by students on all occasions of possible accountability is "Will this count?" My answer is rock bottom and hard: "Everything counts," I say, and silence falls like prayers across the room.

The same is true of writing. Everything counts. Despair is good. Numbness can be excellent. Misery is fine. Ecstasy will work—or pain or sorrow or passion. The only thing that won't work is indifference. A writer refuses to be shocked and appalled by anything going or coming, rising or falling, singing or soundless. The only thing that shocks me, truth to tell, is indifference. How dare you not fight for the right to the crispy end piece on the standing-rib roast? How dare you let the fragrance of Joy go by without taking a whiff of it? How dare you not see the old woman in the snap-front housedress and the rolled-down socks, carrying her Polident and Charmin in a canvas tote that says, simply, elegantly, Le Bag?

After you have lived, paid attention, seen connections, felt the harmony, writhed under the dissonance, fixed a Diet Coke, popped a big stick of Juicy

Fruit in your mouth, gathered your life around you as a mother hen gathers her brood, as a queen settles the folds in her purple robes, you are ready to write. And what you will write about, even if you have one of those teachers who makes you write about, say, Guatemala, will be something very exclusive and intimate — something just between you and Guatemala. All you have to find out is what that small intimacy might be. It is there. And having found it, you have to make it count.

There is no rest for a writer. But there is no boredom either. A Sunday morning with a bottle of extra-strength aspirin within easy reach and an ice bag on your head can serve you very well in writing. So can a fly buzzing at your ear or a heart-stopping siren in the night or an interminable afternoon in a biology lab in front of a frog's innards.

All you need, really, is the audacity to believe, with your whole being, that if you tell it right, tell it truly, tell it so we can all see it, the "it" will play in Peoria, Poughkeepsie, Pompeii, or Podunk. In the South we call that conviction, that audacity, an act of faith. But you can call it writing.

For Discussion

1. What advice does Britt offer a student assigned to write a paper about, say, Guatemala? If you were that student, how would you go about taking her advice?
2. Where in her comment does the author use colorful and effective FIGURES OF SPEECH?
3. What is the TONE of Britt's remarks? Sum up her attitude toward her subject, writing.

DAVE BARRY

DAVE BARRY is a humorist whom the *New York Times* has called "the funniest man in America." Barry was born in 1947 in Armonk, New York, and graduated from Haverford College in 1969. He worked as a journalist for five years and lectured businesspeople on writing for eight years while he began to establish himself as a columnist. His humor writing now appears in several hundred newspapers and has been collected in more than twenty-five books, including *Bad Habits: A 100% Fact Free Book* (1985), *The World According to Dave Barry* (1994), *Dave Barry in Cyberspace* (1996), and *Boogers Are My Beat: More Lies, but Some Actual Journalism* (2003), the last ranging from humorous pieces to serious thoughts on September 11, 2001. In 1988 Barry received the Pulitzer Prize for "distinguished commentary," although, he says, "nothing I've ever written fits the definition." (He thinks he won because his columns stood out from the "earthshakingly important" competition.) Barry lives in Miami with his family.

Batting Clean-Up and Striking Out

This essay from *Dave Barry's Greatest Hits* (1988) illustrates Barry's gift, in the words of critic Alison Teal, "for taking things at face value and rendering them funny on those grounds alone, for rendering every ounce of humor out of a perfectly ordinary experience." Like Suzanne Britt in the previous essay, Barry contrasts two styles of dealing with a mess.

The primary difference between men and women is that women can see 1 extremely small quantities of dirt. Not when they're babies, of course. Babies of both sexes have a very low awareness of dirt, other than to think it tastes better than food.

But somewhere during the growth process, a hormonal secretion takes 2 place in women that enables them to see dirt that men cannot see, dirt at the level of *molecules*, whereas men don't generally notice it until it forms clumps large enough to support agriculture. This can lead to tragedy, as it did in the ill-fated ancient city of Pompeii, where the residents all got killed when the local volcano erupted and covered them with a layer of ash twenty feet deep.[1] Modern people often ask, "How come, when the ashes started falling, the Pompeii people didn't just *leave*?" The answer is that in Pompeii, it was the custom for

[1] Pompeii, in what is now southern Italy, was buried in the eruption of Mount Vesuvius in AD 79. —EDS.

245

the men to do the housework. They never even *noticed* the ash until it had for the most part covered the children. "Hey!" the men said (in Latin). "It's mighty quiet around here!" This is one major historical reason why, to this very day, men tend to do extremely little in the way of useful housework.

What often happens in my specific family unit is that my wife will say to   3
me: "Could you clean Robert's bathroom? It's filthy." So I'll gather up the Standard Male Cleaning Implements, namely a spray bottle of Windex and a wad of paper towels, and I'll go into Robert's bathroom, and it *always looks perfectly fine*. I mean, when I hear the word "filthy" used to describe a bathroom, I think about this bar where I used to hang out called Joe's Sportsman's Lounge, where the men's room had bacteria you could enter in a rodeo.

Nevertheless, because I am a sensitive and caring kind of guy, I "clean" the   4
bathroom, spraying Windex all over everything including the six hundred action figures each sold separately that God forbid Robert should ever take a bath without, and then I wipe it back off with the paper towels, and I go back to whatever activity I had been engaged in, such as doing an important project on the Etch-a-Sketch, and a little while later my wife will say: "I hate to rush you, but could you do Robert's bathroom? It's really *filthy*." She is in there looking at the very walls I *just Windexed*, and she is seeing *dirt! Everywhere!* And if I tell her I already *cleaned* the bathroom, she gives me this look that she has perfected, the same look she used on me the time I selected Robert's outfit for school and part of it turned out to be pajamas.

The opposite side of the dirt coin, of course, is sports. This is an area   5
where men tend to feel very sensitive and women tend to be extremely callous. I have written about this before and I always get irate letters from women who say they are the heavyweight racquetball champion of some place like Iowa and are sensitive to sports to the point where they could crush my skull like a ripe grape, but I feel these women are the exception.

A more representative woman is my friend Maddy, who once invited   6
some people, including my wife and me, over to her house for an evening of stimulating conversation and jovial companionship, which sounds fine except that this particular evening occurred *during a World Series game*. If you can imagine such a social gaffe.

We sat around the living room and Maddy tried to stimulate a conver-   7
sation, but we males could not focus our attention on the various suggested topics because we could actually *feel* the World Series television and radio broadcast rays zinging through the air, penetrating right into our bodies, causing our dental fillings to vibrate, and all the while the women were behaving *as though nothing were wrong*. It was exactly like that story by Edgar Allan Poe where the murderer can hear the victim's heart beating louder and louder even though he (the murder victim) is dead, until finally he (the murderer)

can't stand it anymore, and he just *has* to watch the World Series on television.[2] That was how we felt.

Maddy's husband made the first move, coming up with an absolutely bril-   8
liant means of escape: *He used their baby.* He picked up Justine, their seven-
month-old daughter, who was fussing a little, and announced: "What this
child needs is to have her bottle and watch the World Series." And just like
that he was off to the family room, moving very quickly for a big man holding
a baby. A second male escaped by pretending to clear the dessert plates. Soon
all four of us were in there, watching the Annual Fall Classic, while the
women prattled away about human relationships or something. It turned out
to be an extremely pivotal game.

---

*For a reading quiz, sources on Dave Barry, and annotated links to further readings
on gender differences, visit **bedfordstmartins.com/thebedfordreader**.*

Journal Writing

Are you ever baffled by the behavior of members of the opposite sex — or members of
your own sex, if you often find yourself behaving differently from most of them? List
traits of men or women that you find foreign or bewildering, such as that they do or
do not want to talk about their feelings or that they can spend countless hours watching sports on television or shopping. (To take your journal writing further, see "From
Journal to Essay" on the next page.)

Questions on Meaning

1. What is the PURPOSE of Barry's essay? How do you know?
2. How OBJECTIVE is Barry's portrayal of men and women? Does he seem to understand one sex better than the other? Does he seek to justify and excuse male sloppiness and antisocial behavior?
3. What can you INFER about Barry's attitude toward the differences between the
   sexes? Does he see a way out?

Questions on Writing Strategy

1. Barry's comparison is organized point by point — differences in sensitivity to dirt,
   then differences in sensitivity to sports. What is the EFFECT of this organization?

[2] Except for the World Series ending, Barry refers to Poe's story "The Tell-Tale Heart"
(1843). —EDS.

Or, from another angle, what would have been the effect of a subject-by-subject organization—just men, then just women (or vice versa)?

2. How does Barry set the TONE of this piece from the very first paragraph?
3. The first sentence looks like a THESIS STATEMENT but turns out not to be complete. Where does Barry finish his statement of the essay's thesis? Does it hurt or help the essay that the thesis is divided? Why?
4. How does Barry's ALLUSION to Poe's "The Tell-Tale Heart" (par. 7) enhance Barry's own story?
5. In paragraph 5, how does Barry indicate that he's changing points of comparison?
6. **OTHER METHODS.** How persuasive is the historical EXAMPLE cited in paragraph 2 as EVIDENCE for Barry's claims about men's and women's differing abilities to perceive dirt? Must examples always be persuasive?

Questions on Language

1. Define these words: hormonal (par. 2); implements (3); callous, irate (5); jovial, gaffe (6); prattled, pivotal (8).
2. Paragraph 4 begins with a textbook example of a run-on sentence. Does Barry need a better copyeditor, or is he going for an effect here? If so, what is it?
3. What effect does Barry achieve with frequent italics (for example, *"just Windexed,"* par. 4) and capital letters ("Standard Male Cleaning Implements," 3)?
4. Why does Barry use the word *males* instead of *men* in paragraphs 7 and 8?

Suggestions for Writing

1. **FROM JOURNAL TO ESSAY.** From the list you compiled in your journal, choose the trait of men or women that seems to have the most potential for humor. Write an essay similar to Barry's, exaggerating the difference to the point where it becomes the defining distinction between men and women.
2. How well do you conform to Barry's GENERALIZATIONS about your gender? In what ways are you stereotypically male or female? Do such generalizations amuse or merely annoy you? Why?
3. Considerable research has examined whether the differences between women and men are caused by heredity or by the environment. Explore some of this research, and write an essay ANALYZING what you discover. Based on your reading, do you think gender differences result primarily from biology or from social conditioning?
4. **CRITICAL WRITING.** Barry is obviously not afraid of offending women: He claims to have already done so (par. 5), and yet he persists. Do you take offense at any of this essay's stereotypes of women and men? If so, explain the nature of the offense as coolly as you can. Whether you take offense or not, can you see any virtue in using such stereotypes for humor? For instance, does the humor help undermine the stereotypes or merely strengthen them? Write an essay in which you address these questions, using quotations from Barry as examples and evidence.
5. **CONNECTIONS.** Write an essay about the humor gained from exaggeration, relying on Barry's essay and Suzanne Britt's "Neat People vs. Sloppy People" (p. 239). Why is exaggeration often funny? What qualities does humorous exaggeration have? Quote and PARAPHRASE from Barry's and Britt's essays for your support.

Dave Barry on Writing

For Dave Barry, coming up with ideas for humorous writing is no problem. "Just about anything's a topic for a humor column," he told an interviewer for *Contemporary Authors* in 1990, "any event that occurs in the news, anything that happens in daily life—driving, shopping, reading, eating. You can look at just about anything and see humor in it somewhere."

Writing challenges, for Barry, occur after he has his idea. "Writing has always been hard for me," he says. "The hard part is getting the jokes to come, and it never happens all at once for me. I very rarely have any idea where a column is going to go when it starts. It's a matter of piling a little piece here and a little piece there, fitting them together, going on to the next part, then going back and gradually shaping the whole piece into something. I know what I want in terms of reaction, and I want it to have a certain feel. I know when it does and when it doesn't. But I'm never sure when it's going to get there. That's what writing is. That's why it's so painful and slow. But that's more technique than anything else. You don't rely on inspiration—I don't, anyway, and I don't think most writers do. The creative process is just not an inspirational one for most people. There's a little bit of that and a whole lot of polishing."

A humor writer must be sensitive to readers, trying to make them smile, but Barry warns against catering to an audience. "I think it's a big mistake to write humor for anybody but yourself, to try to adopt any persona other than your own. If I don't at some point think something is funny, then I'm not going to write it." Not that his own sense of humor will always make a piece fly. "Thinking of it in rough form is one thing," Barry confesses, "and shaping and polishing it so that you like the way it reads is so agonizingly slow that by the time you're done, you don't think anything is funny. You think this is something you might use to console a widow."

More often, though, the shaping and polishing—the constant revision—do work. "Since I know how to do that," Barry says, "since I do it every day of the week and have for years and years, I'm confident that if I keep at it I'll get something."

For Discussion

1. Do you agree with Barry that "[y]ou can look at just about anything and see humor in it somewhere"? What topics might be off-limits for humor?
2. What does successful writing depend on, according to Barry? What role does inspiration play?
3. How might Barry's views on writing be relevant to your own experiences as a writer? What can a humor writer teach a college writer?

DAVID SEDARIS

Named Humorist of the Year 2001 by *Time* magazine, DAVID SEDARIS was born in 1957 and grew up in North Carolina. After graduating from the School of the Art Institute of Chicago in 1987, Sedaris taught writing there part-time and then moved to New York City, where he took various odd jobs. One of these jobs—a stint as a department-store Christmas elf—provided Sedaris with material for "The Santaland Diaries," the essay that launched his career as a humorist after he read it on National Public Radio's *Morning Edition* in 1993. Since then, Sedaris has contributed numerous commentaries to public radio's *Morning Edition* and *This American Life*, and his work appears frequently in *The New Yorker, Esquire*, and other magazines. He has published a collection of short fiction, *Barrel Fever* (1994), and the essay collections *Naked* (1996), *Holidays on Ice* (1997), *Me Talk Pretty One Day* (2000), and *Dress Your Family in Corduroy and Denim* (2004). In 2001 Sedaris received the Thurber Prize for American Humor. He lives in France and in New York City.

Remembering My Childhood on the Continent of Africa

Many of Sedaris's essays locate comedy in his basically normal North Carolina childhood. In this essay from *Me Talk Pretty One Day*, Sedaris highlights that normality by contrasting it with the distinctly unusual childhood of his partner.

When Hugh was in the fifth grade, his class took a field trip to an Ethiopian slaughterhouse. He was living in Addis Ababa at the time, and the slaughterhouse was chosen because, he says, "it was convenient." 1

This was a school system in which the matter of proximity outweighed 2 such petty concerns as what may or may not be appropriate for a busload of eleven-year-olds. "What?" I asked. "Were there no autopsies scheduled at the local morgue? Was the federal prison just a bit too far out of the way?"

Hugh defends his former school, saying, "Well, isn't that the whole point 3 of a field trip? To see something new?"

"Technically yes, but . . ." 4

"All right then," he says. "So we saw some new things." 5

One of his field trips was literally a trip to a field where the class watched 6 a wrinkled man fill his mouth with rotten goat meat and feed it to a pack of waiting hyenas. On another occasion they were taken to examine the bloodied bedroom curtains hanging in the palace of the former dictator. There were tamer trips, to textile factories and sugar refineries, but my favorite is always the slaughterhouse. It wasn't a big company, just a small rural enterprise run by a couple of brothers operating out of a low-ceilinged concrete building. Following a brief lecture on the importance of proper sanitation, a small white piglet was herded into the room, its dainty hooves clicking against the concrete floor. The class gathered in a circle to get a better look at the animal, who seemed delighted with the attention he was getting. He turned from face to face and was looking up at Hugh when one of the brothers drew a pistol from his back pocket, held it against the animal's temple, and shot the piglet, execution-style. Blood spattered, frightened children wept, and the man with the gun offered the teacher and bus driver some meat from a freshly slaughtered goat.

When I'm told such stories, it's all I can do to hold back my feelings of   7
jealousy. An Ethiopian slaughterhouse. Some people have all the luck. When I was in elementary school, the best we ever got was a trip to Old Salem or Colonial Williamsburg, one of those preserved brick villages where time supposedly stands still and someone earns his living as a town crier. There was always a blacksmith, a group of wandering patriots, and a collection of bonneted women hawking corn bread or gingersnaps made "the ol'-fashioned way." Every now and then you might come across a doer of bad deeds serving time in the stocks, but that was generally as exciting as it got.

Certain events are parallel, but compared with Hugh's, my childhood was   8
unspeakably dull. When I was seven years old, my family moved to North Carolina. When he was seven years old, Hugh's family moved to the Congo. We had a collie and a house cat. They had a monkey and two horses named Charlie Brown and Satan. I threw stones at stop signs. Hugh threw stones at crocodiles. The verbs are the same, but he definitely wins the prize when it comes to nouns and objects. An eventful day for my mother might have involved a trip to the dry cleaner or a conversation with the potato-chip deliveryman. Asked one ordinary Congo afternoon what she'd done with her day, Hugh's mother answered that she and a fellow member of the Ladies' Club had visited a leper colony on the outskirts of Kinshasa. No reason was given for the expedition, though chances are she was staking it out for a future field trip.

Due to his upbringing, Hugh sits through inane movies never realizing   9
that they're often based on inane television shows. There were no poker-faced sitcom martians in his part of Africa, no oil-rich hillbillies or aproned brides trying to wean themselves from the practice of witchcraft. From time to time a movie would arrive packed in a dented canister, the film scratched and faded from its slow trip around the world. The theater consisted of a few dozen folding chairs arranged before a bedsheet or the blank wall of a vacant hangar out near the airstrip. Occasionally a man would sell warm soft drinks out of a cardboard box, but that was it in terms of concessions.

When I was young, I went to the theater at the nearby shopping center   10
and watched a movie about a talking Volkswagen. I believe the little car had
a taste for mischief but I can't be certain, as both the movie and the afternoon
proved unremarkable and have faded from my memory. Hugh saw the same
movie a few years after it was released. His family had left the Congo by this
time and were living in Ethiopia. Like me, Hugh saw the movie by himself on
a weekend afternoon. Unlike me, he left the theater two hours later, to find a
dead man hanging from a telephone pole at the far end of the unpaved parking lot. None of the people who'd seen the movie seemed to care about the
dead man. They stared at him for a moment or two and then headed home,
saying they'd never seen anything as crazy as that talking Volkswagen. His
father was late picking him up, so Hugh just stood there for an hour, watching
the dead man dangle and turn in the breeze. The death was not reported in
the newspaper, and when Hugh related the story to his friends, they said, "You
saw the movie about the talking car?"

I could have done without the flies and the primitive theaters, but I   11
wouldn't have minded growing up with a houseful of servants. In North Carolina it wasn't unusual to have a once-a-week maid, but Hugh's family had
houseboys, a word that never fails to charge my imagination. They had cooks
and drivers, and guards who occupied a gatehouse, armed with machetes. Seeing as I had regularly petitioned my parents for an electric fence, the business
with the guards strikes me as the last word in quiet sophistication. Having protection suggests that you are important. Having that protection paid for by the
government is even better, as it suggests your safety is of interest to someone
other than yourself.

Hugh's father was a career officer with the US State Department, and   12
every morning a black sedan carried him off to the embassy. I'm told it's not as
glamorous as it sounds, but in terms of fun for the entire family, I'm fairly confident that it beats the sack race at the annual IBM picnic. By the age of three,
Hugh was already carrying a diplomatic passport. The rules that applied to
others did not apply to him. No tickets, no arrests, no luggage search: He was
officially licensed to act like a brat. Being an American, it was expected of
him, and who was he to deny the world an occasional tantrum?

They weren't rich, but what Hugh's family lacked financially they more   13
than made up for with the sort of exoticism that works wonders at cocktail
parties, leading always to the remark "That sounds fascinating." It's a compliment one rarely receives when describing an adolescence spent drinking Icees at the North Hills Mall. No fifteen-foot python ever wandered
onto my school's basketball court. I begged, I prayed nightly, but it just never
happened. Neither did I get to witness a military coup in which forces sympathetic to the colonel arrived late at night to assassinate my next-door

neighbor. Hugh had been at the Addis Ababa teen club when the electricity was cut off and soldiers arrived to evacuate the building. He and his friends had to hide in the back of a jeep and cover themselves with blankets during the ride home. It's something that sticks in his mind for one reason or another.

Among my personal highlights is the memory of having my picture taken   14
with Uncle Paul, the legally blind host of a Raleigh children's television show. Among Hugh's is the memory of having his picture taken with Buzz Aldrin on the last leg of the astronaut's world tour. The man who had walked on the moon placed his hand on Hugh's shoulder and offered to sign his autograph book. The man who led Wake County schoolchildren in afternoon song turned at the sound of my voice and asked, "So what's your name, princess?"

When I was fourteen years old, I was sent to spend ten days with my   15
maternal grandmother in western New York State. She was a small and private woman named Billie, and though she never came right out and asked, I had the distinct impression she had no idea who I was. It was the way she looked at me, squinting through her glasses while chewing on her lower lip. That, coupled with the fact that she never once called me by name. "Oh," she'd say, "are you still here?" She was just beginning her long struggle with Alzheimer's disease, and each time I entered the room, I felt the need to reintroduce myself and set her at ease. "Hi, it's me. Sharon's boy, David. I was just in the kitchen admiring your collection of ceramic toads." Aside from a few trips to summer camp, this was the longest I'd ever been away from home, and I like to think I was toughened by the experience.

About the same time I was frightening my grandmother, Hugh and his   16
family were packing their belongings for a move to Somalia. There were no English-speaking schools in Mogadishu, so, after a few months spent lying around the family compound with his pet monkey, Hugh was sent back to Ethiopia to live with a beer enthusiast his father had met at a cocktail party. Mr. Hoyt installed security systems in foreign embassies. He and his family gave Hugh a room. They invited him to join them at the table, but that was as far as they extended themselves. No one ever asked him when his birthday was, so when the day came, he kept it to himself. There was no telephone service between Ethiopia and Somalia, and letters to his parents were sent to Washington and then forwarded on to Mogadishu, meaning that his news was more than a month old by the time they got it. I suppose it wasn't much different than living as a foreign-exchange student. Young people do it all the time, but to me it sounds awful. The Hoyts had two sons about Hugh's age who were always saying things like "Hey that's *our* sofa you're sitting on" and "Hands off that ornamental stein. It doesn't belong to you."

He'd been living with these people for a year when he overheard Mr. Hoyt   17
tell a friend that he and his family would soon be moving to Munich, Germany, the beer capital of the world.

"And that worried me," Hugh said, "because it meant I'd have to find   18
some other place to live."

Where I come from, finding shelter is a problem the average teenager   19
might confidently leave to his parents. It was just something that came with
having a mom and a dad. Worried that he might be sent to live with his grandparents in Kentucky, Hugh turned to the school's guidance counselor, who
knew of a family whose son had recently left for college. And so he spent
another year living with strangers and not mentioning his birthday. While I
wouldn't have wanted to do it myself, I can't help but envy the sense of fortitude he gained from the experience. After graduating from college, he moved
to France knowing only the phrase "Do you speak French?"—a question guaranteed to get you nowhere unless you also speak the language.

While living in Africa, Hugh and his family took frequent vacations,   20
often in the company of their monkey. The Nairobi Hilton, some suite of
high-ceilinged rooms in Cairo or Khartoum: These are the places his people
recall when gathered at a common table. "Was that the summer we spent in
Beirut or, no, I'm thinking of the time we sailed from Cyprus and took the *Ori-
ent Express* to Istanbul."

Theirs was the life I dreamt about during my vacations in eastern North   21
Carolina. Hugh's family was hobnobbing with chiefs and sultans while I ate
hush puppies at the Sanitary Fish Market in Morehead City, a beach towel
wrapped like a hijab[1] around my head. Someone unknown to me was very
likely standing in a muddy ditch and dreaming of an evening spent sitting
in a clean family restaurant, drinking iced tea and working his way through
an extra-large seaman's platter, but that did not concern me, as it meant I
should have been happy with what I had. Rather than surrender to my bitterness, I have learned to take satisfaction in the life that Hugh has led. His stories have, over time, become my own. I say this with no trace of a kumbaya.[2]
There is no spiritual symbiosis; I'm just a petty thief who lifts his memories the
same way I'll take a handful of change left on his dresser. When my own experiences fall short of the mark, I just go out and spend some of his. It is with
pleasure that I sometimes recall the dead man's purpled face or the report of
the handgun ringing in my ears as I studied the blood pooling beneath the
dead white piglet. On the way back from the slaughterhouse, we stopped for

[1] A headscarf worn by Muslim women.—EDS.
[2] From the gospel-folk song with the line "Kumbaya, my Lord, kumbaya," meaning "Come
by here." Probably because of its popularity in folk music, the word now also has negative connotations of passivity or touchy-feely spiritualism.—EDS.

Cokes in the village of Mojo, where the gas-station owner had arranged a few tables and chairs beneath a dying canopy of vines. It was late afternoon by the time we returned to school, where a second bus carried me to the foot of Coffeeboard Road. Once there, I walked through a grove of eucalyptus trees and alongside a bald pasture of starving cattle, past the guard napping in his gatehouse, and into the waiting arms of my monkey.

*For a reading quiz, sources on David Sedaris, and annotated links to further readings on Americans' experiences among other cultures, visit **bedfordstmartins.com/ thebedfordreader**.*

Journal Writing

When have you envied the life of a friend or relative? Write about what was attractive to you in that person's life. Was it family relationships? educational or employment opportunities? travel experiences? something else? (To take your journal writing further, see "From Journal to Essay" on the next page.)

Questions on Meaning

1. What is the subject of Sedaris's comparison and contrast in this essay?
2. What do you think is the THESIS of this essay? Take into account both Sedaris's obvious envy of Hugh's childhood and Sedaris's awareness that Hugh's life was often lonely and insecure. Is the thesis stated or only implied?
3. There is a certain amount of IRONY in Sedaris's envy of Hugh's childhood. What is this irony? How does Sedaris make this irony explicit in paragraph 21?

Questions on Writing Strategy

1. Does Sedaris develop his comparison and contrast subject by subject or point by point? Briefly outline the essay to explain your answer.
2. Point to some of the TRANSITIONS Sedaris uses in moving between his and Hugh's lives.
3. Sedaris refers to Hugh's monkey in paragraphs 8, 20, and 21. In what sense does he use the monkey as a SYMBOL?
4. The first five paragraphs of the essay include a conversation between Sedaris and Hugh about Hugh's childhood. Why do you think the author opened the essay this way?
5. **OTHER METHODS.** How does Sedaris use NARRATION to develop his comparison and contrast?

Questions on Language

1. How does Sedaris use PARALLEL STRUCTURE in paragraph 8 to highlight the contrast between himself and Hugh? How does he then point up this parallelism?
2. Sedaris offers the image of himself as a "petty thief" in paragraph 21. What is the effect of this IMAGE?
3. Sedaris's language in this essay is notably SPECIFIC and CONCRETE. Point to examples of such language just in paragraph 6.
4. Consult a dictionary if necessary to learn the meanings of the following words: proximity, petty, autopsies, morgue (par. 2); hyenas (6); hawking, stocks (7); leper (8); hangar (9); machetes (11); diplomatic (12); exoticism, coup, evacuate (13); ornamental, stein (16); fortitude (19); hobnobbing, symbiosis, report, canopy, eucalyptus (21).

Suggestions for Writing

1. **FROM JOURNAL TO ESSAY.** Starting from your journal entry, write an essay in which you compare and contrast your own experiences with those of someone whose life you've envied. Have your feelings changed over time? Why, or why not?
2. Hugh's experiences living with strangers gave him a "sense of fortitude" (par. 19), according to Sedaris. When have you ever gone through a difficult experience that left you somehow stronger? Write an essay about such an experience that shows how you were different before and after.
3. In your library or on the Internet, locate and read reviews of Sedaris's book *Me Talk Pretty One Day*, the source of "Remembering My Childhood," or of another essay collection by Sedaris. Write an essay in which you SYNTHESIZE the reviewers' responses to Sedaris's work.
4. **CRITICAL WRITING.** How seriously does Sedaris want the readers of his essay to take him? Write an essay in which you analyze his TONE, citing specific passages from the text to support your conclusions.
5. **CONNECTIONS.** Sherman Alexie, in "Indian Education" (p. 105), writes about a childhood very different from either Sedaris's or Hugh's. In an essay, consider how Sedaris and Alexie might view each other's childhoods.

David Sedaris on Writing

Most of us are contented users of word processors, but not David Sedaris. In "Nutcracker.com," an essay in *Me Talk Pretty One Day*, Sedaris explains why he refuses to give up his typewriter.

I hate computers for any number of reasons, but I despise them most for what they've done to my friend the typewriter. In a democratic country you'd think there would be room for both of them, but computers won't rest until

I'm making my ribbons from torn shirts and brewing Wite-Out in my bathtub. Their goal is to place the IBM Selectric II beside the feather quill and chisel in the museum of antiquated writing implements. They're power hungry, and someone needs to stop them.

When told I'm like the guy still pining for his eight-track tapes, I say, "You have eight-tracks? Where?" In reality I know nothing about them, yet I feel it's important to express some solidarity with others who have had the rug pulled out from beneath them. I don't care if it can count words or rearrange paragraphs at the push of a button, I don't want a computer. Unlike the faint scurry raised by fingers against a plastic computer keyboard, the smack and clatter of a typewriter suggests that you're actually building something. At the end of a miserable day, instead of grieving my virtual nothing, I can always look at my loaded wastepaper basket and tell myself that if I failed, at least I took a few trees down with me.

For Discussion

1. Why does Sedaris prefer writing with a typewriter instead of with a computer?
2. Defend the computerized word processor from Sedaris's attack. What are some advantages of the newer technology?

BRUCE CATTON

BRUCE CATTON (1899–1978) became America's best-known historian of the Civil War. As a boy in Benzonia, Michigan, Catton acted out historical battles on local playing fields. In his memoir *Waiting for the Morning Train* (1972), he recalls how he would listen by the hour to the memories of Union army veterans. His studies at Oberlin College interrupted by service in World War I, Catton never finished his bachelor's degree. Instead, he worked as a reporter, columnist, and editorial writer for the *Cleveland Plain Dealer* and other newspapers, then became a speechwriter and information director for government agencies. Of Catton's eighteen books, seventeen were written after his fiftieth year. *A Stillness at Appomattox* (1953) won him both a Pulitzer Prize for history and a National Book Award; other notable works include *This Hallowed Ground* (1956) and *Gettysburg: The Final Fury* (1974). From 1954 until his death, Catton edited *American Heritage*, a magazine of history. President Gerald Ford awarded him a Medal of Freedom for his life's accomplishment.

Grant and Lee: A Study in Contrasts

"Grant and Lee: A Study in Contrasts" first appeared in *The American Story*, a book of essays written by eminent historians for interested general readers. Contrasting the two great Civil War generals allows Catton to portray not only two very different men but also the conflicting traditions they represented. Catton's essay builds toward the conclusion that, in one outstanding way, the two leaders were more than a little alike.

When Ulysses S. Grant and Robert E. Lee met in the parlor of a modest 1 house at Appomattox Court House, Virginia, on April 9, 1865, to work out the terms for the surrender of Lee's Army of Northern Virginia, a great chapter in American life came to a close, and a great new chapter began.

These men were bringing the Civil War to its virtual finish. To be sure, 2 other armies had yet to surrender, and for a few days the fugitive confederate government would struggle desperately and vainly, trying to find some way to go on living now that its chief support was gone. But in effect it was all over when Grant and Lee signed the papers. And the little room where they wrote out the terms was the scene of one of the poignant, dramatic contrasts in American history.

They were two strong men, these oddly different generals, and they repre- 3 sented the strengths of two conflicting currents that, through them, had come into final collision.

Back of Robert E. Lee was the notion that the old aristocratic concept   4
might somehow survive and be dominant in American life.

Lee was tidewater Virginia, and in his background were family, culture,   5
and tradition . . . the age of chivalry transplanted to a New World which was
making its own legends and its own myths. He embodied a way of life that had
come down through the age of knighthood and the English country squire.
America was a land that was beginning all over again, dedicated to nothing
much more complicated than the rather hazy belief that all men had equal
rights, and should have an equal chance in the world. In such a land Lee stood
for the feeling that it was somehow of advantage to human society to have a
pronounced inequality in the social structure. There should be a leisure class,
backed by ownership of land; in turn, society itself should be keyed to the land
as the chief source of wealth and influence. It would bring forth (according to
this ideal) a class of men with a strong sense of obligation to the community;
men who lived not to gain advantage for themselves, but to meet the solemn
obligations which had been laid on them by the very fact that they were privileged. From them the country would get its leadership; to them it could look
for the higher values—of thought, of conduct, of personal deportment—to
give it strength and virtue.

Lee embodied the noblest elements of this aristocratic ideal. Through   6
him, the landed nobility justified itself. For four years, the Southern states had
fought a desperate war to uphold the ideals for which Lee stood. In the end, it
almost seemed as if the Confederacy fought for Lee; as if he himself was the
Confederacy . . . the best thing that the way of life for which the Confederacy
stood could ever have to offer. He had passed into legend before Appomattox.
Thousands of tired, underfed, poorly clothed Confederate soldiers, long-since
past the simple enthusiasm of the early days of the struggle, somehow considered Lee the symbol of everything for which they had been willing to die. But
they could not quite put this feeling into words. If the Lost Cause, sanctified
by so much heroism and so many deaths, had a living justification, its justification was General Lee.

Grant, the son of a tanner on the Western frontier, was everything Lee   7
was not. He had come up the hard way, and embodied nothing in particular
except the eternal toughness and sinewy fiber of the men who grew up beyond
the mountains. He was one of a body of men who owed reverence and obeisance to no one, who were self-reliant to a fault, who cared hardly anything
for the past but who had a sharp eye for the future.

These frontier men were the precise opposites of the tidewater aristocrats.   8
Back of them, in the great surge that had taken people over the Alleghenies
and into the opening Western country, there was a deep, implicit dissatisfaction with a past that had settled into grooves. They stood for democracy, not

from any reasoned conclusion about the proper ordering of human society, but simply because they had grown up in the middle of democracy and knew how it worked. Their society might have privileges, but they would be privileges each man had won for himself. Forms and patterns meant nothing. No man was born to anything, except perhaps to a chance to show how far he could rise. Life was competition.

Yet along with this feeling had come a deep sense of belonging to a national community. The Westerner who developed a farm, opened a shop, or set up in business as a trader could hope to prosper only as his own community prospered — and his community ran from the Atlantic to the Pacific and from Canada down to Mexico. If the land was settled, with towns and highways and accessible markets, he could better himself. He saw his fate in terms of the nation's own destiny. As its horizons expanded, so did his. He had, in other words, an acute dollars-and-cents stake in the continued growth and development of his country.   9

And that, perhaps, is where the contrast between Grant and Lee becomes most striking. The Virginia aristocrat, inevitably, saw himself in relation to his own region. He lived in a static society which could endure almost anything except change. Instinctively, his first loyalty would go to the locality in which that society existed. He would fight to the limit of endurance to defend it, because in defending it he was defending everything that gave his own life its deepest meaning.   10

The Westerner, on the other hand, would fight with an equal tenacity for the broader concept of society. He fought so because everything he lived by was tied to growth, expansion, and a constantly widening horizon. What he lived by would survive or fall with the nation itself. He could not possibly stand by unmoved in the face of an attempt to destroy the Union. He would combat it with everything he had, because he could only see it as an effort to cut the ground out from under his feet.   11

So Grant and Lee were in complete contrast, representing two diametrically opposed elements in American life. Grant was the modern man emerging; beyond him, ready to come on the stage, was the great age of steel and machinery, of crowded cities and a restless, burgeoning vitality. Lee might have ridden down from the old age of chivalry, lance in hand, silken banner fluttering over his head. Each man was the perfect champion of his cause, drawing both his strengths and his weaknesses from the people he led.   12

Yet it was not all contrast, after all. Different as they were — in background, in personality, in underlying aspiration — these two great soldiers had much in common. Under everything else, they were marvelous fighters. Furthermore, their fighting qualities were really very much alike.   13

Each man had, to begin with, the great virtue of utter tenacity and fidel-   14
ity. Grant fought his way down the Mississippi Valley in spite of acute personal discouragement and profound military handicaps. Lee hung on in the
trenches at Petersburg after hope itself had died. In each man there was an
indomitable quality . . . the born fighter's refusal to give up as long as he can
still remain on his feet and lift his two fists.

Daring and resourcefulness they had, too; the ability to think faster and   15
move faster than the enemy. These were the qualities which gave Lee the daz-
zling campaigns of Second Manassas and Chancellorsville and won Vicksburg
for Grant.

Lastly, and perhaps greatest of all, there was the ability, at the end, to turn   16
quickly from war to peace once the fighting was over. Out of the way these two
men behaved at Appomattox came the possibility of a peace of reconciliation.
It was a possibility not wholly realized, in the years to come, but which did, in
the end, help the two sections to become one nation again . . . after a war
whose bitterness might have seemed to make such a reunion wholly impossible. No part of either man's life became him more than the part he played
in their brief meeting in the McLean house at Appomattox. Their behavior
there put all succeeding generations of Americans in their debt. Two great
Americans, Grant and Lee — very different, yet under everything very much
alike. Their encounter at Appomattox was one of the great moments of
American history.

For a reading quiz, sources on Bruce Catton, and annotated links to further readings on
the American Civil War, Ulysses S. Grant, and Robert E. Lee, visit **bedfordstmartins
.com/thebedfordreader**.

Journal Writing

How do you respond to the opposing political beliefs represented by Grant and Lee?
During the American Civil War, nearly every citizen had an opinion and chose sides.
Do you think Americans today commit themselves as strongly to political and social
causes? In your journal, explain why, or why not. (To take your journal writing further,
see "From Journal to Essay" on p. 263.)

Questions on Meaning

1. What is Bruce Catton's PURPOSE in writing: to describe the meeting of two generals at a famous moment in history; to explain how the two men stood for opposing social forces in America; or to show how the two differed in personality?
2. SUMMARIZE the background and the way of life that produced Robert E. Lee; then do the same for Ulysses S. Grant. According to Catton, what ideals did each man represent?
3. In the historian's view, what essential traits did the two men have in common? Which trait does Catton think most important of all? For what reason?
4. How does this essay help you understand why Grant and Lee were such determined fighters?

Questions on Writing Strategy

1. From the content of this essay, and from knowing where it first appeared, what can you infer about Catton's original AUDIENCE? At what places in "Grant and Lee: A Study in Contrasts" does the writer expect of his readers a familiarity with US history?
2. What effect does the writer achieve by setting both his INTRODUCTION and his CONCLUSION in Appomattox?
3. For what reasons does Catton contrast the two generals *before* he compares them? Suppose he had reversed his outline, and had dealt first with Grant's and Lee's mutual resemblances. Why would his essay have been less effective?
4. Closely read the first sentence of every paragraph and underline each word or phrase in it that serves as a TRANSITION. Then review your underlinings. How much COHERENCE has Catton given his essay?
5. What is the TONE of this essay—that is, what is the writer's attitude toward his two subjects? Is Catton poking fun at Lee by imagining the Confederate general as a knight of the Middle Ages, "lance in hand, silken banner fluttering over his head" (par. 12)?
6. **OTHER METHODS.** In identifying "two conflicting currents," Catton uses CLASSIFICATION to sort Civil War–era Americans into two groups represented by Lee and Grant. Catton then uses ANALYSIS to tease out the characteristics of each current, each type. How do classification and analysis serve Catton's comparison and contrast?

Questions on Language

1. In his opening paragraph, Catton uses a metaphor: American life is a book containing chapters. Find other FIGURES OF SPEECH in his essay (consulting Useful Terms if you need help). What do the figures of speech contribute?
2. Look up *poignant* in the dictionary. Why is it such a fitting word in paragraph 2? Why wouldn't *touching, sad,* or *teary* have been as good?
3. What information do you glean from the sentence "Lee was tidewater Virginia" (par. 5)?
4. Define *aristocratic* as Catton uses it in paragraphs 4 and 6.
5. Define *obeisance* (par. 7); *indomitable* (14).

Suggestions for Writing

1. **FROM JOURNAL TO ESSAY.** Using your journal entry as a starting point, write an essay that offers an explanation for public participation in or commitment to political and social causes today. What fires people up or turns them off? To help focus your essay, zero in on a specific issue, such as education, government spending, health insurance, or gun control.

2. In a brief essay full of specific examples, discuss: Do the "two diametrically opposed elements in American life" (as Catton calls them) still exist in the country today? Are there still any "landed nobility"?

3. In your thinking and your attitudes, whom do you more closely resemble—Grant or Lee? Compare and contrast your outlook with that of one famous American or the other. (A serious tone for this topic isn't required.)

4. **CRITICAL WRITING.** Although slavery, along with other issues, helped precipitate the Civil War, Catton in this particular essay does not deal with it. Perhaps he assumes that his readers will supply the missing context themselves. Is this a fair ASSUMPTION? If Catton had recalled the facts of slavery, would he have undermined any of his assertions about Lee? (Though the general of the pro-slavery Confederacy, Lee was personally opposed to slavery.) In a brief essay, judge whether or not the omission of slavery weakens the essay, and explain why.

5. **CONNECTIONS.** Catton defines two American identities at the time of the Civil War: aristocrats and Westerners. In "The Crisis of National Identity" (p. 400), Samuel P. Huntington discusses contemporary American identities that are very different from Catton's. Based on both essays and on your own observations, write an essay in which you explore how citizens of the United States identify themselves by their relationship with their country.

Bruce Catton on Writing

Most of Bruce Catton's comments on writing, those that have been preserved, refer to the work of others. As editor of *American Heritage*, he was known for his blunt, succinct comments on unsuccessful manuscripts: "This article can't be repaired and wouldn't be much good if it were." Or: "The highwater mark of this piece comes at the bottom of page one, where the naked Indian nymph offers the hero strawberries. Unfortunately, this level is not maintained."

In a memoir published in *Bruce Catton's America* (1979), Catton's associate Oliver Jensen marvels that, besides editing *American Heritage* for twenty-four years (and contributing to nearly every issue), Catton managed to produce so many substantial books. "Concentration was no doubt the secret, that and getting an early start. For many years Catton was always the first person in the office, so early that most of the staff never knew when he did arrive. On his desk the little piles of yellow sheets grew slowly, with much larger piles in the wastebasket. A neat and orderly man, he preferred to type a new page than correct very much in pencil."

His whole purpose as a writer, Catton once said, was "to reexamine [our] debt to the past."

For Discussion

1. To which of Catton's traits does Oliver Jensen attribute the historian's impressive output?
2. Which characteristics of Catton the editor would you expect to have served him well as a writer?

FATEMA MERNISSI

A teacher, writer, and activist, FATEMA MERNISSI was born in 1940 in Fez, Morocco, and was educated at the University of Rabat in Morocco, the Sorbonne in Paris, and Brandeis University in Massachusetts, from which she earned a PhD in sociology. Mernissi soon established herself as both a scholar and a lively writer on subjects ranging from feminism to religion. Her books, originally written in either French or English, include *Beyond the Veil: Male-Female Dynamics in Modern Muslim Society* (1975, revised in 1987), *Islam and Democracy: Fear of the Modern World* (1992), *Dreams of Trespass: Tales of a Harem Girlhood* (1994), and *Women's Rebellion and Islamic Memory* (1996). Mernissi is a professor and research scholar at the University of Mohammed V in Morocco. In 2004 she received the Erasmus Prize for having made an "exceptionally important contribution to European culture, society, or social science."

Size 6: The Western Women's Harem

Mernissi was raised in a harem, an enclave of women within a traditional Muslim household. Traveling outside the Middle East, she encounters common Western misconceptions of a harem as either a "peaceful pleasure-garden" or an "orgiastic feast" in which "men reign supreme over obedient women"—when in fact Muslim men and women both acknowledge the inequality of the harem and women resist men in any way they can. In *Scheherazade Goes West: Different Cultures, Different Harems* (2001), Mernissi explores the "mystery of the Western harem," trying to understand why outsiders imagine harem women as totally compliant and unthreatening to men. In this last chapter from the book, Mernissi finds her answer.

It was during my unsuccessful attempt to buy a cotton skirt in an American department store that I was told my hips were too large to fit into a size 6. That distressing experience made me realize how the image of beauty in the West can hurt and humiliate a woman as much as the veil does when enforced by the state police in extremist nations such as Iran, Afghanistan, or Saudi Arabia. Yes, that day I stumbled onto one of the keys to the enigma of passive beauty in Western harem fantasies. The elegant saleslady in the American store looked at me without moving from her desk and said that she had no skirt my size. "In this whole big store, there is no skirt for me?" I said. "You are joking." I felt very suspicious and thought that she just might be too tired to help me. I could understand that. But then the saleswoman added a condescending judgment, which sounded to me like an imam's fatwa.[1] It left no room for discussion:

---

[1] An *imam* is a Muslim leader. A *fatwa* is a Muslim legal opinion or ruling. —EDS.

"You are too big!" she said.   2

"I am too big compared to what?" I asked, looking at her intently, because   3
I realized that I was facing a critical cultural gap here.

"Compared to a size 6," came the saleslady's reply.   4

Her voice had a clear-cut edge to it that is typical of those who enforce   5
religious laws. "Size 4 and 6 are the norm," she went on, encouraged by my
bewildered look. "Deviant sizes such as the one you need can be bought in
special stores."

That was the first time that I had ever heard such nonsense about my size.   6
In the Moroccan streets, men's flattering comments regarding my particularly
generous hips have for decades led me to believe that the entire planet shared
their convictions. It is true that with advancing age, I have been hearing fewer
and fewer flattering comments when walking in the medina, and sometimes
the silence around me in the bazaars is deafening. But since my face has never
met with the local beauty standards, and I have often had to defend myself
against remarks such as *zirafa* (giraffe), because of my long neck, I learned long
ago not to rely too much on the outside world for my sense of self-worth. In
fact, paradoxically, as I discovered when I went to Rabat as a student, it was
the self-reliance that I had developed to protect myself against "beauty black-
mail" that made me attractive to others. My male fellow students could not
believe that I did not give a damn about what they thought about my body.
"You know, my dear," I would say in response to one of them, "all I need to survive is bread, olives, and sardines. That you think my neck is too long is your
problem, not mine."

In any case, when it comes to beauty and compliments, nothing is too   7
serious or definite in the medina, where everything can be negotiated. But
things seemed to be different in that American department store. In fact, I
have to confess that I lost my usual self-confidence in that New York environment. Not that I am always sure of myself, but I don't walk around the
Moroccan streets or down the university corridors wondering what people are
thinking about me. Of course, when I hear a compliment, my ego expands like
a cheese soufflé, but on the whole, I don't expect to hear much from others.
Some mornings, I feel ugly because I am sick or tired; others, I feel wonderful
because it is sunny out or I have written a good paragraph. But suddenly, in
that peaceful American store that I had entered so triumphantly, as a sovereign consumer ready to spend money, I felt savagely attacked. My hips, until
then the sign of a relaxed and uninhibited maturity, were suddenly being condemned as a deformity. . . .

"And who says that everyone must be a size 6?" I joked to the saleslady   8
that day, deliberately neglecting to mention size 4, which is the size of my
skinny twelve-year-old niece.

At that point, the saleslady suddenly gave me an anxious look. "The norm   9
is everywhere, my dear," she said. "It's all over, in the magazines, on television,
in the ads. You can't escape it. There is Calvin Klein, Ralph Lauren, Gianni
Versace, Giorgio Armani, Mario Valentino, Salvatore Ferragamo, Christian
Dior, Yves Saint-Laurent, Christian Lacroix, and Jean-Paul Gaultier. Big
department stores go by the norm." She paused and then concluded, "If they
sold size 14 or 16, which is probably what you need, they would go bankrupt."

She stopped for a minute and then stared at me, intrigued. "Where on   10
earth do you come from? I am sorry I can't help you. Really, I am." And she
looked it too. She seemed, all of a sudden, interested, and brushed off another
woman who was seeking her attention with a cutting, "Get someone else to
help you, I'm busy." Only then did I notice that she was probably my age, in
her late fifties. But unlike me, she had the thin body of an adolescent girl. Her
knee-length, navy blue, Chanel dress had a white silk collar reminiscent of
the subdued elegance of aristocratic French Catholic schoolgirls at the turn of
the century. A pearl-studded belt emphasized the slimness of her waist. With
her meticulously styled short hair and sophisticated makeup, she looked half
my age at first glance.

"I come from a country where there is no size for women's clothes," I told   11
her. "I buy my own material and the neighborhood seamstress or craftsman
makes me the silk or leather skirt I want. They just take my measurements
each time I see them. Neither the seamstress nor I know exactly what size my
new skirt is. We discover it together in the making. No one cares about my size
in Morocco as long as I pay taxes on time. Actually, I don't know what my size
is, to tell you the truth."

The saleswoman laughed merrily and said that I should advertise my   12
country as a paradise for stressed working women. "You mean you don't watch
your weight?" she inquired, with a tinge of disbelief in her voice. And then,
after a brief moment of silence, she added in a lower register, as if talking to
herself: "Many women working in highly paid fashion-related jobs could lose
their positions if they didn't keep to a strict diet."

Her words sounded so simple, but the threat they implied was so cruel that   13
I realized for the first time that maybe "size 6" is a more violent restriction
imposed on women than is the Muslim veil. Quickly I said good-bye so as not
to make any more demands on the saleslady's time or involve her in any more
unwelcome, confidential exchanges about age-discriminating salary cuts. A
surveillance camera was probably watching us both.

Yes, I thought as I wandered off, I have finally found the answer to my   14
harem enigma. Unlike the Muslim man, who uses space to establish male
domination by excluding women from the public arena, the Western man
manipulates time and light. He declares that in order to be beautiful, a woman

must look fourteen years old. If she dares to look fifty, or worse, sixty, she is beyond the pale. By putting the spotlight on the female child and framing her as the ideal of beauty, he condemns the mature woman to invisibility. In fact, the modern Western man enforces Immanuel Kant's nineteenth-century theories:[2] To be beautiful, women have to appear childish and brainless. When a woman looks mature and self-assertive, or allows her hips to expand, she is condemned as ugly. Thus, the walls of the European harem separate youthful beauty from ugly maturity.

These Western attitudes, I thought, are even more dangerous and cun-   15
ning than the Muslim ones because the weapon used against women is time. Time is less visible, more fluid than space. The Western man uses images and spotlights to freeze female beauty within an idealized childhood, and forces women to perceive aging—that normal unfolding of the years—as a shameful devaluation. "Here I am, transformed into a dinosaur," I caught myself saying aloud as I went up and down the rows of skirts in the store, hoping to prove the saleslady wrong—to no avail. This Western time-defined veil is even crazier than the space-defined one enforced by the ayatollahs.[3]

The violence embodied in the Western harem is less visible than in the   16
Eastern harem because aging is not attacked directly, but rather masked as an aesthetic choice. Yes, I suddenly felt not only very ugly but also quite useless in that store, where, if you had big hips, you were simply out of the picture. You drifted into the fringes of nothingness. By putting the spotlight on the prepubescent female, the Western man veils the older, more mature woman, wrapping her in shrouds of ugliness. This idea gives me the chills because it tattoos the invisible harem directly onto a woman's skin. Chinese foot-binding worked the same way: Men declared beautiful only those women who had small, childlike feet. Chinese men did not force women to bandage their feet to keep them from developing normally—all they did was to define the beauty ideal. In feudal China, a beautiful woman was the one who voluntarily sacrificed her right to unhindered physical movement by mutilating her own feet, and thereby proving that her main goal in life was to please men. Similarly, in the Western world, I was expected to shrink my hips into a size 6 if I wanted to find a decent skirt tailored for a beautiful woman. We Muslim women have only one month of fasting, Ramadan, but the poor Western woman who diets has to fast twelve months out of the year. "Quelle horreur,"[4] I kept repeating to myself, while looking around at the American women shopping. All those my age looked like youthful teenagers. . . .

[2] Kant (1724–1804) was a German philosopher. —EDS.
[3] Among Shiite Muslims, the authorities who interpret religious law. —EDS.
[4] French, "What a horror." —EDS.

Now, at last, the mystery of my Western harem made sense. Framing   17
youth as beauty and condemning maturity is the weapon used against women
in the West just as limiting access to public space is the weapon used in the
East. The objective remains identical in both cultures: to make women feel
unwelcome, inadequate, and ugly.

The power of the Western man resides in dictating what women should   18
wear and how they should look. He controls the whole fashion industry, from
cosmetics to underwear. The West, I realized, was the only part of the world
where women's fashion is a man's business. In places like Morocco, where you
design your own clothes and discuss them with craftsmen and -women, fashion is your own business. Not so in the West. . . .

But how does the system function? I wondered. Why do women accept it?   19

Of all the possible explanations, I like that of the French sociologist Pierre   20
Bourdieu the best. In his latest book, *La Domination Masculine*, he proposes
something he calls *"la violence symbolique"*: "Symbolic violence is a form of
power which is hammered directly on the body, and as if by magic, without
any apparent physical constraint. But this magic operates only because it acti-
vates the codes pounded in the deepest layers of the body."[5] Reading Bourdieu, I had the impression that I finally understood Western man's psyche
better. The cosmetic and fashion industries are only the tip of the iceberg, he
states, which is why women are so ready to adhere to their dictates. Something else is going on on a far deeper level. Otherwise, why would women
belittle themselves spontaneously? Why, argues Bourdieu, would women
make their lives more difficult, for example, by preferring men who are taller
or older than they are? "The majority of French women wish to have a husband who is older and also, which seems consistent, bigger as far as size is concerned," writes Bourdieu.[6] Caught in the enchanted submission characteristic
of the symbolic violence inscribed in the mysterious layers of the flesh, women
relinquish what he calls "les signes ordinaires de la hiérarchie sexuelle," the
ordinary signs of sexual hierarchy, such as old age and a larger body. By so
doing, explains Bourdieu, women spontaneously accept the subservient position. It is this spontaneity Bourdieu describes as magic enchantment.[7]

Once I understood how this magic submission worked, I became very   21
happy that the conservative ayatollahs do not know about it yet. If they did,
they would readily switch to its sophisticated methods, because they are so
much more effective. To deprive me of food is definitely the best way to paralyze my thinking capabilities. . . .

[5] Pierre Bourdieu, *La Domination Masculine* (Paris: Editions du Seuil, 1998), p. 44.
[6] Ibid., p. 41.
[7] Ibid., p. 42.

"I thank you, Allah, for sparing me the tyranny of the 'size 6 harem,'" I   22
repeatedly said to myself while seated on the Paris-Casablanca flight, on my
way back home at last. "I am so happy that the conservative male elite does
not know about it. Imagine the fundamentalists switching from the veil to
forcing women to fit size 6."

How can you stage a credible political demonstration and shout in the   23
streets that your human rights have been violated when you cannot find the
right skirt?

---

*For a reading quiz, sources on Fatema Mernissi, and annotated links to further readings on harems and on cultural ideals of attractiveness, visit **bedfordstmartins.com/
thebedfordreader**.*

Journal Writing

Within your peer group, what constitutes the norm of physical attractiveness for
women and for men? (Don't focus on the ideal here, but on what is expected for a
person not to be considered *un*attractive.) Are the norms similar for women and for
men? (To take your journal writing further, see "From Journal to Essay" on the facing
page.)

Questions on Meaning

1. What two subjects does Mernissi compare? Where does she state her THESIS initially, and where later does she restate and expand on it? What does Mernissi conclude is the same about the two subjects?
2. What is the saleswoman's initial attitude toward Mernissi? How does her attitude seem to change, and how does this change contribute to Mernissi's point?
3. Why does Mernissi believe Western attitudes toward women are "more dangerous and cunning" than Muslim attitudes (par. 15)?

Questions on Writing Strategy

1. What is the PURPOSE of paragraphs 6–7? What do these paragraphs contribute to Mernissi's larger point?
2. What two further comparisons does Mernissi make in paragraph 16? What TRANSITIONS does she use to signal the shift of subject within these comparisons?

3. **OTHER METHODS.** Mernissi devotes considerable attention to a NARRATIVE of her adventure in the department store. Why does she tell this story in such detail? What does it contribute to the essay?

Questions on Language

1. What are the CONNOTATIONS of the saleswoman's word "deviant" (par. 5)?
2. Why is the metaphor of the veil in paragraph 16 especially appropriate? (See *Figures of speech* in Useful Terms if you need a definition of *metaphor*.)
3. Consult a dictionary if you are unsure of the meaning of any of the following: enigma (par. 1); generous, medina, bazaars, paradoxically (6); soufflé, sovereign (7); subdued (10); cunning, devaluation (15); aesthetic, prepubescent, unhindered, mutilating (16).

Suggestions for Writing

1. **FROM JOURNAL TO ESSAY.** Based on your journal entry, draft an essay in which you compare and contrast standards of attractiveness for women and men within your peer group. Be sure to consider how strictly the standards are applied to each gender.
2. Write an essay about a time when your self-confidence was shaken because of how someone else treated or spoke to you. Like Mernissi, explain why you had been confident of yourself before this encounter and what effect it had on you.
3. Mernissi comes from the country of Morocco. Put her essay in context by researching the history and culture of Morocco. Then write an essay in which you discuss what you have learned about the country. How is Morocco different from the more "extremist nations" Mernissi refers to in her first paragraph?
4. **CRITICAL WRITING.** Respond to Mernissi's essay. Do you agree with her views about "the tyranny of the 'size 6 harem'"? Does Mernissi provide enough EVIDENCE to convince you of her views? Even if you agree with her take on her department-store experience, do you think her conclusions apply across the board, as she implies: For instance, do they apply among the poor and working class as well as among the affluent? Write an essay that ANALYZES and EVALUATES Mernissi's thesis and the support for it.
5. **CONNECTIONS.** In "Our Barbies, Ourselves" (p. 353), Emily Prager also writes about ideals of female attractiveness in the United States. In an essay compare and contrast Prager's views and Mernissi's. Do they mainly agree or disagree? Do you find one essay more convincing than another? Why?

ALICE WALKER

ALICE WALKER is best known for her novel *The Color Purple* (1982), which won both a Pulitzer Prize and an American Book Award, was made into a movie by Steven Spielberg, and was adapted to the stage. Born into a share-cropping family in Eatonton, Georgia, in 1944, Walker is the youngest of eight children. She spent two years at Spelman College in Atlanta before transferring to Sarah Lawrence College. Upon graduation in 1965, Walker became active in the civil rights movement, helping to register voters in Georgia by day and pursuing her writing by night. She has won fellowships from the Radcliffe Institute, the Guggenheim Foundation, and the National Endowment for the Arts. In addition to *The Color Purple*, Walker's novels include *The Third Life of Grange Copeland* (1970), *The Temple of My Familiar* (1989), and *Now Is the Time to Open Up Your Heart* (2004). She has also written several volumes of poetry; two short-story collections; a biography of Langston Hughes; an anthology of the work of Zora Neale Hurston; and the essays in the collections *In Search of Our Mothers' Gardens* (1983) and *Living by the Word* (1988). Walker has taught at numerous colleges and universities, including Jackson State College, Wellesley, Yale, and the University of California at Berkeley.

Everyday Use

In this short story about family, Walker reveals two sisters through the eyes of their mother. Published in 1973, the story appeared in *Harper's* magazine and then in Walker's collection *In Love and Trouble: Stories of Black Women*.

I will wait for her in the yard that Maggie and I made so clean and wavy yesterday afternoon. A yard like this is more comfortable than most people know. It is not just a yard. It is like an extended living room. When the hard clay is swept clean as a floor and the fine sand around the edges lined with tiny, irregular grooves, anyone can come and sit and look up into the elm tree and wait for the breezes that never come inside the house. 1

Maggie will be nervous until after her sister goes: She will stand hopelessly in corners, homely and ashamed of the burn scars down her arms and legs, eyeing her sister with a mixture of envy and awe. She thinks her sister has held life always in the palm of one hand, that "no" is a word the world never learned to say to her. 2

You've no doubt seen those TV shows where the child who has "made it" is confronted, as a surprise, by her own mother and father, tottering in weakly from backstage. (A pleasant surprise, of course: What would they do if parent 3 and child came on the show only to curse out and insult each other?) On TV mother and child embrace and smile into each other's faces. Sometimes the mother and father weep, the child wraps them in her arms and leans across the table to tell how she would not have made it without their help. I have seen these programs.

Sometimes I dream a dream in which Dee and I are suddenly brought   4 together on a TV program of this sort. Out of a dark and soft-seated limousine I am ushered into a bright room filled with many people. There I meet a smiling, gray, sporty man like Johnny Carson who shakes my hand and tells me what a fine girl I have. Then we are on the stage and Dee is embracing me with tears in her eyes. She pins on my dress a large orchid, even though she has told me once that she thinks orchids are tacky flowers.

In real life I am a large, big-boned woman with rough, man-working   5 hands. In the winter I wear flannel nightgowns to bed and overalls during the day. I can kill and clean a hog as mercilessly as a man. My fat keeps me hot in zero weather. I can work outside all day, breaking ice to get water for washing; I can eat pork liver cooked over the open fire minutes after it comes steaming from the hog. One winter I knocked a bull calf straight in the brain between the eyes with a sledge hammer and had the meat hung up to chill before nightfall. But of course all this does not show on television. I am the way my daughter would want me to be: a hundred pounds lighter, my skin like an uncooked barley pancake. My hair glistens in the hot bright lights. Johnny Carson has much to do to keep up with my quick and witty tongue.

But that is a mistake. I know even before I wake up. Who ever knew a   6 Johnson with a quick tongue? Who can even imagine me looking a strange white man in the eye? It seems to me I have talked to them always with one foot raised in flight, with my head turned in whichever way is farthest from them. Dee, though. She would always look anyone in the eye. Hesitation was no part of her nature.

"How do I look, Mama?" Maggie says, showing just enough of her thin   7 body enveloped in pink skirt and red blouse for me to know she's there, almost hidden by the door.

"Come out into the yard," I say.   8

Have you ever seen a lame animal, perhaps a dog run over by some care-   9 less person rich enough to own a car, sidle up to someone who is ignorant enough to be kind to him? That is the way my Maggie walks. She has been like this, chin on chest, eyes on ground, feet in shuffle, ever since the fire that burned the other house to the ground.

Dee is lighter than Maggie, with nicer hair and a fuller figure. She's a   10 woman now, though sometimes I forget. How long ago was it that the other house burned? Ten, twelve years? Sometimes I can still hear the flames and feel Maggie's arms sticking to me, her hair smoking and her dress falling off her in little black papery flakes. Her eyes seemed stretched open, blazed open by the flames reflected in them. And Dee. I see her standing off under the sweet gum tree she used to dig gum out of; a look of concentration on her face as she watched the last dingy gray board of the house fall in toward the red-hot brick chimney. Why don't you do a dance around the ashes? I'd wanted to ask her. She had hated the house that much.

I used to think she hated Maggie, too. But that was before we raised the   11
money, the church and me, to send her to Augusta to school. She used to read to us without pity; forcing words, lies, other folks' habits, whole lives upon us two, sitting trapped and ignorant underneath her voice. She washed us in a river of make-believe, burned us with a lot of knowledge we didn't necessarily need to know. Pressed us to her with the serious way she read, to shove us away at just the moment, like dimwits, we seemed about to understand.

Dee wanted nice things. A yellow organdy dress to wear to her graduation   12
from high school; black pumps to match a green suit she'd made from an old suit somebody gave me. She was determined to stare down any disaster in her efforts. Her eyelids would not flicker for minutes at a time. Often I fought off the temptation to shake her. At sixteen she had a style of her own: and knew what style was.

I never had an education myself. After second grade the school was closed   13
down. Don't ask me why: In 1927 colored asked fewer questions than they do now. Sometimes Maggie reads to me. She stumbles along good-naturedly but can't see well. She knows she is not bright. Like good looks and money, quickness passed her by. She will marry John Thomas (who has mossy teeth in an earnest face) and then I'll be free to sit here and I guess just sing church songs to myself. Although I never was a good singer. Never could carry a tune. I was always better at a man's job. I used to love to milk till I was hooked in the side in '49. Cows are soothing and slow and don't bother you, unless you try to milk them the wrong way.

I have deliberately turned my back on the house. It is three rooms, just   14
like the one that burned, except the roof is tin; they don't make shingle roofs anymore. There are no real windows, just some holes cut in the sides, like the portholes in a ship, but not round and not square, with rawhide holding the shutters up on the outside. This house is in a pasture, too, like the other one. No doubt when Dee sees it she will want to tear it down. She wrote me once that no matter where we "choose" to live, she will manage to come see us. But she will never bring her friends. Maggie and I thought about this and Maggie asked me, "Mama, when did Dee ever *have* any friends?"

She had a few. Furtive boys in pink shirts hanging about on washday after   15
school. Nervous girls who never laughed. Impressed with her they worshiped
the well-turned phrase, the cute shape, the scalding humor that erupted like
bubbles in lye. She read to them.

When she was courting Jimmy T she didn't have much time to pay to us,   16
but turned all her faultfinding power on him. He *flew* to marry a cheap city
gal from a family of ignorant flashy people. She hardly had time to recompose
herself.

When she comes I will meet—but there they are!   17

Maggie attempts to make a dash for the house, in her shuffling way, but I   18
stay her with my hand. "Come back here," I say. And she stops and tries to dig
a well in the sand with her toe.

It is hard to see them clearly through the strong sun. But even the first   19
glimpse of leg out of the car tells me it is Dee. Her feet were always neat-
looking, as if God himself had shaped them with a certain style. From the
other side of the car comes a short, stocky man. Hair is all over his head a foot
long and hanging from his chin like a kinky mule tail. I hear Maggie suck in
her breath. "Uhnnnh," is what it sounds like. Like when you see the wriggling
end of a snake just in front of your foot on the road. "Uhnnnh."

Dee next. A dress down to the ground, in this hot weather. A dress so loud   20
it hurts my eyes. There are yellows and oranges enough to throw back the light
of the sun. I feel my whole face warming from the heat waves it throws out.
Earrings gold, too, and hanging down to her shoulders. Bracelets dangling and
making noises when she moves her arm up to shake the folds of the dress out
of her armpits. The dress is loose and flows, and as she walks closer, I like it. I
hear Maggie go "Uhnnnh" again. It is her sister's hair. It stands straight up like
the wool on a sheep. It is black as night and around the edges are two long pig-
tails that rope about like small lizards disappearing behind her ears.

"Wa-su-zo-Tean-o!"[1] she says, coming on in that gliding way the dress   21
makes her move. The short stocky fellow with the hair to his navel is all
grinning and he follows up with "Asalamalakim, my mother and sister!" He
moves to hug Maggie but she falls back, right up against the back of my chair.
I feel her trembling there and when I look up I see the perspiration falling off
her chin.

"Don't get up," says Dee. Since I am stout it takes something of a push.   22
You can see me trying to move a second or two before I make it. She turns,
showing white heels through her sandals, and goes back to the car. Out she

---

[1]"Wa-su-zo-Tean-o" and "Asalamalakim" (next sentence) are greetings spelled as the
mother heard them.—EDS.

peeks next with a Polaroid. She stoops down quickly and lines up picture after picture of me sitting there in front of the house with Maggie cowering behind me. She never takes a shot without making sure the house is included. When a cow comes nibbling around the edge of the yard she snaps it and me *and* the house. Then she puts the Polaroid in the back seat of the car, and comes up and kisses me on the forehead.

Meanwhile Asalamalakim is going through the motions with Maggie's   23 hand. Maggie's hand is as limp as a fish, and probably as cold, despite the sweat, and she keeps trying to pull it back. It looks like Asalamalakim wants to shake hands but wants to do it fancy. Or maybe he don't know how people shake hands. Anyhow, he soon gives up on Maggie.

"Well," I say. "Dee."   24

"No, Mama," she says. "Not 'Dee,' Wangero Leewanika Kemanjo!"   25

"What happened to 'Dee'?" I wanted to know.   26

"She's dead," Wangero said. "I couldn't bear it any longer being named   27 after the people who oppress me."

"You know as well as me you was named after your aunt Dicie," I said.   28 Dicie is my sister. She named Dee. We called her "Big Dee" after Dee was born.

"But who was *she* named after?" asked Wangero.   29

"I guess after Grandma Dee," I said.   30

"And who was she named after?" asked Wangero.   31

"Her mother," I said, and saw Wangero was getting tired. "That's about as   32 far back as I can trace it," I said. Though, in fact, I probably could have carried it back beyond the Civil War through the branches.

"Well," said Asalamalakim, "there you are."   33

"Uhnnnh," I heard Maggie say.   34

"There I was not," I said, "before 'Dicie' cropped up in our family, so why   35 should I try to trace it that far back?"

He just stood there grinning, looking down on me like somebody inspect-   36 ing a Model A car. Every once in a while he and Wangero sent eye signals over my head.

"How do you pronounce this name?" I asked.   37

"You don't have to call me by it if you don't want to," said Wangero.   38

"Why shouldn't I?" I asked. "If that's what you want us to call you, we'll   39 call you."

"I know it might sound awkward at first," said Wangero.   40

"I'll get used to it," I said. "Ream it out again."   41

Well, soon we got the name out of the way. Asalamalakim had a name   42 twice as long and three times as hard. After I tripped over it two or three times he told me to just call him Hakim-a-barber. I wanted to ask him was he a bar- ber, but I didn't really think he was, so I didn't ask.

"You must belong to those beef-cattle peoples down the road," I said.   43
They said "Asalamalakim" when they met you, too, but they didn't shake
hands. Always too busy: feeding the cattle, fixing the fences, putting up salt-
lick shelters, throwing down hay. When the white folks poisoned some of the
herd the men stayed up all night with rifles in their hands. I walked a mile and
a half just to see the sight.

Hakim-a-barber said, "I accept some of their doctrines, but farming and   44
raising cattle is not my style." (They didn't tell me, and I didn't ask, whether
Wangero [Dee] had really gone and married him.)

We sat down to eat and right away he said he didn't eat collards and pork   45
was unclean. Wangero, though, went on through the chitlins and corn bread,
the greens and everything else. She talked a blue streak over the sweet potatoes. Everything delighted her. Even the fact that we still used the benches her
daddy made for the table when we couldn't afford to buy chairs.

"Oh, Mama!" she cried. Then turned to Hakim-a-barber. "I never knew   46
how lovely these benches are. You can feel the rump prints," she said, running
her hands underneath her and along the bench. Then she gave a sigh and her
hand closed over Grandma Dee's butter dish. "That's it!" she said. "I knew
there was something I wanted to ask you if I could have." She jumped up from
the table and went over in the corner where the churn stood, the milk in it
clabber by now. She looked at the churn and looked at it.

"This churn top is what I need," she said. "Didn't Uncle Buddy whittle it   47
out of a tree you all used to have?"

"Yes," I said.   48

"Uh-huh," she said happily. "And I want the dasher,[2] too."   49

"Uncle Buddy whittle that, too?" asked the barber.   50

Dee (Wangero) looked up at me.   51

"Aunt Dee's first husband whittled the dash," said Maggie so low you   52
almost couldn't hear her. "His name was Henry, but they called him Stash."

"Maggie's brain is like an elephant's," Wangero said, laughing. "I can use   53
the churn top as a centerpiece for the alcove table," she said, sliding a plate
over the churn, "and I'll think of something artistic to do with the dasher."

When she finished wrapping the dasher the handle stuck out. I took it for   54
a moment in my hands. You didn't even have to look close to see where hands
pushing the dasher up and down to make butter had left a kind of sink in the
wood. In fact, there were a lot of small sinks; you could see where thumbs and
fingers had sunk into the wood. It was beautiful light yellow wood, from a tree
that grew in the yard where Big Dee and Stash had lived.

After dinner Dee (Wangero) went to the trunk at the foot of my bed and   55

---

[2] The plunger of the butter churn. —EDS.

started rifling through it. Maggie hung back in the kitchen over the dishpan. Out came Wangero with two quilts. They had been pieced by Grandma Dee and then Big Dee and me had hung them on the quilt frames on the front porch and quilted them. One was in the Lone Star pattern. The other was Walk Around the Mountain. In both of them were scraps of dresses Grandma Dee had worn fifty and more years ago. Bits and pieces of Grandpa Jarrell's Paisley shirts. And one teeny faded blue piece, about the size of a penny matchbox, that was from Great Grandpa Ezra's uniform that he wore in the Civil War.

"Mama," Wangero said sweet as a bird. "Can I have these old quilts?"   56

I heard something fall in the kitchen, and a minute later the kitchen door   57
slammed.

"Why don't you take one or two of the others?" I asked. "These old things   58
was just done by me and Big Dee from some tops your grandma pieced before she died."

"No," said Wangero. "I don't want those. They are stitched around the   59
borders by machine."

"That'll make them last better," I said.   60

"That's not the point," said Wangero. "These are all pieces of dresses   61
Grandma used to wear. She did all this stitching by hand. Imagine!" She held the quilts securely in her arms, stroking them.

"Some of the pieces, like those lavender ones, come from old clothes her   62
mother handed down to her," I said, moving up to touch the quilts. Dee (Wangero) moved back just enough so that I couldn't reach the quilts. They already belonged to her.

"Imagine!" she breathed again, clutching them closely to her bosom.   63

"The truth is," I said, "I promised to give them quilts to Maggie, for when   64
she marries John Thomas."

She gasped like a bee had stung her.   65

"Maggie can't appreciate these quilts!" she said. "She'd probably be back-   66
ward enough to put them to everyday use."

"I reckon she would," I said. "God knows I been saving 'em for long   67
enough with nobody using 'em. I hope she will!" I didn't want to bring up how I had offered Dee (Wangero) a quilt when she went away to college. Then she had told me they were old-fashioned, out of style.

"But they're *priceless*!" she was saying now, furiously; for she has a temper.   68
"Maggie would put them on the bed and in five years they'd be in rags. Less than that!"

"She can always make some more," I said. "Maggie knows how to quilt."   69

Dee (Wangero) looked at me with hatred. "You just will not understand.   70
The point is these quilts, *these* quilts!"

"Well," I said, stumped. "What would *you* do with them?"   71

"Hang them," she said. As if that was the only thing you *could* do with   72
quilts.

Maggie by now was standing in the door. I could almost hear the sound   73
her feet made as they scraped over each other.

"She can have them, Mama," she said, like somebody used to never win-   74
ning anything, or having anything reserved for her. "I can 'member Grandma
Dee without the quilts."

I looked at her hard. She had filled her bottom lip with checkerberry snuff   75
and it gave her face a kind of dopey, hangdog look. It was Grandma Dee and
Big Dee who taught her how to quilt herself. She stood there with her scarred
hands hidden in the folds of her skirt. She looked at her sister with something
like fear but she wasn't mad at her. This was Maggie's portion. This was the
way she knew God to work.

When I looked at her like that something hit me in the top of my head   76
and ran down to the soles of my feet. Just like when I'm in church and the
spirit of God touches me and I get happy and shout. I did something I never
had done before: hugged Maggie to me, then dragged her on into the room,
snatched the quilts out of Miss Wangero's hands and dumped them into Maggie's lap. Maggie just sat there on my bed with her mouth open.

"Take one or two of the others," I said to Dee.   77

But she turned without a word and went out to Hakim-a-barber.   78

"You just don't understand," she said, as Maggie and I came out to the car.   79

"What don't I understand?" I wanted to know.   80

"Your heritage," she said. And then she turned to Maggie, kissed her, and   81
said, "You ought to try to make something of yourself, too, Maggie. It's really a
new day for us. But from the way you and Mama still live you'd never know it."

She put on some sunglasses that hid everything above the tip of her nose   82
and her chin.

Maggie smiled; maybe at the sunglasses. But a real smile, not scared. After   83
we watched the car dust settle I asked Maggie to bring me a dip of snuff. And
then the two of us sat there just enjoying, until it was time to go in the house
and go to bed.

*For a reading quiz, sources on Alice Walker, and annotated links to further readings
on African American heritage, visit **bedfordstmartins.com/thebedfordreader**.*

Journal Writing

Do you think the quilts stitched by the narrator's mother should be put to "everyday use," or should they be preserved as a reminder of family and cultural heritage? Write about something owned by you or your family that has been passed down from earlier generations. Is it still in everyday use? Why, or why not? (To take your journal writing further, see "From Journal to Essay" below.)

Questions on Meaning

1. Walker's short story is based on two sets of contrasts, a direct one between people and a more indirect one between attitudes. What are these contrasts?
2. Why has Dee taken on a new name? What is the point of the conversation in which she and her mother discuss the origin of her given name (pars. 24–35)?
3. Why do you think Dee makes sure to include the house when taking photographs of her mother and sister (par. 22)? Why does she want the quilts stitched by her grandmother? What IRONY can you find in her behavior?
4. Why do you think Walker titled this story "Everyday Use"?

Questions on Writing Strategy

1. What might Walker's PURPOSE have been in creating the contrasting sisters? What might the characters represent?
2. In what way does the conclusion of the story echo the beginning? What is the EFFECT of the story's opening and closing in this way?
3. **OTHER METHODS.** Walker's story is, of course, a NARRATIVE. Where does Walker use DESCRIPTION to enhance her narration?

Questions on Language

1. The mother states in paragraph 13 that she is uneducated and earlier says that she doesn't have a "quick tongue" (par. 6). Does the mother's language seem consistent with and appropriate for her educational background? Why, or why not?
2. What is the effect of the mother's referring to her daughter repeatedly as "Dee (Wangero)" and finally, in paragraph 76, as "Miss Wangero"?
3. Be sure you know the meanings of the following words, checking a dictionary if necessary: awe (par. 2); tottering (3); rawhide (14); scalding, lye (15); churn, clabber (46); snuff (75).

Suggestions for Writing

1. **FROM JOURNAL TO ESSAY.** Develop an essay about the family object or objects that you wrote about in your journal entry. Carefully describe the object, and explain its history, significance, and current use.

2. Think of siblings you know who are quite different from each other in looks, interests, behavior, or other attributes. (Your subjects could be you and your own sibling.) In an essay, compare and contrast the two people.

3. Beginning in the late 1960s and early 1970s, many African Americans resembled Walker's character Dee in embracing their heritage—particularly their roots in Africa—to claim a history beyond slavery and segregation. Research the specifics of this movement, and write an essay on how it influenced literature, education, fashion, and other aspects of American life.

4. **CRITICAL WRITING.** ANALYZE the character of Dee/Wangero, in relation to her mother and sister as well as in her own right. How do you think Walker wants readers to respond to this character? How do you respond to her? Be sure to support your analysis with appropriate quotations from the text.

5. **CONNECTIONS.** "Everyday Use" was published ten years after Martin Luther King, Jr., delivered his famous "I Have a Dream" speech (p. 625). How does the story reflect the themes of "I Have a Dream"? How is Walker commenting on the civil rights movement and its aftermath?

Alice Walker on Writing

In an interview with David Bradley in the *New York Times Magazine*, Alice Walker described her method of writing as waiting for friendly spirits to visit her. Usually, she doesn't outline or devote much time to preliminary organization. She plunges in with a passion, and she sees a definite purpose in most of her work: to correct injustices. "I was brought up to try to see what was wrong, and right it. Since I am a writer, writing is how I right it. I was brought up to look at things that are out of joint, out of balance, and to try to bring them into balance. And as a writer that's what I do."

An articulate feminist, Walker has written in support of greater rights for women, including African American women. If most of her works are short—stories, essays, and poems—there is a reason: She sees thick, long-winded volumes as alien to a female sensibility. "The books women write can be more like us—much thinner, much leaner, much cleaner."

Much of Alice Walker's writing has emerged from painful experience: She has written of her impoverished early days on a Georgia sharecropper's farm, a childhood accident with a BB gun that cost her the sight of one eye, a traumatic abortion, years as a civil rights worker in Mississippi. "I think," she says, "writing really helps you heal yourself. I think if you write long enough, you will be a healthy person. That is, if you write what you need to write, as opposed to what will make money or what will make fame."

For Discussion

1. What does the author mean when she speaks of the importance of writing "what you need to write"?
2. What writers can you think of whose work has helped to right the world's wrongs?
3. Can you cite any exceptions to Walker's generalization that long books are alien to women's sensibilities?

ADDITIONAL WRITING TOPICS

Comparison and Contrast

1. In an essay replete with examples, compare and contrast the two subjects in any one of the following pairs:

   The main characters of two films, stories, or novels
   Women and men as consumers
   The styles of two runners
   Liberals and conservatives: their opposing views of the role of government
   How city dwellers and country dwellers spend their leisure time
   The presentation styles of two television news commentators

2. Approach a comparison and contrast essay on one of the following general subjects by explaining why you prefer one thing to the other:

   Computers: Macs and PCs
   Two buildings on campus or in town
   Two football teams
   German-made cars and Detroit-made cars
   Two horror movies
   Television when you were a child and television today
   City life and small-town or rural life
   Malls and main streets
   Two neighborhoods
   Two sports

3. Write an essay in which you compare a reality (what actually exists) with an ideal (what should exist). Some possible topics:

   The affordable car
   Available living quarters
   A job
   The college curriculum
   Public transportation
   Financial aid to college students

8

PROCESS ANALYSIS

Explaining Step by Step

◀ **Process analysis in a photograph**

In a factory in Shenzhen, China, workers create dolls for export to the United States. The single image catches several steps in the doll-making process. At the very back of the assembly line, flat, unstuffed dolls begin the journey past the ranks of workers who stuff the body parts, using material prepared by other workers on the sides. A supervisor, hands behind his or her back, oversees the process. What do you think the photographer, Wally McNamee, wants viewers to understand about this process? What do you imagine the workers themselves think about it?

THE METHOD

A chemist working for a soft-drink firm is asked to improve on a competitor's product, Orange Quench. First, she chemically tests a sample to figure out what's in the drink. This is the method of DIVISION or ANALYSIS, the separation of something into its parts in order to understand it (see the following chapter). Then the chemist writes a report telling her boss how to make a drink like Orange Quench, but better. This recipe is a special kind of analysis, called PROCESS ANALYSIS: explaining step by step how to do something or how something is done.

Like any type of analysis, process analysis divides a subject into its components: It divides a continuous action into stages. Processes much larger and more involved than the making of an orange drink also may be analyzed. When geologists explain how a formation such as the Grand Canyon occurred—a process taking several hundred million years—they describe the successive layers of sediment deposited by oceans, floods, and wind; then the great uplift of the entire region by underground forces; and then the erosion, visible to us today, by the Colorado River and its tributaries, by little streams and flash floods, by crumbling and falling rock, and by wind. Exactly what are the geologists doing in this explanation? They are taking a complicated event (or process) and dividing it into parts. They are telling us what happened first, second, and third, and what is still happening today.

Because it is useful in explaining what is complicated, process analysis is a favorite method of scientists such as geologists. The method, however, may be useful to anybody. Two PURPOSES of process analysis are very familiar to you:

- A *directive process analysis* explains how to do something or make something. You meet it when you read a set of instructions for assembling newly purchased stereo components or follow the directions to an electronics store ("Turn right at the blinker and follow Patriot Boulevard for 2.4 miles . . .").
- An *informative process analysis* explains how something is done or how it takes place. This is the kind we often read out of curiosity. Such an essay may tell of events beyond our control: how atoms behave when split, how lions hunt, how a fertilized egg develops into a child.

In this chapter, you will find examples of both kinds of process analysis—both the "how to" and the "how." For instance, Linnea Saukko offers a directive for destroying the environment (not to be taken literally), while Jessica Mitford spellbindingly informs us of how corpses are embalmed.

Sometimes process analysis is used very imaginatively. Foreseeing that the sun eventually will cool, the earth shrink, the oceans freeze, and all life perish, an astronomer who cannot possibly behold the end of the world nevertheless can write a process analysis of it. An exercise in learned guesswork, such an essay divides a vast and almost inconceivable event into stages that, taken one at a time, become clearer and more readily imaginable.

Whether it is useful or useless (but fun to imagine), an effective process analysis can grip readers and even hold them fascinated. Say you were proposing a change in the procedures for course registration at your school. You could argue your point until you were out of words, but you would get nowhere if you failed to tell your readers exactly how the new process would work: That's what makes your proposal sing. Leaf through a current issue of a newsstand magazine, and you will find that process analysis abounds. You may meet, for instance, articles telling you how to tenderize cuts of meat, sew homemade designer jeans, lose fat, cut hair, arouse a bored mate, and score at Internet stock trading. Less practical, but not necessarily less interesting, are the informative articles: how brain surgeons work, how diamonds are formed, how cities fight crime. Readers, it seems, have an unslakable thirst for process analysis. In every issue of the *New York Times Book Review*, we find an entire best-seller list devoted to "Advice, How-to, and Miscellaneous," including books on how to make money in real estate, how to lose weight, how to find a good mate, and how to lose a bad one. Evidently, if anything will still make an American crack open a book, it is a step-by-step explanation of how he or she, too, can be a success at living.

THE PROCESS

Here are suggestions for writing an effective process analysis of your own. (In fact, what you are about to read is itself a process analysis.)

1. *Understand clearly the process you are about to analyze.* Think it through. This preliminary survey will make the task of writing far easier for you.
2. *Consider your thesis.* What is the point of your process analysis: Why are you bothering to tell readers about it? The THESIS STATEMENT for a process analysis need do no more than say what the subject is and maybe outline its essential stages. For instance:

The main stages in writing a process analysis are listing the steps in the process, drafting to explain the steps, and revising to clarify the steps.

But your readers will surely appreciate something livelier and more pointed, something that says "You can use this" or "This may surprise you" or "Listen up." Here are two thesis statements from essays in this chapter:

[In a mortuary the body] is in short order sprayed, sliced, pierced, pickled, trussed, trimmed, creamed, waxed, painted, rouged, and neatly dressed— transformed from a common corpse into a Beautiful Memory Picture.
                    —Jessica Mitford, "Behind the Formaldehyde Curtain"

Poisoning the earth can be difficult because the earth is always trying to cleanse and renew itself.   —Linnea Saukko, "How to Poison the Earth"

3. *Think about preparatory steps.* If the reader should do something before beginning the process, list these steps. For instance, you might begin, "Remove the packing from around the components," or, "First, lay out three eggs, one pound of Sheboygan bratwurst, and a chopped jalapeño pepper."

4. *List the steps or stages in the process.* Try setting them down in chronological order, one at a time—if this is possible. Some processes, however, do not happen in an orderly sequence, but occur all at once. If, for instance, you are writing an account of a typical earthquake, what do you mention first? The shifting of underground rock strata? Cracks in the earth? Falling houses? Bursting water mains? Toppling trees? Mangled cars? Casualties? Here is a subject for which the method of CLASSIFICA-TION (Chap. 10) may come to your aid. You might sort out apparently simultaneous events into categories: injury to people; damage to homes, to land, to public property.

5. *Check the completeness and order of the steps.* Make sure your list includes *all* the steps in the right order. Sometimes a stage of a process may contain a number of smaller stages. Make sure none has been left out. If any seems particularly tricky or complicated, underline it on your list to remind yourself when you write your essay to slow down and detail it with extra care.

6. *Define your terms.* Ask yourself, "Do I need any specialized or technical terms?" If so, be sure to define them. You'll sympathize with your reader if you have ever tried to work a Malaysian-made VCR that comes with an instruction booklet written in translatorese, full of unexplained technical JARGON, or if you have ever tried to assemble a plastic tricycle according to a directive that begins, "Position sleeve casing on wheel center in fork with shaft in tong groove, and gently but forcibly tap in medium pal nut head."

7. *Use time-markers or TRANSITIONS.* These words or phrases indicate *when* one stage of a process stops and the next begins, and they greatly aid your

reader in following you. Here, for example, is a paragraph of plain medical prose that makes good use of helpful time-markers (underlined). (The paragraph is adapted from Alan Frank Guttmacher's *Pregnancy and Birth: A Book for Expectant Parents.*)

In the human, <u>thirty-six hours after</u> the egg is fertilized, a two-cell egg appears. A twelve-cell development takes place <u>in seventy-two hours.</u> The egg is <u>still</u> round and has increased little in diameter. In this respect it is like a real estate development. <u>At first</u> a road bisects the whole area, <u>then</u> a cross road divides it into quarters, and <u>later</u> other roads divide it into eighths and twelfths. This happens without the taking of any more land, simply by subdivision of the original tract. <u>On the third or fourth day,</u> the egg passes from the Fallopian tube into the uterus. <u>By the fifth day</u> the original single large cell has subdivided into sixty small cells and floats about the slitlike uterine cavity <u>a day or two longer,</u> <u>then</u> adheres to the cavity's inner lining. <u>By the twelfth day</u> the human egg is already firmly implanted. Impregnation is <u>now</u> completed, <u>as yet</u> unbeknown to the woman. <u>At present,</u> she has not even had time to miss her first menstrual period, and other symptoms of pregnancy are <u>still several days distant.</u>

Brief as these time-markers are, they define each stage of the human egg's journey. Note how the writer, after declaring in the second sentence that the egg forms twelve cells, backtracks for a moment and retraces the process by which the egg has subdivided, comparing it (by a brief ANALOGY) to a piece of real estate. When using time-markers, vary them so that they won't seem mechanical. If you can, avoid the monotonous repetition of a fixed phrase (*In the fourteenth stage . . . , In the fifteenth stage . . .*). Even boring time-markers, though, are better than none at all. As in any chronological NARRATIVE, words and phrases such as *in the beginning, first, second, next, then, after that, three seconds later, at the same time,* and *finally* can help a process to move smoothly in the telling and lodge firmly in the reader's mind.

8. *Be specific.* When you write a first draft, state your analysis in generous detail, even at the risk of being wordy. When you revise, it will be easier to delete than to amplify.

9. *Revise.* When your essay is finished, reread it carefully against the checklist on the next page. You might also enlist a friend's help. If your process analysis is a directive ("How to Eat an Ice-Cream Cone Without Dribbling"), see if the friend can follow your instructions without difficulty. If your process analysis is informative ("How a New Word Enters the Dictionary"), ask the friend whether the process unfolds as clearly in his or her mind as it does in yours.

FOCUS ON CONSISTENCY

While drafting a process analysis, you may start off with subjects or verbs in one form and then shift to another form because the original choice feels awkward. In directive analyses, shifts occur most often with the subjects *a person* and *one*:

> INCONSISTENT   To keep the car from rolling while changing the tire, <u>one</u> should first set the car's emergency brake. Then <u>you</u> should block the three other tires with objects like rocks or chunks of wood.

In informative analyses, shifts usually occur from singular to plural as a way to get around *he* when the meaning includes males and females:

> INCONSISTENT   The poll <u>worker</u> first checks each voter against the registration list. Then <u>they</u> ask the voter to sign another list.

To repair inconsistencies, start with a subject that is both comfortable and sustainable:

> CONSISTENT   To keep the car from rolling while changing the tire, <u>you</u> should set the car's emergency brake. Then <u>you</u> should block the three other tires with objects like rocks or chunks of wood.

> CONSISTENT   Poll <u>workers</u> first check each voter against the registration list. Then <u>they</u> ask the voter to sign another list.

Sometimes, writers try to avoid naming or shifting subjects by using PASSIVE verbs that don't require actors:

> INCONSISTENT   To keep the car from rolling while changing the tire, <u>one</u> should first set the car's emergency brake. Then the three other tires <u>should be blocked</u> with objects like rocks or chunks of wood.

> INCONSISTENT   First each voter <u>is checked</u> against the registration list. Then the voter <u>is asked</u> to sign another list.

In directive analyses, avoid passive verbs with *you,* as shown in the consistent example above, or use the commanding form of verbs, in which *you* is understood as the subject:

> CONSISTENT   To keep the car from rolling while changing the tire, first <u>set</u> the car's emergency brake. Then <u>block</u> the three other tires with objects like rocks or chunks of wood.

In informative analyses, passive verbs may be necessary if you don't know who the actor is or want to emphasize the action over the actor. But identifying the actor is generally clearer and more concise:

> CONSISTENT   Poll <u>workers</u> first check each voter against the registration list. Then <u>they</u> ask the voter to sign another list.

For exercises on consistency and passive verbs, visit Exercise Central at *bedfordstmartins.com/thebedfordreader.*

> ### CHECKLIST FOR REVISING A PROCESS ANALYSIS
>
> ✔ **THESIS.** Does your process analysis have a point? Have you made sure readers know what it is?
>
> ✔ **ORGANIZATION.** Have you arranged the steps of your process in a clear chronological order? If steps occur simultaneously, have you grouped them so that readers perceive some order?
>
> ✔ **COMPLETENESS.** Have you included all the necessary steps and explained each one fully? Is it clear how each one contributes to the result?
>
> ✔ **DEFINITIONS.** Have you explained the meanings of any terms your readers may not know?
>
> ✔ **TRANSITIONS.** Do time-markers distinguish the steps of your process and clarify their sequence?
>
> ✔ **CONSISTENCY.** Have you maintained comfortable, consistent, and clear subjects and verb forms?

PROCESS ANALYSIS IN PARAGRAPHS

Writing About Television

The following paragraph, written especially for *The Bedford Reader*, explains the process of setting the timer on a particular VCR. Though composed to be freestanding, the paragraph (ideally with an accompanying illustration) could easily be dropped into a complete set of instructions on how to operate the VCR.

The timer on your videocassette recorder permits you to record   *Process to be explained* up to eight programs over a two-week period even when you are not   *with directive analysis* at home. For each program you wish to record in your absence,   *Step 1* locate an empty program number by pushing the *P* button until a flashing number appears on the TV screen. The next four steps set   *Preview of steps 2–5* the information for the program. First, push the *Day* button until   *Step 2* the day and date show on the screen. The screen will flash *On*. Next set the starting time (be sure the time is set correctly for AM or   *Step 3* PM). Then push the *Off* button and set the ending time (again,   *Step 4* watching AM or PM). When the times have been set, push the *Chan*   *Step 5* button and set the channel using the unit's channel selector. You   *Step 6* may review the program information by pushing the *Check* button. When you are satisfied that the settings are correct, push *Timer* to   *Step 7* set the timer to operate. (The unit cannot be operated manually   *Transitions (underlined)* while the timer is on.)   *clarify steps*

Writing in an Academic Discipline

This paragraph on our descent into sleep comes from a psychology textbook's section on "the most perplexing of our biological rhythms." Before this paragraph the authors review the history of sleep research; after it they continue to analyze the night-long process that follows this initial descent.

When you first climb into bed, close your eyes, and relax, your brain emits bursts of *alpha waves* in a regular, high-amplitude, low-frequency rhythm of 8–12 cycles per second. Alpha is associated with relaxing or not concentrating on anything in particular. Gradually these waves slow down even further and you drift into the Land of Nod, passing through four stages, each deeper than the previous one. *(Steps preceding process)* *(Process to be explained with informative analysis)*

1. *Stage 1.* Your brain waves become small and irregular, indicating activity with low voltage and mixed frequencies. You feel yourself drifting on the edge of consciousness, in a state of light sleep. If awakened, you may recall fantasies or a few visual images. *(Step 1)*
2. *Stage 2.* Your brain emits occasional short bursts of rapid, high-peaking waves called *sleep spindles*. Light sounds or minor noises probably won't disturb you. *(Step 2)*
3. *Stage 3.* In addition to the waves characteristic of stage 2, your brain occasionally emits very slow waves of about 1–3 cycles per second, with very high peaks. These *delta waves* are a sure sign that you will be hard to arouse. Your breathing and pulse have slowed down, your temperature has dropped, and your muscles are relaxed. *(Step 3)*
4. *Stage 4.* Delta waves have now largely taken over, and you are in deep sleep. It will take vigorous shaking or a loud noise to awaken you, and you won't be very happy about it. Oddly enough, though, if you talk or walk in your sleep, this is when you are likely to do so. *(Step 4)*

—Carole Wade and Carol Tavris, Psychology

PROCESS ANALYSIS IN PRACTICE

As a sophomore at Mary Washington College in Virginia, Jennifer Meska was a resident assistant in a freshman dormitory, responsible for students' welfare and, when necessary, for establishing dormitory rules.

In the following memo to the dorm's residents, Meska explained what students must do in the three-times-yearly fire drills. Meska's aim in drafting the memo was to outline the drill procedure so that students could remember and follow it—in other words (though she didn't think of the task this way), to write a clear directive process analysis.

In her first draft, Meska ran the steps of the process together in a paragraph, and for some steps she omitted explanations that might motivate residents to follow them. The bulleted list in her revision and the added explanations make the steps more distinct and memorable.

TO: Residents of Russell Hall
FROM: Jennifer Meska
DATE: September 6, 2004
SUBJECT: Fire-drill procedure

To prepare for the possibility of a fire in our residence hall, we will run three unannounced fire drills throughout the year. These drills will familiarize you with the potentially lifesaving procedures to be used during a real fire.

A loud buzzing noise and flashing lights will signal the start of a fire drill. Each resident has three minutes to complete the following tasks and exit the building:

- Close all bedroom and bathroom windows to prevent additional oxygen from feeding the fire.

- Turn off all electrical appliances, including computers, televisions, fans, radios, and lights. Turning off appliances will prevent electrical surges from starting additional fires.

- Grab a towel to cover your mouth in case you come across any smoke-filled passages, and wear shoes to protect your feet from any dangerous debris.

- Don't take anything else with you. In a real fire, delay could cost you your life.

- Close your door behind you to retard the spread of the fire.

- Go immediately to the nearest exit.

The fire drills are mandated by the state, and all residence halls must pass them in the required three minutes. If you have any questions, please let me know.

LINNEA SAUKKO

LINNEA SAUKKO was born in Warren, Ohio, in 1956. After receiving a degree in environmental quality control from Muskingum Area Technical College, she spent three years as an environmental technician, developing hazardous waste programs and acting as adviser on chemical safety at a large corporation. Concerned about the lack of safe methods for disposing of hazardous waste, Saukko went back to school to earn a BA in geology (Ohio State University, 1985) so that she could help address this issue. She currently lives in Hilliard, Ohio, and works as a groundwater manager at the Ohio Environmental Protection Agency, evaluating various sites for possible contamination of the groundwater.

How to Poison the Earth

"How to Poison the Earth" was written in response to an assignment given in a freshman composition class and was awarded a Bedford Prize in Student Writing. It was subsequently published in *Student Writers at Work: The Bedford Prizes*. Saukko's essay is largely a directive process analysis, but it is also a SATIRE: By outwardly showing us one way to guarantee the fate of the earth, the author implicitly urges us not to do it.

Poisoning the earth can be difficult because the earth is always trying to cleanse and renew itself. Keeping this in mind, we should generate as much waste as possible from substances such as uranium-238, which has a half-life (the time it takes for half of the substance to decay) of one million years, or plutonium, which has a half-life of only 0.5 million years but is so toxic that if distributed evenly, ten pounds of it could kill every person on the earth. Because the United States generates about eighteen tons of plutonium per year, it is about the best substance for long-term poisoning of the earth. It would help if we would build more nuclear power plants because each one generates only 500 pounds of plutonium each year. Of course, we must include persistent toxic chemicals such as polychlorinated biphenyl (PCB) and dichlorodiphenyl trichloroethane (DDT) to make sure we have enough toxins to poison the earth from the core to the outer atmosphere. First, we must develop many different ways of putting the waste from these nuclear and chemical substances in, on, and around the earth.

Putting these substances in the earth is a most important step in the poisoning process. With deep-well injection we can ensure that the earth is poisoned all the way to the core. Deep-well injection involves drilling a hole that is a few thousand feet deep and injecting toxic substances at extremely high pressures so they will penetrate deep into the earth. According to the Envi-

294

ronmental Protection Agency (EPA), there are about 360 such deep injection wells in the United States. We cannot forget the groundwater aquifers that are closer to the surface. These must also be contaminated. This is easily done by shallow-well injection, which operates on the same principle as deep-well injection, only closer to the surface. The groundwater that has been injected with toxins will spread contamination beneath the earth. The EPA estimates that there are approximately 500,000 shallow injection wells in the United States.

Burying the toxins in the earth is the next best method. The toxins from landfills, dumps, and lagoons slowly seep into the earth, guaranteeing that contamination will last a long time. Because the EPA estimates there are only about 50,000 of these dumps in the United States, they should be located in areas where they will leak to the surrounding ground and surface water.   3

Applying pesticides and other poisons on the earth is another part of the poisoning process. This is good for coating the earth's surface so that the poisons will be absorbed by plants, will seep into the ground, and will run off into surface water.   4

Surface water is very important to contaminate because it will transport the poisons to places that cannot be contaminated directly. Lakes are good for long-term storage of pollutants while they release some of their contamination to rivers. The only trouble with rivers is that they act as a natural cleansing system for the earth. No matter how much poison is dumped into them, they will try to transport it away to reach the ocean eventually.   5

The ocean is very hard to contaminate because it has such a large volume and a natural buffering capacity that tends to neutralize some of the contamination. So in addition to the pollution from rivers, we must use the ocean as a dumping place for as many toxins as possible. The ocean currents will help transport the pollution to places that cannot otherwise be reached.   6

Now make sure that the air around the earth is very polluted. Combustion and evaporation are major mechanisms for doing this. We must continuously pollute because the wind will disperse the toxins while rain washes them from the air. But this is good because a few lakes are stripped of all living animals each year from acid rain. Because the lower atmosphere can cleanse itself fairly easily, we must explode nuclear tests bombs that shoot radioactive particles high into the upper atmosphere where they will circle the earth for years. Gravity must pull some of the particles to earth, so we must continue exploding these bombs.   7

So it is that easy. Just be sure to generate as many poisonous substances as possible and be sure they are distributed in, on, and around the entire earth at a greater rate than it can cleanse itself. By following these easy steps we can guarantee the poisoning of the earth.   8

For a reading quiz and annotated links to further readings on pollution, visit **bedfordstmartins.com/thebedfordreader.**

Journal Writing

Saukko's essay is SATIRE—that is, an indirect attack on human follies or flaws, using IRONY to urge behavior exactly opposite what is really desired. In your journal, explore when you have proposed satirical solutions to problems that seem ridiculous or overwhelming—for example, suggesting breaking all the dishes so that they don't have to be washed again or barring pedestrians from city streets so that they don't interfere with cars. What kinds of situations might lead you to make suggestions like these? (To take your journal writing further, see "From Journal to Essay" on the facing page.)

Questions on Meaning

1. Is the author's main PURPOSE to amuse and entertain, to inform readers of ways they can make better use of natural resources, to warn readers about threats to the future of our planet, or to make fun of scientists? Support your answer with EVIDENCE from the essay.
2. Describe at least three of the earth's mechanisms for cleansing its land, water, and atmosphere, as presented in this essay.
3. According to Saukko, many of our actions are detrimental, if not outright destructive, to our environment. Identify these practices and discuss them. If these activities are harmful to the earth, why are they permitted? Do they serve some other important goal or purpose? If so, what? Are there other ways that these goals might be reached?

Questions on Writing Strategy

1. How detailed and specific are Saukko's instructions for poisoning the earth? Which steps in this process would you be able to carry out, once you finished reading the essay? In what instances might an author choose not to provide concrete, comprehensive instructions for a procedure? Relate your answer to the TONE and purpose of this essay.
2. How is Saukko's essay organized? Follow the process carefully to determine whether it happens chronologically, with each step depending on the one before it, or whether it follows another order. How effective is this method of organization and presentation?
3. For what AUDIENCE is this essay intended? How can you tell?

4. What is the tone of this essay? Consider especially the title and the last paragraph as well as examples from the body of the essay. How does the tone contribute to Saukko's satire?
5. What consistent sentence subject does Saukko use in explaining "how to poison the earth"? Who is to perform the process?
6. **OTHER METHODS.** Saukko doesn't mention every possible pollutant but instead focuses on certain EXAMPLES. Why do you think she chooses these particular examples? What serious pollutants can you think of that Saukko doesn't mention specifically?

Questions on Language

1. How do the phrases "next best method" (par. 3), "another part of the poisoning process" (4), and "[l]akes are good for long-term storage of pollutants" (5) signal the tone of this essay? Should they be read literally, ironically, metaphorically, or some other way?
2. Be sure you know how to define the following words: generate, nuclear, toxins (par. 1); lagoons, contamination (3); buffering, neutralize (6); combustion (7).

Suggestions for Writing

1. **FROM JOURNAL TO ESSAY.** Choose one of the solutions you wrote about in your journal, or propose a solution to a problem that your journal entry has suggested. Write an essay detailing this satirical solution, paying careful attention to explaining each step of the process and to maintaining your satiric tone throughout.
2. Write an essay defending and justifying the use of nuclear power plants, pesticides, or another pollutant Saukko mentions. This essay will require some research because you will need to argue that the benefits of these methods outweigh their hazardous and destructive effects. Be sure to support your claims with factual information and statistics. Or approach the issue from the same point of view that Saukko did, and argue against the use of nuclear power plants or pesticides. Substantiate your argument with data and facts, and be sure to propose alternative sources of power or alternative methods of insect control.
3. **CRITICAL WRITING.** What does Saukko gain or lose by using satire and irony to make her point? What would be the comparative strengths and weaknesses of an essay that approached the same pollution problems straightforwardly and sincerely, perhaps urging or pleading with readers to stop polluting?
4. **CONNECTIONS.** Saukko is not the only writer of irony in this book: Among other authors, Suzanne Britt (p. 239), Dave Barry (p. 245), Jessica Mitford (p. 305), Horace Miner (p. 316), Judy Brady (p. 344), Emily Prager (p. 353), and Jonathan Swift (p. 674) also employ it. Based on Saukko's essay and essays by at least two of these others, define *irony*. If you need a boost, supplement the definition in this book's Useful Terms with one in a dictionary of literary or rhetorical terms. But go beyond others' definitions to construct one of your own, using quotations from the essays as your support.

Linnea Saukko on Writing

"After I have chosen a topic," says Linnea Saukko, "the easiest thing for me to do is to write about how I really feel about it. The goal of 'How to Poison the Earth' was to inform people, or, more specifically, to open their eyes.

"As soon as I decided on my topic, I made a list of all the types of pollution and I sat down and basically wrote the paper in less than two hours. The information seemed to pour from me onto the page. Of course I did a lot of editing afterward, but I never changed the idea and the tone that I started with."

For Discussion

When have you had the experience of writing on a subject that compelled your words to pour forth with little effort? What was the subject? What did you learn from this experience?

BILL BRYSON

BILL BRYSON was born in Des Moines, Iowa, in 1951. After graduating from Drake College, he moved to England, where he lives now with his wife and four children. Bryson at first worked in a psychiatric hospital and then embarked on a journalism career in the British press. In 1987 he left regular newspaper work to write books, notably volumes on language, such as *Mother Tongue: English and How It Got That Way* (1990), and perceptive and amusing travel writing, such as *The Lost Continent* (1989), recounting a search for the perfect small American town; *A Walk in the Woods* (1998), detailing an 870-mile hike along the Appalachian Trail; and *In a Sunburned Country* (2000), chronicling travels in Australia. Bryson's latest book, *A Short History of Nearly Everything* (2003), travels through time more than space. It won the Aventis Prize for Science Books.

How You Became You

"How You Became You" (editors' title) is the opening of *A Short History of Nearly Everything*. Providing an eye-popping tour of our own chemical and biological origins, Bryson uses his trademark perceptive humor to make clear and immediate a complex and lengthy process.

Welcome. And congratulations. I am delighted that you could make it. Getting here wasn't easy, I know. In fact, I suspect it was a little tougher than you realize. 1

To begin with, for you to be here now trillions of drifting atoms had somehow to assemble in an intricate and intriguingly obliging manner to create you. It's an arrangement so specialized and particular that it has never been tried before and will only exist this once. For the next many years (we hope) these tiny particles will uncomplainingly engage in all the billions of deft, cooperative efforts necessary to keep you intact and let you experience the supremely agreeable but generally underappreciated state known as existence. 2

Why atoms take this trouble is a bit of a puzzle. Being you is not a gratifying experience at the atomic level. For all their devoted attention, your atoms don't actually care about you—indeed, don't even know that you are there. They don't even know that *they* are there. They are mindless particles, after all, and not even themselves alive. (It is a slightly arresting notion that if you were to pick yourself apart with tweezers, one atom at a time, you would produce a mound of fine atomic dust, none of which had ever been alive but all of which had once been you.) Yet somehow for the period of your existence they will answer to a single overarching impulse: to keep you you. 3

The bad news is that atoms are fickle and their time of devotion is fleet-   4
ing—fleeting indeed. Even a long human life adds up to only about 650,000
hours. And when that modest milestone flashes past, or at some other point
thereabouts, for reasons unknown your atoms will shut you down, silently dis-
assemble, and go off to be other things. And that's it for you.

Still you may rejoice that it happens at all. Generally speaking in the uni-   5
verse it doesn't, so far as we can tell. This is decidedly odd because the atoms
that so liberally and congenially flock together to form living things on Earth
are exactly the same atoms that decline to do it elsewhere. Whatever else it
may be, at the level of chemistry life is curiously mundane: carbon, hydrogen,
oxygen, and nitrogen, a little calcium, a dash of sulfur, a light dusting of other
very ordinary elements—nothing you wouldn't find in any ordinary drugstore—and that's all you need. The only thing special about the atoms that
make you is that they make you. That is of course the miracle of life.

Whether or not atoms make life in other corners of the universe, they   6
make plenty else; indeed, they make everything else. Without them there
would be no water or air or rocks, no stars and planets, no distant gassy clouds
or swirling nebulae or any of the other things that make the universe so use-
fully material. Atoms are so numerous and necessary that we easily overlook
that they needn't actually exist at all. There is no law that requires the universe to fill itself with small particles of matter or to produce light and gravity
and the other physical properties on which our existence hinges. There needn't
actually be a universe at all. For the longest time there wasn't. There were no
atoms and no universe for them to float about in. There was nothing—nothing at all anywhere.

So thank goodness for atoms. But the fact that you have atoms and that   7
they assemble in such a willing manner is only part of what got you here. To
be here now, alive in the twenty-first century and smart enough to know it,
you also had to be the beneficiary of an extraordinary string of biological good
fortune. Survival on Earth is a surprisingly tricky business. Of the billions and
billions of species of living things that have existed since the dawn of time,
most—99.99 percent—are no longer around. Life on Earth, you see, is not
only brief but dismayingly tenuous. It is a curious feature of our existence that
we come from a planet that is very good at promoting life but even better at
extinguishing it.

The average species on Earth lasts for only about 4 million years, so if   8
you wish to be around for billions of years, you must be as fickle as the atoms
that made you. You must be prepared to change everything about yourself—
shape, size, color, species affiliation, everything—and to do so repeatedly.
That's much easier said than done, because the process of change is random. To get from "protoplasmal primordial atomic globule" (as Gilbert and

Sullivan[1] put it) to sentient upright modern human has required you to mutate new traits over and over in a precisely timely manner for an exceedingly long while. So at various periods over the last 3.8 billion years you have abhorred oxygen and then doted on it, grown fins and limbs and jaunty sails, laid eggs, flicked the air with a forked tongue, been sleek, been furry, lived underground, lived in trees, been as big as a deer and as small as a mouse, and a million things more. The tiniest deviation from any of these evolutionary shifts, and you might now be licking algae from cave walls or lolling walruslike on some stony shore or disgorging air through a blowhole in the top of your head before diving sixty feet for a mouthful of delicious sandworms.

Not only have you been lucky enough to be attached since time immemorial to a favored evolutionary line, but you have also been extremely—make that miraculously—fortunate in your personal ancestry. Consider the fact that for 3.8 billion years, a period of time older than the Earth's mountains and rivers and oceans, every one of your forebears on both sides has been attractive enough to find a mate, healthy enough to reproduce, and sufficiently blessed by fate and circumstances to live long enough to do so. Not one of your pertinent ancestors was squashed, devoured, drowned, starved, stranded, stuck fast, untimely wounded, or otherwise deflected from its life's quest of delivering a tiny charge of genetic material to the right partner at the right moment in order to perpetuate the only possible sequence of hereditary combinations that could result—eventually, astoundingly, and all too briefly—in you. 9

For a reading quiz, sources on Bill Bryson, and annotated links to further readings on the evolution of life, visit **bedfordstmartins.com/thebedfordreader**.

Journal Writing

Bryson writes about the chemical and biological process that made you. But other processes have led to your becoming a unique personality with certain abilities, likes and dislikes, quirks, and so forth. In your journal explore the most important stages or events in your personal history that influenced who you are. (To take your journal writing further, see "From Journal to Essay" on the next page.)

[1] The Britons William Gilbert (1836–1911) and Arthur Sullivan (1842–1900) were the librettist and composer of satirical light operas such as *The Pirates of Penzance* and *The Mikado*. —EDS.

Questions on Meaning

1. Bryson describes three stages of the process of creating "you"—the first in paragraphs 2–6, the second in paragraphs 7–8, and the third in paragraph 9. What names would you give to these three stages?
2. Why does Bryson think it is surprising that atoms are the basis of life on Earth?
3. What does Bryson mean when he says "you also had to be the beneficiary of an extraordinary string of biological good fortune" (par. 7)? What other luck does he say was necessary to make you?
4. How does the final sentence of paragraph 2 suggest Bryson's PURPOSE?

Questions on Writing Strategy

1. What is unusual about Bryson's opening? How can his comment "I'm delighted that you could make it" be taken in two ways?
2. Some sentences in paragraphs 6, 8, and 9 contain lists of things or events. What is the EFFECT of these lists?
3. How does Bryson's final phrase ("that could result—eventually, astoundingly, and all too briefly—in you") SUMMARIZE the entire essay?
4. **OTHER METHODS.** What role does CAUSE AND EFFECT play in paragraphs 8 and 9?

Questions on Language

1. Bryson says that atoms are "mindless particles" (par. 3), yet he uses personification to give them human attributes. (For a definition of *personification*, see *Figures of speech* in Useful Terms.) Find examples of personification of atoms. Why do you suppose Bryson chose to describe atoms this way?
2. In paragraph 3 Bryson writes that the work of atoms is "a bit of a puzzle." Where else in the essay does he use language to suggest the "puzzle" of life? How does this language contribute to his overall point?
3. Consult a dictionary if you are unsure of the meaning of any of the following: deft, supremely (par. 2); overarching (3); milestone (4); congenially, mundane (5); dismayingly, tenuous (7); sentient, abhorred, doted, jaunty (8); forebears, perpetuate (9).

Suggestions for Writing

1. **FROM JOURNAL TO ESSAY.** Based on your journal writing, compose an essay in which you trace the process that led to your being the person you are today. Focus on the important milestones in your life that helped shape your personality.
2. Do some research about a scientific process that intrigues you. Consider subjects you've come across in your courses, outside reading, or TV viewing, or try substituting another word for *you* in the title of Bryson's essay—for instance, "How dogs became dogs," "How stars became stars," "How flowers became flowers." Write an essay in which you analyze this process.

3. **CRITICAL WRITING.** Closely examine how Bryson develops the discussion of each stage in his process analysis. In an essay discuss how his approach contributes to his purpose.
4. **CONNECTIONS.** In "How to Poison the Earth" (p. 294), Linnea Saukko also writes about a scientific process. In an essay of your own, COMPARE AND CONTRAST Saukko's purpose and method with Bryson's. What similarities and differences do you find in each writer's approach to explaining his or her subject?

Bill Bryson on Writing

In "Lost in Cyberland," an essay in the collection *I'm a Stranger Here Myself* (1999), Bryson explains his difficulties with computers. This passage from the essay zeros in on his word processor's spelling checker.

Like nearly everything else to do with computers, a spell checker is marvelous in principle. When you have done a piece of work, you activate it and it goes through the text looking for words that are misspelled. Actually, since a computer doesn't understand what words are, it looks for letter clusters it isn't familiar with, and here is where the disappointment begins.

First, it doesn't recognize any proper nouns — names of people, places, corporations, and so on — or nonstandard spellings like *kerb* and *colour*. Nor does it recognize many plurals or other variant forms (like *steps* or *stepped*), or abbreviations or acronyms. Nor, evidently, any word coined since Eisenhower was president. Thus, it recognizes *sputnik* and *beatnik* but not *Internet, fax, cyberspace,* or *butthead,* among many others.

But the really distinctive feature of my spell checker — and here is the part that can provide hours of entertainment for anyone who doesn't have anything approaching a real life — is that it has been programmed to suggest alternatives. These are seldom less than memorable. For this column, for instance, for *Internet* it suggested *internat* (a word that I cannot find in any dictionary, American or British), *internode, interknit,* and *underneath. Fax* prompted no fewer than thirty-three suggested alternatives, including *fab, fays, feats, fuzz, feaze, phase,* and at least two more that are unknown to lexicography: *falx* and *phose. Cyberspace* drew a blank, but for *cyber* it came up with *chubbier* and *scabbier.*

I have tried without success to discern the logic by which a computer and programmer working in tandem could decide that someone who typed *f-a-x* would really have intended to write *p-h-a-s-e,* or why *cyber* might suggest *chubbier* and *scabbier* but not, say, *watermelon* or *full-service gas station*, to name two equally random alternatives. Still less can I explain how nonexistent words like *phose* and *internat* would get into the program. Call me exacting, but I would submit that a computer program that wants to discard a real word in favor of one that does not exist is not ready to be offered for public use.

For Discussion

1. What does Bryson find objectionable about spelling checkers?
2. Have you shared some of Bryson's problems with spelling checkers? Have you had other problems he doesn't mention—for instance, a checker's inability to distinguish among *not* and *now* and *no* or among *their* and *there* and *they're*?
3. What do you think is the remedy for spelling errors when the checking program is flawed? Use the program and hope for the best? Stop using the program and hope for the best? Something else?

JESSICA MITFORD

Born in Batsford Mansion, England, in 1917, the daughter of Lord and Lady Redesdale, JESSICA MITFORD devoted much of her early life to defying her aristocratic upbringing. In her autobiography *Daughters and Rebels* (1960), she tells how she received a genteel schooling at home, then as a young woman moved to Loyalist Spain during the violent Spanish Civil War. Later, she emigrated to America, where for a time she worked in Miami as a bartender. She became one of her adopted country's most noted reporters: *Time* called her "Queen of the Muckrakers." Exposing with her typewriter what she regarded as corruption, abuse, and absurdity, Mitford wrote *The American Way of Death* (1963, revised as *The American Way of Death Revisited* in 1998), *Kind and Unusual Punishment: The Prison Business* (1973), and *The American Way of Birth* (1992). *Poison Penmanship* (1979) collects articles from *The Atlantic Monthly*, *Harper's*, and other magazines. *A Fine Old Conflict* (1976) is the second volume of Mitford's autobiography. And a novel, *Grace Had an English Heart* (1989), examines how the media transform ordinary people into celebrities. Jessica Mitford died in 1996.

Behind the Formaldehyde Curtain

The most famous (or infamous) thing Jessica Mitford wrote is *The American Way of Death*, a critique of the funeral industry. In this selection from the book, Mitford analyzes the twin processes of embalming and restoring a corpse, the practices she finds most objectionable. You may need a stable stomach to enjoy the selection, but in it you'll find a clear, painstaking process analysis, written with masterly style and outrageous wit. (For those who want to know, Mitford herself was cremated after her death.)

For a complementary view of cultural practices, read the essay following Mitford's, Horace Miner's "Body Ritual Among the Nacirema."

The drama begins to unfold with the arrival of the corpse at the mortuary.   1

Alas, poor Yorick! How surprised he would be to see how his counterpart   2
of today is whisked off to a funeral parlor and is in short order sprayed, sliced, pierced, pickled, trussed, trimmed, creamed, waxed, painted, rouged, and neatly dressed—transformed from a common corpse into a Beautiful Memory Picture. This process is known in the trade as embalming and restorative art,

and is so universally employed in the United States and Canada that the funeral director does it routinely, without consulting corpse or kin. He regards as eccentric those few who are hardy enough to suggest that it might be dispensed with. Yet no law requires embalming, no religious doctrine commends it, nor is it dictated by considerations of health, sanitation, or even of personal daintiness. In no part of the world but in Northern America is it widely used. The purpose of embalming is to make the corpse presentable for viewing in a suitably costly container; and here too the funeral director routinely, without first consulting the family, prepares the body for public display.

Is all this legal? The processes to which a dead body may be subjected are after all to some extent circumscribed by law. In most states, for instance, the signature of next of kin must be obtained before an autopsy may be performed, before the deceased may be cremated, before the body may be turned over to a medical school for research purposes; or such provision must be made in the decedent's will. In the case of embalming, no such permission is required nor is it ever sought.[1] A textbook, *The Principles and Practices of Embalming*, comments on this: "There is some question regarding the legality of much that is done within the preparation room." The author points out that it would be most unusual for a responsible member of a bereaved family to instruct the mortician, in so many words, to "embalm" the body of a deceased relative. The very term *embalming* is so seldom used that the mortician must rely upon custom in the matter. The author concludes that unless the family specifies otherwise, the act of entrusting the body to the care of a funeral establishment carries with it an implied permission to go ahead and embalm.

Embalming is indeed a most extraordinary procedure, and one must wonder at the docility of Americans who each year pay hundreds of millions of dollars for its perpetuation, blissfully ignorant of what it is all about, what is done, how it is done. Not one in ten thousand has any idea of what actually takes place. Books on the subject are extremely hard to come by. They are not to be found in most libraries or bookshops.

In an era when huge television audiences watch surgical operations in the comfort of their living rooms, when, thanks to the animated cartoon, the geography of the digestive system has become familiar territory even to the nursery school set, in a land where the satisfaction of curiosity about almost all matters is a national pastime, the secrecy surrounding embalming can, surely,

---

[1] Partly because of Mitford's attack, the Federal Trade Commission now requires the funeral industry to provide families with itemized price lists, including the price of embalming, to state that embalming is not required, and to obtain the family's consent to embalming before charging for it. Shortly before her death, however, Mitford observed that the FTC had "watered down" the regulations and "routinely ignored" consumer complaints about the funeral industry. — EDS.

hardly be attributed to the inherent gruesomeness of the subject. Custom in this regard has within this century suffered a complete reversal. In the early days of American embalming, when it was performed in the home of the deceased, it was almost mandatory for some relative to stay by the embalmer's side and witness the procedure. Today, family members who might wish to be in attendance would certainly be dissuaded by the funeral director. All others, except apprentices, are excluded by law from the preparation room.

A close look at what does actually take place may explain in large measure   6
the undertaker's intractable reticence concerning a procedure that has become his major *raison d'être*. Is it possible he fears that public information about embalming might lead patrons to wonder if they really want this service? If the funeral men are loath to discuss the subject outside the trade, the reader may, understandably, be equally loath to go on reading at this point. For those who have the stomach for it, let us part the formaldehyde curtain. . . .

The body is first laid out in the undertaker's morgue—or rather, Mr. Jones   7
is reposing in the preparation room—to be readied to bid the world farewell.

The preparation room in any of the better funeral establishments has the   8
tiled and sterile look of a surgery, and indeed the embalmer–restorative artist who does his chores there is beginning to adopt the term *dermasurgeon* (appropriately corrupted by some mortician-writers as "demi-surgeon") to describe his calling. His equipment, consisting of scalpels, scissors, augers, forceps, clamps, needles, pumps, tubes, bowls, and basins, is crudely imitative of the surgeon's, as is his technique, acquired in a nine- or twelve-month post-high-school course in an embalming school. He is supplied by an advanced chemical industry with a bewildering array of fluids, sprays, pastes, oils, powders, creams, to fix or soften tissue, shrink or distend it as needed, dry it here, restore the moisture there. There are cosmetics, waxes, and paints to fill and cover features, even plaster of Paris to replace entire limbs. There are ingenious aids to prop and stabilize the cadaver: a Vari-Pose Head Rest, the Edwards Arm and Hand Positioner, the Repose Block (to support the shoulders during the embalming), and the Throop Foot Positioner, which resembles an old-fashioned stocks.

Mr. John H. Eckels, president of the Eckels College of Mortuary Science,   9
thus describes the first part of the embalming procedure: "In the hands of a skilled practitioner, this work may be done in a comparatively short time and without mutilating the body other than by slight incision—so slight that it scarcely would cause serious inconvenience if made upon a living person. It is necessary to remove the blood, and doing this not only helps in the disinfecting, but removes the principal cause of disfigurements due to discoloration."

Another textbook discusses the all-important time element: "The ear-   10
lier this is done, the better, for every hour that elapses between death and em-

balming will add to the problems and complications encountered. . . ." Just how soon should one get going on the embalming? The author tells us, "On the basis of such scanty information made available to this profession through its rudimentary and haphazard system of technical research, we must conclude that the best results are to be obtained if the subject is embalmed before life is completely extinct—that is, before cellular death has occurred. In the average case, this would mean within an hour after somatic death." For those who feel that there is something a little rudimentary, not to say haphazard, about this advice, a comforting thought is offered by another writer. Speaking of fears entertained in early days of premature burial, he points out, "One of the effects of embalming by chemical injection, however, has been to dispel fears of live burial." How true; once the blood is removed, chances of live burial are indeed remote.

To return to Mr. Jones, the blood is drained out through the veins and   11
replaced by embalming fluid pumped in through the arteries. As noted in *The Principles and Practices of Embalming*, "every operator has a favorite injection and drainage point—a fact which becomes a handicap only if he fails or refuses to forsake his favorites when conditions demand it." Typical favorites are the carotid artery, femoral artery, jugular vein, subclavian vein. There are various choices of embalming fluid. If Flextone is used, it will produce a "mild, flexible rigidity. The skin retains a velvety softness, the tissues are rubbery and pliable. Ideal for women and children." It may be blended with B. and G. Products Company's Lyf-Lyk tint, which is guaranteed to reproduce "nature's own skin texture . . . the velvety appearance of living tissue." Suntone comes in three separate tints: Suntan; Special Cosmetic Tint, a pink shade "especially indicated for female subjects"; and Regular Cosmetic Tint, moderately pink.

About three to six gallons of a dyed and perfumed solution of formalde-   12
hyde, glycerin, borax, phenol, alcohol, and water is soon circulating through Mr. Jones, whose mouth has been sewn together with a "needle directed upward between the upper lip and gum and brought out through the left nostril," with the corners raised slightly "for a more pleasant expression." If he should be bucktoothed, his teeth are cleaned with Bon Ami and coated with colorless nail polish. His eyes, meanwhile, are closed with flesh-tinted eye caps and eye cement.

The next step is to have at Mr. Jones with a thing called a trocar. This is   13
a long, hollow needle attached to a tube. It is jabbed into the abdomen, poked around the entrails and chest cavity, the contents of which are pumped out and replaced with "cavity fluid." This done, and the hole in the abdomen sewn up, Mr. Jones's face is heavily creamed (to protect the skin from burns which may be caused by leakage of the chemicals), and he is covered with a

sheet and left unmolested for a while. But not for long—there is more, much more, in store for him. He has been embalmed, but not yet restored, and the best time to start the restorative work is eight to ten hours after embalming, when the tissues have become firm and dry.

The object of all this attention to the corpse, it must be remembered, is to   14
make it presentable for viewing in an attitude of healthy repose. "Our customs require the presentation of our dead in the semblance of normality . . . un-marred by the ravages of illness, disease, or mutilation," says Mr. J. Sheridan Mayer in his *Restorative Art*. This is rather a large order since few people die in the full bloom of health, unravaged by illness and unmarked by some dis-figurement. The funeral industry is equal to the challenge: "In some cases the gruesome appearance of a mutilated or disease-ridden subject may be quite discouraging. The task of restoration may seem impossible and shake the con-fidence of the embalmer. This is the time for intestinal fortitude and determi-nation. Once the formative work is begun and affected tissues are cleaned or removed, all doubts of success vanish. It is surprising and gratifying to discover the results which may be obtained."

The embalmer, having allowed an appropriate interval to elapse, returns   15
to the attack, but now he brings into play the skill and equipment of sculptor and cosmetician. Is a hand missing? Casting one in plaster of Paris is a simple matter. "For replacement purposes, only a cast of the back of the hand is nec-essary; this is within the ability of the average operator and is quite adequate." If a lip or two, a nose, or an ear should be missing, the embalmer has at hand a variety of restorative waxes with which to model replacements. Pores and skin texture are simulated by stippling with a little brush, and over this cos-metics are laid on. Head off? Decapitation cases are rather routinely handled. Ragged edges are trimmed, and head joined to torso with a series of splints, wires, and sutures. It is a good idea to have a little something at the neck—a scarf or a high collar—when time for viewing comes. Swollen mouth? Cut out tissue as needed from inside the lips. If too much is removed, the surface contour can easily be restored by padding with cotton. Swollen necks and cheeks are reduced by removing tissue through vertical incisions made down each side of the neck. "When the deceased is casketed, the pillow will hide the suture incisions . . . as an extra precaution against leakage, the suture may be painted with liquid sealer."

The opposite condition is more likely to present itself—that of emaciation.   16
His hypodermic syringe now loaded with massage cream, the embalmer seeks out and fills the hollowed and sunken areas by injection. In this procedure the backs of the hands and fingers and the under-chin area should not be neglected.

Positioning the lips is a problem that recurrently challenges the ingenuity   17
of the embalmer. Closed too tightly, they tend to give a stern, even disapproving

expression. Ideally, embalmers feel, the lips should give the impression of being ever so slightly parted, the upper lip protruding slightly for a more youthful appearance. This takes some engineering, however, as the lips tend to drift apart. Lip drift can sometimes be remedied by pushing one or two straight pins through the inner margin of the lower lip and then inserting them between the two front upper teeth. If Mr. Jones happens to have no teeth, the pins can just as easily be anchored in his Armstrong Face Former and Denture Replacer. Another method to maintain lip closure is to dislocate the lower jaw, which is then held in its new position by a wire run through holes which have been drilled through the upper and lower jaws at the midline. As the French are fond of saying, *il faut souffrir pour être belle.*[2]

If Mr. Jones has died of jaundice, the embalming fluid will very likely turn   18
him green. Does this deter the embalmer? Not if he has intestinal fortitude. Masking pastes and cosmetics are heavily laid on, burial garments and casket interiors are color-correlated with particular care, and Jones is displayed beneath rose-colored lights. Friends will say "How *well* he looks." Death by carbon monoxide, on the other hand, can be rather a good thing from the embalmer's viewpoint: "One advantage is the fact that this type of discoloration is an exaggerated form of a natural pink coloration." This is nice because the healthy glow is already present and needs but little attention.

The patching and filling completed, Mr. Jones is now shaved, washed, and   19
dressed. Cream-based cosmetic, available in pink, flesh, suntan, brunette, and blond, is applied to his hands and face, his hair is shampooed and combed (and, in the case of Mrs. Jones, set), his hands manicured. For the horny-handed son of toil special care must be taken; cream should be applied to remove ingrained grime, and the nails cleaned. "If he were not in the habit of having them manicured in life, trimming and shaping is advised for better appearance — never questioned by kin."

Jones is now ready for casketing (this is the present participle of the verb   20
"to casket"). In this operation his right shoulder should be depressed slightly "to turn the body a bit to the right and soften the appearance of lying flat on the back." Positioning the hands is a matter of importance, and special rubber positioning blocks may be used. The hands should be cupped slightly for a more lifelike, relaxed appearance. Proper placement of the body requires a delicate sense of balance. It should lie as high as possible in the casket, yet not so high that the lid, when lowered, will hit the nose. On the other hand, we are cautioned, placing the body too low "creates the impression that the body is in a box."

Jones is next wheeled into the appointed slumber room where a few last   21

[2] You have to suffer to be beautiful. — EDS.

touches may be added—his favorite pipe placed in his hand or, if he was a great reader, a book propped into position. (In the case of little Master Jones a Teddy bear may be clutched.) Here he will hold open house for a few days, visiting hours 10 AM to 9 PM.

All now being in readiness, the funeral director calls a staff conference to make sure that each assistant knows his precise duties. Mr. Wilber Kriege writes: "This makes your staff feel that they are a part of the team, with a definite assignment that must be properly carried out if the whole plan is to succeed. You never heard of a football coach who failed to talk to his entire team before they go on the field. They have drilled on the plays they are to execute for hours and days, and yet the successful coach knows the importance of making even the benchwarming third-string substitute feel that he is important if the game is to be won." The winning of *this* game is predicated upon glass-smooth handling of the logistics. The funeral director has notified the pall-bearers whose names were furnished by the family, has arranged for the presence of clergyman, organist, and soloist, has provided transportation for everybody, has organized and listed the flowers sent by friends. In *Psychology of Funeral Service* Mr. Edward A. Martin points out, "He may not always do as much as the family thinks he is doing, but it is his helpful guidance that they appreciate in knowing they are proceeding as they should. . . . The important thing is how well his services can be used to make the family believe they are giving unlimited expression to their own sentiment."

The religious service may be held in a church or in the chapel of the funeral home; the funeral director vastly prefers the latter arrangement, for not only is it more convenient for him but it affords him the opportunity to show off his beautiful facilities to the gathered mourners. After the clergyman has had his say, the mourners queue up to file past the casket for a last look at the deceased. The family is *never* asked whether they want an open-casket ceremony; in the absence of their instruction to the contrary, this is taken for granted. Consequently well over 90 percent of all American funerals feature the open casket—a custom unknown in other parts of the world. Foreigners are astonished by it. An English woman living in San Francisco described her reaction in a letter to the writer:

> I myself have attended only one funeral here—that of an elderly fellow worker of mine. After the service I could not understand why everyone was walking towards the coffin (sorry, I mean casket), but thought I had better follow the crowd. It shook me rigid to get there and find the casket open and poor old Oscar lying there in his brown tweed suit, wearing a suntan makeup and just the wrong shade of lipstick. If I had not been extremely fond of the old boy, I have a horrible feeling that I might have giggled. Then and there I decided that I could never face another American funeral—even dead.

The casket (which has been resting throughout the service on a Classic Beauty Ultra Metal Casket Bier) is now transferred by a hydraulically operated device called Porto-Lift to a balloon-tired, Glide Easy casket carriage which will wheel it to yet another conveyance, the Cadillac Funeral Coach. This may be lavender, cream, light green—anything but black. Interiors, of course, are color-correlated, "for the man who cannot stop short of perfection." 24

At graveside, the casket is lowered into the earth. This office, once the prerogative of friends of the deceased, is now performed by a patented mechanical lowering device. A "Lifetime Green" artificial grass mat is at the ready to conceal the sere earth, and overhead, to conceal the sky, is a portable Steril Chapel Tent ("resists the intense heat and humidity of summer and the terrific storms of winter . . . available in Silver Gray, Rose, or Evergreen"). Now is the time for the ritual scattering of earth over the coffin, as the solemn words "earth to earth, ashes to ashes, dust to dust" are pronounced by the officiating cleric. This can today be accomplished "with a mere flick of the wrist with the Gordon Leak-Proof Earth Dispenser. No grasping of a handful of dirt, no soiled fingers. Simple, dignified, beautiful, reverent! The modern way!" The Gordon Earth Dispenser (at $5) is of nickel-plated brass construction. It is not only "attractive to the eye and long wearing"; it is also "one of the 'tools' for building better public relations" if presented as "an appropriate non-commercial gift" to the clergyman. It is shaped something like a saltshaker. 25

Untouched by human hand, the coffin and the earth are now united. 26

It is in the function of directing the participants through this maze of gadgetry that the funeral director has assigned to himself his relatively new role of "grief therapist." He has relieved the family of every detail, he has revamped the corpse to look like a living doll, he has arranged for it to nap for a few days in a slumber room, he has put on a well-oiled performance in which the concept of *death* has played no part whatsoever—unless it was inconsiderately mentioned by the clergyman who conducted the religious service. He has done everything in his power to make the funeral a real pleasure for everybody concerned. He and his team have given their all to score an upset victory over death. 27

*For a reading quiz, sources on Jessica Mitford, and annotated links to further readings on customs related to death, visit **bedfordstmartins.com/thebedfordreader**.*

Journal Writing

Presumably, morticians embalm and restore corpses, and survivors support the work, because the practices are thought to ease the shock of death. Now that you know what goes on behind the scenes, how do you feel about a loved one's undergoing these procedures? (To take your journal writing further, see "From Journal to Essay" on the next page.)

Questions on Meaning

1. What was your emotional response to this essay? Can you analyze your feelings?
2. To what does the author attribute the secrecy surrounding the embalming process?
3. What, according to Mitford, is the mortician's intent? What common obstacles to fulfilling it must be surmounted?
4. What do you understand from Mitford's remark in paragraph 10, on dispelling fears of live burial: "How true; once the blood is removed, chances of live burial are indeed remote"?
5. Do you find any implied PURPOSE in this essay? Does Mitford seem primarily out to rake muck, or does she offer any positive suggestions to Americans?

Questions on Writing Strategy

1. What is Mitford's TONE? In her opening two paragraphs, exactly what shows her attitude toward her subject?
2. Why do you think Mitford goes into so much grisly detail in analyzing the processes of embalming and restoration? How does the detail serve her purpose?
3. What is the EFFECT of calling the body Mr. Jones (or Master Jones)?
4. Paragraph by paragraph, what TRANSITIONS does the author employ? (If you need a refresher on this point, see the discussion of transitions on pp. 288–89.)
5. To whom does Mitford address her process analysis? How do you know she isn't writing for an AUDIENCE of professional morticians?
6. Consider one of the quotations from the journals and textbooks of professionals and explain how it serves the author's general purpose.
7. Why do you think Mitford often uses PASSIVE verbs to describe the actions of embalmers—for instance, "the blood is drained," "If Flextone is used," and "It may be blended" in paragraph 11? Are the passive verbs effective or ineffective? Why?
8. **OTHER METHODS.** In paragraph 8, Mitford uses CLASSIFICATION in listing the embalmer's equipment and supplies. What groups does she identify, and why does she bother sorting the items at all?

Questions on Language

1. Explain the ALLUSION to Yorick in paragraph 2.
2. What IRONY do you find in this statement in paragraph 7: "The body is first laid out in the undertaker's morgue—or rather, Mr. Jones is reposing in the

preparation room"? Pick out any other words or phrases in the essay that seem ironic. Comment especially on those you find in the essay's last two sentences.

3. Why is it useful to Mitford's purpose that she cites the brand names of morticians' equipment and supplies (the Edwards Arm and Hand Positioner, Lyf-Lyk tint)? List all the brand names in the essay that are memorable.

4. Define the following words or terms: counterpart (par. 2); circumscribed, autopsy, cremated, decedent, bereaved (3); docility, perpetuation (4); inherent, mandatory (5); intractable, reticence, *raison d'être*, formaldehyde (6); "derma- (in *dermasurgeon*)," augers, forceps, distend, stocks (8); somatic (10); carotid artery, femoral artery, jugular vein, subclavian vein, pliable (11); glycerin, borax, phenol, bucktoothed (12); trocar, entrails (13); stippling, sutures (15); emaciation (16); jaundice (18); predicated (22); queue (23); hydraulically (24); cleric, sere (25); therapist (27).

Suggestions for Writing

1. **FROM JOURNAL TO ESSAY.** Drawing on your personal response to Mitford's essay in your journal, write a brief essay that ARGUES either for or against embalming and restoration. Consider the purposes served by these practices, both for the mortician and for the dead person's relatives and friends, as well as their costs and effects.

2. Search the Web or consult a periodical index for sources of information about the phenomenon of quick-freezing the dead. Set forth this process, including its hoped-for result of being able to revive the corpses in the far future.

3. ANALYZE some other process whose operations may not be familiar to everyone. (Have you ever held a job, or helped out in a family business, that has taken you behind the scenes? How is fast food prepared? How are cars serviced? How is a baby sat? How is a house constructed?) Detail it step by step, including transitions to clarify the steps.

4. **CRITICAL WRITING.** In attacking the funeral industry, Mitford also, implicitly, attacks the people who pay for and comply with the industry's attitudes and practices. What ASSUMPTIONS does Mitford seem to make about how we ought to deal with death and the dead? (Consider, for instance, her statements about the "docility of Americans, . . . blissfully ignorant" [par. 4] and the funeral director's making "the funeral a real pleasure for everybody concerned" [27].) Write an essay in which you interpret Mitford's assumptions and agree or disagree with them, based on your own reading and experience. If you like, defend the ritual of the funeral, or the mortician's profession, against Mitford's attack.

5. **CONNECTIONS.** Both Jessica Mitford and the author of the following essay, Horace Miner, use process analysis to reveal something about human behavior. How are the two authors' intentions the same or different? What does each want to accomplish with her or his analysis? Use EXAMPLES from both essays to support your claims.

Jessica Mitford on Writing

"Choice of subject is of cardinal importance," declared Jessica Mitford in *Poison Penmanship*. "One does by far one's best work when besotted by and absorbed in the matter at hand." After *The American Way of Death* was published, Mitford received hundreds of letters suggesting alleged rackets that ought to be exposed, and to her surprise, an overwhelming majority of these letters complained about defective and overpriced hearing aids. But Mitford never wrote a book blasting the hearing aid industry. "Somehow, although there may well be need for such an exposé, I could not warm up to hearing aids as a subject for the kind of thorough, intensive, long-range research that would be needed to do an effective job." She once taught a course at Yale on muckraking, with each student choosing a subject to investigate. "Those who tackled hot issues on campus, such as violations of academic freedom or failure to implement affirmative-action hiring policies, turned in some excellent work; but the lad who decided to investigate 'waste in the Yale dining halls' was predictably unable to make much of this trivial topic." (The editors interject: We aren't sure that the topic is necessarily trivial, but obviously not everyone would burn to write about it!)

The hardest problem Mitford faced in writing *The American Way of Death*, she recalled, was doing her factual, step-by-step account of the embalming process. She felt "determined to describe it in all its revolting details, but how to make this subject palatable to the reader?" Her solution was to cast the whole process analysis in the official JARGON of the mortuary industry, drawing on lists of taboo words and their EUPHEMISMS (or acceptable synonyms), as published in the trade journal *Casket & Sunnyside:* "Mr., Mrs., Miss Blank, not corpse or body; preparation room, not morgue; reposing room, not laying-out room. . . ." The story of Mr. Jones thus took shape, and Mitford's use of jargon, she found, added macabre humor to the proceedings.

For Discussion

1. What seem to be Mitford's criteria for an effective essay or book?
2. What is muckraking? Why do you suppose anyone would want to do it?

HORACE MINER

An anthropologist and teacher, HORACE MINER specialized in the cultures of Africa. He was born in 1912 in Saint Paul, Minnesota, and received degrees from the University of Kentucky (BA, 1933) and the University of Chicago (MA, 1935; PhD, 1937). Miner taught anthropology and sociology at Wayne State University and for many years at the University of Michigan, where he was also a researcher in the Museum of Anthropology. He retired from Michigan in 1980. Based on his field research, Miner wrote numerous journal articles and books, including St. Denis: A French-Canadian Parish (1939), Culture and Agriculture (1953), Oasis and Casbah: Algerian Culture and Personality in Change (1960), and The City in Modern Africa (1967). Miner died in 1993.

Body Ritual Among the Nacirema

As an anthropologist, Miner was adept at *ethnography*, studying and reporting on specific cultures. Miner's specialty was African cultures, but here he turned his ethnographer's eye on a North American culture that may seem familiar to you. Like Jessica Mitford in the previous selection, Miner uses process analysis to reveal and also to poke fun at customs. His essay first appeared in the journal *American Anthropologist* in June 1956 and has often been reprinted.

The anthropologist has become so familiar with the diversity of ways in 1 which different peoples behave in similar situations that he is not apt to be surprised by even the most exotic customs. In fact, if all of the logically possible combinations of behavior have not been found somewhere in the world, he is apt to suspect that they must be present in some yet undescribed tribe. This point has, in fact, been expressed with respect to clan organization by Murdock.[1] In this light, the magical beliefs and practices of the Nacirema present such unusual aspects that it seems desirable to describe them as an example of the extremes to which human behavior can go.

Professor Linton first brought the ritual of the Nacirema to the attention 2 of anthropologists twenty years ago, but the culture of this people is still very poorly understood. They are a North American group living in the territory

---

[1] George Peter Murdock (1897–1985) was an American anthropologist who attempted to identify and classify the cultures of the world. — EDS.

between the Canadian Cree, the Yaqui and Tarahumare of Mexico, and the Carib and Arawak of the Antilles. Little is known of their origin, although tradition states that they came from the east. . . .

Nacirema culture is characterized by a highly developed market economy which has evolved in a rich natural habitat. While much of the people's time is devoted to economic pursuits, a large part of the fruits of these labors and a considerable portion of the day are spent in ritual activity. The focus of this activity is the human body, the appearance and health of which loom as a dominant concern in the ethos of the people. While such a concern is certainly not unusual, its ceremonial aspects and associated philosophy are unique.

The fundamental belief underlying the whole system appears to be that the human body is ugly and that its natural tendency is to debility and disease. Incarcerated in such a body, man's only hope is to avert these characteristics through the use of the powerful influences of ritual and ceremony. Every household has one or more shrines devoted to this purpose. The more powerful individuals in the society have several shrines in their houses and, in fact, the opulence of a house is often referred to in terms of the number of such ritual centers it possesses. Most houses are of wattle and daub construction, but the shrine rooms of the more wealthy are walled with stone. Poorer families imitate the rich by applying pottery plaques to their shrine walls.

While each family has at least one such shrine, the rituals associated with it are not family ceremonies but are private and secret. The rites are normally only discussed with children, and then only during the period when they are being initiated into these mysteries. I was able, however, to establish sufficient rapport with the natives to examine these shrines and to have the rituals described to me.

The focal point of the shrine is a box or chest which is built into the wall. In this chest are kept the many charms and magical potions without which no native believes he could live. These preparations are secured from a variety of specialized practitioners. The most powerful of these are the medicine men, whose assistance must be rewarded with substantial gifts. However, the medicine men do not provide the curative potions for their clients, but decide what the ingredients should be and then write them down in an ancient and secret language. This writing is understood only by the medicine men and by the herbalists who, for another gift, provide the required charm.

The charm is not disposed of after it has served its purpose, but is placed in the charm-box of the household shrine. As these magical materials are specific for certain ills, and the real or imagined maladies of the people are many, the charm-box is usually full to overflowing. The magical packets are so numerous that people forget what their purposes were and fear to use them again. While the natives are very vague on this point, we can only assume that the idea in retaining all the old magical materials is that their presence in the charm-box, before which the body rituals are conducted, will in some way protect the worshipper.

Beneath the charm-box is a small font. Each day every member of the family, in succession, enters the shrine room, bows his head before the charm-box, mingles different sorts of holy water in the font, and proceeds with a brief rite of ablution. The holy waters are secured from the Water Temple of the community, where the priests conduct elaborate ceremonies to make the liquid ritually pure.   8

In the hierarchy of magical practitioners, and below the medicine men in prestige, are specialists whose designation is best translated "holy-mouth-men." The Nacirema have an almost pathological horror of and fascination with the mouth, the condition of which is believed to have a supernatural influence on all social relationships. Were it not for the rituals of the mouth, they believe that their teeth would fall out, their gums bleed, their jaws shrink, their friends desert them, and their lovers reject them. They also believe that a strong relationship exists between oral and moral characteristics. For example, there is a ritual ablution of the mouth for children which is supposed to improve their moral fiber.   9

The daily body ritual performed by everyone includes a mouth-rite. Despite the fact that these people are so punctilious about care of the mouth, this rite involves a practice which strikes the uninitiated stranger as revolting. It was reported to me that the ritual consists of inserting a small bundle of hog hairs into the mouth, along with certain magical powders, and then moving the bundle in a highly formalized series of gestures.   10

In addition to the private mouth-rite, the people seek out a holy-mouth-man once or twice a year. These practitioners have an impressive set of paraphernalia, consisting of a variety of augers, awls, probes, and prods. The use of these objects in the exorcism of the evils of the mouth involves almost unbelievable ritual torture of the client. The holy-mouth-man opens the client's mouth and, using the above mentioned tools, enlarges any holes which decay may have created in the teeth. Magical materials are put into these holes. If there are not naturally occurring holes in the teeth, large sections of one or more teeth are gouged out so that the supernatural substance can be applied. In the client's view, the purpose of these ministrations is to arrest decay and to draw friends. The extremely sacred and traditional character of the rite is evident in the fact that the natives return to the holy-mouth-men year after year, despite the fact that their teeth continue to decay.   11

It is to be hoped that, when a thorough study of the Nacirema is made, there will be careful inquiry into the personality structure of these people.   12

One has but to watch the gleam in the eye of a holy-mouth-man, as he jabs an awl into an exposed nerve, to suspect that a certain amount of sadism is involved. If this can be established, a very interesting pattern emerges, for most of the population shows definite masochistic tendencies. It was to these that Professor Linton referred in discussing a distinctive part of the daily body ritual which is performed only by men. This part of the rite involves scraping and lacerating the surface of the face with a sharp instrument. Special women's rites are performed only four times during each lunar month, but what they lack in frequency is made up in barbarity. As part of this ceremony, women bake their heads in small ovens for about an hour. The theoretically interesting point is that what seems to be a preponderantly masochistic people have developed sadistic specialists.

The medicine men have an imposing temple, or *latipso*, in every commu- 13 nity of any size. The more elaborate ceremonies required to treat very sick patients can only be performed at this temple. These ceremonies involve not only the thaumaturge but a permanent group of vestal maidens who move sedately about the temple chambers in distinctive costume and headdress.

The *latipso* ceremonies are so harsh that it is phenomenal that a fair pro- 14 portion of the really sick natives who enter the temple ever recover. Small children whose indoctrination is still incomplete have been known to resist attempts to take them to the temple because "that is where you go to die." Despite this fact, sick adults are not only willing but eager to undergo the pro- tracted ritual purification, if they can afford to do so. No matter how ill the supplicant or how grave the emergency, the guardians of many temples will not admit a client if he cannot give a rich gift to the custodian. Even after one has gained admission and survived the ceremonies, the guardians will not per- mit the neophyte to leave until he makes still another gift.

The supplicant entering the temple is first stripped of all his or her 15 clothes. In everyday life the Nacirema avoids exposure of his body and its nat- ural functions. Bathing and excretory acts are performed only in the secrecy of the household shrine, where they are ritualized as part of the body-rites. Psy- chological shock results from the fact that body secrecy is suddenly lost upon entry into the *latipso*. A man, whose own wife has never seen him in an excre- tory act, suddenly finds himself naked and assisted by a vestal maiden while he performs his natural functions into a sacred vessel. This sort of ceremonial treatment is necessitated by the fact that the excreta are used by a diviner to ascertain the course and nature of the client's sickness. Female clients, on the other hand, find their naked bodies are subjected to the scrutiny, manipula- tion and prodding of the medicine men.

Few supplicants in the temple are well enough to do anything but lie on 16 their hard beds. The daily ceremonies, like the rites of the holy-mouth-men, involve discomfort and torture. With ritual precision, the vestals awaken their miserable charges each dawn and roll them about on their beds of pain while performing ablutions, in the formal movements of which the maidens are highly trained. At other times they insert magic wands in the supplicant's mouth or force him to eat substances which are supposed to be healing. From time to time the medicine men come to their clients and jab magically treated needles into their flesh. The fact that these temple ceremonies may not cure, and may even kill the neophyte, in no way decreases the people's faith in the medicine men.

There remains one other kind of practitioner, known as a "listener." This   17
witchdoctor has the power to exorcise the devils that lodge in the heads of people who have been bewitched. The Nacirema believe that parents bewitch their own children. Mothers are particularly suspected of putting a curse on children while teaching them the secret body rituals. The counter-magic of the witchdoctor is unusual in its lack of ritual. The patient simply tells the "listener" all his troubles and fears, beginning with the earliest difficulties he can remember. The memory displayed by the Nacirema in these exorcism sessions is truly remarkable. It is not uncommon for the patient to bemoan the rejection he felt upon being weaned as a babe, and a few individuals even see their troubles going back to the traumatic effects of their own birth.

In conclusion, mention must be made of certain practices which have   18
their base in native esthetics but which depend upon the pervasive aversion to the natural body and its functions. There are ritual fasts to make fat people thin and ceremonial feasts to make thin people fat. Still other rites are used to make women's breasts larger if they are small, and smaller if they are large. General dissatisfaction with breast shape is symbolized in the fact that the ideal form is virtually outside the range of human variation. A few women afflicted with almost inhuman hyper-mammary development are so idolized that they make a handsome living by simply going from village to village and permitting the natives to stare at them for a fee.

Reference has already been made to the fact that excretory functions are   19
ritualized, routinized, and relegated to secrecy. Natural reproductive functions are similarly distorted. Intercourse is taboo as a topic and scheduled as an act. Efforts are made to avoid pregnancy by the use of magical materials or by limiting intercourse to certain phases of the moon. Conception is actually very infrequent. When pregnant, women dress so as to hide their condition. Parturition takes place in secret, without friends or relatives to assist, and the majority of women do not nurse their infants.

Our review of the ritual life of the Nacirema has certainly shown them to   20
be a magic-ridden people. It is hard to understand how they have managed to exist so long under the burdens which they have imposed upon themselves.

But even such exotic customs as these take on real meaning when they are viewed with the insight provided by Malinowski[2] when he wrote:

> Looking from far and above, from our high places of safety in the developed civilization, it is easy to see all the crudity and irrelevance of magic. But without its power and guidance early man could not have mastered his practical difficulties as he has done, nor could man have advanced to the higher stages of civilization.

*For a reading quiz, sources on Horace Miner, and annotated links to further readings on body rituals, visit **bedfordstmartins.com/thebedfordreader**.*

Journal Writing

Think about the many little "rituals" you perform regularly: walking the dog, going to the movies or out to clubs with friends, washing dishes or your car. In your journal, write out all the steps of two or three of these routines, in chronological order and in as much detail as you can. (To take your journal writing further, see "From Journal to Essay" on the next page.)

Questions on Meaning

1. At what point did you realize what Miner's true subject is? What tipped you off? Did you see the big hint in the spelling of *Nacirema*?
2. One of Miner's purposes is clearly to amuse readers through social SATIRE. But what other purposes does he seem to have?
3. What stereotype does Miner exploit for its humor at the end of paragraph 6?
4. At the beginning and end of the essay, Miner refers to the Nacirema as having "magical beliefs and practices" (par. 1) and as being "magic-ridden" (20). What kinds of cultures are usually described in this way? Why does Miner use such terms to describe the Nacirema?

Questions on Writing Strategy

1. Miner explains several processes under the umbrella of "body rituals." What are these processes in Americanese—that is, in the words we commonly use for them?

---

[2] Bronislaw Malinowski (1884–1942) was a Polish-born British anthropologist who saw customs in terms of their functions in a culture.—EDS.

2. What is the EFFECT of Miner's opening paragraph? What do the academic TONE and mention of the anthropologist Murdock's work accomplish?
3. This essay originally appeared in *American Anthropologist,* a serious academic journal. In what ways are anthropologists the perfect AUDIENCE for Miner's humor? How do you respond differently to this essay than you think an anthropologist would?
4. This essay was first published more than four decades ago. In what ways does it seem dated? What parts of it still seem fresh?
5. **OTHER METHODS.** Miner's humor involves DEFINITIONS of things that ordinarily need no defining: For instance, he refers to a toothbrush as a "small bundle of hog hairs" (par. 10). Find other examples of bizarre definitions of ordinary things. Other than humor, what is the effect of such definitions?

Questions on Language

1. Why do you think Miner chose the name "Nacirema" for his subjects? What associations does this name call up for you?
2. Explain the IRONY of the last paragraph.
3. Make sure you know the definitions of the following words, including some that are specific to the discipline of anthropology: ethos (par. 3); debility, incarcerated, opulence, wattle and daub (4); curative (6); font, ablution (8); hierarchy (9); punctilious (10); augers, awls, gouged, ministrations (11); sadism, masochistic, lacerating, preponderantly (12); thaumaturge (13); indoctrination, supplicant, neophyte (14); excretory, vestal, vessel, excreta, diviner (15); esthetics (18); parturition (19).

Suggestions for Writing

1. **FROM JOURNAL TO ESSAY.** Imagine that you are an observer from another planet reporting back to your authorities on Earth customs. Write them a letter describing the processes you have detailed in your journal. Remember, you don't understand the language of these earthlings and have no names for the processes you are writing about.
2. Miner satirizes our society's obsession with physical appearance, our hypochondria, our shame over our bodies, our overdependence on psychoanalysis—all in 1956. Evaluate the relevance of this essay today, considering where the concerns with our bodies have brought us. Do you think we are better or worse off, physically and mentally, than we were a hundred or even forty years ago? What's better? What's worse? Be specific.
3. Like other social scientists, anthropologists work under a code of ethics that specifies how they may and may not treat the people they are studying. Read about this subject, perhaps starting with the ethics page of the American Anthropological Association (*aaanet.org/committees/ethics/ethics.htm*) or with the anthropology department at your school. Then write an essay in which you explain the ethical obligations of anthropologists.
4. **CRITICAL WRITING.** Anthropologists have sometimes been criticized for turning the people they study into weird and mysterious "others." How does Miner man-

age to criticize anthropology while working within it, on its own terms, and using its own language and methodology? Focus in particular on the implications of the last paragraph.

5. **CONNECTIONS.** Read or reread Jessica Mitford's "Behind the Formaldehyde Curtain" (p. 305). Taken together, what do Miner's and Mitford's essays say about the importance of the body in our culture? Write an essay either defending or criticizing Americans' obsession with the way they look.

DANIEL OROZCO

DANIEL OROZCO was born in 1957 and grew up in San Francisco. After graduating from Stanford University in 1979, he held temporary positions doing clerical work while studying writing at San Francisco State University and rediscovering a passion for literature. He received an MFA in writing from the University of Washington, was a creative-writing fellow at Stanford, and currently teaches at the University of Idaho. Orozco's stories have appeared in *Harper's, Story,* and other magazines and have been chosen for *The Best American Short Stories* and the *Pushcart Prize Anthology.* Orozco also writes a regular column for the *San Francisco Chronicle Book Review.*

Orientation

Drawing on his experience as an office temp, Orozco created this story in which an employee introduces a newcomer to a company's procedures and people. First published in *Seattle Review* in 1994, "Orientation" appeared in *The Best American Short Stories 1995.* It has also been read on public radio's *This American Life* and even adapted as a dance piece.

Those are the offices and these are the cubicles. That's my cubicle there, and this is your cubicle. This is your phone. Never answer your phone. Let the Voicemail System answer it. This is your Voicemail System Manual. There are no personal phone calls allowed. We do, however, allow for emergencies. If you must make an emergency phone call, ask your supervisor first. If you can't find your supervisor, ask Phillip Spiers, who sits over there. He'll check with Clarissa Nicks, who sits over there. If you make an emergency phone call without asking, you may be let go.

These are your IN and OUT boxes. All the forms in your IN box must be logged in by the date shown in the upper left-hand corner, initialed by you in the upper right-hand corner, and distributed to the Processing Analyst whose name is numerically coded in the lower left-hand corner. The lower right-hand corner is left blank. Here's your Processing Analyst Numerical Code Index. And here's your Forms Processing Procedures Manual.

You must pace your work. What do I mean? I'm glad you asked that. We pace our work according to the eight-hour workday. If you have twelve hours of work in your IN box, for example, you must compress that work into the eight-hour day. If you have one hour of work in your IN box, you must expand that work to fill the eight-hour day. That was a good question. Feel free to ask questions. Ask too many questions, however, and you may be let go.

That is our receptionist. She is a temp. We go through receptionists here. They quit with alarming frequency. Be polite and civil to the temps. Learn

1

2

3

4

their names, and invite them to lunch occasionally. But don't get close to them, as it only makes it more difficult when they leave. And they always leave. You can be sure of that.

The men's room is over there. The women's room is over there. John LaFountaine, who sits over there, uses the women's room occasionally. He says it is accidental. We know better, but we let it pass. John LaFountaine is harmless, his forays into the forbidden territory of the women's room simply a benign thrill, a faint blip on the dull flat line of his life.

Russell Nash, who sits in the cubicle to your left, is in love with Amanda Pierce, who sits in the cubicle to your right. They ride the same bus together after work. For Amanda Pierce, it is just a tedious bus ride made less tedious by the idle nattering of Russell Nash. But for Russell Nash, it is the highlight of his day. It is the highlight of his life. Russell Nash has put on forty pounds, and grows fatter with each passing month, nibbling on chips and cookies while peeking glumly over the partitions at Amanda Pierce, and gorging himself at home on cold pizza and ice cream while watching adult videos on TV.

Amanda Pierce, in the cubicle to your right, has a six-year-old son named Jamie, who is autistic. Her cubicle is plastered from top to bottom with the boy's crayon artwork—sheet after sheet of precisely drawn concentric circles and ellipses, in black and yellow. She rotates them every other Friday. Be sure to comment on them. Amanda Pierce also has a husband, who is a lawyer. He subjects her to an escalating array of painful and humiliating sex games, to which Amanda Pierce reluctantly submits. She comes to work exhausted and freshly wounded each morning, wincing from the abrasions on her breasts, or the bruises on her abdomen, or the second-degree burns on the backs of her thighs.

But we're not supposed to know any of this. Do not let on. If you let on, you may be let go.

Amanda Pierce, who tolerates Russell Nash, is in love with Albert Bosch, whose office is over there. Albert Bosch, who only dimly registers Amanda Pierce's existence, has eyes only for Ellie Tapper, who sits over there. Ellie Tapper, who hates Albert Bosch, would walk through fire for Curtis Lance. But Curtis Lance hates Ellie Tapper. Isn't the world a funny place? Not in the ha-ha sense, of course.

Anika Bloom sits in that cubicle. Last year, while reviewing quarterly reports in a meeting with Barry Hacker, Anika Bloom's left palm began to bleed. She fell into a trance, stared into her hand, and told Barry Hacker when and how his wife would die. We laughed it off. She was, after all, a new employee. But Barry Hacker's wife is dead. So unless you want to know exactly when and how you'll die, never talk to Anika Bloom.

Colin Heavey sits in that cubicle over there. He was new once, just like you. We warned him about Anika Bloom. But at last year's Christmas Potluck, he felt sorry for her when he saw that no one was talking to her. Colin Heavey brought her a drink. He hasn't been himself since. Colin Heavey is doomed. There's nothing he can do about it, and we are powerless to help him. Stay away from Colin Heavey. Never give any of your work to him. If he asks to do something, tell him you have to check with me. If he asks again, tell him I haven't gotten back to you.

This is the Fire Exit. There are several on this floor, and they are marked accordingly. We have a Floor Evacuation Review every three months, and an Escape Route Quiz once a month. We have our Biannual Fire Drill twice a year, and our Annual Earthquake Drill once a year. These are precautions only. These things never happen. 12

For your information, we have a comprehensive health plan. Any catastrophic illness, any unforeseen tragedy is completely covered. All dependents are completely covered. Larry Bagdikian, who sits over there, has six daughters. If anything were to happen to any of his girls, or to all of them, if all six were to simultaneously fall victim to illness or injury—stricken with a hideous degenerative muscle disease or some rare toxic blood disorder, sprayed with semiautomatic gunfire while on a class field trip, or attacked in their bunk beds by some prowling nocturnal lunatic—if any of this were to pass, Larry's girls would all be taken care of. Larry Bagdikian would not have to pay one dime. He would have nothing to worry about. 13

We also have a generous vacation and sick leave policy. We have an excellent disability insurance plan. We have a stable and profitable pension fund. We get group discounts for the symphony, and block seating at the ballpark. We get commuter ticket books for the bridge. We have Direct Deposit. We are all members of Costco. 14

This is our kitchenette. And this, this is our Mr. Coffee. We have a coffee pool, into which we each pay two dollars a week for coffee, filters, sugar, and CoffeeMate. If you prefer Cremora or half-and-half to CoffeeMate, there is a special pool for three dollars a week. If you prefer Sweet 'n Low to sugar, there is a special pool for two-fifty a week. We do not do decaf. You are allowed to join the coffee pool of your choice, but you are not allowed to touch the Mr. Coffee. 15

This is the microwave oven. You are allowed to *heat* food in the microwave oven. You are not, however, allowed to *cook* food in the microwave oven. 16

We get one hour for lunch. We also get one fifteen-minute break in the morning, and one fifteen-minute break in the afternoon. Always take your breaks. If you skip a break, it is gone forever. For your information, your break is a privilege, not a right. If you abuse the break policy, we are authorized to rescind your breaks. Lunch, however, is a right, not a privilege. If you abuse the lunch policy, our hands will be tied, and we will be forced to look the other way. We will not enjoy that. 17

This is the refrigerator. You may put your lunch in it. Barry Hacker, who   18
sits over there, steals food from this refrigerator. His petty theft is an outlet for
his grief. Last New Year's Eve, while kissing his wife, a blood vessel burst in her
brain. Barry Hacker's wife was two months pregnant at the time, and lingered
in a coma for half a year before dying. It was a tragic loss for Barry Hacker. He
hasn't been himself since. Barry Hacker's wife was a beautiful woman. She was
also completely covered. Barry Hacker did not have to pay one dime. But his
dead wife haunts him. She haunts all of us. We have seen her, reflected in the
monitors of our computers, moving past our cubicles. We have seen the dim
shadow of her face in our photocopies. She pencils herself in in the receptionist's appointment book, with the notation: To see Barry Hacker. She has
left messages in the receptionist's Voicemail box, messages garbled by the electronic chirrups and buzzes in the phone line, her voice echoing from an
immense distance within the ambient hum. But the voice is hers. And
beneath her voice, beneath the tidal *whoosh* of static and hiss, the gurgling
and crying of a baby can be heard.

In any case, if you bring a lunch, put a little something extra in the bag for   19
Barry Hacker. We have four Barrys in this office. Isn't that a coincidence?

This is Matthew Payne's office. He is our Unit Manager, and his door is   20
always closed. We have never seen him, and you will never see him. But he is
here. You can be sure of that. He is all around us.

This is the Custodian's Closet. You have no business in the Custodian's   21
Closet.

And this, this is our Supplies Cabinet. If you need supplies, see Curtis   22
Lance. He will log you in on the Supplies Cabinet Authorization Log, then
give you a Supplies Authorization Slip. Present your pink copy of the Supplies
Authorization Slip to Ellie Tapper. She will log you in on the Supplies Cabinet Key Log, then give you the key. Because the Supplies Cabinet is located
outside the Unit Manager's office, you must be very quiet. Gather your supplies quietly. The Supplies Cabinet is divided into four sections. Section One
contains letterhead stationery, blank paper and envelopes, memo and note
pads, and so on. Section Two contains pens and pencils and typewriter and
printer ribbons, and the like. In Section Three we have erasers, correction fluids, transparent tapes, glue sticks, et cetera. And in Section Four we have
paper clips and push pins and scissors and razor blades. And here are the spare
blades for the shredder. Do not touch the shredder, which is located over
there. The shredder is of no concern to you.

Gwendolyn Stich sits in that office there. She is crazy about penguins, and   23
collects penguin knickknacks: penguin posters and coffee mugs and stationery, penguin stuffed animals, penguin jewelry, penguin sweaters and T-shirts
and socks. She has a pair of penguin fuzzy slippers she wears when working late

at the office. She has a tape cassette of penguin sounds which she listens to for relaxation. Her favorite colors are black and white. She has personalized license plates that read PEN GWEN. Every morning, she passes through all the cubicles to wish each of us a *good* morning. She brings Danish on Wednesdays for Hump Day morning break, and doughnuts on Fridays for TGIF afternoon break. She organizes the Annual Christmas Potluck, and is in charge of the Birthday List. Gwendolyn Stich's door is always open to all of us. She will always lend an ear, and put in a good word for you; she will always give you a hand, or the shirt off her back, or a shoulder to cry on. Because her door is always open, she hides and cries in a stall in the women's room. And John LaFountaine—who, enthralled when a woman enters, sits quietly in his stall with his knees to his chest—John LaFountaine has heard her vomiting in there. We have come upon Gwendolyn Stich huddled in the stairwell, shivering in the updraft, sipping a Diet Mr. Pibb and hugging her knees. She does not let any of this interfere with her work. If it interfered with her work, she might have to be let go.

Kevin Howard sits in that cubicle over there. He is a serial killer, the one they call the Carpet Cutter, responsible for the mutilations across town. We're not supposed to know that, so do not let on. Don't worry. His compulsion inflicts itself on strangers only, and the routine established is elaborate and unwavering. The victim must be a white male, a young adult no older than thirty, heavyset, with dark hair and eyes, and the like. The victim must be chosen at random, before sunset, from a public place; the victim is followed home, and must put up a struggle; et cetera. The carnage inflicted is precise: the angle and direction of the incisions; the layering of skin and muscle tissue; the rearrangement of the visceral organs; and so on. Kevin Howard does not let any of this interfere with his work. He is, in fact, our fastest typist. He types as if he were on fire. He has a secret crush on Gwendolyn Stich, and leaves a red-foil-wrapped Hershey's Kiss on her desk every afternoon. But he hates Anika Bloom, and keeps well away from her. In his presence, she has uncontrollable fits of shaking and trembling. Her left palm does not stop bleeding. 24

In any case, when Kevin Howard gets caught, act surprised. Say that he seemed like a nice person, a bit of a loner, perhaps, but always quiet and polite. 25

This is the photocopier room. And this, this is our view. It faces southwest. West is down there, toward the water. North is back there. Because we are on the seventeenth floor, we are afforded a magnificent view. Isn't it beautiful? It overlooks the park, where the tops of those trees are. You can see a segment of the bay between those two buildings there. You can see the sun set in the gap between those two buildings over there. You can see this building reflected in the glass panels of that building across the way. There. See? That's 26 you, waving. And look there. There's Anika Bloom in the kitchenette, waving back.

Enjoy this view while photocopying. If you have problems with the photocopier, see Russell Nash. If you have any questions, ask your supervisor. If you can't find your supervisor, ask Phillip Spiers. He sits over there. He'll check with Clarissa Nicks. She sits over there. If you can't find them, feel free to ask me. That's my cubicle. I sit in there. 27

---

*For a reading quiz, sources on Daniel Orozco, and annotated links to further readings on office culture, visit **bedfordstmartins.com/thebedfordreader**.*

Journal Writing

Think of a situation in which you had to learn new procedures, customs, or people. You may have had a lot of help, as in a training program, or you may have had to go it alone. In your journal write down what you recall most vividly about the process of your orientation. (To take your journal writing further, see "From Journal to Essay" on the next page.)

Questions on Meaning

1. This story seems to be a SATIRE, but what exactly is being satirized?
2. Where does the story's speaker provide information like that in a true job orientation? information that seems appropriate but exaggerated? information that is inappropriate for an orientation, even outrageous? What does this mix of information add to the story?
3. What view of the human condition does Orozco seem to offer in this story?

Questions on Writing Strategy

1. What is the EFFECT of the last paragraph's echo of the first paragraph?
2. What other repetition do you notice in paragraphs 1, 3, 8, and 23? What is its effect?
3. What parts of this story illustrate process analysis?
4. **OTHER METHODS.** What do the EXAMPLES in paragraph 13 suggest about the speaker's interests and attitudes?

Questions on Language

1. How would you describe the speaker's overall TONE? What does this tone contribute to the effect of the story?
2. In paragraph 18 the speaker's tone shifts rather dramatically. What is the shift? How do you account for it?
3. Where does Orozco satirize the language of bureaucracy most obviously?
4. Consult a dictionary if you are uncertain of the meaning of any of the following: cubicles (par. 1); forays, benign (5); autistic, abrasions (7); degenerative, nocturnal (13); rescind (17); TGIF, enthralled (23).

Suggestions for Writing

1. **FROM JOURNAL TO ESSAY.** Compose an essay that explains the process of orientation you wrote about in your journal. Depending on your experience, you may present the process in formal stages or relate what happened in a NARRATIVE.
2. Expand your knowledge about working in an office by interviewing friends and family members who have done so. (If you have worked in an office, add your information to the others'.) Ask about experiences with supervisors, coworkers, procedures, and equipment. In an essay SYNTHESIZE what you discover. What do offices seem to have in common, and how do they differ?
3. **CRITICAL WRITING.** Analyze how Orozco structures his story. How does the speaker move from one stop on the tour to the next? Does the story seem to build in a particular way? What does the organization contribute to the story's effect?
4. **CONNECTIONS.** Both Orozco in this story and Don DeLillo in the story "Videotape" (p. 466) create speakers who address a *you* directly. In an essay consider the similarities and differences between the two authors' speakers and how they seem to conceive of their listeners.

Daniel Orozco on Writing

In an interview with Will Allison for *Novel and Short Story Writer's Market*, Orozco talks about taking his time while writing. "My slowness as a writer seems to be part of a deliberate composition process," he says. "Before I actually begin writing a story, it goes through what I call Gestation and Frustration. Gestation: A story for me begins as an image or situation knocking around in my head, followed by months of notes jotted on scraps of paper, or entered into a file on my PC. This is followed finally by attempts at writing a first draft. Then, Frustration: I can set an unfinished draft aside for anywhere from days to months, during which time I do some reading or research on the story—a great way to avoid actually writing it—or I research or write another story. Eventually, I get back to finishing the first draft, and then I get to revising."

Most of Orozco's process is dedicated to revision, a stage he enjoys more than the initial drafting even though it can be more difficult. In 2001 Orozco published a story that he had worked on intermittently since 1978. "Orientation," which took eleven months, was, Orozco says, "the fastest I'd ever written anything." Asked whether his slow writing process bothers him, Orozco admits, "I used to bitch and moan about . . . how long it would take me to squeeze out a story." But he's learned to accept his writing process as something he can't—and wouldn't—change: "Now I embrace it as simply the way I write stories, stories that I am happy with. I used to wish I wrote faster, but I don't anymore. It's like wishing I were taller—it just ain't gonna happen."

For Discussion

1. Why won't Orozco change his writing process? What does it do for him that another process might not?
2. Do you consider yourself a particularly slow or fast writer? Do you have trouble getting down the first draft, or do you find it more difficult to revise?

ADDITIONAL WRITING TOPICS

Process Analysis

1. Write a *directive* process analysis (a "how-to" essay) in which, drawing on your own knowledge, you instruct someone in doing or making something. Divide the process into steps, and be sure to detail each step thoroughly. Some possible subjects (any of which may be modified or narrowed):

   How to find games (or another kind of software) on the Internet
   How to enlist people's confidence
   How to bake bread
   How to meditate
   How to teach a child to swim
   How to select a science fiction novel
   How to drive a car in snow or rain
   How to prepare yourself to take an intelligence test
   How to compose a photograph
   How to judge cattle
   How to buy a used motorcycle
   How to enjoy an opera
   How to organize your own rock group
   How to eat an artichoke
   How to groom a horse
   How to bellydance
   How to make a movie or videotape
   How to build (or fly) a kite
   How to start weight training
   How to aid a person who is choking
   How to behave on a first date
   How to get your own way
   How to kick a habit
   How to lose weight
   How to win at poker
   How to make an effective protest or complaint

   Or, if you don't like any of those topics, what else do you know that others might care to learn from you?

2. Step by step, working in chronological order, write a careful *informative* analysis of any one of the following processes. (This is not to be a "how-to" essay, but an essay that explains how something works or happens.) Make use of DESCRIPTION wherever necessary, and be sure to include frequent TRANSITIONS. If one of these topics gives you a better idea for a paper, go with your own subject.

   How a student is processed during orientation or registration
   How the student newspaper gets published
   How a particular Web search engine works

How a professional umpire (or an acupuncturist, or some other professional) does his or her job

How an amplifier (or other stereo component) works

How an air conditioner (or other household appliance) works

How birds teach their young (or some other process in the natural world: how sharks feed, how a snake swallows an egg, how the human liver works)

How police control crowds

How people usually make up their minds when shopping for new cars (or new clothes)

3. Write a directive process analysis in which you use a light TONE. Although you need not take your subject in deadly earnest, your humor will probably be effective only if you take the method of process analysis seriously. Make clear each stage of the process and explain it in sufficient detail. Possible topics:

How to get through the month of November (or March)

How to flunk out of college swiftly and efficiently

How to outwit a pinball machine

How to choose a mate

How to go broke

How to sell something that nobody wants

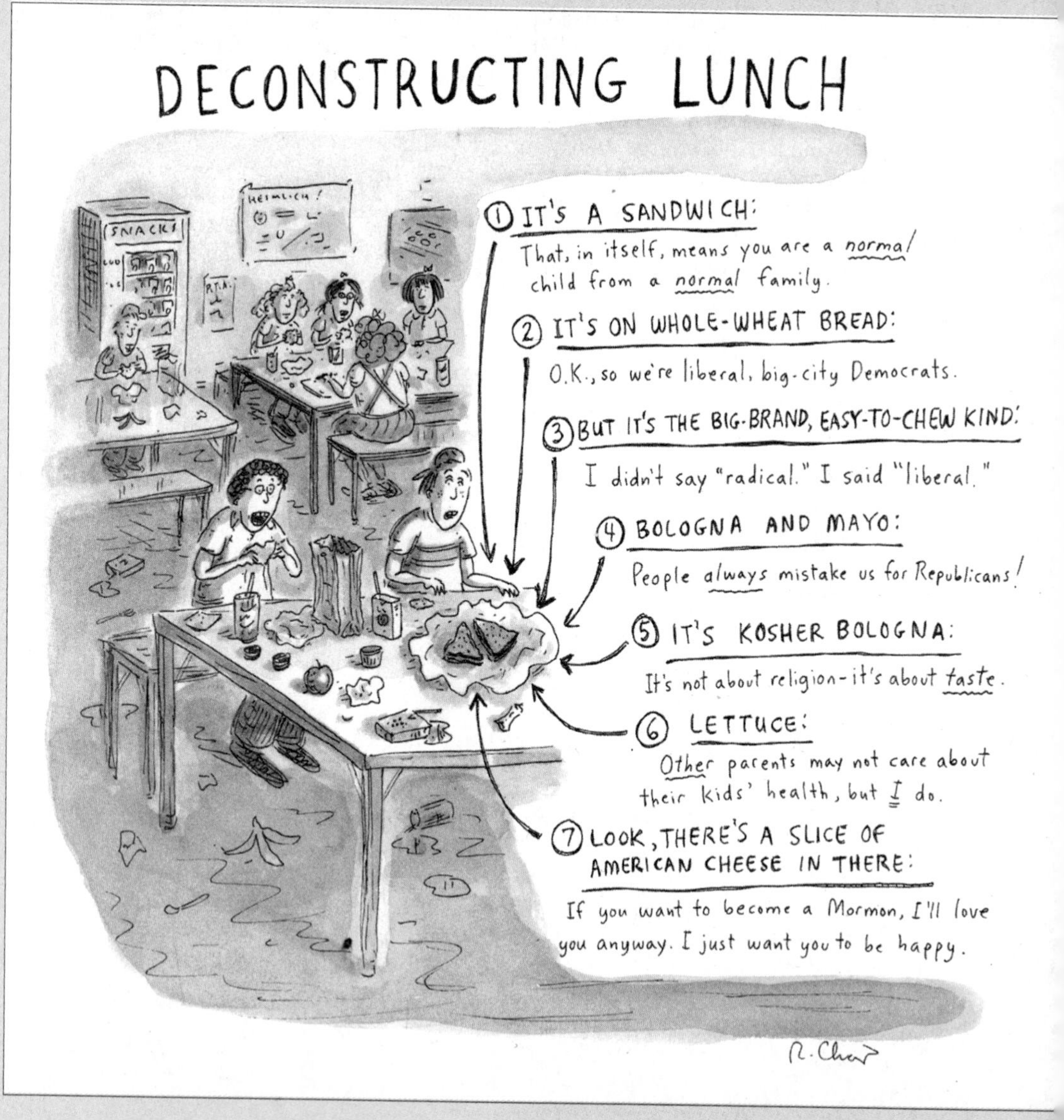
DECONSTRUCTING LUNCH
SNACKS
HEIMLICH!
① IT'S A SANDWICH:
That, in itself, means you are a normal child from a normal family.
② IT'S ON WHOLE-WHEAT BREAD:
O.K., so we're liberal, big-city Democrats.
③ BUT IT'S THE BIG-BRAND, EASY-TO-CHEW KIND:
I didn't say "radical." I said "liberal."
④ BOLOGNA AND MAYO:
People always mistake us for Republicans!
⑤ IT'S KOSHER BOLOGNA:
It's not about religion—it's about taste.
⑥ LETTUCE:
Other parents may not care about their kids' health, but I do.
⑦ LOOK, THERE'S A SLICE OF AMERICAN CHEESE IN THERE:
If you want to become a Mormon, I'll love you anyway. I just want you to be happy.

9

DIVISION OR ANALYSIS

Slicing into Parts

Division or analysis in a cartoon

The cartoonist Roz Chast is well known for witty and percep-tive comments on the everyday, made through words and simple, almost childlike drawings. Dividing or analyzing, this cartoon identifies the elements of a boy's sandwich to discover what the elements can tell about the values and politics of the parent who made the sandwich. The title, "Deconstructing Lunch," refers to a type of analysis that focuses on the multiple meanings of the subject and especially its internal contradic-tions. Summarize what the sandwich reveals about the boy's parent. What contradictions do you spot in his or her values or politics? What might Chast be saying more generally about food choices?

THE METHOD

A chemist working for a soft-drink company is asked to improve on a competitor's product, Orange Quench. (In Chap. 8, the same chemist was working on a different part of the same problem.) To do the job, the chemist first has to figure out what's in the drink. She smells the stuff and tastes it. Then she tests a sample chemically to discover the actual ingredients: water, corn syrup, citric acid, sodium benzoate, coloring. Methodically, the chemist has performed DIVISION or ANALYSIS: She has separated the beverage into its components. Orange Quench stands revealed, understood, ready to be bettered.

Division or analysis (the terms are interchangeable) is a key skill in learning and in life. It is an instrument allowing you to slice a large and complicated subject into smaller parts that you can grasp and relate to one another. With analysis you comprehend — and communicate — the structure of things. And when it works, you find in the parts an idea or conclusion about the subject that makes it clearer, truer, more comprehensive, or more vivid than before you started.

If you have worked with the previous two chapters, you have already used division or analysis in explaining a process (Chap. 8) and in comparing and contrasting (Chap. 7). To make a better Orange Quench (a process), the chemist might prepare a recipe that divides the process into separate steps or actions ("First, boil a gallon of water . . ."). When the batch was done, she might taste-test the two drinks, analyzing and then comparing their orange flavor, sweetness, and acidity. As you'll see in following chapters, too, division or analysis figures in all the other methods of developing ideas, for it is basic to any concerted thought, explanation, or evaluation.

Kinds of Division or Analysis

Although division or analysis always works the same way — separating a whole, singular subject into its elements, slicing it into parts — the method can be more or less difficult depending on how unfamiliar, complex, and abstract the subject is. Obviously, it's going to be much easier to analyze a chicken (wings, legs, thighs . . .) than a poem by T. S. Eliot (this image, that allusion . . .), easier to analyze the structure of a small business than that of a multinational conglomerate. Just about any subject *can* by analyzed and will be the clearer for it. In "I Want a Wife," an essay in this chapter, Judy Brady divides the role of a wife into its various functions or services. In an essay called "Teacher" from his book *Pot Shots at Poetry* (1980), Robert Francis divides the knowledge of poetry he imparted to his class into six pie sections. The first slice is what he told his students that they knew already.

The second slice is what I told them that they could have found out just as well or better from books. What, for instance, is a sestina?

The third slice is what I told them that they refused to accept. I could see it on their faces, and later I saw the evidence in their writing.

The fourth slice is what I told them that they were willing to accept and may have thought they accepted but couldn't accept since they couldn't fully understand. This also I saw in their faces and in their work. Here, no doubt, I was mostly to blame.

The fifth slice is what I told them that they discounted as whimsy or something simply to fill up time. After all, I was being paid to talk.

The sixth slice is what I didn't tell them, for I didn't try to tell them all I knew. Deliberately I kept back something—a few professional secrets, a magic formula or two.

There are always multiple ways to divide or analyze a subject, just as there are many ways to slice a pie. Francis could have divided his knowledge of poetry into knowledge of rhyme, knowledge of meter, knowledge of imagery, and so forth—basically following the components of a poem. In other words, the outcome of an analysis depends on the rule or principle used to do the slicing. This fact accounts for some of the differences among academic disciplines: A psychologist, say, may look at the individual person primarily as a bundle of drives and needs, whereas a sociologist may emphasize the individual's roles in society. Even within disciplines, different factions analyze differently, using different principles of division or analysis. Some psychologists are interested mainly in thought, others mainly in behavior; some psychologists focus mainly on emotional development, others mainly on moral development.

Analysis and Critical Thinking

Analysis plays a fundamental role in CRITICAL THINKING, READING, and WRITING, topics discussed in Chapter 1 (pp. 18–20 and 27–30). In fact, *analysis* and *criticism* are deeply related: The first comes from a Greek word meaning "to undo," the second from a Greek word meaning "to separate."

Critical thinking, reading, and writing go beneath the surface of the object, word, image, or whatever the subject is. When you work critically, you divide the subject into its elements, INFER the buried meanings and ASSUMPTIONS that define its essence, and SYNTHESIZE the parts into a new whole. Say a campaign brochure quotes a candidate as favoring "reasonable government expenditures on reasonable highway projects." The candidate will support new roads, right? Wrong. As a critical reader of the brochure, you quickly sense something fishy in the use (twice) of *reasonable*. As an informed reader, you know (or find out) that the candidate has consistently opposed new roads, so the chances of her finding a highway project "reasonable" are slim. At the same time, her stand has been unpopular, so of course she wants to seem "reasonable" on the issue. Read critically, then, a campaign statement that seems to offer mild support for highways is actually a slippery evasion of any such commitment.

Analysis (a convenient term for the overlapping operations of analysis, inference, and synthesis) is very useful for exposing such evasiveness, but that isn't its only function. If you've read this far in this book, you've already done quite a bit of analytical/critical thinking as you read and analyzed the selections. The method will also help you understand a sculpture, perceive the importance of a case study in sociology, or form a response to an environmental impact report. And the method can be invaluable for straight thinking about popular culture, from TV to toys, as two selections in this chapter demonstrate.

THE PROCESS

Subjects and Theses

Keep an eye out for writing assignments requiring division or analysis — in college and work, they won't be few or hard to find. They will probably include the word *analyze* or a word implying analysis such as *evaluate, examine, explore, interpret, discuss,* or *criticize.* Any time you spot such a term, you know your job is to separate the subject into its elements, to infer their meanings, to explore the relations among them, and to draw a conclusion about the subject.

Almost any coherent entity — object, person, place, concept — is a fit subject for analysis *if* the analysis will add to the subject's meaning or significance. Little is deadlier than the rote analytical exercise that leaves the parts neatly dissected and the subject comatose on the page. As a writer, you have to animate the subject, and that means finding your interest. What about your subject seems curious? What's appealing? or mysterious? or awful? And what will be your PURPOSE in writing about the subject: Do you simply want to explain it, or do you want to argue for or against it?

Such questions can help you find the principle or framework you will use to divide the subject into parts. (As we mentioned before, there's more than one way to slice most subjects.) Say you're contemplating a hunk of bronze in the park. Why do you like the sculpture, or why don't you? What elements of its creation and physical form make it art? What is the point of such public art? What does this sculpture do to this park, or vice versa? Any of these questions could suggest a slant on the subject, a framework for analysis, and a purpose for writing, getting your analysis moving.

Finding your principle of analysis will lead you to your essay's THESIS as well—the main point you want to make about your subject. Expressed in a THESIS STATEMENT, this idea will help keep you focused and help your readers see your subject as a whole rather than a bundle of parts. Here is the thesis statement in one of this chapter's selections:

> [Children's books that ignore] men who share equally in raising their children and show nothing but part-time or no-time fathers are only going to create yet another generation of men who have been told since boyhood— albeit subtly—that mothers are the truer parents and that fathers play, at best, a secondary role in the home.
> —Armin A. Brott, "Not All Men Are Sly Foxes"

See the next page for more on the thesis statement in analysis.

In developing an essay by analysis, having an outline at your elbow can be a help. You don't want to overlook any parts or elements that should be included in your framework. (You needn't mention every feature in your final essay or give them all equal treatment, but any omissions or variations should be conscious.) And you want to use your framework consistently, not switching carelessly (and confusingly) from, say, the form of the sculpture to the cost of public art. In writing her brief essay "I Want a Wife," Judy Brady must have needed an outline to work out carefully the different activities of a wife, so that she covered them all and clearly distinguished them.

Evidence

Making a valid analysis is chiefly a matter of giving your subject thought, but for the result to seem useful and convincing to your readers, it will have to refer to the concrete world. The method requires not only cogitation, but open eyes and a willingness to provide EVIDENCE. The nature of the evidence will depend entirely on what you are analyzing—physical details for a sculpture, quotations for a poem, financial data for a business case study, statistics for a psychology case study, and so forth. The idea is to supply enough evidence to justify and support your particular slant on the subject.

A final caution: It's possible to get carried away with one's own analysis, to become so enamored of the details that the subject itself becomes dim or distorted. You can avoid this danger by keeping the subject literally in front of you as you work (or at least imagining it vividly) and by maintaining an outline. It often helps to reassemble your subject at the end of the essay, placing it in a larger context, speculating on its influence, or affirming its significance.

Division or Analysis

By the end of the essay, your subject must be a coherent whole truly represented by your analysis, not twisted, inflated, or obliterated. The reader should be intrigued by your subject, yes, but also able to recognize it on the street.

FOCUS ON THE THESIS STATEMENT

Readers will have an easier time following your analysis—and will more likely appreciate it—if they have a hook on which to hang the details. Your thesis statement can be that hook if you use it to establish your framework, your principle of analysis.

In each of the following pairs, the first statement is too vague to work as a hook: It conveys the writer's general opinion but not its basis. Each revised statement clarifies the point.

VAGUE　The sculpture is a beautiful piece of work.

REVISED　Although it may not be obvious at first, this smooth bronze sculpture represents the city dweller's relationship with nature.

VAGUE　The sculpture is a waste of money.

REVISED　The huge bronze sculpture in the middle of McBean Park demonstrates that so-called public art may actually undermine the public interest.

A well-focused thesis statement can help you as well, because it gives you a yardstick to judge how complete, consistent, and supportive your analysis is. Don't be discouraged, though, if your thesis statement doesn't come to you until *after* you've written a first draft and had a chance to discover your interest. Writing about your subject may be the best way for you to find its meaning and significance.

CHECKLIST FOR REVISING A DIVISION OR ANALYSIS

✔ **PRINCIPLE OF ANALYSIS AND THESIS.** What is your particular slant on your subject, the rule or principle you have used to divide your subject into its elements? Do you specify it in your thesis statement?

✔ **COMPLETENESS.** Have you considered all the subject's elements required by your principle of analysis?

✔ **CONSISTENCY.** Have you applied your principle of analysis consistently, viewing your subject from a definite slant?

✔ **EVIDENCE.** Is your division or analysis well supported with concrete details, quotations, data, or statistics, as appropriate?

✔ **SIGNIFICANCE.** Why should readers care about your analysis? Have you told them something about your subject that wasn't obvious on its surface?

✔ **TRUTH TO SUBJECT.** Is your analysis faithful to the subject, not distorted, exaggerated, deflated?

DIVISION OR ANALYSIS IN PARAGRAPHS

Writing About Television

The following paragraph analyzes the components of a television laugh track, the recorded chorus that tells us when a comedy is funny. Though written especially for *The Bedford Reader,* not as part of an essay, this brief analysis could itself be one component in an examination of TV comedy. Or, with the related paragraph on pages 380–81, illustrating CLASSIFICATION, it could contribute to an essay on, say, how the producers of TV comedies manipulate viewers.

Most television comedies, even some that boast live audiences, rely on the laugh machine to fill too-quiet moments on the soundtrack. The effect of a canned laugh comes from its four overlapping elements. The first is style, from titter to belly laugh. The second is intensity, the volume, ranging from mild to medium to earsplitting. The third ingredient is duration, the length of the laugh, whether quick, medium, or extended. And finally, there's the number of laughers, from a lone giggler to a roaring throng. According to rumor (for its exact workings are a secret), the machine contains a bank of thirty-two tapes. Furiously working keys and tromping pedals, the operator plays the tapes singly or in combination to blend the four ingredients, as a maestro weaves a symphony out of brass, woodwinds, percussion, and strings.

Principle of analysis: elements creating the effect of a canned laugh

1. *Style*
2. *Intensity*
3. *Duration*
4. *Number*

Details and examples clarify elements

Writing in an Academic Discipline

The next paragraph appeared first in a scholarly journal and then in a textbook on medical ethics. The author discusses four possible models for the doctor-patient relationship, ending with the one detailed below. The careful analysis supports his preference for this model over the others.

The model of social relationship which fits these conditions [of realistic equality between patient and doctor] is that of the contract or covenant. The notion of contract should not be loaded with legalistic implications, but taken in its more symbolic form as in the traditional religious or marriage "contract" or "covenant." Here two individuals or groups are interacting in a way where there are obligations and expected benefits for both parties. The obligations and benefits are limited in scope, though, even if they are expressed in somewhat vague terms. The basic norms of freedom, dignity, truthtelling, promise-keeping, and justice are essential to a contractual relationship. The premise is trust and confidence even though it is recognized that there is not a full mutuality of interests. Social sanc-

Principle of analysis: elements of a contract between doctor and patient

1. *Obligations and benefits for both parties*

2. *Obligations and benefits limited*

3. *Freedom, dignity, and other norms*

4. *Trust and confidence*

Division or Analysis

tions institutionalize and stand behind the relationship, in case there is a violation of the contract, but for the most part the assumption is that there will be a faithful fulfillment of the obligations.
— Robert M. Veatch,
"Models for Medicine in a Revolutionary Age"

5. Support of social sanctions (meaning that society upholds the relationship)

DIVISION OR ANALYSIS IN PRACTICE

During her sophomore year at Boston University, Cortney Keim applied for transfer to Pomona College in California. As part of its application, Pomona requested a statement about Keim, her academic goals, and her reasons for wanting to transfer.

Keim tried several approaches to her statement, struggling to present herself as serious and unique. In one draft, she followed the cue of Pomona's request — providing a brief autobiography, a list of goals, and an explanation for choosing Pomona — but that version seemed obvious and dull. In the end, Keim settled on the fresher approach you see here. She first divides herself into parts and then details each one, showing its relevance to Pomona.

Application Statement of Cortney Keim

In applying for transfer to Pomona, I seek to develop the three main components of myself: actor, student, and explorer.

Pomona's strong theater curriculum will give me the background I need to embark on a career in acting. As unstable a career as it may prove to be, acting is my fire. I have always liked entertaining others (in high school, I was voted class clown), even if it involves making a display of myself. As I have had the chance to act in varied plays over the last few years, I have also found that interpreting an author's text allows me paradoxically to express myself and to lose myself. And, yes, I have loved the appreciation of an audience, the sighs or laughs in the right places, the applause at the end.

Yet acting is not all. In high school and for two years at Boston University, I have also relished the liberal arts courses I've taken and the writing I've done in those courses. The courses have introduced me to worlds of information and ideas I wouldn't have known otherwise, and the writing has let me make up my own text, my own version of reality. Liberal arts courses are hard work, harder in many ways than acting, but the work pays off. Pomona's respected liberal arts curriculum will help me become the rounded, thoughtful, disciplined student I hope to be for the rest of my life.

It's also significant to me that Pomona is a small school in California, so different from the huge university I attend now and so far from the East Coast city where I have lived all my life. The explorer in me needs a new horizon. At Pomona I anticipate the opportunity to be more involved in the activities of the college and to get to know a wider variety of people. In southern California, I expect to become familiar with a new climate, geography, and ecosystem.

Pomona promises to help me fulfill my needs to act, learn, and explore. In return, I promise to contribute whatever I can to the college and the larger community.

Division or Analysis

JUDY BRADY

JUDY BRADY, born in 1937 in San Francisco, where she now lives, earned a BFA in painting from the University of Iowa in 1962. Drawn into political action by her work in the feminist movement, she went to Cuba in 1973, where she studied class relationships as a way of understanding change in a society. When she was diagnosed with cancer in 1980, Brady became an activist against what she calls "the cancer establishment." ("Cancer is, after all, a multibillion dollar business," she says.) In 1991 she published *1 in 3: Women with Cancer Confront an Epidemic*, an anthology of writings by women. She is a board member of Greenaction, an environmental justice organization, and a founding member of the Toxic Links Coalition. She writes articles for Breast Cancer Action in San Francisco and recently provided a chapter for a Canadian book, *Sweeping the Earth: Women Taking Action for a Healthy Planet*.

I Want a Wife

"I Want a Wife" first appeared in the Spring 1972 issue of *Ms.* magazine and has been reprinted often. The essay is one of the best-known manifestos in popular feminist writing. In it, Brady trenchantly divides the work of a wife into its multiple duties and functions, leading to an inescapable conclusion. If you find that Brady stereotypes men, read the essay after hers, Armin A. Brott's "Not All Men Are Sly Foxes," for a different view.

I belong to that classification of people known as wives. I am A Wife. And, not altogether incidentally, I am a mother.

Not too long ago a male friend of mine appeared on the scene fresh from a recent divorce. He had one child, who is, of course, with his ex-wife. He is looking for another wife. As I thought about him while I was ironing one evening, it suddenly occurred to me that I, too, would like to have a wife. Why do I want a wife?

I would like to go back to school so that I can become economically independent, support myself, and, if need be, support those dependent upon me. I want a wife who will work and send me to school. And while I am going to school I want a wife to take care of my children. I want a wife to keep track of the children's doctor and dentist appointments. And to keep track of mine, too. I want a wife to make sure my children eat properly and are kept clean. I want a wife who will wash the children's clothes and keep them mended. I want a wife who is a good nurturant attendant to my children, who arranges for their schooling, makes sure that they have an adequate social life with their peers, takes them to the park, the zoo, etc. I want a wife who takes care of the children when they are sick, a wife who arranges to be around when the children need special care, because, of course, I cannot miss classes at school. My wife must arrange to lose time at work and not lose the job. It may mean a small cut in my wife's income from time to time, but I guess I can tolerate that. Needless to say, my wife will arrange and pay for the care of the children while my wife is working.

I want a wife who will take care of *my* physical needs. I want a wife who will keep my house clean. A wife who will pick up after my children, a wife who will pick up after me. I want a wife who will keep my clothes clean, ironed, mended, replaced when need be, and who will see to it that my personal things are kept in their proper place so that I can find what I need the minute I need it. I want a wife who cooks the meals, a wife who is a *good* cook. I want a wife who will plan the menus, do the necessary grocery shopping, prepare the meals, serve them pleasantly, and then do the cleaning up while I do my studying. I want a wife who will care for me when I am sick and sympathize with my pain and loss of time from school. I want a wife to go along when our family takes vacation so that someone can continue to care for me and my children when I need a rest and change of scene.

I want a wife who will not bother me with rambling complaints about a wife's duties. But I want a wife who will listen to me when I feel the need to explain a rather difficult point I have come across in my course of studies. And I want a wife who will type my papers for me when I have written them.

I want a wife who will take care of the details of my social life. When my wife and I are invited out by my friends, I want a wife who will take care of the babysitting arrangements. When I meet people at school that I like and want to entertain, I want a wife who will have the house clean, will prepare a special meal, serve it to me and my friends, and not interrupt when I talk about things that interest me and my friends. I want a wife who will have arranged that the children are fed and ready for bed before my guests arrive so that the children do not bother us. I want a wife who takes care of the needs of my guests so that they feel comfortable, who makes sure that they have an ashtray, that they are passed the hors d'oeuvres, that they are offered a second helping of the food, that their wine glasses are replenished when necessary, that their coffee is served to them as they like it. And I want a wife who knows that sometimes I need a night out by myself.

I want a wife who is sensitive to my sexual needs, a wife who makes love passionately and eagerly when I feel like it, a wife who makes sure that I am satisfied. And, of course, I want a wife who will not demand sexual attention when I am not in the mood for it. I want a wife who assumes the complete responsibility for birth control, because I do not want more children. I want a wife who will remain sexually faithful to me so that I do not have to clutter up my intellectual life with jealousies. And I want a wife who understands that *my* sexual needs may entail more than strict adherence to monogamy. I must, after all, be able to relate to people as fully as possible.

If, by chance, I find another person more suitable as a wife than the wife I   8
already have, I want the liberty to replace my present wife with another one. Naturally, I will expect a fresh, new life; my wife will take the children and be solely responsible for them so that I am left free.

When I am through with school and have a job, I want my wife to quit   9
working and remain at home so that my wife can more fully and completely take care of a wife's duties.

My God, who *wouldn't* want a wife?   10

---

*For a reading quiz, sources on Judy Brady, and annotated links to further readings on feminism and on gender roles, visit **bedfordstmartins.com/thebedfordreader**.*

Journal Writing

Brady addresses the traditional obligations of a wife and mother. In your journal, jot down parallel obligations of a husband and father. (To take your journal writing further, see "From Journal to Essay" on the facing page.)

Questions on Meaning

1. Sum up the duties of a wife as Brady sees them.
2. To what inequities in the roles traditionally assigned to men and to women does "I Want a Wife" call attention?
3. What is the THESIS of this essay? Is it stated or implied?
4. Is Brady unfair to men?

Questions on Writing Strategy

1. What EFFECT does Brady obtain with the title "I Want a Wife"?
2. What do the first two paragraphs accomplish?

3. What is the TONE of this essay?
4. How do you explain the fact that Brady never uses the pronoun *she* to refer to a wife? Does this make her prose unnecessarily awkward?
5. What principle does Brady use to analyze the role of wife? Can you think of some other principle for analyzing the job?
6. Knowing that this essay was first published in Ms. magazine in 1972, what can you guess about its intended readers? Does "I Want a Wife" strike a college AUDIENCE today as revolutionary?
7. **OTHER METHODS.** Although she mainly divides or analyzes the role of wife, Brady also uses CLASSIFICATION to sort the many duties and responsibilities into manageable groups. What are the groups?

Questions on Language

1. What is achieved by the author's frequent repetition of the phrase "I want a wife"?
2. Be sure you know how to define the following words as Brady uses them: nurturant (par. 3); replenished (6); adherence, monogamy (7).
3. In general, how would you describe the DICTION of this essay? How well does it suit the essay's intended audience?

Suggestions for Writing

1. **FROM JOURNAL TO ESSAY.** Working from your journal entry, write an essay titled "I Want a Husband" in which, using examples as Brady does, you enumerate the roles traditionally assigned to men in our society.
2. Imagining that you want to employ someone to do a specific job, divide the task into its duties and functions. Then, guided by your analysis, write an accurate job description in essay form.
3. **CRITICAL WRITING.** As indicated in the note introducing it, Brady's essay was first published in 1972 in Ms., a feminist magazine. Do some research about the evolving role of women between, say, 1970 and today. How have women's expectations, opportunities, and positions changed? One approach is to locate statistics for then and now about women in higher education (studying and teaching), in medicine and other professions, in the workforce, as wives and mothers, as homemakers, and so on. Based on your research, write an essay in which you SUMMARIZE Brady's view as you understand it and then EVALUATE her essay. Consider: Is Brady fair? If not, is unfairness justified? Is the essay relevant today? If not, what has changed? Provide specific EVIDENCE from your experience, observation, and research.
4. **CONNECTIONS.** Both "I Want a Wife" and Armin A. Brott's "Not All Men Are Sly Foxes" (next page) challenge traditional ideas about how men and women are supposed to divide the labor in a marriage. However, Brady's STYLE is fast paced and her tone is sarcastic, while Brott is more methodical and earnest. Which method of addressing these issues do you find more effective? Why? Write an essay that COMPARES AND CONTRASTS the essays' tones, styles, POINTS OF VIEW, and OBJECTIVE versus SUBJECTIVE language. What conclusions can you draw about the connection between the writers' strategies and their messages?

ARMIN A. BROTT

ARMIN A. BROTT is a writer and parenting expert who lives in Oakland, California. Born in 1958, he received a BA in Russian from San Francisco State University and an MBA that he calls "less useful than the degree in Russian" before embarking on a career in marketing. He turned to writing when his first child was born because he "wanted to be an active, involved father." Since that time he has contributed to the *New York Times Magazine*, the *Washington Post, Reader's Digest, Family Circle, Parenting, Playboy*, and other magazines. He treats issues that affect men: education, health, and especially fatherhood. His six books on fatherhood include *The Expectant Father* (1995, with Jennifer Ash), *The Single Father* (1999), *Throwaway Dads* (1999), and *Father for Life: A Journey of Joy, Challenge, and Change* (2003). Brott also hosts *Positive Parenting*, a weekly radio show that is distributed nationally.

Not All Men Are Sly Foxes

In this essay from a 1992 *Newsweek* magazine, Brott offers a different view of men from that taken by Judy Brady in the previous essay. While acknowledging that women and men are not yet equal in child care, Brott holds that children's books are hardly helping. He uses analysis to show that the Sly Fox remains much more common than the Caring Dad.

If you thought your child's bookshelves were finally free of openly (and 1 not so openly) discriminatory materials, you'd better check again. In recent years groups of concerned parents have persuaded textbook publishers to portray more accurately the roles that women and minorities play in shaping our country's history and culture. *Little Black Sambo* has all but disappeared from library and bookstore shelves; feminist fairy tales by such authors as Jack Zipes have, in many homes, replaced the more traditional (and obviously sexist) fairy tales. Richard Scarry, one of the most popular children's writers, has reissued new versions of some of his classics; now female animals are pictured doing the same jobs as male animals. Even the terminology has changed: Males and females are referred to as mail "carriers" or "firefighters."

There is, however, one very large group whose portrayal continues to fol- 2 low the same stereotypical lines as always: fathers. The evolution of children's literature didn't end with *Goodnight Moon* and *Charlotte's Web*. My local public library, for example, previews 203 new children's picture books (for the under-five set) each *month*. Many of these books make a very conscious effort to take women characters out of the kitchen and the nursery and give them professional jobs and responsibilities.

Despite this shift, mothers are by and large still shown as the primary care-   3
givers and, more important, as the primary nurturers of their children. Men in these books—if they're shown at all—still come home late after work and participate in the child rearing by bouncing baby around for five minutes before putting the child to bed.

In one of my two-year-old daughter's favorite books, *Mother Goose and the*   4
Sly Fox, "retold" by Chris Conover, a single mother (Mother Goose) of seven tiny goslings is pitted against (and naturally outwits) the sly Fox. Fox, a neglectful and presumably unemployed single father, lives with his filthy, hun-gry pups in a grimy hovel littered with the bones of their previous meals. Mother Goose, a successful entrepreneur with a thriving lace business, still finds time to serve her goslings homemade soup in pretty porcelain cups. The story is funny and the illustrations marvelous, but the unwritten message is that women take better care of their kids and men have nothing else to do but hunt down and kill innocent, law-abiding geese.

The majority of other children's classics perpetuate the same negative   5
stereotypes of fathers. Once in a great while, people complain about *Babar's* colonialist slant (little jungle-dweller finds happiness in the big city and brings civilization—and fine clothes—to his backward village). But I've never heard anyone ask why, after his mother is killed by the evil hunter, Babar is automatically an "orphan." Why can he find comfort only in the arms of another female? Why do Arthur's and Celeste's mothers come alone to the city to fetch their children? Don't the fathers care? Do they even have fathers? I need my answers ready for when my daughter asks.

I recently spent an entire day on the children's floor of the local library   6
trying to find out whether these same negative stereotypes are found in the more recent classics-to-be. The librarian gave me a list of the twenty most popular contemporary picture books and I read every one of them. Of the twenty, seven don't mention a parent at all. Of the remaining thirteen, four portray fathers as much less loving and caring than mothers. In *Little Gorilla*, we are told that the little gorilla's "mother loves him" and we see Mama gorilla giving her little one a warm hug. On the next page we're also told that his "father loves him," but in the illustration, father and son aren't even touch-ing. Six of the remaining nine books mention or portray mothers as the only parent, and only three of the twenty have what could be considered "equal" treatment of mothers and fathers.

The same negative stereotypes also show up in literature aimed at the *par-*   7
ents of small children. In *What to Expect the First Year*, the authors answer

almost every question the parents of a newborn or toddler could have in the first year of their child's life. They are meticulous in alternating between references to boys and girls. At the same time, they refer almost exclusively to "mother" or "mommy." Men, and their feelings about parenting, are relegated to a nine-page chapter just before the recipe section.

Unfortunately, it's still true that, in our society, women do the bulk of the child care, and that thanks to men abandoning their families, there are too many single mothers out there. Nevertheless, to say that portraying fathers as unnurturing or completely absent is simply "a reflection of reality" is unacceptable. If children's literature only reflected reality, it would be like prime-time TV and we'd have books filled with child abusers, wife beaters and criminals. 8

Young children believe what they hear—especially from a parent figure. And since, for the first few years of a child's life, adults select the reading material, children's literature should be held to a high standard. Ignoring men who share equally in raising their children and continuing to show nothing but part-time or no-time fathers is only going to create yet another generation of men who have been told since boyhood—albeit subtly—that mothers are the truer parents and that fathers play, at best, a secondary role in the home. We've taken major steps to root out discrimination in what our children read. Let's finish the job. 9

> *For a reading quiz, sources on Armin A. Brott, and annotated links to further readings on gender roles and on children's books, visit **bedfordstmartins.com/ thebedfordreader**.*

Journal Writing

Do you agree with Brott that young children are strongly influenced by the books parents or teachers read to them? In your journal, list particular books from your childhood that stand out in your memory. What made these books come alive so that you still remember them today—the story, the illustrations, the language? (To take your journal writing further, see "From Journal to Essay" on the facing page.)

Questions on Meaning

1. What is the THESIS of Brott's essay? Where is it stated succinctly?

2. What does Brott ASSUME about his AUDIENCE in this essay? To what extent do you fit his assumptions?
3. Brott points out a difference between the illustration of the little gorilla with his mother and the one of him with his father (par. 6). Why is this difference significant?
4. What is the EFFECT of Brott's concluding sentences: "We've taken major steps to root out discrimination in what our children read. Let's finish the job"?

Questions on Writing Strategy

1. What principle of analysis does Brott use in examining the children's books? What elements does he perceive in these books?
2. What purpose does paragraph 7, with its reference to books for parents, serve in this essay about children's books?
3. **OTHER METHODS.** In paragraph 4, Brott provides vivid DESCRIPTION of Mother Goose's and Sly Fox's homes to show the differences between the two parents. What CONCRETE details help explain these differences?

Questions on Language

1. What is the difference between "caregivers" and "nurturers" as Brott uses the words in paragraph 3?
2. How would you analyze Brott's TONE? Give specific words and sentences that you think contribute to the tone.
3. If some of the following words are unfamiliar, look them up in a dictionary: discriminatory (par. 1); stereotypical, evolution (2); goslings, neglectful, hovel, entrepreneur, porcelain (4); perpetuate, colonialist (5); meticulous, exclusively, relegated (7); albeit, subtly (9).

Suggestions for Writing

1. **FROM JOURNAL TO ESSAY.** Working from your journal entry, write a brief essay that explores the messages sent by one of your childhood books. Did the book contain positive role models? negative ones? moral messages? values that you now embrace or reject? Did you learn anything in particular from this book? Based on your recollections, come to your own conclusions about what's appropriate or not in children's books.
2. Write an essay that analyzes another type of writing by examining its elements. You may choose any kind of writing that's familiar to you: news article, sports article, mystery, romance, science fiction, biography, and so on. Be sure to make your principle of analysis clear to your readers.
3. Brott's essay was written some years ago. Have images of fathers in children's books changed since then, or have they remained essentially the same? Read through a sampling of children's books published in the past five years—either in a library or in the children's section of a bookstore. Then write an essay in which you report your findings, being sure to analyze several specific books.

4. **CRITICAL WRITING.** "If children's literature only reflected reality," Brott claims, "it would be like prime-time TV and we'd have books filled with child abusers, wife beaters and criminals" (par. 8). However, Brott also suggests that "reality" contains a significant number of responsible, loving fathers. Does the claim about "reality" being "like prime-time TV" detract from Brott's argument on behalf of good fathers? Write an essay in which you explain how (or whether) Brott resolves this contradiction in his essay. It will probably be helpful to provide a clear DEFINITION of *reality* in this context.

5. **CONNECTIONS.** Look over Judy Brady's "I Want a Wife" (p. 344) and make a list of her implied complaints about the traditional roles of a wife. Now make a list of the responsibilities that Brott implies a good father is happy to take on. How could Brott's essay be viewed as a sort of response or solution to some of the problems Brady raises? Write an essay explaining the changes in traditional gender roles suggested by "I Want a Wife" and "Not All Men Are Sly Foxes" together.

EMILY PRAGER

EMILY PRAGER was first published at age five when the *Houston Post* released her novel *Cinderella Goes to the Ball and Breaks Her Leg*. Born in 1952, she grew up in Houston, Asia, and New York City and graduated from Barnard College with a degree in anthropology. She wrote for *The National Lampoon Magazine*, cowrote and acted in the films *Mr. Mike's Mondo* and *Arena Brains*, and starred for four years in the soap opera *The Edge of Night*. Prager has written humor and social satire for *Saturday Night Live* and for numerous periodicals, collected in *In the Missionary Position* (1999), and she has published four books of fiction: *A Visit from the Footbinder and Other Stories* (1982), *Clea and Zeus Divorce* (1987), *Eve's Tattoo* (1991), and *Roger Fishbite: A Novel* (1999). A recent book, nonfiction, is *Wuhu Diary: On Taking My Adopted Daughter to Her Hometown in China* (2001). Prager teaches fiction and humor writing at New York University.

Our Barbies, Ourselves

The Barbie doll is just a harmless plaything for little girls, right? Prager suspected not, even when she was a child, and some recent information confirmed her hunch. Using division or analysis, she shows here how Barbie represents a twisted ideal of women. The essay first appeared in *Interview* magazine in 1991.

I read an astounding obituary in the *New York Times* not too long ago. It concerned the death of one Jack Ryan. A former husband of Zsa Zsa Gabor, it said, Mr. Ryan had been an inventor and designer during his lifetime. A man of eclectic creativity, he designed Sparrow and Hawk missiles when he worked for the Raytheon Company, and, the notice said, when he consulted for Mattel he designed Barbie.[1]

If Barbie was designed by a man, suddenly a lot of things made sense to me, things I'd wondered about for years. I used to look at Barbie and wonder, What's wrong with this picture? What kind of woman designed this doll? Let's be honest: Barbie looks like someone who got her start at the Playboy Mansion. She could be a regular guest on *The Howard Stern Show*. It is a fact of Barbie's design that her breasts are so out of proportion to the rest of her body that if she were a human woman, she'd fall flat on her face.

---

[1] After Prager wrote this essay, Barbie's thirty-fifth birthday was the occasion for a "biography" asserting that Ryan did not design the doll from scratch but supervised its evolution from a sophisticated adult doll made in Germany. —EDS.

If it's true that a woman didn't design Barbie, you don't know how much   3
saner that makes me feel. Of course, that doesn't ameliorate the damage.
There are millions of women who are subliminally sure that a thirty-nine-inch
bust and a twenty-three-inch waist are the epitome of lovability. Could this
account for the popularity of breast implant surgery?

I don't mean to step on anyone's toes here. I loved my Barbie. Secretly, I   4
still believe that neon pink and turquoise blue are the only colors in which to
decorate a duplex condo. And like many others of my generation, I've never
married, simply because I cannot find a man who looks as good in clam diggers
as Ken.

The question that comes to mind is, of course, Did Mr. Ryan design Bar-   5
bie as a weapon? Because it *is* odd that Barbie appeared about the same time
in my consciousness as the feminist movement — a time when women sought
equality and small breasts were king. Or is Barbie the dream date of weapons
designers? Or perhaps it's simpler than that: Perhaps Barbie is Zsa Zsa if she
were eleven inches tall. No matter what, my discovery of Jack Ryan confirms
what I have always felt: There is something indescribably masculine about
Barbie — dare I say it, phallic. For all her giant breasts and high-heeled feet,
she lacks a certain softness. If you asked a little girl what kind of doll she
wanted for Christmas, I just don't think she'd reply, "Please, Santa, I want a
hard-body."

On the other hand, you could say that Barbie, in feminist terms, is defi-   6
nitely her own person. With her condos and fashion plazas and pools and
beauty salons, she is definitely a liberated woman, a gal on the move. And she
has always been sexual, even totemic. Before Barbie, American dolls were flat-
footed and breastless, and ineffably dignified. They were created in the image
of little girls or babies. Madame Alexander was the queen of doll makers in
the '50s, and her dollies looked like Elizabeth Taylor in *National Velvet*. They
represented the kind of girls who looked perfect in jodhpurs, whose hair was
never out of place, who grew up to be Jackie Kennedy — before she married
Onassis. Her dolls' boyfriends were figments of the imagination, figments with
large portfolios and three-piece suits and presidential aspirations, figments
who could keep dolly in the style to which little girls of the '50s were programmed to become accustomed, a style that spasmed with the '60s and the
appearance of Barbie. And perhaps what accounts for Barbie's vast popularity
is that she was also a '60s woman: into free love and fun colors, anti-class, and
possessed of a real, molded boyfriend, Ken, with whom she could chant a
mantra.

But there were problems with Ken. I always felt weird about him. He had   7
no genitals, and, even at age ten, I found that ominous. I mean, here was Barbie with these humongous breasts, and that was OK with the toy company.

And then, there was Ken with that truncated, unidentifiable lump at his groin. I sensed injustice at work. Why, I wondered, was Barbie designed with such obvious sexual equipment and Ken not? Why was his treated as if it were more mysterious than hers? Did the fact that it was treated as such indicate that somehow his equipment, his essential maleness, was considered more powerful than hers, more worthy of the dignity of concealment? And if the issue in the mind of the toy company was obscenity and its possible damage to children, I still object. How do they think I felt, knowing that no matter how many water beds they slept in, or hot tubs they romped in, or swimming pools they lounged by under the stars, Barbie and Ken could never make love? No matter how much sexuality Barbie possessed, she would never turn Ken on. He would be forever withholding, forever detached. There was a loneliness about Barbie's situation that was always disturbing. And twenty-five years later, movies and videos are still filled with topless women and covered men. As if we're all trapped in Barbie's world and can never escape.

*For a reading quiz, sources on Emily Prager, and annotated links to further readings on gender and toys, visit **bedfordstmartins.com/thebedfordreader**.*

Journal Writing

While growing up, did you play with Barbie or another kind of doll—for instance, baby dolls, action figures like GI Joe, figures based on cartoon or movie characters? In your journal, describe your relationship with such toys, or explain why you never played with them. (To take your journal writing further, see "From Journal to Essay" on the next page.)

Questions on Meaning

1. Why does Prager say that "suddenly a lot of things made sense" when she discovered that Barbie was designed by a man? Is she referring here only to Barbie's looks?
2. Are we supposed to believe the claims that Prager makes in paragraph 4? What is the point she is trying to make?
3. What is Prager's DEFINITION of a *feminist* in this essay? Where do you find this definition?
4. What is Prager's THESIS?

Questions on Writing Strategy

1. What elements of Barbie does Prager's analysis identify? What new picture of the doll does Prager arrive at as a result?
2. Prager refers to four famous women by name. What does each reference suggest? What is the EFFECT of her using these famous names?
3. Prager poses several RHETORICAL QUESTIONS, such as "Could this account for the popularity of breast implant surgery?" (par. 3), "Or is Barbie the dream date of weapons designers?" (5), and "Why . . . was Barbie designed with such obvious sexual equipment and Ken not?" (7). What is the PURPOSE of these rhetorical questions?
4. **OTHER METHODS.** In her last paragraph Prager COMPARES AND CONTRASTS the ways the toy company depicted the sexuality of Barbie and Ken. What are the differences? What ideas of CAUSE AND EFFECT emerge from this comparison?

Questions on Language

1. Prager notes that Barbie is a product of a time when "small breasts were king" (par. 5). What is the significance of the word *king* in this context?
2. Why does Prager call Barbie "masculine" in paragraph 5? Does this description contradict Prager's view of Barbie as an unattainable and inappropriate feminine ideal?
3. Prager describes dolls' boyfriends before Barbie's Ken as "figments with large portfolios and three-piece suits and presidential aspirations" (par. 6). What are the CONNOTATIONS of this description?
4. Consult your dictionary if any of the following words are unfamiliar: eclectic (par. 1); ameliorate, subliminally, epitome (3); phallic (5); totemic, ineffably, jodhpurs (6); humongous, truncated (7).

Suggestions for Writing

1. **FROM JOURNAL TO ESSAY.** Drawing on your journal entry and using your own experiences as EVIDENCE, write an essay that explains the influence of a particular doll or of dolls in general. Your essay may be serious or humorous, but it should include plenty of description and focus on cause and effect.
2. Prager asserts that knowing a man designed Barbie *explains* a lot of problems she always had with Barbie, but it does not *excuse* or *solve* the problems. What new knowledge can you think of that provided a reasonable explanation for a personal problem, while doing nothing to repair the situation? For instance, did you come to understand why your taxes or your rent increased, why you received a disappointing grade in a course, why someone dislikes you, or why a friend is depressed? In an essay, explain the situation, what you now understand about it, and finally, what it would take, in addition to the new information, to solve the problem.
3. **CRITICAL WRITING.** In paragraph 6 Prager suggests, with a tinge of IRONY, several ways to think of Barbie as contributing to the liberation rather than the oppression of women. What do *you* think of Barbie as a role model for girls? Write an

essay supporting or refuting Prager's thesis. (If you haven't seen a Barbie doll in a while, you might visit a toy store.) Is Barbie damaging, as Prager maintains, or liberating, or neither? Much has been written on this question, so you might extend your views with library or Internet research.

4. **CONNECTIONS.** Both Prager and Armin A. Brott, in "Not All Men Are Sly Foxes" (p. 348), examine cultural artifacts that could influence children's ideas of their own and the opposite sex. Consider a cultural artifact that affected you as a child, such as a television show, book, movie, toy, sport, or kind of music. (It may have influenced your views of sex roles but could also have influenced you in other ways—for instance, by contributing to your values, your interests, your ideas about friendship or adult life.) Write an essay that analyzes your subject, identifying the elements that made it influential.

Emily Prager on Writing

Actually, this section should be titled "Emily Prager on *Reading and* Writing." In the Toronto, Canada, *Globe and Mail*, Prager made a passionate case for both:

As a writer, I worry a lot about literacy in the United States. In part, it's purely selfish. If most US high-school graduates can't read above a Grade 5 level, then I'm out of a job in ten years. Without a young, new audience to keep you on your toes, a writer can go stale. Your arteries can harden. You start writing only for your own generation and then you're like a snake eating its own tail: self-involved to the point of stasis. . . .

Americans, given the problems of drugs and dysfunctional school systems, have been left thoroughly, classically illiterate. This, in my estimation, is a form of spiritual bankruptcy—because the ultimate aim of classical literacy (the ability to read and write) is to be able to think, to form ideas, to fantasize goals, to hope, to imagine, to invent and reinvent, to believe in life.

Drugs in school have, of course, contributed mightily to classical illiteracy. By and large, when kids take drugs they do not read. Reading was itself the drug of my generation's childhood. Before we baby boomers found drugs, we read voraciously, addictively. I always say, only half-joking, that if teachers taught reading as the great drug it truly is, kids would want to do it.

But teachers don't. Reading is taught as some dry, dull, meaningless, academic pursuit. No mention is ever made of the high, the physical euphoria and bliss, the fantastic turn-on of intellectual understanding. It seems amazing now that mothers used to fear our reading. Go outside, they'd shout, threatened by our focus and solitude. Little did they know. . . .

It is interesting that the United States, with its national emphasis on freedom, should have come to this strange pass, but it has. The average American
is, at this point, dubious both about the quality of his life and his sense of personal freedom. He is also desperate to rediscover these things, to find his
depth, to relocate some magic and meaning in his existence.

This, television, computers and drug addiction cannot do. Only access
to the great thought and history and art of the planet through reading, and
the formulation of ideas and the sparking of imagination through writing,
can feed the emptiness that we feel. Man cannot live by money and real estate
alone.

Fortunately, Americans are easily bored. I somehow feel they might take
up reading and writing again just because they're bored with everything else
and need a new thrill.

Fine by me. Whatever makes them do it. Readers in their teens never read
my books now and that saddens me. But I can live with it if, when I'm sixty,
there's a whole crop of literate twenty-year-olds to keep my writing young.

For Discussion

1. What, according to Prager, has caused today's "classical illiteracy"? What can
   reading and writing provide that "television, computers and drug addiction"
   cannot?
2. Prager makes some negative GENERALIZATIONS about the teaching of reading
   today. On the basis of your own experience as a student, do you agree or disagree
   with these generalizations? Why?
3. How serious do you think Prager is in hoping for improved literacy because it
   would benefit her own writing (first and last paragraphs)?

LAILA AYAD

Born in 1981, LAILA AYAD grew up in Columbia, Maryland, a planned community based on ideals of racial, social, and economic diversity and balance. "Being exposed at an early age to such a diverse community and coming from a multiethnic family have given me great insight into different cultures and perspectives," says Ayad. After graduating from New York University in 2003 with a degree in theater and English literature, Ayad embarked on an acting career. She recently returned from a ten-month tour with a musical theater company that took her to cities across the United States. When not on stage, Ayad paints and draws and continues to write.

The Capricious Camera

Ayad began college as an art major and produced this essay for a writing class in her sophomore year. The essay first appeared in 2001 in *Mercer Street*, a journal of writing by New York University students. With an artist's eye for detail, Ayad explores the elements of a World War II photograph to find its meaning.

In the years between 1933 and 1945, Germany was engulfed by the rise of a powerful new regime and the eventual spoils of war. During this period, Hitler's quest for racial purification turned Germany not only at odds with itself, but with the rest of the world. Photography as an art and as a business became a regulated and potent force in the fight for Aryan domination, Nazi influence, and anti-Semitism. Whether such images were used to promote Nazi ideology, document the Holocaust, or scare Germany's citizens into accepting their own changing country, the effect of this photography provides enormous insight into the true stories and lives of the people most affected by Hitler's racism. In fact, this photography has become so widespread in our understanding and teaching of the Holocaust that often other factors involved in the Nazi's racial policy have been undervalued in our history textbooks—especially the attempt by Nazi Germany to establish the Nordic Aryans as a master race through the *Lebensborn* experiment, a breeding and adoption program designed to eliminate racial imperfections. It is not merely people of other persecuted races who can become victims in a racial war, but also those we would least expect—the persecuting race itself.

To understand the importance of this often shrouded side of Nazi Germany we might look at the photograph captioned "Mounted Nazi troops on the lookout for likely Polish children." Archived by Catrine Clay and Michael Leapman, this black-and-white photo depicts a young girl in the foreground,

Mounted Nazi troops on the lookout for likely Polish children.

carrying two large baskets and treading across a rural and snow-covered coun-
tryside, while three mounted and armed Nazi soldiers follow closely behind
her. In the distance, we can see farmhouses and a wooden fence, as well as four
other uniformed soldiers or guards. Though the photograph accompanies the
text without the name of the photographer, year, or information as to where it
was found, Clay and Leapman suggest that the photo was taken in Poland
between 1943 and 1945.

Who is this young white girl surrounded by armed soldiers? Is she being   3
protected, watched, persecuted? It would be easy enough to assume that she is
Jewish, but unlike photos documenting the Holocaust, with *this* image the
intent is uncertain. In our general ignorance of the events surrounding this
photo, the picture can be deceiving, and yet it is the picture that can also be
used to shed light on the story.

Looking just at the photo, and ignoring the descriptive caption, there are   4
some interesting visual and artistic effects that help a viewer better understand the circumstances surrounding the image. One of its most prominent
features is the way the photographer decides to focus on only one young child
in the foreground, while including seven Nazi soldiers behind her. The effect
is overwhelming, and in gazing at the image, one is struck by the magnitude
and force of the oppressing men in sharp contrast to the innocence and helplessness of the lone girl. By juxtaposing one child with seven men, the image
comes across strongly as both cruel and terribly frightening. In addition, the
child in the foreground is a young girl, which only adds to the potency of the
image. The photographer makes the soldiers appear far more menacing and
unjust, in that there appears to be no physical way in which a young girl could
possibly defend herself against these men.

What is additionally interesting about this particular aspect of the photo   5
is that the seven men are not grouped together, or in any way concentrated
right next to the child. There are three directly behind the girl, one a little
farther behind and to the left, one even slightly farther behind and to the
right, and two very far off in the distance, walking in the opposite direction.
This placement of the soldiers not only gives the photo an excellent sense of
depth, but also conveys to the viewer a sense that the entire surroundings, not
just the little girl, are being controlled and surveyed. It allows the viewer to
imagine and wonder in what way other children, or perhaps just the other
parts of the village, are being similarly restricted. For the young girl, and the
viewer, it allows no way out; all angles and directions of the photo are covered
by symbols of oppression, producing an eerily suffocating effect.

The child is the only person in the photo looking directly at the photog-   6
rapher. Whether this technique was manipulated on purpose remains to be
seen, but it goes without saying that the effect is dramatic. Her gaze is wistful

and innocent. In contrast, the men occupying the rest of the photo, and most prominently the three mounted ones in the foreground, are gazing either away or down. While it is uncertain what the soldiers behind the child are staring at, their downward stare causes their heads to hang in almost shameful disgrace. They do not look at the child, and yet they do not look at the photographer, who is quite obviously standing in front of them. Is this because they do not see that there is a picture being taken, or perhaps the photographer is another soldier, and this picture is simply routine in recording the progress of their work?

If not a Nazi soldier, the photographer could be a Polish citizen; if this   7
were the case, it might change our interpretation of the photo. Suddenly, the girl's facial expression and direct gaze seem pleading, while, for fear of being caught, the photographer snaps the picture quickly, in the exact moment the soldiers are looking away. Perhaps the soldiers did not mind having their picture taken. Many Polish were considered, after all, their racial equals, and maybe they would have respected and appreciated an amateur photographer's interest in their work.

While all of these scenarios are seemingly plausible, the purpose of the pho-   8
tograph is still uncertain. There are also several possibilities. One is that the Nazis commissioned the photograph, as they did others at the time, to properly record the events surrounding the development of their plan. In an article entitled "The Camera as Weapon: Documentary Photography and the Holocaust," Sybil Milton describes the ways in which Nazi photographers worked:

> Nazi professional photographers produced in excess of one-quarter million images. Their work was officially regulated and licensed. . . . All photos were screened by military censors subservient to official directives of the Propaganda Ministry. . . . Press photographers of World War II rarely showed atrocities and seldom published prints unfavorable to their own side. (1)

However, while the evidence is compelling, Milton recognizes another possibility that significantly changes the motive for the photo: "Portable cameras, and other technical innovations like interchangeable lenses and multiple exposure film, meant that nonprofessionals owned and used cameras with ease. Many soldiers carried small Leica or Ermanox cameras in their rucksacks or pillaged optical equipment from the towns they occupied" (2). While it is possible that the photograph was taken by a soldier seeking to document the work in Poland for his own interests, this probability, against the numerous commissioned photographs and the nature of the subject matter being documented, is unlikely. The photo alone, while intriguing in its image, tells only half of the story, and without a definitive context can become akin to a "choose your own adventure" novel. In other words, the possibilities for a photographic purpose are all laid out, but the true meaning or end remains undetermined. Unlike hand-made art, which in its very purpose begs to be viewed through various interpretations, photography, and particularly photo-journalism, captures a certain moment in time, featuring specific subject matter, under a genuine set of circumstances. The picture is not invented, it is real life, and in being so demands to be viewed alongside its agenda, for without this context, it may never be fully understood.

When we turn to the caption describing the photograph, "Mounted Nazi troops on the lookout for likely Polish children," the book *Master Race* and its accompanying story can now properly be discussed. Instead of typically dealing with the issues of a racist Nazi Germany as it relates to the Holocaust, and the other forms of racial extermination and discrimination that were subsequently involved, Clay and Leapman's book looks at the other side of the coin. It is important in dealing with and understanding the concept of racism to realize that racists are not simply those who dislike others; they are also those who worship themselves. In *Mein Kampf* Hitler outlined the inspiration for his racial tyranny by saying, "The products of human culture, the achievements in art, science and technology . . . are almost exclusively the creative product of the Aryan." He was heavily influenced by the work of racially charged popular science writers, such as H. F. K. Gunther, who in his *Ethnology of the German Nation* wrote: "The man of Nordic race is not only the most gifted but also the most beautiful. . . . The man's face is hard and chiseled, the woman's tender, with rose-pink skin and bright triumphant eyes" (qtd. in Clay and Leapman 17). Through the course of the book, the topic of racism in Nazi Germany focuses intently on the concept of racial purification. By following the work of the carefully selected (meaning those of impeccable Aryan ancestry) members of Himmler's elite SS corps, Clay and Leapman introduce the history of Germany's failed *Lebensborn* experiment and the homes that were created by the Third Reich to breed and raise "perfect Aryans" (ix). 9

In a disturbing segment on Hitler's racial utopia, Clay and Leapman describe the practice of eugenics, improving humankind by eliminating undesirable genetic traits and breeding those that were considered superior. The SS soldiers who are commonly known for forcing the Jews into concentration camps are mentioned, but this time they are discussed as the same men who were ordered to father white babies with volunteer German and Norwegian mothers. However, it is the final fact, the story of the SS soldiers who occupied surrounding countries and then stole children "who looked as if they might further improve the breed," that becomes the focus and ultimate subject matter of the photograph (ix). 10

Looking at the photograph in this context, the soldier no longer appears to be protecting the Polish children, but hunting them. The word "likely" in 11 the caption denotes this. Children who possessed strong Nordic or Aryan qualities were systematically taken from their native countries, adopted by German parents (who were paid by the Nazi regime), taught to forget their families and former lives, and raised to breed not only many children of their own but, above all, families that would uphold Nazi ideology. For Hitler and Heinrich Himmler, who was appointed Commissar for Consolidating German Nationhood, exterminating the racially impure was merely preparation. It was the process of breeding and stealing children that Himmler considered central and key in the ultimate goal for racial purification:

> Obviously in such a mixture of peoples there will always be some racially good types. Therefore I think that it is our duty to take their children with us, to remove them from their environment, if necessary by robbing or steal-ing them. . . . My aim has always been the same, to attract all the Nordic blood in the world and take it for ourselves. (qtd. in Clay and Leapman 91)

Additionally, Himmler's objective in targeting children, rather than adults, was a planned and strategic tool. Through teachings at school, children were used to control their parents by being encouraged to report what they did and said. Himmler realized that older people would be less enthusiastic about his ideas, so he made every effort to win the minds of the next generation.

What is perhaps most compelling about the *Lebensborn* experiment and   12
thus most poignant when viewing the photograph is the reminder that for every child that was stolen from nations like Poland, his or her family was being equally betrayed. One Polish girl recounted the events of her kidnap-ping years later, describing both her and her father's reaction to the incident:

> Three SS men came into the room and put us up against a wall. . . . They immediately picked out the fair children with blue eyes — seven altogether, including me. . . . My father, who tried to stop my being taken away, was threatened by the soldiers. They even said he would be taken to a concen-tration camp. But I have no idea what happened to him later. (qtd. in Clay and Leapman 95)

The girl who spoke above just as easily could have been the young girl being followed by soldiers in the photograph, only moments after she was taken. Such incidents force us to broaden our sense of whom the Nazis victimized. While there is no mistaking the victimization of the Jewish population and other races in Germany, amidst these better-known hate crimes the Nazis were also perpetrating a horrific exploitation of the so-called "white" race.

The complexities surrounding this photograph remind us that the story of   13
any photograph is liable to contain ambiguity. As an art, photography relies on the imagination of the viewer; not *knowing* provides the viewer with a

realm of interesting possibilities. Context matters even with art, and playing with possible contexts gives a photograph diverse meanings. It is in these various viewpoints that we find pleasure, amusement, fear, or wonder. It is perhaps in the shift to photojournalism that determining a particular context becomes even more important. In fact, even if the original photographer saw the image as artistic, subsequent events compel us to try to see the image of the Polish girl with Nazis as journalism. In this endeavor, we must uncover as much as possible about the surrounding context. As much as we can, we need to know this girl's particular story. Without a name, date, place, or relevant data, this girl would fall even further backwards into the chapters of unrecorded history.

Works Cited

"Mounted Nazi Troops on the Lookout for Likely Polish Children." Clay and Leapman, 87.

Clay, Catrine, and Michael Leapman. *Master Race: The* Lebensborn *Experiment in Nazi Germany.* London: Hodder, 1995.

Hitler, Adolf. *Mein Kampf.* Vol. 2, chap. 3. *Hitler Historical Museum.* 1996–2000. 1 Dec. 2000 <http://www.hitler.org/writings/Mein_Kampf>.

Milton, Sybil. "The Camera as Weapon: Documentary Photography and the Holocaust." 1970. *Museum of Tolerance Online.* Simon Wiesenthal Center. 6 Dec. 2000 <http://motlc.wiesenthal.com/resources/books/annual1/chap03.html>.

For a reading quiz and annotated links to further readings on the Holocaust and on the Lebensborn experiment, visit **bedfordstmartins.com/thebedfordreader**.

Journal Writing

Ayad uncovers an aspect of Nazi history that is not well known, perhaps even startling. Think of a time when you learned something that surprised you about history, science, or culture—either in a class or through independent research. In your journal, write about your discovery and how it affected you. (To take your journal writing further, see "From Journal to Essay" on the next page.)

Questions on Meaning

1. Ayad's essay pursues two threads: certain events in German history and certain characteristics of photography, especially photojournalism. Each thread in essence has its own THESIS, stated in paragraphs 1 and 8. What are these theses? Where in the essay does Ayad bring them together?
2. Ayad writes about events in history that she thinks some readers do not know about. What are these events?
3. What do you see as Ayad's PURPOSE in this essay?

Questions on Writing Strategy

1. Why does Ayad devote so much of her essay to discussing the photograph? What is the EFFECT of her speculations about the content and the creation of the photograph?
2. Ayad's AUDIENCE was originally the teacher and students in her writing class. What does she ASSUME readers already know about Nazi Germany? What does she assume they may not know?
3. What is the effect of Ayad's last two sentences? Why does Ayad end this way?
4. **OTHER METHODS.** Where in the essay does Ayad draw on DESCRIPTION? Why is description crucial to Ayad's analysis?

Questions on Language

1. What words and phrases does Ayad use in paragraphs 4–6 to communicate her own feelings about the photograph? What are those feelings?
2. Why does Ayad quote Adolf Hitler and H. F. K. Gunther (par. 9), Heinrich Himmler (11), and the Polish woman who was kidnapped as a child (12)? What does Ayad achieve with these quotations?
3. What is the effect of the word *targeting* in paragraph 11?
4. Consult a dictionary if you are unsure of the meaning of any of the following: capricious (title); Aryan, anti-Semitism, ideology, Nordic (par. 1); shrouded, elucidate (2); juxtaposing (4); suffocating (5); scenarios, plausible, commissioned, pillaged, definitive (8); extermination, tyranny, impeccable (9); poignant (12); ambiguity, subsequent (13).

Suggestions for Writing

1. **FROM JOURNAL TO ESSAY.** Using your journal writing as a starting point, draft an essay about a surprising discovery you made in a class or on your own. If it will be helpful, do some research to extend your knowledge of the subject. Involve your readers in the essay by distinguishing general knowledge—that is, what they probably know already—from the new information.
2. Locate a photograph that you find especially striking, perhaps in a library book or through an online photo collection such as Corbis (*pro.corbis.com*). Write an essay that describes and analyzes the image, using a thesis statement and vivid language to make your interpretation clear.

3. **CRITICAL WRITING.** Some of Ayad's paragraphs are long, especially 1, 8, 9, and 11. How COHERENT are these long paragraphs? Write a brief essay in which you analyze two of them in terms of their organization, the TRANSITIONS or other devices that connect sentences, and any problems with coherence that you see.

4. **CONNECTIONS.** In "Silent Dancing" (p. 162), Judith Ortiz Cofer describes images of a home movie and interprets their meanings. Based on Cofer's and Ayad's essays, write an essay of your own in which you analyze how writers can create meaning through description and analysis of visual images.

JAMAICA KINCAID

JAMAICA KINCAID was born Elaine Potter Richardson in 1949 on the Caribbean island of Antigua. She attended school in Antigua and struggled to
become independent of her mother and her place. "I was supposed to be full
of good manners and good speech," she has recalled. "Where the hell I was
going to go with it I don't know." Kincaid took it to New York, where she
went at age seventeen to work as a family helper. She briefly attended Fran-
conia College on a photography scholarship and did odd jobs in New York.
In the early 1970s, she became friends with George Trow, a writer for *The
New Yorker*. Soon she was contributing to the magazine, and in 1976 she
became a staff writer. Soon after, she began writing fiction, producing a collection of stories, *At the Bottom of the River* (1983), and four novels, *Annie
John* (1985), *Lucy* (1990), *The Autobiography of My Mother* (1996), and *Mr.
Potter* (2002) — all based on her own life on Antigua and as an immigrant.
Her nonfiction books include *A Small Place* (1988), also about Antigua; *My
Brother* (1997), a National Book Award finalist; and *Talk Stories* (2000), a
collection of her "Talk of the Town" pieces from *The New Yorker*. An avid
gardener, Kincaid has also written *My Garden (Book)* (1999) and edited *My
Favorite Plants: Writers and Gardeners on the Plants They Love* (1998). She
lives in Vermont.

Girl

This very short story was collected in *At the Bottom of the River*. Much as Judy
Brady does in "I Want a Wife" (p. 344), Kincaid analyzes the domain of the
title female, both the roles she is expected to fill and the condition of being
in her relationship. The writer Stephanie Vaughn has said that Kincaid's
story "spills out in a single breath. . . . Its exhilarating motion gives me the
sense of a writer carried over the precipice by the energy of her own vision."

Wash the white clothes on Monday and put them on the stone heap; wash   1
the color clothes on Tuesday and put them on the clothesline to dry; don't
walk barehead in the hot sun; cook pumpkin fritters in very hot sweet oil; soak
your little cloths right after you take them off; when buying cotton to make
yourself a nice blouse, be sure that it doesn't have gum on it, because that way
it won't hold up well after a wash; soak salt fish overnight before you cook it;
is it true that you sing benna[1] in Sunday school?; always eat your food in such
a way that it won't turn someone else's stomach; on Sundays try to walk like a
lady and not like the slut you are so bent on becoming; don't sing benna in
Sunday school; you mustn't speak to wharf-rat boys, not even to give direc-

[1] Calypso music. — EDS.

tions; don't eat fruits on the street—flies will follow you; *but I don't sing benna on Sundays at all and never in Sunday school*; this is how to sew on a button; this is how to make a buttonhole for the button you have just sewed on; this is how to hem a dress when you see the hem coming down and so to prevent yourself from looking like the slut I know you are so bent on becoming; this is how you iron your father's khaki shirt so that it doesn't have a crease; this is how you iron your father's khaki pants so that they don't have a crease; this is how you grow okra—far from the house, because okra tree harbors red ants; when you are growing dasheen,[2] make sure it gets plenty of water or else it makes your throat itch when you are eating it; this is how you sweep a corner; this is how you sweep a whole house; this is how you sweep a yard; this is how you smile to someone you don't like too much; this is how you smile to someone you don't like at all; this is how you smile to someone you like completely; this is how you set a table for tea; this is how you set a table for dinner; this is how you set a table for dinner with an important guest; this is how you set a table for lunch; this is how you set a table for breakfast; this is how to behave in the presence of men who don't know you very well, and this way they won't recognize immediately the slut I have warned you against becoming; be sure to wash every day, even if it is with your own spit; don't squat down to play marbles—you are not a boy, you know; don't pick people's flowers—you might catch something; don't throw stones at blackbirds, because it might not be a blackbird at all; this is how to make a bread pudding; this is how to make doukona;[3] this is how to make pepper pot; this is how to make a good medicine for a cold; this is how to make a good medicine to throw away a child before it even becomes a child; this is how to catch a fish; this is how to throw back a fish you don't like, and that way something bad won't fall on you; this is how to bully a man; this is how a man bullies you; this is how to love a man, and if this doesn't work there are other ways, and if they don't work don't feel too bad about giving up; this is how to spit up in the air if you feel like it, and this is how to move quick so that it doesn't fall on you; this is how to make ends meet; always squeeze bread to make sure it's fresh; *but what if the baker won't let me feel the bread?*; you mean to say that after all you are really going to be the kind of woman who the baker won't let near the bread?

For a reading quiz, sources on Jamaica Kincaid, and annotated links to further readings on Kincaid's native Antigua, visit **bedfordstmartins.com/thebedfordreader**.

[2] Taro, a tropical plant with an edible tuber. —EDS.
[3] A pudding made of plantains, fruit similar to bananas. —EDS.

Journal Writing

Are the motherly warnings received by the girl of this story anything like the warnings or instructions that were drilled into you when you were a young adolescent? In your journal, explore the advice you remember receiving while growing up. Who took responsibility for instructing you in "proper" behavior? (To take your journal writing further, see "From Journal to Essay" on the facing page.)

Questions on Meaning

1. What are the CONNOTATIONS of the phrase "wharf-rat boys"? Why is the girl of the title supposed to avoid them?
2. What does it mean to "be the kind of woman who the baker won't let near the bread" (last line)?
3. What do the elements of the mother's advice add up to: What kind of life does she depict for her daughter?

Questions on Writing Strategy

1. Why do you think Kincaid wrote her story as one long sentence? What does she achieve?
2. What does Kincaid convey through the one comment and one question in italics?
3. Toward the end of this story, the mother says, "this is how to spit up in the air if you feel like it, and this is how to move quick so that it doesn't fall on you." What is the EFFECT of this particular piece of advice? What effect would it have if it were the last line of the story?
4. **OTHER METHODS.** The many obligations of a girl/woman can be CLASSIFIED into groups of skills and behaviors. What categories do you see? How do they help organize the story?

Questions on Language

1. What do the repeated directions about how to "sweep," "smile," and "set a table" suggest?
2. What can you conclude about the girl from the mother's scolding, "don't squat down to play marbles—you are not a boy, you know"?
3. Make sure you know the meanings of the following words: fritters, khaki, okra.
4. The fiction writer Stephanie Vaughn advises reading "Girl" aloud. She says, "I find that it is best to stand up when you read this story aloud, and to take a breath from the deepest region of your belly. When your lungs are full, when your shoulders are back, you begin to speak the story, and then you find that you are singing." Try it yourself. How is reading the story aloud different from reading it to yourself?

Suggestions for Writing

1. **FROM JOURNAL TO ESSAY.** "Adolescents' heads are stuffed with advice intended to make them conform to rigid cultural roles and values." Based on your own experience, do you agree or disagree with this statement? Write an essay explaining your position, using EXAMPLES from your journal entry as support.

2. It's fair to assume that "Girl" is at least partly autobiographical because Kincaid has often written or spoken about the influence of her mother. In "Jamaica Kincaid on Writing" (following), the author mentions rebelling against her mother's "magic." Elsewhere, she has said that her mother's close attention made Kincaid's past "a kind of museum. . . . Clearly, the way I became a writer is that my mother wrote my life for me and told it to me." What adult has had a large influence on you? How are you different today because of him or her? Write an essay identifying the parts of yourself that you can attribute to this person—in other words, analyzing yourself as the product of this person's interest (or lack of interest) in you.

3. **CRITICAL WRITING.** The story's speaker repeatedly and gloomily connects her daughter and a "slut." Write an essay analyzing Kincaid's use of *slut*. How does the mother seem to be defining this word? Why does she repeat it so often? Should we ASSUME that the daughter actually is a "slut"? What might be the effect of this repetition on the daughter? What is the effect on you, the reader?

4. **CONNECTIONS.** Judy Brady, in "I Want a Wife" (p. 344), and Kincaid both analyze women's traditional roles, although they have different perspectives on those roles. How are the roles they describe similar? What do the speakers' TONES convey about their attitudes toward their roles? Write an essay explaining how Brady and Kincaid use word choice, sentence structures, repetition, and other elements of tone to clarify their speakers' values and feelings.

Jamaica Kincaid on Writing

In a 1990 interview with Louise Kennedy in the *Boston Globe*, Jamaica Kincaid says that making sense of life is what motivates her writing. "I started out feeling alone," she remarks. "I grew up in a place where I was very alone. I didn't know then that I wanted to write; I didn't have that thought. But even if I had, I would have had no one to tell it to. They would have laughed before they threw me in a pond or something." With this beginning, Kincaid came to believe that the point of writing is not to please the reader. "Sometimes I feel—'I've pushed too far, I don't care, I don't care if you don't like this. I know it and it makes sense to me.'" The point, then, is to understand the world through the self. "I'm trying to discover the secret of myself. . . . For me everything passes through the self."

Kincaid's writing helps her come to terms with the conflicts in her life. "I could be dead or in jail. If you don't know how to make sense of what's happened to you, if you see things but can't express them — it's so painful." Part of Kincaid's pain growing up was the "magic" her mother held over her, a power that fueled Kincaid's rebellion. "That feeling of rebellion is doomed," she says. "You can't succeed. But it's worth trying because you find out that you can't. You have to try, or you die."

Although her native Antigua figures strongly in her writing, Kincaid cannot write there. "When I'm in the place where I'm from, I can't really think. I just absorb it; I take it all in. Then I come back and take it out and unpack it and walk through it." Her need for distance has led her to live in Vermont, "the opposite of where I come from. It changes. It's mountainous. It has seasons." As for Antigua, Kincaid says, "I don't know how to live there, but I don't know how to live without there."

For Discussion

1. How can not caring about the reader's response liberate a writer?
2. What does Kincaid mean by "everything passes through the self"? Do you experience this process from time to time?
3. How does the author view her place of birth? Do you find her last statement contradictory?

ADDITIONAL WRITING TOPICS

Division or Analysis

Write an essay by the method of division or analysis using one of the following subjects (or choose your own subject). In your essay, make sure your purpose and your
principle of division or analysis are clear to your readers. Explain the parts of your subject so that readers know how each relates to the others and contributes to the whole.

1. The slang or technical terminology of a group such as stand-up comedians or
   computer hackers
2. An especially bad movie, television show, or book
3. A doll, game, or other toy from childhood
4. A typical TV commercial for a product such as laundry soap, deodorant, beer, or
   a luxury or economy car
5. An appliance or a machine, such as a stereo speaker, a motorcycle, a microwave
   oven, or a camera
6. An organization or association, such as a social club, a sports league, or a support
   group
7. The characteristic appearance of a rock singer or a classical violinist
8. A year in the life of a student
9. Your favorite poem
10. A short story, an essay, or another work that made you think
11. The government of your community
12. The most popular video store (or other place of business) in town
13. The Bible
14. A band or an orchestra
15. A painting or statue

What Everyone Should Know About The Movie Rating System.

GENERAL AUDIENCES

G

Nothing that would offend parents for viewing by children.

G | GENERAL AUDIENCES
All Ages Admitted

PARENTAL GUIDANCE SUGGESTED

PG

Parents urged to give "parental guidance." May contain some material parents might not like for their young children.

PG | PARENTAL GUIDANCE SUGGESTED
SOME MATERIAL MAY NOT BE SUITABLE FOR CHILDREN

PARENTS STRONGLY CAUTIONED

PG-13

Parents are urged to be cautious. Some material may be inappropriate for pre-teenagers.

PG-13 | PARENTS STRONGLY CAUTIONED
Some Material May Be Inappropriate for Children Under 13

RESTRICTED

R

Contains some adult material. Parents are urged to learn more about the film before taking their young children with them.

R | RESTRICTED
UNDER 17 REQUIRES ACCOMPANYING PARENT OR ADULT GUARDIAN

NO ONE 17 AND UNDER ADMITTED

NC-17

Patently adult. Children are not admitted.

NC-17 | NO ONE 17 AND UNDER ADMITTED

10

CLASSIFICATION

Sorting into Kinds

THE METHOD

To CLASSIFY is to make sense of the world by arranging many units—
trucks, chemical elements, wasps, students—into more manageable groups.
Zoologists classify animals, botanists classify plants—and their classifications
help us to understand a vast and complex subject: life on earth. To help us find
books in a library, librarians classify books into categories: fiction, biography,
history, psychology, and so forth. For the convenience of readers, newspapers
run classified advertising, grouping many small ads into categories such as
Help Wanted and Cars for Sale.

Subjects and Reasons for Classification

The subject of a classification is always a number of things, such as
peaches or political systems. (In contrast, DIVISION or ANALYSIS, the topic of
the preceding chapter, usually deals with a solitary subject, a coherent whole,
such as *a* peach or *a* political system.) The job of classification is to sort the
things into groups or classes based on their similarities and differences. Say, for
instance, you're going to write an essay about how people write. After interviewing a lot of writers, you determine that writers' processes differ widely,
mainly in the amount of planning and rewriting they entail. (Notice that this
determination involves analyzing the process of writing, separating it into
steps. See Chap. 8.) On the basis of your findings, you create groups for planners, one-drafters, and rewriters. Once your groups are defined (and assuming
they are valid), your subjects (the writers) almost sort themselves out.

Classification is done for a PURPOSE. In a New York City guidebook, Joan
Hamburg and Norma Ketay discuss low-priced hotels. (Notice that already
they are examining the members of a group: low-priced as opposed to medium-
and high-priced hotels.) They cast the low-priced hotels into categories:
Rooms for Singles and Students, Rooms for Families, Rooms for Servicepeople,
and Rooms for General Occupancy. Always their purpose is evident: to match
up the visitor with a suitable kind of room. When a classification has no purpose, it seems a silly and hollow exercise.

Just as you can ANALYZE a subject (or divide a pie) in many ways, you can
classify a subject according to many principles. A different New York guidebook might classify all hotels according to price: grand luxury, luxury, commercial, low-priced (Hamburg and Ketay's category), fleabag, and flophouse.
The purpose of this classification would be to match visitors to hotels fitting
their pocketbooks. The principle you use in classifying things depends on your
purpose. A linguist might explain the languages of the world by classifying
them according to their origins (Romance languages, Germanic languages,
Coptic languages . . .), but a student battling with a college language require-

ment might try to entertain fellow students by classifying languages into three groups: hard to learn, harder to learn, and unlearnable.

Kinds of Classification

The simplest classification is binary (or two-part), in which you sort things out into (1) those with a certain distinguishing feature and (2) those without it. You might classify a number of persons, let's say, into smokers and nonsmokers, heavy metal fans and nonfans, runners and nonrunners, believers and nonbelievers. Binary classification is most useful when your subject is easily divisible into positive and negative categories.

Classification can be complex as well. As Jonathan Swift reminds us,

> So, naturalists observe, a flea
> Hath smaller fleas that on him prey,
> And these have smaller yet to bite 'em.
> And so proceed *ad infinitum*.

In being faithful to reality, you will sometimes find that you have to sort out the members of categories into subcategories. Hamburg and Ketay did something of the kind when they subclassified the class of low-priced New York hotels. Writing about the varieties of one Germanic language, such as English, a writer could identify the subclasses of British English, North American English, Australian English, and so on.

As readers, we all enjoy watching a clever writer sort things into categories. We like to meet classifications that strike us as true and familiar. This pleasure may account for the appeal of magazine articles that classify things ("The Seven Common Garden Varieties of Moocher," "Five Embarrassing Types of Social Blunder"). Usefulness as well as pleasure may explain the popularity of classifications that EVALUATE things. The magazine *Consumer Reports* sorts products as varied as computer monitors and canned tuna into groups based on quality (excellent, good, fair, poor, and not acceptable), and then, using DESCRIPTION, discusses each product. (Of a frozen pot pie: "Bottom crust gummy, meat spongy when chewed, with nondescript old-poultry and stale-flour flavor.")

THE PROCESS

Purposes and Theses

Classification will usually come into play when you want to impose order on a complex subject that includes many items. In one essay in this chapter, for instance, Stephanie Ericsson tackles the lies people tell one another.

Sometimes you may use classification humorously, as Russell Baker does in another essay in this chapter, to give a charge to familiar experiences. Whichever use you make of classification, though, do it for a reason. The files of composition instructors are littered with student essays in which nothing was ventured and nothing gained by classification.

Things can be classified into categories that reveal truth or into categories that don't tell us a thing. To sort out ten US cities according to their relative freedom from air pollution or their cost of living or the degree of progress they have made in civil rights might prove highly informative and useful. Such a classification might even tell us where we'd want to live. But to sort out the cities according to a superficial feature such as the relative size of their cat and dog populations wouldn't interest anyone, probably, except a veterinarian looking for a job.

Your purpose, your THESIS, and your principle of classification will all overlap at the point where you find your interest in your subject. Say you're curious about how other students write. Is your interest primarily in the materials they use (word processor, felt-tip pen, pencil), in where and when they write, or in how much planning and rewriting they do? Any of these could lead to a principle for sorting the students into groups. And that principle should be revealed in your THESIS STATEMENT, letting readers know why you are classifying. Here, from the essays in this chapter, are two examples of classification thesis statements:

> Inanimate objects are classified into three major categories—those that don't work, those that break down and those that get lost.
> —Russell Baker, "The Plot Against People"

> [I]t's not easy to entirely eliminate lies from our lives. No matter how pious we may try to be, we will still embellish, hedge, and omit to lubricate the daily machinery of living. But . . . acceptance of lies becomes a cultural cancer that eventually shrouds and reorders reality until moral garbage becomes as invisible to us as water is to a fish.
> —Stephanie Ericsson, "The Ways We Lie"

Categories

For a workable classification, make sure that the categories you choose don't overlap. If you were writing a survey of popular magazines for adults and you were sorting your subject into categories that included women's magazines and sports magazines, you might soon run into trouble. Into which category would you place *Women's Sports*? The trouble is that both categories take in the same item. To avoid this problem, you'll need to reorganize your classification on a different principle. You might sort out the magazines by their audiences: magazines mainly for women, magazines mainly for men, magazines for both women and men. Or you might group them according to subject matter: sports magazines, literary magazines, astrology magazines, fashion magazines, celebrity magazines, trade journals, and so on. *Women's Sports* would fit into either of those classification schemes, but into only *one* category in each scheme.

When you draw up a scheme of classification, be sure also that you include all essential categories. Omitting an important category can weaken the effect of your essay, no matter how well written it is. It would be a major oversight, for example, if you were to classify the residents of a dormitory according to their religious affiliations and not include a category for the numerous non-affiliated. Your reader might wonder if your sloppiness in forgetting a category extended to your thinking about the topic as well.

Some form of outline can be helpful to keep the classes and their members straight as you develop and draft ideas. You might experiment with a diagram in which you jot down headings for the groups, with plenty of space around them, and then let each heading accumulate members as you think of them, the way a magnet attracts paper clips. This kind of diagram offers more flexibility than a vertical list or an outline, and it may be a better aid for keeping categories from overlapping or disappearing.

FOCUS ON PARAGRAPH DEVELOPMENT

A crucial aim of classification is to make sure each group is clear: what's counted in, what's counted out, and why. You'll provide the examples and other details that make the groups clear as you develop the paragraph(s) devoted to each group.

The following paragraph barely outlines one group in a four-part classification of ex-smokers into zealots, evangelists, the elect, and the serene:

> The second group, evangelists, does not condemn smokers but encourages them to quit. Evangelists think quitting is easy, and they preach this message, often earning the resentment of potential converts.

Contrast this bare-bones adaptation with the actual paragraphs written by Franklin E. Zimring in his essay "Confessions of a Former Smoker":

> By contrast, the antismoking evangelist does not condemn smokers. Unlike the zealot, he regards smoking as an easily curable condition, as a social disease, and not a sin. The evangelist spends an enormous amount of time seeking and preaching to the unconverted. He argues that kicking the habit is not *that* difficult. After all, *he* did it; moreover, as he describes it, the benefits of quitting are beyond measure and the disadvantages are nil.

> The hallmark of the evangelist is his insistence that he never misses tobacco. Though he is less hostile to smokers than the zealot, he is resented more. Friends and loved ones who have been the targets of his preachments

frequently greet the resumption of smoking by the evangelist as an occasion for unmitigated glee.

In the second sentence of each paragraph, Zimring explicitly contrasts evangelists with zealots, the group he previously defined. And he does more as well: He provides specific examples of the evangelist's message (first paragraph) and of others' reactions to him (second paragraph). These details pin down the group, making it distinct from other groups and clear in itself.

CHECKLIST FOR REVISING A CLASSIFICATION

✔ **PURPOSE.** Have you classified for a reason? Will readers see why you bothered?

✔ **PRINCIPLE OF CLASSIFICATION.** Will readers also see what rule or principle you have used for sorting individuals into groups? Is this principle apparent in your thesis sentence?

✔ **CONSISTENCY.** Does each representative of your subject fall into one category only, so that categories don't overlap?

✔ **COMPLETENESS.** Have you mentioned all the essential categories suggested by your principle of classification?

✔ **PARAGRAPH DEVELOPMENT.** Have you provided enough examples and other details so that readers can easily distinguish each category from the others?

CLASSIFICATION IN PARAGRAPHS

Writing About Television

Written for *The Bedford Reader*, the following paragraph uses classification to explain how a TV comedy's taped laugh track combines various laughs to sound like an actual rib-tickled audience. With the related paragraph on page 341, which ANALYZES the elements of any particular kind of laugh, this paragraph could be part of a full behind-the-scenes essay on how TV comedies make us laugh, even despite ourselves.

Most canned laughs produced by laugh machines fall into one of five reliable sounds. There are *titters*, light vocal laughs with which an imaginary audience responds to a comedian's least wriggle or grimace. Some producers rely heavily on *chuckles*, deeper, more chesty responses. Most profound of all, *belly laughs* are summoned to acclaim broader jokes and sexual innuendos. When provided at full level of sound and in longest duration, the belly laugh becomes the Big Boffola. There are also *wild howls* or *screamers*, extreme responses used not more than three times per show, lest they seem fake. These

Topic sentence names principle of classification

Categories:
1. *Titters*
2. *Chuckles*
3. *Belly laughs*

4. *Wild howls or screamers*

are crowd laughs, and yet the machine also offers *freaky laughs*, the piercing, eccentric screeches of solitary kooks. With them, a producer affirms that even a canned audience may include one thorny individualist.

5. Freaky laughs

Examples clearly distinguish categories

Writing in an Academic Discipline

This paragraph comes from a textbook on human physical and cultural evolution. The author offers a standard classification of hand grips in order to explain one of several important differences between human beings and their nearest relatives, apes and monkeys.

There are two distinct ways of holding and using tools: the *power grip* and the *precision grip*, as John Napier termed them. Human infants and children begin with the power grip and progress to the precision grip. Think of how a child holds a spoon: first in the power grip, in its fist or between its fingers and palm, and later between the tips of the thumb and first two fingers, in the precision grip. Many primates have the power grip also. It is the way they get firm hold of a tree branch. But neither a monkey nor an ape has a thumb long enough or flexible enough to be completely *opposable* through rotation at the wrist, able to reach comfortably to the tips of all the other fingers, as is required for our delicate yet strong precision grip. It is the opposability of our thumb and the independent control of our fingers that make possible nearly all the movements necessary to handle tools, to make clothing, to write with a pencil, to play a flute.   —Bernard Campbell, *Humankind Emerging*

Topic sentence names principle of classification

Two categories explained side by side

Second category explained in greater detail

CLASSIFICATION IN PRACTICE

The summer between his sophomore and junior years of college, Kharron Reid was seeking an internship in computer networking. After seeing several likely openings posted at his school's placement office, he began compiling a résumé that would make him appealing to potential employers.

Part of Reid's challenge in drafting his résumé was to bring order to what seemed a complex and unwieldy subject, his life. The main solution was to classify his activities and interests into clearly defined groups, such as work experience, education, and special skills. Classification wasn't a conscious choice for Reid: He didn't think, "I must classify." Instead, he recognized from advice he'd seen on résumé writing that some sorting was required.

In his first draft, Reid worked to emphasize his qualifications for the internship he sought. The group that gave him the most trouble was work experience: Should he list his jobs with the specifics of each one? Or should

Classification

he further sort his work experience into skills (such as computer skills, administrative skills, and communication skills) and then list the specifics of his jobs
under each subcategory? He tried the résumé both ways and finally opted for
the former arrangement, which seemed more straightforward, potentially less
confusing to readers.

Before he could prepare his final draft, Reid also needed to decide which
to put first, the category of education or the category of work experience.
Here, he decided on work experience first because it was directly related to the
internships he now sought; his education was more broad based.

Reid's final résumé appears on the facing page. For the cover letter he
wrote to go with the résumé, see pages 193–94.

Kharron Reid
137 Chester Street, Apt. E
Allston, MA 02134
(617) 555-4009
kreid@bu.edu

OBJECTIVE
An internship that offers experience in information systems

EXPERIENCE
Pioneer Networking, Damani, MI, May–September 2003

As an intern, worked as a LAN specialist using a Unix-based server
- Connected eight workstations onto a LAN by laying physical platform and configuring software
- Assisted network engineer in monitoring operations of LAN

NBS Systems Corp., Denniston, MI, June–September 2002

As an intern, helped install seven WANs using Windows 2003
- Planned layout for WANs
- Installed physical platform and configured servers

SPECIAL SKILLS
Computer proficiency:

Windows 98/XP,	QuarkXPress	HTML
Windows NT/2000/2003	Adobe Photoshop	XML
Unix	and InDesign	JavaScript
Linux 2.4 and 2.6		

Internet research

INTERESTS
Building computers, designing Web sites, wrestling

EDUCATION
Boston University, School of Management, 2002 to present

Current standing: sophomore
Double major: business administration and information systems
Courses: introductory and advanced programming, information systems 1 and 2, basic business courses

Lahser High School, Bloomfield Hills, MI, 1998–2002

Graduated with academic, college-preparatory degree

REFERENCES
Available on request from Office of Career Services, Boston University, 19 Deerfield Street, Boston, MA 02215

Classification

RUSSELL BAKER

RUSSELL BAKER is one of America's notable humorists and political satirists. Born in 1925 in Virginia, Baker was raised in New Jersey and Maryland by his widowed mother. After serving in the navy during World War II, he earned a BA from Johns Hopkins University in 1947. He became a reporter for the *Baltimore Sun* that year and then joined the *New York Times* in 1954, covering the State Department, the White House, and Congress. From 1962 until his retirement from the *Times* in 1998, he wrote a popular column that ranged over the merely bothersome (unreadable menus) and the serious (the cold war). Baker has twice received the Pulitzer Prize, once for distinguished commentary and again for the first volume of his autobiography, *Growing Up* (1982). The most recent addition to the autobiography is *Looking Back* (2002). Many of Baker's columns have been collected in books, such as *There's a Country in My Cellar* (1990). Baker has also written fiction and children's books and edited *Russell Baker's Book of American Humor* (1993). In 1993 he began his television career as host of PBS's *Masterpiece Theatre*.

The Plot Against People

The critic R. Z. Sheppard has commented that Baker can "best be appreciated for doing what a good humorist has always done: writing to preserve his sanity for at least one more day." In this piece from the *New York Times* in 1968, Baker uses classification for that purpose, taking aim, as he has often done, at things.

Inanimate objects are classified into three major categories—those that 1 don't work, those that break down and those that get lost.

The goal of all inanimate objects is to resist man and ultimately to defeat 2 him, and the three major classifications are based on the method each object uses to achieve its purpose. As a general rule, any object capable of breaking down at the moment when it is most needed will do so. The automobile is typical of the category.

With the cunning typical of its breed, the automobile never breaks down 3 while entering a filling station with a large staff of idle mechanics. It waits until it reaches a downtown intersection in the middle of the rush hour, or until it is fully loaded with family and luggage on the Ohio Turnpike.

Thus it creates maximum misery, inconvenience, frustration and irritabil- 4 ity among its human cargo, thereby reducing its owner's life span.

Washing machines, garbage disposals, lawn mowers, light bulbs, auto- 5 matic laundry dryers, water pipes, furnaces, electrical fuses, television tubes, hose nozzles, tape recorders, slide projectors—all are in league with the automobile to take their turn at breaking down whenever life threatens to flow smoothly for their human enemies.

Many inanimate objects, of course, find it extremely difficult to break down. Pliers, for example, and gloves and keys are almost totally incapable of breaking down. Therefore, they have had to evolve a different technique for resisting man.   6

They get lost. Science has still not solved the mystery of how they do it, and no man has ever caught one of them in the act of getting lost. The most plausible theory is that they have developed a secret method of locomotion which they are able to conceal the instant a human eye falls upon them.   7

It is not uncommon for a pair of pliers to climb all the way from the cellar to the attic in its single-minded determination to raise its owner's blood pressure. Keys have been known to burrow three feet under mattresses. Women's purses, despite their great weight, frequently travel through six or seven rooms to find hiding space under a couch.   8

Scientists have been struck by the fact that things that break down virtually never get lost, while things that get lost hardly ever break down.   9

A furnace, for example, will invariably break down at the depth of the first winter cold wave, but it will never get lost. A woman's purse, which after all does have some inherent capacity for breaking down, hardly ever does; it almost invariably chooses to get lost.   10

Some persons believe this constitutes evidence that inanimate objects are not entirely hostile to man, and that a negotiated peace is possible. After all, they point out, a furnace could infuriate a man even more thoroughly by getting lost than by breaking down, just as a glove could upset him far more by breaking down than by getting lost.   11

Not everyone agrees, however, that this indicates a conciliatory attitude among inanimate objects. Many say it merely proves that furnaces, gloves and pliers are incredibly stupid.   12

The third class of objects — those that don't work — is the most curious of all. These include such objects as barometers, car clocks, cigarette lighters, flashlights and toy-train locomotives. It is inaccurate, of course, to say that they never work. They work once, usually for the first few hours after being brought home, and then quit. Thereafter, they never work again.   13

In fact, it is widely assumed that they are built for the purpose of not working. Some people have reached advanced ages without ever seeing some of these objects — barometers, for example — in working order.   14

Science is utterly baffled by the entire category. There are many theories about it. The most interesting holds that the things that don't work have attained the highest state possible for an inanimate object, the state to which things that break down and things that get lost can still only aspire.   15

They have truly defeated man by conditioning him never to expect any- 16
thing of them, and in return they have given man the only peace he receives
from inanimate society. He does not expect his barometer to work, his electric
locomotive to run, his cigarette lighter to light or his flashlight to illuminate,
and when they don't it does not raise his blood pressure.

He cannot attain that peace with furnaces and keys and cars and women's 17
purses as long as he demands that they work for their keep.

---

*For a reading quiz, sources on Russell Baker, and annotated links to additional humor writing, visit **bedfordstmartins.com/thebedfordreader**.*

Journal Writing

What other ways can you think of to classify inanimate objects? In your journal, try
expanding on Baker's categories, or create new categories of your own based on a different principle—for example, objects no student can live without or objects no student would want to be caught dead with. (To take your journal writing further, see
"From Journal to Essay" on the facing page.)

Questions on Meaning

1. What is Baker's THESIS?
2. Why don't things that break down get lost, and vice versa?
3. Does Baker have any PURPOSE other than to make his readers smile?
4. How have inanimate objects "defeated man"?

Questions on Writing Strategy

1. What is the EFFECT of Baker's principle of classification? What categories are
   omitted here, and why?
2. In paragraphs 6–10, how does Baker develop the category of things that get lost?
   Itemize the strategies he uses to make the category clear.
3. Find three places where Baker uses hyperbole. (See *Figures of speech* in Useful
   Terms if you need a definition.) What is the effect of the hyperbole?
4. How does the essay's INTRODUCTION help set its TONE? How does the CONCLUSION
   reinforce the tone?
5. **OTHER METHODS.** How does Baker use NARRATION to portray inanimate objects
   in the act of "resisting" people? Discuss how these mini-narratives make his classification more persuasive.

Questions on Language

1. Look up any of these words that are unfamiliar: plausible, locomotion (par. 7); invariably, inherent (10); conciliatory (12).
2. What are the CONNOTATIONS of the word "cunning" (par. 3)? What is its effect in this context?
3. Why does Baker use such expressions as "man," "some people," and "their human enemies" rather than *I* to describe those who come into conflict with inanimate objects? How might the essay have been different if Baker had relied on *I*?

Suggestions for Writing

1. **FROM JOURNAL TO ESSAY.** Write a brief, humorous essay based on one classification system from your journal entry. It may be helpful to use narration or DESCRIPTION in your classification. FIGURES OF SPEECH, especially hyperbole and understatement, can help you to establish a comic tone.
2. Think of a topic that would not generally be considered appropriate for a serious classification (some examples: game-show winners, body odors, stupid pet tricks, knock-knock jokes). Select a principle of classification and write a brief essay sorting the subject into categories. You may want to use a humorous tone; then again, you may want to approach the topic "seriously," counting on the contrast between subject and treatment to make your IRONY clear.
3. **CRITICAL WRITING.** In a short essay, discuss the likely AUDIENCE for "The Plot Against People." (Recall that it was first published in the *New York Times*.) What can you INFER from his EXAMPLES about Baker's own age and economic status? Does he ASSUME his audience is similar? How do the connections between author and audience help establish the essay's humor? Could this humor be seen as excluding some readers?
4. **CONNECTIONS.** Baker adopts a mock-serious tone here, one that pretends to almost scientific precision. How does Baker's tone COMPARE with the tone Horace Miner adopts in "Body Ritual Among the Nacirema" (p. 316)? What similarities and differences can you detect in each writer's STYLE of presentation? How do you think each writer's sense of his intended audience affected this style?

Russell Baker on Writing

In "Computer Fallout," an essay from the October 11, 1987, *New York Times Magazine*, Baker sets out to prove that computers make a writer's life easier, but he ends up somewhere else entirely. The skillful way he takes us along with him is what makes the journey enjoyable — and perhaps familiar.

The wonderful thing about writing with a computer instead of a type-writer or a lead pencil is that it's so easy to rewrite that you can make each sentence almost perfect before moving on to the next sentence.

An impressive aspect of using a computer to write with

One of the plusses about a computer on which to write

Happily, the computer is a marked improvement over both the typewriter and the lead pencil for purposes of literary composition, due to the ease with which rewriting can be effectuated, thus enabling

What a marked improvement the computer is for the writer over the typewriter and lead pencil

The typewriter and lead pencil were good enough in their day, but if Shakespeare had been able to access a computer with a good writing program

If writing friends scoff when you sit down at the computer and say, "The lead pencil was good enough for Shakespeare

One of the drawbacks of having a computer on which to write is the ease and rapidity with which the writing can be done, thus leading to the inclusion of many superfluous terms like "lead pencil," when the single word "pencil" would be completely, entirely and utterly adequate.

The ease with which one can rewrite on a computer gives it an advantage over such writing instruments as the pencil and typewriter by enabling the writer to turn an awkward and graceless sentence into one that is practically perfect, although it

The writer's eternal quest for the practically perfect sentence may be ending at last, thanks to the computer's gift of editing ease and swiftness to those confronting awkward, formless, nasty, illiterate sentences such as

Man's quest is eternal, but what specifically is it that he quests, and why does he

Mankind's quest is

Man's and woman's quest

Mankind's and womankind's quest

Humanity's quest for the perfect writing device

Eternal has been humanity's quest

Eternal have been many of humanity's quests

From the earliest cave writing, eternal has been the quest for a device that will forever prevent writers from using the word "quest," particularly when modified by such adjectives as "eternal," "endless," "tireless" and

Many people are amazed at the ease

Many persons are amazed by the ease

Lots of people are astounded when they see the nearly perfect sentences I write since upgrading my writing instrumentation from pencil and typewriter to

Listen, folks, there's nothing to writing almost perfect sentences with ease and rapidity provided you've given up the old horse-and-buggy writing mentality that says Shakespeare couldn't have written those great plays if he had enjoyed the convenience of electronic compositional instrumentation.

Folks, have you ever realized that there's nothing to writing almost

Have you ever stopped to think, folks, that maybe Shakespeare could have written even better if

To be or not to be, that is the central focus of the inquiry.

In the intrapersonal relationships played out within the mind as to the relative merits of continuing to exist as opposed to not continuing to exist

Live or die, a choice as ancient as humanities' eternal quest, is a tough choice which has confounded mankind as well as womankind ever since the option of dreaming was first perceived as a potentially negating effect of the quiescence assumed to be obtainable through the latter course of action.

I'm sick and tired of Luddites saying pencils and typewriters are just as good as computers for writing nearly perfect sentences when they — the Luddites, that is — have never experienced the swiftness and ease of computer writing which makes it possible to compose almost perfect sentences in practically no time at

Folks, are you sick and tired of

Are you, dear reader

Good reader, are you

A lot of you nice folks out there are probably just as sick and tired as I am of hearing people say they are sick and tired of this and that and

Listen, people, I'm just as sick and tired as you are of having writers and TV commercial performers who oil me in cornpone politician prose addressed to "you nice folks out

A curious feature of computers, as opposed to pencils and typewriters, is that when you ought to be writing something more interesting than a nearly perfect sentence

Since it is easier to revise and edit with a computer than with a typewriter or pencil, this amazing machine makes it very hard to stop editing and revising long enough to write a readable sentence, much less an entire newspaper column.

For Discussion

1. What is Baker's unstated THESIS? Does he convince you?
2. Do you find yourself ever having the problem Baker finally admits to in the last paragraph?

DEBORAH TANNEN

DEBORAH TANNEN is a linguist who is best known for her popular studies of communication between men and women. Born and raised in New York City, Tannen earned a BA from Harpur College (now the State University of New York at Binghamton); MAs from Wayne State University and the University of California at Berkeley; and a PhD in linguistics from Berkeley. She is University Professor at Georgetown University, has published many scholarly articles and books, and has lectured on linguistics all over the world. But her renown is more than academic: With television talk-show appearances, speeches to businesspeople and senators, and best-selling books like *You Just Don't Understand* (1990) and *Talking from 9 to 5* (1994), Tannen has become, in the words of one reviewer, "America's conversational therapist." She is working on a book about the relationships—and miscommunications—between mothers and their adult daughters.

But What Do You Mean?

Why do men and women so often communicate badly, if at all? This question motivates much of Tannen's research and writing, including the essay here. Excerpted in *Redbook* magazine from Tannen's book *Talking from 9 to 5*, "But What Do You Mean?" classifies the conversational areas where men and women have the most difficulty.

Conversation is a ritual. We say things that seem obviously the thing to say, without thinking of the literal meaning of our words, any more than we expect the question "How are you?" to call forth a detailed account of aches and pains.

Unfortunately, women and men often have different ideas about what's appropriate, different ways of speaking. Many of the conversational rituals common among women are designed to take the other person's feelings into account, while many of the conversational rituals common among men are designed to maintain the one-up position, or at least avoid appearing one-down. As a result, when men and women interact—especially at work—it's often women who are at the disadvantage. Because women are not trying to avoid the one-down position, that is unfortunately where they may end up.

Here, the biggest areas of miscommunication.

1. Apologies

Women are often told they apologize too much. The reason they're told to stop doing it is that, to many men, apologizing seems synonymous with putting oneself down. But there are many times when "I'm sorry" isn't self-deprecating, or even an apology; it's an automatic way of keeping both speakers on an equal footing. For example, a well-known columnist once interviewed me and gave me her phone number in case I needed to call her back. I misplaced the number and had to go through the newspaper's main switchboard. When our conversation was winding down and we'd both made ending-type remarks, I added, "Oh, I almost forgot—I lost your direct number, can I get it again?" "Oh, I'm sorry," she came back instantly, even though she had done nothing wrong and *I* was the one who'd lost the number. But I understood she wasn't really apologizing; she was just automatically reassuring me she had no intention of denying me her number.

Even when "I'm sorry" *is* an apology, women often assume it will be the 5 first step in a two-step ritual: I say "I'm sorry" and take half the blame, then you take the other half. At work, it might go something like this:

A: When you typed this letter, you missed this phrase I inserted.

B: Oh, I'm sorry. I'll fix it.

A: Well, I wrote it so small it was easy to miss.

When both parties share blame, it's a mutual face-saving device. But 6 if one person, usually the woman, utters frequent apologies and the other doesn't, she ends up looking as if she's taking the blame for mishaps that aren't her fault. When she's only partially to blame, she looks entirely in the wrong.

I recently sat in on a meeting at an insurance company where the sole 7 woman, Helen, said "I'm sorry" or "I apologize" repeatedly. At one point she said, "I'm thinking out loud. I apologize." Yet the meeting was intended to be an informal brainstorming session, and *everyone* was thinking out loud.

The reason Helen's apologies stood out was that she was the only person 8 in the room making so many. And the reason I was concerned was that Helen felt the annual bonus she had received was unfair. When I interviewed her colleagues, they said that Helen was one of the best and most productive workers—yet she got one of the smallest bonuses. Although the problem might have been outright sexism, I suspect her speech style, which differs from that of her male colleagues, masks her competence.

Unfortunately, not apologizing can have its price too. Since so many 9 women use ritual apologies, those who don't may be seen as hard-edged. What's important is to be aware of how often you say you're sorry (and why), and to monitor your speech based on the reaction you get.

2. Criticism

A woman who cowrote a report with a male colleague was hurt when she   10
read a rough draft to him and he leapt into a critical response—"Oh, that's
too dry! You have to make it snappier!" She herself would have been more
likely to say, "That's a really good start. Of course, you'll want to make it a little
snappier when you revise."

Whether criticism is given straight or softened is often a matter of con-   11
vention. In general, women use more softeners. I noticed this difference when
talking to an editor about an essay I'd written. While going over changes she
wanted to make, she said, "There's one more thing. I know you may not agree
with me. The reason I noticed the problem is that your other points are so
lucid and elegant." She went on hedging for several more sentences until I put
her out of her misery: "Do you want to cut that part?" I asked—and of course
she did. But I appreciated her tentativeness. In contrast, another editor (a
man) I once called summarily rejected my idea for an article by barking, "Call
me when you have something new to say."

Those who are used to ways of talking that soften the impact of criticism   12
may find it hard to deal with the right-between-the-eyes style. It has its own
logic, however, and neither style is intrinsically better. People who prefer criticism given straight are operating on an assumption that feelings aren't
involved: "Here's the dope. I know you're good; you can take it."

3. Thank-Yous

A woman manager I know starts meetings by thanking everyone for com-   13
ing, even though it's clearly their job to do so. Her "thank-you" is simply a
ritual.

A novelist received a fax from an assistant in her publisher's office; it con-   14
tained suggested catalog copy for her book. She immediately faxed him her
suggested changes and said, "Thanks for running this by me," even though her
contract gave her the right to approve all copy. When she thanked the assistant, she fully expected him to reciprocate: "Thanks for giving me such a
quick response." Instead, he said, "You're welcome." Suddenly, rather than an
equal exchange of pleasantries, she found herself positioned as the recipient of
a favor. This made her feel like responding, "Thanks for nothing!"

Many women use "thanks" as an automatic conversation starter and   15
closer; there's nothing literally to say thank you for. Like many rituals typical
of women's conversation, it depends on the goodwill of the other to restore
the balance. When the other speaker doesn't reciprocate, a woman may feel
like someone on a seesaw whose partner abandoned his end. Instead of balancing in the air, she has plopped to the ground, wondering how she got there.

4. Fighting

Many men expect the discussion of ideas to be a ritual fight—explored   16
through verbal opposition. They state their ideas in the strongest possible
terms, thinking that if there are weaknesses someone will point them out, and
by trying to argue against those objections, they will see how well their ideas
hold up.

Those who expect their own ideas to be challenged will respond to   17
another's ideas by trying to poke holes and find weak links—as a way of *helping*. The logic is that when you are challenged you will rise to the occasion:
Adrenaline makes your mind sharper; you get ideas and insights you would
not have thought of without the spur of battle.

But many women take this approach as a personal attack. Worse, they find   18
it impossible to do their best work in such a contentious environment. If
you're not used to ritual fighting, you begin to hear criticism of your ideas as
soon as they are formed. Rather than making you think more clearly, it makes
you doubt what you know. When you state your ideas, you hedge in order to
fend off potential attacks. Ironically, this is more likely to *invite* attack because
it makes you look weak.

Although you may never enjoy verbal sparring, some women find it help-   19
ful to learn how to do it. An engineer who was the only woman among four
men in a small company found that as soon as she learned to argue she was
accepted and taken seriously. A doctor attending a hospital staff meeting
made a similar discovery. She was becoming more and more angry with a male
colleague who'd loudly disagreed with a point she'd made. Her better judgment told her to hold her tongue, to avoid making an enemy of this powerful
senior colleague. But finally she couldn't hold it in any longer, and she rose to
her feet and delivered an impassioned attack on his position. She sat down in
a panic, certain she had permanently damaged her relationship with him. To
her amazement, he came up to her afterward and said, "That was a great rebuttal. I'm really impressed. Let's go out for a beer after work and hash out our
approaches to this problem."

5. Praise

A manager I'll call Lester had been on his new job six months when he   20
heard that the women reporting to him were deeply dissatisfied. When he
talked to them about it, their feelings erupted; two said they were on the verge
of quitting because he didn't appreciate their work, and they didn't want to
wait to be fired. Lester was dumbfounded: He believed they were doing a fine
job. Surely, he thought, he had said nothing to give them the impression he
didn't like their work. And indeed he hadn't. That was the problem. He had

said *nothing*—and the women assumed he was following the adage "If you can't say something nice, don't say anything." He thought he was showing confidence in them by leaving them alone.

Men and women have different habits in regard to giving praise. For ex- 21 ample, Deirdre and her colleague William both gave presentations at a conference. Afterward, Deirdre told William, "That was a great talk!" He thanked her. Then she asked, "What did you think of mine?" and he gave her a lengthy and detailed critique. She found it uncomfortable to listen to his comments. But she assured herself that he meant well, and that his honesty was a signal that she, too, should be honest when he asked for a critique of his performance. As a matter of fact, she had noticed quite a few ways in which he could have improved his presentation. But she never got a chance to tell him because he never asked—and she felt put down. The worst part was that it seemed she had only herself to blame, since she *had* asked what he thought of her talk.

But had she really asked for his critique? The truth is, when she asked for 22 his opinion, she was expecting a compliment, which she felt was more or less required following anyone's talk. When he responded with criticism, she figured, "Oh, he's playing 'Let's critique each other'"—not a game she'd initiated, but one which she was willing to play. Had she realized he was going to criticize her and not ask her to reciprocate, she would never have asked in the first place.

It would be easy to assume that Deirdre was insecure, whether she was 23 fishing for a compliment or soliciting a critique. But she was simply talking automatically, performing one of the many conversational rituals that allow us to get through the day. William may have sincerely misunderstood Deirdre's intention—or may have been unable to pass up a chance to one-up her when given the opportunity.

6. Complaints

"Troubles talk" can be a way to establish rapport with a colleague. You 24 complain about a problem (which shows that you are just folks) and the other person responds with a similar problem (which puts you on equal footing). But while such commiserating is common among women, men are likely to hear it as a request to *solve* the problem.

One woman told me she would frequently initiate what she thought 25 would be pleasant complaint-airing sessions at work. She'd talk about situations that bothered her just to talk about them, maybe to understand them better. But her male office mate would quickly tell her how she could improve the situation. This left her feeling condescended to and frustrated. She was delighted to see this very impasse in a section in my book *You Just Don't*

Understand, and showed it to him. "Oh," he said, "I see the problem. How can we solve it?" Then they both laughed, because it had happened again: He short-circuited the detailed discussion she'd hoped for and cut to the chase of finding a solution.

Sometimes the consequences of complaining are more serious: A man   26
might take a woman's lighthearted griping literally, and she can get a reputation as a chronic malcontent. Furthermore, she may be seen as not up to solving the problems that arise on the job.

7. Jokes

I heard a man call in to a talk show and say, "I've worked for two women   27
and neither one had a sense of humor. You know, when you work with men, there's a lot of joking and teasing." The show's host and the guest (both women) took his comment at face value and assumed the women this man worked for were humorless. The guest said, "Isn't it sad that women don't feel comfortable enough with authority to see the humor?" The host said, "Maybe when more women are in authority roles, they'll be more comfortable with power." But although the women this man worked for *may* have taken themselves too seriously, it's just as likely that they each had a terrific sense of humor, but maybe the humor wasn't the type he was used to. They may have been like the woman who wrote to me: "When I'm with men, my wit or cleverness seems inappropriate (or lost!) so I don't bother. When I'm with my women friends, however, there's no hold on puns or cracks and my humor is fully appreciated."

The types of humor women and men tend to prefer differ. Research has   28
shown that the most common form of humor among men is razzing, teasing, and mock-hostile attacks, while among women it's self-mocking. Women often mistake men's teasing as genuinely hostile. Men often mistake women's mock self-deprecation as truly putting themselves down.

Women have told me they were taken more seriously when they learned   29
to joke the way the guys did. For example, a teacher who went to a national conference with seven other teachers (mostly women) and a group of administrators (mostly men) was annoyed that the administrators always found reasons to leave boring seminars, while the teachers felt they had to stay and take notes. One evening, when the group met at a bar in the hotel, the principal asked her how one such seminar had turned out. She retorted, "As soon as you left, it got much better." He laughed out loud at her response. The playful insult appealed to the men—but there was a trade-off. The women seemed to back off from her after this. (Perhaps they were put off by her using joking to align herself with the bosses.)

There is no "right" way to talk. When problems arise, the culprit may be   30
style differences—and *all* styles will at times fail with others who don't share
or understand them, just as English won't do you much good if you try to speak
to someone who knows only French. If you want to get your message across,
it's not a question of being "right"; it's a question of using language that's
shared—or at least understood.

For a reading quiz, sources on Deborah Tannen, and annotated links to further
readings on gender differences in communication, visit **bedfordstmartins.com/
thebedfordreader**.

Journal Writing

Tannen's ANECDOTE about the newspaper columnist (par. 4) illustrates that much of
what we say is purely automatic. Do you excuse yourself when you bump into inanimate objects? When someone says, "Have a good trip," do you answer, "You too," even
if the other person isn't going anywhere? Do you find yourself overusing certain words
or phrases such as "like" or "you know"? Pay close attention to these kinds of verbal
tics in your own and others' speech. Over the course of a few days, note as many of
them as you can in your journal. (To take your journal writing further, see "From Journal to Essay" on the facing page.)

Questions on Meaning

1. What is Tannen's PURPOSE in writing this essay? What does she hope it will
   accomplish?
2. What does Tannen mean when she writes, "Conversation is a ritual" (par. 1)?
3. What does Tannen see as the fundamental difference between men's and
   women's conversational strategies?
4. Why is "You're welcome" not always an appropriate response to "Thank you"?

Questions on Writing Strategy

1. This essay has a large cast of characters: twenty-three to be exact. What function
   do these characters serve? How does Tannen introduce them to the reader? Does
   she describe them in sufficient detail?

2. Whom does Tannen see as her primary AUDIENCE? ANALYZE her use of the pronoun *you* in paragraphs 9 and 19. Whom does she seem to be addressing here? Why?
3. Analyze how Tannen develops the category of apologies in paragraphs 4–9. Where does she use EXAMPLE, DEFINITION, and COMPARISON AND CONTRAST?
4. How does Tannen's DESCRIPTION of a columnist as "well-known" (par. 4) contribute to the effectiveness of her example?
5. **OTHER METHODS.** For each of her seven areas of miscommunication, Tannen COMPARES AND CONTRASTS male and female communication styles and strategies. SUMMARIZE the main source of misunderstanding in each area.

Questions on Language

1. What is the EFFECT of "I put her out of her misery" (par. 11)? What does this phrase usually mean?
2. What does Tannen mean by a "right-between-the-eyes style" (par. 12)? What is the FIGURE OF SPEECH involved here?
3. What is the effect of Tannen's use of figurative verbs, such as "barking" (par. 11) and "erupted" (20)? Find at least one other example of the use of a verb in a non-literal sense.
4. Look up any of the following words whose meanings you are unsure of: synonymous, self-deprecating (par. 4); lucid, tentativeness (11); intrinsically (12); reciprocate (14); adrenaline, spur (17); contentious, hedge (18); sparring, rebuttal (19); adage (20); soliciting (23); commiserating (24); initiate, condescended, impasse (25); chronic, malcontent (26); razzing (28); retorted (29).

Suggestions for Writing

1. **FROM JOURNAL TO ESSAY.** Write an essay classifying the examples from your journal entry into categories of your own devising. You might sort out the examples by context ("phone blunders," "faulty farewells"), by purpose ("nervous tics," "space fillers"), or by some other principle of classification. Given your subject matter, you might want to adopt a humorous TONE.
2. How well does your style of communication conform to that of your gender as described by Tannen? Write a short essay about a specific communication problem or misunderstanding you have had with someone of the opposite sex (sibling, friend, parent, significant other). How well does Tannen's differentiation of male and female communication styles account for your particular problem?
3. How true do you find Tannen's assessment of miscommunication between the sexes? Consider the conflicts you have observed between your parents, among fellow students or coworkers, in fictional portrayals in books and movies. You could also go beyond your personal experiences and observations by researching the opinions of other experts (linguists, psychologists, sociologists, and so on). Write an essay confirming or questioning Tannen's GENERALIZATIONS, backing up your (and perhaps others') views with your own examples.
4. **CRITICAL WRITING.** Tannen insists that "neither [communication] style is intrinsically better" (par. 12), that "There is no 'right' way to talk" (30). What do you

make of this refusal to take sides in the battle of the sexes? Is Tannen always successful? Is absolute neutrality possible, or even desirable, when it comes to such
divisive issues?

5. **CONNECTIONS.** What pictures of men and women emerge from Tannen's essay
and from Dave Barry's "Batting Clean-Up and Striking Out" (p. 245)? In an essay,
DEFINE each sex as portrayed by these two authors, and then agree or disagree with
the definitions. Support your opinions with examples from your own observations
and experience.

Deborah Tannen on Writing

Though Deborah Tannen's "But What Do You Mean?" is written for a general audience, Tannen is a linguistics scholar who does considerable academic writing. One debate among scholarly writers is whether it is appropriate
to incorporate one's experiences and biases into academic writing, especially given the goal of objectivity in conducting and reporting research. The
October 1996 PMLA (*Publications of the Modern Language Association*) printed
a discussion of the academic uses of the personal, with contributions from
more than two dozen scholars. Tannen's comments, excerpted here, focused
on the first-person *I*.

When I write academic prose, I use the first person, and I instruct my students to do the same. The principle that researchers should acknowledge their
participation in their work is an outgrowth of a humanistic approach to linguistic analysis. . . . Understanding discourse is not a passive act of decoding
but a creative act of imagining a scene (composed of people engaged in culturally recognizable activities) within which the ideas being talked about
have meaning. The listener's active participation in sense making both results
from and creates interpersonal involvement. For researchers to deny their
involvement in their interpreting of discourse would be a logical and ethical
violation of this framework. . . .

[O]bjectivity in the analysis of interactions is impossible anyway.
Whether they took part in the interaction or not, researchers identify with
one or another speaker, are put off or charmed by the styles of participants.
This one reminds you of a cousin you adore; that one sounds like a neighbor
you despise. Researchers are human beings, not atomic particles or chemical
elements. . . .

Another danger of claiming objectivity rather than acknowledging and
correcting for subjectivity is that scholars who don't reveal their participation
in interactions they analyze risk the appearance of hiding it. "Following is an

exchange that occurred between a professor and a student," I have read in articles in my field. The speakers are identified as "A" and "B." The reader is not told that the professor, A (of course the professor is A and the student B), is the author. Yet that knowledge is crucial to contextualizing the author's interpretation. Furthermore, the impersonal designations A and B are another means of constructing a false objectivity. They obscure the fact that human interaction is being analyzed, and they interfere with the reader's understanding. The letters replace what in the author's mind are names and voices and personas that are the basis for understanding the discourse. Readers, given only initials, are left to scramble for understanding by imagining people in place of letters.

Avoiding self-reference by using the third person also results in the depersonalization of knowledge. Knowledge and understanding do not occur in abstract isolation. They always and only occur among people. . . . Denying that scholarship is a personal endeavor entails a failure to understand and correct for the inevitable bias that human beings bring to all their enterprises.

For Discussion

1. In arguing for the use of the first-person *I* in academic prose, Tannen is speaking primarily about its use in her own field, linguistics. From your experience with academic writing, is Tannen's argument applicable to other disciplines as well, such as history, biology, psychology, or government? Why, or why not? What have your teachers in various courses advised you about writing in the first person?

2. Try this experiment on the effects of the first person and third person (*he, she, they*): Write a passage of academic prose in one person or the other. (Tannen's example of professor A and student B can perhaps suggest a direction for your passage, or you may have one already written in a paper you've submitted.) Rewrite the passage in the other person, and ANALYZE the two versions. Does one sound more academic than the other? What are the advantages and disadvantages of each one?

SAMUEL P. HUNTINGTON

SAMUEL PHILLIPS HUNTINGTON was educated at Yale University (BA, 1946), the University of Chicago (MA, 1948), and Harvard University (PhD, 1951) and has been teaching political science at Harvard for more than fifty years. An expert on international relations and domestic policy, Huntington has also served on numerous commissions and as a consultant with the US government; for two years he worked as a policy analyst under President Jimmy Carter. Huntington has contributed to many general and scholarly periodicals, and in 1970 he cofounded *Foreign Policy*, a journal of global politics and economics. His books include *Political Order in Changing Societies* (1968), *American Politics: The Promise of Disharmony* (1981), and *Culture Matters: How Values Shape Human Progress* (with Lawrence E. Harrison, 2000). In the controversial book *The Clash of Civilizations and the Remaking of World Order* (1996), Huntington argues that widening rifts between major "civilizations," particularly between Islam and the West, increasingly shape international politics. (For a comment on Huntington's theory, see Edward Said's "Clashing Civilizations?" on p. 669.)

The Crisis of National Identity

One of Huntington's keenest interests is American national identity—how Americans think of themselves in relation to their country. In these opening pages from his book *Who Are We? The Challenges to America's National Identity* (2004), Huntington classifies the competing identities that, he believes, undermine national unity.

Charles Street, the principal thoroughfare on Boston's Beacon Hill, is a 1 comfortable street bordered by four-story brick buildings with apartments above antique stores and other shops on the ground level. At one time on one block American flags regularly hung over the entrances to the United States Post Office and the liquor store. Then the Post Office stopped displaying the flag, and on September 11, 2001, the liquor store flag flew alone. Two weeks later seventeen flags flew on this block, in addition to a huge Stars and Stripes suspended across the street a short distance away. With their country under attack, Charles Street denizens rediscovered their nation and identified themselves with it.

In their surge of patriotism, Charles Streeters were at one with people 2 throughout America. Since the Civil War, Americans have been a flag-oriented people. The Stars and Stripes has the status of a religious icon and is a more central symbol of national identity for Americans than their flags are for peoples of other nations. Probably never in the past, however, was the flag as omnipresent as it was after September 11. It was everywhere: homes, businesses, automobiles, clothes, furniture, windows, storefronts, lampposts, telephone poles. In early October, 80 percent of Americans said they were displaying the flag, 63 percent at home, 29 percent on clothes, 28 percent on cars.[1] Wal-Mart reportedly sold 116,000 flags on September 11 and 250,000 the next day, "compared with 6,400 and 10,000 on the same days a year earlier." The demand for flags was ten times what it had been during the Gulf War; flag manufacturers went overtime and doubled, tripled, or quintupled production.[2]

The flags were physical evidence of the sudden and dramatic rise in the   3
salience of national identity for Americans compared to their other identities, a transformation exemplified by the comment on October 1 of one young woman:

> When I was 19, I moved to New York City. . . . If you asked me to describe myself then, I would have told you I was a musician, a poet, an artist and, on a somewhat political level, a woman, a lesbian and a Jew. Being an American wouldn't have made my list.
>
> [In my college class Gender and Economics my] girlfriend and I were so frustrated by inequality in America that we discussed moving to another country. On Sept. 11, all that changed. I realized that I had been taking the freedoms I have here for granted. Now I have an American flag on my backpack, I cheer at the fighter jets as they pass overhead and I am calling myself a patriot.[3]

Rachel Newman's words reflect the low salience of national identity for   4
some Americans before September 11. Among some educated and elite Americans, national identity seemed at times to have faded from sight. Globalization, multiculturalism, cosmopolitanism, immigration, subnationalism, and antinationalism had battered American consciousness. Ethnic, racial, and gender identities came to the fore. In contrast to their predecessors, many immigrants were ampersands, maintaining dual loyalties and dual citizenships. A massive Hispanic influx raised questions concerning America's linguistic and cultural unity. Corporate executives, professionals, and Information Age technocrats espoused cosmopolitan over national identities. The teaching of national history gave way to the teaching of ethnic and racial histories. The celebration of diversity replaced emphasis on what Americans had in

---

[1] Luntz Research Co. survey of 1,000 adults, 3 October 2001, reported in *USA Today*, 19–21 October 2001, p. 1.

[2] *New York Times*, 23 September 2001, p. B6.

[3] Rachel Newman, "The Day the World Changed, I Did Too," *Newsweek*, 1 October 2001, p. 9.

common. The national unity and sense of national identity created by work and war in the eighteenth and nineteenth centuries and consolidated in the world wars of the twentieth century seemed to be eroding. By 2000, America was, in many respects, less a nation than it had been for a century. The Stars and Stripes were at half-mast and other flags flew higher on the flagpole of American identities.

The challenges to the salience of American national identity from other-national, subnational, and transnational identities were epitomized in several events of the 1990s.

Other-National Identities

At a Gold Cup soccer game between Mexico and the United States in February 1998, the 91,255 fans were immersed in a "sea of red, white, and green flags"; they booed when "The Star-Spangled Banner" was played; they "pelted" the US players "with debris and cups of what might have been water, beer or worse"; and they attacked with "fruit and cups of beer" a few fans who tried to raise an American flag. This game took place not in Mexico City but in Los Angeles. "Something's wrong when I can't even raise an American flag in my own country," a US fan commented, as he ducked a lemon going by his head. "Playing in Los Angeles is not a home game for the United States," a *Los Angeles Times* reporter agreed.[4]

Past immigrants wept with joy when, after overcoming hardship and risk, they saw the Statue of Liberty; enthusiastically identified themselves with their new country that offered them liberty, work, and hope; and often became the most intensely patriotic of citizens. In 2000 the proportion of foreign-born was somewhat less than in 1910, but the proportion of people in America who were also loyal to and identified with other countries was quite possibly higher than at any time since the American Revolution.

Subnational Identities

In his book *Race Pride and the American Identity*, Joseph Rhea quotes the poetry recited at two presidential inaugurations.[5] At President John F. Kennedy's in 1961, Robert Frost hailed the "heroic deeds" of America's founding that with God's "approval" ushered in "a new order of the ages":

---

[4] *Los Angeles Times*, 16 February 1998, pp. B1, C1; John J. Miller, "Becoming an American," *New York Times*, 26 May 1998, p. A27.

[5] Joseph Tilden Rhea, *Race Pride and the American Identity* (Cambridge: Harvard University Press, 1997), pp. 1–2, 8–9.

Our venture in revolution and outlawry
Has justified itself in freedom's story
Right down to now in glory upon glory.

America, he said, was entering a new "golden age of poetry and power."[6]

Thirty-two years later, Maya Angelou recited a poem at President Bill
Clinton's inauguration that conveyed a different image of America. Without
ever mentioning the words "America" or "American," she identified twenty-
seven racial, religious, tribal, and ethnic groups — Asian, Jewish, Muslim,
Pawnee, Hispanic, Eskimo, Arab, Ashanti among others — and denounced
the immoral repression they suffered, as a result of America's "armed struggles
for profit" and its "bloody sear" of "cynicism." America, she said, may be "wedded forever to fear, yoked eternally to brutishness."[7] Frost saw America's history and identity as glories to be celebrated and perpetuated. Angelou saw the
manifestations of American identity as evil threats to the well-being and real
identities of people with their subnational groups.

A similar contrast in attitudes occurred in a 1997 telephone interview by
a *New York Times* reporter with Ward Connerly, then the leading proponent
of an initiative measure in California prohibiting affirmative action by the
state government. The following exchange occurred:

REPORTER   What are you?
CONNERLY   I am an American.
REPORTER   No, no, no! What *are* you?
CONNERLY   Yes, yes, yes! I am an American.
REPORTER   That is not what I mean. I was told that you are African Ameri-
can. Are you ashamed to be African American?
CONNERLY   No, I am just proud to be an American.

Connerly then explained that his ancestry included Africans, French, Irish,
and American Indians, and the dialog concluded:

REPORTER   What does that make you?
CONNERLY   That makes me all-American![8]

In the 1990s, however Americans like Rachel Newman did not respond
to the question "What are you?" with Ward Connerly's passionate affirmation
of his national identity. They instead articulated subnational racial, ethnic, or
gender identities, as the *Times* reporter clearly expected.

---

[6] Robert Frost, *Selected Poems of Robert Frost* (New York: Holt, Rinehart and Winston,
1963), pp. 297–301, 422.

[7] Maya Angelou, "On the Pulse of Morning," *New York Times*, 21 January 1993, p. A14.

[8] Ward Connerly, "Back to Equality," *Imprimis* 27 (February 1998), p. 3.

Transnational Identities

In 1996 Ralph Nader wrote to the chief executive officers of one hundred   12
of the largest American corporations pointing to the substantial tax benefits
and other subsidies (estimated at $65 billion a year by the Cato Institute) they
received from the federal government and urging them to show their support
for "the country that bred them, built them, subsidized them, and defended
them" by having their directors open their annual stockholders meeting by
reciting the Pledge of Allegiance to the flag and the republic for which it
stands. One corporation (Federated Department Stores) responded favorably;
half the corporations never responded; others rejected it brusquely. The
respondent for Ford explicitly claimed transnational identity: "As a multinational . . . Ford in its largest sense is an Australian company in Australia, a
British company in the United Kingdom, a German company in Germany."
Aetna's CEO called Nader's idea "contrary to the principles on which our
democracy was founded." Motorola's respondent condemned its "political and
nationalistic overtones." Price Costco's CEO asked, "What do you propose
next—personal loyalty oaths?" And Kimberly-Clark's executive asserted that
it was "a grim reminder of the loyalty oaths of the 1950s."[9]

Undoubtedly the vociferous reaction of American corporate leaders was   13
in part because Nader had been hounding them for years and they could not
resist the opportunity to castigate him as a latter-day Joe McCarthy.[10] Yet they
were not alone among American elites in downgrading or disavowing identification with their country. Prominent intellectuals and scholars attacked
nationalism, warned of the dangers of inculcating national pride and commitment to America in students, and argued that a national identity was undesirable. Statements like these reflected the extent to which some people in
American elite groups, business, financial, intellectual, professional, and even
governmental, were becoming denationalized and developing transnational
and cosmopolitan identities superseding their national ones. This was not true
of the American public—and a gap consequently emerged between the pri-
macy of national identity for most Americans and the growth of transnational
identities among the controllers of power, wealth, and knowledge in American society.

September 11 drastically reduced the salience of these other identities   14
and sent Old Glory back to the top of the national flag pole. Will it stay there?

---

[9] Correspondence supplied by Ralph Nader; Jeff Jacoby, "Patriotism and the CEOs," *Boston Globe*, 30 July 1998, p. A15.

[10] As a US senator in the early 1950s, McCarthy (1908–57) used sensationalism and false accusation to exploit anti-Communist fear. — Eds.

The seventeen flags on Charles Street declined to twelve in November, nine in December, seven in January, and five in March, and were down to four by the first anniversary of the attacks, four times the number pre–September 11 but also one-fourth of those displayed immediately afterward. As an index of the salience of national identity, did this represent a modified post–September 11 normalcy, a slightly revised pre–September 11 normalcy, or a new, post–post–September 11 normalcy? Does it take an Osama bin Laden, as it did for Rachel Newman, to make us realize that we are Americans? If we do not experience recurring destructive attacks, will we return to the fragmentation and eroded Americanism before September 11? Or will we find a revitalized national identity that is not dependent on calamitous threats from abroad and that provides the unity lacking in the last decades of the twentieth century?

*For a reading quiz, sources on Samuel P. Huntington, and annotated links to further readings on group identities, visit **bedfordstmartins.com/thebedfordreader**.*

Journal Writing

How do you respond to Huntington's concern about patriotism? What do you think about immigrants maintaining a connection to their native country, about identity based on ethnicity or other characteristics, about valuing a sense of global community? Reflect on these issues in your journal. (To take your journal writing further, see "From Journal to Essay" on the next page.)

Questions on Meaning

1. To what does Huntington attribute "the low salience of national identity for some Americans before September 11" (par. 4)? (What does *salience* mean?)
2. In your own words, define each of Huntington's three categories of identity. How does each differ from the traditional American identity?
3. What is Huntington's THESIS? What is his PURPOSE?

Questions on Writing Strategy

1. Why does Huntington begin and end with the flags flying above Charles Street in Boston?
2. How does Huntington use the example of Rachel Newman in paragraphs 3–4 and 14? What does she represent for him? How does he use the example of Ward Connerly (par. 10) to CONTRAST with that of Rachel Newman?

3. How does Huntington develop the category of subnational identities in paragraphs 8–11?
4. What is the EFFECT of Huntington's phrasing his final sentences as questions?
5. **OTHER METHODS.** Why does Huntington include so many EXAMPLES of corporate
   executives' responses to the suggestion that stockholders' meetings open with the
   Pledge of Allegiance?

Questions on Language

1. How would you describe Huntington's TONE in the essay?
2. What does Huntington achieve by quoting from the two inaugural poems (pars.
   8 and 9)? How does the language of the quotations differ?
3. Consult a dictionary if you are unsure of the meanings of any of the following:
   denizens (par. 1); globalization, predecessors, ampersands (4); manifestations (9);
   brusquely (12); vociferous, inculcating, superseding (13); recurring, revitalized,
   calamitous (14).

Suggestions for Writing

1. **FROM JOURNAL TO ESSAY.** Based on your journal writing, draft an essay in which
   you explain your attitude toward national identity. How would you describe your
   own group identity or identities? Should a national identity always take precedence over other possible identities? As you write, imagine an audience that may
   not entirely agree with you. Can you make a convincing case for your own viewpoint?
2. Identify a current controversy over national policy—health care, Social Security, gun control, education, foreign relations, and so on. Read newspaper and
   weekly magazine editorials, letters to the editor, and other statements on the subject of the controversy. You could also discuss the issue with friends and family.
   Based on your research, write an essay in which you classify people according to
   their stand on the issue. Try to be as objective as possible.
3. **CRITICAL WRITING.** Read the two inaugural poems Huntington refers to, Robert
   Frost's "Dedication" and Maya Angelou's "On the Pulse of Morning." (Both
   poems are widely available on the Internet.) Then write an essay in which you
   consider Huntington's quotations from the poems. Do the quotations accurately
   represent each poet's message? Explain your answer in detail.
4. **CONNECTIONS.** Naomi Klein's "A Web of Brands" (p. 440) and Chitra Divakaruni's "Live Free and Starve" (p. 448) both address effects of global business.
   Write an essay that explores the extent to which these two authors and Huntington might agree or disagree with one another.

STEPHANIE ERICSSON

STEPHANIE ERICSSON is an insightful and frank writer who composes out of her own life. Her book on loss, *Companion Through the Darkness: Inner Dialogues on Grief* (1993), grew out of journal entries and extensive research into the grieving process following the sudden death of her husband while she was pregnant. Ericsson was born in 1953, grew up in San Francisco, and began writing at the age of fifteen. After studying filmmaking in college, she became a screenwriter's assistant and later a writer of situation comedies and advertising. During these years she struggled with substance abuse; after her recovery in 1980 she published *Shamefaced* and *Women of AA: Recovering Together* (both 1985). *Companion into the Dawn: Inner Dialogues on Loving* (1994) is Ericsson's most recent book. She lives in Minneapolis with her two children.

The Ways We Lie

Ericsson wrote this essay from notes for *Companion into the Dawn*, and it was published in the *Utne Reader* for November/December 1992. With classification, Ericsson identifies the kinds of lies we all tell at one time or another. Lying, she finds, may be unavoidable and even sometimes beneficial. But then how do we know when to stop?

William Lutz's "The World of Doublespeak," the essay following Ericsson's, also uses classification to examine types of lies, specifically the verbal substitutions that make "the bad seem good, the negative appear positive."

The bank called today and I told them my deposit was in the mail, even though I hadn't written a check yet. It'd been a rough day. The baby I'm pregnant with decided to do aerobics on my lungs for two hours, our three-year-old daughter painted the living-room couch with lipstick, the IRS put me on hold for an hour, and I was late to a business meeting because I was tired. 1

I told my client that traffic had been bad. When my partner came home, his haggard face told me his day hadn't gone any better than mine, so when he asked, "How was your day?" I said, "Oh, fine," knowing that one more straw might break his back. A friend called and wanted to take me to lunch. I said I was busy. Four lies in the course of a day, none of which I felt the least bit guilty about. 2

We lie. We all do. We exaggerate, we minimize, we avoid confrontation, we spare people's feelings, we conveniently forget, we keep secrets, we justify 3 lying to the big-guy institutions. Like most people, I indulge in small false-hoods and still think of myself as an honest person. Sure I lie, but it doesn't hurt anything. Or does it?

I once tried going a whole week without telling a lie, and it was para-   4
lyzing. I discovered that telling the truth all the time is nearly impossible. It means living with some serious consequences: The bank charges me $60 in overdraft fees, my partner keels over when I tell him about my travails, my client fires me for telling her I didn't feel like being on time, and my friend takes it personally when I say I'm not hungry. There must be some merit to lying.

But if I justify lying, what makes me any different from slick politicians or   5
the corporate robbers who raided the S&L industry? Saying it's okay to lie one way and not another is hedging. I cannot seem to escape the voice deep inside me that tells me: When someone lies, someone loses.

What far-reaching consequences will I, or others, pay as a result of my lie?   6
Will someone's trust be destroyed? Will someone else pay *my* penance because I ducked out? We must consider the *meaning of our actions*. Deception, lies, capital crimes, and misdemeanors all carry meanings. *Webster's* definition of *lie* is specific:

> 1: a false statement or action especially made with the intent to deceive;
> 2: anything that gives or is meant to give a false impression.

A definition like this implies that there are many, many ways to tell a lie.   7
Here are just a few.

The White Lie

A man who won't lie to a woman has very little consideration for her feelings.
                                                    —Bergen Evans

The white lie assumes that the truth will cause more damage than a   8
simple, harmless untruth. Telling a friend he looks great when he looks like hell can be based on a decision that the friend needs a compliment more than a frank opinion. But, in effect, it is the liar deciding what is best for the lied to. Ultimately, it is a vote of no confidence. It is an act of subtle arrogance for anyone to decide what is best for someone else.

Yet not all circumstances are quite so cut-and-dried. Take, for instance,   9
the sergeant in Vietnam who knew one of his men was killed in action but listed him as missing so that the man's family would receive indefinite com-pensation instead of the lump-sum pittance the military gives widows and children. His intent was honorable. Yet for twenty years this family kept their hopes alive, unable to move on to a new life.

Façades

Et tu, Brute?
—Caesar

We all put up façades to one degree or another. When I put on a suit to go   10
to see a client, I feel as though I am putting on another face, obeying the
expectation that serious businesspeople wear suits rather than sweatpants. But
I'm a writer. Normally, I get up, get the kid off to school, and sit at my computer in my pajamas until four in the afternoon. When I answer the phone,
the caller thinks I'm wearing a suit (though the UPS man knows better).

But façades can be destructive because they are used to seduce others into   11
an illusion. For instance, I recently realized that a former friend was a liar.
He presented himself with all the right looks and the right words and offered
lots of new consciousness theories, fabulous books to read, and fascinating
insights. Then I did some business with him, and the time came for him to pay
me. He turned out to be all talk and no walk. I heard a plethora of reasonable
excuses, including in-depth descriptions of the big break around the corner. In
six months of work, I saw less than a hundred bucks. When I confronted him,
he raised both eyebrows and tried to convince me that I'd heard him wrong,
that he'd made no commitment to me. A simple investigation into his past
revealed a crowded graveyard of disenchanted former friends.

Ignoring the Plain Facts

Well, you must understand that Father Porter is only human.
—A Massachusetts priest

In the '60s, the Catholic Church in Massachusetts began hearing com-   12
plaints that Father James Porter was sexually molesting children. Rather
than relieving him of his duties, the ecclesiastical authorities simply moved
him from one parish to another between 1960 and 1967, actually providing
him with a fresh supply of unsuspecting families and innocent children to
abuse. After treatment in 1967 for pedophilia, he went back to work, this
time in Minnesota. The new diocese was aware of Father Porter's obsession
with children, but they needed priests and recklessly believed treatment had
cured him. More children were abused until he was relieved of his duties a year
later. By his own admission, Porter may have abused as many as a hundred
children.

Ignoring the facts may not in and of itself be a form of lying, but con-   13
sider the context of this situation. If a lie is *a false action done with the intent
to deceive,* then the Catholic Church's conscious covering for Porter created
irreparable consequences. The church became a co-perpetrator with Porter.

Deflecting

When you have no basis for an argument, abuse the plaintiff.
—Cicero

I've discovered that I can keep anyone from seeing the true me by being   14
selectively blatant. I set a precedent of being up-front about intimate issues,
but I never bring up the things I truly want to hide; I just let people assume I'm
revealing everything. It's an effective way of hiding.

Any good liar knows that the way to perpetuate an untruth is to deflect   15
attention from it. When Clarence Thomas exploded with accusations that
the Senate hearings were a "high-tech lynching," he simply switched the
focus from a highly charged subject to a radioactive subject.[1] Rather than
defending himself, he took the offensive and accused the country of racism.
It was a brilliant maneuver. Racism is now politically incorrect in official
circles—unlike sexual harassment, which still rewards those who can get
away with it.

Some of the most skilled deflectors are passive-aggressive people who,   16
when accused of inappropriate behavior, refuse to respond to the accusations.
This you-don't-exist stance infuriates the accuser, who, understandably, screams
something obscene out of frustration. The trap is sprung and the act of de-
flection successful, because now the passive-aggressive person can indignantly
say, "Who can talk to someone as unreasonable as you?" The real issue is forgotten and the sins of the original victim become the focus. Feeling guilty of
name-calling, the victim is fully tamed and crawls into a hole, ashamed. I
have watched this fighting technique work thousands of times in disputes
between men and women, and what I've learned is that the real culprit is not
necessarily the one who swears the loudest.

Omission

The cruelest lies are often told in silence.
—R. L. Stevenson

Omission involves telling most of the truth minus one or two key facts   17
whose absence changes the story completely. You break a pair of glasses that
are guaranteed under normal use and get a new pair, without mentioning that
the first pair broke during a rowdy game of basketball. Who hasn't tried something like that? But what about omission of information that could make a difference in how a person lives his or her life?

---

[1] Ericsson refers to the 1991 hearings to confirm Thomas for the Supreme Court, at which
Thomas was accused by Anita Hill of sexual harassment. —EDS.

For instance, one day I found out that rabbinical legends tell of another   18
woman in the Garden of Eden before Eve. I was stunned. The omission of the
Sumerian goddess Lilith from Genesis—as well as her demonization by
ancient misogynists as an embodiment of female evil—felt like spiritual robbery. I felt like I'd just found out my mother was really my stepmother. To take
seriously the tradition that Adam was created out of the same mud as his equal
counterpart, Lilith, redefines all of Judeo-Christian history.

Some renegade Catholic feminists introduced me to a view of Lilith that   19
had been suppressed during the many centuries when this strong goddess was
seen only as a spirit of evil. Lilith was a proud goddess who defied Adam's need
to control her, attempted negotiations, and when this failed, said adios and
left the Garden of Eden.

This omission of Lilith from the Bible was a patriarchal strategy to keep   20
women weak. Omitting the strong-woman archetype of Lilith from Western religions and starting the story with Eve the Rib has helped keep Christian and Jewish women believing they were the lesser sex for thousands of
years.

Stereotypes and Clichés

Where opinion does not exist, the status quo becomes stereotyped and all
originality is discouraged.   —Bertrand Russell

Stereotype and cliché serve a purpose as a form of shorthand. Our need for   21
vast amounts of information in nanoseconds has made the stereotype vital to
modern communication. Unfortunately, it often shuts down original thinking, giving those hungry for the truth a candy bar of misinformation instead of
a balanced meal. The stereotype explains a situation with just enough truth to
seem unquestionable.

All the "isms"—racism, sexism, ageism, et al.—are founded on and   22
fueled by the stereotype and the cliché, which are lies of exaggeration, omission, and ignorance. They are always dangerous. They take a single tree and
make it a landscape. They destroy curiosity. They close minds and separate
people. The single mother on welfare is assumed to be cheating. Any black
male could tell you how much of his identity is obliterated daily by stereotypes. Fat people, ugly people, beautiful people, old people, large-breasted
women, short men, the mentally ill, and the homeless all could tell you
how much more they are like us than we want to think. I once admitted to a
group of people that I had a mouth like a truck driver. Much to my surprise, a
man stood up and said, "I'm a truck driver, and I never cuss." Needless to say,
I was humbled.

Groupthink

Who is more foolish, the child afraid of the dark, or the man afraid of the light?   —Maurice Freehill

Irving Janis, in *Victims of Group Think*, defines this sort of lie as a psycho-   23
logical phenomenon within decision-making groups in which loyalty to the
group has become more important than any other value, with the result that
dissent and the appraisal of alternatives are suppressed. If you've ever worked
on a committee or in a corporation, you've encountered groupthink. It
requires a combination of other forms of lying—ignoring facts, selective
memory, omission, and denial, to name a few.

The textbook example of groupthink came on December 7, 1941. From as   24
early as the fall of 1941, the warnings came in, one after another, that Japan
was preparing for a massive military operation. The navy command in Hawaii
assumed Pearl Harbor was invulnerable—the Japanese weren't stupid enough
to attack the United States' most important base. On the other hand, racist
stereotypes said the Japanese weren't smart enough to invent a torpedo effective in less than 60 feet of water (the fleet was docked in 30 feet); after all, US
technology hadn't been able to do it.

On Friday, December 5, normal weekend leave was granted to all the   25
commanders at Pearl Harbor, even though the Japanese consulate in Hawaii
was busy burning papers. Within the tight, good-ole-boy cohesiveness of the
US command in Hawaii, the myth of invulnerability stayed well entrenched.
No one in the group considered the alternatives. The rest is history.

Out-and-Out Lies

The only form of lying that is beyond reproach is lying for its own sake.   —Oscar Wilde

Of all the ways to lie, I like this one the best, probably because I get tired   26
of trying to figure out the real meanings behind things. At least I can trust the
bald-faced lie. I once asked my five-year-old nephew, "Who broke the fence?"
(I had seen him do it.) He answered, "The murderers." Who could argue?

At least when this sort of lie is told it can be easily confronted. As the per-   27
son who is lied to, I know where I stand. The bald-faced lie doesn't toy with
my perceptions—it argues with them. It doesn't try to refashion reality, it tries
to refute it. *Read my lips.* . . . No sleight of hand. No guessing. If this were the
only form of lying, there would be no such things as floating anxiety or the
adult-children-of-alcoholics movement.

Dismissal

Pay no attention to that man behind the curtain!
I am the Great Oz!	—The Wizard of Oz

Dismissal is perhaps the slipperiest of all lies. Dismissing feelings, percep-	28
tions, or even the raw facts of a situation ranks as a kind of lie that can do as
much damage to a person as any other kind of lie.

The roots of many mental disorders can be traced back to the dismissal of	29
reality. Imagine that a person is told from the time she is a tot that her perceptions are inaccurate. *"Mommy, I'm scared."* "No you're not, darling." *"I
don't like that man next door, he makes me feel icky."* "Johnny, that's a terrible
thing to say, of course you like him. You go over there right now and be nice
to him."

I've often mused over the idea that madness is actually a sane reaction to	30
an insane world. Psychologist R. D. Laing supports this hypothesis in *Sanity,
Madness and the Family*, an account of his investigation into the families of
schizophrenics. The common thread that ran through all of the families he
studied was a deliberate, staunch dismissal of the patient's perceptions from a
very early age. Each of the patients started out with an accurate grasp of reality, which, through meticulous and methodical dismissal, was demolished
until the only reality the patient could trust was catatonia.

Dismissal runs the gamut. Mild dismissal can be quite handy for forgiving	31
the foibles of others in our day-to-day lives. Toddlers who have just learned to
manipulate their parents' attention sometimes are dismissed out of necessity.
Absolute attention from the parents would require so much energy that no
one would get to eat dinner. But we must be careful and attentive about how
far we take our "necessary" dismissals. Dismissal is a dangerous tool, because
it's nothing less than a lie.

Delusion

We lie loudest when we lie to ourselves.
—Eric Hoffer

I could write the book on this one. Delusion, a cousin of dismissal, is the	32
tendency to see excuses as facts. It's a powerful lying tool because it filters out
information that contradicts what we want to believe. Alcoholics who believe
that the problems in their lives are legitimate reasons for drinking rather than
results of the drinking offer the classic example of deluded thinking. Delusion
uses the mind's ability to see things in myriad ways to support what it wants to
be the truth.

But delusion is also a survival mechanism we all use. If we were to fully	33
contemplate the consequences of our stockpiles of nuclear weapons or global

warming, we could hardly function on a day-to-day level. We don't want to incorporate that much reality into our lives because to do so would be paralyzing.

Delusion acts as an adhesive to keep the status quo intact. It shamelessly   34
employs dismissal, omission, and amnesia, among other sorts of lies. Its most cunning defense is that it cannot see itself.

•   •   •

The liar's punishment . . . is that he cannot believe anyone else.
—George Bernard Shaw

These are only a few of the ways we lie. Or are lied to. As I said earlier, it's   35
not easy to entirely eliminate lies from our lives. No matter how pious we may try to be, we will still embellish, hedge, and omit to lubricate the daily machinery of living. But there is a world of difference between telling functional lies and living a lie. Martin Buber once said, "The lie is the spirit committing treason against itself." Our acceptance of lies becomes a cultural cancer that eventually shrouds and reorders reality until moral garbage becomes as invisible to us as water is to a fish.

How much do we tolerate before we become sick and tired of being sick   36
and tired? When will we stand up and declare our *right* to trust? When do we stop accepting that the real truth is in the fine print? Whose lips do we read this year when we vote for president? When will we stop being so reticent about making judgments? When do we stop turning over our personal power and responsibility to liars?

Maybe if I don't tell the bank the check's in the mail I'll be less tolerant of   37
the lies told me every day. A country song I once heard said it all for me: "You've got to stand for something or you'll fall for anything."

*For a reading quiz, sources on Stephanie Ericsson, and annotated links to further readings on lying, visit **bedfordstmartins.com/thebedfordreader**.*

Journal Writing

Ericsson says, "We lie. We all do" (par. 3)—and that must mean you, too. In your journal, write about lies you have told. When is the last time you remember lying? What was the most significant lie you ever told? What circumstances have justified lying? Have you ever been ashamed of a lie or faced consequences for lying? (To take your journal writing further, see "From Journal to Essay" below.)

Questions on Meaning

1. What is Ericsson's THESIS?
2. Does Ericsson think it's possible to eliminate lies from our lives? What EVIDENCE does she offer?
3. If it were possible to eliminate lies from our lives, why would that be desirable?
4. What is this essay's PURPOSE?

Questions on Writing Strategy

1. Ericsson starts out by recounting her own four-lie day (pars. 1–2). What is the EFFECT of this INTRODUCTION?
2. At the beginning of each kind of lie, Ericsson provides an epigraph, a short quotation that forecasts a theme. Which of these epigraphs work best, do you think? What are your criteria for judgment?
3. How does Ericsson develop her discussion of delusion in paragraphs 32–34?
4. What is the message of Ericsson's CONCLUSION? Does the conclusion work well? Why, or why not?
5. **OTHER METHODS.** Examine the way Ericsson uses DEFINITION and EXAMPLE to support her classification. Which definitions are clearest? Which examples are the most effective? Why?

Questions on Language

1. In paragraph 35 Ericsson writes, "Our acceptance of lies becomes a cultural cancer that eventually shrouds and reorders reality until moral garbage becomes as invisible to us as water is to a fish." How do the two FIGURES OF SPEECH in this sentence — cancer and garbage — relate to each other?
2. Occasionally Ericsson's anger shows through, as in paragraphs 12–13 and 18–20. Is the TONE appropriate in these cases? Why, or why not?
3. Look up any of these words you do not know: haggard (par. 2); travails (4); façades (10); plethora (11); ecclesiastical, pedophilia (12); irreparable, co-perpetrator (13); patriarchal, archetype (20); gamut (31); myriad (32); reticent (36).
4. Ericsson uses several words and phrases from the fields of psychology and sociology. Define: passive-aggressive (par. 16); floating anxiety, adult-children-of-alcoholics movement (27); schizophrenics, catatonia (30).

Suggestions for Writing

1. **FROM JOURNAL TO ESSAY.** Develop one or more of the lies you recalled in your journal into an essay. You may choose to elaborate on your lies by classifying according to some principle or by NARRATING the story of a particular lie and its outcome. Give your reader a sense of your motivation for lying in the first place.

2. Ericsson writes, "All the 'isms'—racism, sexism, ageism, et al.—are founded on and fueled by the stereotype and the cliché, which are lies of exaggeration, omission, and ignorance. They are always dangerous. They take a single tree and make it a landscape" (par. 22). Write an essay discussing stereotypes and how they work to encourage prejudice. Use Ericsson's definition as a base, and expand it to include stereotypes you find particularly injurious. How do these stereotypes oversimplify? How are they "dangerous"?

3. Research pathological liars—that is, people who because of a psychological disorder are compelled to tell lies. In an essay, develop an extended definition of the pathological liar.

4. **CRITICAL WRITING.** EVALUATE the success of Ericsson's essay, considering especially how well her evidence supports her GENERALIZATIONS. Are there important categories she overlooks, exceptions she does not account for, gaps in definitions? Offer specific evidence for your own view, whether positive or negative.

5. **CONNECTIONS.** Ericsson begins her essay by acknowledging her own lies, and she often uses the first-person *I* or *we* in explaining her categories. In contrast, the author of the following essay, William Lutz, takes a more distant approach in classifying the dishonest language called *doublespeak*. Which of these two approaches, confessional or more distant, do you find more effective, and why? When, in your view, is it appropriate to inject yourself into your writing, and when is it not?

Stephanie Ericsson on Writing

In an interview on the *Amazon.com* Web site, Stephanie Ericsson discussed when and why she began writing. At first, she said, she did not write to communicate but to find and express herself.

I was fifteen in the year 1968, in the heart of hippie-saturated San Francisco, and like the world, I, too, underwent a major transformation. These spiritual awakenings tend to sound lofty, but the truth is that they are always messy. I began writing regularly then, when I lost my family. There was no one to tell my feelings to, so I turned to the blank white page. The page will never contradict you, never ignore you, and never judge you. I could put the chaos outside of me, and move on. It was a survival tool that I became attached to.

For Discussion

1. Do you agree with Ericsson's assessment of the "blank white page" as benevolent and nonjudgmental?

2. In the passage above, Ericsson is talking about writing for oneself. Is it merely the absence of an audience that makes such writing potentially therapeutic? Why does articulating her thoughts—if only for herself—help Ericsson "move on"?

WILLIAM LUTZ

WILLIAM LUTZ was born in 1940 in Racine, Wisconsin. He received a BA from Dominican College, an MA from Marquette University, a PhD from the University of Nevada at Reno, and a JD from Rutgers School of Law. Since 1971 Lutz has taught at Rutgers University in Camden, New Jersey. For much of his career, Lutz's interest in words and composition has made him an active campaigner against misleading and irresponsible language. He is the author of the best-seller *Doublespeak: From Revenue Enhancement to Terminal Living* (1989) and its sequel, *The New Doublespeak: Why No One Knows What Anyone's Saying Anymore* (1996). For fourteen years, he edited the *Quarterly Review of Doublespeak*. He has written, cowritten, or edited numerous other books, including *The Cambridge Thesaurus of American English* and *Firestorm in Peshtigo: A Town, Its People, and the Deadliest Fire in American History* (with Denise Gess, 2002). In 1996 he received the George Orwell Award for Distinguished Contribution to Honesty and Clarity in Public Language.

The World of Doublespeak

In the previous essay, Stephanie Ericsson examines the damage caused by the outright lies we tell each other every day. But what if our language doesn't lie, exactly, and instead just obscures meanings we'd rather not admit to? Such intentional fudging, or *doublespeak*, is the sort of language Lutz specializes in, and here he uses classification to expose its many guises. "The World of Doublespeak" abridges the first chapter in Lutz's book *Doublespeak*; the essay's title is the chapter's subtitle.

There are no potholes in the streets of Tucson, Arizona, just "pavement deficiencies." The Reagan Administration didn't propose any new taxes, just "revenue enhancement" through new "user's fees." Those aren't bums on the street, just "non-goal oriented members of society." There are no more poor people, just "fiscal underachievers." There was no robbery of an automatic teller machine, just an "unauthorized withdrawal." The patient didn't die because of medical malpractice, it was just a "diagnostic misadventure of a high magnitude." The US Army doesn't kill the enemy anymore, it just "services the target." And the doublespeak goes on.

Doublespeak is language that pretends to communicate but really doesn't. It is language that makes the bad seem good, the negative appear positive, the unpleasant appear attractive or at least tolerable. Doublespeak is language that avoids or shifts responsibility, language that is at variance with its real or purported meaning. It is language that conceals or prevents thought; rather than extending thought, doublespeak limits it.

Doublespeak is not a matter of subjects and verbs agreeing; it is a matter   3
of words and facts agreeing. Basic to doublespeak is incongruity, the incongruity between what is said or left unsaid, and what really is. It is the incongruity between the word and the referent, between seem and be, between the essential function of language—communication—and what doublespeak does—mislead, distort, deceive, inflate, circumvent, obfuscate.

How to Spot Doublespeak

How can you spot doublespeak? Most of the time you will recognize double-   4
speak when you see or hear it. But, if you have any doubts, you can identify doublespeak just by answering these questions: Who is saying what to whom, under what conditions and circumstances, with what intent, and with what results? Answering these questions will usually help you identify as doublespeak language that appears to be legitimate or that at first glance doesn't even appear to be doublespeak.

First Kind of Doublespeak

There are at least four kinds of doublespeak. The first is the euphemism,   5
an inoffensive or positive word or phrase used to avoid a harsh, unpleasant, or distasteful reality. But a euphemism can also be a tactful word or phrase which avoids directly mentioning a painful reality, or it can be an expression used out of concern for the feelings of someone else, or to avoid directly discussing a topic subject to a social or cultural taboo.

When you use a euphemism because of your sensitivity for someone's feel-   6
ings or out of concern for a recognized social or cultural taboo, it is not doublespeak. For example, you express your condolences that someone has "passed away" because you do not want to say to a grieving person, "I'm sorry your father is dead." When you use the euphemism "passed away," no one is misled. Moreover, the euphemism functions here not just to protect the feelings of another person, but to communicate also your concern for that person's feelings during a period of mourning. When you excuse yourself to go to the "restroom," or you mention that someone is "sleeping with" or "involved with" someone else, you do not mislead anyone about your meaning, but you do respect the social taboos about discussing bodily functions and sex in direct

terms. You also indicate your sensitivity to the feelings of your audience, which is usually considered a mark of courtesy and good manners.

However, when a euphemism is used to mislead or deceive, it becomes doublespeak. For example, in 1984 the US State Department announced that it would no longer use the word "killing" in its annual report on the status of human rights in countries around the world. Instead, it would use the phrase "unlawful or arbitrary deprivation of life," which the department claimed was more accurate. Its real purpose for using this phrase was simply to avoid discussing the embarrassing situation of government-sanctioned killings in countries that are supported by the United States and have been certified by the United States as respecting the human rights of their citizens. This use of a euphemism constitutes doublespeak, since it is designed to mislead, to cover up the unpleasant. Its real intent is at variance with its apparent intent. It is language designed to alter our perception of reality.

The Pentagon, too, avoids discussing unpleasant realities when it refers to bombs and artillery shells that fall on civilian targets as "incontinent ordnance." And in 1977 the Pentagon tried to slip funding for the neutron bomb unnoticed into an appropriations bill by calling it a "radiation enhancement device."

Second Kind of Doublespeak

A second kind of doublespeak is jargon, the specialized language of a trade, profession, or similar group, such as that used by doctors, lawyers, engineers, educators, or car mechanics. Jargon can serve an important and useful function. Within a group, jargon functions as a kind of verbal shorthand that allows members of the group to communicate with each other clearly, efficiently, and quickly. Indeed, it is a mark of membership in the group to be able to use and understand the group's jargon.

But jargon, like the euphemism, can also be doublespeak. It can be—and often is—pretentious, obscure, and esoteric terminology used to give an air of profundity, authority, and prestige to speakers and their subject matter. Jargon as doublespeak often makes the simple appear complex, the ordinary profound, the obvious insightful. In this sense it is used not to express but impress. With such doublespeak, the act of smelling something becomes "organoleptic analysis," glass becomes "fused silicate," a crack in a metal support beam becomes a "discontinuity," conservative economic policies become "distributionally conservative notions."

Lawyers, for example, speak of an "involuntary conversion" of property when discussing the loss or destruction of property through theft, accident, or condemnation. If your house burns down or if your car is stolen, you have suffered an involuntary conversion of your property. When used by lawyers in a legal situation, such jargon is a legitimate use of language, since lawyers can be expected to understand the term.

However, when a member of a specialized group uses its jargon to commu-   12
nicate with a person outside the group, and uses it knowing that the non-member does not understand such language, then there is doublespeak. For example, on May 9, 1978, a National Airlines 727 airplane crashed while attempting to land at the Pensacola, Florida, airport. Three of the fifty-two passengers aboard the airplane were killed. As a result of the crash, National made an after-tax insurance benefit of $1.7 million, or an extra 18¢ a share dividend for its stockholders. Now National Airlines had two problems: It did not want to talk about one of its airplanes crashing, and it had to account for the $1.7 million when it issued its annual report to its stockholders. National solved the problem by inserting a footnote in its annual report which explained that the $1.7 million income was due to "the involuntary conversion of a 727." National thus acknowledged the crash of its airplane and the subsequent profit it made from the crash, without once mentioning the accident or the deaths. However, because airline officials knew that most stockholders in the company, and indeed most of the general public, were not familiar with legal jargon, the use of such jargon constituted doublespeak.

Third Kind of Doublespeak

A third kind of doublespeak is gobbledygook or bureaucratese. Basically,   13
such doublespeak is simply a matter of piling on words, of overwhelming the audience with words, the bigger the words and the longer the sentences the better. Alan Greenspan, then chair of President Nixon's Council of Economic Advisors, was quoted in *The Philadelphia Inquirer* in 1974 as having testified before a Senate committee that "It is a tricky problem to find the particular calibration in timing that would be appropriate to stem the acceleration in risk premiums created by falling incomes without prematurely aborting the decline in the inflation-generated risk premiums."

Nor has Mr. Greenspan's language changed since then. Speaking to the   14
meeting of the Economic Club of New York in 1988, Mr. Greenspan, now Federal Reserve chair, said, "I guess I should warn you, if I turn out to be particularly clear, you've probably misunderstood what I've said." Mr. Greenspan's doublespeak doesn't seem to have held back his career.

Sometimes gobbledygook may sound impressive, but when the quote is   15
later examined in print it doesn't even make sense. During the 1988 presidential campaign, vice-presidential candidate Senator Dan Quayle explained the need for a strategic-defense initiative by saying, "Why wouldn't an en-

hanced deterrent, a more stable peace, a better prospect to denying the ones who enter conflict in the first place to have a reduction of offensive systems and an introduction to defense capability? I believe this is the route the country will eventually go."

The investigation into the *Challenger* disaster in 1986 revealed the double-   16
speak of gobbledygook and bureaucratese used by too many involved in the shuttle program. When Jesse Moore, NASA's associate administrator, was asked if the performance of the shuttle program had improved with each launch or if it had remained the same, he answered, "I think our performance in terms of the liftoff performance and in terms of the orbital performance, we knew more about the envelope we were operating under, and we have been pretty accurately staying in that. And so I would say the performance has not by design drastically improved. I think we have been able to characterize the performance more as a function of our launch experience as opposed to it improving as a function of time." While this language may appear to be jargon, a close look will reveal that it is really just gobbledygook laced with jargon. But you really have to wonder if Mr. Moore had any idea what he was saying.

Fourth Kind of Doublespeak

The fourth kind of doublespeak is inflated language that is designed to make   17
the ordinary seem extraordinary; to make everyday things seem impressive; to give an air of importance to people, situations, or things that would not normally be considered important; to make the simple seem complex. Often this kind of doublespeak isn't hard to spot, and it is usually pretty funny. While car mechanics may be called "automotive internists," elevator operators members of the "vertical transportation corps," used cars "pre-owned" or "experienced cars," and black-and-white television sets described as having "non-multicolor capability," you really aren't misled all that much by such language.

However, you may have trouble figuring out that, when Chrysler "initiates   18
a career alternative enhancement program," it is really laying off five thousand workers; or that "negative patient-care outcome" means the patient died; or that "rapid oxidation" means a fire in a nuclear power plant.

The doublespeak of inflated language can have serious consequences. In   19
Pentagon doublespeak, "pre-emptive counterattack" means that American forces attacked first; "engaged the enemy on all sides" means American troops were ambushed; "backloading of augmentation personnel" means a retreat by American troops. In the doublespeak of the military, the 1983 invasion of Grenada was conducted not by the US Army, Navy, Air Force, and Marines, but by the "Caribbean Peace Keeping Forces." But then, according to the Pentagon, it wasn't an invasion, it was a "predawn vertical insertion." . . .

The Dangers of Doublespeak

Doublespeak is not the product of carelessness or sloppy thinking. Indeed,   20
most doublespeak is the product of clear thinking and is carefully designed
and constructed to appear to communicate when in fact it doesn't. It is language designed not to lead but mislead. It is language designed to distort reality and corrupt thought. . . . In the world created by doublespeak, if it's not a
tax increase, but rather "revenue enhancement" or "tax base broadening,"
how can you complain about higher taxes? If it's not acid rain, but rather
"poorly buffered precipitation," how can you worry about all those dead trees?
If that isn't the Mafia in Atlantic City, but just "members of a career-offender
cartel," why worry about the influence of organized crime in the city? If
Supreme Court Justice William Rehnquist wasn't addicted to the pain-killing
drug his doctor prescribed, but instead it was just that the drug had "established an interrelationship with the body, such that if the drug is removed precipitously, there is a reaction," you needn't question that his decisions might
have been influenced by his drug addiction. If it's not a Titan II nuclear-armed
intercontinental ballistic missile with a warhead 630 times more powerful
than the atomic bomb dropped on Hiroshima, but instead, according to air
force colonel Frank Horton, it's just a "very large, potentially disruptive re-
entry system," why be concerned about the threat of nuclear destruction?
Why worry about the neutron bomb escalating the arms race if it's just a "radiation enhancement weapon"? If it's not an invasion, but a "rescue mission" or
a "predawn vertical insertion," you won't need to think about any violations
of US or international law.

Doublespeak has become so common in everyday living that many people   21
fail to notice it. Even worse, when they do notice doublespeak being used on
them, they don't react, they don't protest. Do you protest when you are asked
to check your packages at the desk "for your convenience," when it's not for
your convenience at all but for someone else's? You see advertisements for
"genuine imitation leather," "virgin vinyl," or "real counterfeit diamonds,"
but do you question the language or the supposed quality of the product? Do
you question politicians who don't speak of slums or ghettos but of the "inner
city" or "substandard housing" where the "disadvantaged" live and thus avoid
talking about the poor who have to live in filthy, poorly heated, ramshackle
apartments or houses? Aren't you amazed that patients don't die in the hospital anymore, it's just "negative patient-care outcome"?

Doublespeak such as that noted earlier that defines cab drivers as "urban   22
transportation specialists," elevator operators as members of the "vertical
transportation corps," and automobile mechanics as "automotive internists"
can be considered humorous and relatively harmless. However, when a fire in
a nuclear reactor building is called "rapid oxidation," an explosion in a nuclear

power plant is called an "energetic disassembly," the illegal overthrow of a legitimate government is termed "destabilizing a government," and lies are seen as "inoperative statements," we are hearing doublespeak that attempts to avoid responsibility and make the bad seem good, the negative appear positive, something unpleasant appear attractive; and which seems to communicate but doesn't. It is language designed to alter our perception of reality and corrupt our thinking. Such language does not provide us with the tools we need to develop, advance, and preserve our culture and our civilization. Such language breeds suspicion, cynicism, distrust, and, ultimately, hostility.

Doublespeak is insidious because it can infect and eventually destroy the   23
function of language, which is communication between people and social groups. This corruption of the function of language can have serious and far-reaching consequences. We live in a country that depends upon an informed electorate to make decisions in selecting candidates for office and deciding issues of public policy. The use of doublespeak can become so pervasive that it becomes the coin of the political realm, with speakers and listeners convinced that they really understand such language. After a while we may really believe that politicians don't lie but only "misspeak," that illegal acts are merely "inappropriate actions," that fraud and criminal conspiracy are just "miscertification." President Jimmy Carter in April of 1980 could call the aborted raid to free the American hostages in Teheran an "incomplete success" and really believe that he had made a statement that clearly communicated with the American public. So, too, could President Ronald Reagan say in 1985 that "ultimately our security and our hopes for success at the arms reduction talks hinge on the determination that we show here to continue our program to rebuild and refortify our defenses" and really believe that greatly increasing the amount of money spent building new weapons would lead to a reduction in the number of weapons in the world. If we really believe that we understand such language and that such language communicates and promotes clear thought, then the world of *1984*,[1] with its control of reality through language, is upon us.

---

*For a reading quiz, sources on William Lutz, and annotated links to further readings on doublespeak, visit **bedfordstmartins.com/thebedfordreader**.*

---

[1] In a section omitted from this abridgement of his chapter, Lutz discusses *Nineteen Eighty-Four*, the 1949 novel by George Orwell in which a frightening totalitarian state devises a language, called *newspeak*, to shape and control thought in politically acceptable forms. (For an example of Orwell's writing, see p. 645.) —EDS.

Journal Writing

Now that you know the name for it, when have you read or heard examples of doublespeak? Over the next few days, jot down examples of doublespeak that you recall or that you read and hear—from politicians or news commentators; in the lease for your dwelling or your car; in advertising and catalogs; from bosses, teachers, or other figures of authority; in overheard conversations. (To take your journal writing further, see "From Journal to Essay" on the facing page.)

Questions on Meaning

1. What is Lutz's THESIS? Where does he state it?
2. According to Lutz, four questions can help us identify doublespeak. What are they? How can they help us distinguish between truthful language and doublespeak?
3. What, according to Lutz, are "the dangers of doublespeak"?
4. What ASSUMPTIONS does the author make about his readers' educational backgrounds and familiarity with his subject?

Questions on Writing Strategy

1. What principle does Lutz use for creating his four kinds of doublespeak—that is, what mainly distinguishes the groups?
2. How does Lutz develop the discussion of euphemism in paragraphs 5–8?
3. Lutz quotes Alan Greenspan twice in paragraphs 13–14. What is surprising about the comment in paragraph 14? Why does Lutz include this second quotation?
4. Lutz uses many quotations that were quite current when he first published this piece in 1989 but that now may seem dated—for instance, references to Presidents Carter and Reagan or to the nuclear arms race. Do these EXAMPLES undermine Lutz's essay in any way? Is his discussion of doublespeak still valid today? Explain your answers.
5. **OTHER METHODS.** Lutz's essay is not only a classification but also a DEFINITION of *doublespeak* and an examination of CAUSE AND EFFECT. Where are these other methods used most prominently? What do they contribute to the essay?

Questions on Language

1. How does Lutz's own language compare with the language he quotes as doublespeak? Do you find his language clear and easy to understand?
2. ANALYZE Lutz's language in paragraphs 22 and 23. How do the CONNOTATIONS of words such as "corrupt," "hostility," "insidious," and "control" strengthen the author's message?
3. The following list of possibly unfamiliar words includes only those found in Lutz's own sentences, not those in the doublespeak he quotes. Be sure you can define variance (par. 2); incongruity, referent (3); taboo (5); condolences (6);

esoteric, profundity (10); condemnation (11); ramshackle (21); cynicism (22); insidious (23).

Suggestions for Writing

1. **FROM JOURNAL TO ESSAY.** Choose at least one of the examples of doublespeak noted in your journal, and write an essay explaining why it qualifies as doublespeak. Which of Lutz's categories does it fit under? How did you recognize it? Can you understand what it means?

2. Just about all of us have resorted to doublespeak at one time or another—when making an excuse, when trying to conceal the fact that we're unprepared for an exam, when trying to impress a supervisor or potential employer. Write a NARRATIVE about a time you used deliberately unclear language, perhaps language that you yourself didn't understand. What were the circumstances? Did you consciously decide to use unclear language, or did it just leak out? How did others react to your use of this language?

3. The National Council of Teachers of English has posted a number of articles from the *Quarterly Review of Doublespeak,* which Lutz once edited, on its Web site at *www.ncte.org/about/press/116444.htm.* (Your library may also subscribe to the journal.) Read a few related articles from the journal, and based on them write an essay in which you challenge, expand, or add more examples to Lutz's categories.

4. **CRITICAL WRITING.** Can you determine from his essay who Lutz believes is responsible for the proliferation of doublespeak? Whose responsibility is it to curtail the use of doublespeak: just those who use it? the schools? the government? the media? we who hear it? Write an essay that considers these questions, citing specific passages from the essay and incorporating your own ideas.

5. **CONNECTIONS.** Read Stephanie Ericsson's "The Ways We Lie" (p. 407), which classifies the lies we tell in our daily lives. In what way, if any, do doublespeakers also lie? How, if at all, do the intentions of Ericsson's liars and Lutz's doublespeakers differ? How, if at all, are their intentions the same? Are the results of lying and doublespeak, according to each author, different or the same? Write an essay that answers these questions and that points out any other similarities or differences you notice between liars and doublespeakers. Use EVIDENCE from the two essays or from your own experience to support your thesis.

William Lutz on Writing

In 1989 C-SPAN aired an interview between Brian Lamb and William Lutz. Lamb asked Lutz about his writing process. "I have a rule about writing," Lutz answered, "which I discovered when I wrote my dissertation: You never write a book, you write three pages, or you write five pages. I put off writing my dissertation for a year, because I could not think of writing this whole thing. . . . I had put off doing this book [*Doublespeak*] for quite a while, and my wife said, 'You've got to do the book.' And I said, 'Yes, I am going to, just as soon as I . . . ,' and, of course, I did every other thing I could possibly think of before that, and then I realized one day that she was right, I had to start writing. . . . So one day, I sit down and say, 'I am going to write five pages—that's all—and when I am done with five pages, I'll reward myself.' So I do the five pages, or the next time I will do ten pages or whatever number of pages, but I set a number of pages."

Perhaps wondering just how high Lutz's daily page count might go, Lamb asked Lutz how much he wrote at one time. "It depends," Lutz admitted. "I always begin a writing session by sitting down and rewriting what I wrote the previous day—and that is the first thing, and it does two things. First of all, it makes your writing a little bit better, because rewriting is the essential part of writing. And the second thing is to get you flowing again, get back into the mainstream. Truman Capote[1] once gave the best piece of advice for writers ever given. He said, 'Never pump the well dry; always leave a bucket there.' So, I never stop writing when I run out of ideas. I always stop when I have something more to write about, and write a note to myself, 'This is what I am going to do next,' and then I stop. The worst feeling in the world is to have written yourself dry and have to come back the next day, knowing that you are dry and not knowing where you are going to pick up at this point."

For Discussion

1. Though his work is devoted to words and writing, William Lutz once spent a great deal of time avoiding writing. What finally got him to stop procrastinating? When you are avoiding a writing assignment, is it the length of the project or something else that prevents you from getting to work?
2. Lutz always rewrites before he starts producing new material on the idea that he didn't develop on the previous day. How come? Do you think Lutz's strategy is a good one?

---

[1] Truman Capote (1924–84) was an American journalist and fiction writer. —Eds.

ADDITIONAL WRITING TOPICS

Classification

Write an essay by the method of classification, in which you sort one of the following subjects into categories of your own. Make clear your PURPOSE in classifying and the basis of your classification. Explain each class with DEFINITIONS and EXAMPLES (you may find it helpful to make up a name for each group). Check your classes to be sure they neither gap nor overlap.

1. Commuters, or people who use public transportation
2. Environmental problems or environmental solutions
3. Web sites
4. Vegetarians
5. Talk shows
6. The ills or benefits of city life
7. The recordings you own
8. Families
9. Stand-up comedians
10. Present-day styles of marriage
11. Vacations
12. College students today
13. Movies for teenagers or men or women
14. Waiters you'd never tip
15. Comic strips
16. Movie monsters
17. Sports announcers
18. Inconsiderate people
19. Radio stations
20. Mall millers (people who mill around malls)

GARBAGE IN...

11

CAUSE AND EFFECT

Asking Why

◀ **Cause and effect in a cartoon**

With simple drawings and perhaps a few words, editorial car-
toonists often make striking comments on events. This cartoon
by Mike Thompson, published in the Detroit Free Press, *pro-*
poses a cause to explain a disturbing effect. What is the effect?
What, according to Thompson, is the cause? How does the cap-
tion "Garbage in . . ." reinforce Thompson's explanation? What
other causes might explain the effect depicted here? Do you
agree or disagree with Thompson's view? Why?

THE METHOD

Press the button of a doorbell and, inside the house or apartment, chimes sound. Why? Because the touch of your finger on the button closed an electrical circuit. But why did you ring the doorbell? Because you were sent by your dispatcher: You are a bill collector calling on a customer whose payments are three months overdue.

The touch of your finger on the button is the *immediate cause* of the chimes: the event that precipitates another. That you were ordered by your dispatcher to go ring the doorbell is a *remote cause*: an underlying, more basic reason for the event, not apparent to an observer. Probably, ringing the doorbell will lead to some results: The door will open, and you may be given a check — or a kick in the teeth.

To figure out reasons and results is to use the method of CAUSE AND EFFECT. Either to explain events or to argue for one version of them, you try to answer the question "Why did something happen?" or "What were the consequences?" or "What might be the consequences?" As part of answering such a question, you use DIVISION or ANALYSIS (Chap. 9) to separate the flow of events into causes.

Seeking causes, you can ask, for example, "Why do birds migrate?" "What has caused sales of Detroit-made cars to pick up (or decline) lately?" Looking for effects, you can ask "What have been the effects of the birth-control pill on the typical American family?" "What impact has the personal computer had on the nursing profession?" You can look to a possible future and ask "Of what use might a course in psychology be to me if I become an office manager?" "Suppose an asteroid the size of a sofa were to strike Philadelphia — what would be the probable consequences?" Essay exams in history and economics courses tend often to ask for either causes or effects: "What were the principal causes of America's involvement in the war in Vietnam?" "What were the immediate effects on the world monetary system of Franklin D. Roosevelt's removing the United States from the gold standard?"

Don't, by the way, confuse cause and effect with the method of PROCESS ANALYSIS (Chap. 8). Some process analysis essays, too, deal with happenings; but they focus more on repeatable events (rather than unique ones) and they explain *how* (rather than why) something happened. If you were explaining the process by which the doorbell rings, you might break the happening into stages — (1) the finger presses the button; (2) the circuit closes; (3) the current travels the wire; (4) the chimes make music — and you'd set forth the process in detail. But why did the finger press the button? What happened because the doorbell rang? To answer those questions, you need cause and effect.

In trying to explain why things happen, you can expect to find a whole array of causes — interconnected, perhaps, like the strands of a spiderweb.

You'll want to do an honest job of unraveling, and this may take time. For a jury to acquit or convict an accused slayer, weeks of testimony from witnesses, detectives, and psychiatrists may be required, then days of deliberation. It took a great historian, Jakob Burckhardt, most of his lifetime to set forth a few reasons for the dawn of the Italian Renaissance. To be sure, juries must take great care when a life hangs in the balance; and Burckhardt, after all, was writing an immense book. To produce a college essay, you don't have forty years; but before you start to write, you will need to devote extra time and thought to seeing which facts are the causes, and which matter most.

To answer the questions "Why?" and "What followed as a result?" may sometimes be hard, but it can be satisfying—even illuminating. Indeed, to seek causes and effects is one way for the mind to discover order in a reality that otherwise might seem (as life came to seem to Macbeth) "a tale told by an idiot, full of sound and fury, signifying nothing."

THE PROCESS

Subjects, Purposes, and Theses

The method of cause and effect tends to suggest itself: If you have a subject and soon start thinking "Why?" or "What results?" or "What if?" then you are on the way to analyzing causation. Your subject may be impersonal—like a political victory or a sports defeat—or it may be quite personal. Indeed, an excellent cause-and-effect paper may be written on a subject very near to you. You can ask yourself why you behaved in a certain way at a certain moment. You can examine the reasons for your current beliefs and attitudes. Writing such a paper, you might happen upon a truth you hadn't realized before.

Whether your subject is personal or impersonal, make sure it is manageable: You should be able to get to the bottom of it, given the time and information available. For a 500-word essay due Thursday, the causes of teenage rebellion would be a less feasible topic than why a certain thirteen-year-old you know ran away from home.

Before rushing to list causes or effects, stop a moment to consider what your PURPOSE might be in writing. Much of the time you'll seek simply to explain what did or might occur, discovering and laying out the connections as clearly and accurately as you can. But when reasonable people could disagree over causes or effects, you may want to go further, arguing for one interpretation over others. You'll still need to be clear and accurate in presenting your interpretation, but you'll also need to treat the others fairly. (See Chap. 13 on argument and persuasion.)

When you have a grip on your subject and your purpose, you can draft a

Cause and Effect

tentative THESIS STATEMENT to express the main point of your analysis. The statement may be hypothetical at this stage, before you have gathered EVIDENCE and sorted out the complexity of causes and effects. Still, a statement framed early can help direct your later thinking and research.

The essays in this chapter provide good examples of thesis statements that put across, concisely, the author's central finding about causes and effects. Here are a few examples:

> A bill like the one we've just passed [to ban imports from factories that use child labor] is of no use unless it goes hand in hand with programs that will offer a new life to these newly released children.
> —Chitra Divakaruni, "Live Free and Starve"

> It is possible to stop most drug addiction in the United States within a very short time. Simply make all drugs available and sell them at cost.
> —Gore Vidal, "Drugs"

> My suspicion is, in fact, that very few of us . . . have really responded to the AIDS crisis the way the federal government and educators would like us to believe. My guess is that we're all but ignoring it and that almost anyone who claims otherwise is lying.   —Meghan Daum, "Safe-Sex Lies"

Causal Relations

Your toughest job in writing a cause-and-effect essay may be figuring out what caused what. Sometimes one event will appear to trigger another, and it in turn will trigger yet another, and another still, in an order we call a *causal chain*. A classic example of such a chain is set forth in a Mother Goose rhyme:

> For want of a nail the shoe was lost,
> For want of a shoe the horse was lost,
> For want of a horse the rider was lost,
> For want of a rider the battle was lost,
> For want of a battle the kingdom was lost—
> And all for the want of a nail.

In reality, causes are seldom so easy to find as that missing nail: They tend to be many and complicated. A battle may be lost for more than one reason. Perhaps the losing general had fewer soldiers and had a blinding hangover the morning he mapped out his battle strategy. Perhaps winter set in, expected reinforcements failed to arrive, and a Joan of Arc inspired the winning army. The downfall of a kingdom is not to be explained as though it were the toppling of the last domino in a file. Still, one event precedes another in time, and in discerning causes you don't ignore chronological order; you pay attention to it.

When you can see a number of apparent causes, weigh them and assign each a relative importance. Which do you find matter most? Often, you will see that causes are more important or less so: *major* or *minor*. If Judd acquires a heavy drug habit and also takes up residence in a video arcade, and as a result finds himself penniless, it is probably safe to assume that the drug habit is the major cause of his going broke and his addiction to video games a minor one. If you were writing about his sad case, you'd probably emphasize the drug habit by giving it most of your space, perhaps touching on video games briefly.

When seeking remote causes, look only as far back as necessary. Explaining why a small town has fallen on hard times, you might confine yourself to the immediate cause of the hardship: the closing of a factory. You might explain what caused the shutdown: a dispute between union and management. You might even go back to the cause of the dispute (announced firings) and the cause of the firings (loss of sales to a competitor). For a short essay, that might be far enough back in time to go; but if you were writing a whole book (*Pottsville: Its Glorious Past and Its Present Agony*), you might look to causes still more remote. You could trace the beginning of the decline of Pottsville back to the invention, in 1845, of a better carrot grater. A manageable short paper showing effects might work in the other direction, moving from the factory closing to its impact on the town: unemployment, the closing of stores and the only movie house, people packing up and moving away.

Two cautions about causal relations are in order here. One is to beware of confusing coincidence with cause. In the logical FALLACY called *post hoc* (short for the Latin *post hoc, ergo propter hoc,* "after this, therefore because of this"), one assumes, erroneously, that because A happened before B, A must have caused B. This is the error of the superstitious man who decides that he lost his job because a black cat walked in front of him. Another error is to oversimplify causes by failing to recognize their full number and complexity— claiming, say, that violent crime is simply a result of "all those gangster shows on TV." Avoid such wrong turns in reasoning by patiently looking for evidence before you write, and by giving it careful thought. (For a fuller list of such fallacies, or errors in reasoning, see pp. 524–25.)

Discovery of Causes

To help find causes of actions and events, you can ask yourself a few searching questions. These have been suggested by the work of the literary critic Kenneth Burke:

1. *What act am I trying to explain?*
2. *What is the character, personality, or mental state of whoever acted?*
3. *In what scene or location did the act take place, and in what circumstances?*

4. *What instruments or means did the person use?*
5. *For what purpose did the person act?*

Burke calls these elements a *pentad* (or set of five): the *act*, the *actor*, the *scene*, the *agency*, and the *purpose*. If you are trying to explain, for instance, why a person burned down a liquor shop, it will be revealing to ask about his character and mental state. Was the act committed by the shop's worried, debt-ridden owner? a mentally disturbed anti-alcohol crusader? a drunk who had been denied a purchase? The scene of the burning, too, might tell you something. Was the shop near a church, a mental hospital, or a fireworks factory? And what was the agency (or means of the act): a flaming torch or a flipped-away cigarette butt? To learn the purpose might be illuminating, whether it was to collect insurance on the shop, to get revenge, or to work what the actor believed to be the will of the Lord. You can further deepen your inquiry by seeing relationships between the terms of the pentad. Ask, for instance, what does the actor have to do with this scene? (Is he or she the neighbor across the street, who has been staring at the liquor shop resentfully for years?)[1]

You can use Burke's pentad to help explain the acts of groups as well as those of individuals. Why, for instance, did the sophomore class revel degenerate into a brawl? Here are some possible answers:

1. *Act:* the brawl
2. *Actors:* the sophs were letting off steam after exams, and a mean, tense spirit prevailed
3. *Scene:* a keg-beer party outdoors in the quad at midnight on a sticky and hot May night
4. *Agencies:* fists and sticks
5. *Purpose:* the brawlers were seeking to punish whoever kicked over the keg

Don't worry if not all the questions apply, if not all the answers are immediately forthcoming. Bring the pentad to bear on the sad case of Judd, the drug addict, and probably only the question about his character and mental state would help you much. Even a single hint, though, can help you write. Burke's pentad isn't meant to be a grim rigmarole; it is a means of discovery, to generate a lot of possible material for you—insights, observations, hunches to pursue. It won't solve each and every human mystery, but sometimes it will helpfully deepen your thought.

[1] If you are interested and care to explore the possibilities of Burke's pentad, you can pair up its five terms in ten different ways: act to actor, actor to scene, actor to agency, actor to purpose, act to scene, act to agency, act to purpose, scene to agency, scene to purpose, agency to purpose. This approach can go profoundly deep. We suggest you try writing ten questions (one for each pair) in the form "What does act have to do with actor?" Ask them of some act you'd like to explain.

Final Word

In stating what you believe to be causes and effects, don't be afraid to voice a well-considered hunch. Your instructor doesn't expect you to write, in a short time, a definitive account of the causes of an event or a belief or a phenomenon—only to write a coherent and reasonable one. To discern all causes—including remote ones—and all effects is beyond the power of any one human mind. Still, admirable and well-informed writers on matters such as politics, economics, and world and national affairs are often canny guessers and brave drawers of inferences. At times, even the most cautious and responsible writer has to leap boldly over a void to strike firm ground on the far side. Consider your evidence. Focus your thinking. Look well before leaping. Then take off.

FOCUS ON CLARITY AND CONCISENESS

While drafting a cause-and-effect analysis, you may need to grope a bit to discover just what you think about the sequence and relative importance of reasons and consequences. Your sentences may grope a bit, too, reflecting your initial confusion or your need to circle around your ideas in order to find them. The following draft passage reveals such difficulties:

> WORDY AND UNCLEAR   Employees often worry about suggestive comments from others. The employee may not only worry but feel the need to discuss the situation with coworkers. One thing that is an effect of sexual harassment, even verbal harassment, in the workplace is that productivity is lost. Plans also need to be made to figure out how to deal with future comments. Engaging in these activities is sure to take time and concentration from work.

Drafting this passage, the writer seems to have built up to the idea about lost productivity (third sentence) after providing support for it in the first two sentences. The fourth sentence then adds more support. And sentences 2–4 all show a writer working out his ideas: Sentence subjects and verbs do not focus on the main actors and actions of the sentences, words repeat unnecessarily, and word groups run longer than needed for clarity.

These problems disappear from the edited version below, which moves the idea of the passage up front, uses subjects and verbs to state what the sentences are about (underlined), and cuts unneeded words.

> CONCISE AND CLEAR   Even verbal sexual <u>harassment</u> in the workplace <u>causes</u> a loss of productivity. Worrying about suggestive comments from others, discussing those comments with coworkers, planning how to deal with future comments—these <u>activities</u> <u>consume</u> time and concentration that a harassed employee could spend on work.

For exercises on clarity and conciseness, visit Exercise Central at
bedfordstmartins.com/thebedfordreader.

> ### CHECKLIST FOR REVISING A CAUSE-AND-EFFECT ESSAY
>
> ✔ **SUBJECT.** Have you been able to cover your subject adequately in the time and space available? Should you perhaps narrow the subject so that you can fairly address the important causes and/or effects?
>
> ✔ **THESIS.** For your readers' benefit, have you focused your analysis by stating your main idea succinctly in a thesis statement?
>
> ✔ **COMPLETENESS.** Have you included all relevant causes or effects? Does your analysis reach back to locate remote causes or forward to locate remote effects?
>
> ✔ **CAUSAL RELATIONS.** Have you presented a clear pattern of causes or effects? Have you distinguished the remote from the immediate, the major from the minor?
>
> ✔ **ACCURACY AND FAIRNESS.** Have you avoided the *post hoc* fallacy, assuming that A caused B just because it preceded B? Have you also avoided oversimplifying and instead covered causes or effects in all their complexity?
>
> ✔ **CLARITY AND CONCISENESS.** Have you edited your draft to foreground your main points and tighten your sentences?

CAUSE AND EFFECT IN PARAGRAPHS

Writing About Television

In the following paragraph, the writer poses and concisely answers a question about soccer's near-absence from American TV. The paragraph was written especially for *The Bedford Reader*, but it could serve as a component of a full essay, perhaps one analyzing how television affects sports in general.

Why is it that, despite a growing interest in soccer among American athletes, and despite its ranking as the most popular sport in the world, commercial television all but ignores it? Granted, soccer sometimes makes it to cable, as during the World Cup, but mostly it's shut out. The reason stems partly from the basic nature of commercial television, which exists not to inform and entertain but to sell. During most major sporting events on television—football, baseball, basketball, boxing—producers can take advantage of natural interruptions in the action to broadcast sales pitches; or, if the natural breaks occur too infrequently, the producers can contrive time-outs for the sole purpose of airing lucrative commercials. But soccer is played in two solid halves of forty-five minutes each; not even injury to a player is cause for a time-out. How, then, to insert the requisite number of commercial breaks without resorting to false fouls or other questionable tactics? After CBS aired a soccer match in 1967, players reported, according to Stanley Frank, that before the game the referee had instructed them "to stay down every nine

Topic sentence: question to be answered

Analysis of causes

Commercial TV requires commercial breaks

Soccer is played with only one break

Example of failed attempt to adapt soccer to TV

minutes." The resulting hue and cry rose all the way to the House Communications Subcommittee. From that day to this, no one has been able to figure out how to screen advertising jingles during a televised soccer game. The result is that commercial television has treated soccer almost as if it didn't exist.

Result: little soccer on TV

Writing in an Academic Discipline

This paragraph from a textbook on American history explains the causes of a "fateful decision" in the 1960s—fateful because, as the authors' text goes on to explain, the decision had grave and far-reaching consequences for the United States.

Many factors played a role in [President Lyndon] Johnson's fateful decision [to escalate the Vietnam War]. But the most obvious explanation is that the new president faced many pressures to expand the American involvement and only a very few to limit it.

Topic sentence: summary of causes to be discussed

As the untested successor to a revered and martyred president, he felt obliged to prove his worthiness for the office by continuing the policies of his predecessor. Aid to South Vietnam had been one of the most prominent of those policies. Johnson also felt it necessary to retain in his administration many of the important figures of the Kennedy years. In doing so, he surrounded himself with a group of foreign-policy advisers—Secretary of State Dean Rusk, Secretary of Defense Robert McNamara, National Security Adviser McGeorge Bundy—who strongly believed not only that the United States had an important obligation to resist communism in Vietnam, but that it possessed the ability and resources to make that resistance successful. As a result, Johnson seldom had access to information making clear how difficult the new commitment might become. A compliant Congress raised little protest to, and indeed at one point openly endorsed, Johnson's use of executive powers to lead the nation into war. And for several years at least, public opinion remained firmly behind him—in part because Barry Goldwater's bellicose remarks about the war during the 1964 campaign made Johnson seem by comparison to be a moderate on the issue. Above all, intervention in South Vietnam was fully consistent with nearly twenty years of American foreign policy. An anti-Communist ally was appealing to the United States for assistance; all the assumptions of the containment doctrine seemed to require the nation to oblige. Johnson seemed unconcerned that the government of South Vietnam existed only because the United States had put it there, and that the regime had never succeeded in acquiring the loyalty of its people. Vietnam, he believed, provided a test of American willingness to fight Communist aggression, a test he was determined not to fail.

Causes:

Need to prove worthiness

Advisers urging involvement and shutting off alternative views

Congressional cooperation

Support of public opinion

Consistency with American foreign policy against communism

—Richard N. Current et al., *American History: A Survey*

Cause and Effect

CAUSE AND EFFECT IN PRACTICE

An ardent supporter of her school's track team, Kate Krueger was a sophomore during the team's first winning season in many years. At the end of the
season, the student newspaper published a letter to the editor saying that the
successes were due to a new coach. Krueger found this explanation inadequate
and decided to say so in her own letter. The cause-and-effect analysis below
appeared in the newspaper the following week.

Between the first draft and the final version of her letter, Krueger made
one significant addition. At first, she ignored any contributions of the new
coach, thinking that the original letter writer had more than covered them.
But since Krueger actually agreed that the coach had helped the team, her first
draft did what she accused the letter of doing: It oversimplified. In her revision, Krueger acknowledged the coach's contributions while also detailing the
other causes she saw at work.

May 2, 2004

To the Editor:

I take issue with Tom Boatz's letter that
was printed in the April 30 *Weekly*. Boatz attributes the success of this year's track team
solely to the new coach, John Barak. I have
several close friends who are athletes on the
track team, so as an interested observer and
fan I believe that Boatz oversimplified the
causes of the team's recent success.

To be sure, Coach Barak did improve the
training regimen and overall morale, and
these have certainly contributed to the winning season. Both Coach Barak and the team
members themselves can share credit for an
impressive work ethic and a sense of cama-
raderie unequaled in previous years. However, several factors outside Coach Barak's
control may have been even more influential.

This year's team gained several phenomenal freshman athletes, such as Kristin Hall,
who anchored the 4x400 and 4x800 relays
and played an integral part in setting several school records, and Eric Asper, who was
undefeated in the shot put.

Even more important, and also unmen-
tioned by Tom Boatz, is the college's in-

creased funding for the track program. Last year the school allotted 50 percent more for equipment, and the results have been dramatic. For example, the new vaulting poles are now the correct length and correspond to the weights of the individual athletes, giving them more power and height. Some vaulters have been able to vault as much as a foot higher than their previous records. Similarly, new starting blocks have allowed the team's sprinters to drop valuable seconds off their times.

I agree with Tom Boatz that Coach Barak deserves much credit for the track team's successes. But the athletes do, too, and so does the college for at last supporting its track program.

—KATE KRUEGER '06

NAOMI KLEIN

NAOMI KLEIN was born in Montreal, Canada, in 1970 and attended the University of Toronto. Once a self-described "dedicated mall-rat, fixated on designer labels," she came to prominence with her book *No Logo: Taking Aim at the Brand Bullies* (1999, reissued 2002). Klein was proclaimed as "brilliant" and "prescient" and derided as a "celebrity socialist" for the book's attack on name-brand corporations such as Nike, Coca-Cola, and McDonald's, which, she says, blanket personal and public life. Klein's second book, *Fences and Windows: Dispatches from the Front Lines of the Globalization Debate* (2002), collects articles she wrote for newspapers and magazines in Canada, the United States, and Great Britain. In 2004 she and her husband, the broadcast journalist Avi Lewis, made *The Take*, a film about factory workers in Argentina. Klein has lectured at universities and is currently a fellow at the Nation Institute. She lives in Toronto.

A Web of Brands

Much of Klein's writing focuses on the effects of globalization, the increasing cultural and economic connectedness among the world's societies. To some, globalization is a positive development, promising better allocation of resources and a higher standard of living for everyone. To Klein and others, uncontrolled globalization pits the legal and financial might of multinational corporations against the people who make and consume the corporations' products. In these opening pages from her book *No Logo*, Klein looks at how the transformation of the garment industry in Toronto resonates in the factories of Jakarta, Indonesia. (In the next essay, "Live Free and Starve," Chitra Divakaruni examines yet another effect of globalization.)

Toronto

If I squint, tilt my head, and shut my left eye, all I can see out the window   1
is 1932, straight down to the lake. Brown warehouses, oatmeal-colored smokestacks, faded signs painted on brick walls advertising long-discontinued brands: "Lovely," "Gaywear." This is the old industrial Toronto of garment factories, furriers and wholesale wedding dresses. So far, no one has come up with a way to make a profit out of taking a wrecking ball to these boxes of brick, and in this little eight- or nine-block radius, the modern city has been layered haphazardly on top of the old.

I wrote this book while living in Toronto's ghost of a garment district in a   2
ten-story warehouse. Many other buildings like it have long since been
boarded up, glass panes shattered, smokestacks holding their breath; their
only remaining capitalist function is to hoist large blinking billboards on their
tar-coated roofs, reminding the gridlocked drivers on the lakeshore express-
way of the existence of Molson's beer, Hyundai cars and EZ Rock FM.

In the twenties and thirties, Russian and Polish immigrants darted back   3
and forth on these streets, ducking into delis to argue about Trotsky[1] and the
leadership of the International Ladies' Garment Workers' Union. These days,
old Portuguese men still push racks of dresses and coats down the sidewalk,
and next door you can still buy a rhinestone bridal tiara if the need for such an
item happens to arise (a Hallowe'en costume, or perhaps a school play . . .).
The real action, however, is down the block amid the stacks of edible jewelry
at Sugar Mountain, the retro candy mecca, open until 2 AM to service the late-
night ironic cravings of the club kids. And a store downstairs continues to do
a modest trade in bald naked mannequins, though more often than not it's
rented out as the surreal set for a film school project or the tragically hip backdrop of a television interview.

The layering of decades on Spadina Avenue, like so many urban neigh-   4
borhoods in a similar state of postindustrial limbo, has a wonderful accidental
charm to it. The lofts and studios are full of people who know they are playing
their part in a piece of urban performance art, but for the most part, they do
their best not to draw attention to that fact. If anyone claims too much ownership over "the real Spadina," then everyone else starts feeling like a two-bit
prop, and the whole edifice crumbles.

Which is why it was so unfortunate that City Hall saw fit to commission   5
a series of public art installations to "celebrate" the history of Spadina
Avenue. First came the steel figures perched atop the lampposts: women
hunched over sewing machines and crowds of striking workers waving plac-
ards with indecipherable slogans. Then the worst happened: The giant brass
thimble arrived—right at the corner of my block. There it was: eleven and a
half feet high and eleven feet across. Two giant pastel buttons were plopped
on the sidewalk next to it, with wimpy little saplings growing out of the holes.
Thank goodness Emma Goldman, the famed anarchist and labor organizer
who lived on this street in the late 1930s, wasn't around to witness the transformation of the garment workers' struggle into sweatshop kitsch.

The thimble is only the most overt manifestation of a painful new self-   6
consciousness on the grid. All around me, the old factory buildings are being

---

[1] Leon Trotsky (1879–1940), a Communist theorist and a leader of the Russian Revolution
in 1917.—EDS.

rezoned and converted into "loft-living" complexes with names like "The Candy Factory." The hand-me-downs of industrialization have already been mined for witty fashion ideas — discarded factory workers' uniforms, Diesel's Labor brand jeans and Caterpillar boots. So of course there is also a booming market for condos in secondhand sweatshops, luxuriously reno-ed, with soaking tubs, slate-lined showers, underground parking, skylit gymnasiums and twenty-four-hour concierges.

So far my landlord, who made his fortune manufacturing and selling London Fog overcoats, has stubbornly refused to sell off our building as condominiums with exceptionally high ceilings. He'll relent eventually, but for now he still has a handful of garment tenants left, whose businesses are too small to move to Asia or Central America and who for whatever reason are unwilling to follow the industry trend toward homeworkers paid by the piece. The rest of the building is rented out to yoga instructors, documentary film producers, graphic designers and writers and artists with live/work spaces. The shmata[2] guys still selling coats in the office next door look terribly dismayed when they see the Marilyn Manson clones stomping down the hall in chains and thigh-high leather boots to the communal washroom, clutching tubes of toothpaste, but what can they do? We are all stuck together here for now, caught between the harsh realities of economic globalization and the all-enduring rock-video aesthetic.

Jakarta

"Ask her what she makes — what it says on the label. You know — label?" I said, reaching behind my head and twisting up the collar of my shirt. By now these Indonesian workers were used to people like me: foreigners who come to talk to them about the abysmal conditions in the factories where they cut, sew and glue for multinational companies like Nike, the Gap and Liz Claiborne. But these seamstresses looked nothing like the elderly garment workers I meet in the elevator back home. Here they were all young, some of them as young as fifteen; only a few were over twenty-one.

On this particular day in August 1997, the abysmal conditions in question had led to a strike at the Kaho Indah Citra garment factory on the outskirts of Jakarta in the Kawasan Berikat Nusantar industrial zone. The issue for the Kaho workers, who earn the equivalent of US $2 per day, was that they were being forced to work long hours of overtime but weren't being paid at the legal rate for their trouble. After a three-day walkout, management offered a compromise typical of a region with a markedly relaxed relationship to labor leg-

[2] Yiddish, "rag." — EDS.

islation: overtime would no longer be compulsory but the compensation would remain illegally low. The 2,000 workers returned to their sewing machines; all except 101 young women who—management decided—were the troublemakers behind the strike. "Until now our case is still not settled," one of these workers told me, bursting with frustration and with no recourse in sight.

I was sympathetic, of course, but, being the Western foreigner, I wanted to 10 know what *brand* of garments they produced at the Kaho factory—if I was to bring their story home, I would have to have my journalistic hook. So here we were, ten of us, crowded into a concrete bunker only slightly bigger than a telephone booth, playing an enthusiastic round of labor charades.

"This company produces long sleeves for cold seasons," one worker offered. 11

I guessed: "Sweaters?" 12

"I think not sweaters. If you prepare to go out and you have a cold season 13 you have a . . ."

I got it: "Coat!" 14

"But not heavy. Light." 15

"Jackets!" 16

"Yes, like jackets, but not jackets—long." 17

You can understand the confusion: There isn't much need for overcoats 18 on the equator, not in the closet and not in the vocabulary. And yet increasingly, Canadians get through their cold winters not with clothing manufactured by the tenacious seamstresses still on Spadina Avenue but by young Asian women working in hot climates like this one. In 1997, Canada imported $11.7 million of anoraks and ski jackets from Indonesia, up from $4.7 million in 1993. That much I knew already. But I still didn't know what brand of long coats the Kaho workers sewed before they lost their jobs.

"Long, yes. And what's on the label?" I asked again. 19

There was a bit of hushed consultation, and then, finally, an answer: 20 "London Fog."

A global coincidence, I suppose. I started to tell the Kaho workers that my 21 apartment in Toronto used to be a London Fog coat factory but stopped abruptly when it became clear from their facial expressions that the idea of anyone choosing to live in a garment building was nothing but alarming. In this part of the world, hundreds of workers every year burn to death because their dormitories are located upstairs from firetrap sweatshops.

Sitting cross-legged on the concrete floor of the tiny dorm room, I thought 22 of my neighbors back home: the Ashtanga yoga instructor on two, the commercial animators on four, the aromatherapy candle distributors on eight. It seems the young women in the export processing zone are our roommates of

Percentage Changes in Employment in the Textile, Clothing, Leather, and Footwear
Industries, 1980–93

Country	% Change	Country	% Change
Finland	-71.7	Mauritius	344.6
Sweden	-65.4	Indonesia	177.4
Norway	-64.9	Morocco	166.5
Austria	-51.5	Jordan	160.8
Poland	-51.0	Jamaica	101.7
Syria	-50.0	Malaysia	101.2
France	-45.4	Mexico	85.5
Hungary	-43.1	China	57.3
Netherlands	-41.7	Islamic Republic of Iran	34.0
United Kingdom	-41.5	Turkey	33.7
New Zealand	-40.9	Philippines	31.8
Germany	-40.2	Honduras	30.5
Spain	-35.3	Chile	27.2
Australia	-34.7	Kenya	16.1
Argentina	-32.9	Israel	13.4
United States	-30.1	Venezuela	7.9

Source: United Nations, International Labour Office, Geneva.

sorts, connected, as is so often the case, by a web of fabrics, shoelaces, fran-
chises, teddy bears and brand names wrapped around the planet. Another logo
we had in common was Esprit, also one of the brands manufactured in the
zone. As a teenager I worked as a clerk in a store that sold Esprit clothes. And,
of course, McDonald's: An outlet had just opened near Kaho, frustrating
workers, because this so-called bargain food was squarely out of their price
range.

Usually, reports about this global web of logos and products are couched   23
in the euphoric marketing rhetoric of the global village, an incredible place
where tribespeople in remotest rain forests tap away on laptop computers,
Sicilian grandmothers conduct e-business, and "global teens" share, to borrow
a phrase from a Levi's Web site, "a world-wide style culture." Everyone from
Coke to McDonald's to Motorola has tailored their marketing strategy around
this postnational vision, but it is IBM's long-running "Solutions for a Small
Planet" campaign that most eloquently captures the equalizing promise of the
logo-linked globe.

It hasn't taken long for the excitement inspired by these manic renditions   24
of globalization to wear thin, revealing the cracks and fissures beneath its
high-gloss façade. More and more over the past four years, we in the West

have been catching glimpses of another kind of global village, where the economic divide is widening and cultural choices narrowing.

This is a village where some multinationals, far from leveling the global   25
playing field with jobs and technology for all, are in the process of mining the planet's poorest backcountry for unimaginable profits. This is the village where Bill Gates lives, amassing a fortune of $55 billion while a third of his workforce is classified as temporary workers, and where competitors are either incorporated into the Microsoft monolith or made obsolete by the latest feat in software bundling. This is the village where we are indeed connected to one another through a web of brands, but the underside of that web reveals designer slums like the one I visited outside Jakarta. IBM claims that its technology spans the globe, and so it does, but often its international presence takes the form of cheap Third World labor producing the computer chips and power sources that drive our machines. On the outskirts of Manila, for instance, I met a seventeen-year-old girl who assembles CD-ROM drives for IBM. I told her I was impressed that someone so young could do such high-tech work. "We make computers," she told me, "but we don't know how to operate computers." Ours, it would seem, is not such a small planet after all.

For a reading quiz, sources on Naomi Klein, and annotated links to further readings on globalization and its effects on workers, visit **bedfordstmartins.com/ thebedfordreader**.

Journal Writing

How do you respond to the kind of "small world" or "global village" marketing that Klein cites in paragraph 23? In your journal, write about one such advertisement. (You may want to flip through some fashion or technology magazines to locate some examples.) What do you think is the ad's PURPOSE? How does it affect you? Does it accurately reflect the world we live in today? (To take your journal writing further, see "From Journal to Essay" on the next page.)

Questions on Meaning

1. What is Klein's THESIS in this essay? Where does she state it?
2. What causal relationship does Klein focus on? What is responsible for the "web of brands," and what are its consequences?

3. What does Klein mean by "global coincidence" (par. 21)? What is IRONIC about this coincidence?
4. Why does Klein say that the women working in the Jakarta factory and the neighbors in her Toronto building are "roommates" (par. 22)?

Questions on Writing Strategy

1. Why does Klein open with the lengthy DESCRIPTION of the neighborhood and specific warehouse in which she lives (pars. 1–7)? What purpose does this opening serve?
2. Why do you think Klein writes in detail about the strike of the garment workers and its settlement (par. 9)? What point is she making?
3. Why does Klein mention the seventeen-year-old CD-ROM assembler in paragraph 25?
4. **OTHER METHODS.** Where in the essay does Klein rely extensively on NARRATION? What might be her reason for telling this story in such detail?

Questions on Language

1. In context, what is the EFFECT of the phrase "secondhand sweatshops" in paragraph 6?
2. Why do you think Klein repeats the phrase "abysmal conditions" in paragraphs 8 and 9? What does *abysmal* mean?
3. Why does Klein start the last sentence of paragraph 22 with "And, of course"?
4. Consult a dictionary if you are unsure of the meaning of any of the following: postindustrial, limbo (par. 4); compulsory, compensation, recourse (9); charades (10); tenacious (18); euphoric, eloquently (23); manic (24).

Suggestions for Writing

1. **FROM JOURNAL TO ESSAY.** Write an essay based on your journal writing in which you explore your response to advertising that markets global connectedness and equality. What about the message is appealing or off-putting? To what extent do you see yourself as part of a global culture?
2. Klein focuses on the effect of globalization on workers in developing countries, but these shifts affect American and Canadian workers as well. Research employment changes in the United States that can be attributed to globalization—both in manufacturing and in services such as data processing. (The federal Bureau of Labor Statistics may be a good place to start: *bls.gov/home.htm.*) Write an essay in which, based on your findings, you explain your position on these changes.
3. **CRITICAL WRITING.** In an essay ANALYZE the image that Klein presents of herself. Use specific EXAMPLES of the language she uses and of the things she says about herself. How do you respond to this image?
4. **CONNECTIONS.** In the next essay, "Live Free and Starve," Chitra Divakaruni offers a different perspective on globalization and its effects on workers in developing countries. Write an essay in which you COMPARE AND CONTRAST the views of Klein and Divakaruni. How are their perspectives different? How does this difference affect their conclusions?

Naomi Klein on Writing

In a 2004 radio interview with Yogesh Chawla and Sachin Pandya, Naomi Klein discussed the role of writing in political activism. For herself, she said, research and writing are her main tools. But they serve others as well. She recently spent time among the Zapatistas, a group of Mexicans who use poetry, folk tales, and other nonviolent means to champion the poor and oppose repression. "There's this idea that anything can be a weapon if you use it right," Klein said. "And, you know, that's their famous phrase: 'Our word is our weapon.'" This principle has had a profound effect on Klein and other young activists, "free[ing] us to think about what political writing could be. . . . Creativity is considered once again political—not just a political priority as in dressing up the protests, but at the center of the spirit of how political alternatives will emerge."

For Discussion

1. How might writing serve as a political "weapon"? Can you think of examples when it has?
2. Have you ever written—or thought about writing—a letter of protest or complaint to a newspaper or magazine, a government representative, or a corporation? How have you used or could you use writing to work for change?

CHITRA DIVAKARUNI

Born in 1956 in Calcutta, India, CHITRA BANERJEE DIVAKARUNI spent nineteen years in her homeland before immigrating to the United States. She holds an MA from Wright State University and a PhD from the University of California at Berkeley. Her books, often addressing the immigrant experience in America, include the novels *The Mistress of Spice* (1997), *Sister of My Heart* (1999), *The Vine of Desire* (2002), and *Queen of Dreams* (2004); the story collections *Arranged Marriage* (1995) and *The Unknown Errors of Our Lives* (2001); and the poetry collections *Leaving Yuba City* (1997) and *Black Candle* (2000). Divakaruni has received a number of awards for her work, including the Before Columbus Foundation's 1996 American Book Award. She serves on the boards of two organizations that help victims of domestic abuse: MAITRI, in San Francisco, and Asians Against Domestic Abuse, in Houston.

Live Free and Starve

Many of the consumer goods sold in the United States—shoes, clothing, toys, rugs—are made in countries whose labor practices do not meet US standards for safety and fairness. Americans have been horrified at tales of children put to work by force or under contracts (called *indentures*) with the children's parents. In this essay from *Salon* magazine in 1997, Divakaruni argues that US efforts to stop such practices, though well intentioned, would have dreadful consequences.

For a different perspective on the effects of globalization, see the previous essay, Naomi Klein's "A Web of Brands."

Some days back, the House passed a bill that stated that the United States would no longer permit the import of goods from factories where forced or indentured child labor was used.[1] My liberal friends applauded the bill. It was

[1] The bill Divakaruni seems to refer to, the Sanders Indentured Child Labor Import Ban, was signed into law in 1998. It requires the US Customs Service to issue a detention order on goods that are suspected of having been produced by forced or indentured child labor. However, the goods may still be imported until the service bans them, and the service has ordered few such bans. Various measures have been taken to put more teeth in Sanders, such as a 1999 executive order requiring federal contractors to ensure that the products they provide are not produced with child labor. Meanwhile, a bill that would ban goods made with any kind of child labor has been introduced in Congress every year since 1993 but has not passed.—EDS.

a triumphant advance in the field of human rights. Now children in Third World countries wouldn't have to spend their days chained to their posts in factories manufacturing goods for other people to enjoy while their child-hoods slipped by them. They could be free and happy, like American children.

I am not so sure.   2

It is true that child labor is a terrible thing, especially for those children   3
who are sold to employers by their parents at the age of five or six and have no way to protect themselves from abuse. In many cases it will be decades — perhaps a lifetime, due to the fines heaped upon them whenever they make mistakes — before they can buy back their freedom. Meanwhile these children, mostly employed by rug-makers, spend their days in dark, ill-ventilated rooms doing work that damages their eyes and lungs. They aren't even allowed to stand up and stretch. Each time they go to the bathroom, they suffer a pay cut.

But is this bill, which, if it passes the Senate and is signed by President   4
Clinton, will lead to the unemployment of almost a million children, the answer? If the children themselves were asked whether they would rather work under such harsh conditions or enjoy a leisure that comes without the benefit of food or clothing or shelter, I wonder what their response would be.

It is easy for us in America to make the error of evaluating situations in   5
the rest of the world as though they were happening in this country and pro-pose solutions that make excellent sense — in the context of our society. Even we immigrants, who should know better, have wiped from our minds the memory of what it is to live under the kind of desperate conditions that force a parent to sell his or her child. Looking down from the heights of Maslow's pyramid,[2] it seems inconceivable to us that someone could actually prefer bread to freedom.

When I was growing up in Calcutta, there was a boy who used to work in   6
our house. His name was Nimai, and when he came to us, he must have been about ten or so, just a little older than my brother and I. He'd been brought to our home by his uncle, who lived in our ancestral village and was a field laborer for my grandfather. The uncle explained to my mother that Nimai's parents were too poor to feed their several children, and while his older broth-ers were already working in the fields and earning their keep, Nimai was too frail to do so. My mother was reluctant to take on a sickly child who might prove more of a burden than a help, but finally she agreed, and Nimai lived and worked in our home for six or seven years. My mother was a good

---

[2] The psychologist Abraham Maslow (1908–70) proposed a "hierarchy of needs" in the shape of a five-level pyramid with survival needs at the bottom and "self-actualization" and "self-transcendence" at the top. According to Maslow, one must satisfy the needs at each level before moving up to the next. — EDS.

employer—Nimai ate the same food that we children did and was given new clothes during Indian New Year, just as we were. In the time between his chores—dusting and sweeping and pumping water from the tube-well and running to the market—my mother encouraged him to learn to read and write. Still, I would not disagree with anyone who says that it was hardly a desirable existence for a child.

But what would life have been like for Nimai if an anti–child-labor law   7
had prohibited my mother from hiring him? Every year, when we went to visit our grandfather in the village, we were struck by the many children we saw by the mud roads, their ribs sticking out through the rags they wore. They trailed after us, begging for a few paise.[3] When the hunger was too much to bear, they stole into the neighbors' fields and ate whatever they could find—raw potatoes, cauliflower, green sugar cane and corn torn from the stalk—even though they knew they'd be beaten for it. Whenever Nimai passed these children, he always walked a little taller. And when he handed the bulk of his earnings over to his father, there was a certain pride in his eye. Exploitation, you might be thinking. But he thought he was a responsible member of his family.

A bill like the one we've just passed is of no use unless it goes hand in   8
hand with programs that will offer a new life to these newly released children. But where are the schools in which they are to be educated? Where is the money to buy them food and clothing and medication, so that they don't return home to become the extra weight that capsizes the already shaky raft of their family's finances? Their own governments, mired in countless other problems, seem incapable of bringing these services to them. Are we in America who, with one blithe stroke of our congressional pen, rendered these children jobless, willing to shoulder that burden? And when many of these children turn to the streets, to survival through thievery and violence and begging and prostitution—as surely in the absence of other options they must—are we willing to shoulder that responsibility?

For a reading quiz, sources on Chitra Divakaruni, and annotated links to further readings on globalization and its effects on workers, visit **bedfordstmartins.com/ thebedfordreader**.

---

[3] *Paise* are the smallest unit of Indian currency, worth a fraction of an American penny.—
EDS.

Journal Writing

Write a journal response to Divakaruni's argument against legislation that bans goods produced by forced or indentured child laborers. Do you basically agree or disagree with the author? Why? (To take your journal writing further, see "From Journal to Essay" below.)

Questions on Meaning

1. What do you take to be Divakaruni's PURPOSE in this essay? At what point did it become clear?
2. What is Divakaruni's THESIS? Where is it stated?
3. What are "Third World countries" (par. 1)?
4. From the further information given in the footnote on page 449, what does it mean to be "[l]ooking down from the heights of Maslow's pyramid" (par. 5)? What point is Divakaruni making here?
5. In paragraph 8 Divakaruni suggests some of the reasons that children in other countries may be forced or sold into labor. What are they?

Questions on Writing Strategy

1. In her last paragraph, Divakaruni asks a series of RHETORICAL QUESTIONS. What is the EFFECT of this strategy?
2. How does the structure of paragraph 3 clarify causes and effects?
3. **OTHER METHODS.** What does the extended EXAMPLE of Nimai (pars. 6–7) contribute to Divakaruni's argument? What, if anything, does it add to Divakaruni's authority? What does it tell us about child labor abroad?

Questions on Language

1. Divakaruni says that laboring children could otherwise be "the extra weight that capsizes the already shaky raft of their family's finances" (par. 8). How does this metaphor capture the problem of children in poor families? (See *Figures of speech* in Useful Terms for a definition of *metaphor*.)
2. What do the words in paragraph 7 tell you about Divakaruni's attitude toward the village children? Is it disdain? pity? compassion? horror?
3. Consult a dictionary if you need help in defining the following: indentured (par. 1); inconceivable (5); exploitation (7); mired, blithe (8).

Suggestions for Writing

1. **FROM JOURNAL TO ESSAY.** Starting from your journal entry, write a letter to your congressional representative or one of your senators that takes a position for or against laws such as that opposed by Divakaruni. You can use quotations from

Divakaruni's essay if they serve your purpose, but the letter should center on your own views of the issue. When you've finished your letter, send it. (You can find your representative's and your senators' names and addresses on the Web at *house.gov/writerep* and *senate.gov.*)

2. David Parker, a photographer and doctor, has documented child laborers in a series of powerful photographs (*www.hsph.harvard.edu/gallery/intro.html*). He asks viewers, "Under what circumstances and conditions should children work?" Look at Parker's photographs, and answer his question in an essay. What kind of paid work, for how many hours a week, is appropriate for, say, a ten- or twelve-year-old child? Consider: What about children working in their family's business? Where do you draw the line between occasional babysitting or lawn mowing and full-time factory work?

3. Research the history of child labor in the United States, including the development of child-labor laws. Then write an essay in which you explain how and why the laws evolved and what the current laws are.

4. **CRITICAL WRITING.** Divakaruni's essay depends significantly on appeals to readers' emotions (see pp. 518–19). Locate one emotional appeal that either helps to convince you of the author's point or, in your mind, weakens the argument. What does the appeal ASSUME about the reader's (your) feelings or values? Why are the assumptions correct or incorrect in your case? How, specifically, does the appeal strengthen or undermine Divakaruni's argument?

5. **CONNECTIONS.** In the previous essay, "A Web of Brands" (p. 440), Naomi Klein writes about working conditions for young adults in developing countries. What might Divakaruni have to say about a US ban on goods manufactured under the conditions Klein describes? What are your thoughts about such a ban? How, besides a ban, can importing countries help to improve the situation of workers in developing countries? Write an essay exploring the issues raised by Klein and Divakaruni.

Chitra Divakaruni on Writing

Chitra Divakaruni is both a writer and a community worker, reaching out to refugees and other disadvantaged people through organizations such as MAITRI, which she helped found. In a 1998 interview in *Atlantic Unbound* (the online version of *The Atlantic Monthly*), Katie Bolick asked Divakaruni how her activism and writing affected one another. Here is Divakaruni's response.

Being helpful where I can has always been an important value for me. I did community work in India, and I continue to do it in America, because being involved in my community is something I feel I need to do. Activism has given me enormous satisfaction — not just as a person, but also as a writer. The lives of people I would have only known from the outside, or had stereotyped notions of, have been opened up to me. My hotline work with MAITRI has certainly influenced both my life and my writing immensely. Overall, I have a great deal of sensitivity that I did not have before, and a lot of my preconceptions have changed. I hope that translates into my writing and reaches my readers.

For Discussion

1. What evidence does "Live Free and Starve" give to support Divakaruni's statement about how her activist work has affected her writing?
2. What does Divakaruni mean when she speaks of lives that she "would have only known from the outside"? Of what use is "insider's" knowledge to an activist? to a writer?
3. Do you have a project or activity—comparable to Divakaruni's activism—that you believe positively affects your writing? What is it? How does it help you as you write?

GORE VIDAL

GORE VIDAL was born in 1925 at the US Military Academy at West Point, where his father was an instructor. At the age of nineteen, he wrote his first novel, *Williwaw* (1946), while serving as a warrant officer aboard an army supply ship. Twenty-one other novels followed, including *Burr* (1973), *Duluth* (1983), *Lincoln* (1984), *Hollywood* (1989), and *The Golden Age* (2000). He has also written mysteries under the pen name Edgar Box. As a playwright, he is best known for *Visit to a Small Planet* (1957), which was made into a film. The grandson of Senator T. P. Gore, who represented Oklahoma for thirty years, Vidal twice ran unsuccessfully for Congress, and in 1992 he portrayed a senator in the movie *Bob Roberts*. A provocative and perceptive literary and social critic, Vidal is a frequent contributor to *The New York Review of Books* and other magazines, is a contributing editor of *The Nation* magazine, and has published more than a dozen collections of essays, including *The Essential Gore Vidal* (1999) and *Imperial America: Reflections on the United States of Amnesia* (2004). His books also include a memoir, *Palimpsest* (1995), and several histories, the latest *Inventing a Nation: Washington, Adams, Jefferson* (2003).

Drugs

Vidal first published "Drugs" in 1970 on the *New York Times*'s op-ed page and then included the essay in *Homage to Daniel Shays: Collected Essays 1952–1972*. In just twelve short paragraphs, Vidal analyzes several sets of cause and effect: why making drugs illegal does not work to stop drug addiction and trafficking, why legalizing drugs would work, and why nonetheless legalization is unlikely to occur. "Drugs" is dated in some ways, but the problem it addresses has only worsened. Lately, an increasing number of social scientists, medical professionals, and politicians have urged that we consider just such a radical solution as Vidal proposes.

It is possible to stop most drug addiction in the United States within a very short time. Simply make all drugs available and sell them at cost. Label each drug with a precise description of what effect — good and bad — the drug will have on the taker. This will require heroic honesty. Don't say that marijuana is addictive or dangerous when it is neither, as millions of people know — unlike "speed," which kills most unpleasantly, or heroin, which is addictive and difficult to kick.

For the record, I have tried — once — almost every drug and liked none, disproving the popular Fu Manchu theory that a single whiff of opium will enslave the mind. Nevertheless many drugs are bad for certain people to take and they should be told why in a sensible way.

Along with exhortation and warning, it might be good for our citizens to   3
recall (or learn for the first time) that the United States was the creation of
men who believed that each man has the right to do what he wants with his
own life as long as he does not interfere with his neighbor's pursuit of happiness. (That his neighbor's idea of happiness is persecuting others does confuse
matters a bit.)

This is a startling notion to the current generation of Americans. They   4
reflect a system of public education which has made the Bill of Rights, literally, unacceptable to a majority of high-school graduates (see the annual Pur-
due reports) who now form the "silent majority"—a phrase which that
underestimated wit Richard Nixon took from Homer, who used it to describe
the dead.

Now one can hear the warning rumble begin: If everyone is allowed to   5
take drugs everyone will and the GNP will decrease, the Commies will stop us
from making everyone free, and we shall end up a race of zombies, passively
murmuring "groovy" to one another. Alarming thought. Yet it seems most
unlikely that any reasonably sane person will become a drug addict if he
knows in advance what addiction is going to be like.

Is everyone reasonably sane? No. Some people will always become drug   6
addicts just as some people will always become alcoholics, and it is just too
bad. Every man, however, has the power (and should have the legal right) to
kill himself if he chooses. But since most men don't, they won't be mainliners
either. Nevertheless, forbidding people things they like or think they might
enjoy only makes them want those things all the more. This psychological
insight is, for some mysterious reason, perennially denied our governors.

It is a lucky thing for the American moralist that our country has always   7
existed in a kind of time-vacuum: We have no public memory of anything
that happened before last Tuesday. No one in Washington today recalls what
happened during the years alcohol was forbidden to the people by a Congress
that thought it had a divine mission to stamp out Demon Rum—launching,
in the process, the greatest crime wave in the country's history, causing thousands of deaths from bad alcohol, and creating a general (and persisting) contempt among the citizenry for the laws of the United States.

The same thing is happening today. But the government has learned   8
nothing from past attempts at prohibition, not to mention repression.

Last year when the supply of Mexican marijuana was slightly curtailed by   9
the Feds, the pushers got the kids hooked on heroin and deaths increased dramatically, particularly in New York. Whose fault? Evil men like the Mafiosi?
Permissive Dr. Spock? Wild-eyed Dr. Leary? No.

The government of the United States was responsible for those deaths.   10
The bureaucratic machine has a vested interest in playing cops and robbers.

Both the Bureau of Narcotics and the Mafia want strong laws against the sale and use of drugs because if drugs are sold at cost there would be no money in it for anyone.

If there was no money in it for the Mafia, there would be no friendly play- 11
ground pushers, and addicts would not commit crimes to pay for the next fix.
Finally, if there was no money in it, the Bureau of Narcotics would wither away, something they are not about to do without a struggle.

Will anything sensible be done? Of course not. The American people are 12
as devoted to the idea of sin and its punishment as they are to making money—and fighting drugs is nearly as big a business as pushing them. Since the combination of sin and money is irresistible (particularly to the professional politician), the situation will only grow worse.

For a reading quiz, sources on Gore Vidal, and annotated links to further readings on drug laws and legalization, visit **bedfordstmartins.com/thebedfordreader**.

Journal Writing

Vidal is convinced that the best way to combat the drug problem in this country is to "make all drugs available and sell them at cost." Does this seem like a good idea to you? What do you think would be the practical effects—positive or negative—of legalizing drugs? (To take your journal writing further, see "From Journal to Essay" on the facing page.)

Questions on Meaning

1. What do you take to be Vidal's main PURPOSE in writing this essay? How well does he accomplish it?
2. For what reasons, according to Vidal, is it unlikely that our drug laws will be eased? Can you suggest other possible reasons why the Bureau of Narcotics favors strict drug laws?
3. Vidal's essay was first published more than three decades ago. Do you find the views expressed in it still timely, or out of date?

Questions on Writing Strategy

1. How would you characterize Vidal's humor? Find some EXAMPLES of it.
2. Where in the essay does Vidal appear to anticipate the response of his AUDIENCE? How can you tell?

3. What function do the essay's RHETORICAL QUESTIONS perform?
4. ANALYZE Vidal's opening paragraph. What does it accomplish?
5. **OTHER METHODS.** Study Vidal's use of example in paragraphs 8–10. Does the example of the US government's role in heroin deaths effectively support Vidal's point that restricting drug use does not work? Is Vidal guilty here of oversimplification (p. 524)?

Questions on Language

1. Know the definitions of the following terms: exhortation (par. 3); GNP (5); mainliners, perennially (6); curtailed (9).
2. How do you interpret Vidal's use of the phrase "underestimated wit" to describe Richard Nixon?

Suggestions for Writing

1. **FROM JOURNAL TO ESSAY.** Look back at your journal entry on the effects of legalizing drugs and at Vidal's explanations for why they have *not* been legalized. In an essay, explain why you think the United States resists legalizing drugs. You may support Vidal's moral and economic arguments, you may oppose one or several of his claims, or you may propose new reasons of your own. In any case, be sure to make clear, as Vidal does, the connection between the foreseeable effects of legalization and the reasoning that keeps drugs illegal.
2. Research the situation reported by Vidal in paragraphs 9 and 10. (Begin with the *New York Times Index* for the years 1969 and 1970.) Write an essay that clearly and objectively analyzes the causes of the situation.
3. **CRITICAL WRITING.** How readily do you accept Vidal's statement that "each man has the right to do what he wants with his own life" — including, presumably, to be a drug addict — "as long as he does not interfere with his neighbor's pursuit of happiness" (par. 3)? Do you accept Vidal's implicit ASSUMPTION that people with easy access to drugs are not necessarily threats to their neighbors? Back up your answers with EVIDENCE from your experience and reading.
4. **CONNECTIONS.** Like Vidal, Meghan Daum, in "Safe-Sex Lies" (p. 459), takes a controversial view. Write an essay that COMPARES AND CONTRASTS the ways these two authors present their views. Consider in your essay how each author establishes his or her authority and credibility; uses evidence such as personal experience, facts, and examples; anticipates readers' responses; and addresses readers through TONE.

Gore Vidal on Writing

"Do you find writing easy?" Gerald Clark asked Gore Vidal for the *Paris Review*. "Do you enjoy it?"

Oh, yes, of course I enjoy it. I wouldn't do it if I didn't. Whenever I get up in the morning, I write for about three hours. I write novels in longhand on yellow pads, exactly like the First Criminal Nixon. For some reason I write plays and essays on the typewriter. The first draft usually comes rather fast. One oddity: I never reread a text until I have finished the first draft. Otherwise it's too discouraging. Also, when you have the whole thing in front of you for the first time, you've forgotten most of it and see it fresh. Rewriting, however, is a slow, grinding business.

When I first started writing, I used to plan everything in advance, not only chapter to chapter but page to page. Terribly constricting—like doing a film from someone else's meticulous treatment. About the time of *The Judgment of Paris* [a novel published in 1952] I started improvising. I began with a mood. A sentence. The first sentence is all-important. [My novel] *Washington, D.C.* began with a dream, a summer storm at night in a garden above the Potomac—that was Merrywood, where I grew up.

The most interesting thing about writing is the way that it obliterates time. Three hours seem like three minutes. Then there is the business of surprise. I never know what is coming next. The phrase that sounds in the head changes when it appears on the page. Then I start probing it with a pen, finding new meanings. Sometimes I burst out laughing at what is happening as I twist and turn sentences. Strange business, all in all. One never gets to the end of it. That's why I go on, I suppose. To see what the next sentences I write will be.

For Discussion

1. What is it that Vidal seems to enjoy most about writing?
2. What advantage does he find in not planning every page in advance?

MEGHAN DAUM

Born in 1970 in Palo Alto, California, MEGHAN DAUM is a writer known for provocative, witty essays on American life. Daum graduated from Vassar College with a BA in English (1992) and from Columbia University with an MA in writing (1996). She worked on the staffs of *Allure* magazine and Columbia University Press before turning to writing full-time. On public radio Daum is a contributor to *This American Life* and a commentator for *Morning Edition*. In print she is a contributing writer for *Harper's Bazaar* and has been published in *The New Yorker*, *GQ*, the *New York Times Book Review*, and other magazines. Her collection of essays, *Misspent Youth*, came out in 2001. Her novel, *The Quality of Life Report*, came out in 2003 and was named a *New York Times* Notable Book. Daum lives in Los Angeles.

Safe-Sex Lies

This essay from the *New York Times Magazine* caused a stir when it was first published in January 1996. Daum deftly analyzes several damaging effects of the media's coverage of AIDS, especially the anxiety, shame, mistrust, and dishonesty that she and others of her generation experience.

I have been tested for HIV three times. I've gone to clinics and stuck my arm out for those disposable needles, each time forgetting the fear and nausea that descend upon me before the results come back, those minutes spent in a publicly financed waiting room staring at a video loop about "living with" this thing that kills you. These tests have taken place over five years, and the results have always been negative — not surprisingly in retrospect, since I am not a member of a "high-risk group," don't sleep around and don't take pity on heroin-addicted bass players by going to bed with them in the hopes of being thanked in the liner notes of their first major independent release. Still, getting tested always seemed like the thing to do. Despite my demographic profile, despite the fact that I grew up middle class, attended an elite college and do not personally know any women or straight men within that demographic profile who have the AIDS virus, I am terrified of this disease. I went to a college where condoms and dental dams lay in baskets in dormitory lobbies, where it seemed incumbent on health service counselors to give us the straight talk, to tell us never, ever to have sex without condoms unless we wanted to die; that's right, *die*, shrivel overnight, vomit up our futures, pose a threat to others. (And they'd seen it happen, oh, yes, they had.) They gave us pamphlets, didn't quite explain how to use dental dams, told us where we could get tested, threw us more fistfuls of condoms (even some glow-in-the-dark brands, just for variety). This can actually be fun, they said, if only we'd adopt a better attitude.

We're told we can get this disease and we believe it and vow to protect ourselves, and intend (really, truly) to stick by this rule, until we don't because we just can't, because it's just not fair, because our sense of entitlement exceeds our sense of vulnerability. So we blow off precaution again and again, and then we get scared and get tested, and when it comes out OK, we run out of the clinic, pamphlets in hand, eyes cast upward, promising ourselves we'll never be stupid again. But of course we are stupid, again and again. And the testing is always for the same reasons and with the same results, and soon it becomes more like fibbing about SAT scores ten years after the fact than lying about whether we practice unsafe sex, a lie that sounds like such a breach of contract with ourselves that we might as well be talking about putting a loaded gun under our pillow every night.

Still, I've gone into more than a few relationships with the safest of intentions and discarded them after the fourth or fifth encounter. Perhaps this is a shocking admission, but my hunch is that I'm not the only one doing it. My suspicion is, in fact, that very few of us—"us" being the demographic profile frequently charged with thinking we're immortal, the population accused of being cynical and lazy and weak—have really responded to the AIDS crisis the way the federal government and educators would like us to believe. My guess is that we're all but ignoring it and that almost anyone who claims otherwise is lying.

It seems there is a lot of lying going around. One of the main tenets of the safe-sex message is that ageless mantra "you don't know where he's been," meaning that everyone is a potential threat, that we're all either scoundrels or ignoramuses. "He didn't tell me he was shooting drugs," says an HIV-positive woman on a public-service advertisement. Safe-sex "documentaries" on MTV and call-in radio shows on pop stations give us woman after woman whose boyfriend "claimed he loved me but was sleeping around." The message we receive is that trusting anyone is itself an irresponsible act, that having faith in an intimate partner, particularly women in relation to men, is a symptom of such profound naïveté that we're obviously not mature enough to be having sex anyway.

I find this reasoning almost more troubling than the disease itself. It flies in the face of the social order from which I, as someone born in 1970, was supposed to benefit. That this reasoning runs counter to almost any feminist ideology—the ideology that proclaimed, at least back in the seventies, that women should feel free to ask men on dates and wear jeans and have orgasms—is an admission that no AIDS-concerned citizen is willing to make. Two decades after *The Joy of Sex* made sexual pleasure permissible for both sexes and three decades after the pill put a government-approved stamp on premarital sex, we're still told not to trust each other. We've entered a period where mistrust equals responsibility, where fear signifies health.

Since I spent all of the seventies under the age of ten, I've never known a significantly different sexual and social climate. Supposedly this makes it easier to live with the AIDS crisis. Health educators and AIDS activists like to think that people of my generation can be made to unlearn what we never knew, to break the reckless habits we didn't actually form. But what we have learned thoroughly is how not to enjoy ourselves. Just like our mothers, whose adolescences were haunted by the abstract taboo against being "bad" girls, my contemporaries and I are discouraged from doing what feels good. As it did with our mothers, the onus falls largely on the women. We know that it's much easier for women to contract HIV from a man than the other way around. We know that an "unsafe" man generally means someone who has shot drugs or slept with other men, or possibly slept with prostitutes. We find ourselves wondering about these things over dinner dates. We look for any hints of homosexual tendencies, any references to a hypodermic moment. We try to catch him in the lie we've been told he'll tell.

What could be sadder? We're not allowed to believe anyone anymore. And the reason we're not isn't so much because of AIDS but because of the anxiety that ripples around the disease. The information about AIDS that is supposed to produce "awareness" has been subsumed into the aura of style. AIDS awareness has become so much a part of the pop culture that not only is it barely noticeable, it is largely ineffectual. MTV runs programs about safe sex that are barely distinguishable from documentaries about Madonna. A print advertisement for Benetton features a collage of hundreds of tiny photographs of young people, some of whom are shaded with the word AIDS written across their faces. Many are white and blond and have the tousled, moneyed look common to more traditional fashion spreads or even yearbooks from colleges like the one I attended. There is no text other than the company's slogan. There is no explanation of how these faces were chosen, no public statement of whether these people actually have the disease or not. I called Benetton for clarification and was told that the photographs were supposed to represent people from all over the world and that no one was known to be HIV-positive—just as I suspected. The advertisement was a work of art, which meant I could interpret the image any way I liked. This is how the deliverers of the safe-sex message shoot themselves in the foot. Confronted with arty effects instead of actual information, people like me are going to believe what we want to believe, which, of course, is whatever isn't too scary. So we turn the page.

Since I am pretty sure I do not sleep with bisexual men or IV drug users, my main personal concern about AIDS is that men can get the virus from women and subsequently pass it on to other women. According to the Centers for Disease Control's National AIDS Clearinghouse surveillance report, less than three-quarters of 1 percent of white non-Hispanic men with HIV infection contracted the virus through heterosexual sex with a non–IV drug-using woman. (Interestingly, the CDC labels this category as "risk not specified.") But this statistic seems too dry for MTV and campus health brochures, whose eye-catching "sex kills" rhetoric tells us nothing other than to ignore what we don't feel like thinking about. Obviously, there are still too many cases of HIV; there is a deadly risk in certain kinds of sexual behavior and therefore reason to take precautions. But until more people appear on television, look into the camera and tell me that they contracted HIV through heterosexual sex with someone who had no risk factors, I will continue to disregard the message.

Besides, the very sophistication that allows people like me to filter out   9
much of the hype behind music videos, fashion magazines and television talk shows is what we use to block out the safe-sex message. We are not a population that makes personal decisions based on the public service work of a rock star. We're not going to sacrifice the thing we believe we deserve, the experiences we waited for, because Levi Strauss is a major sponsor of MTV's coverage of World AIDS Day.

So the inconsistent behavior continues, as do the confessions among   10
friends and the lies to health-care providers during routine exams, because we just can't bear the terrifying lectures that ensue when we confess to not always protecting ourselves. Life in your twenties is fraught not only with financial and professional uncertainty, but also with a specter of death that floats above the pursuit of a sex life. And there is no solution, only the conclusion that invariably finishes the hushed conversations: The whole thing simply "sucks." It's a bummer on a grand scale.

Heterosexuals are receiving vague signals. We're told that if we are suffi-   11
ciently vigilant, we will probably be all right. We're being told to assume the worst and to not invite disaster by hoping for the best. We're being encouraged to keep our fantasies on a tight rein, otherwise we'll lose control of the whole buggy, and no one can say we weren't warned. So for us AIDS remains a private hell, smoldering beneath intimate conversations among friends and surfacing on those occasional sleepless nights when it occurs to us to wonder about it, upon which that dark hysteria sets in, and those catalogues of whom we've done it with and whom they might have done it with and oh-my-God-I'll-surely-die seem to project themselves onto the ceiling, the way fanged monsters did when we were children. But we fall asleep and then we wake up. And nothing has changed except our willingness to forget about it, which has become the ultimate survival mechanism. What my peers and I are left with

is a generalized anxiety, a low-grade fear and anger that resides at the core of everything we do. Our attitudes have been affected by the disease by leaving us scared, but our behavior has stayed largely the same. One result is a corrosion of the soul, a chronic dishonesty and fear that will most likely damage us more than the disease itself. In this world, peace of mind is a utopian concept.

For a reading quiz, sources on Meghan Daum, and annotated links to further readings on AIDS, visit **bedfordstmartins.com/thebedfordreader**.

Journal Writing

Writing in her midtwenties, Daum calls herself part of the "demographic profile frequently charged with thinking we're immortal, the population accused of being cynical and lazy and weak" (par. 3). Do you agree that many people in their late teens and twenties fit this description? In your journal, write your own characterization of this age group. (To take your journal writing further, see "From Journal to Essay" on the next page.)

Questions on Meaning

1. What is Daum's PURPOSE in writing this essay? On whom, or what, is she placing blame? Does she offer any solutions in the essay, or is she merely outlining a problem previously unacknowledged?
2. What is Daum's THESIS? Where is it stated?
3. What does Daum mean by "our sense of entitlement exceeds our sense of vulnerability" (par. 2)?
4. Explain how AIDS awareness has become "part of the pop culture" (par. 7).
5. Explain the title's double meaning: What are the two kinds of "Safe-Sex Lies" discussed in the essay?

Questions on Writing Strategy

1. Daum asserts that the media exaggerate the prevalence of AIDS among heterosexuals who are not IV drug users. Explain the chain of causes and effects that she sees as leading from this exaggeration.
2. What is the TONE of the essay?
3. What is the EFFECT of Daum's confession in the second paragraph?

4. What AUDIENCE do you think Daum had in mind when she was writing this essay? Is she targeting all readers of the *New York Times* or a more specific subset of them?
5. What does Daum do to achieve clarity in paragraph 5?
6. **OTHER METHODS.** In paragraph 7 Daum uses an extended EXAMPLE of a Benetton ad to support her assertion that "[t]he information about AIDS that is supposed to produce 'awareness' has been subsumed into the aura of style." Why does it make a difference to Daum that the people represented in the Benetton ad are not known to be HIV-positive?

Questions on Language

1. Look up any of the following words you don't already know: retrospect, demographic, incumbent (par. 1); entitlement, breach (2); cynical (3); mantra, scoundrels, ignoramuses, naïveté (4); ideology (5); abstract, contemporaries, onus (6); subsumed, aura, tousled (7); surveillance (8); fraught, specter (10); vigilant, smoldering (11).
2. What is the effect of the word *those* in "those disposable needles" and "those minutes spent in a publicly financed waiting room" (par. 1)?
3. Daum's language is often quite informal, as in conversation—for instance, "unless we wanted to die; that's right, *die*" and "they'd seen it happen, oh, yes, they had" (par. 1); "It seems there is a lot of lying going around" (4); or "It's a bummer on a grand scale" (10). What is the effect of this language? Is it appropriate to Daum's subject and purpose? Why, or why not?

Suggestions for Writing

1. **FROM JOURNAL TO ESSAY.** Write an essay DEFINING the age group roughly from eighteen to thirty, drawing on your journal entry, Daum's essay, and any other sources that offer ideas. Keep in mind that characterization of such a large and diverse group will require GENERALIZATION on your part. How does your definition compare with other definitions you have heard in the media? Does any attempt to characterize an age group necessarily oversimplify? Do you find some value or interest in the exercise?
2. Write an essay about how AIDS has (or hasn't) changed your life, considering the following questions: Is AIDS something you think about often, or is it something "out there" that happens to other people? How do the media influence your attitudes toward the disease? If a cure for AIDS were discovered tomorrow, would your approach to sexuality and relationships change, or has AIDS permanently affected your attitudes?
3. What are current rates of HIV infection and AIDS-related death in North America and sub-Saharan Africa? Why are these rates different in the two regions? Research the answers to these questions, starting at the Web site of UNAIDS, the Joint United Nations Programme on HIV/AIDS: *www.unaids.org/EN/default.asp*. Then write an essay explaining the difference in the rates.
4. **CRITICAL WRITING.** Analyze how Daum's "demographic profile" (par. 1) determines her perspective on AIDS. Do you find this limited perspective appropriate,

or do you think Daum should have mentioned other views as well—perhaps of those who urge sexual abstinence or who care for AIDS patients or who have AIDS themselves? To what extent does Daum's limited perspective weaken or strengthen her essay?

5. **CONNECTIONS.** Daum and Armin A. Brott, in "Not All Men Are Sly Foxes" (p. 348), are both concerned about the subtle effects of words and pictures on an audience: Daum is interested in the way safe sex is marketed, the face advertising puts on AIDS; Brott is troubled by the negative stereotyping of fathers in books for children. Write an essay criticizing what you consider to be inaccurate or inappropriate media representation of a given group (for example, single mothers, gays and lesbians, lawyers, football players, fashion models). What message do these portrayals send to members of that group and to those outside the group? How might the portrayals be improved?

DON DeLILLO

DON DeLILLO, one of America's preeminent fiction writers, produces dark and often comic works exploring celebrity, consumerism, and other facets of American culture. The son of Italian immigrants, DeLillo was born in 1936 in New York City and grew up in the Bronx. He graduated from Fordham University in 1958 with a degree in communications and then, after searching unsuccessfully for a publishing job, reluctantly accepted work in an advertising agency. Five years later, DeLillo quit copywriting and began working on his first novel, *Americana* (1971). Halfway through the four years it took to write the book, DeLillo says, "it occurred to me almost in a flash that I was a writer. Whatever tentativeness I'd felt about the book dropped away." Since then, DeLillo has published twelve more novels, including *The Names* (1982), *White Noise* (1985), *Libra* (1988), *Mao II* (1991), *Underworld* (1997), *The Body Artist* (2001), and, most recently, *Cosmopolis* (2003). DeLillo received the National Book award for *White Noise*, a PEN/Faulkner award for *Mao II*, and the William Dean Howells Medal from the American Academy of Arts and Letters for *Underworld*.

Videotape

As compelling as fictional TV and movies can be, showing heart-rending tragedy or sickening violence, they can't compare with documentary evidence of the real thing. In this short story from 1994, first published in *Antaeus* magazine, DeLillo's character explores his compulsive fascination with a video slice of life and death.

It shows a man driving a car. It is the simplest sort of family video. You see 1 a man at the wheel of a medium Dodge.

It is just a kid aiming her camera through the rear window of the family 2 car at the windshield of the car behind her.

You know about families and their video cameras. You know how kids 3 get involved, how the camera shows them that every subject is potentially charged, a million things they never see with the unaided eye. They investigate the meaning of inert objects and dumb pets and they poke at family privacy. They learn to see things twice.

It is the kid's own privacy that is being protected here. She is twelve years 4 old and her name is being withheld even though she is neither the victim nor the perpetrator of the crime but only the means of recording it.

It shows a man in a sport shirt at the wheel of his car. There is nothing else 5 to see. The car approaches briefly, then falls back.

You know how children with cameras learn to work the exposed moments 6
that define the family cluster. They break every trust, spy out the undefended
space, catching Mom coming out of the bathroom in her cumbrous robe and
turbaned towel, looking bloodless and plucked. It is not a joke. They will
shoot you sitting on the pot if they can manage a suitable vantage.

The tape has the jostled sort of noneventness that marks the family 7
product. Of course the man in this case is not a member of the family but a
stranger in a car, a random figure, someone who has happened along in the
slow lane.

It shows a man in his forties wearing a pale shirt open at the throat, the 8
image washed by reflections and sunglint, with many jostled moments.

It is not just another video homicide. It is a homicide recorded by a child 9
who thought she was doing something simple and maybe halfway clever,
shooting some tape of a man in a car.

He sees the girl and waves briefly, wagging a hand without taking it off the 10
wheel — an underplayed reaction that makes you like him.

It is unrelenting footage that rolls on and on. It has an aimless determina- 11
tion, a persistence that lives outside the subject matter. You are looking into
the mind of home video. It is innocent, it is aimless, it is determined, it is real.

He is bald up the middle of his head, a nice guy in his forties whose whole 12
life seems open to the hand-held camera.

But there is also an element of suspense. You keep on looking not because 13
you know something is going to happen — of course you do know something
is going to happen and you do look for that reason but you might also keep on
looking if you came across this footage for the first time without knowing the
outcome. There is a crude power operating here. You keep on looking because
things combine to hold you fast — a sense of the random, the amateurish, the
accidental, the impending. You don't think of the tape as boring or interesting. It is crude, it is blunt, it is relentless. It is the jostled part of your mind, the
film that runs through your hotel brain under all the thoughts you know you're
thinking.

The world is lurking in the camera, already framed, waiting for the boy or 14
girl who will come along and take up the device, learn the instrument, shooting old Granddad at breakfast, all stroked out so his nostrils gape, the cereal
spoon baby-gripped in his pale fist.

It shows a man alone in a medium Dodge. It seems to go on forever. 15

There's something about the nature of the tape, the grain of the image, 16
the sputtering black-and-white tones, the starkness — you think this is more
real, truer-to-life, than anything around you. The things around you have a
rehearsed and layered and cosmetic look. The tape is superreal, or maybe
underreal is the way you want to put it. It is what lies at the scraped bottom of

all the layers you have added. And this is another reason why you keep on looking. The tape has a searing realness.

It shows him giving an abbreviated wave, stiff-palmed, like a signal flag at a siding. 17

You know how families make up games. This is just another game in which the child invents the rules as she goes along. She likes the idea of videotaping a man in his car. She has probably never done it before and she sees no reason to vary the format or terminate early or pan to another car. This is her game and she is learning it and playing it at the same time. She feels halfway clever and inventive and maybe slightly intrusive as well, a little bit of brazenness that spices any game. 18

And you keep on looking. You look because this is the nature of the footage, to make a channeled path through time, to give things a shape and a destiny. 19

Of course if she had panned to another car, the right car at the precise time, she would have caught the gunman as he fired. 20

The chance quality of the encounter. The victim, the killer, and the child with a camera. Random energies that approach a common point. There's something here that speaks to you directly, saying terrible things about forces beyond your control, lines of intersection that cut through history and logic and every reasonable layer of human expectation. 21

She wandered into it. The girl got lost and wandered clear-eyed into horror. This is a children's story about straying too far from home. But it isn't the family car that serves as the instrument of the child's curiosity, her inclination to explore. It is the camera that puts her in the tale. 22

You know about holidays and family celebrations and how somebody shows up with a camcorder and the relatives stand around and barely react because they're numbingly accustomed to the process of being taped and decked and shown on the VCR with the coffee and cake. 23

He is hit soon after. If you've seen the tape many times you know from the handwave exactly when he will be hit. It is something, naturally, that you wait for. You say to your wife, if you're at home and she is there, Now here is where he gets it. You say, Janet, hurry up, this is where it happens. 24

Now here is where he gets it. You see him jolted, sort of wire-shocked — then he seizes up and falls toward the door or maybe leans or slides into the door is the proper way to put it. It is awful and unremarkable at the same time. The car stays in the slow lane. It approaches briefly, then falls back. 25

You don't usually call your wife over to the TV set. She has her programs, you have yours. But there's a certain urgency here. You want her to see how it looks. The tape has been running forever and now the thing is finally going to happen and you want her to be here when he's shot. 26

Here it comes, all right. He is shot, head-shot, and the camera reacts, the   27
child reacts—there is a jolting movement but she keeps on taping, there is a
sympathetic response, a nerve response, her heart is beating faster but she
keeps the camera trained on the subject as he slides into the door and even
as you see him die you're thinking of the girl. At some level the girl has to be
present here, watching what you're watching, unprepared—the girl is seeing
this cold and you have to marvel at the fact that she keeps the tape rolling.

It shows something awful and unaccompanied. You want your wife to see   28
it because it is real this time, not fancy movie violence—the realness beneath
the layers of cosmetic perception. Hurry up, Janet, here it comes. He dies so
fast. There is no accompaniment of any kind. It is very stripped. You want to
tell her it is realer than real but then she will ask what that means.

The way the camera reacts to the gunshot—a startled reaction that   29
brings pity and terror into the frame, the girl's own shock, the girl's identification with the victim.

You don't see the blood, which is probably trickling behind his ear and   30
down the back of his neck. The way his head is twisted away from the door,
the twist of the head gives you only a partial profile and it's the wrong side, it's
not the side where he was hit.

And maybe you're being a little aggressive here, practically forcing your   31
wife to watch. Why? What are you telling her? Are you making a little statement? Like I'm going to ruin your day out of ordinary spite. Or a big statement? Like this is the risk of existing. Either way you're rubbing her face in
this tape and you don't know why.

It shows the car drifting toward the guardrail and then there's a jostling   32
sense of two other lanes and part of another car, a split-second blur, and the
tape ends here, either because the girl stopped shooting or because some central authority, the police or the district attorney or the TV station, decided
there was nothing else you had to see.

This is either the tenth or eleventh homicide committed by the Texas   33
Highway Killer. The number is uncertain because the police believe that one
of the shootings may have been a copycat crime.

And there is something about videotape, isn't there, and this particular   34
kind of serial crime? This is a crime designed for random taping and immediate playing. You sit there and wonder if this kind of crime became more possible when the means of taping and playing an event—playing it immediately
after the taping—became part of the culture. The principal doesn't necessarily commit the sequence of crimes in order to see them taped and played. He
commits the crimes as if they were a form of taped-and-played event. The
crimes are inseparable from the idea of taping and playing. You sit there thinking that this is a crime that has found its medium, or vice versa—cheap mass

production, the sequence of repeated images and victims, stark and glary and more or less unremarkable.

It shows very little in the end. It is a famous murder because it is on tape 35
and because the murderer has done it many times and because the crime was recorded by a child. So the child is involved, the Video Kid as she is sometimes called because they have to call her something. The tape is famous and so is she. She is famous in the modern manner of people whose names are strategically withheld. They are famous without names or faces, spirits living apart from their bodies, the victims and witnesses, the underage criminals, out there somewhere at the edges of perception.

Seeing someone at the moment he dies, dying unexpectedly. This is rea- 36
son alone to stay fixed to the screen. It is instructional, watching a man shot dead as he drives along on a sunny day. It demonstrates an elemental truth, that every breath you take has two possible endings. And that's another thing. There's a joke locked away here, a note of cruel slapstick that you are completely willing to appreciate. Maybe the victim's a chump, a dope, classically unlucky. He had it coming, in a way, like an innocent fool in a silent movie.

You don't want Janet to give you any crap about it's on all the time, they 37
show it a thousand times a day. They show it because it exists, because they have to show it, because this is why they're out there. The horror freezes your soul but this doesn't mean that you want them to stop.

For a reading quiz, sources on Don DeLillo, and annotated links to further readings on the effects of seeing real-life violence, visit **bedfordstmartins.com/ thebedfordreader**.

Journal Writing

Do you identify with the NARRATOR's obsession with the videotape of the man being shot? When have you seen documentary footage of a crime or disaster, either once or repeatedly? In your journal, reflect on how the footage affected you. (To take your journal writing further, see "From Journal to Essay" on the facing page.)

Questions on Meaning

1. How does the fact that a twelve-year-old girl accidentally recorded the murder affect the narrator's response?

2. Why does the narrator want his wife to watch the death of the man on the tape?
3. In paragraph 34 the narrator makes a causal connection between certain kinds of serial crimes and the fact that videotaping and instant replay have become "part of the culture." What is this connection? Does it seem reasonable to you?

Questions on Writing Strategy

1. What reasons does the narrator give for his fascination with the replaying videotape?
2. Note how DeLillo's narrator doles out crucial pieces of information. When is it first clear that the video involves a victim? that it records a murder? that a gunshot caused the murder? that the driver was shot? that the video is being run on television? that the crime was committed by a serial killer? What EFFECT does this slow release of details have on your reading of the story?
3. The narrator consistently uses the pronoun *you* rather than *I*. Why do you suppose DeLillo chose this approach? (To see its effect, try rewriting pars. 23–26 with *I* or *me* instead of *you*.)
4. The narrator uses verbs in the present tense—for instance, "It shows" or "Now here is where he gets it." Why is this tense appropriate for the story DeLillo is telling?
5. **OTHER METHODS.** In what way is DESCRIPTION an important part of DeLillo's story?

Questions on Language

1. In paragraph 7 the narrator refers to the victim as "a random figure." Find other references to randomness and words with similar meanings. What do these contribute to the narrator's vision of the event's greater significance?
2. The narrator says the tape has a "sort of noneventness" (par. 7) and that the crime is, in the end, "more or less unremarkable" (34). What do you think he means?
3. The narrator describes the tape as "superreal, or maybe underreal" and having "a searing realness" (par. 16) and being "realer than real" (28). How do you interpret this language?
4. Consult a dictionary if you are unsure of the meanings of any of the following words: inert (par. 3); perpetrator (4); cumbrous, vantage (6); starkness, searing (16); brazenness (18); principal (34); strategically (35); elemental, slapstick (36).

Suggestions for Writing

1. **FROM JOURNAL TO ESSAY.** Expand your journal entry into an essay in which you identify and reflect on your responses to documentary footage of a crime or disaster. Were your responses anything like those of the narrator in DeLillo's story, or were they different? Were your responses affected by how often you saw the footage, whether once, twice, or more often? Why do you think you responded as you did?

2. Think of some important experience you have had—either positive, such as winning an award or having a child, or negative, such as being robbed or being in a car wreck. Write a story about the episode, either true-to-life or fictionalized. Follow DeLillo's example in using the second-person *you* and the present tense of verbs.

3. **CRITICAL WRITING.** ANALYZE DeLillo's use of repetition in "Videotape." What effects does it achieve? In what ways does such repetition echo his theme?

4. **CONNECTIONS.** COMPARE AND CONTRAST the narrator of "Videotape" with the narrator of Alice Walker's "Everyday Use" (p. 272) or Daniel Orozco's "Orientation" (p. 324). How is the narrative voice in each case suitable for the story being told?

Don DeLillo on Writing

In a 1993 interview published in *The Paris Review*, DeLillo defined writing as "a concentrated form of thinking." He explained, "I don't know what I think about certain subjects, even today, until I sit down and try to write about them."

When he sits down to work, his discarded draft pages sit nearby. "I want those pages nearby because there's always a chance I'll have to refer to something that's scrawled at the bottom of a sheet of paper somewhere. Discarded pages mark the physical dimensions of a writer's labor—you know, how many shots it took to get a certain paragraph right. . . . I find I'm more ready to discard pages than I used to be. I used to look for things to keep. I used to find ways to save a paragraph or sentence, maybe by relocating it. Now I look for ways to discard things. If I discard a sentence I like, it's almost as satisfying as keeping a sentence I like. I don't think I've become ruthless or perverse—just a bit more willing to believe that nature will restore itself. The instinct to discard is finally a kind of faith. It tells me there's a better way to do this page even though the evidence is not accessible at the present time."

While drafting, DeLillo types each paragraph on a separate page. When he finishes a paragraph, "even a three-line paragraph," he automatically starts the next one on a fresh page. When he first tried this technique, he said, "[it] enabled me to see a given set of sentences more clearly. It made rewriting easier and more effective. The white space on the page helped me concentrate more deeply on what I'd written."

Uncrowded pages help DeLillo concentrate on sentences. "The words . . . have a sculptural quality. They form odd correspondences. They match up not just through meaning but through sound and look. The rhythm of a sentence will accommodate a certain number of syllables. One syllable too many, I look for another word. There's always another word that means nearly the same thing, and if it doesn't then I'll consider altering the meaning of a sentence to keep the rhythm, the syllable beat. I'm completely willing to let language press meaning upon me. Watching the way in which words match up, keeping the balance in a sentence—these are sensuous pleasures. I might want *very* and *only* in the same sentence, spaced in a particular way, exactly so far apart. I might want *rapture* matched with *danger*—I like to match word endings. I type rather than write longhand because I like the way words and letters look . . .—finished, printed, beautifully formed."

For Discussion

1. Explain DeLillo's definition of *writing* in your own words.
2. Why does DeLillo find satisfaction in his "instinct to discard" parts of his writing that he likes?
3. What does DeLillo mean when he says that writing is filled with "sensuous pleasures"?

ADDITIONAL WRITING TOPICS

Cause and Effect

1. In a short essay, explain *either* the causes *or* the effects of a situation that concerns you. Narrow your topic enough to treat it in some detail, and provide more than a mere list of causes or effects. If seeking causes, you will have to decide carefully how far back to go in your search for remote causes. If stating effects, fill your essay with examples. Here are some topics to consider:

Labor strikes in professional sports

Children searching for pornography on the Internet

State laws mandating the use of seat belts in cars (or the wearing of helmets on motorcycles)

Friction between two roommates, or two friends

The pressure on students to get good grades

Some quirk in your personality, or a friend's

The increasing need for more than one breadwinner per family

The temptation to do something dishonest to get ahead

The popularity of a particular television program, comic strip, rock group, or pop singer

The steady increase in college costs

The scarcity of people in training for employment as skilled workers: plumbers, tool and die makers, electricians, masons, carpenters, to name a few

A decision to enter the ministry or a religious order

The fact that cigarette advertising is banned from television

The absence of a military draft

The fact that more couples are choosing to have only one child, or none

The growing popularity of private elementary and high schools

The fact that most Americans can communicate in no language other than English

Being "born again"

The fact that women increasingly get jobs formerly regarded as being for men only

The pressure on young people to conform to the standards of their peers

The emphasis on competitive sports in high school and college

2. In *Blue Highways* (1982), an account of his rambles around America, William Least Heat Moon explains why Americans, and not the British, settled the vast tract of northern land that lies between the Mississippi and the Rockies. He traces what he believes to be the major cause in this paragraph:

> Were it not for a web-footed rodent and a haberdashery fad in eighteenth-century Europe, Minnesota might be a Canadian province today. The beaver, almost as much as the horse, helped shape the course of early American history. Some *Mayflower* colonists paid their passage with beaver pelts; and a good fur could bring an Indian three steel knives or a five-foot stack could bring a musket. But even more influential were

474

the trappers and fur traders penetrating the great Northern wilderness between the Mississippi River and the Rocky Mountains, since it was their presence that helped hold the Near West against British expansion from the north; and it was their explorations that opened the heart of the nation to white settlement. These men, by making pelts the currency of the wilds, laid the base for a new economy that quickly overwhelmed the old. And all because European men of mode simply had to wear a beaver hat.

In a Least Heat Moon–like paragraph of your own, explain how a small cause produced a large effect. You might generate ideas by browsing in a history book—where you might find, for instance, that a cow belonging to Mrs. Patrick O'Leary is believed to have started the Great Chicago Fire of 1871 by kicking over a lighted lantern—or in a collection of *Ripley's Believe It or Not*. If some small event in your life has had large consequences, you might care to write instead from personal experience.

NEED IS A VERY SUBJECTIVE WORD.

THE NEW H2. **HUMMER** LIKE NOTHING ELSE.

HUMMER.COM

12

DEFINITION

Tracing a Boundary

◀ **Definition in an advertisement**

*This ad for the HUMMER H2 doesn't exactly define need.
Instead, it invites viewers to work the HUMMER into their
own personal definitions of need. The ad appeared in National
Geographic's outdoors magazine* Adventure, *where its colors
were predominantly blue (the background) and yellow (the
HUMMER). What needs in that magazine's readers might the
ad appeal to? How does the HUMMER's cousin, the military
HUMVEE, figure in the ad and in the HUMMER's appeal? Why
is the ad image so stark, and what does each of its few elements
contribute to the appeal? What does the text contribute? At the
same time, what needs in viewers does the ad ignore or even
reject?*

THE METHOD

As a rule, when we hear the word DEFINITION, we immediately think of a dictionary. In that helpful storehouse—a writer's best friend—we find the literal and specific meaning (or meanings) of a word. The dictionary supplies this information concisely: in a sentence, in a phrase, or even in a *synonym*—a single word that means the same thing ("**narrative** [năr-e-tĭv] *n.* **1:** story . . .").

Stating such a definition is often a good way to begin an essay when basic terms may be in doubt. A short definition can clarify your subject to your reader, and perhaps help you to limit what you have to say. If, for instance, you are going to discuss a demolition derby, explaining such a spectacle to readers who may never have seen one, you might offer at the outset a short definition of *demolition derby*, your subject and your key term.

In constructing a short definition, the usual procedure is to state the general class to which the subject belongs and then add any particular features that distinguish it. You could say: "A demolition derby is a contest"—that is its general class—"in which drivers ram old cars into one another until only one car is left running." Short definitions may be useful at *any* moment in an essay, whenever you introduce a technical term that readers may not know.

When a term is really central to your essay and likely to be misunderstood, a *stipulative definition* may be helpful. This fuller explanation stipulates, or specifies, the particular way you are using a term. The paragraph on page 484, defining *TV addiction*, could be a stipulative definition in an essay on the causes and cures of the addiction.

In this chapter, we are mainly concerned with *extended definition*, a kind of expository writing that relies on a variety of other methods. Suppose you wanted to write an essay to make clear what *poetry* means. You would specify its elements—rhythm, IMAGES, and so on—by using DIVISION or ANALYSIS. You'd probably provide EXAMPLES of each element. You might COMPARE AND CONTRAST poetry with prose. You might discuss the EFFECT of poetry on the reader. (Emily Dickinson, a poet herself, once stated the effect that reading a poem had on her: "I feel as if the top of my head were taken off.") In fact, extended definition, unlike other methods of writing discussed in this book, is perhaps less a method in itself than the application of a variety of methods to clarify a purpose. Like DESCRIPTION, extended definition tries to *show* a reader its subject. It does so by establishing boundaries, for its writer tries to differentiate a subject from anything that might be confused with it.

When Gloria Naylor, in her essay in this chapter, seeks to define the freighted word *nigger*, she recalls her experiences of the word as an African

American, recounting exactly what she heard in varying situations. Extended definition examines the nature of the subject, carefully summing up its chief characteristics and drawing boundaries around it, striving to answer the question "What makes this what it is, not something else?"

An extended definition can define a word (like *nigger*), a thing (a laser beam), a concept (TV addiction), or a general phenomenon (the popularity of the demolition derby). Unlike a sentence definition, or any you would find in a standard dictionary, an extended definition takes room: at least a paragraph, often an entire essay. In having many methods of writing at your disposal, you have ample freedom and wide latitude.

Outside an English course, how is this method of writing used? In a newspaper feature, a sportswriter defines what makes a *great team* great. In a journal article, a physician defines the nature of a previously unknown syndrome or disease. In a written opinion, a judge defines not only a word but a concept, *obscenity*. In a book review, a critic defines a newly prevalent kind of poem. In a letter to a younger brother or sister contemplating college, a student might define a *gut course* and how to recognize one.

Unlike a definition in a dictionary that sets forth the literal meaning of a word in an unimpassioned manner, some definitions imply biases. In defining *patron* to the earl of Chesterfield, who had tried to befriend him after ignoring his petitions for aid during his years of grinding poverty, Samuel Johnson wrote scornfully: "Is not a Patron, my Lord, one who looks with unconcern on a man struggling for life in the water, and, when he has reached the ground, encumbers him with help?" IRONY, a FIGURE OF SPEECH (metaphor), and a short definition have rarely been wielded with such crushing power. (*Encumbers*, by the way, is a wonderfully physical word in its context: It means "to burden with dead weight.")

THE PROCESS

Discovery of Meanings

The purpose of almost any extended definition is to explore a topic in its full complexity, to explain its meaning or sometimes to argue for (or against) a particular meaning. To discover this complexity, you may find it useful to ask yourself a series of questions. These questions may be applied both to individual subjects, such as a basketball superstar or a comet, and to collective subjects: institutions (like the American family, a typical savings bank, a university, the Church of Jesus Christ of Latter-Day Saints) and organizations (IBM, the Mafia, a rock band, a Little League baseball team). To illustrate how

Definition

the questions might work, at least in one instance, let's say you plan to write a paper defining *sexism*.[1]

1. *Is this subject unique, or are there others of its kind? If it resembles others, in what ways? How is it different?* As you can see, these last two questions invite you to COMPARE AND CONTRAST. Applied to the concept of sexism, these questions might prompt you to compare sexism with one or two other -isms, such as racism or ageism. Or the questions might remind you that sexists can be both women and men, leading you to note the differences.

2. *In what different forms does it occur, while keeping its own identity?* Specific examples might occur to you: your Uncle George, who won't hire any "damned females" in his auto repair shop, or a girlfriend who is nastily suspicious of all men. Each form—Uncle George and the girlfriend—might rate a description.

3. *When and where do we find it? Under what circumstances and in what situations?* Well, where have you been lately? At any parties where sexism reared its ugly head? In any classroom discussions? Consider other areas of your experience: Did you encounter any sexists while holding a part-time summer job?

4. *What is it at the present moment?* Perhaps you might make the point that sexism was once considered an exclusively male preserve but is now an attribute of women as well. Or you could observe that many men have gone underground with their sexism, refraining from expressing it blatantly while still harboring negative attitudes about women. In either case, you might care to draw examples from life.

5. *What does it do? What are its functions and activities?* Sexists stereotype and sometimes act to exclude or oppress people of the opposite sex. These questions might also invite you to reply with a PROCESS ANALYSIS: You might show, for instance, how a sexist man you know, a personnel director who determines pay scales, systematically eliminates women from better-paying jobs.

6. *How is it put together? What parts make it up? What holds these parts together?* You could apply analysis to the various beliefs and assumptions that, all together, make up sexism. This question might work well in writing about

---

[1] The six questions that follow are freely adapted from those first stated by Richard E. Young, Alton L. Becker, and Kenneth L. Pike, who have applied insights from psychology and linguistics to the writing process. Their procedure for generating ideas and discovering information is called *tagmemics*. To investigate subjects in greater depth, their own six questions may be used in nine possible combinations, as they explain in detail in *Rhetoric: Discovery and Change* (1970).

an organization: the personnel director's company, for instance, with its unfair hiring and promotion policies.

Not all these questions will fit every subject under the sun, and some may lead nowhere, but you will usually find them well worth asking. They can make you aware of points to notice, remind you of facts you already know. They can also suggest interesting points you need to find out more about.

Methods of Development

The preceding questions will give you a good start on using whatever method or methods of writing can best answer the overall question "What is the nature of this subject?" You will probably find yourself making use of much that you have learned earlier from this book. A short definition like the one for *demolition derby* on page 478 may be a good start for your essay, especially if you think your readers need a quick grounding in the subject or in your view of it. (But feel no duty to place a dictionaryish definition in the INTRODUCTION of every essay you write: The device is overused.) In explaining a demolition derby, if your readers already have at least a vague idea of the meaning of the term and need no short, formal definition of it, you could open your extended definition by NARRATING the events at a typical demolition derby, starting with a description of the lineup of old beat-up vehicles:

> One hundred worthless cars—everything from a 1960 Cadillac to a Dodge Dart to a recently wrecked Thunderbird, their glass removed, their radiators leaking—assemble on a racetrack or an open field. Their drivers, wearing crash helmets, buckle themselves into their seats, some pulling at beer cans to soften the blows to come.

You could proceed by example, listing demolition derbies you have known ("The great destruction of 184 vehicles took place at the Orleans County Fair in Barton, Vermont, in the summer of '04 . . ."). If you have enough examples, you could CLASSIFY them; or perhaps you could ANALYZE a demolition derby, dividing it into its components of cars, drivers, judges, first-aid squad, and spectators, and discussing each. You could compare and contrast a demolition derby with that amusement park ride known as Bumper Cars or Dodge-'ems, in which small cars with rubber bumpers bash one another head-on, but (unlike cars in the derby) harmlessly. A process analysis of a demolition derby might help your readers understand the nature of the spectacle: how in round after round, cars are eliminated until one remains. You could ask "What causes the owners of old cars to want to smash them?" or "What causes people to watch the destruction?" or "What are the consequences?" To answer such questions in an essay, you would apply the method of CAUSE AND EFFECT.

Definition

Thesis

Opening up your subject with questions and developing it with various methods are good ways to see what your subject has to offer, but they can also leave you with a welter of ideas and a blurred focus. As in DESCRIPTION, when all your details build to a DOMINANT IMPRESSION, so in definition you want to center all your ideas and evidence about the subject on a single controlling idea, a THESIS. It's not essential to state this idea in a THESIS STATEMENT, although doing so can serve your readers. It is essential that the idea govern.

Here, from the essays in this chapter, are two thesis statements. Notice how each makes an assertion about the subject, and how we can detect the author's bias toward the subject.

> The people in my grandmother's living room took a word [*nigger*] that whites used to signify worthlessness or degradation and rendered it impotent. . . . Meeting the word head-on, they proved it had absolutely nothing to do with the way they were determined to live their lives.
> —Gloria Naylor, "The Meanings of a Word"

> The word *chink* may have been created to harm, ridicule, and humiliate, but for us [Chinese Americans] it may have done the exact opposite.
> —Christine Leong, "Being a Chink"

Evidence

Writing an extended definition, you are like a mapmaker charting a territory, taking in some of what lies within the boundaries and ignoring what lies outside. The boundaries, of course, may be wide; and for this reason, the writing of an extended definition sometimes tempts a writer to sweep across a continent airily and to soar off into abstract clouds. Like any other method of expository writing, though, definition will work only for the writer who remembers the world of the senses and supports every generalization with concrete evidence.

There may be no finer illustration of the perils of definition than the scene, in Charles Dickens's novel *Hard Times*, of the grim schoolroom of a teacher named Gradgrind, who insists on facts but who completely ignores living realities. When a girl whose father is a horse trainer is unable to define a horse, Gradgrind blames her for not knowing what a horse is; and he praises the definition of a horse supplied by a pet pupil: "Quadruped. Graminivorous. Forty teeth, namely twenty-four grinders, four eye-teeth, and twelve incisive. Sheds coat in the spring; in marshy countries, sheds hoofs, too. Hoofs hard, but requiring to be shod with iron. Age known by marks in mouth." To anyone who didn't already know what a horse is, this list of facts would prove of little help. In writing an extended definition, never lose sight of the reality you are attempting to bound, even if its frontiers are as inclusive as those of *psychological burnout* or *human rights*. Give your reader examples, narrate an illustrative story, bring in specific description—in whatever method you use, keep coming down to earth. Without your eyes on the world, you will define no reality. You might define *animal husbandry* till the cows come home and never make clear what it means.

FOCUS ON PARAGRAPH AND ESSAY UNITY

When drafting a definition, you may find yourself being pulled away from your subject by the descriptions, examples, comparisons, and other methods you use to specify meaning. Let yourself explore byways of your subject—doing so will help you discover what you think. But in revising you'll need to direct all paragraphs to your thesis and, within paragraphs, to direct all sentences to the paragraph topic, generally expressed in a TOPIC SENTENCE. In other words, you'll need to ensure the UNITY of your essay and its paragraphs.

Gloria Naylor's "The Meanings of a Word" (p. 486) opens with several paragraphs of background to the definition of the word *nigger* as it was used in Naylor's extended African American family. When Naylor focuses on defining, she proceeds methodically. As shown in the following outline, the paragraphs begin with topic sentences that state parts of the definition, which Naylor then illustrates with examples. (Some parts of the definition require more than a single paragraph, but Naylor keeps the groups of paragraphs focused on a single idea.)

PARAGRAPH 6   In the singular, the word was always applied to . . .

PARAGRAPH 9   When used with a possessive adjective by a woman—"my nigger"—it became a term of . . .

PARAGRAPH 10   In the plural, it became a description of . . .

PARAGRAPH 11   A woman could never be a "nigger" in the singular . . .

PARAGRAPH 13   But if the word was used in a third-person reference or shortened . . . , it always involved . . .

CHECKLIST FOR REVISING A DEFINITION

✔ **MEANINGS.** Have you explored your subject fully, turning up both its obvious and its not-so-obvious meanings?

✔ **METHODS OF DEVELOPMENT.** Have you used an appropriate range of other methods to develop your subject?

✔ **THESIS.** Have you focused your definition and kept within that focus, drawing clear boundaries around your subject?

✔ **EVIDENCE.** Is your definition specific? Do examples, anecdotes, and concrete details both pin the subject down and make it vivid for readers?

✔ **UNITY.** Do all paragraphs focus on your thesis, and do individual paragraphs or groups of paragraphs focus on parts of your definition?

Definition

DEFINITION IN PARAGRAPHS

Writing About Television

The paragraph below SUMMARIZES the definition of *TV addiction* given in Marie Winn's essay on pages 508–09. The paragraph was written for *The Bedford Reader* as an example of definition, but its opening question suggests a broader use than just illustration: In a full essay on the causes and cures of the addiction, the paragraph could serve as a stipulative definition of the essay's key term.

Who is addicted to TV? According to Marie Winn, author of *The Plug-in Drug: Television, Children, and Family Life,* TV addicts are similar to drug or alcohol addicts: They seek a more pleasurable experience than they can get from normal life; they depend on the source of this pleasure; and their lives are damaged by their dependency. TV addicts, says Winn, use TV to screen out the real world of feelings, worries, demands. They watch compulsively—four, five, even six hours on a work day. And they reject (usually passively, sometimes actively) interaction with family or friends, diverting or productive work at hobbies or chores, and chances for change and growth.

Definition of TV addiction

Comparison with drug or alcohol addiction

Analysis is of TV addicts' characteristics

Writing in an Academic Discipline

This paragraph from a biology textbook defines a term, *homology,* that is useful in explaining the evolution of different species from a common ancestor (the topic at this point in the textbook). The paragraph provides a brief definition, a more extensive one, and finally examples of the concept.

When the character traits found in any two species owe their resemblance to a common ancestry, taxonomists say the states are *homologous,* or are *homologues* of each other. *Homology* is defined as correspondence between two structures due to inheritance from a common ancestor. Homologous structures can be identical in appearance and can even be based on identical genes. However, such structures can diverge until they become very different in both appearance and function. Nevertheless, homologous structures usually retain certain basic features that betray a common ancestry. Consider the forelimbs of vertebrates. It is easy to make a detailed, bone-by-bone, muscle-by-muscle comparison of the forearm of a person and a monkey and to conclude that the forearms, as well as the various parts of the forearm, are homologous. The forelimb of a dog, however, shows marked differences from those of primates in both appearance and function. The forelimb is used for locomotion

Definition of homology and related words

Short definition

Refined definition

Examples:

Similar appearance, function, and structure

Dissimilar appearance and function, but similar structure

by dogs but for grasping and manipulation by people and monkeys. Even so, all of the bones can still be matched. The wing of a bird and the flipper of a seal are even more different from each other or from the human forearm, yet they too are constructed around bones that can be matched on a nearly perfect one-to-one basis.
—William K. Purves and Gordon H. Orians,
Life: The Science of Biology

DEFINITION IN PRACTICE

Susan Iessi was a freshman at the State University of New York at New Paltz when she volunteered to become a member of Hall Government, a dormitory association dedicated to student support. Discovering that many dorm residents, especially other freshmen, were unclear about the work of Hall Government, Iessi wrote the following statement.

Iessi's main goal of specifying Hall Government's purposes and responsibilities drew her into defining the mission of the association. After she drafted the statement, she showed it to other members. When one reader suggested that she explain the connections between Hall Government and other campus organizations, Iessi agreed: The change would clarify the boundaries of Hall Government. Iessi's final draft appears below.

The Mission of Hall Government

Hall Government consists of students who volunteer to provide the residents of their dormitory with social and emotional support. Hall Government creates opportunities for residents to meet other residents and build a network of friends through structured discussions, social events, and educational programs. It also mediates in situations such as conflicts between students and teachers or between roommates. The members of Hall Government believe that their support will encourage residents to provide support for each other as well, building a community in which students may learn and thrive during their college years.

Each dormitory's Hall Government functions independently. The groups have no formal relationship with the campus-wide elected student government but are sponsored and funded by the Residence Hall Student Association.

Definition

GLORIA NAYLOR

GLORIA NAYLOR describes herself as "just a girl from Queens who can turn a sentence," but she is well known for bringing African American women vividly within the fold of American literature. She was born in 1950 in New York City and served for some years as a missionary for the Jehovah's Witnesses, working "for better world conditions." While in college, she made her living as a telephone operator. She graduated from Brooklyn College in 1981 and received an MA in African American literature from Yale University in 1983. While teaching at several universities and publishing numerous stories and essays, Naylor has written five interconnected novels: *The Women of Brewster Place* (1982), *Linden Hills* (1985), *Mama Day* (1988), *Bailey's Cafe* (1992), and *The Men of Brewster Place* (1998). *The Women of Brewster Place* won the American Book Award for best first novel, and Naylor has also received fellowships from the National Endowment for the Arts and the Guggenheim Foundation. *Conversations with Gloria Naylor* came out in 2004.

The Meanings of a Word

When she was in third grade, Naylor was stung by a word that seemed new. Only later did she realize that she'd been hearing the word all her life, but in an entirely different context. In "The Meanings of a Word," she uses definition to explore the varying meanings that context creates. The essay first appeared in the *New York Times* in 1986.

The essay following this one, Christine Leong's "Being a Chink," responds directly to Naylor and extends her point about context and meaning.

Language is the subject. It is the written form with which I've managed to 1 keep the wolf away from the door and, in diaries, to keep my sanity. In spite of this, I consider the written word inferior to the spoken, and much of the frustration experienced by novelists is the awareness that whatever we manage to capture in even the most transcendent passages falls far short of the richness of life. Dialogue achieves its power in the dynamics of a fleeting moment of sight, sound, smell, and touch.

I'm not going to enter the debate here about whether it is language that 2 shapes reality or vice versa. That battle is doomed to be waged whenever we seek intermittent reprieve from the chicken and egg dispute. I will simply take the position that the spoken word, like the written word, amounts to a nonsensical arrangement of sounds or letters without a consensus that assigns "meaning." And building from the meanings of what we hear, we order reality. Words themselves are innocuous; it is the consensus that gives them true power.

I remember the first time I heard the word *nigger*. In my third-grade class, our math tests were being passed down the rows, and as I handed the papers to a little boy in back of me, I remarked that once again he had received a much lower mark than I did. He snatched his test from me and spit out that word. Had he called me a nymphomaniac or a necrophiliac, I couldn't have been more puzzled. I didn't know what a nigger was, but I knew that whatever it meant, it was something he shouldn't have called me. This was verified when I raised my hand, and in a loud voice repeated what he had said and watched the teacher scold him for using a "bad" word. I was later to go home and ask the inevitable question that every black parent must face—"Mommy, what does *nigger* mean?" 3

And what exactly did it mean? Thinking back, I realize that this could not have been the first time the word was used in my presence. I was part of a large extended family that had migrated from the rural South after World War II and formed a close-knit network that gravitated around my maternal grandparents. Their ground-floor apartment in one of the buildings they owned in Harlem was a weekend mecca for my immediate family, along with countless aunts, uncles, and cousins who brought along assorted friends. It was a bustling and open house with assorted neighbors and tenants popping in and out to exchange bits of gossip, pick up an old quarrel, or referee the ongoing checkers game in which my grandmother cheated shamelessly. They were all there to let down their hair and put up their feet after a week of labor in the factories, laundries, and shipyards of New York. 4

Amid the clamor, which could reach deafening proportions—two or three conversations going on simultaneously, punctuated by the sound of a baby's crying somewhere in the back rooms or out on the street—there was still a rigid set of rules about what was said and how. Older children were sent out of the living room when it was time to get into the juicy details about "you-know-who" up on the third floor who had gone and gotten herself "p-r-e-g-n-a-n-t!" But my parents, knowing that I could spell well beyond my years, always demanded that I follow the others out to play. Beyond sexual misconduct and death, everything else was considered harmless for our young ears. And so among the anecdotes of the triumphs and disappointments in the various workings of their lives, the word *nigger* was used in my presence, but it was set within contexts and inflections that caused it to register in my mind as something else. 5

In the singular, the word was always applied to a man who had distin- 6
guished himself in some situation that brought their approval for his strength,
intelligence, or drive:

"Did Johnny *really* do that?" 7

"I'm telling you, that nigger pulled in $6,000 of overtime last year. Said he 8
got enough for a down payment on a house."

When used with a possessive adjective by a woman—"my nigger"—it 9
became a term of endearment for her husband or boyfriend. But it could be
more than just a term applied to a man. In their mouths it became the pure
essence of manhood—a disembodied force that channeled their past history
of struggle and present survival against the odds into a victorious statement of
being: "Yeah, that old foreman found out quick enough—you don't mess with
a nigger."

In the plural, it became a description of some group within the commu- 10
nity that had overstepped the bounds of decency as my family defined it. Parents who neglected their children, a drunken couple who fought in public,
people who simply refused to look for work, those with excessively dirty
mouths or unkempt households were all "trifling niggers." This particular circle
could forgive hard times, unemployment, the occasional bout of depression—
they had gone through all of that themselves—but the unforgivable sin was a
lack of self-respect.

A woman could never be a "nigger" in the singular, with its connotation 11
of confirming worth. The noun *girl* was its closest equivalent in that sense, but
only when used in direct address and regardless of the gender doing the
addressing. *Girl* was a token of respect for a woman. The one-syllable word was
drawn out to sound like three in recognition of the extra ounce of wit, nerve,
or daring that the woman had shown in the situation under discussion.

"G-i-r-l, stop. You mean you said that to his face?" 12

But if the word was used in a third-person reference or shortened so that 13
it almost snapped out of the mouth, it always involved some element of communal disapproval. And age became an important factor in these exchanges.
It was only between individuals of the same generation, or from any older person to a younger (but never the other way around), that *girl* would be considered a compliment.

I don't agree with the argument that use of the word *nigger* at this social 14
stratum of the black community was an internalization of racism. The dynamics were the exact opposite: The people in my grandmother's living room took
a word that whites used to signify worthlessness or degradation and rendered
it impotent. Gathering there together, they transformed *nigger* to signify the
varied and complex human beings they knew themselves to be. If the word

was to disappear totally from the mouths of even the most liberal of white society, no one in that room was naive enough to believe it would disappear from white minds. Meeting the word head-on, they proved it had absolutely nothing to do with the way they were determined to live their lives.

So there must have been dozens of times that *nigger* was spoken in front of   15
me before I reached the third grade. But I didn't "hear" it until it was said by a small pair of lips that had already learned it could be a way to humiliate me. That was the word I went home and asked my mother about. And since she knew that I had to grow up in America, she took me in her lap and explained.

*For a reading quiz, sources on Gloria Naylor, and annotated links to further read-ings on the language of stereotypes, visit **bedfordstmartins.com/thebedfordreader.***

Journal Writing

As Naylor shows, the language of stereotypes can be powerful and painful to en-counter. In your journal, recall when you have experienced or witnessed this kind of labeling. What were your reactions? Keep in mind that race is but one object of stereotypes. Consider income, education, body type or other physical attributes, sex-ual preference, activities, or neighborhood, for just a few other characteristics. (To take your journal writing further, see "From Journal to Essay" on the next page.)

Questions on Meaning

1. Why does Naylor think that written language is inferior to spoken language (par. 1)?
2. In paragraph 15, Naylor says that although the word *nigger* had been used in her presence many times, she didn't really "hear" the word until a mean little boy said it. How do you explain this contradiction?
3. Naylor says that "[t]he people in my grandmother's living room . . . transformed *nigger*" (par. 14). How?
4. What is Naylor's primary PURPOSE in this essay?

Questions on Writing Strategy

1. In her first two paragraphs, Naylor discusses language in the ABSTRACT. How are these paragraphs connected to her stories about the word *nigger*? Why do you think she begins the essay this way? Is this INTRODUCTION effective or not? Why?

2. Go through Naylor's essay and note which paragraphs discuss the racist uses of *nigger* and which discuss the nonracist uses. How do Naylor's organization and the space she devotes to each use help Naylor make her point? How does Naylor integrate the two definitions to achieve UNITY?

3. Look back at the last two sentences of Naylor's essay. What is the EFFECT of ending on this idea?

4. **OTHER METHODS.** After each definition of the words *nigger* and *girl*, Naylor gives an EXAMPLE in the form of a quotation. These examples are in paragraphs 7–10 (for instance, "Yeah, that old foreman found out quick enough — you don't mess with a nigger" [9]) and paragraph 12 ("G-i-r-l, stop. You mean you said that to his face?"). What do such examples add to Naylor's definitions?

Questions on Language

1. What is "the chicken and egg dispute" (par. 2)? What does this dispute say about the relationship between language and reality?

2. What do the words *nymphomaniac* and *necrophiliac* CONNOTE in paragraph 3?

3. If you don't know the meanings of the following words, look them up in a dictionary: transcendent, dynamics (par. 1); intermittent, reprieve, consensus, innocuous (2); verified (3); gravitated, mecca (4); clamor, inflections (5); endearment, disembodied (9); unkempt, trifling (10); communal (13); stratum, internalization, degradation, rendered, impotent, naive (14).

Suggestions for Writing

1. **FROM JOURNAL TO ESSAY.** Using as examples the experiences you wrote about in your journal entry, write an essay modeled on Naylor's in which you define "the meanings of a word" (or words). Do you find, too, that meaning varies with context? If so, make the variations clear.

2. Can you think of other labels that may be defined in more than one way? (These might include *smart, childish, old-fashioned, artistic, proud, attractive, heroic*, and so on.) Choose one such label, and write one paragraph for each possible definition. Be sure to explain the contexts for each definition and to give enough examples so that the meanings are clear.

3. Research the history of whites' labels for African Americans, starting when slaves were first brought to the United States. Write an essay in which you discuss the evolution of the labels.

4. **CRITICAL WRITING.** Naylor claims that words are "nonsensical . . . without a consensus that assigns 'meaning'" (par. 2). If so, how do we understand the meaning of a word like *nigger*, when Naylor has shown us that there is more than one consensus about its meaning? Does Naylor contradict herself? Write an essay that either supports or refutes Naylor's claim about meaning and context. You will need to consider how she and you define *consensus*.

5. **CONNECTIONS.** The next essay, Christine Leong's "Being a Chink," identifies a moment when Leong was first struck by the negative power of racist language. Write an essay that COMPARES AND CONTRASTS Naylor's and Leong's reactions to a derogatory label. How did the context help shape their reactions?

Gloria Naylor on Writing

Studying literature in college was somewhat disappointing for Gloria Naylor. "What I wanted to see," she told William Goldstein of *Publishers Weekly*, "were reflections of me and my existence and experience." Then, reading African American literature in graduate school, she discovered that "blacks have been writing in this country since this country has been writing and have a literary heritage of their own. Unfortunately, they haven't had encouragement or recognition for their efforts. . . . What had happened was that when black people wrote, it wasn't quite [considered] serious work—it was race work or protest work."

For Naylor this discovery was a turning point. "I wanted to become a writer because I felt that my presence as a black woman and my perspective as a woman in general had been underrepresented." Her work tries to "articulate experiences that want articulating—for those readers who reflect the subject matter, black readers, and for those who don't, basically white middle-class readers."

For Discussion

1. What does Naylor mean when she says that she tries to "articulate experiences that want articulating"?
2. Naylor is motivated to write by a consciousness of herself as an African American and a woman. How do you see this motivation driving her essay "The Meanings of a Word"?

CHRISTINE LEONG

CHRISTINE LEONG was born in New York City in 1976 and attended Stuyvesant High School there, graduating in 1994. At the Stern School of Business at New York University, she majored in finance and information systems and interned at an investment firm. She graduated with a BS in 1998 and currently works in financial services. In her free time, Leong enjoys a good doughnut and cheering on the New York Yankees. "The one thing I couldn't live without," she says, "is music."

Being a Chink

Leong wrote this essay for her freshman composition class at NYU, and it was published in Mercer Street, 1995–96, a collection of NYU students' essays. As you'll see, Leong was inspired by Gloria Naylor's "The Meanings of a Word" (p. 486) to report her own experiences and to define a word that can be either hurtful or warm, depending on the speaker.

The power of language is something that people often underestimate. It is the one thing that allows people to communicate with each other, to be understood, to be heard. It gives us identity, personality, social status, and it also creates communities, defining both insiders and outsiders. Language has the ability to heal or to harm, to praise or belittle, to promote peace or even to glorify hate. But perhaps most important, language is the tool used to define us and differentiate us from the next person. Names and labels are what separate us from each other. Sometimes these things are innocuous, depending on the particular word and the context in which it is used. Often they serve to ridicule and humiliate.

I remember the first time I saw the word *chink*. I used to work over the summers at my father's Chinese restaurant, the Oriental, to earn a few extra dollars of spending money. It was a warm, sunny Friday morning, and I was busy performing my weekly task of cleaning out the storage area under the cash register at the front of the store. Armed with a large can of Pledge furniture polish and an old cloth, I started attacking the old oak shelves, sorting through junk mail that had accumulated over the last week, separating the bills and other important things that had to be set aside for later, before wiping each wooden panel clean. It was a pretty uneventful chore, that is, until I got to the bottom shelf, the last of three. I always hated cleaning this particular shelf because it required me to get down on my hands and knees behind the counter and reach all the way back into the compartment to dig out all the stuff that managed to get wedged against the wall.

After bending to scoop all the papers out of that third cubicle, I began to   3
sort through them haphazardly. A few old menus, a gum wrapper (I always wondered how little things like that got stuffed in there), some promotional flyers, two capless pens, a dusty scratch pad, and something that appeared to be a little white envelope. Nothing seemed unusual until I examined that last item more closely. It was an old MidLantic envelope from the bank across the street. I was just about to crumple it up and throw it into the trash can when I decided to check if there was any money left in it. Too lazy to deal with the actual "chore" of opening the envelope, I held it up to the light.

As the faint yellow glow from the antique light fixture above me shone   4
through the envelope, turning it transparent, my suspicion that it was empty was confirmed. However, what I found was more shocking than anything I could have imagined. There, outlined by the light, was the word *chink* written backwards. I quickly lowered my arm onto the cool, smooth surface of the counter and flipped the envelope onto its other side, refusing to believe what I had just read. On the back, in dark blue ink with a large circle drawn around it, was the word CHINK written in my father's handwriting.

Up until that moment, I hadn't known that my father knew such words,   5
and thinking again, perhaps he didn't know this one either. After all, it was a habit of his to write down English words he did not know when he heard them and look them up in the dictionary later that day, learning them and adding them to his vocabulary. My mind began spinning with all the possible reasons he had written this particular word down. I wondered if an angry patron who had come in earlier had called him that.

I was shocked at that possibility, but I was not surprised. Being one of only   6
two Asian families living and running a business in a small suburban town predominately inhabited by old Caucasian people was bound to breed some kind of discrimination, if not hatred. I know that my father might not have known exactly what the word *chink* meant, but he must have had a good idea, because he never came to ask me about it as he did with all the other slang words that couldn't be found in the dictionary. It's funny, though, I do not remember the first time I was called a *chink*. I only remember the pain and outrage I felt the first time I saw it in writing, perhaps the first time I discovered that someone had used that hateful word to degrade my father.

In her essay "The Meanings of a Word," Gloria Naylor examines the var-   7
ious meanings of the word *nigger*, definitions that have consensual meanings throughout society and others that vary according to how and when the word

is used. In this piece, Naylor uses personal examples to describe how "[t]he people in [her] grandmother's living room took a word that whites used to signify worthlessness or degradation and rendered it impotent," by transforming *nigger* into a word signifying "the varied and complex human beings that they knew themselves to be." Naylor goes on to add that although none of these people were foolish enough to believe that the word *nigger* would magically be erased from the minds of all humankind, they were convinced that their "head-on" approach of dealing with the label that society had put on them "proved [that] it had absolutely nothing to do with the way they were determined to live their lives."

It has been nearly eight years since that day I stumbled across the bank   8
envelope. Since then we have moved from that suburb in New Jersey to New York City, where the Asian population is much larger, and the word *chink*, although still heard, is either heard less frequently or in a rather "harmless" manner between myself and fellow Chinese (Asian) teenage friends. I do not remember how it happened exactly. I just know that we have been calling each other *chink* for quite a long while now. The word has never been used to belittle or degrade, but rather as a term of endearment, a loving insult between friends, almost but not quite exactly the way *nigger* is sometimes used among black people. It is a practice that we still engage in today, and although we know that there are times when the use of the word *chink* is very inappropriate, it is an accepted term within our circle.

Do not misunderstand us, we are all intelligent Asian youths, all graduat-   9
ing from New York City's top high school, all college students, and we know what the word *chink* truly means. We know, because over the years we have heard it countless times, from strangers on the streets and in stores, from fellow students and peers, and in some instances even from teachers, although it might not have been meant for us to hear.

So you see, even though we may use the term *chink* rather casually, it is   10
only used that way amongst ourselves because we know that when we say it to each other it is truly without malice or harmful intent. I do not think that any of us knows exactly why we do it, but perhaps it is our own way, like the characters in Naylor's piece, of dealing with a label that can never be removed. It is not determined by who we are on the inside, or what we are capable of accomplishing, but instead by what we look like—the shape of our eyes, the color of our skin, the texture of our hair, and our delicate features. Perhaps we intentionally misuse the word as a symbol of our overcoming the stereotypes that American society has imposed upon us, a way of showing that although others have tried to make us feel small, weak, and insignificant, we are the opposite. We are strong, we are determined, we are the voices of the future, and we refuse to let a simple word paralyze us, belittle us, or control us.

The word *chink* may have been created to harm, ridicule, and humiliate, 11 but for us it may have done the exact opposite. In some ways it has helped us find a certain comfort in each other, each of us knowing what the other has gone through, a common thread of racism binding us all together, a strange union born from the word *chink* that was used against us, and a shared goal of perseverance.

For a reading quiz and annotated links to further readings on the language of stereotypes, visit **bedfordstmartins.com/thebedfordreader**.

Journal Writing

Although children often assume they will be protected by their parents, Leong presents a situation in which she felt the need to protect her father. Can you identify with Leong's feelings? Have you ever felt particularly angry or defensive on behalf of a parent? In your journal, explore why and what happened as a result. (To take your journal writing further, see "From Journal to Essay" on the next page.)

Questions on Meaning

1. In paragraph 9 Leong says that she and her friends "know what the word *chink* truly means." Where in her essay does she explain this "true" meaning?
2. What has the word *chink* come to mean when Leong and her friends use it? Where in the essay does Leong explain this?
3. One might argue that the THESIS of Leong's essay is that language is not absolute. Is her PURPOSE, then, to propose a new DEFINITION for a word, to teach the reader something about how labels work, or to explain how adapting a racist term can be a form of gaining power? How do you know?

Questions on Writing Strategy

1. Look carefully at Gloria Naylor's essay "The Meanings of a Word" (p. 486). What structural similarities do you notice between it and Leong's? Why do you think Leong adapts these features of Naylor's essay?
2. In paragraph 3 Leong details all the forgotten items she finds under the counter. What is the EFFECT of ending with the "old MidLantic envelope from the bank across the street"?
3. What is the main purpose of the extended example from Naylor's essay in paragraph 7?

4. Why is Leong so careful to explain that she and her friends are all intelligent and educated (par. 9)?

5. **OTHER METHODS.** Leong suggests CAUSE AND EFFECT when she expresses shock and disbelief at seeing the word *chink* in writing (par. 4). Why does Leong react so strongly to the writing on the envelope?

Questions on Language

1. In paragraph 10 Leong explains that she and her friends are "dealing with a label that can never be removed." What other words does she use in this paragraph to suggest the potential helplessness of being permanently labeled?

2. What do the CONNOTATIONS of "term of endearment" (par. 8) indicate about the way Leong and her friends have redefined *chink*?

3. Make sure you know the meanings of the following words: status, belittle, innocuous (par. 1); cubicle, haphazardly (3); Caucasian, degrade (6); consensual (7); malice (10); perseverance (11).

Suggestions for Writing

1. **FROM JOURNAL TO ESSAY.** Write an essay that explores why and how children might feel compelled to act like parents toward their own parents. Is this a shift that comes with age? with specific circumstances? out of the blue? Make some GENERALIZATIONS about this process, using as EVIDENCE the personal recollections from your journal entry.

2. As Leong explains in her INTRODUCTION, not all labels are intended to be hurtful. Often they are shorthand ways for our families and friends to identify us, perhaps reflecting something about our appearance ("Red," "Slim") or our interests ("Sport," "Chef"). What do your family or friends call you? Write several paragraphs giving a careful definition of this label. Where did it come from? Why is it appropriate (or not)?

3. Research the history of Chinese Americans. When and why did the initial wave of immigration occur? What forces have led to other patterns of immigration over the years? Have Chinese Americans faced different kinds of discrimination than other immigrants have? In an essay, answer these or other questions that occur to you.

4. **CRITICAL WRITING.** In her opening paragraph Leong says that "language is the tool used to define us." But she goes on to explain how she and her friends *refuse* to be defined by racist language. Does this apparent contradiction weaken her essay? Why, or why not? (To answer this question, consider the purpose of Leong's essay; see "Meaning" question 3.)

5. **CONNECTIONS.** Both Leong and Gloria Naylor, in "The Meanings of a Word" (p. 486), show that racist language can be taken over by those against whom it is directed. They also show that for groups or communities to redefine, and thus to own, these racist slurs can be empowering. Do you find their ARGUMENTS convincing, or do these redefinitions reveal what Naylor denies — namely, "an internalization of racism" (par. 14)? In an essay, explain your opinion on this issue, using as evidence passages from Naylor's and Leong's essays as well as insights and EXAMPLES from your own observations and experience.

Christine Leong on Writing

For *The Bedford Reader*, Christine Leong commented on the difficulties of writing and the rewards that can ensue.

Writing is something that comes easily for many people, but unfortunately I am not one of them. For me the writing process is one of the hardest and quite possibly is *the* most nerve-wracking thing that I have ever experienced. I can't even begin to count all the hours I have spent throughout the course of my life staring at a blank computer screen, trying desperately to come up with the right combination of words to express my thoughts and feelings, and although after many hours of frustration I eventually end up with something, I am never happy with it because I am undoubtedly my own worst critic. Perhaps my mentality of "it's not good enough yet" stems from my belief that writing can never really be completed; to me it has no beginning and no end but is rather a small representation of who I am at a given moment in time, and I believe that the more things I experience in life, the more I am able to contribute to my writing. Thus, whatever I write always has the potential of being better; there's always room for improvement via more revisions, greater insight, and about a hundred more drafts.

I used to believe that writing always had to make sense, but since then I have learned that there are many things in this life that do not adhere to this "rule." I now realize that writing doesn't necessarily have to be grammatically correct or even sensible, and the only thing that really matters is that whatever is written is truly inspired. Passion comes through very clearly in a writer's words, and the more emotion that goes into a piece, the more impact it will ultimately have on the reader. In recent years I have learned that there are no real writing guidelines, and that writing is much like any other art form: It can be abstract or it can follow more traditional "themes." However, in order for a piece of writing to be effective, in the sense that it can differentiate itself from any other writing sample and hopefully have some significance to the reader, I believe that it has to come from within.

The majority of what I write about, and that which I feel is worth reading, is inspired by actual experiences that I have had. For example, "Being a Chink" began as an assignment in a freshman writing workshop class in college. When first presented with the task of writing it, I was at a complete loss for words and had absolutely no clue where to start. However, after reading Gloria Naylor's "The Meanings of a Word," I was reminded of one of the most traumatic and memorable events in my life. The piece triggered a very strong memory, and before long I found myself writing down anything that came into my head, letting my thoughts and emotions flow freely in the form of words without thinking about whether or not they made any kind of sense. Many hours later I discovered that I had written the basic structure of what would eventually be my final product. I must honestly say that I can't really recall the actual process of writing "Being a Chink"; it was just an essay that seemed to take on a life and form of its own. Perhaps that, along with its universal theme, is what makes it such a strong piece. It not only is a recollection from my adolescence but is something that defines the very essence of the person that I have become since then.

In retrospect, I now realize that writing "Being a Chink" was not only about completing an essay and fulfilling a writing requirement; it was also about the acknowledgment of my own growth as a person. In many ways, without my initially being aware of it, the piece has helped me come to terms with one of the most controversial issues that I have ever been faced with.

For Discussion

1. Does Leong's characterization of writing as "nerve-wracking" ring bells with you? How do you overcome writer's block?
2. What do you think about Leong's statement that "writing doesn't necessarily have to be grammatically correct or even sensible, and the only thing that really matters is that whatever is written is truly inspired"? In your experience with writing, what are the roles of correctness, sense, and inspiration? What matters most to you? What matters most to readers?

THOMAS SOWELL

THOMAS SOWELL has been called "perhaps the leading black scholar among conservatives." His support for free markets and corresponding disdain for government regulations and social programs has endeared him to those on the right of center, while his logic and clarity have earned him respect from those on the left. Born in North Carolina in 1930, Sowell attended a segregated high school and went on to earn three degrees in economics: a BA from Harvard College (1958), an MA from Columbia University (1959), and a PhD from the University of Chicago (1968). He has taught at Harvard, Cornell University, Amherst College, and other schools; served as an economist in government and business; and held positions at several research centers, since 1980 at the Hoover Institution at Stanford University. Sowell writes a syndicated newspaper column and has published over two dozen books on economics, education, and race, the latest *Controversial Essays* (2002), *Applied Economics: Thinking Beyond Stage One* (2003), and *Affirmative Action Around the World: An Empirical Study* (2004).

"Needs"

What do we really need? In this essay from his collection *Is Reality Optional?* (1993), Sowell distinguishes between *want* and *need* because, he believes, by not distinguishing we all suffer.

1   A group of UCLA economists were having lunch together one day at the faculty club. One of them, named Mike, got up to get himself some more coffee. Being a decent sort, he asked:

2   "Does anybody else here need coffee?"

3   "Need?!" another economist cried out in astonishment and outrage.

4   The other economists around the table also pounced on this unfortunate word, while poor Mike retreated to the coffee maker, like someone who felt lucky to escape with his life.

5   Partly this was good clean fun — or what passes for good clean fun among economists. But partly it was a very serious issue.

6   Someone is always talking about what we "need" — more child care centers, more medical research, more housing, more environmental protection. The list goes on and on. All the things we "need" would add up to far more than the gross national product. Obviously we cannot and will not get all the things we "need."

7   Why call them "needs" then? We obviously get along without them, simply because we have no choice. These "needs" are simply things we want — or

that some of us want. Given that we cannot possibly have all the things we want, we have to make trade-offs. That is what economics is all about.

Words like *needs, rights,* or *entitlements* try to put some things on a pedestal, so that they don't have to face the reality of trade-offs. This is part of the higher humbug of politics. 8

Surely some things are really needs, you might say. If that is true, food must be one of those needs, since we would die without it. Huge agricultural surpluses are one result of this kind of mushy thinking. 9

There is obviously some amount of food that is urgently required to keep body and soul together. But the average American already takes in far more food than is necessary to sustain life — and in fact so much food as to make his lifespan shorter than it would be at a lower weight. 10

Like virtually everything else, food beyond some point ceases to be as urgently demanded and even ceases to be a benefit. When it reaches the point of being positively harmful, it can hardly be called a "need." That is why rigid words like *need* spread so much confusion in our thinking and havoc in our policies. 11

Prices force us into trade-offs, which is one of many reasons why the marketplace operates so much more efficiently than political allocation according to "need," "entitlement," "priorities" or other such rigid notions. 12

The real issue is almost never whether we should have nothing at all or some unlimited amount, or even some fixed amount of a particular good. The real issue is what kind of trade-off makes sense. That usually means having some of many things but not all we want of anything. 13

Prices tell us what the terms of the trade-offs are. Do we "need" more clothing? At some prices we do and at other prices we can get along with what we have. I happen to own three suits. But if clothing prices were one-tenth of what they are, I might have a wardrobe that would knock you dead. 14

My daughter used to make snide remarks about an old car that I drove for eight years. She stopped only when I told her that I could easily afford to get a new car, just by not paying her tuition. That's what trade-offs are all about. 15

If the government were giving out cars to those who "needed" them, I could have written an application that would have brought tears to your eyes. I could have gone on talk shows and worked up public sympathy over the ways my old jalopy was messing up my life — even threatening my life because the brakes failed completely twice. 16

If the taxpayers were paying for it, I would have "needed" a new car. But, since it was my money that was being spent, I had a brake job instead. 17

Politicians take advantage of our mushy thinking by promising to meet our "need" or by giving us a "right" or "entitlement" to this or that. But let's 18 go back to square one. Politicians don't manufacture anything except hot air. Every "need" they meet takes away from some other "need" somewhere else.

Every job the government creates is supported by resources taken out of   19 the private sector, where those same resources could have created another job — or maybe two other jobs, given the wastefulness of government.

"Needs" are a dangerous concept. Mike the economist suffered only a   20 momentary embarrassment from using the word. Our whole economy and society suffer much more from the mindless policies based on such misconceptions.

For a reading quiz, sources on Thomas Sowell, and annotated links to further readings on the concepts of wants and needs in economics, visit ***bedfordstmartins.com/ thebedfordreader***.

Journal Writing

How would you define your own personal needs? In your journal, write about what you require for a comfortable and fulfilled life. (To take your journal writing further, see "From Journal to Essay" on the next page.)

Questions on Meaning

1. How does Sowell define the customary use of *needs*? What is distinctive about this definition?
2. What would you say is Sowell's underlying PURPOSE in offering his definition?
3. What does Sowell mean when he talks about "trade-offs" (pars. 12–15)?

Questions on Writing Strategy

1. Why do you think Sowell begins his essay with the story of Mike and the other UCLA economists? How does this story support his point about *needs*?
2. Why does Sowell put quotations marks around *need* in his title and throughout the essay?
3. What is Sowell's reason for writing about food in paragraphs 9–11 and his old car in paragraphs 15–17? Do you think these EXAMPLES help clarify his point?
4. **OTHER METHODS.** How does Sowell use CAUSE AND EFFECT in paragraphs 18–20?

Questions on Language

1. Check a dictionary for the meanings of *humbug* (par. 8). Why do you think Sowell chose to use this word?
2. If you don't know the meanings of *allocation* and *entitlement* (par. 12), look them up in a dictionary.
3. Sowell refers to *needs* as a "rigid" word (par. 11). What is his point in using this adjective?
4. Point to some examples of informal language in the essay. What is the EFFECT of such language?

Suggestions for Writing

1. **FROM JOURNAL TO ESSAY.** Based on your journal writing, compose an essay in which you define your own needs. Which needs do you share with most other people, and which are particular to yourself? What trade-offs must you make among your needs?
2. Because government cannot provide everything we think we need, Sowell says, we have to establish priorities for allocating public funds. Write an essay that lays out what you believe should be the priorities in government spending. What must government provide, and what should it not be responsible for? If you wish to do some research into current spending allocations of the federal government, a summary appears at *home.att.net/~davis2/budintro.html* and the detailed US budget appears at *gpoaccess.gov/usbudget*.
3. **CRITICAL WRITING.** Write an essay in which you ANALYZE the UNITY of Sowell's essay. What methods does Sowell use to create unity? Does he digress at all?
4. **CONNECTIONS.** Consider Sowell's essay in COMPARISON with Anna Quindlen's "Homeless" (p. 200), which focuses on the need for a home, and the HUMMER advertisement at the start of this chapter (p. 476), whose theme is need. Using all three works as examples, write your definition of *need*.

DAGOBERTO GILB

DAGOBERTO GILB was born in Los Angeles in 1950 to a Mexican mother and a German American father. Though he admits to getting into trouble as a teen and says that he "wasn't the best student at all," he enrolled in junior college and went on to earn a BA in philosophy and an MA in religion from the University of California at Santa Barbara. From 1976 to 1991 Gilb pursued a dual career as a carpenter and writer. The stories he wrote then and later, often focusing on working-class Latinos in the Southwest, have been collected in *Winners on the Pass Line* (1985), *The Magic of Blood* (1993), which received a PEN/Hemingway award, and *Woodcuts of Women* (2001). Gilb has also written a novel, *The Last Known Residence of Mickey Acuna* (1994), which was named a *New York Times* Notable Book, and a collection of essays, *Gritos* (2003). Gilb has been a visiting writer at several universities and currently teaches in the creative writing program at Southwest Texas State University.

Pride

Gritos, Gilb's essay collection and the source of this piece, takes its title from a Spanish word that translates loosely as "shouts" but more precisely, Gilb explains, as exclamations of "defiance and freedom," "joy and support." All these feelings figure in Gilb's definition of *pride* through the lives of Mexican Americans in El Paso, Texas.

It's almost time to close at the northwest corner of Altura and Copia in El Paso. That means it is so dark that it is as restful as the deepest unremembering sleep, dark as the empty space around this spinning planet, as a black star. Headlights that beam a little cross-eyed from a fatso American car are feeling around the asphalt road up the hill toward the Good Time Store, its yellow plastic smiley face bright like a sugary suck candy. The loose muffler holds only half the misfires, and, dry springs squeaking, the automobile curves slowly into the establishment's lot, swerving to avoid the new self-serve gas pump island. Behind it, across the street, a Texas flag — out too late this and all the nights — pops and slaps in a summer wind that finally is cool.

A good man, gray on the edges, an assistant manager in a brown starched and ironed uniform, is washing the glass windows of the store, lit up by as many watts as Venus, with a roll of paper towels and the blue liquid from a spray bottle. Good night, m'ijo![1] he tells a young boy coming out after playing the video game, a Grande Guzzler the size of a wastebasket balanced in one hand, an open bag of Flaming Hot Cheetos, its red dye already smearing his

---

[1] Spanish slang, "my son." —EDS.

503

mouth and the hand not carrying the weight of the soda, his white T-shirt, its short sleeves reaching halfway down his wrists, the whole XXL of it billowing and puffing in the outdoor gust.

A plump young woman steps out of that car. She's wearing a party dress, 3 wide scoops out of the top, front, and back, its hemline way above the knees.

Did you get a water pump? the assistant manager asks her. Are you going 4 to make it to Horizon City? He's still washing the glass of the storefront, his hand sweeping in small hard circles.

The young woman is patient and calm like a loving mother. I don't know 5 yet, she tells him as she stops close to him, thinking. I guess I should make a call, she says, and her thick-soled shoes, the latest fashion, slap against her heels to one of the pay phones at the front of the store.

Pride is working a job like it's as important as art or war, is the happiness 6 of a new high score on a video arcade game, of a pretty new black dress and shoes. Pride is the deaf and blind confidence of the good people who are too poor but don't notice.

A son is a long time sitting on the front porch where he played all those 7 years with the squirmy dog who still licks his face, both puppies then, even before he played on the winning teams of Little League baseball and City League basketball. They sprint down the sidewalk and across streets, side by side, until they stop to rest on the park grass, where a red ant, or a spider, bites the son's calf. It swells, but he no longer thinks to complain to his mom about it — he's too old now — when he comes home. He gets ready, putting on the shirt and pants his mom would have ironed but he wanted to iron himself. He takes the ride with his best friend since first grade. The hundreds of moms and dads, abuelos y abuelitas, the tios and primos,[2] baby brothers and older married sisters, all are at the Special Events Center for the son's high school graduation. His dad is a man bigger than most, and when he walks in his dress eel-skin boots down the cement stairs to get as close to the hardwood basketball-court floor and ceremony to see — m'ijo! — he feels an embarrassing sob bursting from his eyes and mouth. He holds it back, and with his hands, hides the tears that do escape, wipes them with his fingers, because the chavalitos[3] in his aisle are playing and laughing and they are so small and he is so big next to them. And when his son walks to the stage to get his high school diploma and his dad wants to scream his name, he hears how many others, from the floor in caps and gowns and from around the arena, are already screaming it — could be any name, it could be any son's or daughter's: Alex! Vanessa! Carlos! Veronica! Ricky! Tony! Estella! Isa! — and sees his boy waving back to all of them.

---

[2] Spanish, "grandfathers and grandmothers," "aunts and uncles," and "cousins." — EDS.
[3] Spanish slang, "little kids." — EDS.

Pride hears gritty dirt blowing against an agave whose stiff fertile stalk, so   8
tall, will not bend—the love of land, rugged like the people who live on it.
Pride sees the sunlight on the Franklin Mountains in the first light of morning
and listens to a neighbor's gallo[4]—the love of culture and history. Pride smells
a sweet, musky drizzle of rain and eats huevos con chile[5] in corn tortillas
heated on a cast-iron pan—the love of heritage.

Pride is the fearless reaction to disrespect and disregard. It is knowing the   9
future will prove that wrong.

Seeing the beauty: Look out there from a height of the mountain and on   10
the north and south of the Rio Grande, to the far away and close, the so many
miles more of fuzz on the wide horizon, knowing how many years the people
have passed and have stayed, the ancestors, the ones who have medaled,
limped back on crutches or died or were heroes from wars in the Pacific or
Europe or Korea or Vietnam or the Persian Gulf, the ones who have raised the
fist and dared to defy, the ones who wash the clothes and cook and serve the
meals, who stitch the factory shoes and the factory slacks, who assemble and
sort, the ones who laugh and the ones who weep, the ones who care, the ones
who want more, the ones who try, the ones who love, those ones with shame-
less courage and hardened wisdom, and the old ones still so alive, holding
their grandchildren, and the young ones in their glowing prime, strong and
gorgeous, holding each other, the ones who will be born from them. The
desert land is rock-dry and ungreen. It is brown. Brown like the skin is brown.
Beautiful brown.

---

*For a reading quiz, sources on Dagoberto Gilb, and annotated links to further read-
ings on Mexican Americans in the United States, visit **bedfordstmartins.com/
thebedfordreader**.*

Journal Writing

In your journal, jot down images of pride that occur to you based on your own experiences and observations. Then try briefly to create your own definition—or definitions—of *pride*. (To take your journal writing further, see "From Journal to Essay" on
the next page.)

---

[4] Spanish, "rooster."—EDS.
[5] Traditional Mexican dish of eggs and peppers.—EDS.

Questions on Meaning

1. In your own words, SUMMARIZE Gilb's definition of *pride*.
2. How do paragraphs 8–10 contribute to Gilb's definition?
3. What point does Gilb make in his concluding paragraph? How does his final IMAGE serve as a sort of summary?
4. What would you say is Gilb's PURPOSE in this essay?

Questions on Writing Strategy

1. Why do you think Gilb opens the essay as he does? What impression does he create with the three people in the Good Time Store parking lot?
2. Following paragraphs 1–5, Gilb specifically defines the pride of the people about whom he has just written; however, after paragraph 7 his definition does not apply specifically to the father and son just described. Why do you think he varied his strategy here?
3. ANALYZE Gilb's development of paragraph 7. How would you describe its movement? its ultimate EFFECT?
4. How does Gilb achieve UNITY and COHERENCE in paragraph 8?
5. **OTHER METHODS.** Paragraphs 1–5 rely heavily on DESCRIPTION. Why do you think Gilb describes this scene in such detail?

Questions on Language

1. In paragraph 1 how does Gilb use specific language to create a distinct impression of the car that pulls into the store's parking lot?
2. What is striking about the verbs Gilb uses in paragraph 8?
3. The first sentence of paragraph 10 is unusually long. How does Gilb manage to maintain its clarity and readability?

Suggestions for Writing

1. **FROM JOURNAL TO ESSAY.** Using your journal writing as a springboard, write an essay in which you develop your own definition of *pride*. Like Gilb, present specific images and *examples* in addition to statements of your definition.
2. Using Gilb's essay as a model, write an essay of your own that defines another human feeling or characteristic—*happiness*, for example, or *sadness* or *fear* or *courage*. As Gilb does, present a wide range of examples to suggest various aspects of your subject.
3. Research the current situation of Mexican Americans in the United States: population, incomes, living conditions, education levels, occupations, and so forth. Then write an essay in which you present your findings.
4. **CRITICAL WRITING.** Write an essay in which you analyze Gilb's use of language in this essay or in a portion of it. What is the level of his DICTION? What are some especially effective uses of language? What overall impression does Gilb give of himself based on the language he uses?

5. **CONNECTIONS.** In "Indian Education" (p. 105), Sherman Alexie writes about the experiences of another ethnic group in the United States, Native Americans. Write an essay in which you COMPARE AND CONTRAST Gilb's presentation of Mexican Americans with Alexie's of Native Americans.

Dagoberto Gilb on Writing

In the introduction to his essay collection, *Gritos,* Dagoberto Gilb describes the pleasure he gets from writing.

[N]ot only has writing saved my life, . . . it has offered me joy and fun. . . . I assure you, every one of [these essays] has given me such pleasure and satisfaction, the same kind I had when I used to cut wood with my skilsaw and drive nails and build, watch a building rise huge, a fun of the kind that trowels the back of a tile with adhesive and sets it in, a pattern mounting. Each word is a rock I've placed personally into a wall—five go in and I pick through a pile and find another, shift them all around until it's right. I've chipped and nicked at most so they look to me like good sentences, good paragraphs. If I don't think of myself as the smartest, I do feel a strength in my working of the craft, so that every time I finish something, I'm maybe too proud of myself, can hardly believe I did it, that I could. The words are beyond my own physical self or nature, because I was not born to be a writer, I've just done it anyway. Often this work is outright fun, almost as fun as a good construction job where we were all muscles sweating and laughing and building . . . and getting paid at the same time—living and working—except writing work is alone, only an imaginary crew. Sometimes you see that laughter in these essays, but even when it's not haha, when it's like the drudgery of any job, it's still so good when it's finally gone through, completed—that pleasure, that joy.

For Discussion

1. How is carpentry a metaphor of the writing process for Gilb? (If you need a definition of *metaphor*, see *Figures of speech* in Useful Terms.)
2. What do you think Gilb means by "The words are beyond my own physical self or nature, because I was not born to be a writer"?

MARIE WINN

MARIE WINN was born in Czechoslovakia in 1936. As a child she immigrated with her family to New York City, where she attended public school. She graduated from Radcliffe College and went on to Columbia University for further study. She has contributed articles to the *New York Times Magazine*, the *New York Times Book Review*, *Smithsonian*, and the *Wall Street Journal*, where for twelve years she wrote a column on nature and bird watching. She is also the author of eleven books for adults and children, including *The Fireside Book of Fun and Game Songs* (1974). Several of her books raise difficult issues of child rearing and have attracted much attention: *The Plug-In Drug: Television, Computers, and Family Life* (1977, revised 2002), *Children Without Childhood* (1983), and *Unplugging the Plug-In Drug* (1987). Winn's book *Red-Tails in Love: A Wildlife Drama in Central Park* (1998) tells the story of a pair of red-tailed hawks nesting on a New York high-rise and the community of people who observed them. Winn continues to track the hawks and publishes photographs and a progress report on her Web site at *mariewinn.com*.

Cookies or Heroin?

Do you know someone who can't stop watching television? In this excerpt from *The Plug-In Drug*, Winn defines the troubling malady of TV addiction.

The word *addiction* is often used loosely and wryly in conversation. People will refer to themselves as "mystery-book addicts" or "cookie addicts." E. B. White[1] wrote of his annual surge of interest in gardening: "We are hooked and are making an attempt to kick the habit." Yet nobody really believes that reading mysteries or ordering seeds by catalogue is serious enough to be compared with addictions to heroin or alcohol. In these cases the word *addiction* is used jokingly to denote a tendency to overindulge in some pleasurable activity.

People often refer to being "hooked on TV." Does this, too, fall into the lighthearted category of cookie eating and other pleasures that people pursue with unusual intensity? Or is there a kind of television viewing that falls into the more serious category of destructive addiction?

Not unlike drugs or alcohol, the television experience allows the participant to blot out the real world and enter into a pleasurable and passive mental state. To be sure, other experiences, notably reading, also provide a temporary respite from reality. But it's much easier to stop reading and return

[1] See page 686. —EDS.

to reality than to stop watching television. The entry into another world offered by reading includes an easily accessible return ticket. The entry via television does not. In this way television viewing, for those vulnerable to addiction, is more like drinking or taking drugs—once you start it's hard to stop.

Just as alcoholics are only vaguely aware of their addiction, feeling that they control their drinking more than they really do ("I can cut it out any time I want—I just like to have three or four drinks before dinner"), many people overestimate their control over television watching. Even as they put off other activities to spend hour after hour watching television, they feel they could easily resume living in a different, less passive style. But somehow or other while the television set is present in their homes, it just stays on. With television's easy gratifications available, those other activities seem to take too much effort.

A heavy viewer (a college English instructor) observes:

> I find television almost irresistible. When the set is on, I cannot ignore it. I can't turn it off. I feel sapped, will-less, enervated. As I reach out to turn off the set, the strength goes out of my arms. So I sit there for hours and hours.

Self-confessed television addicts often feel they "ought" to do other things—but the fact that they don't read and don't plant their garden or sew or crochet or play games or have conversations means that those activities are no longer as desirable as television viewing. In a way, the lives of heavy viewers are as unbalanced by their television "habit" as drug addicts' or alcoholics' lives. They are living in a holding pattern, as it were, passing up the activities that lead to growth or development or a sense of accomplishment. This is one reason people talk about their television viewing so ruefully, so apologetically. They are aware that it is an unproductive experience, that by any human measure almost any other endeavor is more worthwhile.

It is the adverse effect of television viewing on the lives of so many people that makes it feel like a serious addiction. The television habit distorts the sense of time. It renders other experiences vague and curiously unreal while taking on a greater reality for itself. It weakens relationships by reducing and sometimes eliminating normal opportunities for talking, for communicating.

And yet television does not satisfy, else why would the viewer continue to watch hour after hour, day after day? "The measure of health," wrote the psychiatrist Lawrence Kubie, "is flexibility . . . and especially the freedom to cease when sated." But heavy television viewers can never be sated with their television experiences. These do not provide the true nourishment that satiation requires, and thus they find that they cannot stop watching.

*For a reading quiz, sources on Marie Winn, and annotated links to further readings on the effects of television viewing, visit **bedfordstmartins.com/thebedfordreader**.*

Journal Writing

If you like to watch television, Winn's essay may seem exaggerated. After all, isn't turning on the TV a great way to unwind or to be entertained? In your journal, write about your own relationship to television. How often do you watch? Does TV viewing interfere with your life, or do you have it under control? What does TV viewing do for (or to) your life? If you don't watch TV at all, write instead about why you don't. (To take your journal writing further, see "From Journal to Essay" on the facing page.)

Questions on Meaning

1. What distinction does Winn make between "lighthearted" addiction and destructive addiction?
2. In paragraph 2 Winn poses questions that lead to her THESIS. What are the answers to these questions? Do you find them explicitly stated anywhere?
3. What does Winn think are the main problems caused by excessive TV viewing?
4. Does Winn think there can be anything good about watching television? How do you know?

Questions on Writing Strategy

1. Why does Winn take care to give the nonserious meanings of *addiction* (par. 1)? What do these definitions do for the essay?
2. Winn does not answer her thesis question immediately after she asks it (par. 2). Why, do you think? What is the EFFECT of this delay?
3. Winn puts a number of words and phrases in quotation marks—for example, "hooked on TV" (par. 2), "ought" (6), and "habit" (6). What does this punctuation contribute to Winn's essay?
4. How does Winn maintain UNITY in her essay?
5. **OTHER METHODS.** Study Winn's COMPARISON between drug or alcohol addiction and TV addiction. How are the two similar? Are they different in any way?

Questions on Language

1. In paragraph 8 Winn uses a metaphor of eating to explain addiction. (See *Figures of speech* in Useful Terms if you need a definition of *metaphor*.) If you do not know

the meanings of *sated, nourishment,* or *satiation,* look them up in a dictionary. What is the effect of using such terms to define addiction?

2. What does Winn mean when she describes addiction as "living in a holding pattern" (par. 6)?

3. Consult a dictionary if you don't know the meaning of any of the following words: wryly, denote (par. 1); respite, vulnerable (3); gratifications (4); sapped, enervated (5); ruefully, apologetically, endeavor (6); adverse, renders (7).

Suggestions for Writing

1. **FROM JOURNAL TO ESSAY.** If you are a TV watcher, write an essay that compares and contrasts your relationship with TV and Winn's definition of *TV addiction.* Would Winn consider you a television addict? Do you consider yourself one? Is it possible to watch a lot of television without being an addict? If you are not a TV watcher (or not much of one), write an essay that compares and contrasts your life with that of a frequent watcher (not necessarily an addict): How do you benefit? What might you be missing?

2. As Winn's opening paragraph points out, people often claim to be "addicted" to all kinds of things. From your experience, you probably know that such addictions can include everything from spy novels to Snickers candy bars to driving dangerously. Write an essay defining an addiction (but not to cigarettes, drugs, alcohol, or television). Your essay's TONE may be serious or humorous, but you should give your readers a sense of the addiction's CAUSES AND EFFECTS as well as EXAMPLES of its sufferers.

3. Many researchers have studied the effects on people of watching a lot of television. Locate a number of these studies, and write an essay in which you explain the extent to which they support Winn's thesis—or don't support it.

4. **CRITICAL WRITING.** "It is the adverse effect of television viewing on the lives of so many people that makes it feel like a serious addiction" (par. 7). Do you agree with this statement? Does the number of people affected define an addiction as "serious"? If fewer people suffered the "adverse effect" of TV viewing, would it not be a serious addiction? Or, in contrast, do the huge numbers of TV viewers remove the behavior from addicted to normal? Write an essay that either confirms or refutes Winn's assertion, using examples to support your opinion.

5. **CONNECTIONS.** Gore Vidal's "Drugs" (p. 454) proposes legalizing drugs as a solution to the problem of drug addiction and its effects on our society. Following Vidal's model (though not his precise recommendations, of course, since television is already legal), propose a solution to the problem of TV addiction. Your solution may be serious or humorous, and it may approach the problem at the level of the individual addict or at the level of society as a whole.

Marie Winn on Writing

For Marie Winn, the most enjoyable part of writing is making improvements. "I love spending an hour or two with a dictionary and a thesaurus looking for a more nearly perfect word," she declares in an account of her working habits written for *The Bedford Reader*. "Or taking my pen and ruthlessly pruning all the unnecessary adjectives (a practice I can wholeheartedly recommend to you), or fooling around with the rhythm of a sentence or a paragraph by changing a verb into a participle, or making any number of little changes that a magazine editor I work with ruefully calls 'mouse milking.'"

But the proportion of time Winn spends at this "delightful occupation" is small. "For me, the pleasure and pain of writing go on simultaneously. Once I have finally forced myself to bite the bullet and get to work, as soon as the flow of writing stops—after a few sentences or paragraphs or, if I am extraordinarily lucky, a few pages—then, as a little reward for having actually written something and also as a procrastinating measure to delay the painful necessity of having to write something again, I play with the words and sentences on the page.

"That's the trouble, of course: There have to be words and sentences on the page before I can enjoy the pleasure of playing with them. Somehow I have to transform the vague and confused tangle of ideas in my head into an orderly and logical sequence on a blank piece of paper. That's the real hell of writing: the inescapable need to think clearly. . . . You have to figure it out, make it all hang together, consider the implications, the alternatives, eliminate the contradictions, the extraneous thoughts, the illogical conclusions. I *hate* that part of writing and I have a feeling you know perfectly well what I'm talking about."

For Discussion

1. For Winn, what is the most difficult part of the writing process? What part does she most enjoy?
2. What does the author see as the role that thinking plays in writing?

ADDITIONAL WRITING TOPICS

Definition

1. Write an essay in which you define an institution, trend, phenomenon, or abstraction as specifically and concretely as possible. Following are some suggestions designed to stimulate ideas. Before you begin, limit your subject.

Responsibility	Leadership
Fun	Leisure
Sorrow	Originality
Unethical behavior	Character
The environment	Imagination
Education	Democracy
Progress	A smile
Advertising	A classic (of music, literature, art,
Happiness	or film)
Fads	Dieting
Feminism	Meditation
Marriage	Friendship
Sportsmanship	

2. In a brief essay, define one of the following. In each instance, you have a choice of something good or something bad to talk about.

   A good or bad boss
   A good or bad parent
   A good or bad host
   A good or bad TV newscaster
   A good or bad physician
   A good or bad nurse
   A good or bad minister, priest, or rabbi
   A good or bad roommate
   A good or bad driver
   A good or bad disk jockey

3. In a paragraph, define one of the following slang expressions for someone who has never heard the term: *bling-bling, sick, hook up, wack, dis, awesome, wimp, druggie, snob, freak, loser, quack, chill, pig out, gross out, winging it, sweet.*

13

ARGUMENT AND PERSUASION

Stating Opinions and Proposals

◄ **Argument and persuasion in an image**

Adbusters Media Foundation, an activist group "concerned about the erosion of our physical and cultural environments by commercial forces," launched its Corporate America flag in 1999. This version appeared in a full-page advertisement in the New York Times in 2004. Replacing the American flag's stars with well-known corporate logos, the image adapts a symbol that many Americans revere to make a strong argument about the United States. What is the argument? How do you respond to the image: Are you offended? persuaded? amused? Why? Whatever your view, do you understand why others might think differently? (For a written view on the effects of commercial forces, see Naomi Klein's "A Web of Brands," p. 440.)

THE METHOD

Practically every day, we try to persuade ourselves or someone else. We usually attempt such persuasion without being aware that we follow any special method at all. Often, we'll state an *opinion:* We'll tell someone our own way of viewing things. We say to a friend, "I'm starting to like Senator Clark. Look at all she's done to help people with disabilities. Look at her voting record on toxic waste." And, having stated these opinions, we might go on to make a *proposal,* to recommend that some action be taken. Addressing our friend, we might suggest, "Hey, Senator Clark is talking on campus at four-thirty. Want to come with me and listen to her?"

Sometimes you try to convince yourself that a certain way of interpreting things is right. You even set forth an opinion in writing—as in a letter to a friend who has asked, "Now that you're at New Age College, how do you like the place?" You may write a letter of protest to a landlord who wants to raise your rent, pointing out that the bathroom hot water faucet doesn't work. As a concerned citizen, you may wish to speak your mind in an occasional letter to a newspaper or to your elected representatives.

In many professions, one is expected to persuade people in writing. Before arguing a case in court, a lawyer prepares briefs setting forth all the points in favor of his or her side. Businesspeople regularly put in writing their ideas for new products and ventures, for improvements in cost control and job efficiency. Researchers write proposals for grants to obtain money to support their work. Scientists write and publish papers to persuade the scientific community that their findings are valid, often stating hypotheses, or tentative opinions.

Even if you never produce a single persuasive work (which is very unlikely), you will certainly encounter such works directed at you. In truth, we live our lives under a steady rain of opinions and proposals. Organizations that work for causes campaign with posters and direct mail, all hoping that we will see things their way. Moreover, we are bombarded with proposals from people who wish us to act. Religious leaders urge us to lead more virtuous lives. Advertisers urge us to rush right out and buy the large economy size.

Small wonder, then, that argument and persuasion—and CRITICAL THINKING about argument and persuasion—may be among the most useful skills a college student can acquire. Time and again, your instructors will ask you to criticize or to state opinions, either in class or in writing. You may be asked to state your view of anything from the electoral college to animal rights. You may be asked to judge the desirability or undesirability of compulsory testing for drugs or the revision of existing immigration laws. On an examination in, say, sociology, you may be asked, "Suggest three practical approaches to the most pressing needs of disadvantaged people in urban areas." Critically reading other people's arguments and composing your own, you will find, helps you discover what you think, refine it, and share what you believe.

Is there a difference between argument and persuasion? It is, admittedly, not always clear. Strictly speaking, PERSUASION aims to influence readers' actions, or their support for an action, by engaging their beliefs and feelings, while ARGUMENT aims to win readers' agreement with an assertion or claim by engaging their powers of reasoning. But most effective persuasion or argument contains elements of both methods; hence the confusion. In this book we tend to use the terms interchangeably.

One other point: We tend to talk here about *writing* argument and persuasion, but most of what we say has to do with *reading* them as well. When we discuss your need, as a writer, to support your assertions, we are also discussing your need, as a reader, to question the support other authors provide for their assertions. In reading arguments critically, you apply the critical-thinking skills we discussed in Chapter 1 — ANALYSIS, INFERENCE, SYNTHESIS, EVALUATION — to a particular kind of writing.

Transaction Between Writer and Reader

Unlike some television advertisers, responsible writers of argument and persuasion do not try to storm people's minds. In writing a paper for a course, you persuade by gentler means: by sharing your view with readers willing to consider it. You'll want to learn how to express your view clearly and vigorously. But to be fair and persuasive, it is important to understand your readers' views as well.

In stating your opinion, you present the truth as you see it: "The immigration laws discourage employers from hiring nonnative workers" or "The immigration laws protect legal aliens." To persuade your readers that your view makes sense, you need not begin by proclaiming that, by Heaven, your view is absolutely right and should prevail. Instead, you might begin by trying to state what your readers probably think, as best you can infer it. You don't consider views that differ from your own merely to flatter your readers. You do so to correct your own view and make it more accurate. Regarded in this light, argument and persuasion aren't cynical ways to pull other people's strings. Writer and reader become two sensible people trying to find a common ground. This view will relieve you, whenever you have to state your opinions in writing, of the terrible obligation to be 100 percent right at all times.

Thesis Statement

In an argument you champion or defend your opinion about something. This opinion is the THESIS, or *claim,* of your argument, and it will probably appear in your essay as your THESIS STATEMENT. Usually, but not always, you'll state your thesis statement at the beginning of your essay, making a play for readers' attention and clueing them in to your purpose. But if you think readers may have difficulty accepting your thesis until they've heard some or all of your argument, then you might save the thesis statement for the middle or end.

The essays in this chapter provide a variety of thesis statements as models. Here are four examples:

> Today there is more pressure placed on students to do well [in school]. . . . This new pressure is what is causing the increase in cheating.
> > —Colleen Wenke, "Too Much Pressure"

> I think the observable reluctance of the majority of Americans to assert themselves in minor matters is related to our increased sense of helplessness in an age of technology and centralized political and economic power.
> > —William F. Buckley, Jr., "Why Don't We Complain?"

> Racial profiling is an ugly business. . . . But I'm not opposed to allowing— no, requiring—airlines to pay closer attention to passengers who fit a terrorist profile, which includes national origin.
> > —Linda Chavez, "Everything Isn't Racial Profiling"

> Giving up privacy rights [to government surveillance] can't guarantee physical safety, but it will almost certainly inhibit intellectual freedom and limit cognitive liberty. We Americans who cherish our freedoms should seriously consider whether or not this is a compromise we are willing to make.
> > —Zara Gelsey, "The FBI Is Reading over Your Shoulder"

Evidence and Appeals

To support the thesis of your argument, you need EVIDENCE—anything that demonstrates what you're claiming. Evidence may include facts, statistics (facts expressed in numbers), expert opinions, examples, reported experience. It should be accurate, should fairly represent the available facts and opinions, should relate directly to your claims, and should be ample to convince readers of your claims. (For concise examples of using evidence effectively, see the paragraphs and letter on pp. 529–31.)

Even the best-supported argument also must appeal to readers' intelligence and to their feelings. In appealing to reason—a RATIONAL APPEAL— you'll want to rely on conventional methods of reasoning (see the facing page) and supply evidence according to the criteria stated above. In appealing to feelings—an EMOTIONAL APPEAL—you'll want to acknowledge what you know of readers' sympathies and beliefs and also show how your argument relates to them.

Emotional appeal requires vigilance, from both writers and readers, because it can be manipulative. "Do you really want to deprive your children of what's best for them?" asks a pitch for a certain learn-to-read program, appealing to pride or shame while neglecting to provide evidence that the program works. Another kind of writing, generally not cynical, relies heavily on emotional appeal for the purpose of inspiring readers who are already partial to the writer's message. (An impressive example is "I Have a Dream" by Martin Luther King, Jr., reprinted on pp. 625–29.) But even in an argument directed at a skeptical audience and based largely on reason and evidence, an emotional appeal can stir readers by fair means to constructive belief and action. Such an appeal recognizes that we are not intellectual robots but creatures with feelings. Indeed, in any effective argument, a writer had better engage the feelings of readers or they may reply, "True enough, but who cares?" Argument, to succeed in persuading, makes us feel that a writer's views are close to our own.

Yet another resource in argument is ETHICAL APPEAL: impressing your reader that you are a well-informed person of good will, good sense, and good moral character—and, therefore, to be believed. You make such an appeal by collecting ample evidence, reasoning carefully, using an appropriate emotional appeal, and minding your TONE (see pp. 527–28). You can also cite or quote respected authorities. If you don't know whether an authority is respected, you can ask a reference librarian for tips on finding out, or talk to an instructor who is a specialist in that field.

In arguing, you don't prove your assertion in the same irrefutable way in which a chemist demonstrates that hydrogen will burn. If you say, "Health coverage for the uninsured should be given top priority in Congress," that kind of claim isn't clearly either true or false. Argument takes place in areas that invite more than one opinion. In writing an argument, you help your reader see and understand just one open-eyed, open-minded view of reality.

Reasoning

When we argue rationally, we reason—that is, we make statements that lead to a conclusion. From the time of the ancient Greeks down to our own day, distinctly different methods of proceeding from statements to conclusions have been devised. This section will tell you of a recent, informal method of reasoning and also of two traditional methods. Understanding these methods, knowing how to use them, and being able to recognize when they are misused will make you a better writer *and* reader.

The Toulmin Method

Data, claim, and warrant   In recent decades, a simple, practical method of reasoning has been devised by the British philosopher Stephen Toulmin.[1] Helpfully, Toulmin has divided a typical argument into three parts:

DATA   The evidence to prove something

CLAIM   What you are proving with the data

WARRANT   The assumption or principle that connects the data to the claim

Any clear, explicit argument has to have all three parts. Toulmin's own example of such an argument is this:

Harry was born in Bermuda ─────────→ So Harry is a British subject
        (*Data*)   (*Claim*)

Since a man born in Bermuda
will be a British subject
(*Warrant*)

Of course, the data for a larger, more controversial claim will be more extensive. Here are some claims that would call for many more data, perhaps thousands of words.

The war on drugs is not winnable.

The United States must help to destroy drug production in South America.

Drug addiction is a personal matter.

The warrant at the center   The warrant, that middle term, is often crucially important. It is usually an ASSUMPTION or a GENERALIZATION that explains *why* the claim follows from the data. Often a writer won't bother to state a warrant because it is obvious: "In his bid for reelection, Mayor Perkins failed miserably. Out of 5,000 votes cast for both candidates, he received only 200." The warrant might be stated, "To make what I would consider a strong showing, he would have had to receive 2,000 votes or more," but it is clear that 200 out of 5,000 is a small minority, and no further explanation seems necessary.

A flaw in many arguments, though, is that the warrant is not clear. A clear warrant is essential. To be persuaded, a reader needs to understand your assumptions and the thinking that follows from them. If you were to argue, "Drug abuse is a serious problem in the United States. Therefore, the United States must

---

[1] *The Uses of Argument* (1958, updated 2003) sets forth Toulmin's system in detail. His views are further explained and applied by Douglas Ehninger and Wayne Brockriede in *Decision by Debate* (2nd ed., 1978) and by Toulmin himself, with Richard Rieke and Allan Janik, in *An Introduction to Reasoning* (2nd ed., 1984).

help to destroy drug production in Latin America," then your reader might well be left wondering why the second statement follows from the first. But if you were to add, between the statements, "As long as drugs are manufactured in Latin America, they will be smuggled into the United States, and drug abuse will continue," then you supply a warrant. You show why your claim follows from your data—which, of course, you must also supply to make your case.

The unstated warrant can pitch an argument into trouble—whether your own or another writer's. Since warrants are usually assumptions or generalizations, rather than assertions of fact, they are valid only if readers accept or agree that they are valid. With stated warrants, any weaknesses are more likely to show. Suppose someone asserts that a certain woman should not be elected mayor because women cannot form ideas independently of their husbands and this woman's husband has bad ideas on how to run the city. At least the warrant—that women cannot form ideas independently of their husbands—is out there on the table, exposed for all to inspect. But unstated warrants can be just as absurd, or even just doubtful, and pass unnoticed because they are not exposed. Here's the same argument without its warrant: "She shouldn't be elected mayor because her husband has bad ideas on how to run the city."

Here's another argument with an unstated warrant, this one adapted from a magazine advertisement: "Scientists have no proof, just statistical correlations, linking smoking and heart disease, so you needn't worry about the connection." Now, the fact that this ad was placed by a cigarette manufacturer would tip off any reasonably alert reader to beware of bias in the claim. To discover the slant, we need to examine the unstated warrant, which runs something like this: "Since they are not proof, statistical correlations are worthless as guides to behavior." It is true that statistical correlations are not scientific proof, by which we generally mean repeated results obtained under controlled laboratory conditions—the kind of conditions to which human beings cannot ethically be subjected. But statistical correlations *can* establish connections and in fact inform much of our healthful behavior, such as getting physical exercise, avoiding fatty foods, brushing our teeth, and not driving while intoxicated. The advertiser's unstated warrant isn't valid, so neither is the argument.

Example of a Toulmin argument   Let's look at how the data-claim-warrant scheme can work in constructing an argument. In an assignment for her course in English composition, Maire Flynn was asked to produce a condensed argument in three short paragraphs. The first paragraph was to set forth some data; the second, a claim; and the third, a warrant. The result became a kind of outline that the writer could then expand into a whole essay. Following is Flynn's argument.

DATA   Over the past five years, assistance in the form of food stamps has not had the effect of decreasing the number of people on welfare. Despite this help, 95 percent of long-term recipients remain below the poverty line today.

CLAIM   The present system of distributing food stamps is a dismal failure, a less effective way to help the needy than other possible ways.

WARRANT   No one is happy to receive charity. We need to encourage people to quit the welfare rolls; we need to make sure that government aid goes only to the deserving. More effective than giving out food stamps would be to help untrained young people learn job skills; to help single mothers with small children to obtain child care, freeing them for the job market; and to enlarge and improve our state employment counseling and job-placement services. The problem of poverty will be helped only if more people will find jobs and become self-sufficient.

In her warrant paragraph, Flynn spells out her reasons for holding her opin-ion—the one she states in her claim. "The warrant," she found, "was the hardest part to write," but hers turned out to be clear. Like any good warrant, hers expresses those thoughts that her data set in motion. Another way of looking at the warrant: It is the thinking that led the writer on to the opinion she holds. In this statement of her warrant, Flynn makes clear her assump-tions: that people who can support themselves don't deserve food stamps and that a person is better off (and happier) holding a job than receiving charity. By generating more ideas and evidence, she was easily able to expand both the data paragraph and the warrant paragraph, and the result was a coherent essay of seven hundred words.

How, by the way, would someone who didn't accept Flynn's warrant argue with her? What about old, infirm, or disabled persons who cannot work? What quite different assumptions about poverty might be possible?

Deductive and Inductive Reasoning

Stephen Toulmin's method of argument is a fairly recent—and very help-ful—way to analyze and construct arguments. Two other reliable methods date back to the Greek philosopher Aristotle, who identified the complemen-tary processes of INDUCTIVE REASONING (induction) and DEDUCTIVE REASON-ING (deduction). In *Zen and the Art of Motorcycle Maintenance*, Robert M. Pirsig gives examples of deductive and inductive reasoning:

> If the cycle goes over a bump and the engine misfires, and then goes over another bump and the engine misfires, and then goes over another bump and the engine misfires, and then goes over a long smooth stretch of road and there is no misfiring, and then goes over a fourth bump and the engine misfires

again, one can logically conclude that the misfiring is caused by the bumps. That is induction: reasoning from particular experiences to general truths.

Deductive inferences do the reverse. They start with general knowledge and predict a specific observation. For example if, from reading the hierarchy of facts about the machine, the mechanic knows the horn of the cycle is powered exclusively by electricity from the battery, then he can logically infer that if the battery is dead the horn will not work. That is deduction.

In inductive reasoning, the method of the sciences, we collect bits of evidence on which to base generalizations. From interviews with a hundred self-identified conservative Republicans (the evidence), you might conclude that conservative Republicans favor less government regulation of business (the generalization). The more evidence you have, the more trustworthy your generalization is, but it would never be airtight unless you talked to every conservative Republican in the country. Since such thoroughness is impractical if not impossible, inductive reasoning involves making an *inductive leap* from the evidence to the conclusion. The smaller the leap — the more evidence you have — the better.

Deductive reasoning works the other way, from a general statement to particular cases. The basis of deduction is the SYLLOGISM, a three-step form of reasoning practiced by Aristotle:

> All men are mortal.
>
> Socrates is a man.
>
> Therefore, Socrates is mortal.

The first statement (the major premise) is a generalization about a large group: It is the result of inductive reasoning. The second statement (the minor premise) says something about a particular member of that large group. The third statement (the conclusion) follows inevitably from the premises and applies the generalization to the particular: If the premises are true, then the conclusion must be true. Here is another syllogism:

> MAJOR PREMISE   Conservative Republicans favor less government regulation of business.
>
> MINOR PREMISE   William F. Buckley, Jr., is a conservative Republican.
>
> CONCLUSION   Therefore, William F. Buckley, Jr., favors less government regulation of business.

Problems with deductive reasoning start in the premises. In 1633, Scipio Chiaramonti, professor of philosophy at the University of Pisa, came up with this untrustworthy syllogism: "Animals, which move, have limbs and muscles. The earth has no limbs and muscles. Hence, the earth does not move." This is bad deductive reasoning, and its flaw is to assume that all things need limbs and muscles to move — ignoring raindrops, rivers, and many other moving things. In the next pages, we'll look at some of the things that can go wrong with any kind of reasoning.

Logical Fallacies

In arguments we read and hear, we often meet logical FALLACIES: errors in reasoning that lead to wrong conclusions. From the time when you start thinking about your proposition or claim and planning your paper, you'll need to watch out for them. To help you recognize logical fallacies when you see them or hear them, and so guard against them when you write, here is a list of the most common.

- *Non sequitur* (from the Latin, "it does not follow"): stating a conclusion that doesn't follow from the first premise or premises. "I've lived in this town a long time — why, my grandfather was the first mayor — so I'm against putting fluoride in the drinking water."
- *Oversimplification:* supplying neat and easy explanations for large and complicated phenomena. "No wonder drug abuse is out of control. Look at how the courts have hobbled police officers." Oversimplified solutions are also popular: "All these teenage kids that get in trouble with the law — why, they ought to ship 'em over to China. That would straighten 'em out!" (See also p. 433.)
- *Hasty generalization:* leaping to a generalization from inadequate or faulty evidence. The most familiar hasty generalization is the stereotype: "Men aren't sensitive enough to be day-care providers." "Women are too emotional to fight in combat."
- *Either/or reasoning:* assuming that a reality may be divided into only two parts or extremes; assuming that a given problem has only one of two possible solutions. "What's to be done about the trade imbalance with Asia? Either we ban all Asian imports, or American industry will collapse." Obviously, either/or reasoning is a kind of extreme oversimplification.
- *Argument from doubtful or unidentified authority:* "We ought to castrate all sex offenders; Uncle Oswald says we should." Or: "According to reliable sources, my opponent is lying."
- *Argument ad hominem* (from the Latin, "to the man"): attacking a person's views by attacking his or her character. "Mayor Burns is divorced and estranged from his family. How can we listen to his pleas for a city nursing home?"
- *Begging the question:* taking for granted from the start what you set out to demonstrate. When you reason in a *logical* way, you state that because

something is true, then, as a result, some other truth follows. When you beg the question, however, you repeat that what is true is true. If you argue, for instance, that dogs are a menace to people because they are dangerous, you don't prove a thing, since the idea that dogs are dangerous is already assumed in the statement that they are a menace. Beggars of questions often just repeat what they already believe, only in different words. This fallacy sometimes takes the form of arguing in a circle, or demonstrating a premise by a conclusion and a conclusion by a premise: "I am in college because that is the right thing to do. Going to college is the right thing to do because it is expected of me."

- *Post hoc, ergo propter hoc* (from the Latin, "after this, therefore because of this"), or *post hoc* for short: assuming that because B follows A, B was caused by A. "Ever since the city suspended height restrictions on skyscrapers, the city budget has been balanced." (See also p. 433.)

- *False analogy:* the claim of persuasive likeness when no significant likeness exists. An ANALOGY asserts that because two things are comparable in some respects, they are comparable in other respects as well. Analogies cannot serve as evidence in a rational argument because the differences always outweigh the similarities; but analogies can reinforce such arguments *if* the subjects are indeed similar in some ways. If they aren't, the analogy is false. Many observers see the "war on drugs" as a false and damaging analogy because warfare aims for clear victory over a specific, organized enemy, whereas the complete eradication of illegal drugs is probably unrealistic and, in any event, the "enemy" isn't well defined: the drugs themselves? users? sellers? producers? the producing nations? (These critics urge approaching drugs as a social problem to be skillfully managed and reduced.)

THE PROCESS

In stating an opinion, you set forth and support a claim—a truth you believe. You may find such a truth by thinking and feeling, by reading, by talking to your instructors or fellow students, by listening to a discussion of some problem or controversy.

In stating a proposal, you already have an opinion in mind, and from there, you go on to urge an action or a solution to a problem. Usually, these two statements will take place within the same piece of writing: A writer will first set forth a view ("Compact discs are grossly overpriced") and then go right on to a proposal ("Compact discs should be discounted in the college store").

Whether your essay states an opinion, a proposal, or both, it is likely to contain similar ingredients. One essential is your THESIS—the proposition or claim you are going to defend. As we noted earlier (p. 518), the likeliest spot for your thesis statement is near the start of your essay, where you might also explain why you think the thesis worth upholding, perhaps showing how it concerns your readers. If you plan to include both an opinion and a proposal in your essay, you may wish to set forth your opinion first, saving your proposal for later, perhaps for your conclusion.

Your thesis stated, introduce your least important point first. Then build in a crescendo to the strongest point you have. This structure will lend emphasis to your essay and perhaps make your chain of ideas more persuasive as the reader continues to follow it.

For every point, give EVIDENCE: facts, figures, examples, expert opinions. If you introduce statistics, make sure that they are up to date and fairly repre-sented. In an essay advocating a law against smoking, it would be unfair to declare that "in Pottsville, Illinois, last year, 50 percent of all deaths were caused by lung cancer" if only two people died in Pottsville last year—one of them struck by a car.

If you are arguing fairly, you should be able to face potential criticisms fairly, and give your critics due credit, by recognizing the objections you expect your assertion will meet. This is the strategy Linda Chavez uses in "Everything Isn't Racial Profiling" by maintaining, more than once, that racial profiling based on prejudice is wrong and by sympathizing with an Arab American who was not allowed to board a plane because of his ethnicity. As Chavez does, you can tackle possible objections throughout your essay, or you can discuss them early on or near the end. Also like Chavez, you should take pains to reason with opponents, not just dismiss them.

In your CONCLUSION, briefly restate your claim, if possible in a fresh, pointed way. (For example, see the concluding sentence in the essay by William F. Buckley, Jr., in this chapter.) In an essay with a strong emotional component, you may want to end with an appeal to feelings.

Finally, don't forget the power of humor in argument. You don't have to crack gratuitous jokes, but there is often an advantage in having a reader or listener who laughs on your side. When Abraham Lincoln debated Stephen Douglas, he triumphed in his reply to Douglas's snide remark that Lincoln had once been a bartender. "I have long since quit my side of the bar," Lincoln declared, "while Mr. Douglas clings to his as tenaciously as ever."

In arguing—doing everything you can to bring your reader around to your view—you can draw on any method of writing discussed in this book. Arguing for or against further reductions in welfare funding, you might give EXAMPLES of wasteful spending, or of neighborhoods where welfare funds are still needed. You might analyze the CAUSES of social problems that call for wel-fare funds, or foresee the likely EFFECTS of cutting welfare programs or of keeping them. You might COMPARE AND CONTRAST the idea of slashing welfare funds with the idea of increasing them. You could use NARRATION to tell a pointed story; you could use DESCRIPTION to portray certain welfare recipients and their neighborhoods. If it suited your purposes, you could employ several of these methods in writing a single argument.

You will rarely find, when you begin to write a persuasive paper, that you have too much evidence to support your claim. But unless you're writing a term paper and have months to spend on it, you're limited in how much evidence you can gather. Begin by stating your claim. Make it narrow enough to support in the time you have available. For a paper due a week from now, the opinion that "our city's downtown area has a serious litter problem" can probably be backed up in part by your own eyewitness reports. But to support the claim "Litter is one of the worst environmental problems of North American cities," you would surely need to spend time in a library.

In rewriting, you may find yourself tempted to keep all the evidence you have collected with such effort. Of course, some of it may not support your claim; some may seem likely to persuade the reader only to go to sleep. If so, throw it out. A stronger argument will remain.

FOCUS ON TONE

Readers are most likely to be persuaded by an argument when they sense a writer who is reasonable, trustworthy, and sincere. Sound reasoning, strong evidence, and acknowledgment of opposing views do much to convey these attributes, but so does TONE, the attitude implied by choice of words and sentence structures.

Generally, you should try for a tone of moderation in your view of your subject and a tone of respectfulness and goodwill toward readers and opponents.

- State opinions and facts calmly:

  OVEREXCITED   One clueless administrator was quoted in the newspaper as saying she thought many students who claim learning disabilities are faking their difficulties to obtain special treatment! Has she never heard of dyslexia, attention-deficit disorders, and other well-established disabilities?

  CALM   Particularly worrisome was one administrator's statement, quoted in the newspaper, that many students who claim learning disabilities may be "faking" their difficulties to obtain special treatment.

- Replace arrogance with deference and sarcasm with plain speaking:

  ARROGANT   I happen to know that many students would rather party or just bury their heads in the sand than get involved in a serious, worthy campaign against the school's unjust learning-disabled policies.

  DEFERENTIAL   Time pressures and lack of information about the issues may be what prevents students from joining the campaign against the school's unjust learning-disabled policies.

SARCASTIC   Of course, the administration knows even without meeting students what is best for every one of them.

PLAIN   The administration should agree to meet with each learning-disabled student to learn about his or her needs.

- Choose words whose CONNOTATIONS convey reasonableness rather than anger, hostility, or another negative emotion:

  HOSTILE   The administration *coerced* some students into dropping their lawsuits. [*Coerced* implies the use of threats or even violence.]

  REASONABLE   The administration *convinced* some students to drop their lawsuits. [*Convinced* implies the use of reason.]

For exercises on language, visit Exercise Central at *bedfordstmartins.com/ thebedfordreader.*

CHECKLIST FOR REVISING ARGUMENT OR PERSUASION

✔ **AUDIENCE.** Have you taken account of your readers' probable views? Have you reasoned with readers, not attacked them? Are your emotional appeals appropriate to readers' likely feelings? Do you acknowledge opposing views?

✔ **THESIS.** Does your argument have a thesis, a claim about how your subject is or should be? Is the thesis narrow enough to argue convincingly in the space and time available? Is it stated clearly? Is it reasonable?

✔ **EVIDENCE.** Is your thesis well supported with facts, statistics, expert opinions, and examples? Is your evidence accurate, representative, relevant, and ample?

✔ **WARRANT.** Have you made sound connections between your evidence and your thesis or claim?

✔ **LOGICAL FALLACIES.** Have you avoided common errors in reasoning, such as oversimplifying or begging the question? (See pp. 524–25 for a list of fallacies.)

✔ **STRUCTURE.** Does your organization lead readers through your argument step by step, building to your strongest ideas and frequently connecting your evidence to your central claim?

✔ **TONE.** Is the tone of your argument reasonable and respectful?

ARGUMENT AND PERSUASION IN PARAGRAPHS

Writing About Television

This self-contained paragraph, written for *The Bedford Reader*, argues that TV news aims for entertainment at the expense of serious coverage of events and issues. The argument here could serve a number of different purposes in full essays: For instance, in a paper claiming that television is our least reliable source of news, the paragraph would give one cause of unreliability; or in an essay analyzing television news, the paragraph would examine one element.

Television news has a serious failing: It's show business. Unlike a newspaper, its every image has to entertain the average beer drinker. To score high ratings and win advertisers, the visual medium favors the spectacular: riots, tornados, air crashes. Now that satellite transmission invites live coverage, newscasters go for the fast-breaking story at the expense of thoughtful analysis. "The more you can get data out instantly," says media critic Jeff Greenfield, "the more you rely on instant data to define the news." TV zooms in on people who make news, but, to avoid boredom, won't let them argue or explain. (How can they, in speeches limited to fifteen seconds?) In 1996, as American missiles bombed military sites in Iraq, President Clinton held a press conference to explain the action. His lengthy remarks were clipped to twenty seconds on one news broadcast, and then an anchorwoman digested the opposition to a single line: "Republicans tonight were critical of the president's actions." During the 2004 presidential election, both candidates sometimes deliberately packaged bad news so that it could not be distilled to a sound bite on the evening news — and thus would not make the evening news at all. Americans who rely on television for their news (two-thirds, according to recent polls) exist on a starvation diet.

Topic sentence: the claim

Evidence:
    Expert opinion

Facts and examples

Statistic

Writing in an Academic Discipline

Taken from a textbook on public relations, the following paragraph argues that lobbyists (who work to persuade public officials in behalf of a cause) are not slick manipulators but something else. The paragraph falls in the textbook's section on lobbying as a form of public relations, and its purpose is to correct a mistaken definition.

Although the public stereotypes a lobbyist as a fast-talking person twisting an elected official's arm to get special concessions, the reality is quite different. Today's lobbyist, who may be fully employed by one industry or represent a variety of clients, is often a quiet-spoken, well-educated man or woman armed with statistics and research reports. Robert Gray, former head of Hill and Knowlton's Washington office and a public affairs expert for thirty years, adds, "Lobbying is no longer a booze and buddies business. It's presenting honest facts and convincing Congress that your side has more merit than the other." He rejects lobbying as being simply "influence peddling and button-holing" top administration officials. Although the public has the perception that lobbying is done only by big business, Gray correctly points out that a variety of special interests also do it.

Topic sentence: the claim

Evidence:
    Expert opinion

These may include such groups as the Sierra Club, Mothers Against   *Facts and examples*
Drunk Driving, the National Association of Social Workers, the
American Civil Liberties Union, and the American Federation of
Labor. Even the American Society of Plastic and Reconstructive
Surgeons hired a Washington public relations firm in their battle
against restrictions on breast implants. Lobbying, quite literally, is
an activity in which widely diverse groups and organizations engage
as an exercise of free speech and representation in the marketplace
of ideas. Lobbyists often balance each other and work toward legislative compromises that not only benefit their self-interests but
society as a whole.

—Dennis L. Wilcox, Phillip H. Ault, and Warren K. Agee,
Public Relations: Strategies and Tactics

ARGUMENT AND PERSUASION IN PRACTICE

As a college freshman, Kristen Corcoran commuted to school at night. In
the following letter, she appealed to her college's president to have a parking
ticket canceled because legal parking was unavailable.

Corcoran's letter is a model of argument for a specific purpose, but it
didn't start out that way. In her much longer first draft, she let her anger push
her into detailing every one of her five previous parking difficulties and criticizing the president personally for not solving the problem. She did not get to
her request to have the ticket canceled until the very end.

Reviewing her draft, Corcoran realized that she was trying to negotiate
with the president, not tell her off, and for that a more direct, conciliatory
approach was needed. In the revision you see here, Corcoran focuses immediately on her purpose for writing, summarizes her problems with parking, and
takes the tack of informing, rather than criticizing, the president.

1073 Dogwood Terrace
North Andover, MA 01845
May 2, 2004

President Delores Reed
North State College
755 Little Road
Danvers, MA 01923

Dear President Reed:

I write to ask you to rescind a ten-dollar citation I received on April
4 for parking in North State's Lot E. I know that this lot is reserved
for faculty use, but flooding in three of the four commuter lots left

me with no reasonable parking alternatives. The campus police have not been able to help me, so I turn to you.

As you know, flooding is a recurring problem at North State, but perhaps you don't know how it affects commuting students. April 4 was one of six evenings this semester when I arrived to find Lots A, C, and D overrun by nearby marshes. On the other nights, Lot B filled quickly with cars and I was forced on two occasions to hunt for parking in the crowded residential areas off-campus. On April 4, I chose not to spend a half-hour finding a space and parked in Lot E. Many of its spaces are vacant at night when there are fewer classes and most campus offices are closed.

I understand from the campus police that North State has no plan for solving this seasonal problem. I, like hundreds of other commuter students, paid fifty dollars for a parking permit in the beginning of the semester and should be able to expect convenient parking like that described in North State's brochures. The parking problem is a serious one that affects not only commuters, who make up more than half of the student body, but also North State's neighbors, who are inconvenienced by crowds of cars monopolizing their streets each spring.

Please rescind my ticket and try to create some solutions to this problem. As a first step, may I suggest amending the school's parking policy to allow commuter use of Lot E in emergencies?

Sincerely,

Kristen Corcoran

Kristen Corcoran

COLLEEN WENKE

COLLEEN WENKE was born in 1979 and grew up in Queens, New York. After graduating from Boston College in 2001 with a degree in psychology, she moved back to New York City and took a job as a project coordinator at a real estate investment and development firm. She was recently promoted to project manager at the same firm and is currently pursuing an MA in real estate at New York University. An avid traveler, Wenke spent a semester at the University of New South Wales in Sydney, Australia, and she has taken trips to Europe and Southeast Asia. She is also an enthusiast of extreme sports, such as skydiving, rappelling, white-water rafting, and scuba diving.

Too Much Pressure

Why do students cheat in school? In this essay written when she was a college freshman, Wenke explores several reasons, finding one especially compelling. "Too Much Pressure" was published in the 1998 edition of *Fresh Ink*, a collection of work by students in Boston College's first-year writing course.

You hear the clock ticking in your head, and your teacher keeps erasing, in ten-minute decrements, the time you have left to complete the test. You do not remember anything from the last month of class. You probably should have studied more, watched less television, and spent less time on the phone. All the "should haves" are not important now. You need to finish the test and get out of here. The thought of a big fat F and a "See me" on the top of your midterm scares you. You remember the small piece of paper you have hidden in your pocket just in case. For a fleeting moment you think about what will happen if you are caught; then you slip the paper from your pocket onto the desktop. You transfer all the required information onto the test in time. You smile in anticipation of the A you are going to get. You think of how easy it was to cheat. All that matters is getting the grade.

Cheating is taking work done by somebody else, be it a friend or someone you do not know, and writing your name on it and saying it is your work. Any time I walked through my high school cafeteria or the hallways, I saw people cheating. It came in many forms, from copying homework to giving out copies of the exam. Students even wrote the answers to a Scantron exam down the sides of number-2 pencils and gave the pencils to their friends. My history teacher freshman year had a name for these students: "cafeteria scholars." These were the students who pulled 90s by knowing what the test questions were before they got to the classroom. Their friends who had taken the exam earlier in the day would tell them the questions and answers during lunch.

532

The teachers knew that these things went on, yet nobody seemed to do anything about them. I thought this was the way school went. The people who were cheating were doing the best in all of my classes. I would study for hours and still pull Bs. They would pull As.

I remember conversations over the dinner table with my parents on the subject of cheating. My parents were disgusted at the apathetic views my brothers and I held. We really didn't think it was a big deal to copy homework. I thought everyone cheated, probably even my parents and teachers when they were my age. But my parents swore that they had never cheated. Did I believe them? Not really. I thought that they were giving us the "it was so much better when we were growing up" speech.

I soon learned differently. In the article "When the Ends Justify the Means," written by Robin Stansbury, a reporter for the Connecticut newspaper *The Courant*, I found that my parents were telling the truth. Stansbury reports that "cheating in school has probably been around since the first exam was given." But he goes on to say, "State and national statistics show cheating among high-school students has risen dramatically during the past fifty years."[1] Reading this upset me and made me think about what had caused this increase. I hoped this was not a reflection of moral decline in the people who would soon be running my country. I blamed our school system for not instilling the proper values in its students. I figured that the dramatic change in the role of the family over the past generation, from two-parent homes with a working father and a mother who stayed at home and watched her children to families which have only a single parent or in which both parents work outside the home, meant schools needed to include moral standards in the curriculum. I believed schools were not fulfilling their role and therefore were producing students who do not know the difference between right and wrong.

An article written by Robert L. Maginnis, a policy analyst in the Cultural Studies Project at the Family Research Council, indicates my hypothesis had some truth to it. Maginnis states that "the erosion of values is traceable largely to changes in institutions which have traditionally been responsible for imparting them to our youth." He defines "these key institutions [to] include family, school, church, media and government." I agree with Maginnis, but I can't accept these factors as the only sources in the increase of cheating in the classroom. The facts seem contradictory. If my parents' generation had such high morals and wouldn't cheat, wouldn't they teach their children the same? My parents had taught me that cheating was wrong, yet I seemed to accept it.

---

[1] Wenke uses the MLA style of source citation, discussed on pages 56–67. Here and later, she does not provide parenthetical text citations because she names the authors in the text and because her sources — two Web documents and a television program — did not have numbered pages she could cite. — EDS.

There is a new "class" of cheaters today. In the past, as one would expect,   6
the students who cheated were the ones who could not pass or did not do the
work. They were the lazy students. But today the majority of the students who
admit to cheating are college-bound overachievers. The students who are trying to juggle too many activities are resorting to compromising their integrity
for a good grade. There is too much competition between students, which
leads to increased pressure to do well. Cheating becomes a way to get the edge
over the other students in the class. In addition, penalties for getting caught
are mild. If you were caught cheating at my high school, you received a zero
for the test. Your parents were not called, and you were not suspended. True,
a zero would hurt your grade severely if all grades for each quarter counted.
But there was a loophole in the system: Each quarter the lowest grade was
dropped. If the zero grade was dropped, it made no difference; the average was
not affected. Students who cheated on all the tests but only got caught once
still received good grades.

A main difference between school today and school when my parents   7
were enrolled is that we are now very goal-oriented and will compromise our
values to achieve these goals. Stansbury sees this compromise of values and
reports in his article that "cheating is a daily occurrence in high school. . . .
What this says is that many of our students today do not have much internal
integrity." Stansbury argues that students "want a goal, and how to get the
goal is somewhat irrelevant." Today there is more pressure placed on students
to do well. They are expected to receive good grades, play a sport, and volunteer if they are to be looked at by a good college. With a B tainting your tran-
script, a college might not look at you. This new pressure is what is causing the
increase in cheating. Maginnis agrees with Stansbury and goes further, reporting, "A national survey found a shift in motivation away from altruism and
toward concern with making money and getting power and status." Like
Stansbury, Maginnis says that "students are finding it easier to rationalize lying
or cheating in pursuit of their goals." And what goals are these students pursuing? They want the best grades so that they can get into the best schools and
get the highest-paying jobs. Starting in the classroom, we are sending the message that it is acceptable to cheat as long as you do not get caught and you do
the best.

Dean Morton, a broadcaster for *Good Morning America*, reported that   8
according to a national survey conducted in 1997 by *Who's Who in American
High School Students*, as many as 98 percent of students who participated in the
survey admitted to cheating. The segment of the show was even entitled
"Guess What? Cheaters Do Prosper." Like Stansbury and Maginnis, this survey also concluded that it is now the common belief among students that
cheaters are getting ahead in life. Stansbury interviewed several high-school

students in his article and discovered that many of them feel cheaters do get ahead in the classroom: "In high school, the cheaters always win. They don't get caught and they are the ones getting 100 on the exams when the noncheaters are getting 80s and 90s. Cheaters do win." We are sending a message to our youth that it is acceptable to cheat as long as you don't get caught and you are getting As. In this kind of society, morals take a back seat to how much you earn and how prosperous you are.

Students who would not usually cheat get sucked into believing it is the 9 only way to get ahead in school: If the cheaters are doing better than they are and not getting caught, then they had better try it. Stansbury proposes that there is such an enormous increase in cheating because more students are joining in: "They see others cheating and they think they are being unfairly disadvantaged." He adds that the "only way many of them feel they can keep in the game, to get into the right schools, is to cheat." In high school I always felt at a disadvantage, because everybody else was cheating and doing better than I was, even if only by a few points. My friends felt the same way, that copying work or cheating was the only way to keep up with the rest of the class. It frustrated me, because the cheaters were not earning their grades. But there were plenty of times when I was in a jam and copied homework from friends. Thinking about this now, I wonder what allowed me to push aside my conviction that cheating was wrong. I wasn't bringing in cheat sheets and didn't know the questions to tests before I got there, but I was cheating nonetheless.

How should we respond to the huge increase in cheating over the past 10 generation? We need to step back and look at the broader picture. We are creating a society in which people feel it is acceptable to cheat. This attitude will not stop in the classroom, but will carry on into the business world. Those who are cheating are the ones getting the grades and getting into the best schools. They are the "smart" ones. They in turn are the ones who will be running our country. They will become the heads of businesses and presidents of big corporations. Are these the people we want to have the power? In all likelihood they will not stop cheating once they get to the top. They become the people we idolize and aspire to be like. Because they are powerful, we consider them clever, highly respectable people. I do not hold any respect for a dishonest cheater. The phrase "honest businessman" will truly be an oxymoron. I am scared to think of the consequences of having cheaters rule our country. Is our society teaching that this is the only way to get ahead in life? Does obtaining status and power make you good? Schools are drifting away from emphasizing learning and are emphasizing the grade instead. When the thirst for knowledge is replenished in a student's mind, the desire for the grade without the work will dissolve. Only then will cheating decline.

Works Cited

Maginnis, Robert L. "Cheating Scandal Points to Moral Decline." Family Research Council, 1994. 3 May 1997 <http://www.frc.org/perspeceivelpv94dled.html>.

Morton, Dean. "Guess What? Cheaters Do Prosper." Good Morning America. ABC. WCVB, Boston. 16 Apr. 1997.

Stansbury, Robin. "Cheating in Connecticut's Classrooms: When the Ends Justify the Means." Hartford Courant 2 Mar. 1997. 2 May 1997 <http://www.ctnow.com/news/hc-specialUcheating/daY1.html>.

*For a reading quiz and annotated links to further readings on cheating in school, visit **bedfordstmartins.com/thebedfordreader**.*

Journal Writing

Do you agree with Wenke that most students think cheating is acceptable? In your journal, write down your views of how common cheating is in your school and what students' attitudes are toward it. (To take your journal writing further, see "From Journal to Essay" on the facing page.)

Questions on Meaning

1. What reasons does Wenke suggest for the increase in cheating among students?
2. What does Wenke see as a possible negative consequence of cheating among students today?
3. What solution does Wenke offer for the problem of student cheating?

Questions on Writing Strategy

1. How effective do you find Wenke's opening paragraph? What does it suggest to you about her intended AUDIENCE?
2. Wenke cites several outside sources in the course of her essay. What do these sources contribute to her argument?
3. What is the EFFECT of Wenke's admission that she herself copied homework from friends in high school (par. 9)? Does this admission add to or detract from Wenke's ethical appeal? Why?
4. **OTHER METHODS.** Wenke's argument is based largely on CAUSE AND EFFECT ANALYSIS. Does her analysis seem sound to you? Do you think she overemphasizes some causes or overlooks others? Explain.

Questions on Language

1. Find examples of COLLOQUIAL EXPRESSIONS in Wenke's essay. What is the effect of such language? Does it strike you as appropriate for her argument?
2. What does Wenke mean when she says, "The phrase 'honest businessman' will truly be an oxymoron" (par. 10)? What is an *oxymoron*?
3. Use a dictionary if necessary to help you define any of the following words: decrements (par. 1); apathetic (3); hypothesis (5); integrity (6); altruism, rationalize (7); replenished (10).

Suggestions for Writing

1. **FROM JOURNAL TO ESSAY.** Based on your journal entry, write an essay in which you analyze the problem of student cheating at your school. Who does it? Why? What do others think about it? What does the school do about it? If cheating is uncommon at your school, analyze why.
2. Wenke refers to the intense pressure students are under today to get good grades as well as to participate in sports and other extracurricular activities. Besides cheating, what are some other consequences of the pressure faced by contemporary students — including positive consequences, if you think there are any? Drawing on your own experiences as well as the experiences of people you know, write an essay about what happens to students when they feel they are under pressure to excel.
3. Wenke wrote her essay in 1998. Has the problem of student cheating improved or worsened since then? Research the problem in several studies published since 1998 — the more recent the better. Then write an essay in which you explain the current trend in cheating and what you think causes it.
4. **CRITICAL WRITING.** In an essay, EVALUATE Wenke's argument. How well does she convince you of the extent of the problem of student cheating and of its causes? How well do you think she develops her proposed solutions?
5. **CONNECTIONS.** In "The Ways We Lie" (p. 407), Stephanie Ericsson categorizes the kinds of lies people tell in everyday life. In what sense is cheating a form of lying? Which of Ericsson's categories might it belong to? On the scale of lying, how bad is cheating? Are cheaters likely to lie in other ways as well?

WILLIAM F. BUCKLEY, JR.

Born in New York in 1925, WILLIAM FRANK BUCKLEY, JR., is one of the most articulate proponents of American conservatism. Shortly after his graduation from Yale, he published *God and Man at Yale* (1951), a memoir espousing conservative political values and traditional Christian principles. Since then, he has written more than twenty works on politics and government, published a syndicated newspaper column, and founded and edited *The National Review*, a magazine of conservative opinion. His latest nonfiction books are *Miles Gone by: A Literary Autobiography* and *The Fall of the Berlin Wall* (both 2004). He has also written several books on sailing and more than fifteen novels, most recently *Getting It Right* (2004). In 1991 Buckley was awarded the Presidential Medal of Freedom. On *Firing Line*, a weekly television debate program that Buckley hosted from 1966 to 1999, he gained popular recognition as a man of wry charm. When he was half-seriously running for mayor of New York City in 1965, someone asked him what he would do if elected. "Demand a recount," he replied.

Why Don't We Complain?

Most people riding in an overheated commuter train would perspire quietly. For Buckley, this excess of warmth sparks an indignant essay, first published in *Esquire* in 1961, in which he takes to task both himself and his fellow Americans. Does the essay appeal mainly to reason or to emotion? And what would happen if everyone were to do as Buckley urges?

It was the very last coach and the only empty seat on the entire train, so there was no turning back. The problem was to breathe. Outside, the temperature was below freezing. Inside the railroad car the temperature must have been about 85 degrees. I took off my overcoat, and a few minutes later my jacket, and noticed that the car was flecked with the white shirts of the passengers. I soon found my hand moving to loosen my tie. From one end of the car to the other, as we rattled through Westchester County, we sweated; but we did not moan.

I watched the train conductor appear at the head of the car. "Tickets, all tickets, please!" In a more virile age, I thought, the passengers would seize the conductor and strap him down on a seat over the radiator to share the fate of his patrons. He shuffled down the aisle, picking up tickets, punching commutation cards. *No one addressed a word to him.* He approached my seat, and I drew a deep breath of resolution. "Conductor," I began with a considerable edge to my voice. Instantly the doleful eyes of my seatmate turned tiredly from his newspaper to fix me with a resentful stare: What question could be so important as to justify my sibilant intrusion into his stupor? I was shaken by those eyes. I am incapable of making a discreet fuss, so I mumbled a question about what time we were due in Stamford (I didn't even ask whether it would be before or after dehydration could be expected to set in), got my reply, and went back to my newspaper and to wiping my brow.

The conductor had nonchalantly walked down the gauntlet of eighty sweating American freemen, and not one of them had asked him to explain why the passengers in that car had been consigned to suffer. There is nothing to be done when the temperature *outdoors* is 85 degrees, and indoors the air conditioner has broken down; obviously when that happens there is nothing to do, except perhaps curse the day that one was born. But when the temperature outdoors is below freezing, it takes a positive act of will on somebody's part to set the temperature *indoors* at 85. Somewhere a valve was turned too far, a furnace overstocked, a thermostat maladjusted: something that could easily be remedied by turning off the heat and allowing the great outdoors to come indoors. All this is so obvious. What is not obvious is what has happened to the American people.

It isn't just the commuters, whom we have come to visualize as a supine breed who have got on to the trick of suspending their sensory faculties twice a day while they submit to the creeping dissolution of the railroad industry. It isn't just they who have given up trying to rectify irrational vexations. It is the American people everywhere.

A few weeks ago at a large movie theater I turned to my wife and said, "The picture is out of focus." "Be quiet," she answered. I obeyed. But a few minutes later I raised the point again, with mounting impatience. "It will be all right in a minute," she said apprehensively. (She would rather lose her eyesight than be around when I make one of my infrequent scenes.) I waited. It was *just* out of focus—not glaringly out, but out. My vision is 20-20, and I assume that is the vision, adjusted, for most people in the movie house. So, after hectoring my wife throughout the first reel, I finally prevailed upon her to admit that it *was* off, and very annoying. We then settled down, coming to rest on the presumption that: a) someone connected with the management of the theater must soon notice the blur and make the correction; or b) that someone seated near the rear of the house would make the complaint in behalf of those of us up front; or c) that—any minute now—the entire house would explode into catcalls and foot stamping, calling dramatic attention to the irksome distortion.

What happened was nothing. The movie ended, as it had begun, *just* out of focus, and as we trooped out, we stretched our faces in a variety of contortions to accustom the eye to the shock of normal focus.

I think it is safe to say that everybody suffered on that occasion. And I   7
think it is safe to assume that everyone was expecting someone else to take the
initiative in going back to speak to the manager. And it is probably true even
that if we had supposed the movie would run right through the blurred image,
someone surely would have summoned up the purposive indignation to get up
out of his seat and file his complaint.

But notice that no one did. And the reason no one did is because we are   8
all increasingly anxious in America to be unobtrusive, we are reluctant to
make our voices heard, hesitant about claiming our rights; we are afraid that
our cause is unjust, or that if it is not unjust, that it is ambiguous; or if not even
that, that it is too trivial to justify the horrors of a confrontation with Authority; we will sit in an oven or endure a racking headache before undertaking a
head-on, I'm-here-to-tell-you complaint. That tendency to passive compliance,
to a heedless endurance, is something to keep one's eyes on — in sharp focus.

I myself can occasionally summon the courage to complain, but I cannot,   9
as I have intimated, complain softly. My own instinct is so strong to let the
thing ride, to forget about it — to expect that someone will take the matter up,
when the grievance is collective, in my behalf — that it is only when the
provocation is at a very special key, whose vibrations touch simultaneously a
complexus of nerves, allergies, and passions, that I catch fire and find the
reserves of courage and assertiveness to speak up. When that happens, I get
quite carried away. My blood gets hot, my brow wet, I become unbearably and
unconscionably sarcastic and bellicose; I am girded for a total showdown.

Why should that be? Why could not I (or anyone else) on that railroad   10
coach have said simply to the conductor, "Sir" — I take that back: that sounds
sarcastic — "Conductor, would you be good enough to turn down the heat?
I am extremely hot. In fact, I tend to get hot every time the temperature
reaches 85 degr—." Strike that last sentence. Just end it with the simple
statement that you are extremely hot, and let the conductor infer the cause.

Every New Year's Eve I resolve to do something about the Milquetoast in   11
me and vow to speak up, calmly, for my rights, and for the betterment of our
society, on every appropriate occasion. Entering last New Year's Eve I was fortified in my resolve because that morning at breakfast I had had to ask the
waitress three times for a glass of milk. She finally brought it — after I had finished my eggs, which is when I don't want it anymore. I did not have the man-
liness to order her to take the milk back, but settled instead for a cowardly
sulk, and ostentatiously refused to drink the milk — though I later paid for
it — rather than state plainly to the hostess, as I should have, why I had not
drunk it, and would not pay for it.

So by the time the New Year ushered out the Old, riding in on my morn-   12
ing's indignation and stimulated by the gastric juices of resolution that flow so

faithfully on New Year's Eve, I rendered my vow. Henceforward I would con-
quer my shyness, my despicable disposition to supineness. I would speak out
like a man against the unnecessary annoyances of our time.

Forty-eight hours later, I was standing in line at the ski repair store in Pico   13
Peak, Vermont. All I needed, to get on with my skiing, was the loan, for one
minute, of a small screwdriver, to tighten a loose binding. Behind the counter
in the workshop were two men. One was industriously engaged in servicing
the complicated requirements of a young lady at the head of the line, and
obviously he would be tied up for quite a while. The other—"Jiggs," his work-
mate called him—was a middle-aged man, who sat in a chair puffing a pipe,
exchanging small talk with his working partner. My pulse began its telltale
acceleration. The minutes ticked on. I stared at the idle shopkeeper, hoping to
shame him into action, but he was impervious to my telepathic reproof and
continued his small talk with his friend, brazenly insensitive to the nervous
demands of six good men who were raring to ski.

Suddenly my New Year's Eve resolution struck me. It was now or never.   14
I broke from my place in line and marched to the counter. I was going to control
myself. I dug my nails into my palms. My effort was only partially successful.

"If you are not too busy," I said icily, "would you mind handing me a screw-   15
driver?"

Work stopped and everyone turned his eyes on me, and I experienced that   16
mortification I always feel when I am the center of centripetal shafts of curiosity, resentment, perplexity.

But the worst was yet to come. "I am sorry, sir," said Jiggs deferentially,   17
moving the pipe from his mouth. "I am not supposed to move. I have just
had a heart attack." That was the signal for a great whirring noise that de-
scended from heaven. We looked, stricken, out the window, and it appeared
as though a cyclone had suddenly focused on the snowy courtyard between
the shop and the ski lift. Suddenly a gigantic army helicopter materialized,
and hovered down to a landing. Two men jumped out of the plane carrying a
stretcher, tore into the ski shop, and lifted the shopkeeper onto the stretcher.
Jiggs bade his companion good-bye and was whisked out the door, into the
plane, up to the heavens, down—we learned—to a nearby army hospital. I
looked up manfully—into a score of man-eating eyes. I put the experience
down as a reversal.

As I write this, on an airplane, I have run out of paper and need to reach   18
into my briefcase under my legs for more. I cannot do this until my empty
lunch tray is removed from my lap. I arrested the stewardess as she passed
empty-handed down the aisle on the way to the kitchen to fetch the lunch
trays for the passengers up forward who haven't been served yet. "Would you
please take my tray?" "Just a *moment*, sir!" she said, and marched on sternly.

Shall I tell her that since she is headed for the kitchen *anyway*, it could not delay the feeding of the other passengers by more than two seconds necessary to stash away my empty tray? Or remind her that not fifteen minutes ago she spoke unctuously into the loudspeaker the words undoubtedly devised by the airline's highly paid public relations counselor: "If there is anything I or Miss French can do for you to make your trip more enjoyable, *please* let us—" I have run out of paper.

I think the observable reluctance of the majority of Americans to assert   19
themselves in minor matters is related to our increased sense of helplessness in an age of technology and centralized political and economic power. For generations, Americans who were too hot, or too cold, got up and did something about it. Now we call the plumber, or the electrician, or the furnace man. The habit of looking after our own needs obviously had something to do with the assertiveness that characterized the American family familiar to readers of American literature. With the technification of life goes our direct responsibility for our material environment, and we are conditioned to adopt a position of helplessness not only as regards the broken air conditioner, but as regards the overheated train. It takes an expert to fix the former, but not the latter; yet these distinctions, as we withdraw into helplessness, tend to fade away.

Our notorious political apathy is a related phenomenon. Every year,   20
whether the Republican or the Democratic Party is in office, more and more power drains away from the individual to feed vast reservoirs in far-off places; and we have less and less say about the shape of events which shape our future. From this alienation of personal power comes the sense of resignation with which we accept the political dispensations of a powerful government whose hold upon us continues to increase.

An editor of a national weekly news magazine told me a few years ago that   21
as few as a dozen letters of protest against an editorial stance of his magazine was enough to convene a plenipotentiary meeting of the board of editors to review policy. "So few people complain, or make their voices heard," he explained to me, "that we assume a dozen letters represent the inarticulated views of thousands of readers." In the past ten years, he said, the volume of mail has noticeably decreased, even though the circulation of his magazine has risen.

When our voices are finally mute, when we have finally suppressed the   22
natural instinct to complain, whether the vexation is trivial or grave, we shall have become automatons, incapable of feeling. When Premier Khrushchev[1] first came to this country late in 1959 he was primed, we are informed, to experience the bitter resentment of the American people against his tyranny,

---

[1] Nikita Khrushchev (1894–1971) was premier of the former Soviet Union from 1958 to 1964. —EDS.

against his persecutions, against the movement which is responsible for the great number of American deaths in Korea, for billions in taxes every year, and for life everlasting on the brink of disaster; but Khrushchev was pleasantly surprised, and reported back to the Russian people that he had been met with overwhelming cordiality (read: apathy), except, to be sure, for "a few fascists who followed me around with their wretched posters, and should be horse-whipped."

I may be crazy, but I say there would have been lots more posters in a society where train temperatures in the dead of winter are not allowed to climb to 85 degrees without complaint.   23

For a reading quiz, sources on William F. Buckley, Jr., and annotated links to further readings on apathy, visit **bedfordstmartins.com/thebedfordreader**.

Journal Writing

One reason we don't complain, according to Buckley, is that we expect someone else to do so for us. Do you agree? Do you ever "take the initiative" (par. 7) to complain about big or little hassles, or do you too sit in silent annoyance? Answer in your journal, explaining why. (To take your journal writing further, see "From Journal to Essay" on the next page.)

Questions on Meaning

1. How does Buckley account for his failure to complain to the train conductor? What reasons does he give for not taking action when he notices that the movie he is watching is out of focus?
2. Where does Buckley finally place the blame for the average American's reluctance to try to "rectify irrational vexations"?
3. By what means does the author bring his argument around to the subject of political apathy?
4. What THESIS does Buckley attempt to support? What is his PURPOSE?

Questions on Writing Strategy

1. In taking to task not only his fellow Americans but also himself, does Buckley strengthen or weaken his charge that, as a people, Americans do not complain enough?

2. Judging from the vocabulary displayed in this essay, would you say that Buckley is writing for a highly specialized AUDIENCE or an educated but nonspecialized general audience?
3. As a whole, is Buckley's essay an example of appeal to emotion or reasoned argument or both? Give EVIDENCE for your answer.
4. **OTHER METHODS.** Buckley includes as evidence four NARRATIVES of his personal experiences. What is the point of the narrative about Jiggs (pars. 13–17)?

Questions on Language

1. Define the following words: virile, doleful, sibilant (par. 2); supine (4); hectoring (5); unobtrusive, ambiguous (8); intimated, unconscionably, bellicose (9); ostentatiously (11); despicable (12); impervious (13); mortification, centripetal (16); deferentially (17); unctuously (18); notorious, dispensations (20); plenipotentiary, inarticulated (21); automatons (22).
2. What does Buckley's use of the capital A in *Authority* (par. 8) contribute to the sentence in which he uses it?
3. What is Buckley talking about when he alludes to "the Milquetoast in me" (par. 11)? (Notice how well the ALLUSION fits into the paragraph, with its emphasis on breakfast and a glass of milk.)

Suggestions for Writing

1. **FROM JOURNAL TO ESSAY.** Write an essay about one moment when you either spoke up against an annoyance or didn't complain when you should have. Narrate this incident, also using the information from your journal entry to help explain why you did or did not act.
2. Think of some disturbing incident you have witnessed, or some annoying treatment you have received in a store or other public place, and write a letter of complaint to whomever you believe responsible. Be specific in your evidence, be temperate in your language, make clear what you would like to come of your complaint (your proposal), and be sure to put your letter in the mail.
3. **CRITICAL WRITING.** Write a paper in which you ANALYZE and EVALUATE any one of Buckley's ideas. For instance: Do we feel as helpless as Buckley says (par. 19)? Are we politically apathetic, and if so should the government be blamed (par. 20)? For that matter, do we not complain? Support your view with evidence from your experience, observation, or reading.
4. **CONNECTIONS.** Both Buckley and Viet D. Dinh, in "How the USA Patriot Act Defends Democracy" (p. 585), make a strong ETHICAL APPEAL (see p. 519), going out of their way to convince readers of their goodwill, reasonableness, and authority. Write an essay in which you analyze the ethical appeal of both authors, using quotations and PARAPHRASES from both essays to support your analysis.

William F. Buckley, Jr., on Writing

In the autobiographical *Overdrive*, Buckley recalls a conversation with a friend and fellow columnist: "George Will once told me how deeply he loves to write. 'I wake in the morning,' he explained to me, 'and I ask myself: Is this one of the days I have to write a column? And if the answer is yes, I rise a happy man.' I, on the other hand, wake neither particularly happy nor unhappy, but to the extent that my mood is affected by the question whether I need to write a column that morning, the impact of Monday-Wednesday-Friday"—the days when he must write a newspaper column—"is definitely negative. Because I do not like to write, for the simple reason that writing is extremely hard work, and I do not 'like' extremely hard work."

Still, in the course of a "typical year," Buckley produces scores of newspaper columns, longer articles, and speeches, as well as a book or two. "Why do I do so much? . . . It is easier to stay up late working for hours than to take one tenth the time to inquire into the question whether the work is worth performing."

In the introduction to another book, A *Hymnal: The Controversial Arts*, Buckley states an attitude toward writing that most other writers would not share. "I have discovered, in sixteen years of writing columns," he declares, "that there is no observable difference in the quality of that which is written at very great speed (twenty minutes, say), and that which takes three or four times as long. . . . Pieces that take longer to write sometimes, on revisiting them, move along grumpily."

For Discussion

1. Given that he so dislikes writing, why does Buckley do it?
2. Buckley's attitude toward giving time to writing is unusual. What is the more usual view of writing?

LAURA FRASER

LAURA FRASER was born in 1961 in Denver, Colorado. Since graduating from Wesleyan University (BA, 1982), she has been a freelance writer whose work has appeared in numerous publications, including *Glamour*, *Vogue*, and *Mother Jones*. A recovered bulimic, Fraser was motivated to write her first book after struggling for many years with her weight. In that book, *Losing It: False Hopes and Fat Profits in the Diet Industry* (1997), Fraser investigates America's obsession with thinness and the businesses that cater to it. Fraser's latest book is *An Italian Affair* (2001), a travelog and memoir of an intermittent two-year romance. She has taught magazine writing at the University of California at Berkeley and currently lives in San Francisco.

Why I Stopped Being a Vegetarian

As its title indicates, Fraser's essay is part explanation — a funny and self-revealing one at that — but it also offers an argument both for and ultimately against vegetarianism. The essay was published in the January 7, 2000, issue of the online magazine *Salon*. For a view opposing Fraser's, see the next essay, Peter Singer's "A Vegetarian Philosophy" (p. 552).

Until a few months ago, I had been a vegetarian for fifteen years. Like 1 most people who call themselves vegetarians (somewhere between 4 and 10 percent of us, depending on the definition; only 1 percent of Americans are vegans, eating no animal products at all), I wasn't strict about it. I ate dairy products and eggs as well as fish. That made me a pesco-ovo-lacto-vegetarian, which isn't a category you can choose for special meals on airlines.

About a year ago, in Italy, it dawned on me that a little pancetta was 2 really good in pasta, too. After failing to convince myself that pancetta was a vegetable, I became a pesco-ovo-lacto-pancetta-vegetarian, with a "Don't Ask, Don't Tell" policy about chicken broth. It was a slippery slope from there.

Nevertheless, for most of those fifteen years, hardly a piece of animal flesh 3 crossed my lips. Over the course of that time, many people asked me why I became a vegetarian. I came up with vague answers: my health, the environment, the impracticality and heartlessness of killing animals for food when we can survive perfectly well on soy burgers. It was political, it was emotional and it made me special, not to mention slightly morally superior to all those blood-thirsty carnivores out there.

The truth is, I became a vegetarian in college for two reasons. One was   4
that meat was more expensive than lentils, and I was broke, or broke enough
to choose to spend my limited budget on other classes of ingestibles. The
other was that I was not a lesbian.

This is not to say that all lesbians are carnivores; in fact, there's probably   5
a higher percentage of vegetarians among lesbians than most other groups.
But there was a fair amount of political pressure to be something in those days.
Since, as a privileged white girl from suburban Denver, I couldn't really identify with any oppressed minority group, I was faced with becoming a lesbian in
order to prove my political mettle. I had to decide between meat and men,
and for better or worse, I became a vegetarian.

The identity stuck, even though the political imperative for my label   6
faded. It wasn't an identity that ever really fit: My friends thought it odd that
such an otherwise hedonistic woman should have that one ascetic streak. It
was against my nature, they said. But by then, I'd started to believe the other
arguments about vegetarianism.

First was health. There's a lot of evidence that vegetarians live longer,   7
have lower cholesterol levels and are thinner than meat eaters. This is somewhat hard to believe, since for the first few years of not eating meat, I was basically a cheesetarian. Try leafing through some of those vegetarian recipe books
from the early '80s: You added three cups of grated cheddar to everything but
the granola. Then vegetarianism went through that mathematical phase
where you had to figure out which proteins you had to combine with which in
order to get a complete protein. Since many nutritionists will tell you people
don't need that much protein anyway, I gave up, going for days and days without so much as contemplating beans or tofu.

For whatever haphazard combination of proteins I ate, being a vegetarian   8
did seem to have a stunning effect on my cholesterol level. This, of course,
could be genetic. But when I had a very involved physical exam once at the
Cooper Institute for Aerobic Fitness in Dallas, my total cholesterol level was
a super-low 135, and my ratio of HDL (good) cholesterol to LDL (evil) was so
impressive that the doctor drawled, "Even if you had heart disease, you would
be reversing it." This good news, far from reassuring me that I could well afford
a few barbecued ribs now and then, spurred me on in my vegetarianism,
mainly because my cholesterol numbers effectively inoculated me against the
doctor's advice that I also needed to lose fifteen pounds.

"Why?" I asked. "Don't you lose weight to lower your cholesterol?"   9

He couldn't argue with that. Whether or not most vegetarians are leaner   10
than carnivores, in my case I was happy to more than make up the calories
with carbohydrates, which, perhaps not coincidentally, I always craved.

After the health rationale came the animal rights one. Like most vegetar-   11 ians, I cracked Peter Singer's philosophical treatise on animal rights, and bought his utilitarian line that if you don't have to kill animals, and it potentially causes suffering, you shouldn't do it.[1] (Singer, now at Princeton, has recently come under attack for saying that if a human being's incapacitated life causes more suffering than good, it is OK to kill him.)

It's hard to know where to stop with utilitarianism. Do I need a cashmere   12
sweater more than those little shorn goats need to be warm themselves? Do animals really suffer if they have happy, frolicking lives before a quick and painless end? Won't free-range[2] do?

My animal rights philosophy had a lot of holes from the start. First of all,   13
I excluded fish from the animal kingdom—not only because fish taste delicious grilled with a little butter and garlic, but also because they make it a lot easier to be a vegetarian when you go out to restaurants. Now that's utilitarian. Besides, as soon as you start spending your time fretting about the arguments that crowd the inner pens of animal rights philosophy—do fish think?—then you know you're experiencing a real protein deficiency.

I rationalized the fish thing by telling myself I would eat anything I would   14
kill myself. I had been fly-fishing with my dad and figured a few seconds of flopping around was outweighed by the merits of trout almondine. (Notice that I, not the fish, was doing the figuring.) But who was I kidding? If I were hungry enough, I'd kill a cow in a heartbeat. I'd practically kill a cow just for a great pair of shoes.

Which brings me to the leather exception. As long as other people are   15
eating cow, I decided, I might as well recycle the byproducts and diminish the harm by wearing leather jackets and shoes. When everyone stopped eating meat, I'd stop buying leather jackets and shoes. In the meantime, better stock up.

Then there's the environmental rationale. There is no doubt, as Frances   16
Moore Lappe first pointed out in her 1971 book *Food First*, that there is a huge loss of protein resources going from grain to meat, and that some animals, especially cattle and Americans, use up piggish amounts of water, grain and crop land.

But the problem really isn't meat, but too much meat—overgrazing, over-   17
fishing and overconsumption. If Americans just ate less meat—like driving cars less often—the problem could be alleviated without giving up meat entirely. That approach has worked for centuries, and continues to work in Europe.

---

[1] See page 552 for a biography of Singer. His book on animal rights is *Animal Liberation* (1975). *Utilitarianism*, as he defines it, is a standard that "judges whether acts are right or wrong by their consequences."—EDS.

[2] Free-range animals are not penned up in a small space but are allowed to move about freely in ample space.—EDS.

All my deep vegetarian questioning was silenced one day when a friend   18
ordered roasted rosemary chicken for two. I thought I'd try "just a bite," and
then I was ripping into it like a starving hyena. Roasted chicken, I realized, is
wonderful. Meat is good.

From a culinary point of view, that's obvious. Consider that most vegetar-   19
ians live in America and England, places tourists do not visit for the food. You
don't find vegetarians in France, and rarely in Italy. Enough said.

As for health, if nutritionists are always telling you to "listen to your   20
body," mine was definitely shouting for more meat. One roasted bird unleashed
fifteen years' worth of cravings. All of a sudden I felt like I had a bass note
playing in my body to balance out all those soprano carbohydrates. Forget
about winning the low-cholesterol Olympics. For the first time in a long time,
I felt satisfied.

As a vegetarian, not only had I denied myself something I truly enjoyed, I   21
had been antisocial. How many times had I made a hostess uncomfortable by
refusing the main course at a dinner party, lamely saying I'd "eat around it"?
How often did my vegetarianism cause other people to go to extra trouble to
make something special for me to eat, and why did it never occur to me that
that was selfish? How about the time, in a small town in Italy, when the chef
had presented me with a plate of very special local sausage, since I was the
American guest — and I had refused it, to the mortification of my Italian
friends? Or when a then-boyfriend, standing in the meat section of the grocery
store, forlornly told a friend, "If only I had a girlfriend who ate meat"? If eating is a socially conscious act, you have to be conscious of the society of your
fellow *Homo sapiens* along with the animals. And we humans, as it happens,
are omnivores.

---

*For a reading quiz, sources on Laura Fraser, and annotated links to further readings
on vegetarianism, visit **bedfordstmartins.com/thebedfordreader**.*

Journal Writing

In her conclusion Fraser says that her refusal to eat meat was sometimes rude and even
selfish. Do you agree? In your journal, write about a time when you may have behaved
rudely or selfishly — or maybe just coolly — because you were upholding a personal
principle such as never lying or never cheating or, for that matter, never eating meat.
(To take your journal writing further, see "From Journal to Essay" on the next page.)

Questions on Meaning

1. Fraser offers three general arguments for not eating meat. What are they? How does she question the validity of these arguments?
2. What, for Fraser, are the strongest arguments in favor of eating meat, at least occasionally? How do they relate to her THESIS?
3. What is Fraser's apparent PURPOSE here? What makes you think so?

Questions on Writing Strategy

1. Fraser focuses almost exclusively on herself in this essay. How does she expand on her own experiences to apply her argument to vegetarians more generally? Does her largely personal approach damage her argument? Why, or why not?
2. How would you describe Fraser's TONE in this essay? What is its EFFECT on you as a reader?
3. **OTHER METHODS.** In what sense is Fraser's essay an argument based on EXAMPLE?

Questions on Language

1. In paragraph 2 Fraser writes that she "became a pesco-ovo-lacto-pancetta-vegetarian, with a 'Don't Ask, Don't Tell' policy about chicken broth." What points is she making in this sentence?
2. What is the effect of Fraser calling herself a "cheesetarian" in paragraph 7?
3. How does Fraser use the word *inoculated* in paragraph 8 for comic effect? How about the word *recycle* in paragraph 15?
4. Be sure that you know the meaning of the following words, checking a dictionary if necessary: pancetta (par. 2); carnivores (3); ingestibles (4); mettle (5); imperative, hedonistic, ascetic (6); cholesterol, tofu (7); carbohydrates (10); incapacitated (11); frolicking (12); deficiency (13); rationalized, almondine (14); alleviated (17); culinary (19); mortification, forlornly, *Homo sapiens*, omnivores (21).

Suggestions for Writing

1. **FROM JOURNAL TO ESSAY.** Picking up from your journal writing, explain when, if ever, your principles should be compromised in order to accommodate the feelings of others. For example, if you believe in always telling the truth, are there still times when it is better to lie? Or does the principle of telling the truth always outweigh other concerns? Use specific examples to develop your thesis.
2. Fraser refers to the argument based on animal rights as a rationale for not eating meat. Do you think animals have rights that are abused for the sake of human self-interest? Or do you believe that human self-interest generally takes precedence? In an essay, argue for or against the idea of animal rights. You might consider issues such as experimenting on animals to test potentially life-saving medical procedures, protecting endangered species to the detriment of economic interests, and capturing and confining wild animals for people to observe in zoos.

3. **CRITICAL WRITING.** ANALYZE Fraser's use of humor in this essay. Do you think the humor contributes positively to her argument, or does it undercut the points she is trying to make? Cite specific passages to support your view.
4. **CONNECTIONS.** In the next essay Peter Singer argues in favor of vegetarianism. Write an essay in which you consider how Fraser and Singer might respond to each other. To what extent do the authors address each other's arguments? What if any holes would either identify in the other's essay? To what extent do the authors' different purposes explain the differences in their arguments?

Laura Fraser on Writing

Since publishing *An Italian Affair* about a romantic relationship she was involved in, Laura Fraser has often been asked, "How could you write something so personal?" She answers in "On Writing a Book About One's Personal Life," an essay appearing in the online magazine *Bold Type*. "*An Italian Affair* began simply as something I wrote for myself, for my journal," Fraser writes. "I've always kept a journal, to blow off steam, tell my secrets, sort through personal conundrums, and to try to get to the heart of matters I'm muddling through in my ever-vexing romantic life. I've always thought it was a little strange, and even sad, that for the most part, I've considered the writing I've done for myself to be better than the writing I've done for magazines, where often you can't use your true voice — or heart. In my journal, I write with a stripped-down emotionalism that isn't very useful in the world of investigative journalism."

When she wrote of her Italian experience in her journal, Fraser realized that she had "what writers are always looking for, and rarely stumble across — a story." She started publishing short pieces about the experience in *Salon* and eventually turned the pieces into a full-length book. She was nervous about publishing such personal work, but, she says, "I was having fun — for the first time, publishing stories in my real, formerly secret journal voice."

For Discussion

1. How would you define VOICE in writing? (If you need help, see the definition in Useful Terms.)
2. How has Fraser's journal writing differed from her writing as an investigative journalist?
3. How is your writing for yourself different from your writing for others, such as in papers for your courses? How does knowing that you will have an AUDIENCE affect your voice?

PETER SINGER

The philosopher PETER SINGER is both greatly influential and hotly controversial. He was born in 1946 in Melbourne, Australia, and received degrees
from the University of Melbourne (BA, 1967; MA, 1969) and Oxford University (B.Phil., 1971). He has taught philosophy at a number of schools, and
in 1999 he became a professor of bioethics at Princeton University. Singer's
philosophy "is shaped," he says, "by an abhorrence of suffering and cruelty."
His book *Animal Liberation* (1975) helped found the modern animal-rights
movement and gained Singer international attention. In the book Singer
argues against human cruelty to other animals and even against humans having any better claim to life than other animals. As Singer has put it elsewhere, "A human being doesn't have value just by virtue of being a human."
Singer has written many other controversial books and essays in which he
applies severe reason — some say inhumane coldness — to euthanasia, test-
tube babies, cloning, genetic engineering, and other ethical dilemmas. His
works include *Practical Ethics* (1979), *Should the Baby Live? The Problem of
Handicapped Infants* (1985), *Rethinking Life and Death* (1995), *One World:
Ethics of Globalization* (2002), and *Pushing Time Away: My Grandfather and
the Tragedy of Jewish Vienna* (2003).

A Vegetarian Philosophy

In this essay Singer takes on the Big Mac, arguing against the factory farms
that produce it and against meat eating in general. The essay appeared in
Singer's collection *Writings on an Ethical Life* (2000). It is based on a longer
version that he wrote for *Consuming Passions: Food in the Age of Anxiety*
(1988), various authors' takes on our eating habits. For a different view of
vegetarianism, see the preceding essay by Laura Fraser (p. 546).

Issues regarding eating meat were highlighted in 1997 by the longest trial 1
in British legal history. *McDonald's Corporation and McDonald's Restaurants
Limited v. Steel and Morris*, better known as the "McLibel" trial, ran for 313
days and heard 180 witnesses. In suing Helen Steel and David Morris, two
activists involved with the London Greenpeace organization, McDonald's put
on trial the way in which its fast-food products are produced, packaged, advertised, and sold, as well as their nutritional value, the environmental impact of
producing them, and the treatment of the animals whose flesh and eggs are
made into that food. . . .

The case provided a remarkable opportunity for weighing up evidence for 2
and against modern agribusiness methods. The leaflet "What's Wrong with
McDonald's" that provoked the defamation suit had a row of McDonald's
arches along the top of each page. Two of these arches bore the words
"McMurder" and "McTorture." One section below was headed "In what way
are McDonald's responsible for torture and murder?" The leaflet answered the
question as follows:

> The menu at McDonald's is based on meat. They sell millions of burgers
> every day in thirty-five countries throughout the world. This means the con-
> stant slaughter, day by day, of animals born and bred solely to be turned into
> McDonald's products. Some of them—especially chickens and pigs—spend
> their lives in the entirely artificial conditions of huge factory farms, with no
> access to air or sunshine and no freedom of movement. Their deaths are
> bloody and barbaric.

McDonald's claimed that the leaflet meant that the company was respon- 3
sible for the inhumane torture and murder of cattle, chickens, and pigs, and
that this was defamatory. In considering this claim, Mr. Justice Bell based his
judgment on what he took to be attitudes that were generally accepted in
Britain. Thus for the epithet "McTorture" to be justified, he held, it would not
be enough for Steel and Morris to show that animals were under stress or suffered some pain or discomfort:

> Merely containing, handling, and transporting an animal may cause it stress;
> and taking it to slaughter certainly may do so. But I do not believe that
> the ordinary reasonable person believes any of these things to be cruel, pro-
> vided that the necessary stress, or discomfort or even pain is kept to a rea-
> sonably acceptable level. That ordinary person may know little about the
> detail of farming and slaughtering methods but he must find a certain
> amount of stress, discomfort, or even pain acceptable and not to be criticised
> as cruel.

By the end of the trial, however, Mr. Justice Bell found that the stress, dis- 4
comfort, and pain inflicted on some animals amounted to more than this
acceptable level, and hence did constitute a "cruel practice" for which
McDonald's was "culpably responsible." Chickens, laying hens, and sows, he
said, kept in individual stalls suffered from "severe restriction of movement"
which "is cruel." He also found a number of other cruel practices in the production of chickens, including the restricted diet fed to breeding birds, which
leaves them permanently hungry; the injuries inflicted on chickens by catch-
ers stuffing 600 birds an hour into crates to take them to slaughter; and the
failure of the stunning apparatus to ensure that all birds are stunned before
they have their throats cut. Judging by entirely conventional moral standards,

Mr. Justice Bell held these practices to be cruel, and McDonald's to be culpably responsible for them.

It was not libelous to describe McDonald's as "McTorture," because the   5
charge was substantially true. What follows from this judgment about the
morality of buying and eating intensively raised chickens, pig products that
come from the offspring of sows kept in stalls, or eggs laid by hens kept in battery cages? Surely that, too, must be wrong?

This claim has been challenged. At a conference dinner some years ago I   6
found myself sitting opposite a Buddhist philosopher from Thailand. As we
helped ourselves to the lavish buffet, I avoided the various forms of meat being
offered, but the Thai philosopher did not. When I asked him how he reconciled the dinner he had chosen with the first precept of Buddhism, which tells
us to avoid harming sentient beings, he told me that in the Buddhist tradition
it is wrong to eat meat only if you have reason to believe that the animal was
killed specially for you. The meat he had taken, however, was not from animals killed specially for him; the animals would have died anyway, even if he
were a strict vegetarian or had not been in that city at all. Hence, by eating it,
he was not harming any animals.

I was unable to convince my dinner companion that this defense of meat   7
eating was better suited to a time when a peasant family might kill an animal especially to have something to put in the begging bowl of a wandering monk than it is to our own era. The flaw in the defense is the disregard
of the link between the meat I eat today and the future killing of animals.
Granted, the chicken lying in the supermarket freezer today would have died
even if I had never existed; but the fact that I take the chicken from the
freezer, and ignore the tofu on a nearby shelf, has something to do with the
number of chickens, or blocks of tofu, the supermarket will order next week
and thus contributes, in a small way, to the future growth or decline of the
chicken and tofu industries. That is what the laws of supply and demand are
all about.

Some defenders of a variant of the ancient Buddhist line may still want to   8
argue that one chicken fewer sold makes no perceptible difference to the
chicken producers, and therefore there can be nothing wrong with buying
chicken. The division of moral responsibility in a situation of this kind does
raise some interesting issues, but it is a fallacy to argue that a person can do
wrong only by making a perceptible harm. The Oxford philosopher Jonathan
Glover has explored the implications of this refusal to accept the divisibility
of responsibility in an entertaining article called "It makes no difference
whether or not I do it" (*Proceedings of the Aristotelian Society*, 1975).

Glover imagines that in a village, 100 people are about to eat lunch. Each   9
has a bowl containing 100 beans. Suddenly, 100 hungry bandits swoop down

on the village. Each bandit takes the contents of the bowl of one villager, eats it, and gallops off. Next week, the bandits plan to do it again, but one of their number is afflicted by doubts about whether it is right to steal from the poor. These doubts are set to rest by another of their number who proposes that each bandit, instead of eating the entire contents of the bowl of one villager, should take one bean from every villager's bowl. Since the loss of one bean cannot make a perceptible difference to any villager, no bandit will have harmed anyone. The bandits follow this plan, each taking a solitary bean from 100 bowls. The villagers are just as hungry as they were the previous week, but the bandits can all sleep well on their full stomachs, knowing that none of them has harmed anyone.

Glover's example shows the absurdity of denying that we are each respon- 10 sible for a share of the harms we collectively cause, even if each of us makes no perceptible difference. McDonald's has a far bigger impact on the practices of the chicken, egg, and pig industries than any individual consumer; but McDonald's itself would be powerless if no one ate at its restaurants. Collectively, all consumers of animal products are responsible for the existence of the cruel practices involved in producing them. In the absence of special circumstances, a portion of this responsibility must be attributed to each purchaser.

Without in any way departing from a conventional moral attitude toward 11 animals, then, we have reached the conclusion that eating intensively produced chicken, battery eggs, and some pig products is wrong. This is, of course, well short of an argument for vegetarianism. Mr. Justice Bell found "cruel practices" only in these areas of McDonald's food production. But he did not find that McDonald's beef is "cruelty-free." He did not consider that question, because he drew a distinction between McDonald's responsibility for practices in the beef and dairy industries and those in the chicken, egg, and pig industries. McDonald's chickens, eggs, and pig products are supplied by a relatively small number of very large producers, over whose practices the corporation could quite easily have a major influence. On the other hand, McDonald's beef and dairy requirements came from a very large number of producers; and in respect of whose methods, Mr. Justice Bell held, "there was no evidence from which I could infer that [McDonald's] would have any effective influence, should it try to exert it." Whatever one may think of that view—it seems highly implausible to me—the judge, in accepting it, decided not to address the evidence presented to him of cruelty in the raising of cattle, so that no conclusions either way can be drawn.

This does not mean that the trial itself had nothing to say about animal 12 suffering in general. McDonald's called as a witness Mr. David Walker, chief executive of one of McDonald's major United Kingdom suppliers, McKey

Food Services Ltd. In cross-examination, Helen Steel asked Walker whether it was true that, "as the result of the meat industry, the suffering of animals is inevitable." Walker replied: "The answer to that must be 'yes.'"

Walker's admission raises a serious question about the ethics of the meat   13
industry: How much suffering are we justified in inflicting on animals in order to turn them into meat, or to use their eggs or milk?

The case for vegetarianism is at its strongest when we see it as a moral   14
protest against our use of animals as mere things, to be exploited for our convenience in whatever way makes them most cheaply available to us. Only the tiniest fraction of the tens of billions of farm animals slaughtered for food each year—the figure for the United States alone is nine billion—were treated during their lives in ways that respected their interests. Questions about the wrongness of killing in itself are not relevant to the moral issue of eating meat or eggs from factory-farmed animals, as most people in developed countries do. Even when animals are roaming freely over large areas, as sheep and cattle do in Australia, operations like hot-iron branding, castration, and dehorning are carried out without any regard for the animals' capacity to suffer. The same is true of handling and transport prior to slaughter. In the light of these facts, the issue to focus on is not whether there are some circumstances in which it could be right to eat meat, but on what we can do to avoid contributing to this immense amount of animal suffering.

The answer is to boycott all meat and eggs produced by large-scale com-   15
mercial methods of animal production, and encourage others to do the same. Consideration for the interests of animals alone is enough justification for this response, but the case is further strengthened by the environmental problems that the meat industry causes. Although Mr. Justice Bell found that the allegations directed at McDonald's regarding its contribution to the destruction of rain forests were not true, the meat industry as a whole can take little comfort from that, because Bell accepted evidence that cattle ranching, particularly in Brazil, had contributed to the clearing of vast areas of rain forest. The problem for David Morris and Helen Steel was that they did not convince the judge that the meat used by McDonald's came from these regions. So the meat industry as a whole remains culpable for the loss of rain forest and for all the consequences of that, from global warming to the deaths of indigenous people fighting to defend their way of life.

Environmentalists are increasingly recognizing that the choice of what we   16
eat is an environmental issue. Animals raised in sheds or on feedlots eat grains or soybeans, and they use most of the food value of these products simply in order to maintain basic functions and develop unpalatable parts of the body like bones and skin. To convert eight or nine kilos of grain protein into a

single kilo of animal protein wastes land, energy, and water. On a crowded planet with a growing human population, that is a luxury that we are becoming increasingly unable to afford.

Intensive animal production is a heavy user of fossil fuels and a major source of pollution of both air and water. It releases large quantities of methane and other greenhouse gases into the atmosphere. We are risking unpredictable changes to the climate of our planet—which means, ultimately, the lives of billions of people, not to mention the extinction of untold thousands of species of plants and animals unable to cope with changing conditions— for the sake of more hamburgers. A diet heavy in animal products, catered to by intensive animal production, is a disaster for animals, the environment, and the health of those who eat it.   17

*For a reading quiz, sources on Peter Singer, and annotated links to further readings on vegetarianism, visit **bedfordstmartins.com/thebedfordreader**.*

Journal Writing

In your journal respond to Singer's contention that we should all become vegetarians because of the suffering of animals during meat production. What do you think of Singer's recommendation that people should participate in a "moral protest against our use of animals as mere things, to be exploited for our convenience in whatever way makes them most cheaply available to us" (par. 14)? Do you believe animals have rights that humans currently exploit? (To take your journal writing further, see "From Journal to Essay" on the next page.)

Questions on Meaning

1. What meat-production practices did the judge in the "McLibel" trial rule to be cruel to animals? Why did he rule against McDonald's claim that the pamphlet by Steel and Morris was libelous on this point?
2. Why does Singer discuss the ANALOGY created by Jonathan Glover (par. 9)?
3. Why did the British judge not hold McDonald's responsible for cruelty in the beef and dairy industries? What does Singer seem to think of this decision?
4. What further arguments does Singer make against eating meat in his final two paragraphs?
5. What is Singer's THESIS? What is his PURPOSE?

Questions on Writing Strategy

1. Why does Singer devote so much attention to the "McLibel" trial? Do you find this strategy effective for his argument? Why, or why not?
2. For what purpose does Singer relate his encounter with the Buddhist philosopher in paragraph 6?
3. How do you think Singer defined his AUDIENCE for this essay? Why do you think as you do?
4. **OTHER METHODS.** Where does Singer use EXAMPLES to illustrate the cruelty to animals caused by meat production? What do these examples contribute to the argument?

Questions on Language

1. How would you describe Singer's TONE in the essay? How does his choice of language help achieve this tone?
2. The pamphlet criticizing McDonald's used the coined terms "McMurder" and "McTorture." Do you think these coinages are effective, or do they trivialize the issue?
3. Consult a dictionary if you are unsure of the meaning of any of the following: agribusiness, defamation (par. 2); culpably (4); fallacy (8); perceptible (9); implausible (11); castration (14); indigenous (15); kilo (16).

Suggestions for Writing

1. **FROM JOURNAL TO ESSAY.** Expand your journal writing into an essay in which you respond personally to Singer's argument that we should "boycott all meat and eggs produced by large-scale commercial methods of animal production" and that "[c]onsideration for the interests of animals alone is enough justification for this response" (par. 15). If you generally agree with Singer, what can you add to convince others who do not? If you generally disagree, how do you answer Singer's arguments?
2. Do some research for an essay about alternatives to "large-scale commercial methods of animal production." What are the alternatives? Are any of them cruelty-free? How does alternative production affect the prices consumers pay? How available to consumers are meat and poultry produced by alternative methods? How feasible is widespread consumption of such products?
3. **CRITICAL WRITING.** Write an essay in which you ANALYZE the main CLAIMS of Singer's argument. What EVIDENCE does he provide to back up these claims? Do you find the evidence adequate?
4. **CONNECTIONS.** In the preceding essay, "Why I Stopped Being a Vegetarian" (p. 546), Laura Fraser refers to the utilitarian philosophy of Peter Singer (pars. 11–12). Although Singer doesn't use the term *utilitarian*, his argument nonetheless exemplifies the philosophy. From Fraser's and Singer's essays and from research in an encyclopedia, write a one- or two-paragraph DEFINITION of *utilitarianism* in your own words. Add examples of your own (that is, don't use vegetarianism).

Peter Singer on Writing

Unlike most modern philosophers, Peter Singer has a large general audience outside the academic world, an audience he carefully considers when writing. "We philosophers often forget that the ordinary reader is not so used to abstract thinking," Singer told Richard Atcheson in an interview for the *Princeton Weekly*. "I always strive to be clear and to eliminate unnecessary jargon." Singer also makes his writing more accessible by using concrete examples from real-life situations: "Putting real people and real examples into the work helps the reader to follow what you're doing."

In his clear, concrete writing, Singer approaches delicate issues with a cold precision that feeds the rage of some critics. For example, Singer believes that parents should have the right to end the life of a severely disabled newborn: "Killing a disabled infant is not morally equivalent to killing a person. Very often it is not wrong at all." Asked about the angry attacks on such statements, Singer told Bob Abernathy of *Religion and Ethics Newsweekly*, "What I'm saying is controversial. Clearly, it goes against an ethic that has been around for a long time. I think that ethic is in the process of change, anyway, but I have, perhaps, brought out a little more clearly and bluntly than some people the way in which that ethic needs to change. And I've refused to try to disguise or camouflage what I'm saying behind a veil which says, for example, 'We're not killing; we're merely letting die.' . . . I think it's my refusal to draw that nice veil over things that makes them look better that has led to some of this opposition."

For Discussion

1. How is Singer's awareness of his audience reflected in his writing? Do you find what he says true of "A Vegetarian Philosophy"? Why, or why not?
2. Leaving aside his opinions on the issues themselves, what do you think of Singer's aim to write bluntly about difficult ethical issues? Judging from "A Vegetarian Philosophy," how effective is his approach?

KATHA POLLITT

KATHA POLLITT is a poet and essayist. Her poetry has been praised for its "serious charm" and "spare delicacy" in capturing thought and feeling. Her essays have contained strong and convincing commentary on such topics as surrogate motherhood and women in the media. Pollitt was born in New York City in 1949 and earned a BA from Radcliffe College in 1972. Her verse began appearing in the 1970s in such magazines as *The New Yorker* and *The Atlantic Monthly*; it was collected in the book *Antarctic Traveler* (1982), which won the National Book Critics Circle award in 1983. Pollitt has received several other awards as well, including a grant from the National Endowment for the Arts and a Guggenheim fellowship. Her essays and criticism have appeared in *Mother Jones*, the *New York Times*, *The New Yorker*, and *The Nation*, where she currently writes a regular column. *Reasonable Creatures: Essays on Women and Feminism* appeared in 1994. *Subject to Debate: Sense and Dissent on Women, Politics, and Culture*, a collection of her columns from *The Nation*, appeared in 2001. Pollitt lives in New York City.

What's Wrong with Gay Marriage?

In her *Nation* column Pollitt regularly takes on controversial topics from a fresh, unabashedly liberal perspective. In this 2003 essay she counters arguments against marriage between homosexuals, including those posed by Charles Colson in the next essay, "Gay 'Marriage': Societal Suicide" (p. 566).

Both Pollitt and Colson refer to the 2003 decision of the Massachusetts Supreme Judicial Court granting gays and lesbians the right to marry under the state constitution. A constitutional amendment banning same-sex marriage but permitting same-sex civil unions passed the Massachusetts state legislature in 2004 and could go before voters in late 2006. Partly in response to the Massachusetts decision and to other efforts to legitimate gay marriage, opponents are pressing for an amendment to the US Constitution that would define *marriage* as strictly between a man and a woman, and in November 2004 eleven states passed constitutional amendments either defining marriage as heterosexual or banning same-sex marriage.

Will someone please explain to me how permitting gays and lesbians to marry threatens the institution of marriage? Now that the Massachusetts Supreme Court has declared gay marriage a constitutional right, opponents really have to get their arguments in line. The most popular theory, advanced by David Blankenhorn, Jean Bethke Elshtain and other social conservatives, is that under the tulle and orange blossom, marriage is all about procreation. There's some truth to this as a practical matter—couples often live together and tie the knot only when baby's on the way. But whether or not marriage is the best framework for child rearing, having children isn't a marital requirement. As many have pointed out, the law permits marriage to the infertile, the elderly, the impotent and those with no wish to procreate; it allows married couples to use birth control, to get sterilized, to be celibate. There's something creepily authoritarian and insulting about reducing marriage to procreation, as if intimacy mattered less than biological fitness. It's not a view that anyone outside a right-wing think tank, a Catholic marriage tribunal or an ultra-Orthodox rabbi's court is likely to find persuasive.

So scratch procreation. How about: Marriage is the way women domesticate men. This theory, a favorite of right-wing writer George Gilder, has some statistical support—married men are much less likely than singles to kill people, crash the car, take drugs, commit suicide—although it overlooks such husbandly failings as domestic violence, child abuse, infidelity and abandonment. If a man rapes his wife instead of his date, it probably won't show up on a police blotter, but has civilization moved forward? Of course, this view of marriage as a barbarian-adoption program doesn't explain why women should undertake it—as is obvious from the state of the world, they haven't been too successful at it anyway. Nor does it explain why marriage should be restricted to heterosexual couples. The gay men and lesbians who want to marry don't impinge on the male-improvement project one way or the other. Surely not even Gilder believes that a heterosexual pothead with plans for murder and suicide would be reformed by marrying a lesbian?

What about the argument from history? According to this, marriage has been around forever and has stood the test of time. Actually, though, marriage as we understand it—voluntary, monogamous, legally egalitarian, based on love, involving adults only—is a pretty recent phenomenon. For much of human history, polygyny was the rule—read your Old Testament—and in much of Africa and the Muslim world, it still is. Arranged marriages, forced marriages, child marriages, marriages predicated on the subjugation of women—gay marriage is like a fairy-tale romance compared with most chapters of the history of wedlock.

The trouble with these and other arguments against gay marriage is that they overlook how loose, flexible, individualized and easily dissolved the bonds of marriage already are. Virtually any man and woman can marry, no matter how ill assorted or little acquainted. An eighty-year-old can marry an eighteen-year-old; a john can marry a prostitute; two terminally ill patients can marry each other from their hospital beds. You can get married by proxy, like medieval royalty, and not see each other in the flesh for years. Whatever may have been the case in the past, what undergirds marriage in most people's minds today is not some sociobiological theory about reproduction or male socialization. Nor is it the enormous bundle of privileges society awards to married people. It's love, commitment, stability.

Speaking just for myself, I don't like marriage. I prefer the old-fashioned   5
ideal of monogamous free love, not that it worked out particularly well in my case. As a social mechanism, moreover, marriage seems to me a deeply unfair way of distributing social goods like health insurance and retirement checks, things everyone needs. Why should one's marital status determine how much you pay the doctor, or whether you eat cat food in old age, or whether a child gets a government check if a parent dies? It's outrageous that, for example, a working wife who pays Social Security all her life gets no more back from the system than if she had married a male worker earning the same amount and stayed home. Still, as long as marriage is here, how can it be right to deny it to those who want it? In fact, you would think that, given how many heterosexuals are happy to live in sin, social conservatives would welcome maritally minded gays with open arms. Gays already have the baby — they can adopt in many states, and lesbians can give birth in all of them — so why deprive them of the marital bathwater?

At bottom, the objections to gay marriage are based on religious prej-   6
udice: The marriage of man and woman is "sacred," and opening it to same-sexers violates its sacral nature. That is why so many people can live with civil unions but draw the line at marriage — spiritual union. In fact, polls show a striking correlation of religiosity, especially evangelical Protestant-ism, with opposition to gay marriage and with belief in homosexuality as a choice, the famous "gay lifestyle." For these people gay marriage is wrong because it lets gays and lesbians avoid turning themselves into the straights God wants them to be. As a matter of law, however, marriage is not about Adam and Eve versus Adam and Steve. It's not about what God blesses; it's about what the government permits. People may think *marriage* is a word wholly owned by religion, but actually it's wholly owned by the state. No mat-ter how big your church wedding, you still have to get a marriage license from city hall. And just as divorced people can marry even if the Catholic Church considers it bigamy, and Muslim and Mormon men can marry only one woman even if their holy books tell them they can wed all the girls in Apart-ment 3G, two men or two women should be able to marry, even if religions oppose it and it makes some heterosexuals, raised in those religions, uncom-fortable.

Gay marriage — it's not about sex, it's about separation of church and   7
state.

*For a reading quiz, sources on Katha Pollitt, and annotated links to further readings on same-sex marriage, visit **bedfordstmartins.com/thebedfordreader**.*

Journal Writing

Write in your journal about your thoughts on marriage—not necessarily who should be allowed to marry or what you see as the ideal marriage, but rather why you think people marry. What do they hope to gain? What do they give up? How is being married different from simply living together as a couple? Base your entry on your observations and experiences. (To take your journal writing further, see "From Journal to Essay" on the next page.)

Questions on Meaning

1. What three arguments against same-sex marriage does Pollitt summarize in her first three paragraphs, and how does she refute each argument?
2. What, according to Pollitt, is the common understanding of what marriage is? What is Pollitt's own attitude toward marriage?
3. What does Pollitt believe to be the most basic reason why people object to same-sex marriage?
4. What is Pollitt's THESIS, and where does she state it directly?

Questions on Writing Strategy

1. What is the EFFECT of Pollitt's opening her essay with the question that she does? of her asking several questions in paragraphs 2 and 5?
2. Why, in paragraphs 1 and 2, does Pollitt admit "some truth" to the point that "marriage is all about procreation" and admit "some statistical support" for the point that "[m]arriage is the way women domesticate men"? How do these concessions affect her argument?
3. ANALYZE Pollitt's TRANSITIONS between paragraphs 1 and 2, 2 and 3, 3 and 4, and 5 and 6. How do they work?
4. Why do you think Pollitt spends a paragraph on her own negative views of marriage? Does this paragraph strengthen or weaken Pollitt's argument?
5. **OTHER METHODS.** How does Pollitt use DIVISION or ANALYSIS to structure her argument?

Questions on Language

1. Some of the language in paragraph 2 is deliberately humorous. Point to EXAMPLES of humor in the paragraph. Why do you think Pollitt chose to use such language at this point in the essay?

2. In the second-to-last sentence of paragraph 5, why does Pollitt use the phrase "live in sin" rather than, say, "live together without being married"? Does she believe such living situations are sinful?
3. What is Pollitt's point in putting some words in paragraph 6 in quotation marks?
4. Notice the PARALLELISM and repetition in the passage beginning "As a matter of law" in the middle of paragraph 6. What is the effect of the writing here?
5. Consult a dictionary if you are unsure of the meaning of any of the following: tulle, procreation, celibate, authoritarian (par. 1); impinge (2); monogamous, egalitarian, polygyny, subjugation (3); proxy, undergirds (4).

Suggestions for Writing

1. **FROM JOURNAL TO ESSAY.** Using your journal writing as a starting point, write an essay that presents a detailed view of the function of marriage in contemporary society. Refer to specific examples from your experience as appropriate. If you wish, use your observations and reflections to make a point about same-sex marriage.
2. Pollitt writes in paragraph 3 that "marriage as we understand it . . . is a pretty recent phenomenon." Research the history of marriage, beginning with its earliest forms and including marriage in non-Western cultures. Use your research in an essay to amplify or dispute Pollitt's CLAIM.
3. **CRITICAL WRITING.** Write an essay in which you analyze Pollitt's TONE in the essay. How does she present herself and her attitudes toward others (gays, women, men, opponents of gay marriage)? How do you respond to her tone?
4. **CONNECTIONS.** The next essay, by Charles Colson, argues against same-sex marriage. Write an essay in which you evaluate both Pollitt's and Colson's arguments for their EVIDENCE, reasonableness, fairness, response to opposing views, tone, and overall success. Be as OBJECTIVE as possible: Imagine yourself (if you aren't in fact) undecided on the issue of same-sex marriage.

―――――――――

Katha Pollitt on Writing

Katha Pollitt began writing early. "I started writing poetry when I was in about sixth grade," she told Ruth Coniff of *The Progressive* magazine in 1994. "I used to come home from school and go up to my room and sit on my bed and write my poems. And I was writing angry letters to the newspaper. . . . I recently came across a letter I had written when I was twelve years old to the *New York Times*. It was about some complicated legal case involving someone who was accused of being a spy, but I have absolutely no memory of writing this letter or of what this case was. It was actually like something I would write today. I thought, . . . have I been doing this for that long?"

Coniff observed that Pollitt's poetry is not political and asked why. "Well," Pollitt replied, "I was always a two-track writer. I always wrote poetry and prose. . . . I have to say that I see poetry and political writing as different endeavors. What I want in a poem is not an argument, it's not a statement, it has to do with language. I'm looking for a kind of energized, fresh, alive perception. . . . To me it's much more interesting to read that than to read a poem with whose politics I would agree, but that doesn't have a lot of depth of language and imagination in it. . . . What I like about poetry is the verbal concentration and levels of meaning. A poem with only one level of meaning is not a very interesting poem."

For Discussion

1. What are your earliest memories of writing? When have you written on your own (that is, not for a school assignment)? What moves you to write?

2. Explore Pollitt's ideas about poetry versus political prose by comparing two works earlier in this book: the poem "Edward Hopper's *Nighthawks*, 1942" by Joyce Carol Oates (p. 178) and the essay "Not All Men Are Sly Foxes" by Armin A. Brott (p. 348). Both are about women and men, but how do they differ in their use of language? Does this difference make one "better" than the other? Why?

CHARLES COLSON

Born in Boston in 1931, CHARLES COLSON graduated from Brown University in 1953 and earned a law degree from George Washington University. He served in the US Marine Corps and was a partner in a law firm before rising to national prominence—and notoriety—as special counsel to President Richard Nixon during the Watergate scandal that caused Nixon to resign. Colson ended up serving seven months in prison for his involvement in the scandal. After his release in 1974, he founded Prison Fellowship Ministries, an outreach group that provides support both for prisoners and for victims of crime. Colson's many books include the autobiographies *Born Again* (1976) and *Life Sentence* (1979) as well as *Kingdoms in Conflict: An Insider's Challenging View of Politics, Power, and the Pulpit* (1987), *Why America Doesn't Work* (1991), *Justice that Restores* (2001), and *Science and Evolution: Developing a Christian Worldview of Science and Evolution* (with Nancy R. Pearcey, 2001). Colson is a contributing editor of *Christianity Today* magazine and a commentator on the radio program *BreakPoint*, which takes a Christian perspective on current issues. In 1991 he was awarded the Templeton Prize for Progress in Religion and donated the $1 million prize money to Prison Fellowship Ministries.

Gay "Marriage": Societal Suicide

Written with Anne Morse for *Christianity Today* in 2004, this essay presents a case against same-sex marriage and thus counters the preceding essay, Katha Pollitt's "What's Wrong with Gay Marriage?" For a summary of the legal status of gay marriage as of this writing, see the headnote to Pollitt's essay on page 560.

Is America witnessing the end of marriage? The Supreme Judicial Court 1
of Massachusetts has ordered that the state issue marriage licenses to same-sex couples. (By late March, the Massachusetts legislature voted to recognize same-sex civil unions instead.) An unprecedented period of municipal lawlessness has followed, with officials in California, New York, Oregon, and New Mexico gleefully mocking their state constitutions and laws. The result: Thousands of gays rushed to these municipalities to "marry," while much of the news media egged them on.

In the midst of the chaos, President Bush announced his support for a Fed- 2
eral Marriage Amendment, which assures that this contentious issue will be

debated in every quarter of American life. It should be, because the consequences of having "gay marriage" forced on us by judicial (or mayoral) fiat will fall on all Americans—not just those who embrace it.

As a supporter of the amendment, I'm well aware of the critical arguments. As the president noted, "After more than two centuries of American jurisprudence, and millennia of human experience, a few judges and local authorities are presuming to change the most fundamental institution of civilization. Their action has created confusion on an issue that requires clarity."

He's right. Here's the clarity: Marriage is the traditional building block of human society, intended both to unite couples and bring children into the world. Tragically, the sexual revolution led to the decoupling of marriage and procreation; same-sex "marriage" would pull them completely apart, leading to an explosive increase in family collapse, out-of-wedlock births—and crime.

How do we know this? In nearly thirty years of prison ministry, I've witnessed the disastrous consequences of family breakdown—in the lives of thousands of delinquents. Dozens of studies now confirm the evidence I've seen with my own eyes. Boys who grow up without fathers are at least twice as likely as other boys to end up in prison. Sixty percent of rapists and 72 percent of adolescent murderers never knew or lived with their fathers. Even in the toughest inner-city neighborhoods, just 10 percent of kids from intact families get into trouble, but 90 percent of those from broken families do. Girls raised without a father in the home are five times more likely to become mothers while still adolescents. Children from broken homes have more academic and behavioral problems at school and are nearly twice as likely to drop out of high school.

Critics agree with this but claim gay "marriage" will not weaken heterosexual marriage. The evidence says they're wrong. Stanley Kurtz of the Hoover Institution writes: "It follows that once marriage is redefined to accommodate same-sex couples, that change cannot help but lock in and reinforce the very cultural separation between marriage and parenthood that makes gay marriage conceivable to begin with." He cites Norway, where courts imposed same-sex "marriage" in 1993—a time when Norwegians enjoyed a low out-of-wedlock birth rate. After the imposition of same-sex "marriage," Norway's out-of-wedlock birth rate shot up as the link between marriage and childbearing was broken and cohabitation became the norm.

Gay "marriage" supporters argue that most family tragedies occur because of broken *heterosexual* marriages—including those of many Christians. They are right. We ought to accept our share of the blame, repent, and clean up our own house. But the fact that we have badly served the institution of marriage is not a reflection on the institution itself; it is a reflection on us.

As we debate the wisdom of legalizing gay "marriage," we must remember 8 that, like it or not, there is a natural moral order for the family. History and tradition—and the teachings of Jews, Muslims, and Christians—support the overwhelming empirical evidence: The family, led by a married mother and father, is the best available structure for both child rearing and cultural health. This is why, although some people will always pair off in unorthodox ways, society as a whole must never legitimize any form of marriage other than that of one man and one woman, united with the intention of permanency and the nurturing of children.

Marriage is not a private institution designed solely for the individual 9 gratification of its participants. If we fail to enact a Federal Marriage Amendment, we can expect, not just more family breakdown, but also more criminals behind bars and more chaos in our streets.

*For a reading quiz, sources on Charles Colson, and annotated links to further readings on same-sex marriage, visit **bedfordstmartins.com/thebedfordreader**.*

Journal Writing

In paragraph 5 Colson makes a number of claims about the effect on children of being raised by single parents, particularly single mothers. Write in your journal about friends and family members—or the children of friends and family members—who have been raised by a single parent. (If you were raised by a single parent, consider yourself as well.) What have been the effects? (To take your journal writing further, see "From Journal to Essay" on the facing page.)

Questions on Meaning

1. What is Colson's THESIS? Where does he state it directly?
2. What evidence does Colson present to link same-sex marriage to an increase in out-of-wedlock births? to link single-parent households to increases in crime, early parenthood, and other problems of young people? How effective do you find this evidence?
3. What other argument does Colson make against same-sex marriage?

Questions on Writing Strategy

1. ANALYZE the reasoning in Colson's argument. What are its CLAIM and WARRANT, in the Toulmin scheme (see pp. 520–22)? What is the DEDUCTIVE SYLLOGISM (pp. 523–24)?

2. Why does Colson use quotation marks around *marriage* when referring to same-sex unions?
3. What is the EFFECT of the question with which Colson opens his essay?
4. What is the purpose of paragraph 7? Why do you think Colson includes it?
5. **OTHER METHODS.** What role does CAUSE AND EFFECT play in the essay?

Questions on Language

1. How do the words Colson uses in paragraphs 1 and 2 reinforce his opinion of recent moves to legitimate same-sex marriage?
2. Why do you think Colson uses the words *imposed* and *imposition* in the last two sentences of paragraph 6?
3. Consult a dictionary if you are unsure of the meaning of any of the following: unprecedented, gleefully (par. 1); millennia (3); decoupling, procreation (4); intact (5); unorthodox (8).

Suggestions for Writing

1. **FROM JOURNAL TO ESSAY.** Using your journal entry as a starting point, write an essay in which you explain what you think are the effects on children of being raised in single-parent households. From what you have seen, do such children fit the patterns described by Colson? If your observations do not coincide with Colson's, how do you account for the differences?
2. Research the current status of same-sex marriage in the United States, including both state laws and constitutional amendments and the proposed amendment to the US Constitution. Then write an essay in which you discuss your findings and predict what you believe will be the future of legally recognized unions between same-sex couples.
3. **CRITICAL WRITING.** Write an essay in which you examine the TONE of Colson's essay. How does the author present himself, his issue, and his opponents? How reasonable do you find his language?
4. **CONNECTIONS.** In the previous essay, Katha Pollitt addresses many of the arguments raised by opponents of same-sex marriage, including those of Colson. Draw on Pollitt's and Colson's essays as you see fit to argue your own views on same-sex marriage.

ADNAN R. KHAN

ADNAN R. KHAN is a freelance photojournalist based in Toronto, Canada. He is a contributing editor of *Maclean's*, a Canadian magazine of business, politics, and world news, and travels extensively on assignment for the magazine. Khan recently reported from Iraq, covering the abuses in Abu Ghraib prison and the search for Saddam Hussein.

Close Encounters with US Immigration

As a journalist, Khan frequently crosses national borders. As a Pakistani Canadian and a Muslim, he receives an especially close look from the guards at US borders. In this essay from *Maclean's* in 2002, Khan uses personal experience as evidence in arguing against racial and ethnic profiling—that is, singling out people as suspicious solely because of religious affiliation or physical characteristics such as skin color.

The fairness and necessity of profiling have been widely debated, especially since the terrorist attacks of September 11, 2001. The issue is one of the many that center on the trade-offs between making the United States more secure from terrorism, on the one hand, and preserving the liberties guaranteed by the US Constitution, on the other. For a different view of profiling, see the next essay, "Everything Isn't Racial Profiling," by Linda Chavez (p. 575). The two essays after that, by Zara Gelsey and Viet D. Dinh, debate another facet of security versus liberty, the 2001 USA Patriot Act.

I'm getting accustomed to people asking me where I was born. Since 9/11, my brown skin's been a sort of blinking light to many curiosity seekers, my sleepy left eye a source of worry for the growing list of morphological profilers roaming the streets of North America. I usually respond offhandedly. "Pakistan," I say, and turn my attention elsewhere as if that should be enough. It never is. So when an American border official posed the same question to me on a recent trip to the United States, I tried to sound as casual as if it were just another inebriated yokel slurring out a barely comprehensible "Where you from?" It didn't work.

I know America has a right to defend its border, but Muslims are increasingly under suspicion these days, even comfortably hyphenated Canadian ones like myself. We should resign ourselves, I suppose, to the cold sterility of waiting rooms at American border crossings where towering models of the

Statue of Liberty singe the ceilings and the depressingly happy faces of missing children stare out from dingy bulletin boards. It's our lot, I fatalistically think, to be subjected to overzealous immigration officials, grilling us to the point of near panic, ignoring language barriers, goading and prodding until we stumble over our words. That's more than enough to make us look suspicious, besides our place of birth, of course.

For the group of Muslims milling about for hours in the waiting room with me at the Lewiston-Queenston Bridge near Niagara Falls, the experience was enough to make them pull a Rohinton Mistry[1] and refuse, as did the author, to enter the United States. "I'm never going back," one Pakistani father of four fumed after being fingerprinted and photographed. Another Middle Eastern man, after having his wallet unceremoniously emptied onto a counter before he was whisked away and locked in a back room, only to be released an hour later and told to go back to Canada, refused to discuss his ordeal with me. Both men were Canadian citizens and neither could understand why they were singled out. A few other visible minorities came in and left within an hour, but for Muslims, it would not be so simple.

By the time my interrogation began, I'd lost all hope of making it into the States before nightfall. The stock questions were asked by a droopy-eyed, uniformed immigration official who finally reached the inevitable one: "What were you doing in Afghanistan?" I explained that I'm a freelance photojournalist and I was working for *Maclean's* at the time. I pointed out the "journalist" credentials clearly marked on the Afghan visa in my passport, which elicited an ambiguous "Hmmm" from my interlocutor. Every answer was recorded on a sheet of foolscap. I asked why and he responded cryptically, "What's real is unreal and what's unreal is real."

That could be the slogan for contemporary America—a fraying of reality in the post–9/11 world. And when my car was searched by two white-gloved officials, I felt as if I'd slipped into a David Lynch[2] movie. They dissected my defenseless little Honda and its contents with a zeal that seemed utterly over the top. My notebook and personal organizer were confiscated, and I worried whether I had any cheesy love poetry scribbled into my notes (how embarrassing!) or if my friends' phone numbers would be copied and filed away for future reference.

When the immigration official ushered me into a back room, drably furnished with a rectangular table and four chairs, my anxiety level skyrocketed. Two casually dressed men entered the room and introduced themselves as members of the Joint Terrorism Task Force.

[1] Fiction writer born in India (1952) and living in Canada. —EDS.
[2] American filmmaker (born 1946), known for creating vivid characters and surreal situations. —EDS.

Now I was scared.   7

They pulled the chairs close together, crowding one corner of the table   8
and asked me to sit down between them. The border patrol agent and his New
York State trooper counterpart rifled through a set of prepared questions.
Their knowledge of Pakistani culture and geography seemed minimal, but I
thought this might be a ploy. (Was I becoming paranoid?) At one point, the
border patrol agent casually asked if I spoke Pakistani, and I was tempted to
respond that while my Pakistani was a bit rough, I could speak Canadian flaw-
lessly. But I refrained. Why tempt fate, I thought, especially when fate's
accomplices had me cornered in a back office of a foreign country.

During the three-hour ordeal, I'd been made to feel like an unwanted out-   9
sider, as if I were guilty of some heinous crime and now it was my responsibility to prove my innocence. The alienation I felt was relatively minor for
someone with few ties to America, but for the thousands of Canadian Muslims
who have loved ones living south of the border, America's rejection of their
kind wounds deeply.

When it was all over, I couldn't help but laugh as I drove back over the   10
bridge, picturing my personal profile wasting kilobytes in an FBI database. I'd
been grilled by three levels of American security and for what? Had America's
national interest really been served?

Back at the Canadian border, a uniformed official inquired about how   11
long I'd stayed in the United States. Just a few hours, I responded, too
ashamed to go into the details.

"And the value of goods you're bringing over?" he asked.   12

"Zero," I replied.   13

"Okay, go home."   14

Gladly.   15

---

*For a reading quiz and annotated links to further readings on the use of profiling to
guard against terrorism, visit bedfordstmartins.com/thebedfordreader.*

Journal Writing

Write about a time when you were regarded suspiciously or made to feel unwelcome for
reasons you felt were unjustified. How did you respond? How did you feel afterward?
(To take your journal writing further, see "From Journal to Essay" on the facing page.)

Questions on Meaning

1. What does Khan say results from the actions of "overzealous immigration officials" (par. 2) who single out people like himself for interrogation? Why does he see this practice as problematic?
2. What does Khan think made him especially suspicious to the immigration officials? Why weren't these suspicions justified?
3. What is Khan's point in paragraph 9? in paragraph 10?
4. What is Khan's THESIS? What seems to be his PURPOSE?

Questions on Writing Strategy

1. What is the EFFECT of the opening of paragraph 2?
2. What does Khan accomplish in paragraph 3? What does this paragraph contribute to his central point?
3. Why do you think Khan mentions the contents of his notebook and personal organizer (par. 5)?
4. What is the effect of the single sentence in paragraph 7? How would the effect change if Khan had attached this sentence to the preceding paragraph?
5. **OTHER METHODS.** This argument is unusual in that it is developed almost entirely by NARRATION. How does Khan's story serve his argumentative purpose?

Questions on Language

1. ANALYZE the language Khan uses to describe the "waiting rooms at American border crossings" (par. 2).
2. How would you characterize Khan's TONE in this essay? Is it appropriate for his argument? Why, or why not?
3. Consult a dictionary if you are unsure of the meaning of any of the following: morphological, inebriated (par. 1); singe, fatalistically (2); unceremoniously (3); credentials, elicited, ambiguous, foolscap (4); heinous (9).

Suggestions for Writing

1. **FROM JOURNAL TO ESSAY.** Based on your journal entry, write an essay in which you relate your experience of being regarded suspiciously or made to feel unwelcome. Follow Khan's model in telling your story as evidence in an argument against such treatment.
2. Draft an essay in which you respond directly to Khan, explaining what you think about his and other Canadian Muslims' experiences at the US border. If you wish, write your essay in the form of a letter to Khan.
3. How common is Khan's experience, not just at Canadian borders but at other points of entry to the United States, including airports? Are people with an ethnic and/or physical resemblance to the September 11 terrorists generally stopped? Are many such people turned away? What is current US policy on racial or ethnic profiling? Research the answers to these questions, and write an argument based on your findings.

4. **CRITICAL WRITING.** Write an essay in which you analyze Khan's ETHICAL APPEAL — the sense of himself presented in his essay. Base your analysis on the language Khan uses as well as the way he tells his story.

5. **CONNECTIONS.** In the following essay Linda Chavez takes a different view of profiling. Write an essay in which you COMPARE AND CONTRAST Khan's and Chavez's arguments. Where do they agree? Where do they disagree? In your view, whose case is stronger? Why?

LINDA CHAVEZ

An outspoken voice on issues of civil rights and affirmative action, LINDA CHAVEZ was born in 1947 in Albuquerque, New Mexico, to a Spanish American family long established in the Southwest. She graduated from the University of Colorado (BA, 1970) and did graduate work at the University of California, Los Angeles, and at the University of Maryland. She has held a number of government positions, including director of the White House Office of Public Liaison under President Ronald Reagan and chair of the National Commission on Migrant Education under the first President George Bush. She has published three books: *Out of the Barrio: Toward a New Politics of Hispanic Assimilation* (1991), which argues against affirmative action and bilingual education; *An Unlikely Conservative: The Transformation of a Renegade Democrat (Or How I Became The Most Hated Hispanic in America)* (2002); and *Betrayal: How Union Bosses Shake Down Their Members and Corrupt American Politics* (with Daniel Gray, 2004). Chavez is currently president of the Center for Equal Opportunity, a public-policy research organization. She also writes a syndicated newspaper column, hosts a syndicated radio show, and is a political analyst for Fox News.

Everything Isn't Racial Profiling

In this piece written in 2002 for *townhall.com*, a conservative news and information Web site, Chavez draws in part on her own experiences as a Latina to condemn racial and ethnic profiling in general but to condone its use as a tool against terrorism. For Chavez, the need for security in this case outweighs the need for liberty, a view that opposes her to Adnan R. Khan in the previous essay, "Close Encounters with US Immigration."

Racial profiling is an ugly business—and I have been on record opposing it   1
for years. But I'm not opposed to allowing—no, requiring—airlines to pay closer attention to passengers who fit a terrorist profile, which includes national origin. The problem is distinguishing between what is permissible, indeed prudent, behavior and what is merely bigotry. As the Christmas day incident involving an Arab American Secret Service agent who was denied passage on American Airlines makes clear, it's not always easy to tell the difference.

Racial profiling entails picking someone out for special scrutiny simply be-   2
cause of his race. It happens when highway patrolmen pull over blacks who've committed no traffic violations for spot checks but ignore other drivers who

share similar characteristics, say, out-of-state plates or expensive cars. It happens when security guards at a mall tail black customers in stores or insist on inspecting only their bags, ignoring whites. The underlying presumption in these cases is that blacks are more likely to be involved in criminal acts because of the color of their skin.

This kind of racial profiling is both morally wrong and ineffective. But there are times when it makes sense to include race or national origin in a larger criminal profile, particularly if you're dealing with a crime that has already been committed or is ongoing and the participants all come from a single ethnic or racial group.   3

It would make no sense if witnesses identified a six-foot-tall, blond male fleeing a homicide but police stopped females, short men, or blacks or Latinos for questioning. Likewise, if you stopped every tall, blond man, a lot of innocent people would be inconvenienced, if only temporarily. Which brings us to the case of the Arab American Secret Service agent.   4

Walid Shater was allowed initially to board an American Airlines plane in Baltimore headed for Texas, carrying a loaded gun, but then was pulled off the plane, along with a handful of other passengers, for questioning. In the intervening ninety minutes, Shater's lawyers allege that he was mistreated and denied the right to fly because he was an Arab American, while the pilot claims that the agent became loud and abusive, leading him to keep Shater off the flight.   5

I can fully sympathize with the agent's anger—but I don't think the airline acted improperly. I've had encounters similar to Shater's, largely because of my appearance. When I used to travel frequently in Europe from the mid-'80s to the mid-'90s, I was routinely questioned more than other passengers, I suspect because I look vaguely Middle Eastern—or as one airline agent put it, "Your passport's American, but you don't look American."   6

On a trip from Israel in 1985, where I was an official government guest of the Israelis, security agents at Tel Aviv Airport questioned me for almost an hour. "But you can't keep me from leaving Israel," I protested. "No, but we can keep you from doing so on an airplane," the guard responded. They finally let me go when another passenger, who recognized me from the newspapers, vouched for me.   7

On another flight, this time from Switzerland, I was asked to deboard the plane after the passengers were in their seats and was questioned about items in my checked luggage. It was humiliating to be called off the plane and to have the passengers told the flight would be delayed because of concerns about one of the passenger's bags.   8

But I didn't rush to file a discrimination complaint. I didn't like being singled out, but I understood why I was being subjected to more scrutiny. At   9 the time I was hassled, Middle Eastern terrorism was very prevalent in Europe, and female terrorists were operating as well as men, usually on stolen or phony passports. It wasn't unreasonable for airlines to look at me a little more closely than other passengers given these facts.

In Shater's case, nineteen Arab terrorists killed more than three thousand   10
Americans on September 11, and several of the hijackers possessed stolen identification cards and pilots' uniforms. It wasn't unreasonable for the American Airlines pilot to be extra cautious with Shater under the circumstances, despite his official ID. As a law enforcement officer himself, Shater might have cut these guys a little more slack.

Sure it's unpleasant to be a suspect when you're innocent. But it's worse to   11
overlook terrorists because we ignored their pertinent characteristics. I sometimes felt annoyed when I was singled out, but I also felt safer because the airlines were doing their job.

For a reading quiz, sources on Linda Chavez, and annotated links to further readings on the use of profiling to guard against terrorism, visit **bedfordstmartins.com/ thebedfordreader**.

Journal Writing

How likely are you to be suspicious of another person based on his or her appearance? Can you think of instances when people's looks (skin color, manner of dress, body type, or whatever) led you to feel you had something to fear from them — or might lead you to feel that way? In your journal, explore your thoughts about such "profiling." (To take your journal writing further, see "From Journal to Essay" on the next page.)

Questions on Meaning

1. What incident apparently prompted Chavez's essay?
2. How does Chavez distinguish between racial profiling that is "morally wrong and ineffective" and profiling that "include[s] race or national origin in a larger criminal profile" (par. 3)?
3. Why does Chavez say that denying air passage to Walid Shater was reasonable?
4. What is Chavez's THESIS?

Questions on Writing Strategy

1. What is Chavez's point in describing the search for the hypothetical "six-foot-tall, blond male" in paragraph 4?
2. Why does Chavez relate ANECDOTES about herself in paragraphs 7 and 8?
3. What is the EFFECT of Chavez's final sentence?
4. **OTHER METHODS.** Where does Chavez make prominent use of COMPARISON AND CONTRAST and DEFINITION? Why does she rely on these methods?

Questions on Language

1. What modifiers does Chavez use to describe the kinds of racial profiling that she finds unacceptable and acceptable? How do these modifiers further her argument?
2. How would you describe Chavez's TONE in the essay?
3. Consult a dictionary if you are unsure of the meaning of any of the following: prudent (par. 1); scrutiny, presumption, (2); prevalent (9).

Suggestions for Writing

1. **FROM JOURNAL TO ESSAY.** Based on your journal entry, write an essay exploring the features of other people's appearance that do or might arouse your suspicions. What justifies your suspicions? What might be prejudice on your part?
2. How can airlines make their planes secure without infringing on the liberty of passengers who fit a terrorist profile? Or should all such passengers be singled out for scrutiny? Write an essay answering these questions, addressing an AUDIENCE that includes both people who might be profiled as potential terrorists and people who advocate broad profiling.
3. Research the case of Walid Shater and several other cases since September 11, 2001, in which Arab Americans have been removed from airplanes, detained, or otherwise profiled as terrorists and then have been cleared of suspicion. Write an essay in which you use these examples to argue for or against the right of those profiled to sue the authorities who targeted them.
4. **CRITICAL WRITING.** Write an essay examining the organization of Chavez's essay. What does Chavez accomplish in each paragraph? How effectively does she use TRANSITIONS to move from paragraph to paragraph?
5. **CONNECTIONS.** In paragraph 6 Chavez reports once being told by an airline agent, "Your passport's American, but you don't look American." Adnan R. Khan may not have heard "you don't look American" at the US border, but the experience he reports in "Close Encounters with US Immigration" (p. 570) conveyed that message. What does it mean to "look American" in a country as diverse as the United States? In an essay, define or dispute this phrase. Should an American look be used to determine who enters the United States without difficulty and who doesn't? Why, or why not?

ZARA GELSEY

ZARA GELSEY is a pen name for Stephanie Anderson, who was born in 1979 in California's Central Valley. (See "Zara Gelsey on Writing" for more on her use of a pen name.) She graduated from the University of California at Davis (BA, 2001) and did graduate work in English literature at the University of Sussex, England (MA, 2003). Until recently she was the director of communications at the Center for Cognitive Liberty and Ethics, an organization focusing on the law, policy, and ethics of freedom of thought. At the center she managed the *Journal of Cognitive Liberties* and edited the newsletter *Mind Matters*. Currently a freelance writer, she has written for a number of publications, including *The Humanist*, *Media Bypass*, and Boston's *Weekly Dig*. She lives in Davis, California, with her husband.

The FBI Is Reading over Your Shoulder

The loud debate over security versus liberty since September 11, 2001, found an early focus in the USA Patriot Act, passed by Congress and signed into law just weeks after the terrorist attacks. "USA Patriot" is actually an acronym for the law's full title, Uniting and Strengthening America by Providing Appropriate Tools Required to Intercept and Obstruct Terrorism. As its title suggests, the law broadens the government's ability to collect information through surveillance and other means. Its opponents, including Gelsey, maintain that the law erodes constitutional rights of freedom of speech and protection from unreasonable search and seizure of individuals and their property. The proponents of the law, including Viet D. Dinh, the author of the next essay, hold that it safeguards against government abuses while significantly improving the ability to fight terrorism. Gelsey's essay first appeared in *The Humanist* in 2002.

I hate the feeling of someone reading over my shoulder. Not only is it 1 superficially distracting, but it often affects how I respond to the text. Being conscious of being watched inhibits my thinking because I find myself reading through my watcher's eyes. It makes me suddenly self-conscious wondering if the observer is making faulty suppositions about me based on the material I'm reading. The bored businessperson next to me on the train isn't a big deal, but the thought of the FBI peering over my shoulder in the public library definitely puts me on edge.

Ever since the USA Patriot Act was passed by Congress in October 2001,   2
the FBI has been reading over our shoulders by visiting libraries across the
country to demand library patrons' reading records and other files. Under the
Patriot Act, the FBI doesn't have to demonstrate "probable cause" of criminal
activity to request records; in fact, the so-called search warrant is issued by a
secret court. Once granted, it entitles the FBI to procure any library records
pertaining to book circulation, Internet use, or patron registration. Librarians
can even be compelled to cooperate with the FBI in monitoring Internet
usage.

This sort of secrecy is not only chilling, it is ripe for potential abuse. A   3
similar Cold War version of library monitoring was called the Library Awareness Program, through which FBI agents specifically targeted Soviet and Eastern European nationals. The American Library Association effectively fought
the LAP then and is now standing up to the Patriot Act searches. ALA policy on governmental intimidation, established in 1981, unequivocally opposes
"the use of any governmental prerogative which leads to the intimidation of
the individual or the citizenry from the exercise of free expression." The ALA
sees the new FBI policy for what it is: blatant intimidation of patrons.

But beyond FBI intimidation tactics, the new library surveillance program   4
is bound to backfire. What one reads does say something about one's interests — but it may say different things to different people. If one only sees a few
details about someone else's life, his or her actions can easily be contorted to
fit the observer's version of reality.

This is a classic sitcom plotline: An observer misconstrues a sequence of   5
unrelated details and then has a skewed perception of the protagonist. Perhaps the observer reads a personal letter that is lying on a coffee table but
doesn't realize it is part of a novel-in-progress. Based on this bit of information, the observer constructs conclusions, with a succession of trivial actions
seemingly reinforcing the observer's misperceptions, all to the delight of the
omniscient audience.

By seeking to discover what books certain people are reading, the FBI falls   6
right into the role of the ill-informed observer in a similar plotline being
played out in libraries across the country. Only it's not so delightful when the
FBI concludes you're a terrorist because you're doing research at your local
library for an article on suicide bombings and have amassed a circulation
record it deems suspicious. A person who reads a book intending to make a
bomb could be a suspect — as could anyone researching terrorist bombings in
order to prevent them.

The same knowledge can be used for "good" or "evil." The fateful tree in   7
the Garden of Eden represented the knowledge of good and evil — opposing
values intertwined on one tree. The FBI can't possibly know the intent of

knowledge harvested from books, and affording the agency the opportunity to pretend it can is incredibly dangerous. Just as a person wearing rose-colored glasses sees everything rosy, so the FBI is predisposed to find suspicious facts. If the FBI wants to scour libraries looking for "suspicious" reading records, it's going to find them—but its perception is inherently skewed by its intent.

I view reading as access to information; the FBI views it as an indictment. 8 Government suddenly fears domestic suicide bombings, so reading lists are examined and suddenly an innocent researcher is a suspect. In the worst case scenario, details could be dragged from one's past which seemingly support such suspicions. In the best case scenario, the FBI has wasted a lot of time and tax dollars on tracking a nonexistent threat. Meanwhile, all of us feel the presence of Big Brother reading over our shoulders.

Yes, we want protection from terrorists and we want our government to 9 root out those who intend to harm us. But surveillance always spreads beyond its original purpose, justified each step of the way by manufactured fear and better-safe-than-sorry rationales. . . .

While the FBI may never visit your library—not that you'll know if they 10 do, as librarians are barred by law from disclosing the FBI's presence—this program of surveillance still has a chilling effect on cognitive liberty. The feeling of being monitored inhibits freedom of thought.

Take for instance Winston Smith in George Orwell's *Nineteen Eighty-* 11 *Four*.[1] When Winston gets up the nerve to hide from the omnipresent telescreen to indulge in writing with pen and paper—an act not expressly forbidden but punishable nonetheless—he "seemed not merely to have lost the power of expressing himself, but even to have forgotten what it was he originally intended to say." Excessive surveillance trained him to self-censor, thereby stifling his creative and cognitive abilities. Likewise, the FBI's surveillance is bound to have a chilling effect on seekers of knowledge who rely on the public library system. It's implied that you'd better watch what you read because the FBI will be watching too. Intimidating readers in such a manner is, in effect, controlling what we read and how we think.

Freedom of thought and the freedom to read are intertwined. And while 12 monitoring library records isn't as direct as banning books, it is bound to cause self-censorship among readers—which may be the intended result anyway. The government may not be able to ban a book, so instead it will make it suspect to read that book. Thus, the FBI circumvents the First Amendment[2] by threatening readers rather than prohibiting what they read.

---

[1] Published in 1949, Orwell's futuristic novel warns about the dangers of totalitarian government. Winston Smith is the novel's main character. For more on Orwell, see page 645.—EDS.

[2] The First Amendment of the US Constitution protects freedom of speech, the press, assembly, and petition.—EDS.

We may not always like what people do with some of the information they   13
glean, but their right to do so is what ensures everybody's right of access to
information. As Supreme Court Justice Anthony M. Kennedy recently
observed in the majority opinion in *Ashcroft v. Free Speech Coalition:*

> The mere tendency of speech to encourage unlawful acts is not sufficient
> reason for banning it. . . . First Amendment freedoms are most in danger
> when the government seeks to control thought or to justify its laws for that
> impermissible end. The right to think is the beginning of freedom, and
> speech must be protected from the government because speech is the begin-
> ning of thought.

Under the guise of protecting us from terrorism, these surveillance activi-   14
ties intimidate library patrons by spying over their shoulders, collecting reading
lists, and tracking Internet usage. The FBI is policing our minds by purporting
to read them. Of course we want to be kept safe—but not to the extent that
we are patrolled and treated as suspect. Giving up privacy rights can't guarantee physical safety, but it will almost certainly inhibit intellectual freedom and
limit cognitive liberty. We Americans who cherish our freedoms should seriously consider whether or not this is a compromise we are willing to make.

---

*For a reading quiz and annotated links to further readings on the USA Patriot Act,
visit **bedfordstmartins.com/thebedfordreader**.*

Journal Writing

Gelsey writes in paragraph 4, "If one only sees a few details about someone else's life,
his or her actions can easily be contorted to fit the observer's version of reality." Think
of a time when you came to incorrect conclusions about another person based on just
a little knowledge about the person. Write about the situation in your journal. (To
take your journal writing further, see "From Journal to Essay" on the facing page.)

Questions on Meaning

1. What provisions of the Patriot Act does Gelsey object to?
2. What argument against the Patriot Act does Gelsey present in paragraph 3? in
   paragraphs 4–9? in paragraphs 11–12?
3. What is Gelsey's THESIS, and where does she state it directly? What does this
   statement reveal about Gelsey's PURPOSE?

Questions on Writing Strategy

1. Why do you think Gelsey opens her argument as she does? What is the EFFECT of this opening?
2. Why might Gelsey have introduced the ANALOGY of the sitcom plotline in paragraph 5? How does she connect this plotline to FBI surveillance allowed by the Patriot Act?
3. Where does Gelsey acknowledge the opposing side of her argument? Do these concessions seem adequate to you? Why, or why not?
4. Why does Gelsey quote Supreme Court Justice Kennedy in paragraph 13?
5. **OTHER METHODS.** How does the EXAMPLE in paragraph 11 support Gelsey's argument?

Questions on Language

1. What does Gelsey intend by "so-called" in paragraph 2? What point is she trying to make?
2. Gelsey uses the word *harvested* in an unusual sense in paragraph 7. How does the word work in context?
3. At several points in the essay, Gelsey refers to "intimidation" when discussing FBI surveillance of library patrons. Do you agree with this word choice? Why, or why not?
4. Consult a dictionary if you are unsure of the meaning of any of the following: suppositions (par. 1); unequivocally, prerogative, blatant (3); misconstrues, omniscient (5); amassed (6); predisposed, inherently, skewed (7); indictment (8); surveillance (9); omnipresent, circumvents (12); guise, purporting (14).

Suggestions for Writing

1. **FROM JOURNAL TO ESSAY.** Write an essay based on your journal entry in which you relate what happened when you misjudged someone because you had only limited information about the person. What did you observe initially about the person? What did you mistakenly believe? What were the consequences of your misjudgment? What, if anything, did you learn from the experience?
2. At the end of her essay, Gelsey asks readers to consider what compromises in freedom they are willing to make in order to be safe. What do you think? What limits on your freedom would you be willing to endure in exchange for security from terror? (Consider not just freedom of library use but also, perhaps, freedom of movement, speech, and religion, a free press, and the protections of criminal law.) Write an essay explaining where you draw the line.
3. Visit the Web site of the American Library Association to learn more about the organization's response to the USA Patriot Act (*ala.org/ala/pio/mediarelations/patriotactmedia.htm*). Then write an essay in which you provide an overview of this response and agree or disagree with it.
4. **CRITICAL WRITING.** Write an ANALYSIS of Gelsey's argument in which you consider the facts she presents, the organization of her main points, and the overall development of her case against the USA Patriot Act's provisions regarding libraries. How successful do you find her argument?

5. **CONNECTIONS.** The following essay by Viet D. Dinh defends the USA Patriot Act, including its provisions regarding libraries. Write an essay in which you consider how the points raised in Gelsey's and Dinh's arguments differ. How might Gelsey respond to Dinh?

Zara Gelsey on Writing

Zara Gelsey was the pen name used by the writer Stephanie Anderson during the year in which she wrote "The FBI Is Reading over Your Shoulder." In comments written especially for *The Bedford Reader*, she explains her decision to use a pen name.

Voice is an important consideration in any style of writing, particularly when you are trying to persuade an audience to see things from your perspective. I was always hopeless in high school debates because I could usually see good points on both sides of any argument. While it's important to acknowledge opposing viewpoints and a nuanced perspective is often the most authentic, persuasive writing demands a less complicated approach. In order to write compelling op-ed pieces and essays, I found a new voice to tap into by creating a pen name. The character I created with the pen name was, of course, much less complicated than myself; writing under a pen name helped me commit to a single viewpoint, helped me become more able to persuade a reader. When writing under my pen name, Zara Gelsey, I am able to enter the persona of my created character, a persona with fewer complications and reservations. Over time, the confidence of this new voice has improved my weaker attributes and strengthened many aspects of my writing—all through the simple act of renaming myself.

For Discussion

1. Anderson/Gelsey created a separate identity for herself as a writer. Based on her comments, how do you think she would define VOICE? Do you consider voice a matter of identity, style, or a combination of both?
2. Why do you think Gelsey argues for simplicity over complexity in making a persuasive argument, especially for op-ed pieces and essays?
3. Have you ever written under a pen name or wished you could? What were the circumstances?

VIET D. DINH

In 1978 ten-year-old VIET D. DINH immigrated to the United States from Vietnam with his mother and six of his siblings. His father was imprisoned in Vietnam until he escaped in 1983 and joined his family. Dinh reports learning English from Hardy Boys and Nancy Drew mysteries. From that beginning, he went on to graduate from Harvard College in political science, earn a law degree from Harvard Law School, and clerk for Supreme Court Justice Sandra Day O'Connor. His career has blended teaching at Georgetown University Law Center with significant work in the federal government, notably as special counsel to Senator Pete Domenici for the impeachment trial of President Bill Clinton and as assistant attorney general in the Department of Justice. In the latter role, he became the ranking Vietnamese American in the administration of George W. Bush. Dinh started the job early in 2001 and after September 11 of that year took responsibility for the drafting and implementation of the USA Patriot Act. He continues to consult with the Justice and Homeland Security departments on national security while teaching at Georgetown.

How the USA Patriot Act Defends Democracy

Passed soon after September 11, 2001, the USA Patriot Act expands the surveillance powers of government to improve its ability to predict and prevent terrorist activity. As the chief architect of the law, Dinh is ideally suited to explain it and to defend it from opponents who maintain that it erodes constitutional rights. Much of Dinh's essay directly addresses the concerns expressed by Zara Gelsey in the previous essay, "The FBI Is Reading over Your Shoulder" (p. 579).

"How the USA Patriot Act Defends Democracy" is an abridgment of a longer paper published in 2004 by the Foundation for the Defense of Democracy.

Passed soon after the terrorist attacks of 9/11, the USA Patriot Act[1] is one of the most important legislative measures in American history. The act

---

[1] Uniting and Strengthening America by Providing Appropriate Tools Required to Intercept and Obstruct Terrorism (USA Patriot) Act of 2001, Pub. L, No. 107-56, 115 Stat. 272, available at *http://frwebgate.access.gpo.gov/cgi-bin/getdoc.cgi?dbname=107_cong_public_laws&docid =f:publ056.107.pdf* (PDF file) and *http://frwebgate.access.gpo.gov/cgi-bin/getdoc.cgi?dbname=107 _cong_public_laws&docid=f:publ056.107* (text file) (last viewed May 21, 2004).

enables the government to fight what will undoubtedly be a long and difficult war against international terrorism. At the same time, the act constrains the government, preventing any government attempt to unjustifiably extend its powers.

Yet the Patriot Act, despite its near-unanimous passage through Congress, has also become one of the most vilified pieces of legislation in living memory. Critics charge that the act allows for extensive domestic surveillance of US citizens engaged in peaceful, law-abiding activities, that the act could potentially turn the United States into a police state. While some of the rhetoric deployed against the Patriot Act is hyperbolic, the concerns expressed about official surveillance of US citizens are reasonable and should be addressed. The vehemence of many of those who oppose the Patriot Act is a reflection of their attachment to our Constitution, even if, as this paper will argue, many of their fears about government surveillance are unfounded. . . .

The fundamental question facing Americans today is not the false trade-off between security and liberty, but rather how we can use security to protect liberty. Any debate over security and liberty must start with the recognition that the primary threat to American freedom comes from al-Qaeda and other groups that seek to kill Americans, not from the men and women of law enforcement agencies who protect them from that danger. That the American homeland has not suffered another terrorist attack since September 11, 2001, is a testament to the remarkable efforts of law enforcement, intelligence, and homeland security personnel. Their hard work, dedication, and increased coordination have been greatly aided by the tools, resources, and guidance that Congress provided in the Patriot Act. . . .

There has been widespread condemnation of Section 215 of the Patriot Act, the so-called library records provision. The debate over Section 215 illustrates how awry the direction of the debate has gone. Critics have railed against the provision as allowing a return to J. Edgar Hoover's[2] monitoring of private citizens' reading habits. The American Civil Liberties Union (ACLU) has sued the government, claiming that the provision, through its mere existence, foments a chilling fear among Muslim organizations and activists.[3] Others, more fancifully, have claimed that Section 215 allows the government to act as Big Brother, snooping on innocent citizens in a manner reminiscent of George Orwell's *Nineteen Eighty-Four*.[4]

---

[2] Hoover (1895–1972) was director of the FBI from 1924 until his death. — EDS.

[3] United States District Court, Eastern District of Michigan, Southern Division, Complaint for Declaratory and Injunctive Relief. *Muslim Community Association of Ann Arbor et al. v. Ashcroft and Mueller.* Filed by American Civil Liberties Union Foundation and American Civil Liberties Union Fund of Michigan (July 30, 2003), available at *http://news.findlaw.com/ cnn/docs/aclu/mcaa2ash73003cmp.pdf* (last viewed May 21, 2004).

[4] See page 645. — EDS.

These fears are sincere. They are also historically and legally unfounded. 5
Not only does the Patriot Act end the anomaly that allows such records to be
routinely seen by investigators in criminal cases while preventing their access
by counter-terrorism officials, the legislation provides more protections than
usually occur when records are subject to subpoena. For years, grand juries
have issued subpoenas to businesses to hand over records relevant to criminal
inquiries. Section 215 of the Patriot Act gives courts, for national security
investigations, the same power to issue similar orders to businesses, from
chemical makers to explosives dealers. Section 215 is not aimed at bookstores
or libraries. Like its criminal grand jury equivalent, Section 215 orders are
written with business records in mind but could, if necessary, be applied to
reading materials acquired by a terrorist suspect.

Contrary to what the critics claim, Section 215 is narrow in scope. The 6
FBI cannot use Section 215 to investigate garden-variety crimes, nor even
domestic terrorism. Instead, Section 215 can be used only to "obtain foreign
intelligence information not concerning a United States person," or to "protect against international terrorism or clandestine intelligence activities."
The records of average Americans, and even not-so-average criminals, are
simply beyond the reach of Section 215.

The fact that Section 215 applies uniquely to national security investiga- 7
tions means that the orders are confidential. As such secrecy raises legitimate concerns, Congress embedded significant checks into the issuing Section
215 warrants. First, a federal judge alone can issue and supervise a Section 215
order. By contrast, grand jury subpoenas for records are routinely issued by
the court clerk. Second, the government must report to Congress every six
months the number of times, and the manner, of the provision's use. On October 17, 2002, the House Judiciary Committee stated that its review of the
information "has not given rise to any concern that the authority is being misused or abused."[5] Moreover, in September 2003, the attorney general made
public the previously classified information that Section 215 had not been
used once since its passage.[6]

It may well be that the clamor over Section 215 reflects a different con- 8
cern, closely related to the cherished American tradition of free speech. Some
seem to fear the government can use ordinary criminal investigative tools to

[5] Press Release, US House of Representatives, Committee on the Judiciary, Sensenbrenner
Statement and Release of Justice Department's Answers to USA Patriot Act Oversight Questions (October 17, 2002), available at *http://www.house.gov/judiciary/news101702.htm* (last
viewed May 21, 2004).
[6] See, for example, Dan Eggen, "Patriot Monitoring Claims Dismissed; Government Has
Not Tracked Bookstore or Library Activity, Ashcroft Says," *Washington Post*, September 19,
2003.

easily obtain records from purveyors of First Amendment activities, such as libraries and bookstores. Again the fundamental concern is as understandable as the specific fear related to Section 215 is unjustified. The prohibition in Section 215 that investigations "not be conducted of a United States person solely upon the basis of activities protected by the first amendment of the Constitution of the United States" addresses this problem directly and makes the Patriot Act more protective of civil liberties than ordinary criminal procedure. . . .

One of the most serious criticisms after 9/11 was that US security agencies   9
failed to pool intelligence that could have prevented the attacks. The Patriot Act addressed this issue while being sensitive to concerns about the capabilities these agencies have for monitoring citizens. Section 218 of the Act amended the Foreign Intelligence Surveillance Act (FISA)[7] to facilitate increased cooperation between agents gathering intelligence about foreign threats and investigators prosecuting foreign terrorists—liaison previously barred by administrative and judicial interpretations of FISA. Even the most strident of opponents of the Patriot Act would not want another terrorist attack to occur because a quarter of a century–old provision prevented the law enforcement and intelligence communities from talking to each other.

Section 218, essential as it is, raises important questions about law enforce-   10
ment and domestic intelligence. The drafters of the act grappled with questions such as whether the change is consistent with the Fourth Amendment protection against unreasonable search and seizure, whether criminal prosecutors should initiate and direct intelligence operations and whether there is adequate process for defendants to seek exclusion of intelligence evidence from their trial. In the end, Congress decided that Section 218 complies with the Fourth Amendment and that defendants have sufficient recourse to exclude evidence gathered by intelligence agencies from their trials. . . .

The Patriot Act's surveillance provisions are not the executive grab for   11
power and extension of government that many portray them to be. Rather the act sensibly updates the law to keep pace with changing technology, tidies up confused legal interpretations, and standardizes powers while restraining them. The act gives the government the tools it needs to fight terrorism while observing the cherished liberties of Americans. Counterterrorism is a dynamic process, and the Patriot Act is not written in stone. It will be scrutinized by the courts, debated by the citizenry, and amended by Congress.

[7]Foreign Intelligence Surveillance Act (FISA) of 1978, Pub. L, No. 95-511, 92 Stat. 1783, available at *http://www4.law.cornell.edu/uscode/50/ch36.html* (last viewed May 21, 2004).

We have to recognize that our nation is navigating uncharted waters. We have been forced to fight an unprovoked conflict, a war declared against us by nihilistic terrorists, not by our traditional adversary, a nation-state. During these times, when the foundation of liberty is under attack, it is critical that we both reaffirm the ideals of our constitutional democracy and also discern the techniques necessary to secure those ideals against the threat of terrorism. As Karl Llewellyn, the renowned law professor, once observed: "Ideals without technique are a mess. But technique without ideals is a menace."[8] The Patriot Act, by combining ideals and technique, is the domestic shield of American democracy, a protection deserving of renewal by our Congress.   12

*For a reading quiz, sources on Viet D. Dinh, and annotated links to further readings on the USA Patriot Act, visit **bedfordstmartins.com/thebedfordreader**.*

Journal Writing

What are your attitudes toward the federal government? Are you interested in its workings, or do you not follow politics closely? Do you trust elected and appointed officials to act in your best interest, or do you distrust them? In a journal entry, consider your answers to questions such as these and why you feel as you do. If you are not a US citizen, you may wish to write about your home country's government. (To take your journal writing further, see "From Journal to Essay" on the next page.)

Questions on Meaning

1. What is Dinh's THESIS, and where does he first state it? Does he rephrase it at any point?
2. What does Dinh mean in paragraph 3 by asking "how we can use security to protect liberty"?
3. What is Dinh's point in paragraph 5? What clarification of the point does he make in the last sentence of the paragraph?
4. In paragraph 6 how does Dinh explain what he calls the narrow scope of Section 215 of the Patriot Act?

[8]Karl Llewellyn, "On What Is Wrong with So-Called Legal Education," *Columbia Law Review* 35 (1935): 651.

5. In paragraphs 7 and 8 Dinh addresses critics' concerns about the secrecy of Section 215 warrants and the section's effects on free speech. How does he refute these concerns?

Questions on Writing Strategy

1. In paragraph 2 and in several other places, Dinh says that concerns about the Patriot Act are "reasonable" and are guided by respect for the US Constitution. Why does he make this point when he clearly wants to show that the "fears about government surveillance are unfounded"?
2. What is Dinh's PURPOSE in paragraph 4? What does the beginning of paragraph 5 tell you about his purpose?
3. Why do you suppose Dinh covers Section 218 of the Patriot Act last in the essay (pars. 9–10)—the provision allowing US intelligence agencies to share information?
4. **OTHER METHODS.** What assertion of CAUSE AND EFFECT does Dinh make at the end of paragraph 3? Do you accept this assertion?

Questions on Language

1. How does Dinh use PARALLELISM to set up a contrast in paragraphs 1 and 2? What do you think he intends by this contrast?
2. How do the verbs in the second sentence of paragraph 11 reinforce the point Dinh is making there?
3. In his concluding paragraph, Dinh first quotes Karl Llewellyn and then in his final sentence echoes Llewellyn's language. What is the EFFECT of this pairing?
4. Consult a dictionary if you are unsure of the meaning of any of the following: vilified, hyperbolic, vehemence (par. 2); awry, railed, foments, fancifully (4); anomaly, subpoena (5); clandestine (6); liaison, strident (9); grappled, recourse (10); scrutinized (11); uncharted, nihilistic (12).

Suggestions for Writing

1. **FROM JOURNAL TO ESSAY.** Based on your journal entry, write an essay explaining your attitudes toward your country's government. If you wish, focus specifically on current officeholders or issues of government. You could also cast your essay as an argument—for example, making the case that people should pay closer attention than most do to the workings of the government or making the case that politics does not really affect the lives of most individuals.
2. Do you feel more or less secure from terrorism than in the months immediately following September 11, 2001? What since then has contributed to your feeling: government actions? news reports? discussions with friends and family? the simple passage of time? Write an essay explaining your current attitudes and their causes.
3. **CRITICAL WRITING.** Write an essay in which you ANALYZE Dinh's essay for clarity and persuasiveness. What do you see as the essay's strengths and weaknesses? Support your response with specific quotations and PARAPHRASES from the essay.

4. **CONNECTIONS.** Zara Gelsey in the previous essay and Viet D. Dinh in this one both take strong positions about Section 215 of the USA Patriot Act. In your library or on the Internet, locate more neutral analyses of Section 215. (One starting point can be found at *slate.msn.com/id/2087984.*) Or better yet read the act itself at *thomas.loc.gov/cgi~bin/query/D?c107:4:/temp/~c107UXzHbo::* (note the final colons), clicking on "Text of Legislation," or at one of the sites given by Dinh in the footnote on page 585. Based on your research, write an argument for your own view of Section 215.

Viet D. Dinh on Writing

In a 2004 interview with Kim Zetter of *Wired News*, Viet D. Dinh discussed the USA Patriot Act and its effect on civil liberties. At one point Zetter asked Dinh, "What do you say to Americans who feel that the Patriot Act has shrunk their zone of liberty?" Dinh's response: "If indeed that is your fear or that is your perception, then engage in the democratic process. Back up your argument, back up your belief with facts, marshal evidence in order to convince those who are engaged in the process of governance. . . . Somebody once said that democracy is not a spectator sport. We should all applaud each other for getting into the game and risking injury, because at the end of the day we all win if we do engage."

For Discussion

1. Dinh calls for citizens to participate in government by using a crucial strategy of argument and persuasion. What is it?
2. In Dinh's terms, are you a participant in democracy or a spectator?
3. Dinh says that "we all win if we do engage" in democracy. How might you and others win if you were to participate, as he suggests, through well-supported argument?

ADDITIONAL WRITING TOPICS

Argument and Persuasion

1. Write a persuasive essay in which you express a deeply felt opinion. In it, address a particular person or audience. For instance, you might direct your essay

   To a friend unwilling to attend a ballet performance (or a wrestling match) with you on the grounds that such an event is a waste of time
   To a teacher who asserts that more term papers, and longer ones, are necessary for students to master academic writing
   To a state trooper who intends to give you a ticket for speeding
   To a developer who plans to tear down a historic house
   To someone who sees no purpose in studying a foreign language
   To a high-school class whose members don't want to go to college
   To an older generation skeptical of the value of "all that noise" (meaning current popular music)
   To an atheist who asserts that religion just distracts us from the here and now
   To the members of a library board who want to ban a book you love

2. Write a letter to your campus newspaper or a city newspaper in which you argue for or against a certain cause or view. You may wish to object to a particular feature or editorial in the paper. Send your letter and see if it is published.

3. Write a short letter to your congressional or state representative, arguing in favor of (or against) the passage of some pending legislation. See a news magazine or a newspaper for a worthwhile bill to write about. Or else write in favor of some continuing cause: for instance, requiring (or not requiring) cars to reduce exhaust emissions, reducing (or increasing) military spending, providing (or reducing) aid to the arts, expanding (or reducing) government loans to college students.

4. Write an essay arguing that something you believe strongly about should be changed, removed, abolished, enforced, repeated, revised, reinstated, or reconsidered. Be sure to propose some plan for carrying out whatever suggestions you make. Possible topics, listed to start you thinking, are these:

   Gun laws
   Graduation requirements
   ROTC programs in schools and colleges
   Movie ratings (G, PG, PG-13, R, NC-17, X)
   School prayer
   Fraternities and sororities
   Dress codes in primary and secondary schools

5. On the model of Maire Flynn's three-part condensed argument on pages 521–22, write a condensed argument in three paragraphs demonstrating data, claim, and warrant. For a topic, consider any of the preceding ideas or any problem or controversy in this morning's newspaper.

PART THREE

MIXING THE
METHODS

Everywhere in this book, we have tried to prove how flexible the methods of development are. All the preceding essays offer superb examples of DESCRIPTION or CLASSIFICATION or DEFINITION or ARGUMENT, but every one also illustrates other methods, too—description in PROCESS ANALYSIS, ANALYSIS and NARRATION in COMPARISON, EXAMPLES and CAUSE AND EFFECT in argument.

In this part of the book, we take this point even further by abandoning the individual methods. Instead, we offer a collection of twelve essays, many of them considered classics, all of them by well-known writers. The selections range widely in their subjects and approaches, but they share a significant feature: All the authors draw on whatever methods of development, at whatever length, will help them achieve their PURPOSES with readers. (To show how the writers combine methods, we have highlighted the most significant ones in the note preceding each essay.)

You have already begun to command the methods by focusing on them individually, making each a part of your kit of writing tools. Now, when you face a writing assignment, you can consider whether and how each method may help you sharpen your focus, develop your ideas, and achieve your aim. Indeed, as we noted in Chapter 2, one way to approach a subject is to apply each method to it, one by one. The following list distills the discussion on pages 36–37 to a set of questions that you can ask about any subject:

1. *Narration:* Can you tell a story about the subject?
2. *Description:* Can you use your senses to illuminate the subject?
3. *Example:* Can you point to instances that will make the subject concrete and specific?
4. *Comparison and contrast:* Will setting the subject alongside another generate useful information?
5. *Process analysis:* Will a step-by-step explanation of how the subject works add to the reader's understanding?
6. *Division or analysis:* Can slicing the subject into its parts produce a clearer vision of it?
7. *Classification:* Is it worthwhile to sort the subject into kinds or groups?
8. *Cause and effect:* Does it add to the subject to ask why it happened or what its results are?
9. *Definition:* Can you trace a boundary that will clarify the meaning of the subject?
10. *Argument and persuasion:* Can you state an opinion or make a proposal about the subject?

Rarely will every one of these questions produce fruit for a given essay, but inevitably two or three or four will. Try the whole list when you're stuck at the beginning of an assignment or when you're snagged in the middle of a draft. You'll find the questions are as good at removing obstacles as they are at generating ideas.

SANDRA CISNEROS

Born in 1954 in Chicago, SANDRA CISNEROS attended Loyola University, where she received a BA in 1976. Two years later, she earned an MFA from the University of Iowa Writers' Workshop. While at Iowa, she embraced her Chicano heritage in her writing, turning to her childhood for inspiration. Most of her published work deals explicitly with issues of ethnic heritage, poverty, and personal identity. She is the author of two novels, *The House on Mango Street* (1984), for which she won the American Book Award, and *Caramelo* (2003); a collection of short stories, *Woman Hollering Creek* (1991); and four books of poetry, including *My Wicked, Wicked Ways* (1987) and *Loose Woman* (1994). Cisneros has received numerous awards, including two from the National Endowment for the Arts and the Lannan Foundation Literary Award. In 1995 she was named a MacArthur fellow.

Only Daughter

How could a man who had little interest in reading, whose only ambition for his daughter was marriage, prove to be the main reason that his daughter became a writer? In this essay from a 1990 *Glamour* magazine, Cisneros explains.

"Only Daughter" mixes several methods of development to show the difficult yet fruitful bond between daughter and father:

Narration (Chap. 4): paragraphs 9–12, 15–22
Description (Chap. 5): paragraphs 7, 13, 16–21
Cause and effect (Chap. 11): paragraphs 3, 5, 7, 8
Definition (Chap. 12): paragraphs 1–2

Once, several years ago, when I was just starting out my writing career, I 1
was asked to write my own contributor's note for an anthology I was part of. I wrote: "I am the only daughter in a family of six sons. *That* explains everything."

Well, I've thought about that ever since, and yes, it explains a lot to me, 2
but for the reader's sake I should have written: "I am the only daughter in a *Mexican* family of six sons." Or even: "I am the only daughter of a Mexican father and a Mexican-American mother." Or: "I am the only daughter of a working-class family of nine." All of these had everything to do with who I am today.

I was/am the only daughter and *only* a daughter. Being an only daughter in 3
a family of six sons forced me by circumstance to spend a lot of time by myself because my brothers felt it beneath them to play with a *girl* in public. But that aloneness, that loneliness, was good for a would-be writer—it allowed me time to think and think, to imagine, to read and prepare myself.

Being only a daughter for my father meant my destiny would lead me to become someone's wife. That's what he believed. But when I was in fifth grade and shared my plans for college with him, I was sure he understood. I remember my father saying, *"Que bueno, mi'ja,* that's good." That meant a lot to me, especially since my brothers thought the idea hilarious. What I didn't realize was that my father thought college was good for girls — for finding a husband. After four years in college and two more in graduate school, and still no husband, my father shakes his head even now and says I wasted all that education. 4

In retrospect, I'm lucky my father believed daughters were meant for husbands. It meant it didn't matter if I majored in something silly like English. After all, I'd find a nice professional eventually, right? This allowed me the liberty to putter about embroidering my little poems and stories without my father interrupting with so much as a "What's that you're writing?" 5

But the truth is, I wanted him to interrupt. I wanted my father to understand what it was I was scribbling, to introduce me as "My only daughter, the writer." Not as "This is my only daughter. She teaches." *El maestra* — teacher. Not even *profesora.* 6

In a sense, everything I have ever written has been for him, to win his approval even though I know my father can't read English words, even though my father's only reading includes the brown-ink *Esto* sports magazines from Mexico City and the bloody *¡Alarma!* magazines that feature yet another sighting of *La Virgen de Guadalupe* on a tortilla or a wife's revenge on her philandering husband by bashing his skull in with a *molcajete* (a kitchen mortar made of volcanic rock). Or the *fotonovelas,* the little picture paperbacks with tragedy and trauma erupting from the characters' mouths in bubbles. 7

My father represents, then, the public majority. A public who is uninterested in reading, and yet one whom I am writing about and for, and privately trying to woo. 8

When we were growing up in Chicago, we moved a lot because of my father. He suffered periodic bouts of nostalgia. Then we'd have to let go our flat, store the furniture with mother's relatives, load the station wagon with baggage and bologna sandwiches, and head south. To Mexico City. 9

We came back, of course. To yet another Chicago flat, another Chicago neighborhood, another Catholic school. Each time, my father would seek out the parish priest in order to get a tuition break, and complain or boast: "I have seven sons." 10

He meant *siete hijos,* seven children, but he translated it as "sons." "I have seven sons." To anyone who would listen. The Sears Roebuck employee who sold us the washing machine. The short-order cook where my father ate his ham-and-eggs breakfasts. "I have seven sons." As if he deserved a medal from the state. 11

My papa. He didn't mean anything by that mistranslation, I'm sure. But [12] somehow I could feel myself being erased. I'd tug my father's sleeve and whisper: "Not seven sons. Six! and *one daughter*."

When my oldest brother graduated from medical school, he fulfilled my [13] father's dream that we study hard and use this—our heads, instead of this—our hands. Even now my father's hands are thick and yellow, stubbed by a history of hammer and nails and twine and coils and springs. "Use this," my father said, tapping his head, "and not this," showing us those hands. He always looked tired when he said it.

Wasn't college an investment? And hadn't I spent all those years in college? And if I didn't marry, what was it all for? Why would anyone go to college [14] and then choose to be poor? Especially someone who had always been poor.

Last year, after ten years of writing professionally, the financial rewards [15] started to trickle in. My second National Endowment for the Arts Fellowship. A guest professorship at the University of California, Berkeley. My book, which sold to a major New York publishing house.

At Christmas, I flew home to Chicago. The house was throbbing, same as [16] always; hot *tamales* and sweet *tamales* hissing in my mother's pressure cooker, and everybody—mother, six brothers, wives, babies, aunts, cousins—talking too loud and at the same time, like in a Fellini[1] film, because that's just how we are.

I went upstairs to my father's room. One of my stories had just been trans-[17] lated into Spanish and published in an anthology of Chicano writing, and I wanted to show it to him. Ever since he recovered from a stroke two years ago, my father likes to spend his leisure hours horizontally. And that's how I found him, watching a Pedro Infante movie on Galavision and eating rice pudding.

There was a glass filmed with milk on the bedside table. There were sev-[18] eral vials of pills and balled Kleenex. And on the floor, one black sock and a plastic urinal that I didn't want to look at but looked at anyway. Pedro Infante was about to burst into song, and my father was laughing.

I'm not sure if it was because my story was translated into Spanish, or [19] because it was published in Mexico, or perhaps because the story dealt with Tepeyac, the *colonia* my father was raised in, but at any rate, my father punched the mute button on his remote control and read my story.

I sat on the bed next to my father and waited. He read it very slowly. As if [20] he were reading each line over and over. He laughed at all the right places and read lines he liked out loud. He pointed and asked questions: "Is this So-and-so?" "Yes," I said. He kept reading.

---

[1] Federico Fellini (1920–93), an Italian, directed *La Strada, La Dolce Vita, Satyricon*, and other movies. —EDS.

When he was finally finished, after what seemed like hours, my father   21
looked up and asked: "Where can we get more copies of this for the relatives?"

Of all the wonderful things that happened to me last year, that was the   22
most wonderful.

For a reading quiz, sources on Sandra Cisneros, and annotated links to further readings on parent-child relationships, visit **bedfordstmartins.com/thebedfordreader**.

Journal Writing

Cisneros's father thinks of success primarily in terms of financial rewards. Do you agree? In your journal, consider the meaning of *success*, focusing on these questions: Whom in your own life do you consider to be successful, and why? Where do your ideas of success come from — your parents? your friends? your schooling? the media? (To take your journal writing further, see "From Journal to Essay" on the next page.)

Questions on Meaning

1. What do you take to be Cisneros's main PURPOSE in this essay?
2. Cisneros writes, "I am the only daughter in a family of six sons. *That* explains everything" (par. 1). What does it explain in this essay?
3. What are some of the parallels Cisneros draws between her father and "the public majority" (par. 8)?
4. Why do you think her father's appreciation of her story was, for Cisneros, "the most wonderful" thing that happened to her in a year that was already good?

Questions on Writing Strategy

1. Does Cisneros seem to be writing mainly for other Mexican Americans or for a wider AUDIENCE? Cite passages from the essay to support your answer.
2. What can you INFER about Cisneros's stories and poems from the information about her education (par. 4), the details about her father's reading (7–8), and the list of her successes (15)?
3. **MIXED METHODS.** Cisneros's INTRODUCTION (pars. 1–2) gives a DEFINITION of the author. How effective is this introduction for setting up the essay that follows?
4. **MIXED METHODS.** Perhaps a third of Cisneros's essay is devoted to a NARRATIVE and DESCRIPTION of a Christmas visit home (pars. 16–22). Why do you think Cisneros relates this incident in so much detail? What do we gain from knowing what was cooking, what her father was watching on TV, or what questions he asked as he read Cisneros's story?

Questions on Language

1. What are the contrasting ideas in Cisneros's paired phrases "the only daughter and *only* a daughter" (par. 3)?
2. How do Cisneros's words convey her feeling about her father's translation of *siete hijos* as "seven sons" (pars. 11–12)?
3. Consult a dictionary if you need help in defining the following: retrospect, putter (par. 5); philandering, mortar (7); woo (8).

Suggestions for Writing

1. **FROM JOURNAL TO ESSAY.** Write an extended definition of *success* that also examines the sources of your definition, as you explored them in your journal. (The sources could be negative as well as positive — that is, your own ideas may have formed in reaction *against* others' ideas as well as in agreement *with* them.) Be sure your essay has a clear THESIS and plenty of EXAMPLES to make your definition precise.
2. Cisneros writes of differences from her father that frustrated her but that also motivated her to achieve. In a narrative and descriptive essay, relate some aspect of a relationship with a parent or other figure of authority that you found troubling or even maddening at the time but that now seems to have shaped you in positive ways. Did a parent (or someone else) push you to study when you wanted to play sports or hang out with your friends? make you attend religious services when they seemed unimportant? refuse to acknowledge accomplishments you were proud of? try to direct you onto a path you didn't care to take?
3. **CRITICAL WRITING.** Cisneros attributes many of her father's attitudes to his Mexican heritage. As an extension of the previous assignment, consider whether Cisneros's experiences are particular to Mexican American families or are common in all families, whatever their ethnicity. Are conflicts between children and their parents inevitable, do you think? Why, or why not?
4. **CONNECTIONS.** Both Cisneros's "Only Daughter" and Richard Rodriguez's "Aria" (p. 655) examine relationships with parents. How are the two authors' parents similar and different? How are the authors' feelings about their parents similar and different? Write an essay of COMPARISON AND CONTRAST that quotes or PARAPHRASES passages from both essays as EVIDENCE.
5. **CONNECTIONS.** Several authors in this book recall interaction with a parent and use dialog to make the interaction vivid. Examples include Amy Tan's "Fish Cheeks" (p. 94), Brad Manning's "Arm Wrestling with My Father" (p. 144), Sarah Vowell's "Shooting Dad" (p. 152), and Maxine Hong Kingston's "No Name Woman" (p. 631). Try your hand at using dialog in a brief narrative that recalls a significant incident between yourself and a parent. Then write briefly about your experience using dialog: How easy or difficult was it to remember who said what? How easy or difficult was it to make the speakers sound like themselves?

Sandra Cisneros on Writing

A bilingual author, Sandra Cisneros writes primarily in English. Yet Spanish influences her English sentences, and she frequently uses Spanish words in her prose. She spoke with Feroza Jussawalla and Reed Way Dasenbrock about how Spanish affects her writing:

"What it does is change the rhythm of my writing. I think that incorporating the Spanish, for me, allows me to create new expressions in English — to say things that have never been said before. And I get to do that by translating literally. I love calling stories by Spanish expressions. I have this story called 'Salvador, Late or Early.' It's a nice title. It means 'sooner or later,' *tarde o temprano,* which literally translates as 'late or early.' All of a sudden something happens to the English, something really new is happening, a new spice is added to the English language."

In some of her work, Cisneros uses Spanish and then offers a translation for English readers. At other times, she thinks complete translation is unnecessary: "See, sometimes, you don't have to say the whole thing. Now I'm learning how you can say something in English so that you know the person is saying it in Spanish. I like that. You can say a phrase in Spanish, and you can choose not to translate it, but you can make it understood through the context. 'And then my *abuelita* called me a *sin verguenza* and cried because I am without shame,' you see? Just in the sentence you can weave it in. To me it's really fun to be doing that; to me it's like I've uncovered this whole mother lode that I haven't tapped into. All the *expresiones* in Spanish when translated make English wonderful."

That said, Cisneros believes that "[t]he readers who are going to like my stories the best and catch all the subtexts and all the subtleties, that even my editor can't catch, are Chicanas. When there are Chicanas in the audience, and they laugh, they are laughing at stuff that we talk about among ourselves. And there's no way that my editor at Random House is ever going to get those jokes." This seems particularly true, she finds, when she's making use of Mexican and Southwestern myths and legends about which the general public might not be aware. "That's why I say the real ones who are going to get it are the Latinos, the Chicanos. They're going to get it in that they're going to understand the myth and how I've revised it. When I talked to someone at *Interview* magazine, I had to explain to him what I was doing with *la llorona, La Malinche,* and the Virgin of Guadalupe in the story ['Woman Hollering Creek']. But he said, 'Hey, I didn't know that, but I still got the story.' You can get it at some other level. He reminded me, 'Sandra, if you're from Ireland, you're going to get a lot more out of Joyce than if you're not, but just because you're not Irish doesn't mean you're not going to get it at another level.'"

For Discussion

1. In the passages quoted here, Sandra Cisneros is talking about her fiction writing. Do her thoughts about Spanish apply to the kind of English she uses when she writes a nonfiction piece like "Only Daughter"?

2. In "Only Daughter," Sandra Cisneros writes of her father: "In a sense, everything I have ever written has been for him, to win his approval, even though I know my father can't read English words. . . ." How does this square with her claim that Chicana readers are her best readers?

3. Who is the reader who would best understand your essays?

JOAN DIDION

A writer whose fame is fourfold—as novelist, essayist, journalist, and screen-writer—JOAN DIDION was born in 1934 in California, where her family has lived for five generations. After graduation from the University of California, Berkeley, she spent a few years in New York, working as a feature editor for *Vogue*, a fashion magazine. In 1964 she returned to California, where she worked as a freelance journalist and wrote four much-discussed novels: *River Run* (1963), *Play It as It Lays* (1971), *A Book of Common Prayer* (1977), and *Democracy* (1984). *Salvador* (1983), her book-length essay based on a visit to war-torn El Salvador, and *Miami* (1987), a study of Cuban exiles in Florida, also received wide attention. With her late husband, John Gregory Dunne, Didion coauthored a number of screenplays, notably for *A Star Is Born* (1976), *True Confessions* (1981), and *Up Close and Personal* (1996). Her latest books are *After Henry* (1992), a collection of essays; *The Last Thing He Wanted* (1996), a novel; *Political Fictions* (2001) and *Fixed Ideas: America Since 9.11* (2003), both critiques of US politics; and *Where I Was From* (2003), a memoir and an assessment of Didion's native California.

Earthquakes

Long a resident of California, Didion knows firsthand the experience of earthquakes and the peculiar blend of dread and denial with which most Californians view seismic catastrophe. This piece is a self-contained excerpt from a longer essay, "Los Angeles Days," that appeared first in 1988 in *The New Yorker* and then in Didion's collection *After Henry*.

"Earthquakes" relies on a range of methods to depict the attitudes of Didion herself and of her fellow Californians to "the Big One":

Narration (Chap. 4): paragraphs 1, 2–7, 8, 9
Description (Chap. 5): paragraphs 1, 2, 9
Example (Chap. 6): paragraphs 1, 2, 8, 9
Process analysis (Chap. 8): paragraph 2
Cause and effect (Chap. 11): paragraphs 1, 7–9
Definition (Chap. 12): paragraphs 1, 8, 9

During one of the summer weeks I spent in Los Angeles in 1988 there was [1] a cluster of small earthquakes, the most noticeable of which, on the Garlock Fault, a major lateral-slip fracture that intersects the San Andreas in the Tehachapi range north of Los Angeles, occurred at six minutes after four on a Friday afternoon when I happened to be driving in Wilshire Boulevard from the beach. People brought up to believe that the phrase *terra firma*[1] has real

---

[1] Latin, "solid earth."—EDS.

meaning often find it hard to understand the apparent equanimity with which earthquakes are accommodated in California, and tend to write it off as regional spaciness. In fact it is less equanimity than protective detachment, the useful adjustment commonly made in circumstances so unthinkable that psychic survival precludes preparation. I know very few people in California who actually set aside, as instructed, a week's supply of water and food. I know fewer still who could actually lay hands on the wrench required to turn off, as instructed, the main gas valve; the scenario in which this wrench will be needed is a catastrophe, and something in the human spirit rejects planning on a daily basis for catastrophe. I once interviewed, in the late sixties, someone who did prepare: a Pentecostal minister who had received a kind of heavenly earthquake advisory, and on its quite specific instructions was moving his congregation from Port Hueneme, north of Los Angeles, to Murfreesboro, Tennessee. A few months later, when a small earthquake was felt not in Port Hueneme but in Murfreesboro, an event so novel that it was reported nationally, I was, I recall, mildly gratified.

A certain fatalism comes into play. When the ground starts moving all bets are off. Quantification, which in this case takes the form of guessing where the movement at hand will rank on the Richter scale, remains a favored way of regaining the illusion of personal control, and people still crouched in the nearest doorjamb will reach for a telephone and try to call Caltech, in Pasadena, for a Richter reading. "Rock and roll," the DJ said on my car radio that Friday afternoon at six minutes past four. "This console is definitely shaking . . . no word from Pasadena yet, is there?"

"I would say this is a three," the DJ's colleague said.

"Definitely a three, maybe I would say a little higher than a three."

"Say an eight . . . just joking."

"It felt like a six where I was."

What it turned out to be was a five-two, followed by a dozen smaller aftershocks, and it had knocked out four of the six circuit breakers at the A. D. Edmonston pumping plant on the California Aqueduct, temporarily shutting down the flow of Northern California water over the Tehachapi range and cutting off half of Southern California's water supply for the weekend. This was all within the range not only of the predictable but of the normal. No one had been killed or seriously injured. There was plenty of water for the weekend in the system's four southern reservoirs, Pyramid, Castaic, Silverwood, and Perris lakes. A five-two earthquake is not, in California, where the movements people remember tend to have Richter numbers well over six, a major event, and the probability of earthquakes like this one had in fact been built into the aqueduct: The decision to pump the water nineteen hundred feet over the Tehachapi was made precisely because the aqueduct's engineers rejected the idea of tunneling through an area so geologically complex, periodically wrenched by opposing displacements along the San Andreas and the Garlock, that it has been called California's structural knot.

Still, this particular five-two, coming as it did when what Californians call 8 "the Big One" was pretty much overdue (the Big One is the eight, the Big One is the seven in the wrong place or at the wrong time, the Big One could even be the six-five centered near downtown Los Angeles at nine on a weekday morning), made people a little uneasy. There was some concern through the weekend that this was not merely an ordinary five-two but a "foreshock," an earthquake prefiguring a larger event (the chances of this, according to Caltech seismologists, run about one in twenty), and by Sunday there was what seemed to many people a sinister amount of activity on other faults: a three-four just east of Ontario at twenty-two minutes past two in the afternoon, a three-six twenty-two minutes later at Lake Berryessa, and, four hours and one minute later, northeast of San Jose, a five-five on the Calaveras Fault. On Monday, there was a two-three in Playa del Rey and a three in Santa Barbara.

Had it not been for the five-two on Friday, very few people would have reg- 9 istered these little quakes (the Caltech seismological monitors in Southern California normally record from twenty to thirty earthquakes a day with magnitudes below three), and in the end nothing came of them, but this time people did register them, and they lent a certain moral gravity to the way the city happened to look that weekend, a temporal dimension to the hard white edges and empty golden light. At odd moments during the next few days people would suddenly clutch at tables, or walls. "Is it going," they would say, or "I think it's moving." They almost always said *it*, and what they meant by *it* was not just the ground but the world as they knew it. I have lived all my life with the promise of the Big One, but when it starts going now even I get the jitters.

---

*For a reading quiz, sources on Joan Didion, and annotated links to further readings on earthquakes in California, visit **bedfordstmartins.com/thebedfordreader**.*

Journal Writing

What potential threat or threats in your life most give you "the jitters"? Write a journal entry exploring your specific worries. (To take your journal writing further, see "From Journal to Essay" on the next page.)

Questions on Meaning

1. What does Didion mean by "protective detachment" in referring to Californians' attitude toward earthquakes (par. 1)?
2. How, according to Didion, do Californians maintain the illusion of personal control during earthquakes?
3. Why was the earthquake Didion writes about a cause of special concern, even though it was not a major disturbance?
4. What is the ultimate threat of "the Big One"? Why does its possibility give Didion "the jitters"?

Questions on Writing Strategy

1. Why in paragraphs 1 and 8 is Didion so specific about the times of the earthquakes?
2. How does Didion use IRONY in paragraph 1?
3. Why do you suppose Didion quotes the on-air conversation between the radio DJ and his associate in paragraphs 2–6?
4. **MIXED METHODS.** What other method does Didion use in paragraph 8 to DEFINE "the Big One"?
5. **MIXED METHODS.** What CAUSE AND EFFECT relationship does Didion explore in paragraph 9?

Questions on Language

1. What is the effect of Didion's use of "as instructed" twice in the middle of paragraph 1?
2. Throughout the essay Didion refers to specific Richter-scale numbers when describing earthquakes. Why does she do so?
3. What does Didion mean by the phrase "temporal dimension" in paragraph 9? What does *temporal* mean?
4. Check a dictionary if any of the following are unfamiliar to you: equanimity, precludes, scenario (par. 1); fatalism (2); displacements (7); seismologists (8); magnitudes (9).

Suggestions for Writing

1. **FROM JOURNAL TO ESSAY.** Expand your journal entry into an essay in which you explore your concerns about a potential threat in your life. What has led you to feel the way you do? Do you think many other people share your concern? How do you cope with your feelings? What might you do if the threat became real?
2. Do some research about the incidence and probability of earthquakes in the United States. (A good starting point is the Geologic Hazards Team of the US Geological Survey: *geohazards.cr.usgs.gov/research.html*). Is California the only state vulnerable to earthquakes? (The answer may surprise you.) What kinds of damage and loss of life have been caused by earthquakes in this country? Write a report about earthquakes in which you answer these questions and others that interest you.

3. **CRITICAL READING.** Didion is noted for a distinctive STYLE of writing. In an essay, ANALYZE Didion's style in "Earthquakes." What seems notable about the words Didion chooses and the ways she structures her sentences? What is her TONE? What does her style say about her? How do you respond to it?

4. **CONNECTIONS.** In "Fly-Fishing for Doctors" (p. 173), Ethan Canin writes about an incident that crystallized his attitudes toward his surroundings. Write an essay that COMPARES AND CONTRASTS Didion's and Canin's essays: How are the authors' experiences, conclusions, and self-presentations similar and different?

5. **CONNECTIONS.** Like that in "Earthquakes," Didion's reporting often involves herself as part of the story. In "A Web of Brands" (p. 440), Naomi Klein is also involved in the situations she reports. Write an essay that considers how the presence of the writer affects each essay. How would the essays be different if they had been written from a completely OBJECTIVE perspective?

Joan Didion on Writing

In "Why I Write," an essay published by the *New York Times Book Review,* adapted from her Regents' Lecture at the University of California at Berkeley, Joan Didion writes, "I stole the title for this talk, from George Orwell [see p. 653]. One reason I stole it was that I like the sound of the words: Why I Write. There you have three short unambiguous words that share a sound, and the sound they share is this:

I

I

I

In many ways writing is the act of saying *I*, of imposing oneself upon other people, of saying *listen to me, see it my way, change your mind. . . .*"

Didion's "way," though, comes not from notions of how the world works or should work but from its observable details. She writes, "I am not in the least an intellectual, which is not to say that when I hear the word 'intellectual' I reach for my gun, but only to say that I do not think in abstracts. During the years when I was an undergraduate at Berkeley I tried, with a kind of hopeless late-adolescent energy, to buy some temporary visa into the world of ideas, to forge for myself a mind that could deal with the abstract. . . . In short, I tried to think. I failed. My attention veered inexorably back to the specific, to the tangible, to what was generally considered, by everyone I knew then and for that matter have known since, the peripheral. I would try to contemplate the Hegelian dialectic and would find myself concentrating instead on the flowering pear tree outside my window and the particular way the petals fell on my floor."

Later in the essay, Didion writes, "During those years I was traveling on what I knew to be a very shaky passport, forged papers: I knew that I was no legitimate resident in any world of ideas. I knew I couldn't think. All I knew then was what I wasn't, and it took me some years to discover what I was.

"Which was a writer.

"By which I mean not a 'good' writer or a 'bad' writer but simply a writer, a person whose most absorbed and passionate hours are spent arranging words on pieces of paper. Had my credentials been in order I would never have become a writer. Had I been blessed with even limited access to my own mind there would have been no reason to write. I write entirely to find out what I'm thinking, what I'm looking at, what I see, and what it means. What I want and what I fear. . . . *What is going on in these pictures in my mind?*"

In the essay, Didion emphasizes that these mental pictures have a grammar. "Grammar is a piano I play by ear, since I seem to have been out of school the year the rules were mentioned. All I know about grammar is its infinite power. To shift the structure of a sentence alters the meaning of that sentence, as definitely and inflexibly as the position of a camera alters the meaning of the object photographed. Many people know about camera angles now, but not so many know about sentences. The arrangement of the words matters, and the arrangement you want can be found in the picture in your mind. The picture dictates the arrangement. The picture dictates whether this will be a sentence with or without clauses, a sentence that ends hard or a dying-fall sentence, long or short, active or passive. The picture tells you how to arrange the words and the arrangement of the words tells you, or tells me, what's going on in the picture."

For Discussion

1. What is Didion's definition of thinking? Do you agree with it?
2. To what extent does Didion's writing support her remarks about how and why she writes?
3. What does Didion mean when she says that grammar has "infinite power"? Power to do what?

BARBARA EHRENREICH

Born in 1941 in Butte, Montana, BARBARA EHRENREICH is an essayist and investigative journalist known for sharp political and social criticism. After graduating from Reed College, she received a PhD in biology from Rockefeller University and taught briefly while becoming an activist and writer. She has contributed to dozens of periodicals, among them *The New Republic*, *Mother Jones*, *Time*, and *The Atlantic Monthly*. She currently writes a column for *The Progressive*. Her many books include *Poverty in the American Dream: Women and Children First* (1983), *Fear of Falling: The Inner Life of the Middle Class* (1989), and *Blood Rites: Origins and History of the Passions of War* (1997). For her 2001 best-seller, *Nickel and Dimed: On (Not) Getting By in America*, Ehrenreich worked as a waiter, housecleaner, and Wal-Mart clerk, among other jobs, to investigate how unskilled workers manage financially. The recipient of numerous grants and awards, Ehrenreich is also a fellow at the New York Institute for the Humanities and a scholar at the Institute for Policy Studies.

The Roots of War

Why do human beings make war? In this essay written for *The Progressive* in April 2003, Ehrenreich tackles this vast subject with typical clarity and force.

"The Roots of War" mainly analyzes causes and effects to argue for a particular explanation of human warfare and a particular approach to warfare. But Ehrenreich draws on several other methods as well to develop the essay.

Example (Chap. 6): paragraphs 3, 4, 6, 7
Comparison and contrast (Chap. 7): paragraphs 4, 6, 8–9
Process analysis (Chap. 8): paragraphs 4, 6
Division or analysis (Chap. 9): paragraphs 2–4
Cause and effect (Chap. 11): throughout
Definition (Chap. 12): paragraph 4
Argument and persuasion (Chap. 13): paragraphs 9–10

Only three types of creatures engage in warfare—humans, chimpanzees, and ants. Among humans, warfare is so ubiquitous and historically commonplace that we are often tempted to attribute it to some innate predisposition for slaughter—a gene, perhaps, manifested as a murderous hormone. The earliest archeological evidence of war is from 12,000 years ago, well before such innovations as capitalism and cities and at the very beginning of settled, agricultural life. Sweeping through recorded history, you can find a predilection for warfare among hunter-gatherers, herding and farming peoples, industrial and even postindustrial societies, democracies, and dictatorships. The good old pop-feminist explanation — testosterone — would seem, at first sight, to fit the facts.

But war is too complex and collective an activity to be accounted for by any warlike instinct lurking within the individual psyche. Battles, in which the violence occurs, are only one part of war, most of which consists of preparation for battle — training, the manufacture of weapons, the organization of supply lines, etc. There is no plausible instinct, for example, that could impel a man to leave home, cut his hair short, and drill for hours in tight formation.

Contrary to the biological theories of war, it is not easy to get men to fight. In recent centuries, men have often gone to great lengths to avoid war — fleeing their homelands, shooting off their index fingers, feigning insanity. So unreliable was the rank and file of the famed eighteenth-century Prussian army that military rules forbade camping near wooded areas: The troops would simply melt away into the trees. Even when men are duly assembled for battle, killing is not something that seems to come naturally to them. As Lieutenant Colonel Dave Grossman argued in his book *On Killing: The Psychological Cost of Learning to Kill in War and Society*, one of the great challenges of military training is to get soldiers to shoot directly at individual enemies.

What is it, then, that has made war such an inescapable part of the human experience? Each war, of course, appears to the participants to have an immediate purpose — to crush the "Hun," preserve democracy, disarm Saddam, or whatever — that makes it noble and necessary. But those who study war dispassionately, as a recurrent event with no moral content, have observed a certain mathematical pattern: that of "epidemicity," or the tendency of war to spread in the manner of an infectious disease. Obviously, war is not a symptom of disease or the work of microbes, but it does spread geographically in a diseaselike manner, usually as groups take up warfare in response to warlike neighbors. It also spreads through time, as the losses suffered in one war call forth new wars of retaliation. Think of World War I, which breaks out for no good reason at all, draws in most of Europe as well as the United States, and then "reproduces" itself, after a couple of decades, as World War II.

In other words, as the Dutch social scientist Henk Houweling puts it, "one of the causes of war is war itself." Wars produce warlike societies, which, in turn, make the world more dangerous for other societies, which are thus recruited into being war-prone themselves. Just as there is no gene for war, neither is there a single type or feature of society — patriarchy or hierarchy — that generates it. War begets war and shapes human societies as it does so.

In general, war shapes human societies by requiring that they possess two things: one, some group or class of men (and, in some historical settings, women) who are trained to fight; and, two, the resources to arm and feed them. These requirements have often been compatible with patriarchal cultures dominated by a warrior elite—knights or samurai—as in medieval Europe or Japan. But not always: Different ways of fighting seem to lead to different forms of social and political organization. Historian Victor Hansen has argued that the phalanx formation adopted by the ancient Greeks, with its stress on equality and interdependence, was a factor favoring the emergence of democracy among nonslave Greek males. And there is no question but that the mass, gun-wielding armies that appeared in Europe in the seventeenth century contributed to the development of the modern nation-state—if only as a bureaucratic apparatus to collect the taxes required to support these armies.

Marx[1] was wrong, then: It is not only the "means of production" that shape societies, but the means of destruction. In our own time, the costs of war, or war readiness, are probably larger than at any time in history, in relation to other human needs, due to the pressure on nations not only to maintain a mass standing army—the United States supports about a million men and women at arms—but to keep up with an extremely expensive, ever-changing technology of killing. The cost squeeze has led to a new type of society, perhaps best termed a "depleted" state, in which the military has drained resources from all other social functions. North Korea is a particularly ghoulish example, where starvation coexists with nuclear-weapons development. But the USSR also crumbled under the weight of militarism, and the United States brandishes its military might around the world while, at this moment, cutting school lunches and health care for the poor.   7

"Addiction" provides only a pallid and imprecise analogy for the human relationship to war; parasitism—or even predation—is more to the point. However and whenever war began, it has persisted and propagated itself with the terrifying tenacity of a beast attached to the neck of living prey, feeding on human effort and blood.   8

If this is what we are up against, it won't do much good to try to uproot whatever warlike inclinations may dwell within our minds. Abjuring violent speech and imagery, critiquing masculinist culture, and promoting respect for human diversity—all of these are worthy projects, but they will make little contribution to the abolition of war. It would be far better to think of war as something external to ourselves, something which has to be uprooted, everywhere, down to the last weapon and bellicose pageant.   9

The "epidemicity" of war has one other clear implication: War cannot be used as a means to prevent or abolish war. True, for some time to come, urgent   10

---

[1]Karl Marx (1818–93), German political philosopher and founder of modern socialism, maintained that a society's mode of economic production—how goods are produced, who produces them, and who profits from their production—determines the society's politics, culture, and stability.—EDS.

threats from other heavily armed states will require at least the threat of armed force in response. But these must be very urgent threats and extremely restrained responses. To indulge, one more time, in the metaphor of war as a kind of living thing, a parasite on human societies: The idea of a war to end war is one of its oldest, and cruelest, tricks.

*For a reading quiz, sources on Barbara Ehrenreich, and annotated links to further readings on human warfare, visit **bedfordstmartins.com/thebedfordreader**.*

Journal Writing

Ehrenreich dismisses the idea of "some innate predisposition for slaughter" in human beings (par. 1). Take this point about biology down to the level of the individual: To what extent were you born with a predisposition toward your characteristics — kindness, aggressiveness, athleticism, intelligence, shyness, musical talent, and so on? (To take your journal writing further, see "From Journal to Essay" on the facing page.)

Questions on Meaning

1. In paragraph 3 Ehrenreich refers to "biological theories of war." What are these theories, and why does she dismiss them?
2. Ehrenreich's THESIS develops over the course of the essay. What is it?
3. According to Ehrenreich, why are the costs of war higher today than in the past?
4. What point does Ehrenreich make with the examples of North Korea and the former Soviet Union in paragraph 7?

Questions on Writing Strategy

1. Ehrenreich published this essay about a month after the United States and its allies invaded Iraq in 2003. How might the timing relate to her PURPOSE in writing the essay? What do you think her purpose is?
2. What ANALOGY does Ehrenreich use to explain the root cause of war (par. 4)? What is her purpose in using it?
3. Where in the essay does Ehrenreich cite the opinions of experts? What does this strategy contribute to the essay?
4. **MIXED METHODS.** What does Ehrenreich COMPARE AND CONTRAST in paragraph 6? What purpose does the comparison serve?
5. **MIXED METHODS.** Explain how Ehrenreich uses CAUSE AND EFFECT to build to the ARGUMENT in paragraphs 9–10.

Questions on Language

1. Why do you think Ehrenreich prefers the words *parasitism* and *predation* over *addiction* to describe our relationship to war (par. 8)? What do the CONNOTATIONS of these words suggest about her viewpoint?
2. How does Ehrenreich's TONE shift between paragraphs 1–6 and paragraphs 7–10? What is the EFFECT of this shift?
3. If any of the following words are unfamiliar, be sure to look them up in a dictionary: ubiquitous, predilection, testosterone (par. 1); feigning, duly (3); microbes (4); patriarchy, hierarchy, begets (5); phalanx (6); brandishes (7); pallid, propagated, tenacity (8); abjuring, bellicose (9).

Suggestions for Writing

1. **FROM JOURNAL TO ESSAY.** Working from your journal entry, write an essay that explores the debate about heredity versus environment, nature versus nurture, as it applies to you. Using specific EXAMPLES, discuss the extent to which you think genes or your surroundings have shaped who you are.
2. Ehrenreich writes about the causes of warfare in general. In the library or on the Web, research the causes proposed for a particular war that interests you. How, if at all, do the various explanations jibe with Ehrenreich's explanation? Which explanations do you find most compelling, and why? Write an essay that explores and takes a position on the various causal explanations.
3. **CRITICAL WRITING.** Respond to Ehrenreich's conclusion that "[w]ar cannot be used as a means to prevent or abolish war" (par. 10). How well does Ehrenreich support this claim? In an essay, ANALYZE and EVALUATE Ehrenreich's argument, looking in particular at her EVIDENCE, her reasoning, and whether and how she considers possible opposing arguments.
4. **CONNECTIONS.** In paragraph 7 Ehrenreich implies that governments should spend less money on their military and more on social programs. In an essay, discuss how Ehrenreich's point about the trade-off between military and social spending corresponds to the ideas in Thomas Sowell's "'Needs'" (p. 499).
5. **CONNECTIONS.** As Ehrenreich points out in paragraph 7, nations pay huge costs "to keep up with an extremely expensive, ever-changing technology of killing." Write an essay in which you discuss how Chet Raymo might respond to this point, based on the main idea of his essay "A Measure of Restraint" (p. 212).

Barbara Ehrenreich on Writing

The printed word, in the view of Barbara Ehrenreich, should be a powerful instrument for reform. In an article in *Mother Jones*, though, she complains about a tacit censorship in American magazines that has sometimes prevented her from fulfilling her purpose as a writer. Ehrenreich recalls the difficulties she had in trying to persuade the editor of a national magazine to assign her a story on the plight of Third World women refugees. "Sorry," said the editor, "Third World women have never done anything for me."

Ehrenreich infers that writers who write for such magazines must follow a rule: "You must learn not to stray from your assigned sociodemographic stereotype." She observes, "As a woman, I am generally asked to write on 'women's topics,' such as cooking, divorce, how to succeed in business, diet fads, and the return of the bustle. These are all fine topics and give great scope to my talents, but when I ask, in faltering tones, for an assignment . . . on the trade deficit, I am likely to be told that *anyone* (Bill, Gerry, Bob) could cover that, whereas my 'voice' is *essential* for the aerobic toothbrushing story. This is not, strictly speaking, 'censorship'—just a division of labor in which white men cover politics, foreign policy, and the economy, and the rest of us cover what's left over, such as the bustle."

Over the years Ehrenreich has had many manuscripts rejected by editors who comment, "too angry," "too depressing," and "Where's the bright side?" She agrees with writer Herbert Gold, who once deduced that the American media want only "happy stories about happy people with happy problems." She concludes, "You can write about anything—death squads, AIDS . . . —so long as you make it 'upbeat.'" Despite such discouragements, Ehrenreich continues her battle to "disturb the stupor induced by six straight pages of Calvin Klein ads."

For Discussion

1. Is Ehrenreich right about "a tacit censorship in American magazines"? Check a recent issue of a magazine that prints signed articles. How many of the articles *not* on "women's topics" are written by women? How many are written by men?
2. To what extent do you agree with Ehrenreich—and with Herbert Gold—that the American media are interested only in "upbeat" stories?

STEPHEN JAY GOULD

A paleontologist and collector of snails, STEPHEN JAY GOULD was born in New York City in 1941, went to Antioch College, and took a doctorate from Columbia University. From the age of twenty-five, Gould taught biology, geology, and the history of science at Harvard, where his courses were among the most popular. Although he often wrote for specialists (*Ontogeny and Phylogeny*, 1977), Gould is best known for essays that explore science in prose a layperson can enjoy. For twenty-seven years, until 2000, he wrote a monthly column for *Natural History* magazine. These and other essays have been collected in many books, including *Hens' Teeth and Horses' Toes* (1983), *Eight Little Piggies* (1993), *Dinosaur in a Haystack* (1995), and *Leonardo's Mountain of Clams and the Diet of Worms* (1998). His most recent books are *Rocks of Ages* (1999), which attempts to heal the rift between science and religion; *The Structure of Evolutionary Theory* (2002), in which he proposes a new framework for thinking about Darwinism; and *I Have Landed: Splashes and Reflections from a Life in Natural History* (2002), a collection of essays. In 1981 Gould received a grant from the MacArthur Foundation. In 1999 he became president of the American Association for the Advancement of Science. He died in 2002 at the age of sixty.

A Biological Homage to Mickey Mouse

In this selection from *The Panda's Thumb*, a 1980 collection of *Natural History* essays, Gould takes the fiftieth birthday of Mickey Mouse as the occasion for witty yet serious observations about human evolution. The original Mickey changed greatly over the years, growing not older and wiser but younger and better behaved. How, you might ask, does the evolution of Mickey apply to us humans? Gould tells all.

Gould draws on a number of methods to trace Mickey's evolution, and our own:

Narration (Chap. 4): paragraphs 3, 7
Description (Chap. 5): paragraphs 1, 2, 6, 8, 13
Comparison and contrast (Chap. 7): paragraphs 11, 13, 16–18, 20
Process analysis (Chap. 8): paragraphs 5–6, 10, 17–18
Division or analysis (Chap. 9): paragraphs 4, 7–8, 10, 15
Cause and effect (Chap. 11): paragraphs 3–4, 7–8, 12–15, 18–19
Definition (Chap. 12): paragraphs 16–17

Age often turns fire to placidity. Lytton Strachey, in his incisive portrait of Florence Nightingale,[1] writes of her declining years:

---

[1] Strachey (1880–1932) was an English historian. Nightingale (1820–1910) was an English nurse who founded the modern practice of nursing. —EDS.

Destiny, having waited very patiently, played a queer trick on Miss Nightingale. The benevolence and public spirit of that long life had only been equalled by its acerbity. Her virtue had dwelt in hardness. . . . And now the sarcastic years brought the proud woman her punishment. She was not to die as she had lived. The sting was to be taken out of her; she was to be made soft; she was to be reduced to compliance and complacency.

I was therefore not surprised—although the analogy may strike some people   2
as sacrilegious—to discover that the creature who gave his name as a synonym for insipidity had a gutsier youth. Mickey Mouse turned a respectable fifty last year. To mark the occasion, many theaters replayed his debut performance in *Steamboat Willie* (1928). The original Mickey was a rambunctious, even slightly sadistic fellow. In a remarkable sequence, exploiting the exciting new development of sound, Mickey and Minnie pummel, squeeze, and twist the animals on board to produce a rousing chorus of "Turkey in the Straw." They honk a duck with a tight embrace, crank a goat's tail, tweak a pig's nipples, bang a cow's teeth as a stand-in xylophone, and play bagpipe on her udder.

Christopher Finch, in his semiofficial pictorial history of Disney's work,   3
comments: "The Mickey Mouse who hit the movie houses in the late twenties was not quite the well-behaved character most of us are familiar with today. He was mischievous, to say the least, and even displayed a streak of cruelty." But Mickey soon cleaned up his act, leaving to gossip and speculation only his unresolved relationship with Minnie and the status of Morty and Ferdie.

Mickey's Evolution During Fifty Years (left to right)   As Mickey became increasingly well behaved over the years, his appearance became more youthful. Measurements of three stages in his development revealed a larger relative head size, larger eyes, and an enlarged cranium—all traits of juvenility. © Disney Enterprises, Inc.

Finch continues: "Mickey . . . had become virtually a national symbol, and as such he was expected to behave properly at all times. If he occasionally stepped out of line, any number of letters would arrive at the studio from citizens and organizations who felt that the nation's moral well-being was in their hands. . . . Eventually he would be pressured into the role of straight man."[2]

As Mickey's personality softened, his appearance changed. Many Disney fans are aware of this transformation through time, but few (I suspect) have recognized the coordinating theme behind all the alterations—in fact, I am not sure that the Disney artists themselves explicitly realized what they were doing, since the changes appeared in such a halting and piecemeal fashion. In short, the blander and inoffensive Mickey became progressively more juvenile in appearance. (Since Mickey's chronological age never altered—like most cartoon characters he stands impervious to the ravages of time—this change in appearance at a constant age is a true evolutionary transformation. Progressive juvenilization as an evolutionary phenomenon is called *neoteny*. More on this later.)

4

The characteristic changes of form during human growth have inspired a substantial biological literature. Since the head-end of an embryo differentiates first and grows more rapidly in utero than the foot-end (an anteroposterior gradient, in technical language), a newborn child possesses a

5

[2] Finch's book is *The Art of Walt Disney: From Mickey Mouse to the Magic Kingdom* (1975, rev. 2004).—EDS.

relatively large head attached to a medium-sized body with diminutive legs and feet. This gradient is reversed through growth as legs and feet overtake the front end. Heads continue to grow but so much more slowly than the rest of the body that relative head size decreases.

In addition, a suite of changes pervades the head itself during human growth. The brain grows very slowly after age three, and the bulbous cranium of a young child gives way to the more slanted, lower-browed configuration of adulthood. The eyes scarcely grow at all and relative eye size declines precipitously. But the jaw gets bigger and bigger. Children, compared with adults, have larger heads and eyes, smaller jaws, a more prominent, bulging cranium, and smaller, pudgier legs and feet. Adult heads are altogether more apish, I'm sorry to say.   6

Mickey, however, has traveled this ontogenetic pathway in reverse during his fifty years among us. He has assumed an ever more childlike appearance as the ratty character of *Steamboat Willie* became the cute and inoffensive host to a magic kingdom. By 1940, the former tweaker of a pig's nipples gets a kick in the ass for insubordination (as the *Sorcerer's Apprentice* in *Fantasia*). By 1953, his last cartoon, he has gone fishing and cannot even subdue a squirting clam.   7

The Disney artists transformed Mickey in clever silence, often using suggestive devices that mimic nature's own changes by different routes. To give him the shorter and pudgier legs of youth, they lowered his pants line and covered his spindly legs with a baggy outfit. (His arms and legs also thickened substantially—and acquired joints for a floppier appearance.) His head grew relatively larger and its features more youthful. The length of Mickey's snout has not altered, but decreasing protrusion is more subtly suggested by a pronounced thickening. Mickey's eye has grown in two modes: first, by a major, discontinuous evolutionary shift as the entire eye of ancestral Mickey became the pupil of his descendants, and second, by gradual increase thereafter.   8

Mickey's improvement in cranial bulging followed an interesting path since his evolution has always been constrained by the unaltered convention of representing his head as a circle with appended ears and an oblong snout. The circle's form could not be altered to provide a bulging cranium directly. Instead, Mickey's ears moved back, increasing the distance between nose and ears, and giving him a rounded, rather than a sloping, forehead.   9

To give these observations the cachet of quantitative science, I applied my best pair of dial calipers to three stages of the official phylogeny—the thin-nosed, ears-forward figure of the early 1930s (stage 1), the latter-day Jack of *Mickey and the Beanstalk* (1947, stage 2), and the modern mouse (stage 3). I measured three signs of Mickey's creeping juvenility: increasing eye size (maximum height) as a percentage of head length (base of the nose to top of rear ear); increasing head length as a percentage of body length; and increasing cranial vault size measured by rearward displacement of the front ear   10

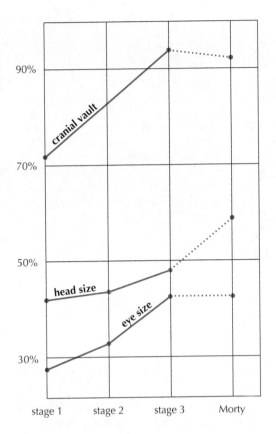

90%

70%

cranial vault

50%

head size

eye size

30%

stage 1   stage 2   stage 3   Morty

The "Evolution" of Mickey Mouse At an early stage in his evolution, Mickey had a smaller head, cranial vault, and eyes. He evolved toward the characteristics of his young nephew Morty (connected to Mickey by a dotted line).

(base of the nose to top of front ear as a percentage of base of the nose to top of rear ear).

All three percentages increased steadily — eye size from 27 to 42 percent of head length; head length from 42.7 to 48.1 percent of body length; and nose to front ear from 71.7 to a whopping 95.6 percent of nose to rear ear. For comparison, I measured Mickey's young "nephew" Morty Mouse. In each case, Mickey has clearly been evolving toward youthful stages of his stock, although he still has a way to go for head length.

You may, indeed, now ask what an at least marginally respectable scientist has been doing with a mouse like that. In part, fiddling around and having fun, of course. (I still prefer *Pinocchio* to *Citzen Kane*.) But I do have a serious point — two, in fact — to make. We must first ask why Disney chose to change his most famous character so gradually and persistently in the same direction? National symbols are not altered capriciously and market researchers (for the doll industry in particular) have spent a good deal of time and practical effort learning what features appeal to people as cute and friendly. Biologists also

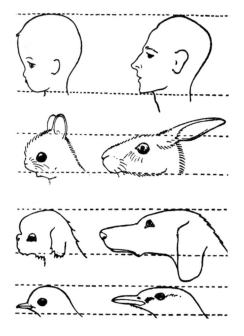

Humans feel affection for animals with juvenile features: large eyes, bulging craniums, retreating chins (left column). Small-eyed, long-snouted animals (right column) do not elicit the same response. From *Studies in Animal and Human Behavior*, vol. 2, by Konrad Lorenz (London: Methuen, 1971).

have spent a great deal of time studying a similar subject in a wide range of animals.

In one of his most famous articles, Konrad Lorenz[3] argues that humans use the characteristic differences in form between babies and adults as important behavioral cues. He believes that features of juvenility trigger "innate releasing mechanisms" for affection and nurturing in adult humans. When we see a living creature with babyish features, we feel an automatic surge of disarming tenderness. The adaptive value of this response can scarcely be questioned, for we must nurture our babies. Lorenz, by the way, lists among his releasers the very features of babyhood that Disney affixed progressively to Mickey: "a relatively large head, predominance of the brain capsule, large and low-lying eyes, bulging cheek region, short and thick extremities, a springy elastic consistency, and clumsy movements." . . .

Lorenz emphasizes the power that juvenile features hold over us, and the abstract quality of their influence, by pointing out that we judge other animals by the same criteria—although the judgment may be utterly inappropriate in an evolutionary context. We are, in short, fooled by an evolved response to our own babies, and we transfer our reaction to the same set of features in other animals. . . .

[3] Lorenz (1903–89) was an Austrian psychologist, winner of a Nobel Prize. —EDS.

I submit that Mickey Mouse's evolutionary road down the course of his   15
own growth in reverse reflects the unconscious discovery of this biological
principle by Disney and his artists. In fact, the emotional status of most Disney characters rests on the same set of distinctions. To this extent, the Magic
Kingdom trades on a biological illusion—our ability to abstract and our
propensity to transfer inappropriately to other animals the fitting responses we
make to changing form in the growth of our own bodies. . . .

As a second, serious biological comment on Mickey's odyssey in form, I   16
note that his path to eternal youth repeats, in epitome, our own evolutionary
story. For humans are neotenic. We have evolved by retaining to adulthood
the originally juvenile features of our ancestors. Our australopithecine forebears,[4] like Mickey in *Steamboat Willie,* had projecting jaws and low vaulted
craniums.

Our embryonic skulls scarcely differ from those of chimpanzees. And we   17
follow the same path of changing form through growth: relative decrease of
the cranial vault since brains grow so much more slowly than bodies after
birth, and continuous relative increase of the jaw. But while chimps accentuate these changes, producing an adult strikingly different in form from a baby,
we proceed much more slowly down the same path and never get nearly so far.
Thus, as adults, we retain juvenile features. To be sure, we change enough to
produce a notable difference between baby and adult, but our alteration is far
smaller than that experienced by chimps and other primates.

A marked slowdown of developmental rates has triggered our neoteny.   18
Primates are slow developers among mammals, but we have accentuated the
trend to a degree matched by no other mammal. We have very long periods of
gestation, markedly extended childhoods, and the longest life span of any
mammal. The morphological features of eternal youth have served us well.
Our enlarged brain is, at least in part, a result of extending rapid prenatal
growth rates to later ages. (In all mammals, the brain grows rapidly in utero
but often very little after birth. We have extended this fetal phase into post-
natal life.)

But the changes in timing themselves have been just as important. We are   19
preeminently learning animals, and our extended childhood permits the
transference of culture by education. Many animals display flexibility and
play in childhood but follow rigidly programmed patterns as adults. Lorenz
writes . . . : "The characteristic which is so vital for the human peculiarity of
the true man—that of always remaining in a state of development—is quite
certainly a gift which we owe to the neotenous nature of mankind."

---

[4] *Australopithecus,* an extinct ancestor of humans, lived about 4 million to 1.5 million years
ago. — EDS.

In short, we, like Mickey, never grow up although we, alas, do grow old.   20
Best wishes to you, Mickey, for your next half-century. May we stay as young
as you, but grow a bit wiser.

*For a reading quiz, sources on Stephen Jay Gould, and annotated links to further
readings on Mickey Mouse and on evolution, visit **bedfordstmartins.com/
thebedfordreader**.*

Journal Writing

Gould writes, paraphrasing Konrad Lorenz, that innately "[w]hen we see a living creature with babyish features, we feel an automatic surge of disarming tenderness" (par.
13). How do you respond to this statement? In your experience is it true of people generally, or are some people more predisposed to such feelings than others? What is your
own reaction to babies and young animals? Write a journal entry in which you consider these questions. (To take your journal writing further, see "From Journal to
Essay" on the facing page.)

Questions on Meaning

1. How, according to Gould, did Mickey Mouse change in terms of behavior over
   the years? To what does Gould attribute this change?
2. What basic point does Gould make about changes to Mickey Mouse's appearance
   over the years? How are these changes related to the concept of neoteny (pars. 4,
   16)?
3. How exactly did Mickey Mouse's appearance change? In addition to Gould's
   statements about the changes, what do you observe yourself in the illustration on
   pages 616–17?
4. What are Gould's two "serious" comments (pars. 12 and 16)? State his points in
   your own words.

Questions on Writing Strategy

1. What is the PURPOSE of each visual image included by Gould? Does each seem
   necessary?
2. What is the point of paragraphs 10–11? Is Gould serious? How do you respond to
   these paragraphs?
3. **MIXED METHODS.** How does PROCESS ANALYSIS serve Gould in paragraphs 5–6?
   Why does he explain human physical development in such detail?

4. **MIXED METHODS.** How is Gould's third illustration (p. 620) a model of COMPARISON AND CONTRAST? What subjects does Gould compare and contrast in paragraphs 17–18?

Questions on Language

1. In what sense is Mickey Mouse, as Gould claims, "a synonym for insipidity" (par. 2)? What do *synonym* and *insipidity* mean? In everyday speech, what does *Mickey Mouse* mean?
2. Gould uses vivid verbs in the last two sentences of paragraph 2. What is their EFFECT?
3. How would you characterize Gould's DICTION in this essay? What does his diction suggest about his intended AUDIENCE? Does he assume that readers are scientists like himself?
4. Consult a dictionary if you are uncertain of the meaning of any of the following: homage (title); sacrilegious, rambunctious, sadistic, pummel (par. 2); mischievous (3); explicitly, piecemeal, impervious (4); in utero, gradient (5); suite, pervades, bulbous, cranium (6); ontogenetic (7); protrusion (8); oblong (9); cachet, quantitative, calipers, phylogeny (10); innate (13); odyssey, epitome (16); accentuate (17); morphological (18); preeminently (19).

Suggestions for Writing

1. **FROM JOURNAL TO ESSAY.** Based on your journal entry, write an essay that examines people's responses to animals (including humans) with babyish features. Does everyone respond the same way, in your experience? If you see variation, what do you think accounts for it: upbringing? gender? heredity? personality? distraction? Use EXAMPLES from your experience to illustrate and support your ideas.
2. At a library or video store, locate a sampling of Mickey Mouse cartoons from the original *Steamboat Willie* (1928) through the last of the series in the 1950s. Write an essay that traces the evolution of Mickey's personality and behavior over the years. You might also consider his stature today as a symbol for the Walt Disney Company. For more information on Mickey Mouse, visit the "ultimate unofficial site," maintained by Chris Gibson, at *www.mickey-mouse.com* (the URL must include *www*).
3. Research the work of Stephen Jay Gould, looking for reviews of his books as well as interviews with him. In an essay, consider Gould's achievements as a scientist and a writer.
4. **CONNECTIONS.** "A Measure of Restraint" by Chet Raymo (p. 212) is another essay by a scientist written for a nonspecialist audience. In an essay compare and contrast Gould's essay with Raymo's. Do both writers succeed equally well in presenting complex concepts in ways that most readers can understand? Use quotations and PARAPHRASES from both essays to support your ideas.
5. **CONNECTIONS.** In "How You Became You" (p. 299), Bill Bryson writes about the chemical and biological evolution of the human species. Write an essay that integrates Gould's and Bryson's presentations of human evolution. How do the physical changes that Gould describes fit into Bryson's longer view?

Stephen Jay Gould on Writing

In his prologue to *The Flamingo's Smile*, Stephen Jay Gould positions himself in a long and respectable tradition of writers who communicate scientific ideas to a general audience. To popularize, he says, does not mean to trivialize, cheapen, or adulterate. "I follow one cardinal rule in writing these essays," he insists. "No compromises. I will make language accessible by defining or eliminating jargon; I will not simplify concepts. I can state all sorts of highfalutin, moral justifications for this approach (and I do believe in them), but the basic reason is simple and personal. I write these essays primarily to aid my own quest to learn and understand as much as possible about nature in the short time allotted."

In his own view, Gould was lucky: He was a writer carried along by a single, fascinating theme. "If my volumes work at all, they owe their reputation to coherence supplied by the common theme of evolutionary theory. I have a wonderful advantage among essayists because no other theme so beautifully encompasses both the particulars that fascinate and the generalities that instruct. . . . Each essay is both a single long argument and a welding together of particulars."

For Discussion

1. What differences would occur naturally between the work of a scientist writing for other scientists and the work of Gould, who wrote about science for a general AUDIENCE?
2. How does the author defend himself against the possible charge that, as a popularizer of science, he trivializes his subject?

MARTIN LUTHER KING, JR.

MARTIN LUTHER KING, JR. (1929–68), was born in Atlanta, the son of a Baptist minister, and was himself ordained in the same denomination. Stepping to the forefront of the civil rights movement in 1955, King led African Americans in a boycott of segregated city buses in Montgomery, Alabama; became the first president of the Southern Christian Leadership Conference; and staged sit-ins and mass marches that helped bring about the Civil Rights Act passed by Congress in 1964 and the Voting Rights Act of 1965. He received the Nobel Peace Prize in 1964. While King preached "nonviolent resistance," he was himself the target of violence. He was stabbed in New York, pelted with stones in Chicago; his home in Montgomery was bombed; and ultimately he was assassinated in Memphis by a sniper. On his tombstone near Atlanta's Ebenezer Baptist Church are these words from the spiritual he quotes at the conclusion of "I Have a Dream": "Free at last, free at last, thank God almighty, I'm free at last." Martin Luther King's birthday, January 15, is now a national holiday.

I Have a Dream

In Washington, DC, on August 28, 1963, King's campaign of nonviolent resistance reached its historic climax. On that date, commemorating the centennial of Lincoln's Emancipation Proclamation freeing the slaves, King led a march of 200,000 persons, black and white, from the Washington Monument to the Lincoln Memorial. Before this throng, and to millions who watched on television, he delivered this unforgettable speech.

Intended to inspire and motivate its audience, King's speech is a model of a certain kind of persuasion. To make his point, King draws on a number of methods:

Narration (Chap. 4): paragraphs 1–2
Description (Chap. 5): paragraphs 2, 4
Example (Chap. 6): paragraphs 6–9, 12–16, 21–22
Comparison and contrast (Chap. 7): paragraphs 3–4, 6
Cause and effect (Chap. 11): paragraphs 5, 7, 19
Argument and persuasion (Chap. 13): throughout

Five score years ago, a great American, in whose symbolic shadow we   1
stand, signed the Emancipation Proclamation. This momentous decree came as a great beacon light of hope to millions of Negro slaves who had been seared in the flames of withering injustice. It came as a joyous daybreak to end the long night of captivity.

But one hundred years later, we must face the tragic fact that the Negro   2
is still not free. One hundred years later, the life of the Negro is still sadly

crippled by the manacles of segregation and the chains of discrimination. One hundred years later, the Negro lives on a lonely island of poverty in the midst of a vast ocean of material prosperity. One hundred years later, the Negro is still languishing in the corners of American society and finds himself in exile in his own land. So we have come here today to dramatize an appalling condition.

In a sense we have come to our nation's capital to cash a check. When the architects of our republic wrote the magnificent words of the Constitution and the Declaration of Independence, they were signing a promissory note to which every American was to fall heir. This note was a promise that all men would be guaranteed the unalienable rights of life, liberty, and the pursuit of happiness.

It is obvious today that America has defaulted on this promissory note insofar as her citizens of color are concerned. Instead of honoring this sacred obligation, America has given the Negro people a bad check; a check which has come back marked "insufficient funds." But we refuse to believe that the bank of justice is bankrupt. We refuse to believe that there are insufficient funds in the great vaults of opportunity of this nation. So we have come to cash this check—a check that will give us upon demand the riches of freedom and the security of justice. We have also come to this hallowed spot to remind America of the fierce urgency of *now*. This is no time to engage in the luxury of cooling off or to take the tranquilizing drugs of gradualism. *Now* is the time to make real the promises of Democracy. *Now* is the time to rise from the dark and desolate valley of segregation to the sunlit path of racial justice. *Now* is the time to open the doors of opportunity to all of God's children. *Now* is the time to lift our nation from the quicksands of racial injustice to the solid rock of brotherhood.

It would be fatal for the nation to overlook the urgency of the moment and to underestimate the determination of the Negro. This sweltering summer of the Negro's legitimate discontent will not pass until there is an invigorating autumn of freedom and equality; 1963 is not an end, but a beginning. Those who hope that the Negro needed to blow off steam and will now be content will have a rude awakening if the nation returns to business as usual. There will be neither rest nor tranquillity in America until the Negro is granted his citizenship rights. The whirlwinds of revolt will continue to shake the foundations of our nation until the bright day of justice emerges.

But there is something that I must say to my people who stand on the warm threshold which leads into the palace of justice. In the process of gaining our rightful place we must not be guilty of wrongful deeds. Let us not seek to satisfy our thirst for freedom by drinking from the cup of bitterness and hatred. We must forever conduct our struggle on the high plane of dignity and discipline. We must not allow our creative protest to degenerate into physical violence. Again and again we must rise to the majestic heights of meeting physical force with soul force. The marvelous new militancy which has engulfed the Negro community must not lead us to a distrust of all white people, for many of our white brothers, as evidenced by their presence here today, have come to realize that their destiny is tied up with our destiny and their freedom is inextricably bound to our freedom. We cannot walk alone.

And as we walk, we must make the pledge that we shall march ahead. We 7 cannot turn back. There are those who are asking the devotees of civil rights, "When will you be satisfied?" We can never be satisfied as long as the Negro is the victim of the unspeakable horrors of police brutality. We can never be satisfied as long as our bodies, heavy with the fatigue of travel, cannot gain lodging in the motels of the highways and the hotels of the cities. We cannot be satisfied as long as the Negro's basic mobility is from a smaller ghetto to a larger one. We can never be satisfied as long as a Negro in Mississippi cannot vote and a Negro in New York believes he has nothing for which to vote. No, no, we are not satisfied, and we will not be satisfied until justice rolls down like waters and righteousness like a mighty stream.

I am not unmindful that some of you have come here out of great trials 8 and tribulations. Some of you have come fresh from narrow jail cells. Some of you have come from areas where your quest for freedom left you battered by the storms of persecution and staggered by the winds of police brutality. You have been the veterans of creative suffering. Continue to work with the faith that unearned suffering is redemptive.

Go back to Mississippi, go back to Alabama, go back to South Carolina, 9 go back to Georgia, go back to Louisiana, go back to the slums and ghettos of our northern cities, knowing that somehow this situation can and will be changed. Let us not wallow in the valley of despair.

I say to you today, my friends, that in spite of the difficulties and frustra- 10 tions of the moment I still have a dream. It is a dream deeply rooted in the American dream.

I have a dream that one day this nation will rise up and live out the true 11 meaning of its creed: "We hold these truths to be self-evident; that all men are created equal."

I have a dream that one day on the red hills of Georgia the sons of former 12 slaves and the sons of former slaveowners will be able to sit down together at the table of brotherhood.

I have a dream that one day even the state of Mississippi, a desert state 13 sweltering with the heat of injustice and oppression, will be transformed into an oasis of freedom and justice.

I have a dream that my four little children will one day live in a nation   14
where they will not be judged by the color of their skin but by the content of
their character.

I have a dream today.   15

I have a dream that one day the state of Alabama, whose governor's lips   16
are presently dripping with the words of interposition and nullification, will
be transformed into a situation where little black boys and black girls will be
able to join hands with little white boys and white girls and walk together as
sisters and brothers.

I have a dream today.   17

I have a dream that one day every valley shall be exalted, every hill and   18
mountain shall be made low, the rough places will be made plain, and the
crooked places will be made straight, and the glory of the Lord shall be
revealed, and all flesh shall see it together.

This is our hope. This is the faith with which I return to the South. With   19
this faith we will be able to hew out of the mountain of despair a stone of
hope. With this faith we will be able to transform the jangling discords of
our nation into a beautiful symphony of brotherhood. With this faith we
will be able to work together, to pray together, to struggle together, to go to
jail together, to stand up for freedom together, knowing that we will be free
one day.

This will be the day when all of God's children will be able to sing with   20
new meaning

> My country, 'tis of thee,
> Sweet land of liberty,
> Of thee I sing:
> Land where my fathers died,
> Land of the pilgrims' pride,
> From every mountainside
> Let freedom ring.

And if America is to be a great nation this must become true. So let free-   21
dom ring from the prodigious hilltops of New Hampshire. Let freedom ring
from the mighty mountains of New York. Let freedom ring from the height-
ening Alleghenies of Pennsylvania!

Let freedom ring from the snowcapped Rockies of Colorado!   22

Let freedom ring from the curvaceous peaks of California!   23

But not only that; let freedom ring from Stone Mountain of Georgia!   24

Let freedom ring from Lookout Mountain of Tennessee!   25

Let freedom ring from every hill and molehill of Mississippi. From every   26
mountainside, let freedom ring.

When we let freedom ring, when we let it ring from every village and   27
every hamlet, from every state and every city, we will be able to speed up that
day when all of God's children, black men and white men, Jews and Gentiles,
Protestants and Catholics, will be able to join hands and sing in the words of
the old Negro spiritual, "Free at last! free at last! thank God almighty, we are
free at last!"

*For a reading quiz, sources on Martin Luther King, Jr., and annotated links to further
readings on the civil rights movement in the United States, visit **bedfordstmartins
.com/thebedfordreader**.*

Journal Writing

Do you think we have moved closer to fulfilling King's dream in the decades since he
gave this famous speech? In your journal, explore why or why not. (To take your journal writing further, see "From Journal to Essay" on the next page.)

Questions on Meaning

1. What is the apparent PURPOSE of this speech?
2. What THESIS does King develop in his first four paragraphs?
3. What does King mean by the "marvelous new militancy which has engulfed the
   Negro community" (par. 6)? Does this contradict King's nonviolent philosophy?
4. In what passages of his speech does King notice events of history? Where does he
   acknowledge the historic occasion on which he is speaking?

Questions on Writing Strategy

1. What indicates that King's words were meant primarily for an AUDIENCE of listeners, and only secondarily for a reading audience? To hear these indications, try
   reading the speech aloud. What uses of PARALLELISM do you notice?
2. Where in the speech does King acknowledge that not all of his listeners are
   African American?
3. How much EMPHASIS does King place on the past? How much does he place on
   the future?
4. **MIXED METHODS.** Analyze the ETHICAL APPEAL of King's ARGUMENT (see p. 519).
   Where in the speech, for instance, does he present himself as reasonable despite
   his passion? To what extent does his personal authority lend power to his words?

5. **MIXED METHODS.** The DESCRIPTION in paragraphs 2 and 4 depends on metaphor, a FIGURE OF SPEECH in which one thing is said to be another thing. How do the metaphors in these paragraphs work for King's purpose?

Questions on Language

1. In general, is the language of King's speech ABSTRACT or CONCRETE? How is this level appropriate to his message and to the span of history with which he deals?
2. Point to memorable figures of speech besides those examined in the "Mixed Methods" question on the preceding page.
3. Define momentous (par. 1); manacles, languishing (2); promissory note, unalienable (3); defaulted, hallowed, gradualism (4); inextricably (6); mobility, ghetto (7); tribulations, redemptive (8); interposition, nullification (16); prodigious (21); curvaceous (23); hamlet (27).

Suggestions for Writing

1. **FROM JOURNAL TO ESSAY.** Use your journal entry to write an essay that explains your sense of how well the United States has progressed toward realizing King's dream. You may choose to focus on America as a whole or on your particular community, but you should use specific EVIDENCE to support your opinion.
2. Propose some course of action in a situation that you consider an injustice. Racial injustice is one possible area, or unfairness to any minority, or to women, children, the elderly, ex-convicts, the disabled, the poor. If possible, narrow your subject to a particular incident or a local situation on which you can write knowledgeably.
3. **CRITICAL WRITING.** What can you INFER from this speech about King's own attitudes toward oppression and injustice? Does he follow his own injunction not "to satisfy our thirst for freedom by drinking from the cup of bitterness and hatred" (par. 6)? Explain your answer, using evidence from the speech.
4. **CONNECTIONS.** King's "I Have a Dream" and Edward Said's "Clashing Civilizations?" (p. 669) both seek to influence readers, either to cause them to act or to change their views. Yet the two authors take very different approaches to achieve their purposes. COMPARE AND CONTRAST the authors' persuasive strategies, considering especially their effectiveness for the situation each writes about and the audience each addresses.
5. **CONNECTIONS.** King's speech was delivered in 1963. Brent Staples's essay "Black Men and Public Space" (p. 205) was first published in 1986. In an essay, explore the changes, if any, that are evident in the ASSUMPTIONS the authors make about their audiences' attitudes, about race in general, and about racism.

MAXINE HONG KINGSTON

MAXINE HONG KINGSTON grew up caught between two complex and very different cultures: the China of her parents and the America of her surroundings. In her first two books, *The Woman Warrior: Memoirs of a Girlhood Among Ghosts* (1976) and *China Men* (1980), Kingston combines Chinese myth and history with family tales to create a dreamlike world that shifts between reality and fantasy. Born in 1940 in Stockton, California, Kingston was the first American-born child of a scholar and a medical practitioner who became laundry workers in this country. After graduating from the University of California at Berkeley (BA, 1962), Kingston taught English at California and Hawaii high schools, at the University of Hawaii, and for many years at UC Berkeley. She has contributed essays, poems, and stories to *The New Yorker*, the *New York Times Magazine*, *Ms.*, and other periodicals. Other books by Kingston include a collection of essays, *Hawai'i One Summer* (1987); a novel, *Tripmaster Monkey: His Fake Book* (1989); and a collection of lectures and verse, *To Be a Poet* (2002). Her most recent publication, *The Fifth Book of Peace* (2003), rose from the ashes of a manuscript that was destroyed, along with her home and possessions, in a 1991 fire—a tragedy Kingston turned into a story of "loss, reconciliation, and peace."

No Name Woman

"No Name Woman" is part of *The Woman Warrior*. Like much of Kingston's writing, it blends the "talk-stories" of Kingston's elders, her own vivid imaginings, and the reality of her experience—this time to discover why her Chinese aunt drowned herself in the family well.

Kingston develops "No Name Woman" with four main methods, all intertwined: In the context of narrating her own experiences, she seeks the causes of her aunt's suicide by comparing various narratives of it, and she employs description to make the narratives concrete and vivid. The main uses of these methods appear below:

Narration (Chap. 4): paragraphs 1–8, 14, 16–20, 23, 28–30, 34–35, 37–46
Description (Chap. 5): paragraphs 4–8, 21, 23–27, 31, 37, 40–46
Comparison and contrast (Chap. 7): paragraphs 15–18, 20–24, 27–28, 31
Cause and effect (Chap. 11): paragraphs 10–11, 15–18, 21–25, 29–31,
    33–39, 44–48

"You must not tell anyone," my mother said, "what I am about to tell you. 1
In China your father had a sister who killed herself. She jumped into the family well. We say that your father has all brothers because it is as if she had never been born.

"In 1924 just a few days after our village celebrated seventeen hurry-up 2
weddings—to make sure that every young man who went 'out on the road'

would responsibly come home—your father and his brothers and your grandfather and his brothers and your aunt's new husband sailed for America, the Gold Mountain. It was your grandfather's last trip. Those lucky enough to get contracts waved good-bye from the decks. They fed and guarded the stowaways and helped them off in Cuba, New York, Bali, Hawaii. 'We'll meet in California next year,' they said. All of them sent money home.

"I remember looking at your aunt one day when she and I were dressing; 3 I had not noticed before that she had such a protruding melon of a stomach. But I did not think, 'She's pregnant,' until she began to look like other pregnant women, her shirt pulling and the white tops of her black pants showing. She could not have been pregnant, you see, because her husband had been gone for years. No one said anything. We did not discuss it. In early summer she was ready to have the child, long after the time when it could have been possible.

"The village had also been counting. On the night the baby was to be 4 born the villagers raided our house. Some were crying. Like a great saw, teeth strung with lights, files of people walked zigzag across our land, tearing the rice. Their lanterns doubled in the disturbed black water, which drained away through the broken bunds. As the villagers closed in, we could see that some of them, probably men and women we knew well, wore white masks. The people with long hair hung it over their faces. Women with short hair made it stand up on end. Some had tied white bands around their foreheads, arms, and legs.

"At first they threw mud and rocks at the house. Then they threw eggs 5 and began slaughtering our stock. We could hear the animals scream their deaths—the roosters, the pigs, a last great roar from the ox. Familiar wild heads flared in our night windows; the villagers encircled us. Some of the faces stopped to peer at us, their eyes rushing like searchlights. The hands flattened against the panes, framed heads, and left red prints.

"The villagers broke in the front and the back doors at the same time, 6 even though we had not locked the doors against them. Their knives dripped with the blood of our animals. They smeared blood on the doors and walls. One woman swung a chicken, whose throat she had slit, splattering blood in red arcs about her. We stood together in the middle of our house, in the family hall with the pictures and tables of the ancestors around us, and looked straight ahead.

"At that time the house had only two wings. When the men came back, 7 we would build two more to enclose our courtyard and a third one to begin a second courtyard. The villagers pushed through both wings, even your grandparents' rooms, to find your aunt's, which was also mine until the men returned. From this room a new wing for one of the younger families would grow. They ripped up her clothes and shoes and broke her combs, grinding them underfoot. They tore her work from the loom. They scattered the cooking fire and rolled the new weaving in it. We could hear them in the kitchen breaking our bowls and banging the pots. They overturned the great waist-high earthenware jugs; duck eggs, pickled fruits, vegetables burst out and mixed in acrid torrents. The old woman from the next field swept a broom through the air and loosed the spirits-of-the-broom over our heads. 'Pig.' 'Ghost.' 'Pig,' they sobbed and scolded while they ruined our house.

"When they left, they took sugar and oranges to bless themselves. They 8 cut pieces from the dead animals. Some of them took bowls that were not broken and clothes that were not torn. Afterward we swept up the rice and sewed it back up into sacks. But the smells from the spilled preserves lasted. Your aunt gave birth in the pigsty that night. The next morning when I went up for the water, I found her and the baby plugging up the family well.

"Don't let your father know that I told you. He denies her. Now that you 9 have started to menstruate, what happened to her could happen to you. Don't humiliate us. You wouldn't like to be forgotten as if you had never been born. The villagers are watchful."

Whenever she had to warn us about life, my mother told stories that ran 10 like this one, a story to grow up on. She tested our strength to establish realities. Those in the emigrant generations who could not reassert brute survival died young and far from home. Those of us in the first American generations have had to figure out how the invisible world the emigrants built around our childhoods fit in solid America.

The emigrants confused the gods by diverting their curses, misleading 11 them with crooked streets and false names. They must try to confuse their offspring as well, who, I suppose, threaten them in similar ways—always trying to get things straight, always trying to name the unspeakable. The Chinese I know hide their names; sojourners take new names when their lives change and guard their real names with silence.

Chinese-Americans, when you try to understand what things in you are 12 Chinese, how do you separate what is peculiar to childhood, to poverty, insanities, one family, your mother who marked your growing with stories, from what is Chinese? What is Chinese tradition and what is the movies?

If I want to learn what clothes my aunt wore, whether flashy or ordinary, 13 I would have to begin, "Remember Father's drowned-in-the-well sister?" I cannot ask that. My mother has told me once and for all the useful parts. She will add nothing unless powered by Necessity, a riverbank that guides her life. She plants vegetable gardens rather than lawns; she carries the odd-shaped tomatoes home from the fields and eats food left for the gods.

Whenever we did frivolous things, we used up energy; we flew high kites. 14
We children came up off the ground over the melting cones our parents
brought home from work and the American movie on New Year's Day—*Oh,
You Beautiful Doll* with Betty Grable one year, and *She Wore a Yellow Ribbon*
with John Wayne another year. After the one carnival ride each, we paid in
guilt; our tired father counted his change on the dark walk home.

Adultery is extravagance. Could people who hatch their own chicks and 15
eat the embryos and the heads for delicacies and boil the feet in vinegar for
party food, leaving only the gravel, eating even the gizzard lining—could
such people engender a prodigal aunt? To be a woman, to have a daughter in
starvation time was a waste enough. My aunt could not have been the lone
romantic who gave up everything for sex. Women in the old China did not
choose. Some man had commanded her to lie with him and be his secret evil.
I wonder whether he masked himself when he joined the raid on her family.

Perhaps she encountered him in the fields or on the mountain where the 16
daughters-in-law collected fuel. Or perhaps he first noticed her in the marketplace. He was not a stranger because the village housed no strangers. She had
to have dealings with him other than sex. Perhaps he worked an adjoining
field, or he sold her the cloth for the dress she sewed and wore. His demand
must have surprised, then terrified her. She obeyed him; she always did as she
was told.

When the family found a young man in the next village to be her husband, 17
she stood tractably beside the best rooster, his proxy, and promised before they
met that she would be his forever. She was lucky that he was her age and she
would be the first wife, an advantage secure now. The night she first saw him,
he had sex with her. Then he left for America. She had almost forgotten what
he looked like. When she tried to envision him, she only saw the black and
white face in the group photograph the men had had taken before leaving.

The other man was not, after all, much different from her husband. They 18
both gave orders: she followed. "If you tell your family, I'll beat you. I'll kill
you. Be here again next week." No one talked sex, ever. And she might have
separated the rapes from the rest of living if only she did not have to buy her
oil from him or gather wood in the same forest. I want her fear to have lasted
just as long as rape lasted so that the fear could have been contained. No
drawn-out fear. But women at sex hazarded birth and hence lifetimes. The fear
did not stop but permeated everywhere. She told the man, "I think I'm pregnant." He organized the raid against her.

On nights when my mother and father talked about their life back home, 19
sometimes they mentioned an "outcast table" whose business they still seemed
to be settling, their voices tight. In a commensal tradition, where food is precious, the powerful older people made wrongdoers eat alone. Instead of letting

them start separate new lives like the Japanese, who could become samurais and geishas, the Chinese family, faces averted but eyes glowering sideways, hung on to the offenders and fed them leftovers. My aunt must have lived in the same house as my parents and eaten at an outcast table. My mother spoke about the raid as if she had seen it, when she and my aunt, a daughter-in-law to a different household, should not have been living together at all. Daughters-in-law lived with their husbands' parents, not their own; a synonym for marriage in Chinese is "taking a daughter-in-law." Her husband's parents could have sold her, mortgaged her, stoned her. But they had sent her back to her own mother and father, a mysterious act hinting at disgraces not told me. Perhaps they had thrown her out to deflect the avengers.

She was the only daughter; her four brothers went with her father, hus- 20 band, and uncles "out on the road" and for some years became western men. When the goods were divided among the family, three of the brothers took land, and the youngest, my father, chose an education. After my grandparents gave their daughter away to her husband's family, they had dispensed all the adventure and all the property. They expected her alone to keep the traditional ways, which her brothers, now among the barbarians, could fumble without detection. The heavy, deep-rooted women were to maintain the past against the flood, safe for returning. But the rare urge west had fixed upon our family, and so my aunt crossed boundaries not delineated in space.

The work of preservation demands that the feelings playing about in one's 21 guts not be turned into action. Just watch their passing like cherry blossoms. But perhaps my aunt, my forerunner, caught in a slow life, let dreams grow and fade and after some months or years went toward what persisted. Fear at the enormities of the forbidden kept her desires delicate, wire and bone. She looked at a man because she liked the way the hair was tucked behind his ears, or she liked the question-mark line of a long torso curving at the shoulder and straight at the hip. For warm eyes or a soft voice or a slow walk—that's all—a few hairs, a line, a brightness, a sound, a pace, she gave up family. She offered us up for a charm that vanished with tiredness, a pigtail that didn't toss when the wind died. Why, the wrong lighting could erase the dearest thing about him.

It could very well have been, however, that my aunt did not take subtle 22 enjoyment of her friend, but, a wild woman, kept rollicking company. Imagining her free with sex doesn't fit, though. I don't know any women like that, or men either. Unless I see her life branching into mine, she gives me no ancestral help.

To sustain her being in love, she often worked at herself in the mirror, 23 guessing at the colors and shapes that would interest him, changing them frequently in order to hit on the right combination. She wanted him to look back.

On a farm near the sea, a woman who tended her appearance reaped a   24
reputation for eccentricity. All the married women blunt-cut their hair in
flaps about their ears or pulled it back in tight buns. No nonsense. Neither
style blew easily into heart-catching tangles. And at their weddings they displayed themselves in their long hair for the last time. "It brushed the backs of
my knees," my mother tells me. "It was braided, and even so, it brushed the
backs of my knees."

At the mirror my aunt combed individuality into her bob. A bun could   25
have been contrived to escape into black streamers blowing in the wind or in
quiet wisps about her face, but only the older women in our picture album wear
buns. She brushed her hair back from her forehead, tucking the flaps behind her
ears. She looped a piece of thread, knotted into a circle between her index fingers and thumbs, and ran the double strand across her forehead. When she
closed her fingers as if she were making a pair of shadow geese bite, the string
twisted together catching the little hairs. Then she pulled the thread away from
her skin, ripping the hairs out neatly, her eyes watering from the needles of pain.
Opening her fingers, she cleaned the thread, then rolled it along her hairline
and the tops of her eyebrows. My mother did the same to me and my sisters and
herself. I used to believe that the expression "caught by the short hairs" meant a
captive held with a depilatory string. It especially hurt at the temples, but my
mother said we were lucky we didn't have to have our feet bound when we were
seven. Sisters used to sit on their beds and cry together, she said, as their mothers or their slave removed the bandages for a few minutes each night and let the
blood gush back into their veins. I hope that the man my aunt loved appreciated
a smooth brow, that he wasn't just a tits-and-ass man.

Once my aunt found a freckle on her chin, at a spot that the almanac said   26
predestined her for unhappiness. She dug it out with a hot needle and washed
the wound with peroxide.

More attention to her looks than these pullings of hairs and pickings at   27
spots would have caused gossip among the villagers. They owned work clothes
and good clothes, and they wore good clothes for feasting the new seasons.
But since a woman combing her hair hexes beginnings, my aunt rarely found
an occasion to look her best. Women looked like great sea snails—the corded
wood, babies, and laundry they carried were the whorls on their backs. The
Chinese did not admire a bent back; goddesses and warriors stood straight.
Still there must have been a marvelous freeing of beauty when a worker laid
down her burden and stretched and arched.

Such commonplace loveliness, however, was not enough for my aunt. She   28
dreamed of a lover for the fifteen days of New Year's, the time for families to
exchange visits, money, and food. She plied her secret comb. And sure
enough she cursed the year, the family, the village, and herself.

Even as her hair lured her imminent lover, many other men looked at her.   29
Uncles, cousins, nephews, brothers would have looked, too, had they been
home between journeys. Perhaps they had already been restraining their
curiosity, and they left, fearful that their glances, like a field of nesting birds,
might be startled and caught. Poverty hurt, and that was their first reason for
leaving. But another, final reason for leaving the crowded house was the
never-said.

She may have been unusually beloved, the precious only daughter, spoiled   30
and mirror gazing because of the affection the family lavished on her. When
her husband left, they welcomed the chance to take her back from the in-laws;
she could live like the little daughter for just a while longer. There are stories
that my grandfather was different from other people, "crazy ever since the little
Jap bayoneted him in the head." He used to put his naked penis on the dinner
table, laughing. And one day he brought home a baby girl, wrapped up inside
his brown western-style greatcoat. He had traded one of his sons, probably my
father, the youngest, for her. My grandmother made him trade back. When he
finally got a daughter of his own, he doted on her. They must have all loved
her, except perhaps my father, the only brother who never went back to
China, having once been traded for a girl.

Brothers and sisters, newly men and women, had to efface their sexual   31
color and present plain miens. Disturbing hair and eyes, a smile like no other,
threatened the ideal of five generations living under one roof. To focus blurs,
people shouted face to face and yelled from room to room. The immigrants I
know have loud voices, unmodulated to American tones even after years away
from the village where they called their friendships out across the fields. I have
not been able to stop my mother's screams in public libraries or over tele-
phones. Walking erect (knees straight, toes pointed forward, not pigeon-toed,
which is Chinese-feminine) and speaking in an inaudible voice, I have tried
to turn myself American-feminine. Chinese communication was loud, public.
Only sick people had to whisper. But at the dinner table, where the family
members came nearest one another, no one could talk, not the outcasts nor
any eaters. Every word that falls from the mouth is a coin lost. Silently they
gave and accepted food with both hands. A preoccupied child who took his
bowl with one hand got a sideways glare. A complete moment of total attention is due everyone alike. Children and lovers have no singularity here, but
my aunt used a secret voice, a separate attentiveness.

She kept the man's name to herself throughout her labor and dying; she   32
did not accuse him that he be punished with her. To save her inseminator's
name she gave silent birth.

He may have been somebody in her own household, but intercourse with   33
a man outside the family would have been no less abhorrent. All the village

were kinsmen, and the titles shouted in loud country voices never let kinship be forgotten. Any man within visiting distance would have been neutralized as a lover — "brother," "younger brother," "older brother" — one hundred and fifteen relationship titles. Parents researched birth charts probably not so much to assure good fortune as to circumvent incest in a population that has but one hundred surnames. Everybody has eight million relatives. How useless then sexual mannerisms, how dangerous.

As if it came from an atavism deeper than fear, I used to add "brother"   34 silently to boys' names. It hexed the boys, who would or would not ask me to dance, and made them less scary and as familiar and deserving of benevolence as girls.

But, of course, I hexed myself also — no dates. I should have stood up,   35 both arms waving, and shouted out across libraries, "Hey, you! Love me back." I had no idea, though, how to make attraction selective, how to control its direction and magnitude. If I made myself American-pretty so that the five or six Chinese boys in the class fell in love with me, everyone else — the Caucasian, Negro, and Japanese boys — would too. Sisterliness, dignified and honorable, made much more sense.

Attraction eludes control so stubbornly that whole societies designed to   36 organize relationships among people cannot keep order, not even when they bind people to one another from childhood and raise them together. Among the very poor and the wealthy, brothers married their adopted sisters, like doves. Our family allowed some romance, paying adult brides' prices and providing dowries so that their sons and daughters could marry strangers. Marriage promises to turn strangers into friendly relatives — a nation of siblings.

In the village structure, spirits shimmered among the live creatures, bal-   37 anced and held in equilibrium by time and land. But one human being flaring up into violence could open up a black hole, a maelstrom that pulled in the sky. The frightened villagers, who depended on one another to maintain the real, went to my aunt to show her a personal, physical representation of the break she made in the "roundness." Misallying couples snapped off the future, which was to be embodied in true offspring. The villagers punished her for acting as if she could have a private life, secret and apart from them.

If my aunt had betrayed the family at a time of large grain yields and   38 peace, when many boys were born, and wings were being built on many houses, perhaps she might have escaped such severe punishment. But the men — hungry, greedy, tired of planting in dry soil, cuckolded — had been forced to leave the village in order to send food-money home. There were ghost plagues, bandit plagues, wars with the Japanese, floods. My Chinese brother and sister had died of an unknown sickness. Adultery, perhaps only a mistake during good times, became a crime when the village needed food.

The round moon cakes and round doorways, the round tables of graduated   39
size that fit one roundness inside another, round windows and rice bowls—
these talismans had lost their power to warn this family of the law: A family
must be whole, faithfully keeping the descent line by having sons to feed the
old and the dead who in turn look after the family. The villagers came to show
my aunt and lover-in-hiding a broken house. The villagers were speeding up
the circling of events because she was too shortsighted to see that her infidelity had already harmed the village, that waves of consequences would
return unpredictably, sometimes in disguise, as now, to hurt her. This roundness had to be made coin-sized so that she would see its circumference: punish
her at the birth of her baby. Awaken her to the inexorable. People who refused
fatalism because they could invent small resources insisted on culpability.
Deny accidents and wrest fault from the stars.

After the villagers left, their lanterns now scattering in various directions   40
toward home, the family broke their silence and cursed her. "Aiaa, we're going
to die. Death is coming. Death is coming. Look what you've done. You've
killed us. Ghost! Dead Ghost! Ghost! You've never been born." She ran out
into the fields, far enough from the house so that she could no longer hear
their voices, and pressed herself against the earth, her own land no more.
When she felt the birth coming, she thought that she had been hurt. Her body
seized together. "They've hurt me too much," she thought. "This is gall, and it
will kill me." With forehead and knees against the earth, her body convulsed
and then relaxed. She turned on her back, lay on the ground. The black well
of sky and stars went out and out and out forever; her body and her complexity seemed to disappear. She was one of the stars, a bright dot in blackness,
without home, without a companion, in eternal cold and silence. An agoraphobia rose in her, speeding higher and higher, bigger and bigger; she would
not be able to contain it; there would be no end to fear.

Flayed, unprotected against space, she felt pain return, focusing her body.   41
This pain chilled her—a cold, steady kind of surface pain. Inside, spasmodically, the other pain, the pain of the child, heated her. For hours she lay
on the ground, alternately body and space. Sometimes a vision of normal
comfort obliterated reality: She saw the family in the evening gambling at
the dinner table, the young people massaging their elders' backs. She saw
them congratulating one another, high joy on the mornings the rice shoots
came up. When these pictures burst, the stars drew out further apart. Black
space opened.

She got to her feet to fight better and remembered that old-fashioned   42
women gave birth in their pigsties to fool the jealous, pain-dealing gods, who
do not snatch piglets. Before the next spasms could stop her, she ran to the
pigsty, each step a rushing out into emptiness. She climbed over the fence and

knelt in the dirt. It was good to have a fence enclosing her, a tribal person alone.

Laboring, this woman who had carried her child as a foreign growth that 43 sickened her every day, expelled it at last. She reached down to touch the hot, wet, moving mass, surely smaller than anything human, and could feel that it was human after all—fingers, toes, nails, nose. She pulled it up on to her belly, and it lay curled there, butt in the air, feet precisely tucked one under the other. She opened her loose shirt and buttoned the child inside. After resting, it squirmed and thrashed and she pushed it up to her breast. It turned its head this way and that until it found her nipple. There, it made little snuffling noises. She clenched her teeth at its preciousness, lovely as a young calf, a piglet, a little dog.

She may have gone to the pigsty as a last act of responsibility: She would 44 protect this child as she had protected its father. It would look after her soul, leaving supplies on her grave. But how would this tiny child without family find her grave when there would be no marker for her anywhere, neither in the earth nor the family hall? No one would give her a family hall name. She had taken the child with her into the wastes. At its birth the two of them had felt the same raw pain of separation, a wound that only the family pressing tight could close. A child with no descent line would not soften her life but only trail after her, ghostlike, begging her to give it purpose. At dawn the villagers on their way to the fields would stand around the fence and look.

Full of milk, the little ghost slept. When it awoke, she hardened her 45 breasts against the milk that crying loosens. Toward morning she picked up the baby and walked to the well.

Carrying the baby to the well shows loving. Otherwise abandon it. Turn 46 its face into the mud. Mothers who love their children take them along. It was probably a girl; there is some hope of forgiveness for boys.

"Don't tell anyone you had an aunt. Your father does not want to hear her 47 name. She has never been born." I have believed that sex was unspeakable and words so strong and fathers so frail that "aunt" would do my father mysterious harm. I have thought that my family, having settled among immigrants who had also been their neighbors in the ancestral land, needed to clean their name, and a wrong word would incite the kinspeople even here. But there is more to this silence: They want me to participate in her punishment. And I have.

In the twenty years since I heard this story I have not asked for details nor 48 said my aunt's name; I do not know it. People who comfort the dead can also chase after them to hurt them further—a reverse ancestor worship. The real punishment was not the raid swiftly inflicted by the villagers, but the family's deliberately forgetting her. Her betrayal so maddened them, they saw to it that she would suffer forever, even after death. Always hungry, always needing, she would have to beg food from other ghosts, snatch and steal it from those whose living descendants give them gifts. She would have to fight the ghosts massed at crossroads for the buns a few thoughtful citizens leave to decoy her away from village and home so that the ancestral spirits could feast unharassed. At peace, they could act like gods, not ghosts, their descent lines providing them with paper suits and dresses, spirit money, paper houses, paper automobiles, chicken, meat, and rice into eternity — essences delivered up in smoke and flames, steam and incense rising from each rice bowl. In an attempt to make the Chinese care for people outside the family, Chairman Mao encourages us now to give our paper replicas to the spirits of outstanding soldiers and workers, no matter whose ancestors they may be. My aunt remains forever hungry. Goods are not distributed evenly among the dead.

My aunt haunts me — her ghost drawn to me because now, after fifty years   49
of neglect, I alone devote pages of paper to her, though not origamied into houses and clothes. I do not think she always means me well. I am telling on her, and she was a spite suicide, drowning herself in the drinking water. The Chinese are always very frightened of the drowned one, whose weeping ghost, wet hair hanging and skin bloated, waits silently by the water to pull down a substitute.

For a reading quiz, sources on Maxine Hong Kingston, and annotated links to further readings on Chinese culture and on Chinese American culture, visit **bedfordstmartins.com/thebedfordreader.**

Journal Writing

Most of us have heard family stories that left lasting impressions — ghost stories like Kingston's, biographies of ancestors, explanations for traditions, family superstitions, and so on. Write in your journal about a family story you remember vividly from your childhood. (To take your journal writing further, see "From Journal to Essay" on the next page.)

Questions on Meaning

1. What PURPOSE does Kingston have in telling her aunt's story? How does this differ from her mother's purpose in relating the tale?

2. According to Kingston, who could have been the father of her aunt's child? Who could not?
3. Kingston says that her mother told stories "to warn us about life." What warning does this story provide?
4. Why is Kingston so fascinated by her aunt's life and death?

Questions on Writing Strategy

1. Whom does Kingston seem to include in her AUDIENCE: her family and other older Chinese? second-generation Chinese Americans like herself? other Americans? How might she expect each of these groups to respond to her essay?
2. Why is Kingston's opening line—her mother's "You must not tell anyone"— especially fitting for this essay? What secrets are being told? Why does Kingston divulge them?
3. As Kingston tells her tale of her aunt, some events are based on her mother's story or her knowledge of Chinese customs, and some are wholly imaginary. What is the EFFECT of blending these several threads of reality, perception, and imagination?
4. **MIXED METHODS.** Examine the details in the two contrasting NARRATIVES of how Kingston's aunt became pregnant: one in paragraphs 15–18 and the other in paragraphs 21–28. How do the details create different realities? Which version does Kingston seem more committed to? Why?
5. **MIXED METHODS.** Kingston COMPARES AND CONTRASTS various versions of her aunt's story, trying to find the CAUSES that led her aunt to drown in the well. In the end, what causes does Kingston seem to accept?

Questions on Language

1. How does Kingston's language—lyrical, poetic, full of FIGURES OF SPEECH and other IMAGES—reveal her relationship to her Chinese heritage? Find phrases that are especially striking.
2. Look up any of these words you do not know: bunds (par. 4); acrid (7); frivolous (14); tractably, proxy (17); hazarded (18); commensal (19); delineated (20); depilatory (25); plied (28); miens (31); abhorrent, circumvent (33); atavism (34); maelstrom (37); talismans, inexorable, fatalism, culpability (39); gall, agoraphobia (40); spasmodically (41).
3. Sometimes Kingston indicates that she is reconstructing or imagining events through verbs like "would have" and words like "maybe" and "perhaps" ("Perhaps she encountered him in the fields," par. 16). Other times she presents obviously imaginary events as if they actually happened ("Once my aunt found a freckle on her chin," 26). What effect does Kingston achieve with these apparent inconsistencies?

Suggestions for Writing

1. **FROM JOURNAL TO ESSAY.** Develop the family story from your journal into a narrative essay. Build in the context of the story as well: Who told it to you? What

purpose did he or she have in telling it to you? How does it illustrate your family's beliefs and values?

2. Write an essay explaining the role of ancestors in Chinese family and religious life, supplementing what Kingston says with research in the library or on the Web or (if you are Chinese American) drawing on your own experiences.

3. **CRITICAL WRITING.** ANALYZE the ideas about gender roles revealed in "No Name Woman," both in China and in the Chinese American culture Kingston grew up in. How have these ideas affected Kingston? Do you perceive any semblance of them in contemporary American culture?

4. **CONNECTIONS.** Both Kingston and Gloria Naylor, in "The Meanings of a Word" (p. 486), examine communication within their families. Relate an incident or incidents from your own childhood that portray something about the communication within your family. You might want to focus on the language of communication, such as the words used to discuss (or not discuss) a taboo topic, the special family meanings for familiar words, a misunderstanding between you and an adult about something the adult said. Use dialog and as much CONCRETE detail as you can to clarify your experience and its significance.

5. **CONNECTIONS.** Amy Tan in "Fish Cheeks" (p. 94) and Christine Leong in "Being a Chink" (p. 492) also write about relationships between parents and children in Chinese American families. In an essay, analyze what these two essays along with Kingston's suggest about the experiences of the children of Chinese immigrants to the United States.

Maxine Hong Kingston on Writing

In an interview with Jean W. Ross published in *Contemporary Authors* in 1984, Maxine Hong Kingston discusses the writing and revising of *The Woman Warrior*. Ross asks Kingston to clarify an earlier statement that she had "no idea how people who don't write endure their lives." Kingston replies: "When I said that, I was thinking about how words and stories create order. Some of the things that happen to us in life seem to have no meaning, but when you write them down you find the meanings for them; or, as you translate life into words, you force a meaning. Meaning is intrinsic in words and stories."

Ross then asks if Kingston used an outline and planned to blend fact with legend in *The Woman Warrior*. "Oh no, no," Kingston answers. "What I have at the beginning of a book is not an outline. I have no idea of how stories will end or where the beginning will lead. Sometimes I draw pictures. I draw a blob and then I have a little arrow and it goes to this other blob, if you want to call that an outline. It's hardly even words; it's like a doodle. Then when it turns into words, I find the words lead me to various scenes and stories which I don't know about until I get there. I don't see the order until very late in the writing and sometimes the ending just comes. I just run up against it. All of a sudden the book's over and I didn't know it would be over."

A question from Ross about whether her emotions enter her writing leads Kingston to talk about revision. "Well, when I first set something down I feel the emotions I write about. But when I do a second draft, third draft, ninth draft, then I don't feel very emotional. The rewriting is very intellectual; all my education and reading and intellect are involved. The mechanics of sentences, how one phrase or word goes with another one—all that happens in later drafts. There's a very emotional first draft and a very technical last draft."

For Discussion

1. Do you agree with Kingston that when you write things down you find their meaning? Give examples of when the writing process has or hasn't clarified an experience for you.
2. Kingston doodles as a way to discover her material. How do you discover what you have to say?
3. What does Kingston mean by "[t]he mechanics of sentences"? Do you consider this element as you revise?

GEORGE ORWELL

GEORGE ORWELL was the pen name of Eric Blair (1903–50), born in Bengal, India, the son of an English civil servant. After attending Eton on a scholarship, he joined the British police in Burma, where he acquired a distrust for the methods of the empire. Then followed years of tramping, odd jobs, and near-starvation—recalled in *Down and Out in Paris and London* (1933). From living on the fringe of society and from reporting on English miners and factory workers, Orwell deepened his sympathy with underdogs. Severely wounded while fighting in the Spanish civil war, he wrote a memoir, *Homage to Catalonia* (1938), voicing disillusionment with Loyalists who, he claimed, sought not to free Spain but to exterminate their political enemies. A socialist by conviction, Orwell kept pointing to the dangers of a collective state run by totalitarians. In *Animal Farm* (1945), he satirized Soviet bureaucracy; and in his famous novel *Nineteen Eighty-Four* (1949), he foresaw a regimented England whose government perverts truth and spies on citizens by two-way television. (The motto of the state and its leader: Big Brother Is Watching You.)

Shooting an Elephant

Orwell wrote compellingly of his experiences as a police officer in Burma. In this selection from *Shooting an Elephant and Other Essays* (1950), he combines personal experience and piercing insight to expose both an oppressive government and himself as the government's hireling.

"Shooting an Elephant" is foremost a narrative, but Orwell uses description, example, and cause and effect as well to develop and give significance to his tale.

Narration (Chap. 4): throughout
Description (Chap. 5): paragraphs 2, 4–12
Example (Chap. 6): paragraphs 1–2, 4, 14
Cause and effect (Chap. 11): paragraphs 1–2, 6–7

In Moulmein, in Lower Burma, I was hated by large numbers of people— 1 the only time in my life that I have been important enough for this to happen to me. I was subdivisional police officer of the town, and in an aimless, petty kind of way anti-European feeling was very bitter. No one had the guts to raise a riot, but if a European woman went through the bazaars alone somebody would probably spit betel juice over her dress. As a police officer I was an obvious target and was baited whenever it seemed safe to do so. When a nimble Burman tripped me up on the football field and the referee (another Burman) looked the other way, the crowd yelled with hideous laughter. This happened more than once. In the end the sneering yellow faces of young men that met me everywhere, the insults hooted after me when I was at a safe distance, got badly on my nerves. The young Buddhist priests were the worst of all. There were several thousands of them in the town and none of them seemed to have anything to do except stand on street corners and jeer at Europeans.

All this was perplexing and upsetting. For at that time I had already made up my mind that imperialism was an evil thing and the sooner I chucked up my job and got out of it the better. Theoretically—and secretly, of course—I was all for the Burmese and all against the oppressors, the British. As for the job I was doing, I hated it more bitterly than I can perhaps make clear. In a job like that you see the dirty work of Empire at close quarters. The wretched prisoners huddling in the stinking cages of the lockups, the grey, cowed faces of the long-term convicts, the scarred buttocks of the men who had been flogged with bamboos—all these oppressed me with an intolerable sense of guilt. But I could get nothing into perspective. I was young and ill-educated and I had had to think out my problems in the utter silence that is imposed on every Englishman in the East. I did not even know that the British Empire is dying, still less did I know that it is a great deal better than the younger empires that are going to supplant it. All I knew was that I was stuck between my hatred of the empire I served and my rage against the evil-spirited little beasts who tried to make my job impossible. With one part of my mind I thought of the British Raj[1] as an unbreakable tyranny, as something clamped down, in *saecula saeculorum*,[2] upon the will of prostrate peoples; with another part I thought that the greatest joy in the world would be to drive a bayonet into a Buddhist priest's guts. Feelings like these are the normal by-products of imperialism; ask any Anglo-Indian official, if you can catch him off duty.

One day something happened which in a roundabout way was enlightening. It was a tiny incident in itself, but it gave me a better glimpse than I had had before of the real nature of imperialism—the real motives for which despotic governments act. Early one morning the subinspector at a police station the other end of town rang me up on the phone and said that an elephant was ravaging the bazaar. Would I please come and do something about it? I did not know what I could do, but I wanted to see what was happening and I got on to a pony and started out. I took my rifle, an old .44 Winchester and much too small to kill an elephant, but I thought the noise might be useful *in terrorem*.[3] Various Burmans stopped me on the way and told me about the elephant's doings. It was not, of course, a wild elephant, but a tame one which

2

3

---

[1] British imperial government. *Raj* in Hindi means "reign," a word similar to *rajah*, "ruler."—EDS.

[2] Latin, "world without end."—EDS.

[3] Latin, "to give warning."—EDS.

had gone "must." It had been chained up, as tame elephants always are when their attack of "must" is due, but on the previous night it had broken its chain and escaped. Its mahout,[4] the only person who could manage it when it was in that state, had set out in pursuit, but had taken the wrong direction and was now twelve hours' journey away, and in the morning the elephant had suddenly reappeared in the town. The Burmese population had no weapons and were quite helpless against it. It had already destroyed somebody's bamboo hut, killed a cow and raided some fruit stalls and devoured the stock; also it had met the municipal rubbish van and, when the driver jumped out and took to his heels, had turned the van over and inflicted violences upon it.

The Burmese subinspector and some Indian constables were waiting for   4
me in the quarter where the elephant had been seen. It was a very poor quarter, a labyrinth of squalid bamboo huts, thatched with palmleaf, winding all over a steep hillside. I remember that it was a cloudy, stuffy morning at the beginning of the rains. We began questioning the people as to where the elephant had gone and, as usual, failed to get any definite information. That is invariably the case in the East; a story always sounds clear enough at a distance, but the nearer you get to the scene of events the vaguer it becomes. Some of the people said that the elephant had gone in one direction, some said that he had gone in another, some professed not even to have heard of any elephant. I had almost made up my mind that the whole story was a pack of lies, when we heard yells a little distance away. There was a loud, scandalized cry of "Go away, child! Go away this instant!" and an old woman with a switch in her hand came round the corner of a hut, violently shooing away a crowd of naked children. Some more women followed, clicking their tongues and exclaiming; evidently there was something that the children ought not to have seen. I rounded the hut and saw a man's dead body sprawling in the mud. He was an Indian, a black Dravidian coolie, almost naked, and he could not have been dead many minutes. The people said that the elephant had come suddenly upon him round the corner of the hut, caught him with its trunk, put its foot on his back and ground him into the earth. This was the rainy season and the ground was soft, and his face had scored a trench a foot deep and a couple of yards long. He was lying on his belly with arms crucified and head sharply twisted to one side. His face was coated with mud, the eyes wide open, the teeth bared and grinning with an expression of unendurable agony. (Never tell me, by the way, that the dead look peaceful. Most of the corpses I have seen looked devilish.) The friction of the great beast's foot had stripped the skin from his back as neatly as one skins a rabbit. As soon as I saw the dead man I sent an orderly to a friend's house nearby to borrow an elephant rifle. I

---

[4] Keeper or groom, a servant of the elephant's owner. —EDS.

had already sent back the pony, not wanting it to go mad with fright and throw me if it smelled the elephant.

The orderly came back in a few minutes with a rifle and five cartridges,   5
and meanwhile some Burmans had arrived and told us that the elephant was in the paddy fields below, only a few hundred yards away. As I started forward practically the whole population of the quarter flocked out of the houses and followed me. They had seen the rifle and were all shouting excitedly that I was going to shoot the elephant. They had not shown much interest in the ele-phant when he was merely ravaging their homes, but it was different now that he was going to be shot. It was a bit of fun to them, as it would be to an En-glish crowd; besides they wanted the meat. It made me vaguely uneasy. I had no intention of shooting the elephant—I had merely sent for the rifle to defend myself if necessary—and it is always unnerving to have a crowd fol-lowing you. I marched down the hill, looking and feeling a fool, with the rifle over my shoulder and an ever-growing army of people jostling at my heels. At the bottom, when you got away from the huts, there was a metalled road and beyond that a miry waste of paddy fields a thousand yards across, not yet ploughed but soggy from the first rains and dotted with coarse grass. The ele-phant was standing eight yards from the road, his left side towards us. He took not the slightest notice of the crowd's approach. He was tearing up bunches of grass, beating them against his knees to clean them and stuffing them into his mouth.

I had halted on the road. As soon as I saw the elephant I knew with per-   6
fect certainty that I ought not to shoot him. It is a serious matter to shoot a working elephant—it is comparable to destroying a huge and costly piece of machinery—and obviously one ought not to do it if it can possibly be avoided. And at that distance, peacefully eating, the elephant looked no more dangerous than a cow. I thought then and I think now that his attack of "must" was already passing off; in which case he would merely wander harm-lessly about until the mahout came back and caught him. Moreover, I did not in the least want to shoot him. I decided that I would watch him for a little while to make sure that he did not turn savage again, and then go home.

But at that moment, I glanced round at the crowd that had followed me.   7
It was an immense crowd, two thousand at the least and growing every minute. It blocked the road for a long distance on either side. I looked at the sea of yellow faces above the garish clothes—faces all happy and excited over this bit of fun, all certain that the elephant was going to be shot. They were watching me as they would watch a conjuror about to perform a trick. They did not like me, but with the magical rifle in my hands I was momentarily worth watching. And suddenly I realized that I should have to shoot the ele-phant after all. The people expected it of me and I had got to do it; I could feel

their two thousand wills pressing me forward, irresistibly. And it was at this moment, as I stood there with the rifle in my hands, that I first grasped the hollowness, the futility of the white man's dominion in the East. Here was I, the white man with his gun, standing in front of the unarmed native crowd — seemingly the leading actor of the piece; but in reality I was only an absurd puppet pushed to and fro by the will of those yellow faces behind. I perceived in this moment that when the white man turns tyrant it is his own freedom that he destroys. He becomes a sort of hollow, posing dummy, the conventionalized figure of a sahib. For it is the condition of his rule that he shall spend his life in trying to impress the "natives," and so in every crisis he has got to do what the "natives" expect of him. He wears a mask, and his face grows to fit it. I had got to shoot the elephant. I had committed myself to doing it when I sent for the rifle. A sahib has got to act like a sahib; he has got to appear resolute, to know his own mind and do definite things. To come all that way, rifle in hand, with two thousand people marching at my heels, and then to trail feebly away, having done nothing — no, that was impossible. The crowd would laugh at me. And my whole life, every white man's life in the East, was one long struggle not to be laughed at.

But I did not want to shoot the elephant. I watched him beating his   8
bunch of grass against his knees, with that preoccupied grandmotherly air that elephants have. It seemed to me that it would be murder to shoot him. At that age I was not squeamish about killing animals, but I had never shot an elephant and never wanted to. (Somehow it always seems worse to kill a *large* animal.) Besides, there was the beast's owner to be considered. Alive, the elephant was worth at least a hundred pounds; dead, he would only be worth the value of his tusks, five pounds, possibly. But I had got to act quickly. I turned to some experienced-looking Burmans who had been there when we arrived, and asked them how the elephant had been behaving. They all said the same thing: He took no notice of you if you left him alone, but he might charge if you went too close to him.

It was perfectly clear to me what I ought to do. I ought to walk up to   9
within, say, twenty-five yards of the elephant and test his behavior. If he charged, I could shoot; if he took no notice of me, it would be safe to leave him until the mahout came back. But also I knew that I was going to do no such thing. I was a poor shot with a rifle and the ground was soft mud into which one would sink at every step. If the elephant charged and I missed him, I should have about as much chance as a toad under a steamroller. But even then I was not thinking particularly of my own skin, only of the watchful yellow faces behind. For at that moment, with the crowd watching me, I was not afraid in the ordinary sense, as I would have been if I had been alone. A white man mustn't be frightened in front of "natives"; and so, in general, he isn't

frightened. The sole thought in my mind was that if anything went wrong those two thousand Burmans would see me pursued, caught, trampled on, and reduced to a grinning corpse like that Indian up the hill. And if that happened it was quite probable that some of them would laugh. That would never do. There was only one alternative. I shoved the cartridges into the magazine and lay down on the road to get a better aim.

The crowd grew very still, and a deep, low, happy sigh, as of people who see the theater curtain go up at last, breathed from innumerable throats. They were going to have their bit of fun after all. The rifle was a beautiful German thing with cross-hair sights. I did not then know that in shooting an elephant one would shoot to cut an imaginary bar running from ear-hole to ear-hole. I ought, therefore, as the elephant was sideways on, to have aimed straight at his ear-hole; actually I aimed several inches in front of this, thinking the brain would be further forward.

When I pulled the trigger I did not hear the bang or feel the kick—one never does when a shot goes home—but I heard the devilish roar of glee that went up from the crowd. In that instant, in too short a time, one would have thought, even for the bullet to get there, a mysterious, terrible change had come over the elephant. He neither stirred nor fell, but every line of his body had altered. He looked suddenly stricken, shrunken, immensely old, as though the frightful impact of the bullet had paralyzed him without knocking him down. At last, after what seemed a long time—it might have been five seconds, I dare say—he sagged flabbily to his knees. His mouth slobbered. An enormous senility seemed to have settled upon him. One could have imagined him thousands of years old. I fired again into the same spot. At the second shot he did not collapse but climbed with desperate slowness to his feet and stood weakly upright, with legs sagging and head drooping. I fired a third time. That was the shot that did for him. You could see the agony of it jolt his whole body and knock the last remnant of strength from his legs. But in falling he seemed for a moment to rise, for as his hind legs collapsed beneath him he seemed to tower upward like a huge rock toppling, his trunk reaching skywards like a tree. He trumpeted, for the first and only time. And then down he came, his belly towards me, with a crash that seemed to shake the ground even where I lay.

I got up. The Burmans were already racing past me across the mud. It was obvious that the elephant would never rise again, but he was not dead. He was breathing very rhythmically with long rattling gasps, his great mound of a side painfully rising and falling. His mouth was wide open. I could see far down into caverns of pale pink throat. I waited a long time for him to die, but his breathing did not weaken. Finally I fired my two remaining shots into the spot where I thought his heart must be. The thick blood welled out of him like red velvet, but still he did not die. His body did not even jerk when the shots hit him, the tortured breathing continued without a pause. He was dying, very slowly and in great agony, but in some world remote from me where not even a bullet could damage him further. I felt I had got to put an end to that dreadful noise. It seemed dreadful to see the great beast lying there, powerless to move and yet powerless to die, and not even to be able to finish him. I sent back for my small rifle and poured shot after shot into his heart and down his throat. They seemed to make no impression. The tortured gasps continued as steadily as the ticking of a clock.

In the end I could not stand it any longer and went away. I heard later that it took him half an hour to die. Burmans were bringing dahs and baskets even before I left, and I was told they had stripped his body almost to the bones by the afternoon.   13

Afterwards, of course, there were endless discussions about the shooting of the elephant. The owner was furious, but he was only an Indian and could do nothing. Besides, legally I had done the right thing, for a mad elephant has to be killed, like a mad dog, if its owner fails to control it. Among the Europeans opinion was divided. The older men said I was right, the younger men said it was a damn shame to shoot an elephant for killing a coolie, because the elephant was worth more than any damn Coringhee coolie. And afterwards I was very glad that the coolie had been killed; it put me legally in the right and it gave me sufficient pretext for shooting the elephant. I often wondered whether any of the others grasped that I had done it solely to avoid looking a fool.   14

*For a reading quiz, sources on George Orwell, and annotated links to further readings on British imperial rule in Burma, visit **bedfordstmartins.com/ thebedfordreader**.*

Journal Writing

How do you respond to Orwell's decision to shoot the elephant even though he believed it unnecessary to do so? Do you have any sympathy for his action? Recall a time when you acted against your better judgment in order to save face in front of others. Write as honestly as you can about what motivated you and what mistakes you made. (To take your journal writing further, see "From Journal to Essay" on the next page.)

Questions on Meaning

1. How would you answer the exasperated student who, after reading this essay, exploded, "Why didn't Orwell just leave his gun at home?"
2. Why did Orwell shoot the elephant?
3. Describe the epiphany that Orwell experiences in the course of the event he writes about. (An *epiphany* is a sudden realization of a truth.)
4. In the last paragraph of his essay, Orwell says he was "glad that the coolie had been killed." How do you account for this remark?
5. What is the PURPOSE of this essay?

Questions on Writing Strategy

1. In addition to serving as an INTRODUCTION to Orwell's essay, what function is performed by paragraphs 1 and 2?
2. From what circumstances does the IRONY of Orwell's essay spring?
3. What does "Shooting an Elephant" gain from having been written years after the events it recounts?
4. **MIXED METHODS.** What does the blend of NARRATION and DESCRIPTION in paragraphs 11–12 contribute to the story? How does it further Orwell's purpose?
5. **MIXED METHODS.** How do the EXAMPLES in paragraphs 1 and 2 illustrate Orwell's conflict about his work as a police officer in Burma?

Questions on Language

1. What do you understand by Orwell's statement that the elephant had "gone 'must'" (par. 3)? Look up *must* or its variant *musth* in your dictionary.
2. What examples of English (as opposed to American) usage do you find in Orwell's essay?
3. Define, if necessary, bazaars, betel (par. 1); intolerable, supplant, prostrate (2); despotic (3); labyrinth, squalid, invariably (4); dominion, sahib (7); magazine (9); innumerable (10); senility (11).

Suggestions for Writing

1. **FROM JOURNAL TO ESSAY.** Write a narrative essay from your journal entry. Tell the story of your action, and consider what the results were, what you might have done differently, and what you learned from the experience.
2. With what examples of governmental face-saving are you familiar? If none leaps to mind, read a newspaper or watch the news on television to catch public officials in the act of covering themselves. (Not only national government but also local or student government may provide examples.) In an essay, ANALYZE two or three examples: What do you think was really going on that needed covering? Did the officials succeed in saving face, or did their efforts fail? Were the efforts harmful in any way?
3. **CRITICAL WRITING.** Orwell is honest with himself and his readers in acknowledging his mistakes as a government official. Write an essay that examines the degree to which confession may, or may not, erase blameworthiness for misdeeds. Does

Orwell remain just as guilty as he would have been if he had not taken responsibility for his actions? Why, or why not? Feel free to supplement your analysis of Orwell's case with examples from your own life or from the news.

4. **CONNECTIONS.** Read William Lutz's "The World of Doublespeak" (p. 417), which CLASSIFIES language that deliberately conceals or misleads. In an essay, examine which of Lutz's categories of doublespeak seem to arise from the motives Orwell describes in paragraph 7: the need "to impress," to do what is expected of one, "to appear resolute," "not to be laughed at." Use specific examples from Lutz's essay — or from your own experience — to support your ideas.

5. **CONNECTIONS.** Like "Shooting an Elephant," Maya Angelou's "Champion of the World" (p. 88) also blends narration and description. COMPARE AND CONTRAST the two essays, not on their purposes, which are vastly different, but on this blending. What senses do the authors rely on? How do they keep their narratives moving? How much of themselves do they inject into their essays?

George Orwell on Writing

George Orwell explains the motives for his own writing in the essay "Why I Write" (1946), from which we reprint the following excerpts.

What I have most wanted to do throughout the past ten years is to make political writing into an art. My starting point is always a feeling of partisanship, a sense of injustice. When I sit down to write a book, I do not say to myself, "I am going to produce a work of art." I write it because there is some lie that I want to expose, some fact to which I want to draw attention, and my initial concern is to get a hearing. But I could not do the work of writing a book, or even a long magazine article, if it were not also an esthetic experience. Anyone who cares to examine my work will see that even when it is downright propaganda it contains much that a full-time politician would consider irrelevant. I am not able, and I do not want, completely to abandon the worldview that I acquired in childhood. So long as I remain alive and well I shall continue to feel strongly about prose style, to love the surface of the earth, and to take a pleasure in solid objects and scraps of useless information. It is no use trying to suppress that side of myself. The job is to reconcile my ingrained likes and dislikes with the essentially public, nonindividual activities that this age forces on all of us.

It is not easy. It raises problems of construction and of language, and it raises in a new way the problem of truthfulness. Let me give just one example of the cruder kind of difficulty that arises. My book about the Spanish civil war, *Homage to Catalonia*, is, of course, a frankly political book, but in the main it is written with a certain detachment and regard for form. I did try very hard in it to tell the whole truth without violating my literary instincts. But among other things it contains a long chapter, full of newspaper quotations and the like, defending the Trotskyists who were accused of plotting with Franco. Clearly such a chapter, which after a year or two would lose its interest for any ordinary reader, must ruin the book. A critic whom I respect read me a lecture about it. "Why did you put in all that stuff?" he said. "You've turned what might have been a good book into journalism." What he said was true, but I could not have done otherwise. I happened to know, what very few people in England had been allowed to know, that innocent men were being falsely accused. If I had not been angry about that I should never have written the book.

In one form or another this problem comes up again. The problem of language is subtler and would take too long to discuss. I will only say that of late years I have tried to write less picturesquely and more exactly. In any case I find that by the time you have perfected any style of writing, you have always outgrown it. *Animal Farm* was the first book in which I tried, with full consciousness of what I was doing, to fuse political purpose and artistic purpose into the whole. . . .

Looking back through the last page or two, I see that I have made it appear as though my motives in writing were wholly public-spirited. I don't want to leave that as the final impression. All writers are vain, selfish, and lazy, and at the very bottom of their motives there lies a mystery. Writing a book is a horrible, exhausting struggle, like a long bout of some painful illness. One would never undertake such a thing if one were not driven on by some demon whom one can neither resist nor understand. For all one knows that demon is simply the same instinct that makes a baby squall for attention. And yet it is also true that one can write nothing readable unless one constantly struggles to efface one's own personality. Good prose is like a windowpane. I cannot say with certainty which of my motives are the strongest, but I know which of them deserve to be followed. And looking back through my work, I see that it is invariably where I lacked a *political* purpose that I wrote lifeless books and was betrayed into purple passages, sentences without meaning, decorative adjectives, and humbug generally.

For Discussion

1. What does Orwell mean by his "political purpose" in writing? by his "artistic purpose"? How did he sometimes find it hard to fulfill both purposes?
2. Think about Orwell's remark that "one can write nothing readable unless one constantly struggles to efface one's own personality." From your own experience, have you found any truth in this observation, or any reason to think otherwise?

RICHARD RODRIGUEZ

The son of Spanish-speaking Mexican Americans, RICHARD RODRIGUEZ was born in 1944 in San Francisco. After graduation from Stanford in 1967, he earned an MA from Columbia, studied at the Warburg Institute in London, and received a PhD in English literature from the University of California at Berkeley. He once taught but now devotes himself to writing and lecturing. Rodriguez's essays have appeared in *The American Scholar, Change*, and many other magazines. He is an editor at Pacific News Service and a contributing editor for *US News & World Report, Harper's*, and the *Los Angeles Times*. His on-air essays for PBS's *Newshour with Jim Lehrer* won him the George Foster Peabody Award in 1997. In 1982 he published *Hunger of Memory*, a widely discussed book of autobiographical essays. *Mexico's Children* (1991) is a study of Mexicans in America, and *Days of Obligation: An Argument with My Mexican Father* (1992) is also a memoir. Rodriguez's latest book is *Brown* (2002), in which he explores color and race in American society.

Aria: A Memoir of a Bilingual Childhood

"Aria: A Memoir of a Bilingual Childhood" is taken from *Hunger of Memory*. First published in *The American Scholar* in 1981, this poignant memoir sets forth the author's views of bilingual education. To the child Rodriguez, Spanish was a private language, English a public one. Would the boy have learned faster and better if his teachers had allowed him the use of his native language in school?

In this essay, four main methods of development serve a fifth, argument. The argument is pervasive but most explicit in the paragraphs listed below.

Narration (Chap. 4): paragraphs 1–3, 5–9, 13, 16–18, 21, 23–37
Description (Chap. 5): paragraphs 7–11, 13, 16–18, 21, 23–29
Comparison and contrast (Chap. 7): paragraphs 10–11, 14, 22, 29–30, 33–35, 38–40
Cause and effect (Chap. 11): paragraphs 12, 15, 18–20, 28–32, 36, 38–40
Argument and persuasion (Chap. 13): paragraphs 4, 19–20, 38–39

I remember, to start with, that day in Sacramento, in a California now 1 nearly thirty years past, when I first entered a classroom—able to understand about fifty stray English words. The third of four children, I had been preceded by my older brother and sister to a neighborhood Roman Catholic school. But neither of them had revealed very much about their classroom experiences. They left each morning and returned each afternoon, always together, speaking Spanish as they climbed the five steps to the porch. And their mysterious books, wrapped in brown shopping-bag paper, remained on the table next to the door, closed firmly behind them.

An accident of geography sent me to a school where all my classmates 2
were white and many were the children of doctors and lawyers and business
executives. On that first day of school, my classmates must certainly have
been uneasy to find themselves apart from their families, in the first institution
of their lives. But I was astonished. I was fated to be the "problem student"
in class.

The nun said, in a friendly but oddly impersonal voice: "Boys and girls, 3
this is Richard Rodriguez." (I heard her sound it out: *Rich-heard Road-ree-
guess.*) It was the first time I had heard anyone say my name in English.
"Richard," the nun repeated more slowly, writing my name down in her book.
Quickly I turned to see my mother's face dissolve in a watery blur behind the
pebbled-glass door.

Now, many years later, I hear of something called "bilingual education" — 4
a scheme proposed in the late 1960s by Hispanic-American social activists,
later endorsed by a congressional vote. It is a program that seeks to permit
non–English-speaking children (many from lower class homes) to use their
"family language" as the language of school. Such, at least, is the aim its supporters announce. I hear them, and am forced to say no: It is not possible for
a child, any child, ever to use his family's language in school. Not to understand this is to misunderstand the public uses of schooling and to trivialize the
nature of intimate life.

Memory teaches me what I know of these matters. The boy reminds the 5
adult. I was a bilingual child, but of a certain kind: "socially disadvantaged,"
the son of working-class parents, both Mexican immigrants.

In the early years of my boyhood, my parents coped very well in America. 6
My father had steady work. My mother managed at home. They were nobody's
victims. When we moved to a house many blocks from the Mexican-American
section of town, they were not intimidated by those two or three neighbors
who initially tried to make us unwelcome. ("Keep your brats away from my
sidewalk!") But despite all they achieved, or perhaps because they had so
much to achieve, they lacked any deep feeling of ease, of belonging in public.
They regarded the people at work or in crowds as being very distant from us.
Those were the others, *los gringos.* That term was interchangeable in their
speech with another, even more telling: *los americanos.*

I grew up in a house where the only regular guests were my relations. On 7
a certain day, enormous families of relatives would visit us, and there would be
so many people that the noise and the bodies would spill out to the backyard
and onto the front porch. Then for weeks no one would come. (If the doorbell
rang, it was usually a salesman.) Our house stood apart — gaudy yellow in a
row of white bungalows. We were the people with the noisy dog, the people

who raised chickens. We were the foreigners on the block. A few neighbors would smile and wave at us. We waved back. But until I was seven years old, I did not know the name of the old couple living next door or the names of the kids living across the street.

In public, my father and mother spoke a hesitant, accented, and not   8 always grammatical English. And then they would have to strain, their bodies tense, to catch the sense of what was rapidly said by *los gringos*. At home, they returned to Spanish. The language of their Mexican past sounded in counterpoint to the English spoken in public. The words would come quickly, with ease. Conveyed through those sounds was the pleasing, soothing, consoling reminder that one was at home.

During those years when I was first learning to speak, my mother and   9 father addressed me only in Spanish; in Spanish I learned to reply. By contrast, English (*inglés*) was the language I came to associate with gringos, rarely heard in the house. I learned my first words of English overhearing my parents speaking to strangers. At six years of age, I knew just enough words for my mother to trust me on errands to stores one block away—but no more.

I was then a listening child, careful to hear the very different sounds of   10 Spanish and English. Wide-eyed with hearing, I'd listen to sounds more than to words. First, there were English (gringo) sounds. So many words still were unknown to me that when the butcher or the lady at the drugstore said something, exotic polysyllabic sounds would bloom in the midst of their sentences. Often the speech of people in public seemed to me very loud, booming with confidence. The man behind the counter would literally ask, "What can I do for you?" But by being so firm and clear, the sound of his voice said that he was a gringo; he belonged in public society. There were also the high, nasal notes of middle-class American speech—which I rarely am conscious of hearing today because I hear them so often, but could not stop hearing when I was a boy. Crowds at Safeway or at bus stops were noisy with the birdlike sounds of *los gringos*. I'd move away from them all—all the chirping chatter above me.

My own sounds I was unable to hear, but I knew that I spoke English   11 poorly. My words could not extend to form complete thoughts. And the words I did speak I didn't know well enough to make distinct sounds. (Listeners would usually lower their heads to hear better what I was trying to say.) But it was one thing for *me* to speak English with difficulty; it was more troubling to hear my parents speaking in public: their high-whining vowels and guttural consonants; their sentences that got stuck with "eh" and "ah" sounds; the confused syntax; the hesitant rhythm of sounds so different from the way gringos spoke. I'd notice, moreover, that my parents' voices were softer than those of gringos we would meet.

I am tempted to say now that none of this mattered. (In adulthood I am   12 embarrassed by childhood fears.) And, in a way, it didn't matter very much that my parents could not speak English with ease. Their linguistic difficulties had no serious consequences. My mother and father made themselves understood at the county hospital clinic and at government offices. And yet, in another way, it mattered very much. It was unsettling to hear my parents struggle with English. Hearing them, I'd grow nervous, and my clutching trust in their protection and power would be weakened.

There were many times like the night at a brightly lit gasoline station (a   13
blaring white memory) when I stood uneasily hearing my father talk to a teenage attendant. I do not recall what they were saying, but I cannot forget the sounds my father made as he spoke. At one point his words slid together to form one long word—sounds as confused as the threads of blue and green oil in the puddle next to my shoes. His voice rushed through what he had left to say. Toward the end, he reached falsetto notes, appealing to his listener's understanding. I looked away at the lights of passing automobiles. I tried not to hear any more. But I heard only too well the attendant's reply, his calm, easy tones. Shortly afterward, headed for home, I shivered when my father put his hand on my shoulder. The very first chance that I got, I evaded his grasp and ran on ahead into the dark, skipping with feigned boyish exuberance.

But then there was Spanish: *español*, the language rarely heard away from   14
the house; *español*, the language which seemed to me therefore a private language, my family's language. To hear its sounds was to feel myself specially recognized as one of the family, apart from *los otros*. A simple remark, an inconsequential comment could convey that assurance. My parents would say something to me and I would feel embraced by the sounds of their words. Those sounds said: *I am speaking with ease in Spanish. I am addressing you in words I never use with los gringos. I recognize you as someone special, close, like no one outside. You belong with us. In the family. Ricardo.*

At the age of six, well past the time when most middle-class children no   15
longer notice the difference between sounds uttered at home and words spoken in public, I had a different experience. I lived in a world compounded of sounds. I was a child longer than most. I lived in a magical world, surrounded by sounds both pleasing and fearful. I shared with my family a language enchantingly private—different from that used in the city around us.

Just opening or closing the screen door behind me was an important expe-   16
rience. I'd rarely leave home all alone or without feeling reluctance. Walking down the sidewalk, under the canopy of tall trees, I'd warily notice the (suddenly) silent neighborhood kids who stood warily watching me. Nervously, I'd arrive at the grocery store to hear there the sounds of the gringo, reminding me that in this so-big world I was a foreigner. But if leaving home was never routine, neither was coming back. Walking toward our house,

climbing the steps from the sidewalk, in summer when the front door was open, I'd hear voices beyond the screen door talking in Spanish. For a second or two I'd stay, linger there listening. Smiling, I'd hear my mother call out, saying in Spanish, "Is that you, Richard?" Those were her words, but all the while her sounds would assure me: *You are home now. Come close inside. With us.* "*Sí,*" I'd reply.

Once more inside the house, I would resume my place in the family. The sounds would grow harder to hear. Once more at home, I would grow less conscious of them. It required, however, no more than the blurt of the door-bell to alert me all over again to listen to sounds. The house would turn instantly quiet while my mother went to the door. I'd hear her hard English sounds. I'd wait to hear her voice turn to soft-sounding Spanish, which assured me, as surely as did the clicking tongue of the lock on the door, that the stranger was gone.

Plainly it is not healthy to hear such sounds so often. It is not healthy to distinguish public from private sounds so easily. I remained cloistered by sounds, timid and shy in public, too dependent on the voices at home. I remember many nights when my father would come back from work, and I'd hear him call out to my mother in Spanish, sounding relieved. In Spanish, his voice would sound the light and free notes that he never could manage in English. Some nights I'd jump up just hearing his voice. My brother and I would come running into the room where he was with our mother. Our laugh-ing (so deep was the pleasure!) became screaming. Like others who feel the pain of public alienation, we transformed the knowledge of our public sepa-rateness into a consoling reminder of our intimacy. Excited, our voices joined in a celebration of sounds. *We are speaking now the way we never speak out in public—we are together,* the sounds told me. Some nights no one seemed willing to loosen the hold that sounds had on us. At dinner we invented new words that sounded Spanish, but made sense only to us. We pieced together new words by taking, say, an English verb and giving it Spanish endings. My mother's instructions at bedtime would be lacquered with mock-urgent tones. Or a word like *sí,* sounded in several notes, would convey added mea-sures of feeling. Tongues lingered around the edges of words, especially fat vowels, and we happily sounded that military drum roll, the twirling roar of the Spanish *r.* Family language, my family's sounds: the voices of my parents and sisters and brother. Their voices insisting: *You belong here. We are family members. Related. Special to one another. Listen!* Voices singing and sighing, ris-ing and straining, then surging, teeming with pleasure which burst syllables into fragments of laughter. At times it seemed there was steady quiet only when, from another room, the rustling whispers of my parents faded and I edged closer to sleep.

17

18

Supporters of bilingual education imply today that students like me miss a   19
great deal by not being taught in their family's language. What they seem not
to recognize is that, as a socially disadvantaged child, I regarded Spanish as a
private language. It was a ghetto language that deepened and strengthened my
feeling of separateness. What I needed to learn in school was that I had the
right, and the obligation, to speak the public language. The odd truth is that
my first-grade classmates could have become bilingual, in the conventional
sense of the word, more easily than I. Had they been taught early (as upper-
middle-class children often are taught) a "second language" like Spanish or
French, they could have regarded it simply as another public language. In my
case, such bilingualism could not have been so quickly achieved. What I did
not believe was that I could speak a single public language.

Without question, it would have pleased me to have heard my teachers   20
address me in Spanish when I entered the classroom. I would have felt much
less afraid. I would have imagined that my instructors were somehow "related"
to me; I would indeed have heard their Spanish as my family's language.
I would have trusted them and responded with ease. But I would have
delayed—postponed for how long?—having to learn the language of public
society. I would have evaded—and for how long?—learning the great lesson
of school: that I had a public identity.

Fortunately, my teachers were unsentimental about their responsibility.   21
What they understood was that I needed to speak public English. So their voices
would search me out, asking me questions. Each time I heard them I'd look up
in surprise to see a nun's face frowning at me. I'd mumble, not really meaning
to answer. The nun would persist. "Richard, stand up. Don't look at the floor.
Speak up. Speak to the entire class, not just to me!" But I couldn't believe English could be my language to use. (In part, I did not want to believe it.) I continued to mumble. I resisted the teacher's demands. (Did I somehow suspect
that once I learned this public language my family life would be changed?)
Silent, waiting for the bell to sound, I remained dazed, diffident, afraid.

Because I wrongly imagined that English was intrinsically a public lan-   22
guage and Spanish was intrinsically private, I easily noted the difference
between classroom language and the language at home. At school, words were
directed to a general audience of listeners. ("Boys and girls . . .") Words were
meaningfully ordered. And the point was not self-expression alone, but to
make oneself understood by many others. The teacher quizzed: "Boys and
girls, why do we use that word in this sentence? Could we think of a better
word to use there? Would the sentence change its meaning if the words were
differently arranged? Isn't there a better way of saying much the same thing?"
(I couldn't say. I wouldn't try to say.)

Three months passed. Five. A half year. Unsmiling, ever watchful, my   23
teachers noted my silence. They began to connect my behavior with the slow
progress my brother and sisters were making. Until, one Saturday morning,
three nuns arrived at the house to talk to our parents. Stiffly they sat on the
blue living-room sofa. From the doorway of another room, spying on the visitors, I noted the incongruity, the clash of two worlds, the faces and voices of
school intruding upon the familiar setting of home. I overheard one voice
gently wondering, "Do your children speak only Spanish at home, Mrs.
Rodriguez?" While another voice added, "That Richard especially seems so
timid and shy."

That Rich-heard!   24

With great tact, the visitors continued, "Is it possible for you and your   25
husband to encourage your children to practice their English when they are
home?" Of course my parents complied. What would they not do for their
children's well-being? And how could they question the Church's authority
which those women represented? In an instant they agreed to give up the language (the sounds) which had revealed and accentuated our family's closeness. The moment after the visitors left, the change was observed. "*Ahora,*
speak to us only *en inglés,*" my father and mother told us.

At first, it seemed a kind of game. After dinner each night, the family   26
gathered together to practice "our" English. It was still then *inglés,* a language
foreign to us, so we felt drawn to it as strangers. Laughing, we would try to
define words we could not pronounce. We played with strange English sounds,
often overanglicizing our pronunciations. And we filled the smiling gaps of
our sentences with familiar Spanish sounds. But that was cheating, somebody
shouted, and everyone laughed.

In school, meanwhile, like my brother and sisters, I was required to attend   27
a daily tutoring session. I needed a full year of this special work. I also needed
my teachers to keep my attention from straying in class by calling out, "*Rich-
heard*"—their English voices slowly loosening the ties to my other name, with
its three notes, *Ri-car-do.* Most of all, I needed to hear my mother and father
speak to me in a moment of seriousness in "broken"—suddenly heartbreak-
ing—English. This scene was inevitable. One Saturday morning I entered the
kitchen where my parents were talking, but I did not realize that they were
talking in Spanish until, the moment they saw me, their voices changed and
they began speaking English. The gringo sounds they uttered startled me.
Pushed me away. In that moment of trivial misunderstanding and profound
insight, I felt my throat twisted by unsounded grief. I simply turned and left
the room. But I had no place to escape to where I could grieve in Spanish. My
brother and sisters were speaking English in another part of the house.

Again and again in the days following, as I grew increasingly angry, I was   28
obliged to hear my mother and father encouraging me: "Speak to us *en inglés*."
Only then did I determine to learn classroom English. Thus, sometime afterward it happened: One day in school, I raised my hand to volunteer an answer
to a question. I spoke out in a loud voice and I did not think it remarkable
when the entire class understood. That day I moved very far from being the
disadvantaged child I had been only days earlier. Taken hold at last was the
belief, the calming assurance, that I *belonged* in public.

Shortly after, I stopped hearing the high, troubling sounds of *los gringos*. A   29
more and more confident speaker of English, I didn't listen to how strangers
sounded when they talked to me. With so many English-speaking people around
me, I no longer heard American accents. Conversations quickened. Listening
to persons whose voices sounded eccentrically pitched, I might note their
sounds for a few seconds, but then I'd concentrate on what they were saying.
Now when I heard someone's tone of voice—angry or questioning or sarcastic or happy or sad—I didn't distinguish it from the words it expressed. Sound
and word were thus tightly wedded. At the end of each day I was often bemused, and always relieved, to realize how "soundless," though crowded with
words, my day in public had been. An eight-year-old boy, I finally came to accept what had been technically true since my birth: I was an American citizen.

But diminished by then was the special feeling of closeness at home. Gone   30
was the desperate, urgent, intense feeling of being at home among those with
whom I felt intimate. Our family remained a loving family, but one greatly
changed. We were no longer so close, no longer bound tightly together by the
knowledge of our separateness from *los gringos*. Neither my older brother nor
my sisters rushed home after school anymore. Nor did I. When I arrived home,
often there would be neighborhood kids in the house. Or the house would be
empty of sounds.

Following the dramatic Americanization of their children, even my par-   31
ents grew more publicly confident—especially my mother. First she learned
the names of all the people on the block. Then she decided we needed to have
a telephone in our house. My father, for his part, continued to use the word
gringo, but it was no longer charged with bitterness or distrust. Stripped of any
emotional content, the word simply became a name for those Americans not
of Hispanic descent. Hearing him, sometimes, I wasn't sure if he was pro-
nouncing the Spanish word *gringo*, or saying gringo in English.

There was a new silence at home. As we children learned more and more   32
English, we shared fewer and fewer words with our parents. Sentences needed
to be spoken slowly when one of us addressed our mother or father. Often the
parent wouldn't understand. The child would need to repeat himself. Still the
parent misunderstood. The young voice, frustrated, would end up saying,

"Never mind"—the subject was closed. Dinners would be noisy with the clinking of knives and forks against dishes. My mother would smile softly between her remarks; my father, at the other end of the table, would chew and chew his food while he stared over the heads of his children.

My mother! My father! After English became my primary language, I no   33
longer knew what words to use in addressing my parents. The old Spanish words (those tender accents of sound) I had earlier used—*mamá* and *papá*—I couldn't use anymore. They would have been all-too-painful reminders of how much had changed in my life. On the other hand, the words I heard neighborhood kids call their parents seemed equally unsatisfactory. "Mother" and "father," "ma," "pa," "dad," "pop" (how I hated the all-American sound of that last word)—all these I felt were unsuitable terms of address for my parents. As a result, I never used them at home. Whenever I'd speak to my parents, I would try to get their attention by looking at them. In public conversations, I'd refer to them as my "parents" or my "mother" and "father."

My mother and father, for their part, responded differently, as their chil-   34
dren spoke to them less. My mother grew restless, seemed troubled and anxious at the scarceness of words exchanged in the house. She would question me about my day when I came home from school. She smiled at my small talk. She pried at the edges of my sentences to get me to say something more. ("What . . . ?") She'd join conversations she overheard, but her intrusions often stopped her children's talking. By contrast, my father seemed to grow reconciled to the new quiet. Though his English somewhat improved, he tended more and more to retire into silence. At dinner he spoke very little. One night his children and even his wife helplessly giggled at his garbled English pronunciation of the Catholic "Grace Before Meals." Thereafter he made his wife recite the prayer at the start of each meal, even on formal occasions when there were guests in the house.

Hers became the public voice of the family. On official business it was she,   35
not my father, who would usually talk to strangers on the phone or in stores. We children grew so accustomed to his silence that years later we would routinely refer to his "shyness." (My mother often tried to explain: Both of his parents died when he was eight. He was raised by an uncle who treated him as little more than a menial servant. He was never encouraged to speak. He grew up alone—a man of few words.) But I realized my father was not shy whenever I'd watch him speaking Spanish with relatives. Using Spanish, he was quickly effusive. Especially when talking with other men, his voice would spark, flicker, flare alive with varied sounds. In Spanish he expressed ideas and feelings he rarely revealed when speaking English. With firm Spanish sounds he conveyed a confidence and authority that English would never allow him.

The silence at home, however, was not simply the result of fewer words   36 passing between parents and children. More profound for me was the silence created by my inattention to sounds. At about the time I no longer bothered to listen with care to the sounds of English in public, I grew careless about listening to the sounds made by the family when they spoke. Most of the time I would hear someone speaking at home and didn't distinguish his sounds from the words people uttered in public. I didn't even pay much attention to my parents' accented and ungrammatical speech—at least not at home. Only when I was with them in public would I become alert to their accents. But even then their sounds caused me less and less concern. For I was growing increasingly confident of my own public identity.

I would have been happier about my public success had I not recalled,   37
sometimes, what it had been like earlier, when my family conveyed its intimacy through a set of conveniently private sounds. Sometimes in public, hearing a stranger, I'd hark back to my lost past. A Mexican farm worker approached me one day downtown. He wanted directions to some place. "*Hijito, . . .*" he said. And his voice stirred old longings. Another time I was standing beside my mother in the visiting room of a Carmelite convent, before the dense screen which rendered the nuns shadowy figures. I heard several of them speaking Spanish in their busy, singsong, overlapping voices, assuring my mother that, yes, yes, we were remembered, all our family was remembered, in their prayers. Those voices echoed faraway family sounds. Another day a dark-faced old woman touched my shoulder lightly to steady herself as she boarded a bus. She murmured something to me I couldn't quite comprehend. Her Spanish voice came near, like the face of a never-before-seen relative in the instant before I was kissed. That voice, like so many of the Spanish voices I'd hear in public, recalled the golden age of my childhood.

Bilingual educators say today that children lose a degree of "individuality"   38
by becoming assimilated into public society. (Bilingual schooling is a program popularized in the seventies, that decade when middle-class "ethnics" began to resist the process of assimilation—the "American melting pot.") But the bilingualists oversimplify when they scorn the value and necessity of assimilation. They do not seem to realize that a person is individualized in two ways. So they do not realize that, while one suffers a diminished sense of *private* individuality by being assimilated into public society, such assimilation makes possible the achievement of *public* individuality.

Simplistically again, the bilingualists insist that a student should be   39
reminded of his difference from others in mass society, of his "heritage." But they equate mere separateness with individuality. The fact is that only in private—with intimates—is separateness from the crowd a prerequisite for individuality; an intimate "tells" me that I am unique, unlike all others, apart from

the crowd. In public, by contrast, full individuality is achieved, paradoxically, by those who are able to consider themselves members of the crowd. Thus it happened for me. Only when I was able to think of myself as an American, no longer an alien in gringo society, could I seek the rights and opportunities necessary for full public individuality. The social and political advantages I enjoy as a man began on the day I came to believe that my name is indeed *Rich-heard Road-ree-guess*. It is true that my public society today is often impersonal; in fact, my public society is usually mass society. But despite the anonymity of the crowd, and despite the fact that the individuality I achieve in public is often tenuous—because it depends on my being one in a crowd—I celebrate the day I acquired my new name. Those middle-class ethnics who scorn assimilation seem to me filled with decadent self-pity, obsessed by the burden of public life. Dangerously, they romanticize public separateness and trivialize the dilemma of those who are truly socially disadvantaged.

If I rehearse here the changes in my private life after my Americanization,   40
it is finally to emphasize a public gain. The loss implies the gain. The house I returned to each afternoon was quiet. Intimate sounds no longer greeted me at the door. Inside there were other noises. The telephone rang. Neighborhood kids ran past the door of the bedroom where I was reading my schoolbooks— covered with brown shopping-bag paper. Once I learned the public language, it would never again be easy for me to hear intimate family voices. More and more of my day was spent hearing words, not sounds. But that may only be a way of saying that on the day I raised my hand in class and spoke loudly to an entire roomful of faces, my childhood started to end.

*For a reading quiz, sources on Richard Rodriguez, and annotated links to further readings on bilingual education, visit **bedfordstmartins.com/thebedfordreader**.*

Journal Writing

Rodriguez remembers thinking as a child, "We are speaking now the way we never speak out in public—we are together" (par. 18). In your journal, write about any aspect of language spoken by you and your family when you were a child—language different from what you heard in public. Perhaps, like Rodriguez's family, your family spoke a language other than the dominant one in the larger culture. Or perhaps your private language consisted of a special vocabulary, inside jokes, ALLUSIONS, particular tones of voice, or other differences. (To take your journal writing further, see "From Journal to Essay" on the next page.)

Questions on Meaning

1. Rodriguez's essay is both memoir and ARGUMENT. What is the thrust of the author's argument?
2. How did the child Rodriguez react when, in his presence, his parents had to struggle to make themselves understood by *"los gringos"*?
3. What does the author mean when he says, "I was a child longer than most" (par. 15)?
4. According to the author, what impact did the Rodriguez children's use of English have on relationships within the family?
5. Contrast the child Rodriguez's view of the nuns who insisted he speak English with his adult view.

Questions on Writing Strategy

1. How effective an INTRODUCTION is Rodriguez's first paragraph?
2. Several times in his essay Rodriguez shifts from memoir to argument and back again. What is the overall EFFECT of these shifts? Do they strengthen or weaken the author's stance against bilingual education?
3. Twice in his essay (in pars. 1 and 40) the author mentions schoolbooks wrapped in shopping-bag paper. How does the use of this detail enhance his argument?
4. What AUDIENCE probably would not like this essay? Why would they not like it?
5. **MIXED METHODS.** Examine how Rodriguez uses DESCRIPTION to COMPARE AND CONTRAST the sounds of Spanish and English (pars. 10, 11, 13, 14, 18, 33, 37). What sounds does he evoke? What are the differences among them?
6. **MIXED METHODS.** Rodriguez's essay is an argument supported mainly by personal NARRATIVE — Rodriguez's own experience. What kind of ETHICAL APPEAL (p. 519) does the narrative make? What can we INFER about Rodriguez's personality, intellect, fairness, and trustworthiness?

Questions on Language

1. Consult the dictionary if you need help defining these words: counterpoint (par. 8); polysyllabic (10); guttural, syntax (11); falsetto, exuberance (13); inconsequential (14); cloistered, lacquered (18); diffident (21); intrinsically (22); incongruity (23); bemused (29); effusive (35); assimilated (38); paradoxically, tenuous, decadent (39).
2. In Rodriguez's essay, how do the words *public* and *private* relate to the issue of bilingual education? What important distinction does the author make between *individuality* and *separateness* (par. 39)?
3. What exactly does the author mean when he says, "More and more of my day was spent hearing words, not sounds" (par. 40)?

Suggestions for Writing

1. **FROM JOURNAL TO ESSAY.** Expanding on your journal entry, write an essay DEFINING the distinctive quality of the language spoken in your home when you were a child. What effect, if any, did this language have on you when you went out into

   public? Does it influence your memories of childhood? Do you revert to this private language when you are with your family?
2. Bilingual education is a controversial issue with EVIDENCE and strong feelings on
   both sides. In a page or so of preliminary writing, respond to Rodriguez's essay
   with your own gut feelings on the issue. Then do some library research to extend,
   support, or refute your views. (Consult a periodical database such as *InfoTrac* as a
   first step.) In a well-reasoned and well-supported essay, give your opinion on
   whether or not public schools should teach children in their "family language."
3. **CRITICAL WRITING.** In his argument against bilingual education, Rodriguez offers
   no data from studies, no testimony from education experts, indeed no evidence at
   all except his personal experience. In an essay, ANALYZE and EVALUATE this evidence: How convincing do you find it? Is it adequate to support the argument? (In
   your essay consider Rodriguez's ethical appeal, the topic of the sixth question on
   writing strategy, previous page.)
4. **CONNECTIONS.** Rodriguez's mother and father seem to have had a definite idea of
   their parental obligations to their children. Look at Jamaica Kincaid's story "Girl"
   (p. 368) and write a COMPARISON between that mother's sense of parental obligations and the Rodriguezes'. What, for example, is the connection between good
   parenting and teaching one's child to conform? In both cases, you will have to
   infer the parents' values from their actions and words. Use evidence from both
   works to support your inferences.
5. **CONNECTIONS.** In "Indian Education" (p. 105) Sherman Alexie also writes about
   the effect of schooling on his relationship to his family and his ethnic culture. In
   an essay, compare and contrast the experiences of Rodriguez and Alexie, focusing
   on how the two writers' views of education are similar and different.

Richard Rodriguez on Writing

For *The Bedford Reader*, Richard Rodriguez described the writing of "Aria."

From grammar school to college, my teachers offered perennial encouragement: "Write about what you know." Every year I would respond with the
student's complaint: "I have nothing to write about . . . I haven't done anything." (Writers, real writers, I thought, lived in New York or Paris; they
smoked on the back jackets of library books, their chores done.)

   Stories die for not being told. My story got told because I had received an
education; my teachers had given me the skill of stringing words together in a
coherent line. But it was not until I was a man that I felt any need to write my
story. A few years ago I left graduate school, quit teaching for political reasons
(to protest affirmative action). But after leaving the classroom, as the months
passed, I grew desperate to talk to serious people about serious things. In the

great journals of the world, I noticed, there was conversation of a sort, glamorous company of a sort, and I determined to join it. I began writing to stay alive—not as a job, but to stay alive.

Even as you see my essay now, in cool printer's type, I look at some pages and cannot remember having written them. Or else I can remember earlier versions—unused incident, character, description (rooms, faces)—crumbled and discarded. Flung from possibility. They hit the wastebasket, those pages, and yet, defying gravity with a scratchy, starchy resilience, tried to reopen themselves. Then they fell silent. I read certain other sentences now and they recall the very day they were composed—the afternoon of rain or the telephone call that was to come a few moments after, the house, the room where these sentences were composed, the pattern of the rug, the wastebasket. (In all there were about thirty or forty versions that preceded this final "Aria.") I tried to describe my experiences exactly, at once to discover myself and to reveal myself. Always I had to write against the fear I felt that no one would be able to understand what I was saying.

As a reader, I have been struck by the way those novels and essays that are most particular, most particularly about one other life and time (Hannibal, Missouri; one summer; a slave; the loveliness of a muddy river) most fully achieve universality and call to be cherished. It is a paradox apparently: The more a writer unearths the detail that makes a life singular, the more a reader is led to feel a kind of sharing. Perhaps the reason we are able to respond to the life that is so different is because we all, each of us, think privately that we are different from one another. And the more closely we examine another life in its misery or wisdom or foolishness, the more it seems we take some version of ourselves.

It is, in any case, finally you that I end up having to trust not to laugh, not to snicker. Even as you regard me in these lines, I try to imagine your face as you read. You who read "Aria," especially those of you with your theme-divining yellow felt pen poised in your hand, you for whom this essay is yet another assignment, please do not forget that it is my life I am handing you in these pages—memories that are as personal for me as family photographs in an old cigar box.

For Discussion

1. What seems to be Rodriguez's attitude toward his AUDIENCE when he writes? Do you think he writes chiefly for his readers, or for himself? Defend your answer.
2. Rodriguez tells us what he said when, as a student, he was told, "Write about what you know." What do you think he would say now?

EDWARD SAID

EDWARD SAID was born in Jerusalem in 1935 and educated at Victoria College in Cairo, Egypt. As a boy he attended boarding school in Massachusetts, and then he went to Princeton and Harvard universities, taking a PhD from Harvard in 1964. Until his death in 2003, Said was professor of English and comparative literature at Columbia University. He wrote much literary criticism during his life, but his fame and notoriety came from his political writing. His book *Orientalism* (1978) was nominated for the National Book Critics Circle Award, translated into thirty-six languages, and acclaimed for its unblinkered view of the ideology and racism behind Western attitudes toward Islam. But that work and others also brought Said virulent attacks in print, occasional death threats, and, for his support of the Palestinian cause, the label "professor of terror." In his lifetime Said received many awards, including the Picasso Medal (1994), the Spinoza Prize (1999), and the Lannan Foundation Lifetime Achievement Award (2001). His memoir, *Out of Place* (1999), received *The New Yorker*'s award for nonfiction. An accomplished pianist, Said also wrote frequently on music and was music critic for *The Nation*.

Clashing Civilizations?

Just after the terrorist attacks of September 11, 2001, Said published an essay, "We All Swim Together," in *New Statesman*. This excerpt from the essay takes strong issue with the view of Samuel P. Huntington and others that the West and Islam are definable, inevitably opposed "civilizations." (For a biography of Huntington and an essay by him, see p. 400.) To Said, such concepts are not only misleading but also dangerous.

Said's essay is overall an argument against a certain comparison, classification, and definition, developed by other methods as well:

Narration (Chap. 4): paragraphs 1, 6
Example (Chap. 6): paragraphs 3, 4, 6
Comparison and contrast (Chap. 7): paragraphs 2–4, 6–7
Division or analysis (Chap. 9): paragraphs 2–7
Classification (Chap. 10): paragraphs 1–3, 6–7
Cause and effect (Chap. 11): paragraphs 1, 3–7
Definition (Chap. 12): paragraphs 5–7
Argument and persuasion (Chap. 13): throughout

Samuel Huntington's article "The Clash of Civilizations?" appeared in the summer 1993 issue of *Foreign Affairs*, where it immediately attracted a surprising amount of attention and reaction. Because the article was intended to supply Americans with an original thesis about "a new phase" in world politics after the end of the Cold War, Huntington's terms of argument seemed compellingly large, bold, even visionary. "It is my hypothesis," he wrote,

> that . . . the great divisions among humankind and the dominating source of conflict will be cultural. Nation-states will remain the most powerful actors in world affairs, but the principal conflicts of global politics will occur between nations and groups of different civilizations. The clash of civilizations will dominate global politics. The fault lines between civilizations will be the battle lines of the future.

Most of the argument in the pages that followed relied on a vague notion   2
of something Huntington called "civilization identity" and "the interactions among seven or eight [*sic*] major civilizations," of which the conflict between two of them, Islam and the West, gets the lion's share of his attention. In this belligerent kind of thought, he relies heavily on a 1990 article by the veteran orientalist Bernard Lewis, whose ideological colors are manifest in its title, "The Roots of Muslim Rage." In both articles, the personification of enormous entities called "the West" and "Islam" is recklessly affirmed, as if hugely complicated matters such as identity and culture existed in a cartoonlike world where Popeye and Bluto bash each other mercilessly, with one always more virtuous pugilist getting the upper hand over his adversary. Certainly neither Huntington nor Lewis has much time to spare for the internal dynamics and plurality of every civilization; or for considering that the major contest in most modern cultures concerns the definition or interpretation of each culture; or for the unattractive possibility that a great deal of demagogy and downright ignorance is involved in presuming to speak for a whole religion or civilization. No, the West is the West, and Islam is Islam.

The basic model of west versus the rest (the Cold War opposition refor-   3
mulated) is what has persisted, often insidiously and implicitly, in discussion since the terrible events of September 11. The carefully planned and horrendous, pathologically motivated suicide attack and mass slaughter by a small group of deranged militants has been turned into proof of Huntington's thesis. Instead of seeing it for what it is — the capture of big ideas (I use the word loosely) by a tiny band of crazed fanatics for criminal purposes — international luminaries from the former Pakistani prime minister Benazir Bhutto to the Italian prime minister, Silvio Berlusconi, have pontificated about Islam's troubles and, in the latter's case, have used Huntington's ideas to rant on about the West's superiority, how "we" have Mozart and Michelangelo and they don't.

But why not instead see parallels, admittedly less spectacular in their   4
destructiveness, to Osama Bin Laden and his followers in such cults as the Branch Davidians, or the disciples of the Reverend Jim Jones in Guyana, or the Japanese Aum Shinrikyo? Even *The Economist*, in its issue of September

22–28, 2001, couldn't resist reaching for the vast generalization, praising Huntington extravagantly for his "cruel and sweeping, but nonetheless acute" observations about Islam. "Today," the journal says, Huntington writes that "the world's billion or so Muslims are 'convinced of the superiority of their culture, and obsessed with the inferiority of their power.'" Did he canvass one hundred Indonesians, two hundred Moroccans, five hundred Egyptians and fifty Bosnians? Even if he did, what sort of sample is that?

Uncountable are the editorials in every American and European news- 5
paper and magazine of note adding to this vocabulary of gigantism and apoc-
alypse, each use of which is plainly designed to inflame the reader's indignant passion as a member of the "West," and what we need to do. Churchillian rhetoric[1] is used inappropriately by self-appointed combatants in the West's, and especially America's, war against its haters, despoilers, destroyers, with scant attention to complex histories that defy such reductiveness and have seeped from one territory into another, overriding the boundaries that are supposed to separate us all into divided armed camps.

This is the problem with unedifying labels such as *Islam* and *the West:* 6
They mislead and confuse the mind, which is trying to make sense of a disor-
derly reality that won't be pigeonholed. I remember interrupting a man who, after a lecture I had given at a West Bank[2] university in 1994, rose from the audience and started to attack my ideas as "Western," as opposed to the strict Islamic ones he espoused. "Why are you wearing a suit and tie?" was the first retort that came to mind. "They're Western, too." He sat down with an embarrassed smile on his face, but I recalled the incident when information on the September 11 terrorists started to come in: how they had mastered all the technical details required to inflict their homicidal evil on the World Trade Center, the Pentagon and the aircraft they had commandeered. Where does one draw the line between "Western" technology and, as Berlusconi declared, "Islam's" inability to be a part of "modernity"?

One cannot easily do so. How finally inadequate are the labels, general- 7
izations and cultural assertions. At some level, for instance, primitive passions and sophisticated know-how converge in ways that give the lie to a fortified boundary not only between "West" and "Islam," but also between past and present, us and them, to say nothing of the very concepts of identity and nationality about which there is unending debate. A unilateral decision made to undertake crusades, to oppose their evil with our good, to extirpate terrorism

---

[1] A statesman and gifted orator, Winston Churchill (1874–1965) was British prime minis-
ter during World War II, when his stirring speeches fortified his embattled nation's resolve to fight the Germans. —Eds.

[2] Disputed territory adjacent to Israel, controlled partly by Israel and partly by the Palestinian Authority. —Eds.

and, in Paul Wolfowitz's[3] nihilistic vocabulary, to end nations entirely, doesn't make the supposed entities any easier to see; rather, it speaks to how much simpler it is to make bellicose statements for the purpose of mobilizing collective passions than to reflect, examine, sort out what it is we are dealing with in reality, the interconnectedness of innumerable lives, "ours" as well as "theirs."

---

*For a reading quiz, sources on Edward Said, and annotated links to further readings on Western views of Islam, visit **bedfordstmartins.com/thebedfordreader.***

Journal Writing

Write in your journal about the images of Islam that you see in the US media. Based on news reports and other media presentations, what view would an average American have of Islam? (To take your journal writing further, see "From Journal to Essay" on the facing page.)

Questions on Meaning

1. SUMMARIZE the views to which Said responds. How were these views affected by the events of September 11, 2001?
2. Summarize Said's ARGUMENT in response to Huntington's and others' views on the West and Islam.
3. What is Said's point in paragraph 6?
4. What is Said's THESIS? Where does he state it?

Questions on Writing Strategy

1. What is Said's point in referring to Popeye and Bluto in paragraph 2?
2. Why does Said compare Osama Bin Laden and his followers to "such cults as the Branch Davidians, or the disciples of the Reverend Jim Jones in Guyana, or the Japanese Aum Shinrikyo" (par. 4)?
3. Look for places where Said puts words in quotation marks though not actually quoting anyone in particular. What do the quotation marks signify?
4. **MIXED METHODS.** What does Said use DIVISION or ANALYSIS for in paragraph 2? What PURPOSE does this paragraph serve in Said's argument?
5. **MIXED METHODS.** How does Said's EXAMPLE and NARRATION about the West Bank man who challenged him contribute to his point in paragraph 6?

[3] Deputy secretary of defense under President George W. Bush. —EDS.

Questions on Language

1. What words does Said use to characterize the attitude of those he is criticizing? What is the EFFECT of his language? How do you respond to it?
2. In quoting Huntington in paragraph 2, what does Said intend by the use of *sic* in brackets?
3. In paragraph 3 Said refers to the September 11 terrorist attack as "the capture of big ideas (I use the word loosely) by a tiny band of crazed fanatics for criminal purposes." What does he mean by the sentence in parentheses?
4. Consult a dictionary if you are unsure of the meaning of any of the following: visionary (par. 1); belligerent, personification, pugilist, plurality, demagogy (2); insidiously, luminaries, pontificated (3); gigantism, apocalypse, reductiveness (5); unedifying (6); unilateral, extirpate, nihilistic, bellicose, mobilizing (7).

Suggestions for Writing

1. **FROM JOURNAL TO ESSAY.** Based on your journal writing, write an essay in which you analyze images of Islam presented by the US media. (You may want to supplement your current knowledge with research among news magazines and television and radio news and talk shows.) EVALUATE the accuracy of these images.
2. Do you think that there is an inevitable "clash of civilizations" between Islam and the West? Write an essay in which you respond to the view of Samuel P. Huntington, Bernard Lewis, and others quoted by Said.
3. **CRITICAL WRITING.** Write an essay in which you analyze the TONE of Said's essay. Does the tone reinforce Said's argument? Is it effective? Why, or why not?
4. **CONNECTIONS.** Samuel P. Huntington's "The Crisis of National Identity" (p. 400) raises questions about the American national identity. Read that selection, and write an essay on one of the following: (1) how Huntington might respond to Said; (2) how the ideas in "The Crisis of National Identity" fit into Huntington's ideas about clashing civilizations, at least as Said presents them; (3) how Said might respond to "The Crisis of National Identity."
5. **CONNECTIONS.** Adnan R. Khan, in "Close Encounters with US Immigration" (p. 570), and Linda Chavez, in "Everything Isn't Racial Profiling" (p. 575), both address attitudes toward Muslims since September 11, 2001. In an essay bring these two authors face to face with Said. Where might the three writers agree? Where might they disagree?

JONATHAN SWIFT

JONATHAN SWIFT (1667–1745), the son of English parents who had settled in Ireland, divided his energies among literature, politics, and the Church of England. Dissatisfied with the quiet life of an Anglican parish priest, Swift spent much of his time in London hobnobbing with writers and producing pamphlets in support of the Tory Party. In 1713 Queen Anne rewarded his political services with an assignment the London-loving Swift didn't want: to supervise St. Patrick's Cathedral in Dublin. There, as Dean Swift, he ended his days—beloved by the Irish, whose interests he defended against the English government. Although Swift's chief works include the remarkable satires *The Battle of the Books* and *A Tale of a Tub* (both 1704) and scores of fine poems, he is best remembered for *Gulliver's Travels* (1726), an account of four imaginary voyages. This classic is always abridged when it is given to children because of its frank descriptions of human filth and viciousness. In *Gulliver's Travels*, Swift pays tribute to the reasoning portion of "that animal called man," and delivers a stinging rebuke to the rest of him.

A Modest Proposal

Three consecutive years of drought and sparse crops had worked hardship upon the Irish when Swift wrote this ferocious essay in the summer of 1729. At the time, there were said to be thirty-five thousand wandering beggars in the country: Whole families had quit their farms and had taken to the roads. Large landowners, of English ancestry, preferred to ignore their tenants' sufferings and lived abroad to dodge taxes and payment of church duties. Swift had no special fondness for the Irish, but he hated the inhumanity he witnessed.

Although printed as a pamphlet in Dublin, Swift's essay is clearly meant for English readers as well as Irish ones. When circulated, the pamphlet caused a sensation in both Ireland and England and had to be reprinted seven times in the same year. Swift is an expert with plain, vigorous English prose, and "A Modest Proposal" is a masterpiece of SATIRE and IRONY. (If you are uncertain what Swift argues for, see the discussion of these devices in Useful Terms.)

"A Modest Proposal" is an argument developed chiefly by process analysis and cause and effect. These two methods mix with notable uses of description, example, and comparison and contrast.

Description (Chap. 5): paragraphs 1–2, 19
Example (Chap. 6): paragraphs 1–2, 6, 10, 14, 18, 32
Comparison and contrast (Chap. 7): paragraph 17
Process analysis (Chap. 8): paragraphs 4, 6–7, 10–17
Cause and effect (Chap. 11): paragraphs 4–5, 13, 21–29, 31, 33
Argument and persuasion (Chap. 13): throughout

*For Preventing the Children of Poor People in Ireland
from Being a Burden to Their Parents or Country,
and for Making Them Beneficial to the Public*

It is a melancholy object to those who walk through this great town[1] or
travel in the country, when they see the streets, the roads, and cabin doors,
crowded with beggars of the female sex, followed by three, four, or six children, all in rags and importuning every passenger for an alms. These mothers,
instead of being able to work for their honest livelihood, are forced to employ
all their time in strolling to beg sustenance for their helpless infants, who, as
they grow up, either turn thieves for want of work, or leave their dear native
country to fight for the Pretender in Spain, or sell themselves to the Barbados.[2]

I think it is agreed by all parties that this prodigious number of children in
the arms, or on the backs, or at the heels of their mothers, and frequently of
their fathers, is in the present deplorable state of the kingdom a very great
additional grievance; and therefore whoever could find out a fair, cheap, and
easy method of making these children sound, useful members of the commonwealth would deserve so well of the public as to have his statue set up for a pre-
server of the nation.

But my intention is very far from being confined to provide only for the
children of professed beggars; it is of a much greater extent, and shall take
in the whole number of infants at a certain age who are born of parents in effect as little able to support them as those who demand our charity in the
streets.

As to my own part, having turned my thoughts for many years upon this
important subject, and maturely weighed the several schemes of other projectors,[3] I have always found them grossly mistaken in their computation. It is
true, a child just dropped from its dam may be supported by her milk for a solar
year, with little other nourishment; at most not above the value of two
shillings, which the mother may certainly get, or the value in scraps, by her
lawful occupation of begging; and it is exactly at one year that I propose to
provide for them in such a manner as instead of being a charge upon their parents or the parish, or wanting food and raiment for the rest of their lives, they
shall on the contrary contribute to the feeding, and partly to the clothing, of
many thousands.

1

2

3

4

---

[1] Dublin. — EDS.

[2] The Pretender was James Stuart, exiled in Spain; in 1718 many Irishmen had joined an
army seeking to restore him to the English throne. Others wishing to emigrate had signed
papers as indentured servants, agreeing to work for a number of years in the Barbados or other
British colonies in exchange for their ocean passage. — EDS.

[3] Planners. — EDS.

There is likewise another great advantage in my scheme, that it will pre-   5
vent those voluntary abortions, and that horrid practice of women murdering
their bastard children, alas, too frequent among us, sacrificing the poor innocent babes, I doubt, more to avoid the expense than the shame, which would
move tears and pity in the most savage and inhuman breast.

The number of souls in this kingdom being usually reckoned one million   6
and a half, of these I calculate there may be about two hundred thousand
couples whose wives are breeders; from which number I subtract thirty thousand couples who are able to maintain their own children, although I apprehend there cannot be so many under the present distress of the kingdom; but
this being granted, there will remain an hundred and seventy thousand breeders. I again subtract fifty thousand for those women who miscarry, or whose
children die by accident or disease within the year. There only remain an hundred and twenty thousand children of poor parents annually born. The question therefore is, how this number shall be reared and provided for, which, as
I have already said, under the present situation of affairs, is utterly impossible
by all the methods hitherto proposed. For we can neither employ them in
handicraft or agriculture; we neither build houses (I mean in the country) nor
cultivate land. They can very seldom pick up a livelihood stealing till they
arrive at six years old, except where they are of towardly parts;[4] although I
confess they learn the rudiments much earlier, during which time they can
however be looked upon only as probationers, as I have been informed by a
principal gentleman in the country of Cavan, who protested to me that he
never knew above one or two instances under the age of six, even in a part of
the kingdom so renowned for the quickest proficiency in that art.

I am assured by our merchants that a boy or a girl before twelve years old   7
is no salable commodity; and even when they come to this age they will not
yield above three pounds, or three pounds and half a crown at most on the
Exchange; which cannot turn to account either to the parents or the kingdom, the charge of nutriment and rags having been at least four times that
value.

I shall now therefore humbly propose my own thoughts, which I hope will   8
not be liable to the least objection.

I have been assured by a very knowing American of my acquaintance in   9
London, that a young healthy child well nursed is at a year old a most delicious, nourishing, and wholesome food, whether stewed, roasted, baked, or
boiled; and I make no doubt that it will equally serve in a fricassee or a ragout.[5]

I do therefore humbly offer it to public consideration that of the hundred   10

---

[4] Teachable wits, innate abilities. —EDS.
[5] Stew. —EDS.

and twenty thousand children, already computed, twenty thousand may be reserved for breed, whereof only one fourth part to be males, which is more than we allow to sheep, black cattle, or swine; and my reason is that these children are seldom the fruits of marriage, a circumstance not much regarded by our savages, therefore one male will be sufficient to serve four females. That the remaining hundred thousand may at a year old be offered in sale to the persons of quality and fortune through the kingdom, always advising the mother to let them suck plentifully in the last month, so as to render them plump and fat for a good table. A child will make two dishes at an entertainment for friends; and when the family dines alone, the fore or hind quarter will make a reasonable dish, and seasoned with a little pepper or salt will be very good boiled on the fourth day, especially in winter.

11   I have reckoned upon a medium that a child just born will weigh twelve pounds, and in a solar year it tolerably nursed increaseth to twenty-eight pounds.

12   I grant this food will be somewhat dear, and therefore very proper for landlords, who, as they have already devoured most of the parents, seem to have the best title to the children.

13   Infant's flesh will be in season throughout the year, but more plentiful in March, and a little before and after. For we are told by a grave author, an eminent French physician,[6] that fish being a prolific diet, there are more children born in Roman Catholic countries about nine months after Lent than at any other season; therefore, reckoning a year after Lent, the markets will be more glutted than usual, because the number of popish infants is at least three to one in this kingdom; and therefore it will have one other collateral advantage, by lessening the number of Papists among us.

14   I have already computed the charge of nursing a beggar's child (in which list I reckon all cottagers, laborers, and four-fifths of the farmers) to be about two shillings per annum, rags included; and I believe no gentleman would repine to give ten shillings for the carcass of a good fat child, which, as I have said, will make four dishes of excellent nutritive meat, when he hath only some particular friend or his own family to dine with him. Thus the squire will learn to be a good landlord, and grow people among the tenants; the mother will have eight shillings net profit, and be fit for work till she produces another child.

15   Those who are more thrifty (as I must confess the times require) may flay the carcass; the skin of which artificially[7] dressed will make admirable gloves for ladies, and summer boots for fine gentlemen.

---

[6] Swift's favorite French writer, François Rabelais, sixteenth-century author; not "grave" at all, but a broad humorist. — EDS.

[7] With art or craft. — EDS.

As to our city of Dublin, shambles[8] may be appointed for this purpose in   16
the most convenient parts of it, and butchers we may be assured will not be
wanting; although I rather recommend buying the children alive, and dressing
them hot from the knife as we do roasting pigs.

A very worthy person, a true lover of his country, and whose virtues I   17
highly esteem, was lately pleased in discoursing on this matter to offer a
refinement upon my scheme. He said that many gentlemen of his kingdom,
having of late destroyed their deer, he conceived that the want of venison
might be well supplied by the bodies of young lads and maidens, not exceed-
ing fourteen years of age nor under twelve, so great a number of both sexes in
every county being now ready to starve for want of work and service; and these
to be disposed of by their parents, if alive, or otherwise by their nearest relations. But with due deference to so excellent a friend and so deserving a
patriot, I cannot be altogether in his sentiments; for as to the males, my American acquaintance assured me from frequent experience that their flesh was
generally tough and lean, like that of our schoolboys, by continual exercise,
and their taste disagreeable; and to fatten them would not answer the charge.
Then as to the females, it would, I think with humble submission, be a loss to
the public, because they soon would become breeders themselves; and besides,
it is not improbable that some scrupulous people might be apt to censure such
a practice (although indeed very unjustly) as a little bordering upon cruelty;
which, I confess, hath always been with me the strongest objection against
any project, how well soever intended.

But in order to justify my friend, he confessed that this expedient was put   18
into his head by the famous Psalmanazar,[9] a native of the island Formosa, who
came from thence to London above twenty years ago, and in conversation
told my friend that in his country when any young person happened to be put
to death, the executioner sold the carcass to persons of quality as a prime
dainty; and that in his time the body of a plump girl of fifteen, who was crucified for an attempt to poison the emperor, was sold to his Imperial Majesty's
prime minister of state, and other great mandarins of the court, in joints from
the gibbet, at four hundred crowns. Neither indeed can I deny that if the same
use were made of several plump young girls in this town, who without one
single groat to their fortunes cannot stir abroad without a chair, and appear at
the playhouse and assemblies in foreign fineries which they never will pay for,
the kingdom would not be the worse.

---

[8] Butcher shops or slaughterhouses. —EDS.
[9] Georges Psalmanazar—a Frenchman who pretended to be Japanese, the author of a completely imaginary *Description of the Isle Formosa* (1705)—had become a well-known figure in
gullible London society. —EDS.

Some persons of a desponding spirit are in great concern about that vast   19
number of poor people who are aged, diseased, or maimed, and I have been
desired to employ my thoughts what course may be taken to ease the nation of
so grievous an encumbrance. But I am not in the least pain upon that matter,
because it is very well known that they are every day dying and rotting by cold
and famine, and filth and vermin, as fast as can be reasonably expected. And
as to the younger laborers, they are now in almost as hopeful a condition.
They cannot get work, and consequently pine away for want of nourishment
to a degree that if any time they are accidentally hired to common labor, they
have not strength to perform it; and thus the country and themselves are happily delivered from the evils to come.

I have too long digressed, and therefore shall return to my subject. I think   20
the advantages by the proposal which I have made are obvious and many, as
well as of the highest importance.

For first, as I have already observed, it would greatly lessen the number of   21
Papists, with whom we are yearly overrun, being the principal breeders of the
nation as well as our most dangerous enemies; and who stay at home on purpose to deliver the kingdom to the Pretender, hoping to take their advantage
by the absence of so many good Protestants, who have chosen rather to leave
their country than to stay at home and pay tithes against their conscience to
an Episcopal curate.

Secondly, the poorer tenants will have something valuable of their own,   22
which by law may be made liable to distress,[10] and help to pay their landlord's
rent, their corn and cattle being already seized and money a thing unknown.

Thirdly, whereas the maintenance of an hundred thousand children, from   23
two years old and upwards, cannot be computed at less than ten shillings a
piece per annum, the nation's stock will be thereby increased fifty thousand
pounds per annum, besides the profit of a new dish introduced to the tables of
all gentlemen of fortune in the kingdom who have any refinement in taste.
And the money will circulate among ourselves, the goods being entirely of our
own growth and manufacture.

Fourthly, the constant breeders, besides the gain of eight shillings sterling   24
per annum by the sale of their children, will be rid of the charge of maintaining them after the first year.

Fifthly, this food would likewise bring great custom to taverns, where the   25
vintners will certainly be so prudent as to procure the best receipts for dressing it to perfection, and consequently have their houses frequented by all the
fine gentlemen, who justly value themselves upon their knowledge in good

[10] Subject to seizure by creditors. —EDS.

eating; and a skillful cook, who understands how to oblige his guests, will contrive to make it as expensive as they please.

Sixthly, this would be a great inducement to marriage, which all wise 26
nations have either encouraged by rewards or enforced by laws and penalties. It would increase the care and tenderness of mothers toward their children, when they were sure of a settlement for life to the poor babes, provided in some sort by the public, to their annual profit instead of expense. We should see an honest emulation among the married women, which of them could bring the fattest child to the market. Men would become as fond of their wives during the time of their pregnancy as they are now of their mares in foal, their cows in calf, or sows when they are ready to farrow; nor offer to beat or kick them (as is too frequent a practice) for fear of a miscarriage.

Many other advantages might be enumerated. For instance, the addition 27
of some thousand carcasses in our exportation of barreled beef, the propagation of swine's flesh, and improvements in the art of making good bacon, so much wanted among us by the great destruction of pigs, too frequent at our tables, which are no way comparable in taste or magnificence to a well-grown, fat, yearling child, which roasted whole will make a considerable figure at a lord mayor's feast or any other public entertainment. But this and many others I omit, being studious of brevity.

Supposing that one thousand families in this city would be constant cus- 28
tomers for infants' flesh, besides others who might have it at merry meetings, particularly weddings and christenings, I compute that Dublin would take off annually about twenty thousand carcasses, and the rest of the kingdom (where probably they will be sold somewhat cheaper) the remaining eighty thousand.

I can think of no one objection that will possibly be raised against this 29
proposal, unless it should be urged that the number of people will be thereby much lessened in the kingdom. This I freely own, and it was indeed one principal design in offering it to the world. I desire the reader will observe, that I calculate my remedy for this one individual kingdom of Ireland and for no other that ever was, is, or I think ever can be upon earth. Therefore let no man talk to me of other expedients: of taxing our absentees at five shillings a pound: of using neither clothes nor household furniture except what is of our own growth and manufacture: of utterly rejecting the materials and instruments that promote foreign luxury: of curing the expensiveness of pride, vanity, idleness, and gaming in our women: of introducing a vein of parsimony, prudence, and temperance: of learning to love our country, in the want of which we differ even from Laplanders and the inhabitants of Topinamboo:[11]

[11] A district of Brazil. — EDS.

of quitting our animosities and factions, nor acting any longer like the Jews, who were murdering one another at the very moment their city was taken:[12] of being a little cautious not to sell our country and conscience for nothing: of teaching landlords to have at least one degree of mercy toward their tenants: lastly, of putting a spirit of honesty, industry, and skill into our shopkeepers; who, if a resolution could now be taken to buy only our native goods, would immediately unite to cheat and exact upon us in the price, the measure, and the goodness, nor could ever yet be brought to make one fair proposal of just dealing, though often and earnestly invited to it.

Therefore I repeat, let no man talk to me of these and the like expedients, till he hath at least some glimpse of hope that there will ever be some hearty and sincere attempt to put them in practice. 30

But as to myself, having been wearied out for many years with offering vain, idle, visionary thoughts, and at length utterly despairing of success, I fortunately fell upon this proposal, which, as it is wholly new, so it hath something solid and real, of no expense and little trouble, full in our own power, and whereby we can incur no danger in disobliging England. For this kind of commodity will not bear exportation, the flesh being of too tender a consistence to admit a long continuance in salt, although perhaps I could name a country which would be glad to eat up our whole nation without it. 31

After all, I am not so violently bent upon my own opinion as to reject any offer proposed by wise men, which shall be found equally innocent, cheap, easy, and effectual. But before something of that kind shall be advanced in contradiction to my scheme, and offering a better, I desire the author or authors will be pleased maturely to consider two points. First, as things now stand, how they will be able to find food and raiment for an hundred thousand useless mouths and backs. And secondly, there being a round million of creatures in human figure throughout this kingdom, whose sole subsistence put into a common stock would leave them in debt two millions of pounds sterling, adding those who are beggars by profession to the bulk of farmers, cottagers, and laborers, with their wives and children who are beggars in effect; I desire those politicians who dislike my overture, and may perhaps be so bold to attempt an answer, that they will first ask the parents of these mortals whether they would not at this day think it a great happiness to have been sold for food at a year old in this manner I prescribe, and thereby have avoided such a perpetual scene of misfortunes as they have since gone through by the oppression of landlords, the impossibility of paying rent without money or trade, the want of common sustenance, with neither house nor clothes to 32

---

[12] During the Roman siege of Jerusalem (AD 70), prominent Jews were executed on the charge of being in league with the enemy. — EDS.

cover them from the inclemencies of the weather, and the most inevitable prospect of entailing the like or greater miseries upon their breed forever.

I profess, in the sincerity of my heart, that I have not the least personal   33
interest in endeavoring to promote this necessary work, having no other motive than the public good of my country, by advancing our trade, providing for infants, relieving the poor, and giving some pleasure to the rich. I have no children by which I can propose to get a single penny; the youngest being nine years old, and my wife past childbearing.

---

*For a reading quiz, sources on Jonathan Swift, and annotated links to further readings on eighteenth-century Ireland, visit **bedfordstmartins.com/thebedfordreader**.*

Journal Writing

Swift's proposal is aimed at a serious social problem of his day. In your journal, consider a contemporary problem that—like the poverty and starvation Swift describes—seems to require drastic action. For instance, do you believe that a particular group of people is neglected, mistreated, or victimized? Turn to the news media for ideas if no problem comes immediately to mind. (To take your journal writing further, see "From Journal to Essay" on the facing page.)

Questions on Meaning

1. On the surface, what is Swift proposing?
2. Beneath his IRONY, what is Swift's argument?
3. What do you take to be the PURPOSE of Swift's essay?
4. How does the introductory paragraph serve Swift's purpose?
5. Comment on the statement "I can think of no one objection that will possibly be raised against this proposal" (par. 29). What objections can you think of?

Questions on Writing Strategy

1. Describe the mask of the personage through whom Swift writes.
2. By what means does the writer attest to his reasonableness?
3. At what point in the essay did it become clear to you that the proposal isn't modest but horrible?
4. **MIXED METHODS.** As an ARGUMENT, does "A Modest Proposal" appeal primarily to reason or to emotion? (See pp. 518–19 for a discussion of the distinction.)

5. **MIXED METHODS.** What does Swift's argument gain by his careful attention to PROCESS ANALYSIS and to CAUSE AND EFFECT?

Questions on Language

1. How does Swift's choice of words enforce the monstrousness of his proposal? Note especially words from the vocabulary of breeding and butchery.
2. Consult your dictionary for the meanings of any of the following words not yet in your vocabulary: importuning, sustenance (par. 1); prodigious, commonwealth (2); computation, raiment (4); apprehend, rudiments, probationers (6); nutriment (7); fricassee (9); repine (14); flay (15); scrupulous, censure (17); mandarins (18); desponding, encumbrance (19); per annum (23); vintners (25); emulation, foal, farrow (26); expedients, parsimony, animosities (29); disobliging, consistence (31); overture, inclemencies (32).

Suggestions for Writing

1. **FROM JOURNAL TO ESSAY.** Write an essay in which you propose a solution to the problem raised in your journal. Your essay may be either of the following:
   a. A straight argument, giving EVIDENCE, in which you set forth possible solutions to the problem.
   b. An ironic proposal in the manner of Swift. If you do this one, find a device other than cannibalism to eliminate the victims or their problems. You don't want to imitate Swift too closely; he is probably inimitable.
2. In an encyclopedia, look into what has happened in Ireland since Swift wrote. Choose a specific contemporary aspect of Irish-English relations, research it in books and periodicals, and write a report on it.
3. **CRITICAL WRITING.** Choose several examples of irony in "A Modest Proposal" that you find particularly effective. In a brief essay, ANALYZE Swift's use of irony. Do your examples of irony depend on understating, overstating, or saying the opposite of what is meant? How do they improve on literal statements? What is the value of irony in argument?
4. **CONNECTIONS.** Read Jessica Mitford's "Behind the Formaldehyde Curtain" (p. 305) alongside "A Modest Proposal," and analyze the use of irony and humor in these two essays. How heavily does each author depend on irony and humor to make his or her argument? Do these elements strengthen both authors' arguments? What evidence does each offer that would also work in a more straightforward argument?
5. **CONNECTIONS.** Analyze the ways Swift and Martin Luther King, Jr., in "I Have a Dream" (p. 625), create sympathy for the oppressed groups they are concerned about. Concentrate not only on what they say but on the words they use and their TONE. Then write a process analysis explaining techniques for portraying oppression so as to win the reader's sympathy. Use quotations or PARAPHRASES from Swift's and King's essays as EXAMPLES. If you can think of other techniques that neither author uses, by all means include and illustrate them as well.

Jonathan Swift on Writing

Although surely one of the most inventive writers in English literature, Swift voiced his contempt for writers of his day who bragged of their newness and originality. In *The Battle of the Books,* he compares such a self-professed original to a spider who "spins and spits wholly from himself, and scorns to own any obligation or assistance from without." Swift has the fable-writer Aesop praise that writer who, like a bee gathering nectar, draws from many sources.

> Erect your schemes with as much method and skill as you please; yet if the materials be nothing but dirt, spun out of your own entrails (the guts of modern brains), the edifice will conclude at last in a cobweb. . . . As for us Ancients, we are content, with the bee, to pretend to nothing of our own beyond our wings and our voice, that is to say, our flights and our language. For the rest, whatever we have got has been by infinite labor and search and ranging through every corner of nature; the difference is, that, instead of dirt and poison, we have rather chosen to fill our hives with honey and wax, thus furnishing mankind with the two noblest of things, which are sweetness and light.

Swift's advice for a writer would seem to be: Don't just invent things out of thin air; read the best writers of the past. Observe and converse. Do legwork.

Interestingly, when in *Gulliver's Travels* Swift portrays his ideal beings, the Houyhnhnms, a race of noble and intelligent horses, he includes no writers at all in their society. "The Houyhnhnms have no letters," Gulliver observes, "and consequently their knowledge is all traditional." Still, "in poetry they must be allowed to excel all other mortals; wherein the justness of their description are indeed inimitable." (Those very traits—striking comparisons and detailed descriptions—make much of Swift's own writing memorable.)

In his great book, in "A Modest Proposal," and in virtually all he wrote, Swift's purpose was forthright and evident. He declared in "Verses on the Death of Dr. Swift,"

> As with a moral view designed
> To cure the vices of mankind:
> Yet malice never was his aim;
> He lashed the vice but spared the name.
> No individual could resent,
> Where thousands equally were meant.
> His satire points at no defect
> But what all mortals may correct.

For Discussion

1. Try applying Swift's parable of the spider and the bee to our own day. How much truth is left in it?
2. Reread thoughtfully the quotation from Swift's poem. According to the poet, what faults or abuses can a satiric writer fall into? How may these be avoided?
3. What do you take to be Swift's main PURPOSE as a writer? In your own words, SUM-MARIZE it.

E. B. WHITE

Elwyn Brooks White (1899–1985) for half a century was a regular contributor to *The New Yorker*, and his essays, editorials, anonymous features for "The Talk of the Town," and fillers helped build the magazine a reputation for wit and good writing. If as a child you read *Charlotte's Web* (1952), you have met E. B. White before. The book reflects some of his own life on a farm in North Brooklin, Maine. His *Letters* were collected in 1976, his *Essays* in 1977, and his *Poems and Sketches* in 1981. On July 4, 1963, President Kennedy named White in the first group of Americans to receive the Presidential Medal of Freedom, with a citation that called him "an essayist whose concise comment . . . has revealed to yet another age the vigor of the English sentence."

Once More to the Lake

"Once More to the Lake" first appeared in *Harper's* magazine in 1941. Perhaps if a duller writer had written the essay, or an essay with the same title, we wouldn't much care about it, for at first its subject seems as personal and ordinary as a letter home. White's loving and exact portrayal, however, brings this lakeside camp to life for us. In the end, the writer arrives at an awareness that shocks him—shocks us, too, with a familiar sensory detail.

"Once More to the Lake" is a stunning mixture of description and narration, but it is also more. To make his observations and emotions clear and immediate, White relies extensively on several other methods of development as well.

Narration (Chap. 4): throughout
Description (Chap. 5): throughout
Example (Chap. 6): paragraphs 2, 7–8, 11, 12
Comparison and contrast (Chap. 7): paragraphs 4–7, 9–10, 11–12
Process analysis (Chap. 8): paragraphs 9, 10, 12

August 1941

One summer, along about 1904, my father rented a camp on a lake in Maine and took us all there for the month of August. We all got ringworm from some kittens and had to rub Pond's Extract on our arms and legs night and morning, and my father rolled over in a canoe with all his clothes on; but outside of that the vacation was a success and from then on none of us ever thought there was any place in the world like that lake in Maine. We returned summer after summer—always on August 1 for one month. I have since become a salt-water man, but sometimes in summer there are days when the restlessness of the tides and the fearful cold of the sea water and the incessant wind that blows across the afternoon and into the evening make me wish for the placidity of a lake in the woods. A few weeks ago this feeling got so strong I bought myself a couple of bass hooks and a spinner and returned to the lake where we used to go, for a week's fishing and to revisit old haunts.

I took along my son, who had never had any fresh water up his nose and who had seen lily pads only from train windows. On the journey over to the lake I began to wonder what it would be like. I wondered how time would have marred this unique, this holy spot—the coves and streams, the hills that the sun set behind, the camps and the paths behind the camps. I was sure that the tarred road would have found it out, and I wondered in what other ways it would be desolated. It is strange how much you can remember about places like that once you allow your mind to return into the grooves that lead back. You remember one thing, and that suddenly reminds you of another thing. I guess I remembered clearest of all the early mornings, when the lake was cool and motionless, remembered how the bedroom smelled of the lumber it was made of and of the wet woods whose scent entered through the screen. The partitions in the camp were thin and did not extend clear to the top of the rooms, and as I was always the first up I would dress softly so as not to wake the others, and sneak out into the sweet outdoors and start out in the canoe, keeping close along the shore in the long shadows of the pines. I remembered being very careful never to rub my paddle against the gunwale for fear of disturbing the stillness of the cathedral.

The lake had never been what you would call a wild lake. There were cottages sprinkled around the shores, and it was in farming country although the shores of the lake were quite heavily wooded. Some of the cottages were owned by nearby farmers, and you would live at the shore and eat your meals at the farmhouse. That's what our family did. But although it wasn't wild, it was a fairly large and undisturbed lake and there were places in it that, to a child at least, seemed infinitely remote and primeval.

I was right about the tar: It led to within half a mile of the shore. But when I got back there, with my boy, and we settled into a camp near a farmhouse and into the kind of summertime I had known, I could tell that it was going to be pretty much the same as it had been before—I knew it, lying in bed the first morning smelling the bedroom and hearing the boy sneak quietly out and go off along the shore in a boat. I began to sustain the illusion that he was I, and therefore, by simple transposition, that I was my father. This sensation persisted, kept cropping up all the time we were there. It was not an entirely new feeling, but in this setting it grew much stronger. I seemed to be living a dual existence. I would be in the middle of some simple act, I would be picking up a bait box or laying down a table fork, or I would be saying something and suddenly it would be not I but my father who was saying the words or making the gesture. It gave me a creepy sensation.

We went fishing the first morning. I felt the same damp moss covering the worms in the bait can, and saw the dragonfly alight on the tip of my rod as it hovered a few inches from the surface of the water. It was the arrival of this fly that convinced me beyond any doubt that everything was as it always had been, that the years were a mirage and that there had been no years. The small waves were the same, chucking the rowboat under the chin as we fished at anchor, and the boat was the same boat, the same color green and the ribs broken in the same places, and under the floorboards the same fresh water leavings and debris—the dead hellgrammite, the wisps of moss, the rusty discarded fishhook, the dried blood from yesterday's catch. We stared silently at the tips of our rods, at the dragonflies that came and went. I lowered the tip of mine into the water, tentatively, pensively dislodging the fly, which darted two feet away, poised, darted two feet back, and came to rest again a little farther up the rod. There had been no years between the ducking of this dragonfly and the other one—the one that was part of memory. I looked at the boy, who was silently watching his fly, and it was my hands that held his rod, my eyes watching. I felt dizzy and didn't know which rod I was at the end of.

We caught two bass, hauling them in briskly as though they were mackerel, pulling them over the side of the boat in a businesslike manner without any landing net, and stunning them with a blow on the back of the head. When we got back for a swim before lunch, the lake was exactly where we had left it, the same number of inches from the dock, and there was only the merest suggestion of a breeze. This seemed an utterly enchanted sea, this lake you could leave to its own devices for a few hours and come back to, and find that it had not stirred, this constant and trustworthy body of water. In the shallows, the dark, water-soaked sticks and twigs, smooth and old, were undulating in clusters on the bottom against the clean ribbed sand, and the track of the mussel was plain. A school of minnows swam by, each minnow with its small individual shadow, doubling the attendance, so clear and sharp in the sunlight. Some of the other campers were in swimming, along the shore, one of them with a cake of soap, and the water felt thin and clear and unsubstantial. Over the years there had been this person with the cake of soap, this cultist, and here he was. There had been no years.

Up to the farmhouse to dinner through the teeming dusty field, the road under our sneakers was only a two-track road. The middle track was missing, the one with the marks of the hooves and the splotches of dried, flaky manure. There had always been three tracks to choose from in choosing which track to walk in; now the choice was narrowed down to two. For a moment I missed terribly the middle alternative. But the way led past the tennis court, and something about the way it lay there in the sun reassured me; the tape had loosened along the backline, the alleys were green with plantains and other weeds, and the net (installed in June and removed in September) sagged in the dry noon, and the whole place steamed with midday heat and hunger and emptiness. There was a choice of pie for dessert, and one was blueberry and one was apple, and the waitresses were the same country girls, there having been no passage of time, only the illusion of it as in a dropped curtain — the waitresses were still fifteen; their hair had been washed, that was the only difference — they had been to the movies and seen the pretty girls with the clean hair.

Summertime, oh, summertime, pattern of life indelible, the fade-proof lake, the woods unshatterable, the pasture with the sweetfern and the juniper forever and ever, summer without end; this was the background, and the life along the shore was the design, the cottages with their innocent and tranquil design, their tiny docks with the flagpole and the American flag floating against the white clouds in the blue sky, the little paths over the roots of the trees leading from camp to camp and the paths leading back to the outhouses and the can of lime for sprinkling, and at the souvenir counters at the store the miniature birchbark canoes and the postcards that showed things looking a little better than they looked. This was the American family at play, escaping the city heat, wondering whether the newcomers in the camp at the head of the cove were "common" or "nice," wondering whether it was true that the people who drove up for Sunday dinner at the farmhouse were turned away because there wasn't enough chicken. 8

It seemed to me, as I kept remembering all this, that those times and those summers had been infinitely precious and worth saving. There had been jollity and peace and goodness. The arriving (at the beginning of August) had been so big a business in itself, at the railway station the farm wagon drawn up, the first smell of the pine-laden air, the first glimpse of the smiling farmer, and the great importance of the trunks and your father's enormous authority in such matters, and the feel of the wagon under you for the long ten-mile haul, and at the top of the last long hill catching the first view of the lake after eleven months of not seeing this cherished body of water. The shouts and cries of the other campers when they saw you, and the trunks to be unpacked, to give up their rich burden. (Arriving was less exciting nowadays, when you sneaked up in your car and parked it under a tree near the camp and took out the bags and in five minutes it was all over, no fuss, no loud wonderful fuss about trunks.) 9

Peace and goodness and jollity. The only thing that was wrong now, really, was the sound of the place, an unfamiliar nervous sound of the outboard motors. This was the note that jarred, the one thing that would sometimes 10 break the illusion and set the years moving. In those other summertimes all motors were inboard; and when they were at a little distance, the noise they made was a sedative, an ingredient of summer sleep. They were one-cylinder and two-cylinder engines, and some were make-and-break and some were jump-spark, but they all made a sleepy sound across the lake. The one-lungers throbbed and fluttered, and the twin-cylinder ones purred and purred, and that was a quiet sound, too. But now the campers all had outboards. In the daytime, in the hot mornings, these motors made a petulant irritable sound; at night in the still evening when the afterglow lit the water, they whined about one's ears like mosquitoes. My boy loved our rented outboard, and his great desire was to achieve single-handed mastery over it, and authority, and he soon learned the trick of choking it a little (but not too much), and the adjustment of the needle valve. Watching him I would remember the things you could do with the old one-cylinder engine with the heavy flywheel, how you could have it eating out of your hand if you got really close to it spiritually. Motorboats in those days didn't have clutches, and you would make a landing by shutting off the motor at the proper time and coasting in with a dead rudder. But there was a way of reversing them, if you learned the trick, by cutting the switch and putting it on again exactly on the final dying revolution of the flywheel, so that it would kick back against compression and begin reversing. Approaching a dock in a strong following breeze, it was difficult to slow up sufficiently by the ordinary coasting method, and if a boy felt he had complete mastery over his motor, he was tempted to keep it running beyond its time and then reverse it a few feet from the dock. It took a cool nerve, because if you threw the switch a twentieth of a second too soon you would catch the flywheel when it still had speed enough to go up past center, and the boat would leap ahead, charging bull-fashion at the dock.

We had a good week at the camp. The bass were biting well and the sun shone endlessly, day after day. We would be tired at night and lie down in the accumulated heat of the little bedrooms after the long hot day and the breeze would stir almost imperceptibly outside and the smell of the swamp drift in through the rusty screens. Sleep would come easily and in the morning the red squirrel would be on the roof, tapping out his gay routine. I kept remembering everything, lying in bed in the mornings — the small steamboat that had a long rounded stern like the lip of a Ubangi, and how quietly she ran on the moonlight sails, when the older boys played their mandolins and the girls sang and we ate doughnuts dipped in sugar, and how sweet the music was on the water in the shining night, and what it had felt like to think about girls then. After breakfast we would go up to the store and the things were in the same place — the minnows in a bottle, the plugs and spinners disarranged and pawed over by the youngsters from the boys' camp, the Fig Newtons and the

Beeman's gum. Outside, the road was tarred and cars stood in front of the store. Inside, all was just as it had always been, except there was more Coca-Cola and not so much Moxie and root beer and birch beer and sarsaparilla. We would walk out with a bottle of pop apiece and sometimes the pop would backfire up our noses and hurt. We explored the streams, quietly, where the turtles slid off the sunny logs and dug their way into the soft bottom; and we lay on the town wharf and fed worms to the tame bass. Everywhere we went I had trouble making out which was I, the one walking at my side, the one walking in my pants.

One afternoon while we were at the lake a thunderstorm came up. It was   12
like the revival of an old melodrama that I had seen long ago with childish awe. The second-act climax of the drama of the electrical disturbance over a lake in America had not changed in any important respect. This was the big scene, still the big scene. The whole thing was so familiar, the first feeling of oppression and heat and a general air around camp of not wanting to go very far away. In midafternoon (it was all the same) a curious darkening of the sky, and a lull in everything that had made life tick; and then the way the boats suddenly swung the other way at their moorings with the coming of a breeze out of the new quarter, and the premonitory rumble. Then the kettle drum, then the snare, then the bass drum and cymbals, then crackling light against the dark, and the gods grinning and licking their chops in the hills. Afterward the calm, the rain steadily rustling in the calm lake, the return of light and hope and spirits, and the campers running out in joy and relief to go swimming in the rain, their bright cries perpetuating the deathless joke about how they were getting simply drenched, and the children screaming with delight at the new sensation of bathing in the rain, and the joke about getting drenched linking the generations in a strong indestructible chain. And the comedian who waded in carrying an umbrella.

When the others went swimming my son said he was going in, too. He   13
pulled his dripping trunks from the line where they had hung all through the shower and wrung them out. Languidly, and with no thought of going in, I watched him, his hard little body, skinny and bare, saw him wince slightly as he pulled up around his vitals the small, soggy, icy garment. As he buckled the swollen belt, suddenly my groin felt the chill of death.

For a reading quiz, sources on E. B. White, and annotated links to further readings on vacation memories and on fatherhood, visit **bedfordstmartins.com/thebedfordreader**.

Journal Writing

White strongly evokes the lake camp as a place that was important to him as a child. What place or places were most important to you as a child? In your journal, jot down some memories. (To take your journal writing further, see "From Journal to Essay" on the facing page.)

Questions on Meaning

1. How do you account for the distortions that creep into the author's sense of time?
2. What does the discussion of inboard and outboard motors (par. 10) have to do with the author's divided sense of time?
3. To what degree does White make us aware of his son's impression of this trip to the lake?
4. What do you take to be White's main PURPOSE in the essay? At what point do you become aware of it?

Questions on Writing Strategy

1. In paragraph 4 the author first introduces his confused feeling that he has gone back in time to his own childhood, an idea that he repeats and expands throughout his account. What is the function of these repetitions?
2. Try to describe the impact of the essay's final paragraph. By what means is it achieved?
3. To what extent is this essay written to appeal to any but middle-aged readers? Is it comprehensible to anyone whose vacations were never spent at a Maine summer cottage?
4. What is the TONE of White's essay?
5. **MIXED METHODS.** White's DESCRIPTION depends on many IMAGES that are not FIGURES OF SPEECH but literal translations of sensory impressions. Locate four such images.
6. **MIXED METHODS.** Within White's description and NARRATION of his visit to the lake, what purpose is served by the COMPARISON AND CONTRAST between the lake now and when he was a boy?

Questions on Language

1. Be sure you know the meanings of the following words: incessant, placidity (par. 1); gunwale (2); primeval (3); transposition (4); hellgrammite (5); undulating, cultist (6); indelible, tranquil (8); petulant (10); imperceptibly (11); premonitory (12); languidly (13).
2. Comment on White's DICTION in his reference to the lake as "this unique, this holy spot" (par. 2).
3. Explain what White is describing in the sentence that begins, "Then the kettle drum" (par. 12). Where else does the author use figures of speech?

Suggestions for Writing

1. **FROM JOURNAL TO ESSAY.** Choose one of the places suggested by your journal entry, and write an essay describing the place now, revisiting it as an adult. (If you haven't visited the place since childhood, you can imagine what seeing it now would be like.) Your description should draw on your childhood memories, making them as vivid as possible for the reader, but you should also consider how your POINT OF VIEW toward the place differs now.

2. In a descriptive paragraph about a real or imagined place, try to appeal to each of your reader's five senses.

3. **CRITICAL WRITING.** While on the vacation he describes, White wrote to his wife, Katharine, "This place is as American as a drink of Coca Cola. The white collar family having its annual liberty." Obviously, not everyone has a chance at the lakeside summers White enjoyed. To what extent, if at all, does White's privileged point of view deprive his essay of universal meaning and significance? Write an essay answering this question. Back up your ideas with EVIDENCE from White's essay.

4. **CONNECTIONS.** In White's "Once More to the Lake" and Brad Manning's "Arm Wrestling with My Father" (p. 144), the writers reveal a changing sense of what it means to be a father. Write an essay that examines the similarities and differences in their definitions of fatherhood. How does a changing idea of what it means to be a son connect with this redefinition of fatherhood?

5. **CONNECTIONS.** White's essay is full of images that place his audience in a setting important to him in childhood. David Sedaris, in "Remembering My Childhood on the Continent of Africa" (p. 250), also uses vivid images to evoke childhood, both his own and Hugh's. After reading these two essays, write an essay of your own ANALYZING four or five images from each that strike you as especially evocative. What sense impression does each image draw on? What does each one tell you about the author's feelings?

E. B. White on Writing

"You asked me about writing—how I did it," E. B. White replied to a seventeen-year-old who had written to him, wanting to become a professional writer but feeling discouraged. "There is no trick to it. If you like to write and want to write, you write, no matter where you are or what else you are doing or whether anyone pays any heed. I must have written half a million words (mostly in my journal) before I had anything published, save for a couple of short items in *St. Nicholas*.[1] If you want to write about feelings, about the end of the summer, about growing, write about it. A great deal of writing is not

---

[1] A magazine for children, popular early in the twentieth century. —EDS.

.ted' — most of my essays have no plot structure, they are a ramble in the woods, or a ramble in the basement of my mind. You ask, 'Who cares?' Everybody cares. You say, 'It's been written before.' Everything has been written before. . . . Henry Thoreau, who wrote *Walden*, said, 'I learned this at least by my experiment: that if one advances confidently in the direction of his dreams and endeavors to live the life which he has imagined, he will meet with a success unexpected in common hours.' The sentence, after more than a hundred years, is still alive. So, advance confidently."

In trying to characterize his own writing, White was modest in his claims. To his brother Stanley Hart White, he once remarked, "I discovered a long time ago that writing of the small things of the day, the trivial matters of the heart, the inconsequential but near things of this living, was the only kind of creative work which I could accomplish with any sincerity or grace. As a reporter, I was a flop, because I always came back laden not with facts about the case, but with a mind full of the little difficulties and amusements I had encountered in my travels. Not till *The New Yorker* came along did I ever find any means of expressing those impertinences and irrelevancies. Thus yesterday, setting out to get a story on how police horses are trained, I ended by writing a story entitled 'How Police Horses Are Trained' which never even mentions a police horse, but has to do entirely with my own absurd adventures at police headquarters. The rewards of such endeavor are not that I have acquired an audience or a following, as you suggest (fame of any kind being a Pyrrhic victory[2]), but that sometimes in writing of myself — which is the only subject anyone knows intimately — I have occasionally had the exquisite thrill of putting my finger on a little capsule of truth, and heard it give the faint squeak of mortality under my pressure, an antic sound."

For Discussion

1. Sometimes young writers are counseled to study the market and then try to write something that will sell. How would you expect E. B. White to have reacted to such advice?
2. What, exactly, does White mean when he says, "Everything has been written before"? How might an aspiring writer take this remark as encouragement?
3. What interesting distinction does White make between reporting and essay writing?

---

[2] A victory won at great cost. The Greek king Pyrrhus defeated the Romans in 279 BC but exclaimed afterward, "One more such victory and I am lost." — EDS.

VIRGINIA WOOLF

Generally regarded as one of the greatest twentieth-century writers, VIRGINIA WOOLF earned her acclaim by producing uncommon fiction and nonfiction, the first sensitive and complex, the second poetic and immediate. Born Virginia Stephen in London in 1882, Woolf and her sister Vanessa were educated at home, largely by their father, Sir Leslie Stephen, an author and editor. The two sisters were central to the Bloomsbury Group, an informal society of writers and artists that included the economist John Maynard Keynes and the novelist E. M. Forster. Virginia married Leonard Woolf, a member of the group, in 1912, and the two soon founded the Hogarth Press, publisher of Virginia Woolf and many other notable writers of the day. Woolf's most innovative novels include *Mrs. Dalloway* (1925), *To the Lighthouse* (1927), *Orlando* (1928), *The Waves* (1931), and *Between the Acts* (1941). Her exemplary critical and meditative essays appear in *The Common Reader* (1925), *The Second Common Reader* (1933), and many other collections. Subject to severe depression all her adult life, in 1941 Woolf committed suicide.

The Death of the Moth

One of Woolf's most famous works of nonfiction, this essay was published in *The Death of the Moth and Other Essays* (1942). Though as brief as the life of the moth Woolf observes, the essay is typically evocative, intense, and enduring.

"The Death of the Moth" is a seamless blend of narration (Chap. 4) and description (Chap. 5). It is also implicitly a comparison and contrast (Chap. 7) between the moth in life and in death and between the author's responses to these states.

Moths that fly by day are not properly to be called moths; they do not excite that pleasant sense of dark autumn nights and ivy-blossom which the commonest yellow-underwing asleep in the shadow of the curtain never fails to rouse in us. They are hybrid creatures, neither gay like butterflies nor somber like their own species. Nevertheless the present specimen, with his narrow hay-colored wings, fringed with a tassel of the same color, seemed to be content with life. It was a pleasant morning, mid-September, mild, benignant, yet with a keener breath than that of the summer months. The plough was already scoring the field opposite the window, and where the share had been, the earth was pressed flat and gleamed with moisture. Such vigor came rolling in from the fields and the down beyond that it was difficult to keep the eyes strictly turned upon the book. The rooks too were keeping one of their annual festivities; soaring round the tree tops until it looked as if a vast net with thousands of black knots in it had been cast up into the air; which, after a few moments sank slowly down upon the trees until every twig seemed to have a knot at the end of it. Then, suddenly, the net would be thrown into the air again in a wider circle this time, with the utmost clamor and vociferation, as though to be thrown into the air and settle slowly down upon the tree tops were a tremendously exciting experience.

The same energy which inspired the rooks, the ploughmen, the horses, and even, it seemed, the lean bare-backed downs, sent the moth fluttering from side to side of his square of the windowpane. One could not help watching him. One, was, indeed, conscious of a queer feeling of pity for him. The possibilities of pleasure seemed that morning so enormous and so various that to have only a moth's part in life, and a day moth's at that, appeared a hard fate, and his zest in enjoying his meager opportunities to the full, pathetic. He flew vigorously to one corner of his compartment, and, after waiting there a second, flew across to the other. What remained for him but to fly to a third corner and then to a fourth? That was all he could do, in spite of the size of the downs, the width of the sky, the far-off smoke of houses, and the romantic voice, now and then, of a steamer out at sea. What he could do he did. Watching him, it seemed as if a fiber, very thin but pure, of the enormous energy of the world had been thrust into his frail and diminutive body. As often as he crossed the pane, I could fancy that a thread of vital light became visible. He was little or nothing but life.

Yet, because he was so small, and so simple a form of the energy that was rolling in at the open window and driving its way through so many narrow and intricate corridors in my own brain and in those of other human beings, there was something marvelous as well as pathetic about him. It was as if someone had taken a tiny bead of pure life and decking it as lightly as possible with down and feathers, had set it dancing and zigzagging to show us the true nature of life. Thus displayed one could not get over the strangeness of it. One is apt to forget all about life, seeing it humped and bossed and garnished and cumbered so that it has to move with the greatest circumspection and dignity. Again, the thought of all that life might have been had he been born in any other shape caused one to view his simple activities with a kind of pity.

After a time, tired by his dancing apparently, he settled on the window ledge in the sun, and, the queer spectacle being at an end, I forgot about him. Then, looking up, my eye was caught by him. He was trying to resume his dancing, but seemed either so stiff or so awkward that he could only flutter to the bottom of the windowpane; and when he tried to fly across it he failed. Being intent on other matters I watched these futile attempts for a time without thinking, unconsciously waiting for him to resume his flight, as one waits for a machine, that has stopped momentarily, to start again without considering the reason of its failure. After perhaps a seventh attempt he slipped from the wooden ledge and fell, fluttering his wings, on to his back on the windowsill. The helplessness of his attitude roused me. It flashed upon me that he was in difficulties; he could no longer raise himself; his legs struggled vainly. But, as I stretched out a pencil, meaning to help him to right himself, it came over me that the failure and awkwardness were the approach of death. I laid the pencil down again.

The legs agitated themselves once more. I looked as if for the enemy   5 against which he struggled. I looked out of doors. What had happened there? Presumably it was midday, and work in the fields had stopped. Stillness and quiet had replaced the previous animation. The birds had taken themselves off to feed in the brooks. The horses stood still. Yet the power was there all the same, massed outside, indifferent, impersonal, not attending to anything in particular. Somehow it was opposed to the little hay-colored moth. It was useless to try to do anything. One could only watch the extraordinary efforts made by those tiny legs against an oncoming doom which could, had it chosen, have submerged an entire city, not merely a city, but masses of human beings; nothing, I knew had any chance against death. Nevertheless after a pause of exhaustion the legs fluttered again. It was superb this last protest, and so frantic that he succeeded at last in righting himself. One's sympathies, of course, were all on the side of life. Also, when there was nobody to care or to know, this gigantic effort on the part of an insignificant little moth, against a power of such magnitude, to retain what no one else valued or desired to keep, moved one strangely. Again, somehow, one saw life, a pure bead. I lifted the pencil again, useless though I knew it to be. But even as I did so, the unmistakable tokens of death showed themselves. The body relaxed, and instantly grew stiff. The struggle was over. The insignificant little creature now knew death. As I looked at the dead moth, this minute wayside triumph of so great a force over so mean an antagonist filled me with wonder. Just as life had been strange a few minutes before, so death was now as strange. The moth having righted himself now lay most decently and uncomplainingly composed. O yes, he seemed to say, death is stronger than I am.

*For a reading quiz, sources on Virginia Woolf, and annotated links to further readings on human responses to death, visit **bedfordstmartins.com/thebedfordreader**.*

Journal Writing

Try thinking from Woolf's perspective, recognizing the struggle and life force within creatures we generally consider insignificant. In your journal, sketch out some ideas. What do you find admirable about turtles, mosquitoes, minnows, or ants? (To take your journal writing further, see "From Journal to Essay" on the facing page.)

Questions on Meaning

1. Why does Woolf choose to write about something as insignificant as a moth's death? Does she have a PURPOSE other than relating a simple observation?
2. Why, in paragraph 2, does Woolf say that the moth was "little or nothing but life"? Why is the moth pitiable?
3. What does the moth in his square windowpane represent to the author? How does Woolf's DESCRIPTION in the essay make this clear?
4. How does Woolf's outlook change in paragraph 5? Why?

Questions on Writing Strategy

1. Is Woolf's essay an OBJECTIVE or a SUBJECTIVE description? Give details from the essay to support your answer.
2. What is the EFFECT of Woolf's scene-setting in paragraph 1? How does this description influence our perception of the moth?
3. **MIXED METHODS.** Which of the five senses does Woolf's description principally rely on? Why, do you think?
4. **MIXED METHODS.** This essay is a description in the framework of a NARRATIVE. SUMMARIZE the changes in Woolf's perceptions of the moth that occur in the narrative.

Questions on Language

1. ANALYZE the writing in paragraph 5. How do sentence structure and words create a mood different from that in earlier paragraphs?
2. Analyze Woolf's IMAGES in describing the moth and her substitutions for the word *moth*, such as "the present specimen" in paragraph 1. How do these reinforce Woolf's changing perceptions as you outlined them in question 4 on writing strategy?
3. You may find Woolf's vocabulary more difficult than that of some other writers in this book. Look up any unfamiliar words in the following list: rouse, hybrid, benignant, plough, share, down, rooks, clamor, vociferation (par. 1); zest, meager, pathetic, diminutive (2); decking, cumbered, circumspection (3); spectacle, futile, vainly (4); animation, righting, magnitude, minute, mean, antagonist (5).

Suggestions for Writing

1. **FROM JOURNAL TO ESSAY.** Write a brief essay from your journal entry, using ample descriptive details to depict both the creature and its significance. What lessons does the creature have to offer?

2. Find a place to write, and begin working on this assignment. Examine your surroundings: What could conceivably distract you from your work? Peeling paint? An uncomfortable chair? A funny smell? A noise? The view out your window? Your blinking computer cursor? Write a description of what you see, hear, feel, smell, taste.

3. **CRITICAL WRITING.** Respond to the ideas about life and death in Woolf's essay. First explain what you understand these ideas to be. Then use EXAMPLES from your reading and experience to support or contest Woolf's ideas.

4. **CONNECTIONS.** Human responses to death also figure in Jessica Mitford's "Behind the Formaldehyde Curtain" (p. 305). Write an essay in which you explore your perceptions of what happens at death and how that affects what should happen to the body afterward. Draw on the views of Woolf and Mitford if they seem relevant. If you have been directly affected by the death of a loved one or its aftermath, you might reflect on that experience as well.

5. **CONNECTIONS.** COMPARE Woolf's "The Death of the Moth" with Anna Quindlen's "Homeless" (p. 200). Of these two highly subjective essays, which is more personal? Write a brief essay answering this question, and support your answer with quotations and PARAPHRASES from Woolf and Quindlen.

Virginia Woolf on Writing

A journal keeper from her youth, Virginia Woolf used the form not only to record and reflect on events but also to do a kind of "rough & random" writing she otherwise had little chance for. (See p. 35 for more on journal writing.) Woolf wrote in her journal on April 20, 1919, that "the habit of writing thus for my own eye only is good practice. It loosens the ligaments. Never mind the misses & the stumbles. Going at such a pace as I do I must make the most direct & instant shots at my object, & thus have to lay hands on words, choose them, & shoot them with no more pause than is needed to put my pen in the ink. I believe that during the past year I can trace some increase of ease in my professional writing which I attribute to my casual half hours after tea."

Thirteen years later, Woolf felt just as strongly about the value of writing freely, without censorship. In "A Letter to a Young Poet," she advises against writing solely for "a severe and intelligent public." Follow the excitement of "actual life," she urges. "Write then, now that you are young, nonsense by the ream. Be silly, be sentimental, imitate Shelley, imitate Samuel Smiles; give the rein to every impulse; commit every fault of style, grammar, taste, and syntax; pour out; tumble over; loose anger, love, satire, in whatever words you can catch, coerce, or create, in whatever meter, prose, poetry, or gibberish that comes to hand. Thus you will learn to write."

For Discussion

1. What does Woolf gain from journal writing? What does she mean when she says that such writing "loosens the ligaments"?
2. Do you think Woolf seriously believed that young writers should write "nonsense by the ream"? (A *ream*, incidentally, is about five hundred sheets of paper.) What might the young writer learn from such freedom?
3. These excerpts do not discuss the writer's work needed to turn the loose, private writing Woolf recommends into writing that can be understood and appreciated by others. In your view, what does that work consist of?

USEFUL TERMS

Abstract and concrete   Two kinds of language. *Abstract* words refer to ideas, conditions, and qualities we cannot directly perceive: *truth, love, courage, evil, poverty, progressive*. *Concrete* words indicate things we can know with our senses: *tree, chair, bird, pen, motorcycle, perfume, thunderclap*. Concrete words lend vigor and clarity to writing, for they help a reader to picture things. See IMAGE.

Writers of expository and argumentative essays tend to shift back and forth from one kind of language to the other. They often begin a paragraph with a general statement full of abstract words ("There is *hope* for the *future* of *motoring*"). Then they usually go on to give examples and present evidence in sentences full of concrete words ("Inventor *Jones* claims his *car* will go from *Fresno* to *Los Angeles* on a *gallon* of *peanut oil*"). Inexperienced writers often use too many abstract words and not enough concrete ones. (See also pp. 140–41.)

Active voice   The form of the verb when the sentence subject is the actor: *Trees* [subject] *shed* [active verb] *their leaves in autumn*. Contrast PASSIVE VOICE.

Allude, allusion   To refer to a person, place, or thing believed to be common knowledge (*allude*), or the act or result of doing so (*allusion*). An allusion may point to a famous event, a familiar saying, a noted personality, a well-known story or song. Usually brief, an allusion is a space-saving way to convey much meaning. For example, the statement "The game was Coach Johnson's Waterloo" informs the reader that, like Napoleon meeting defeat in a celebrated battle, the coach led a confrontation resulting in his downfall and that of his team. If the writer is also

701

showing Johnson's character, the allusion might further tell us that the coach is a man of Napoleonic ambition and pride. To make an effective allusion, you have to ensure that it will be clear to your audience. Not every reader, for example, would understand an allusion to a neighbor, to a seventeenth-century Russian harpsichordist, or to a little-known stock-car driver.

Analogy   An extended comparison based on the like features of two unlike things: one familiar or easily understood, the other unfamiliar, abstract, or complicated. For instance, most people know at least vaguely how the human eye works: The pupil adjusts to admit light, which registers as an image on the retina at the back of the eye. You might use this familiar information to explain something less familiar to many people, such as how a camera works: The aperture (like the pupil) adjusts to admit light, which registers as an image on the film (like the retina) at the back of the camera. Analogies are especially helpful for explaining technical information in a way that is nontechnical, more easily grasped. For example, the spacecraft *Voyager 2* transmitted spectacular pictures of Saturn to Earth. To explain the difficulty of their achievement, NASA scientists compared their feat to a golfer sinking a putt from five hundred miles away. Because it can make abstract ideas vivid and memorable, analogy is also a favorite device of philosophers, politicians, and preachers. In his celebrated speech "I Have a Dream" (p. 625), Martin Luther King, Jr., draws a remarkable analogy to express the anger and disappointment of African Americans that, one hundred years after Lincoln's Emancipation Proclamation, their full freedom has yet to be achieved. "It is obvious today," declares King, "that America has defaulted on this promissory note"; and he compares the founding fathers' written guarantee — of the rights of life, liberty, and the pursuit of happiness — to a bad check returned for insufficient funds.

Analogy is similar to the method of COMPARISON AND CONTRAST. Both identify the distinctive features of two things and then set the features side by side. But a comparison explains two obviously similar things — two Civil War generals, two responses to a mess — and considers both their differences and their similarities. An analogy yokes two apparently unlike things (eye and camera, spaceflight and golf, guaranteed human rights and bad checks) and focuses only on their major similarities. Analogy is thus an extended *metaphor*, the FIGURE OF SPEECH that declares one thing to be another — even though it isn't, in a strictly literal sense — for the purpose of making us aware of similarity: "Hope," says the poet Emily Dickinson, "is the thing with feathers / That perches in the soul."

In an ARGUMENT, analogy can make readers more receptive to a point or inspire them, but it can't prove anything because in the end the subjects are dissimilar. A false analogy is a logical FALLACY that claims a fundamental likeness when none exists. See page 525.

Analyze, analysis   To separate a subject into its parts (*analyze*), or the act or result of doing so (*analysis*, also called *division*). Analysis is a key skill in CRITICAL THINKING, READING, AND WRITING; see pages 18–19. It is also considered a method of development; see Chapter 9.

Anecdote   A brief NARRATIVE, or retelling of a story or event. Anecdotes have many uses: as essay openers or closers, as examples, as sheer entertainment. See Chapter 4.

Appeals   Resources writers draw on to connect with and persuade readers:

- A **rational appeal** asks readers to use their intellects and their powers of reasoning. It relies on established conventions of logic and evidence.
- An **emotional appeal** asks readers to respond out of their beliefs, values, or feelings. It inspires, affirms, frightens, angers.
- An **ethical appeal** asks readers to look favorably on the writer. It stresses the writer's intelligence, competence, fairness, morality, and other qualities desirable in a trustworthy debater or teacher.

See also pages 518–19.

Argument   A mode of writing intended to win readers' agreement with an assertion by engaging their powers of reasoning. Argument often overlaps PERSUASION. See Chapter 13.

Assume, assumption   To take something for granted (*assume*), or a belief or opinion taken for granted (*assumption*). Whether stated or unstated, assumptions influence a writer's choices of subject, viewpoint, evidence, and even language. See also pages 19 and 520–21.

Audience   A writer's readers. Having in mind a particular audience helps the writer in choosing strategies. Imagine, for instance, that you are writing two reviews of a new movie, one for the students who read the campus newspaper, the other for amateur and professional filmmakers who read *Millimeter*. For the first audience, you might write about the actors, the plot, and especially dramatic scenes. You might judge the picture and urge your readers to see it — or to avoid it. Writing for *Millimeter*, you might discuss special effects, shooting techniques, problems in editing and in mixing picture and sound. In this review, you might use more specialized and technical terms. Obviously, an awareness of the interests and knowledge of your readers, in each case, would help you decide how to write. If you told readers of the campus paper too much about filming techniques, you would lose most of them. If you told *Millimeter*'s readers the film's plot in detail, probably you would put them to sleep.

  You can increase your awareness of your audience by asking yourself a few questions before you begin to write. Who are to be your readers? What is their age level? background? education? Where do they live? What are their beliefs and attitudes? What interests them? What, if anything, sets them apart from most people? How familiar are they with your subject? Knowing your audience can help you write so that your readers will not only understand you better but care more deeply about what you say.

Cause and effect   A method of development in which a writer ANALYZES reasons for an action, event, or decision, or analyzes its consequences. See Chapter 11. See also EFFECT.

Chronological order   The arrangement of events as they occurred or occur in time, first to last. Most NARRATIVES and PROCESS ANALYSES use chronological order.

Claim   The proposition that an ARGUMENT demonstrates. Stephen Toulmin favors this term in his system of reasoning. See pages 520–22. In some discussions of argument, the term THESIS is used instead.

Classification   A method of development in which a writer sorts out plural things (contact sports, college students, kinds of music) into categories. See Chapter 10.

Cliché   A worn-out, trite expression that a writer employs thoughtlessly. Although at one time the expression may have been colorful, from heavy use it has lost its luster. It is now "old as the hills." In conversation, most of us sometimes use clichés, but in writing they "stick out like sore thumbs." Alert writers, when they revise, replace a cliché with a fresh, concrete expression. Writers who have trouble recognizing clichés should be suspicious of any phrase they've heard before and should try to read more widely. Their problem is that, so many expressions being new to them, they do not know which ones are full of moths.

Coherence   The clear connection of the parts in effective writing so that the reader can easily follow the flow of ideas between sentences, paragraphs, and larger divisions, and can see how they relate successively to one another.

In making your essay coherent, you may find certain devices useful. Transitions, for instance, can bridge ideas. Reminders of points you have stated earlier are helpful to a reader who may have forgotten them—as readers tend to do sometimes, particularly if your essay is long. However, a coherent essay is not one merely pasted together with transitions and reminders. It derives its coherence from the clear relationship between its Thesis (or central idea) and all its parts. (See also pp. 234–35.)

Colloquial expressions   Words and phrases occurring primarily in speech and in informal writing that seeks a relaxed, conversational tone. "My favorite chow is a burger and a shake" or "This math exam has me wired" may be acceptable in talking to a roommate, in corresponding with a friend, or in writing a humorous essay for general readers. Such choices of words, however, would be out of place in formal writing—in, say, a laboratory report or a letter to your senator. Contractions (*let's, don't, we'll*) and abbreviated words (*photo, sales rep, ad*) are the shorthand of spoken language. Good writers use such expressions with an awareness that they produce an effect of casualness.

Comparison and contrast   Two methods of development usually found together. Using them, a writer examines the similarities and differences between two things to reveal their natures. See Chapter 7.

Conclusion   The sentences or paragraphs that bring an essay to a satisfying and logical end. A conclusion is purposefully crafted to give a sense of unity and completeness to the whole essay. The best conclusions evolve naturally out of what has gone before and convince the reader that the essay is indeed at an end, not that the writer has run out of steam.

Conclusions vary in type and length depending on the nature and scope of the essay. A long research paper may require several paragraphs of summary to review and emphasize the main points. A short essay, however, may benefit from a few brief closing sentences.

In concluding an essay, beware of diminishing the impact of your writing by finishing on a weak note. Don't apologize for what you have or have not written, or cram in a final detail that would have been better placed elsewhere.

Although there are no set formulas for closing, the following list presents several options:

- Restate the thesis of your essay, and perhaps your main points.
- Mention the broader implications or significance of your topic.
- Give a final example that pulls all the parts of your discussion together.

- Offer a prediction.
- End with the most important point as the culmination of your essay's development.
- Suggest how the reader can apply the information you have just imparted.
- End with a bit of drama or flourish. Tell an ANECDOTE, offer an appropriate quotation, ask a question, make a final insightful remark. Keep in mind, however, that an ending shouldn't sound false and gimmicky. It truly has to conclude.

Concrete   See ABSTRACT AND CONCRETE.

Connotation and denotation   Two types of meanings most words have. *Denotation* is the explicit, literal, dictionary definition of a word. *Connotation* refers to a word's implied meaning, resonant with associations. The denotation of *blood* is "the fluid that circulates in the vascular system." The connotations of *blood* range from *life force* to *gore* to *family bond*. A doctor might use the word *blood* for its denotation, and a mystery writer might rely on the word's connotations to heighten a scene.

Because people have different experiences, they bring to the same word different associations. A conservative's emotional response to the word *welfare* is not likely to be the same as a liberal's. And referring to your senator as a *diplomat* evokes a different response, from the senator and from others, than would *baby-kisser*, *political hack*, or even *politician*. The effective use of words involves knowing both what they mean literally and what they are likely to suggest.

Critical thinking, reading, and writing   A group of interlocking skills that are essential for college work and beyond. Each seeks the meaning beneath the surface of a statement, poem, editorial, picture, advertisement, Web site, or other "text." Using ANALYSIS, INFERENCE, SYNTHESIS, and often EVALUATION, the critical thinker, reader, and writer separates this text into its elements in order to see and judge meanings, relations, and ASSUMPTIONS that might otherwise remain buried. See also pages 18–20, 26–30, 49–52, 337–38.

Data   The name for EVIDENCE favored by logician Stephen Toulmin in his system of reasoning. See pages 520–22.

Deductive reasoning, deduction   The method of reasoning from the general to the particular: From information about what we already know, we deduce what we need or want to know. See Chapter 13, pages 522–24.

Definition   A statement of the literal and specific meaning or meanings of a word, or a method of developing an essay. In the latter, the writer usually explains the nature of a word, a thing, a concept, or a phenomenon. Such a definition may employ NARRATION, DESCRIPTION, or any other method. See Chapter 12.

Denotation   See CONNOTATION AND DENOTATION.

Description   A mode of writing that conveys the evidence of the senses: sight, hearing, touch, taste, smell. See Chapter 5.

Diction   The choice of words. Every written or spoken statement contains diction of some kind. To describe certain aspects of diction, the following terms may be useful:

- **Standard English:** the common American language, words and grammatical forms that are used and expected in school, business, and other sites.
- **Nonstandard English:** words and grammatical forms such as *theirselves* and *ain't* that are used mainly by people who speak a dialect other than standard English.

- **Dialect:** a variety of English based on differences in geography, education, or social background. Dialect is usually spoken but may be written. Maya Angelou's essay in Chapter 4 transcribes the words of dialect speakers ("He gone whip him till that white boy call him Momma").
- **Slang:** certain words in highly informal speech or writing, or in the speech of a particular group—for example, *blow off, dis, dweeb.*
- **Colloquial expressions:** words and phrases from conversation. See COLLOQUIAL EXPRESSIONS for examples.
- **Regional terms:** words heard in a certain locality, such as *spritzing* for "raining" in Pennsylvania Dutch country.
- **Technical terms:** words and phrases that form the vocabulary of a particular discipline (*monocotyledon* from botany), occupation (*drawplate* from die-making), or avocation (*interval training* from running). See also JARGON.
- **Archaisms:** old-fashioned expressions, once common but now used to suggest an earlier style, such as *ere* and *forsooth.*
- **Obsolete diction:** words that have passed out of use (such as the verb *werien,* "to protect or defend," and the noun *isetnesses,* "agreements"). *Obsolete* may also refer to certain meanings of words no longer current (*fond* for foolish, *clipping* for hugging or embracing).
- **Pretentious diction:** use of words more numerous and elaborate than necessary, such as *institution of higher learning* for college, and *partake of solid nourishment* for eat.

Archaic, obsolete, and pretentious diction usually has no place in good writing unless for ironic or humorous effect: the journalist and critic H. L. Mencken delighted in the hifalutin use of *tonsorial studio* instead of barber shop. Still, any diction may be the right diction for a certain occasion: The choice of words depends on a writer's PURPOSE and AUDIENCE.

Discovery   The stage of the writing process before the first draft. It may include deciding on a topic, narrowing the topic, creating or finding ideas, doing reading and other research, defining PURPOSE and AUDIENCE, planning and arranging material. Discovery may follow from daydreaming or meditation, reading, or perhaps carefully ransacking memory. In practice, though, it usually involves considerable writing and is aided by the act of writing. The operations of discovery—reading, research, further idea creation, and refinement of subject, purpose, and audience—may all continue well into drafting as well. See also pages 34–37, 41.

Division   See ANALYZE, ANALYSIS.

Dominant impression   The main idea a writer conveys about a subject through DESCRIPTION—that an elephant is gigantic, for example, or an experience scary. See also Chapter 5.

Drafting   The stage of the writing process during which a writer expresses ideas in complete sentences, links them, and arranges them in a sequence. See also pages 37, 41–42.

Effect   The result of an event or action, usually considered together with CAUSE as a method of development. See the discussion of cause and effect in Chapter 11. In discussing writing, the term *effect* also refers to the impression a word, sentence, paragraph, or entire work makes on the reader: how convincing it is, whether it elicits an emotional response, what associations it conjures up, and so on.

Emotional appeal   See APPEALS.

Emphasis The stress or special importance given to a certain point or element to make it stand out. A skillful writer draws attention to what is most important in a sentence, paragraph, or essay by controlling emphasis in any of the following ways:

- **Proportion:** Important ideas are given greater coverage than minor points.
- **Position:** The beginnings and ends of sentences, paragraphs, and larger divisions are the strongest positions. Placing key ideas in these spots helps draw attention to their importance. The end is the stronger position, for what stands last stands out. A sentence in which less important details precede the main point is called a **periodic sentence:** "Having disguised himself as a guard and walked through the courtyard to the side gate, the prisoner made his escape." A sentence in which the main point precedes less important details is a **loose sentence:** "Autumn is orange: gourds in baskets at roadside stands, the harvest moon hanging like a pumpkin, and oak leaves flashing like goldfish."
- **Repetition:** Careful repetition of key words or phrases can give them greater importance. (Careless repetition, however, can cause boredom.)
- **Mechanical devices:** Italics (underlining), capital letters, and exclamation points can make words or sentences stand out. Writers sometimes fall back on these devices, however, after failing to show significance by other means. Italics and exclamation points can be useful in reporting speech, but excessive use sounds exaggerated or bombastic.

Essay A short nonfiction composition on one central theme or subject in which the writer may offer personal views. Essays are sometimes classified as either formal or informal. In general, a **formal essay** is one whose DICTION is that of the written language (not colloquial speech), serious in TONE, and usually focused on a subject the writer believes is important. (For example, see Bruce Catton's "Grant and Lee.") An **informal essay,** in contrast, is more likely to admit COLLOQUIAL EXPRESSIONS; the writer's tone tends to be lighter, perhaps humorous, and the subject is likely to be personal, sometimes even trivial. (See Dave Barry's "Batting Clean-Up and Striking Out.") These distinctions, however, are rough ones: An essay such as Judy Brady's "I Want a Wife" uses colloquial language and speaks of personal experience, but its tone is serious and its subject imporant.

Ethical appeal See APPEALS.

Euphemism The use of inoffensive language in place of language that readers or listeners may find hurtful, distasteful, frightening, or otherwise objectionable—for instance, a police officer's announcing that someone *passed on* rather than *died,* or a politician's calling for *revenue enhancement* rather than *taxation.* Writers sometimes use euphemism out of consideration for readers' feelings, but just as often they use it to deceive readers or shirk responsibility. (For more on euphemism, see William Lutz's "The World of Doublespeak" in Chap. 10.)

Evaluate, evaluation To judge the merits of something (*evaluate*), or the act or result of doing so (*evaluation*). Evaluation is often part of CRITICAL THINKING, READING, AND WRITING. In evaluating a work of writing, you base your judgment on your ANALYSIS of it and your sense of its quality or value. See also pages 20, 30, 49–52.

Evidence The factual basis for an argument or an explanation. In a courtroom, an attorney's case is only as good as the evidence marshaled to support it. In an essay, a writer's opinions and GENERALIZATIONS also must rest upon evidence. The common forms of evidence are **facts**, verifiable statements; **statistics**, facts stated numerically; **examples**, specific instances of a generalization; **reported experience**, usually eyewitness accounts; **expert testimony**, the opinions of people considered very skilled or knowledgeable in the field; and, in CRITICAL WRITING about other writing, **quotations** or **paraphrases** from the work being discussed. (See PARAPHRASE.)

Example   Also called **exemplification** or **illustration**, a method of development in which the writer provides instances of a general idea. See Chapter 6. *An example* is a verbal illustration.

Exposition   The mode of prose writing that explains (or exposes) its subject. Its function is to inform, to instruct, or to set forth ideas: the major trade routes in the Middle East, how to make a dulcimer, why the United States consumes more energy than it needs. Exposition may call various methods to its service: EXAMPLE, COMPARISON AND CONTRAST, PROCESS ANALYSIS, and so on. Most college writing is at least partly exposition, and so are most of the essays in this book.

Fallacies   Errors in reasoning. See pages 524–25 for a list and examples.

Figures of speech   Expressions that depart from the literal meanings of words for the sake of emphasis or vividness. To say "She's a jewel" doesn't mean that the subject of praise is literally a kind of shining stone; the statement makes sense because its CONNOTATIONS come to mind: rare, priceless, worth cherishing. Some figures of speech involve comparisons of two objects apparently unlike:

- A **simile** (from the Latin, "likeness") states the comparison directly, usually connecting the two things using *like, as,* or *than:* "The moon is like a snowball," "He's as lazy as a cat full of cream," "My feet are flatter than flyswatters."
- A **metaphor** (from the Greek, "transfer") declares one thing to *be* another: "A mighty fortress is our God," "The sheep were bolls of cotton on the hill." (A **dead metaphor** is a word or phrase that, originally a figure of speech, has come to be literal through common usage: "the *hands* of a clock.")
- **Personification** is a simile or metaphor that assigns human traits to inanimate objects or abstractions: "A stoop-shouldered refrigerator hummed quietly to itself," "The solution to the math problem sat there winking at me."

Other figures of speech consist of deliberate misrepresentations:

- **Hyperbole** (from the Greek, "throwing beyond") is a conscious exaggeration: "I'm so hungry I could eat a saddle," "I'd wait for you a thousand years."
- The opposite of hyperbole, **understatement**, creates an ironic or humorous effect: "I accepted the ride. At the moment, I didn't feel like walking across the Mojave Desert."
- A **paradox** (from the Greek, "conflicting with expectation") is a seemingly self-contradictory statement that, on reflection, makes sense: "Children are the poor person's wealth" (wealth can be monetary, or it can be spiritual). *Paradox* may also refer to a situation that is inexplicable or contradictory, such as the restriction of one group's rights in order to secure the rights of another group.

Flashback   A technique of NARRATIVE in which the sequence of events is interrupted to recall an earlier period.

Focus   The narrowing of a subject to make it manageable. Beginning with a general subject, you concentrate on a certain aspect of it. For instance, you may select crafts as a general subject, then decide your main interest lies in weaving. You could focus your essay still further by narrowing it to operating a hand loom. You also focus your writing according to who will read it (AUDIENCE) or what you want it to achieve (PURPOSE).

General and specific   Terms that describe the relative number of instances or objects included in the group signified by a word. *General* words name a group or class (*flowers*); *specific* words limit the class by naming its individual members (*rose, violet, dahlia, marigold*). Words may be arranged in a series from more general to more specific: *clothes, pants, jeans, Levis*. The word *cat* is more specific than *animal*, but less specific than *tiger cat*, or *Garfield*. See also ABSTRACT AND CONCRETE and pages 140–41.

Generalization   A statement about a class based on an examination of some of its members: "Lions are fierce." The more members examined and the more representative they are of the class, the sturdier the generalization. The statement "Solar heat saves home owners money" would be challenged by home owners who have yet to recover their installation costs. "Solar heat can save home owners money in the long run" would be a sounder generalization. Insufficient or nonrepresentative EVIDENCE often leads to a hasty generalization, such as "All freshmen hate their roommates" or "Men never express their feelings." Words such as *all, every, only, never,* and *always* have to be used with care: "Some men don't express their feelings" is more credible. Making a trustworthy generalization involves the use of INDUCTIVE REASONING (discussed on pp. 522–23).

Hyperbole   See FIGURES OF SPEECH.

Illustration   Another name for EXAMPLE. See Chapter 6.

Image   A word or word sequence that evokes a sensory experience. Whether literal ("We picked two red apples") or figurative ("His cheeks looked like two red apples, buffed and shining"), an image appeals to the reader's memory of seeing, hearing, smelling, touching, or tasting. Images add concreteness to fiction — "The farm looked as tiny and still as a seashell, with the little knob of a house surrounded by its curved furrows of tomato plants" (Eudora Welty in a short story, "The Whistle") — and are an important element in poetry. But writers of essays, too, use images to bring ideas down to earth. See also FIGURES OF SPEECH.

Inductive reasoning, induction   The process of reasoning to a conclusion about an entire class by examining some of its members. See pages 522–23.

Infer, inference   To draw a conclusion (*infer*), or the act or result of doing so (*inference*). In CRITICAL THINKING, READING, AND WRITING, inference is the means to understanding a writer's meaning, ASSUMPTIONS, PURPOSE, fairness, and other attributes. See also pages 19 and 29.

Introduction   The opening of a written work. Often it states the writer's subject, narrows it, and communicates the writer's main idea (THESIS). Introductions vary in length, depending on their purposes. A research paper may need several paragraphs to set forth its central idea and its plan of organization; a brief, informal essay may need only a sentence or two for an introduction. Whether long or short, good introductions tell readers no more than they need to know when they begin reading. Here are a few possible ways to open an essay effectively:

- State your central idea, or thesis, perhaps showing why you care about it.
- Present startling facts about your subject.
- Tell an illustrative ANECDOTE.
- Give background information that will help your reader understand your subject, or see why it is important.
- Begin with an arresting quotation.
- Ask a challenging question. (In your essay, you'll go on to answer it.)

Irony   A manner of speaking or writing that does not directly state a discrepancy, but implies one. **Verbal irony** is the intentional use of words to suggest a meaning other than literal: "What a mansion!" (said of a shack); "There's nothing like sunshine" (said on a foggy morning). (For more examples, see the essays by Jessica Mitford, Linnea Saukko, and Judy Brady.) If irony is delivered contemptuously with an intent to hurt, we call it **sarcasm:** "Oh, you're a real friend!" (said to someone who refuses to lend the speaker the coins to make a phone call). With **situational irony,** the circumstances themselves are incongruous, run contrary to expectations, or twist fate: Juliet regains consciousness only to find that Romeo, believing her dead, has stabbed himself. See also SATIRE.

Jargon   Strictly speaking, the special vocabulary of a trade or profession. The term has also come to mean inflated, vague, meaningless language of any kind. It is characterized by wordiness, ABSTRACTIONS galore, pretentious DICTION, and needlessly complicated word order. Whenever you meet a sentence that obviously could express its idea in fewer words and shorter ones, chances are that it is jargon. For instance: "The motivating force compelling her to opt continually for the most labor-intensive mode of operation in performing her functions was consistently observed to be the single constant and regular factor in her behavior patterns." Translation: "She did everything the hard way." (For more on such jargon, see William Lutz's "The World of Doublespeak" in Chap. 10.)

Journal   A record of one's thoughts, kept daily or at least regularly. Keeping a journal faithfully can help a writer gain confidence and develop ideas. See also page 35.

Metaphor   See FIGURES OF SPEECH.

Narration   The mode of writing that tells a story. See Chapter 4.

Narrator   The teller of a story, usually either in the first PERSON (*I*) or in the third (*he, she, it, they*). See pages 78–79.

Nonstandard English   See DICTION.

Objective and subjective   Kinds of writing that differ in emphasis. In *objective* writing, the emphasis falls on the topic; in *subjective* writing, it falls on the writer's view of the topic. Objective writing occurs in factual journalism, science reports, certain PROCESS ANALYSES (such as recipes, directions, and instructions), and logical arguments in which the writer attempts to downplay personal feelings and opinions. Subjective writing sets forth the writer's feelings, opinions, and interpretations. It occurs in friendly letters, journals, bylined feature stories and columns in newspapers, personal essays, and ARGUMENTS that appeal to emotion. Few essays, however, contain one kind of writing exclusive of the other.

Paradox   See FIGURES OF SPEECH.

Paragraph   A group of closely related sentences that develop a central idea. In an essay, a paragraph is the most important unit of thought because it is both self-contained and part of the larger whole. Paragraphs separate long and involved ideas into smaller parts that are more manageable for the writer and easier for the reader to take in. Good paragraphs, like good essays, possess UNITY and COHERENCE. The central idea is usually stated in a TOPIC SENTENCE, often found at the beginning of the paragraph that relates directly to the essay's THESIS. All other sentences in the paragraph relate to this topic sentence, defining it, explaining it, illustrating it, providing it with evidence and support. If you meet a unified and coherent paragraph that has no topic sentence, it will contain a central idea that no sentence in it explicitly states, but that every sentence in it clearly implies. See also pages 234 (paragraph coherence), 379 (paragraph development), and 483 (paragraph unity).

Parallelism, parallel structure   A habit of good writers: keeping ideas of equal importance in similar grammatical form. A writer may place nouns side by side ("*Trees* and *streams* are my weekend tonic") or in a series ("Give me *wind, sea, and stars*"). Phrases, too, may be arranged in parallel structure ("*Out of my bed, into my shoes, up to my classroom*—that's my life"); or clauses ("Ask not what your country can do for you; ask what you can do for your country").

   Parallelism may be found not only in single sentences, but in larger units as well. A paragraph might read: "Rhythm is everywhere. It throbs in the rain forests of Brazil. It vibrates ballroom floors in Vienna. It snaps its fingers on street corners in Chicago." In a whole essay, parallelism may be the principle used to arrange ideas in a balanced or harmonious structure. See the famous speech given by Martin Luther King, Jr. (p. 625), in which paragraphs 11–18 all begin with the words "I have a dream" and describe an imagined future. Not only does such a parallel structure organize ideas, but it also lends them force.

Paraphrase   Putting another writer's thoughts into your own words. In writing a research paper or an essay containing EVIDENCE gathered from your reading, you will find it necessary to paraphrase—unless you are using another writer's very words with quotation marks around them—and to acknowledge your sources. Contrast SUMMARY. And see pages 52–53.

Passive voice   The form of the verb when the sentence subject is acted upon: *The report* [subject] *was published* [passive verb] *anonymously*. Contrast ACTIVE VOICE.

Person   A grammatical distinction made between the speaker, the one spoken to, and the one spoken about. In the first person (*I, we*), the subject is speaking. In the second person (*you*), the subject is being spoken to. In the third person (*he, she, it*), the subject is being spoken about. The point of view of an essay or work of fiction is often specified according to person: "This short story is told from a first-person point of view." See POINT OF VIEW.

Personification   See FIGURES OF SPEECH.

Persuasion   A mode of writing intended to influence people's actions by engaging their beliefs and feelings. Persuasion often overlaps ARGUMENT. See Chapter 13.

Plagiarism   The use of someone else's ideas or words as if they were your own, without acknowledging the original author. See pages 55–56.

Point of view   In an essay, the physical position or the mental angle from which a writer beholds a subject. On the subject of starlings, the following three writers would likely have different points of view: An ornithologist might write OBJECTIVELY about the introduction of these birds into North America, a farmer might advise other farmers how to prevent the birds from eating seed, and a bird-watcher might SUBJECTIVELY describe a first glad sighting of an unusual species. Furthermore, the PERSON of each essay would probably differ: The scientist might present a scholarly paper in the third person, the farmer might offer advice in the second, and the bird-watcher might recount the experience in the first.

Premise   A proposition or ASSUMPTION that supports a conclusion. See pages 523–24 for examples.

Process analysis   A method of development that most often explains step by step how something is done or how to do something. See Chapter 8.

Purpose   A writer's reason for trying to convey a particular idea (THESIS) about a particular subject to a particular AUDIENCE of readers. Though it may emerge gradually during the writing process, in the end purpose should govern every element of a piece of writing.

In trying to define the purpose of an essay you read, ask yourself "Why did the writer write this?" or "What was this writer trying to achieve?" Even though you cannot know the writer's intentions with absolute certainty, an effective essay will make some purpose clear.

Rational appeal   See APPEALS.

Revision   The stage of the writing process during which a writer "re-sees" a draft from the viewpoint of a reader. Revision usually involves two steps, first considering fundamental matters such as PURPOSE and organization, and then editing for surface matters such as smooth TRANSITIONS and error-free sentences. See pages 39–40, 43–45.

Rhetoric   The study (and the art) of using language effectively. *Rhetoric* also has a negative CONNOTATION of empty or pretentious language meant to waffle, stall, or even deceive. This is the meaning in "The president had nothing substantial to say about taxes, just the usual rhetoric."

Rhetorical question   A question posed for effect, one that requires no answer. Instead, it often provokes thought, lends emphasis to a point, asserts or denies something without making a direct statement, launches further discussion, introduces an opinion, or leads the reader where the writer intends. Sometimes a writer throws one in to introduce variety in a paragraph full of declarative sentences. The following questions are rhetorical: "When will the United States learn that sending people into space does not feed them on the earth?" "Shall I compare thee to a summer's day?" "What is the point of making money if you've no one but yourself to spend it on?" Both reader and writer know what the answers are supposed to be. (1) Someday, if the United States ever wises up. (2) Yes. (3) None.

Sarcasm   See IRONY.

Satire   A form of writing that employs wit to attack folly. Unlike most comedy, the purpose of satire is not merely to entertain, but to bring about enlightenment — even reform. Usually, satire employs irony — as in Linnea Saukko's "How to Poison the Earth" and Jonathan Swift's "A Modest Proposal." See also IRONY.

Scene   In a NARRATIVE, an event retold in detail to re-create an experience. See Chapter 4.

Sentimentality   A quality sometimes found in writing that fails to communicate. Such writing calls for an extreme emotional response on the part of an AUDIENCE, although its writer fails to supply adequate reason for any such reaction. A sentimental writer delights in waxing teary over certain objects: great-grandmother's portrait, the first stick of chewing gum baby chewed (now a shapeless wad), an empty popcorn box saved from the World Series of 1996. Sentimental writing usually results when writers shut their eyes to the actual world, preferring to snuffle the sweet scents of remembrance.

Simile   See FIGURES OF SPEECH.

Slang   See DICTION.

Specific   See GENERAL AND SPECIFIC.

Standard English   See DICTION.

Strategy   Whatever means a writer employs to write effectively. The methods set forth in this book are strategies; but so are narrowing a subject, organizing ideas clearly, using TRANSITIONS, writing with an awareness of your reader, and other effective writing practices.

Style   The distinctive manner in which a writer writes. Style may be seen especially in the writer's choice of words and sentence structures. Two writers may write on the same subject, even express similar ideas, but it is style that gives each writer's work a personality.

Subjective   See OBJECTIVE AND SUBJECTIVE.

Summarize, summary   To condense a work (essay, movie, news story) to its essence (*summarize*), or the act or result of doing so (*summary*). Summarizing a piece of writing in one's own words is an effective way to understand it. (See pp. 17–18.) Summarizing (and acknowledging) others' writing in your own text is a good way to support your ideas. (See pp. 52–53.) Contrast PARAPHRASE.

Suspense   Often an element in NARRATION: the pleasurable expectation or anxiety we feel that keeps us reading a story. In an exciting mystery story, suspense is constant: How will it all turn out? Will the detective get to the scene in time to prevent another murder? But there can be suspense in less melodramatic accounts as well.

Syllogism   A three-step form of reasoning that employs DEDUCTION. See page 523 for an illustration.

Symbol   A visible object or action that suggests further meaning. The flag suggests country, the crown suggests royalty—these are conventional symbols familiar to us. Life abounds in such clear-cut symbols. Football teams use dolphins and rams for easy identification; married couples symbolize their union with a ring.

In writing, symbols usually do not have such a one-to-one correspondence, but evoke a whole constellation of associations. In Herman Melville's *Moby-Dick*, the whale suggests more than the large mammal it is. It hints at evil, obsession, and the untamable forces of nature. Such a symbol carries meanings too complex or elusive to be neatly defined.

Although more common in fiction and poetry, symbols can be used to good purpose in nonfiction because they often communicate an idea in a compact and concrete way.

Synthesize, synthesis   To link elements into a whole (*synthesize*), or the act or result of doing so (*synthesis*). In CRITICAL THINKING, READING, AND WRITING, synthesis is the key step during which you reassemble a work you have ANALYZED or connect the work with others. See pages 19 and 29–30.

Thesis   The central idea in a work of writing, to which everything else in the work refers. In some way, each sentence and PARAGRAPH in an effective essay serves to support the thesis and to make it clear and explicit to readers. Good writers, while writing, often set down a **thesis statement** or **thesis sentence** to help them define their purpose. They also often include this statement in their essay as a promise and a guide to readers. See also pages 21, 37–38, and 340.

Tone   The way a writer expresses his or her regard for subject, AUDIENCE, or self. Through word choice, sentence structures, and what is actually said, the writer conveys an attitude and sets a prevailing spirit. Tone in writing varies as greatly as tone of voice varies in conversation. It can be serious, distant, flippant, angry, enthusiastic, sincere, sympathetic. Whatever tone a writer chooses, usually it informs an entire essay and helps a reader decide how to respond. For works of strong tone, see the essays by Maya Angelou, Jessica Mitford, Judy Brady, Russell Baker, Dagoberto Gilb, and Martin Luther King, Jr. See also pages 527–28.

Topic sentence   The statement of the central idea in a PARAGRAPH, usually asserting one aspect of an essay's THESIS. Often the topic sentence will appear at (or near) the beginning of the paragraph, announcing the idea and beginning its development. Because all other sentences in the paragraph explain and support this central idea, the topic sentence is a way to create UNITY.

Transitions   Words, phrases, sentences, or even paragraphs that relate ideas. In moving from one topic to the next, a writer has to bring the reader along by showing how the ideas are developing, what bearing a new thought or detail has on an earlier discussion, or why a new topic is being introduced. A clear purpose, strong ideas, and logical development certainly aid COHERENCE, but to ensure that the reader is following along, good writers provide signals, or transitions.

To bridge sentences or paragraphs and to point out relationships within them, you can use some of the following devices of transition:

- Repeat or restate words or phrases to produce an echo in the reader's mind.
- Use PARALLEL STRUCTURES to produce a rhythm that moves the reader forward.
- Use pronouns to refer back to nouns in earlier passages.
- Use transitional words and phrases. These may indicate a relationship of time (*right away, later, soon, meanwhile, in a few minutes, that night*), proximity (*beside, close to, distant from, nearby, facing*), effect (*therefore, for this reason, as a result, consequently*), comparison (*similarly, in the same way, likewise*), or contrast (*yet, but, nevertheless, however, despite*). Some words and phrases of transition simply add on: *besides, too, also, moreover, in addition to, second, last, in the end*.

Understatement   See FIGURES OF SPEECH.

Unity   The quality of good writing in which all parts relate to the THESIS. In a unified essay, all words, sentences, and PARAGRAPHS support the single central idea. Your first step in achieving unity is to state your thesis; your next step is to organize your thoughts so that they make your thesis clear. See also page 483.

Voice   In writing, the sense of the author's character, personality, and attitude that comes through the words. See TONE.

Warrant   The name in Stephen Toulmin's system of reasoning for the thinking, or ASSUMPTION, that links DATA and CLAIM. See pages 520–22.

Acknowledgments

Sherman Alexie. "Indian Education" from *The Lone Ranger and Tonto Fistfight in Heaven*. Copyright © 1993 by Sherman Alexie. Reprinted with the permission of Grove/Atlantic, Inc. "Sherman Alexie on Writing," excerpted from Pam Lambert, "Poetry and Three-pointers," from *People*, May 8, 1995. Copyright © 1995 by Time, Inc. Reprinted with the permission of Time, Inc. Excerpt from Doug Marx, "Sherman Alexie: A Reservation of the Mind," from *Publishers Weekly*, September 16, 1996. Reprinted with the permission of *Publishers Weekly*. Excerpt from E. K. Caldwell, "Interview: Sherman Alexie," from *Dreaming the Dawn*. Reprinted with the permission of University of Nebraska Press. Excerpt from Joel McNally, "Profile: Sherman Alexie," from http://www.writermag.com.

Maya Angelou. "Champion of the World" from *I Know Why the Caged Bird Sings*. Copyright © 1969 and renewed 1997 by Maya Angelou. Reprinted with the permission of Random House, Inc. "Maya Angelou on Writing," excerpted from Sheila Weller, "Work in Progress/ Maya Angelou," from *Intellectual Digest*, June 1973. Reprinted with the permission of Sheila Weller.

Barbara Lazear Ascher. "On Compassion" from *The Habit of Loving*. Copyright © 1986, 1987, 1989 by Barbara Lazear Ascher. Reprinted with the permission of Random House, Inc. "Barbara Lazear Ascher on Writing," excerpted from Barbara Lazear Ascher selection in *Contemporary Authors Online*. Copyright © 1999. Reprinted with the permission of The Gale Group, http://www.galegroup.com.

Russell Baker. "The Plot Against People," *New York Times*, January 1, 1951. Copyright © 1951 by The New York Times Company. Reprinted with permission. "Russell Baker on Writing," previously appeared as "Computer Fallout" in *New York Times Magazine*, October 11, 1987. Copyright © 1987 by The New York Times Company. Reprinted with permission.

Dave Barry. "Batting Clean-Up and Striking Out" from *Dave Barry's Greatest Hits*. Copyright © 1988 by Dave Barry. Reprinted with the permission of Crown Publishers, Inc. "Dave Barry on Writing," excerpts from Dave Barry selection in *Contemporary Authors, New Revision Series*, vol. 134. Copyright © 1992. Reprinted with the permission of The Gale Group, http://www.galegroup.com.

Judy Brady. "I Want a Wife," copyright © 1970 by Judy Brady. Reprinted with the permission of the author.

Suzanne Britt. "Neat People vs. Sloppy People" from *Show and Tell*. Copyright © 1982 by Suzanne Britt. Reprinted with the permission of the author. "Suzanne Britt on Writing," copyright © 1984 by St. Martin's Press. Reprinted with permission.

Armin A. Brott. "Not All Men Are Sly Foxes" from *Newsweek* (1992). Reprinted with the permission of the author.

Bill Bryson. "How You Became You" (editors' title), formerly the introduction to *A Short History of Nearly Everything*. Copyright © 2003 by Bill Bryson. Reprinted with the permission of Broadway Books, a division of Random House, Inc. "Bill Bryson on Writing" excerpted from Bill Bryson, "Lost in Cyberspace," from *I'm a Stranger Here Myself*. Copyright © 1999 by Bill Bryson. Reprinted with the permission of Random House, Inc.

William F. Buckley, Jr. "Why Don't We Complain?" from *Esquire* (1960). Copyright © 1960 by *Esquire*. "William F. Buckley, Jr., on Writing," excerpts from *Overdrive: A Personal Documentary*. Copyright © 1981, 1983 by N. R. Resources, Inc. Excerpt from *A Hymnal: The Controversial Arts*, copyright © 1978 by William F. Buckley, Jr. All reprinted with the permission of the Wallace Literary Agency.

Ethan Canin. "Fly-Fishing for Doctors" from *The New Yorker*, June 22–29, 1998. Copyright © 1998 by Ethan Canin. Reprinted with the permission of Maxine Groffsky Literary

chives. Reprinted with permission. "Chitra Divakaruni on Writing" excerpted from "Women's Places" interview by Katie Bolick from *Atlantic Unbound*, April 8, 1998, http://www.theatlantic.com/unbound/factfict/ff9804.html. Reprinted with permission.

Barbara Ehrenreich. "The Roots of War," *The Progressive*, April 10, 2003. Reprinted with the permission of *The Progressive*, 409 East Main Street, Madison, WI 53703.

Stephanie Ericsson. "The Ways We Lie," *Utne Reader*, November/December 1992. Copyright © 1992 by Stephanie Ericsson. Reprinted with the permission of Dunham Literary Agency as agents for the author. "Stephanie Ericsson on Writing," excerpted from "Amazon.com Talks to Stephanie Ericsson," http://www.amazon.com/exec/obidos/show-interview/e-s-ricssontephanie.

Robert Francis. Excerpt from "Teacher" from *The Satirical Rogue on Poetry*. Copyright © 1968 by Robert Francis. Reprinted with the permission of The University of Massachusetts Press.

Laura Fraser. "Why I Stopped Being a Vegetarian" from *Salon.com*, January 7, 2000, http://dir.salon.com/travel/food/feature/2000/01/07/vegetarian/index.html. An online version remains in the *Salon* Archives. Reprinted with permission. "Laura Fraser on Writing" excerpted from "An Interview with Laura Fraser," http://www.randomhouse.com. Reprinted with permission.

Zara Gelsey. "The FBI Is Reading over Your Shoulder" (editors' title; originally titled "Who's Reading over Your Shoulder?"), Civil Liberties Watch, *The Humanist*, September/October 2002. Copyright © 2002 by The American Humanist Association. Reprinted with permission.

Dagoberto Gilb. "Pride" from *Gritos: Essays by Dagoberto Gilb* (New York: Grove/Atlantic, 2003). Copyright © 2003 by Dagoberto Gilb. Reprinted with the permission of Witherspoon Associates. "Dagoberto Gilb on Writing" excerpted from Dagoberto Gilb, *Gritos*. Copyright © 2003 by Dagoberto Gilb. Reprinted with the permission of Grove/Atlantic, Inc.

Stephen Jay Gould. "A Biological Homage to Mickey Mouse" from *The Panda's Thumb: More Reflections in Natural History*. Copyright © 1980 by Stephen Jay Gould. "Steven Jay Gould on Writing" excerpted from *The Flamingo's Smile: Reflections in Natural History*, copyright © 1985 by Stephen Jay Gould. All reprinted with the permission of W. W. Norton & Company, Inc.

Samuel P. Huntington. "The Crisis of National Identity" (editors' title; originally titled "Are the Flags Still There?") from *Who Are We? The Challenges to America's National Identity*. Copyright © 2004 by Samuel P. Huntington. Reprinted with the permission of Simon & Schuster Adult Publishing Group. This selection contains material from Rachel Newman, excerpt from "The Day the World Changed, I Did Too," *Newsweek*, October 1, 2001. Copyright © 2001 by Newsweek, Inc. All rights reserved. Reprinted by permission. Robert Frost, excerpt from "Dedication" from *The Poetry of Robert Frost*, edited by Edward Connery Lathem. Copyright © 1969 by Henry Holt and Company, LLC. Reprinted with the permission of Henry Holt and Co., LLC. Maya Angelou, excerpts from "On the Pulse of Morning" from *The Complete Collected Poems of Maya Angelou*. Copyright © 1993 by Maya Angelou. Reprinted with the permission of Random House, Inc.

Shirley Jackson. "The Lottery" from *The Lottery and Other Stories*. Copyright 1948, 1949 by Shirley Jackson, renewed © 1976, 1977 by Laurence Hyman, Barry Hyman, Mrs. Sarah Webster, and Mrs. Joanne Schnurer. Reprinted with the permission of Farrar, Straus & Giroux, LLC.

H. W. Janson. Excerpt from *The History of Art*, 5th ed., p. 482. Copyright © 1997 by Harry N. Abrams, Inc. Reprinted with the permission of Pearson Education, Upper Saddle River, New Jersey.

David Sedaris. "Remembering My Childhood on the Continent of Africa" from *Me Talk Pretty One Day*. Copyright © 2000 by David Sedaris. Reprinted with the permission of Little, Brown and Company, Inc.

Peter Singer. "A Vegetarian Philosophy" from *Consuming Passions: Food in the Age of Anxiety*. Copyright © 1998 by Peter Singer. Reprinted with the permission of Manchester University Press. "Peter Singer on Writing" excerpted from Richard Atcheson, "Of Animals and Ethics," *Princeton Alumni Weekly*, November 16, 2000. Reprinted with the permission of *Princeton Alumni Weekly*.

Michael Sorkin. Excerpt from "Faking It" in *Watching Television: A Pantheon Guide to Popular Culture*, edited by Todd Gitlin. Copyright © 1986 by Todd Gitlin. Reprinted with the permission of Pantheon Books, a division of Random House, Inc.

Thomas Sowell. " 'Needs' " from *Is Reality Optional? and Other Essays* (Stanford, Calif.: Hoover Institution Press, 1993). Copyright © 1993 by Thomas Sowell. Reprinted with the permission of the author.

Brent Staples. "Black Men and Public Space," *Harper's*, December 1986. Reprinted with the permission of the author. "Brent Staples on Writing," copyright © 1991 by St. Martin's Press. Reprinted with permission.

Amy Tan. "Fish Cheeks" from *Seventeen*. Copyright © 1987 by Amy Tan. Digitalized with the permission of the author and the Sandra Dijkstra Literary Agency. "Amy Tan on Writing" excerpted from "Mother Tongue" from *Threepenny Review* (1990). Copyright © 1990 by Amy Tan. Reprinted with the permission of the author and the Sandra Dijkstra Literary Agency.

Deborah Tannen. "But What Do You Mean?" from *Talking 9 to 5*. Copyright © 1994 by Deborah Tannen. Reprinted with the permission of HarperCollins Publishers, Inc. "Deborah Tannen on Writing" excerpted from *Publication of the Modern Language Association of America* (October 1996). Reprinted with permission.

Edward J. Tarbuck and Frederick K. Lutgens. Excerpt from *The Earth: An Introduction to Physical Geology*. Reprinted with the permission of Pearson Education, Upper Saddle River, New Jersey.

Robert M. Veatch. Excerpt from "Models for Medicine in a Revolutionary Age" from *Hastings Center Report 2* (1972): 5–7. Copyright © 1972 by The Hastings Center. Reprinted with the permission of the author and The Hastings Center.

Gore Vidal. "Drugs" from *Homage to Daniel Shays: Collected Essays, 1952–1972*. Copyright © 1970 by Gore Vidal. Reprinted with the permission of Random House, Inc. "Gore Vidal on Writing" excerpted from *Writers at Work*, 5th ed., edited by George Plimpton. Copyright © 1981 by the *Paris Review*. Reprinted with the permission of Viking Penguin, a division of Penguin Group (USA) Inc.

Sarah Vowell. "Shooting Dad" from *Take the Cannoli*. Copyright © 2000 by Sarah Vowell. Reprinted with the permission of Simon & Schuster Adult Publishing Group. "Sarah Vowell on Writing" excerpted from "Sarah Vowell's Topic" from *Transom.org*. Copyright © 2001 by Atlantic Public Media. Reprinted with permission.

Carole Wade and Carol Tavris. Excerpts from *Psychology*. Reprinted with the permission of Pearson Education, Upper Saddle River, New Jersey.

Alice Walker. "Everyday Use" from *In Love and Trouble: Stories of Black Women*. Copyright © 1973 by Alice Walker. Reprinted with the permission of Harcourt, Inc. "Alice Walker on Writing" excerpted from David Bradley, "Alice Walker: Telling the Black Woman's Story," *New York Times Magazine*, January 8, 1984: 24. Reprinted with permission.

Colleen Wenke. "Too Much Pressure" from *Fresh Ink: Essays from Boston College's First-Year Writing Seminar, 1998*. Reprinted with the permission of the author.

E. B. White. "Once More to the Lake" from *One Man's Meat*. Copyright © 1941 by E. B. White. Copyright renewed. Reprinted with the permission of Tilbury House, Publishers, Gardiner, Maine. "E. B. White on Writing" excerpted from *The Letters of E. B. White*, edited by Dorothy Lobrano Guth. Copyright © 1976 by E. B. White. Reprinted with the permission of HarperCollins Publishers, Inc.

Dennis L. Wilcox, Phillip H. Ault, and Warren K. Agee. Excerpt from *Public Relations: Strategies and Tactics*. Reprinted with the permission of Longman.

Marie Winn. "Cookies or Heroin?" from *The Plug-In Drug*, rev. ed. Copyright © 1977, 1985, 2002 by Marie Winn. Reprinted with the permission of Viking Penguin, a division of Penguin Group (USA) Inc. "Marie Winn on Writing," copyright © 1986 by St. Martin's Press. Reprinted with permission.

Virginia Woolf. "The Death of the Moth" from *The Death of the Moth and Other Essays*. Copyright 1942 by Harcourt, Inc., renewed © 1970 by Marjorie T. Parsons, Executrix. Reprinted with the permission of the publisher. "Virginia Woolf on Writing" excerpted from *The Diary of Virginia Woolf*. Copyright © by Harcourt, Inc., and The Hogarth Press. Excerpt from "Letter to a Young Poet," copyright 1932 by Virginia Woolf. Reprinted with the permission of Harcourt, Inc., and The Society of Authors, as the Literary Representatives of the Estate of Virginia Woolf.

Visual Images

Page 28: "Trust," advertisement for the Saint Paul Companies. Reprinted by permission of Saint Paul Travelers, Inc., St. Paul, Minnesota.

Page 74: Charles Atlas®, "How Joe's Body Brought Him Fame Instead of Shame©," copyright 2005, under license from Charles Atlas, Ltd., http://www.charlesatlas.com.

Page 134: Doug and Mizan's House, East River, 1993. © Margaret Morton from *Fragile Dwellings*, Aperture, 2000. Reprinted by permission.

Page 179: Nighthawks, 1942, painting by Edward Hopper, oil on canvas, 84.1 × 152.4 cm. Friends of American Art Collection, 1942.51. © The Art Institute of Chicago. All rights reserved.

Page 186: "Cellular Phones of the Future," cartoon by Barry Blitt, from the May/June 2000 issue of *Mother Jones*. Reprinted by permission of the artist.

Page 228: American Gothic, painting by Grant Wood, 1930, oil on beaverboard, 30 11/16 × 25 11/16 in. unframed, Friends of American Art Collection, 1930.934. © The Art Institute of Chicago. Licensed by VAGA, New York. All rights reserved. *Rural Rehabilitation Client*, photograph by Ben Shahn/CORBIS.

Page 284: "Workers Making Dolls." © Wally McNamee/CORBIS.

Page 334: "Deconstructing Lunch," cartoon by Roz Chast, from *The New Yorker*. © The New Yorker Collection, 2000, Roz Chast, from *cartoonbank.com*. All rights reserved.

Page 360: "Mounted Nazi Troops on the Lookout for Likely Polish Children," photograph reproduced from *Master Race: The Lebensborn Experiment in Nazi Germany* by Catrine Clay and Michael Leapman. Copyright © 1995 by Hodder and Stoughton.

Page 374: "What Everyone Should Know About the Movie Rating System." Courtesy Motion Picture Association of America.

Page 428: "Garbage In . . . ," cartoon by Mike Thompson. Reprinted by permission of Mike Thompson, *Detroit Free Press*.

Page 476: "Need Is a Very Subjective Word." Reprinted by permission of HUMMER Advertising, General Motors Corporation.

Page 514: "Corporate America Flag." Courtesy *Adbusters.org.*

Pages 616–17: "Mickey Mouse's Evolution During 50 Years." © Disney Enterprises, Inc.

Page 619: "The 'Evolution' of Mickey Mouse" from *The Panda's Thumb: More Reflections in Natural History.* Copyright © 1994 by W. W. Norton and Company, Inc.

Page 620: "Humans feel affection for animals with juvenile features" from *Studies in Animal and Human Behavior,* vol. 2, by Konrad Lorenz, 1971. Methuen & Co. Ltd. Used by permission of Thomson Publishing Services, United Kingdom.

INDEX

e help with writing and research?
Ne Visit our Web sites.

,y of Web sites designed to help students with their most common
ive a wu'll find advice from experts, models you can rely on, and exercises
g conght away how you're doing. And it's all free and available any hour of
will te'
: day.

,h grammar problems?
Need hCentral   (bedfordstmartins.com/exercisecentral)
    Ex

ee what papers for your other courses look like?
Wanlel Documents Gallery   (bedfordstmartins.com/modeldocs)

, somewhere in the research process? (Maybe at the beginning?)
S The Bedford Research Room   (bedfordstmartins.com/researchroom)

Vondering whether a Web site is good enough to use in your paper?
Tutorial for Evaluating Online Sources
(bedfordstmartins.com/onlinesourcetutorial)

Having trouble figuring out how to cite a source?
Research and Documentation Online   (bedfordstmartins.com/resdoc)

Confused about plagiarism?
The St. Martin's Tutorial on Avoiding Plagiarism
(bedfordstmartins.com/plagiarismtutorial)

Want to get more out of your word processor?
Using Your Word Processor   (bedfordstmartins.com/wordprocessor)

Trying to improve the look of your paper?
Using Your Word Processor to Design Documents
(bedfordstmartins.com/docdesigntutorial)

Need to create slides for a presentation?
Preparing Presentation Slides Tutorial
(bedfordstmartins.com/presentationslidetutorial)

Interested in creating a Web site?
Web Design Tutorial   (bedfordstmartins.com/webdesigntutorial)

Want to see what else *The Bedford Reader* has to offer?
Visit our companion Web site.

The companion Web site for *The Bedford Reader* is designed to help you get more out of the book, especially when it comes time to write papers.

bedfordstmartins.com/thebedfordreader

Web boxes throughout the book point you to the site's variety of useful resources:

- **Exercise Central,** the largest online collection of editing exercises, helps you improve your grammar and usage skills.

- **Reading quizzes** for each essay in the book test comprehension skills. Electronic scoring, which can be monitored by instructors, offers immediate feedback.

- **TopLinks** is a database of links to reliable Web sites related to the readings and topics in the book. You can search by chapter or by topic, and each link has a brief annotation telling you about the site.

- **Author Links** direct you to further reading on the authors in the book.